ORIGINAL ART WANTED

X-Men #111

Avengers #189

Jungle Action #14

Justice League #207

All-Star #70

Green Lantern #92

Captain America #202

SSSV #8

Brave & Bold #136

Human Fly #10

Marvel 2-in-1 #55

NEAL ADAMS
Action #466
DC 1978 Calendar
Cover - Disasters

ROSS ANDRU
Superman #334, 338, 341, 349

JIM APARO
Adventure #452 (Aquaman)
Aquaman #62, 63
Batman #294
Brave & Bold #130, 136, 139
Manbat #2
Showcase #94, 95, 96 (Doom Patrol)

RICH BUCKLER
Action #478, 483
All-Star Comics #69
Astonishing Tales #26, 27 (Deathlok)
DC Super Stars #10 (Strange Sports)
Freedom Fighters #9, 10, 14
Iron Man Annual #3
Justice League #148, 158
Kamandi #42-50, 52, 56, 60
Secret Society Super Villians Spectacular (DC Special Series #6)
Superman #327
Super Team Family #8 (Challengers)
New Gods #14, 15
Teen Titans (old) #50-53
X-Men #97

BOB BUDIANSKY
Ghost Rider #40, 43
Marvel 2-in-1 #49
X-Men #120

JOHN BUSCEMA
Fantastic Four #202
Thor #262

SAL BUSCEMA
Hulk #207 *(interior pages)*
What If? #17 (old)

JOHN BYRNE
****Avengers #181 *(interiors)*, 186-190
****(No one will pay more for Byrne Avengers covers /interiors)
Capt. America #248
Champions #11 *(Pages 1-3)*
Fantastic Four (ANY covers #211-267!)

Iron Man #109
Marvel Team-Up (ANY covers!)
Marvel 2-in-1 (ANY covers), *any interiors #53-58*
Secret Origins Annual #1 (Doom Patrol)
Spec. Spider-Man #17
Super Villain Team-Up #14
X-Men #108-142 (ANY covers & interiors)

ERNIE CHAN(CHUA)
Batman #282
Champions #17
DC Super Stars #8 (Of Space), #9 (Man Behind the Gun)
Flash #243
Invaders #29
Justice League #132
Kamandi #45, 48, 49
Secret Society Super Villains #1-5
Teen Titans (old) #44

DAVE COCKRUM
Avengers #169, 175
Battlestar Galactica #2, 3
Hulk #207
Human Fly #3
Iron Man #110
Star Wars #17
Super Villain Team-Up #12
****X-Men Giant Size #1, #94-126, 145-147 (ANY covers/pages)

GENE COLAN
Dr. Strange #27
Tomb of Dracula #64
What If? #17 (old) (Ghost Rider/Capt. Marvel/Spiderwoman)

DICK DILLIN
DC Presents #13, 14
DC Super Stars #10 (Strange Sports) *(interior pages)*
Justice League #144, 147, 148 *(also interiors #144, 147), 168, 172, 173*

STEVE DITKO
Shade #3, 7

KEITH GIFFEN
Defenders #44 (ANY interior pages)

DICK GIORDANO
Batman #300
Superboy & Legion #253

MIKE GOLDEN
Micronauts #3-17

MIKE GRELL
Green Lantern #92, 100
Superboy & Legion #228, 230, 231

BOB HALL
Champions #16 *(Interiors)*
Human Fly #17
ANY Squadron Supreme Covers
Super Villain Team-Up #14 (ANY Interior Pages)

RICK HOBERG
Star Wars #2

CARMINE INFANTINO
Star Wars #14, 15, 19, 22

GIL KANE
Avengers #130, 141
Captain America #216
Champions #11, 16
Jungle Action (Black Panther) #14
Marvel Team-Up #23
Star Wars #8

MIKE KALUTA
Batman Family #17

JACK KIRBY
Capt. America #202 (cover + page 14)
Defenders #44
Invaders #14, 15
Kamandi (ANY covers)
Weird Wonder Tales #18

ALAN KUPPERBERG
Invaders #37, 38
Marvel's Greatest Comics #81

BOB LAYTON
Iron Man #121, 127, 135, 139 (others considered)
Marvel Premiere #47 (Ant Man)
Marvel 2-in-1 #42
Squadron Supreme (ANY covers)
What If? #32 (old)

GARCIA LOPEZ
Action #481, 482, 484
DC Special Series #5 (Superman Specs.), #11 (Flash Spectacular)
Untold Legend of Batman #2

AL MILGROM
Al Star Comics #70

Amazing Spider-Man #194
Defenders #74
Firestorm (old) #2, 3
Flash #268
Invaders #41
Secret Society Super Villains #10
Shogun Warriors (ANY covers)
Skull the Slayer #1

FRANK MILLER
Daredevil #158-181 (Covers & Splashes)
Dark Knight (ANY pgs)
X-Men Annual #4

MIKE NASSER
Kobra #6, 7
Spectacular Spider-Man #37

DON NEWTON
Avengers Annual #9
New Gods #12 (Splash page)

GEORGE PEREZ
****AVENGERS
#160-168, 170-174, 181, 183-185, 191, 192, 194-201, Avengers Ann. #8 (especially #161, 181), *interiors wanted #161, 162, 167,*
Korvac TPB Cover,
****(No one will pay/trade more for Perez Avengers covers!)
Batman Outsiders #5
Fantastic Four (ANY cover)
Infinity Gauntlet (ANY cover)
Justice League #184, 195, 196, 197, 207, 209, 219, 220 (any other covers considered)
Marvel Fanfare #10-12
Marvel Premiere #45-46 (Manwolf)
Marvel 2-in-1 #42, 50,51,57,58,61-63 (ANY interiors #53-58)
New Teen Titans #1-50, Annual #3
New Titans (Baxter) #1-5
War of Gods #1
X-Men #112, Annual #3 *(interior pages)*
Also looking for "oddball" titles Perez did from 1975-1987

KEITH POLLARD
Iron Man #108, 111, 112 Marvel 2-in-1 #55

FRANK ROBBINS
Human Fly #10

MARSHALL ROGERS
Mr. Miracle (DC House Ad Page-1977), #19-25

JOHN ROMITA, JR.
Avengers #176
Defenders #62
Iron Man #114-117

ALEX ROSS
Marvels #0-4 (ANY splashes/pages)
Kingdom Come (various pages)

PAUL RYAN
Squadron Supreme (ANY covers)

KURT SCHAFFENBERGER
Action #474

ALEX SCHOMBURG
Invaders Ann. #1 (Also Human Torch pages)

JIM STARLIN
Justice League #185

JOE STATON
All Star Comics #71-73 "DC Explosion" (DC House Ad page -1978)
New Gods #19
Showcase #97, 99 (Power Girl)
Superboy & Legion #249

CHIC STONE
Marvel 2-in-1 #48

HERB TRIMPE
Godzilla #3
Marvel Spotlight #12 (Son of Satan)

DAVE WENZEL
Avengers #177 *(interiors)*

ALAN WEISS
Human Fly #7
Shazam! (1977) #34

WALLY WOOD
All-Star Comics #64

RON WILSON
Marvel Premiere #55
Marvel 2-in-1 #37
Captain America #230

ARTISTS

Please Contact: JONATHAN MANKUTA
75 McArthur Lane, Smithtown, NY 11
Phone –1-631-864-2281 (Leave message if
e-mail JONMANKUTA@AOL.COM

INTRODUCING
Comics Guaranty, L.L.C.

A Revolution for Comic Books

COMICS

GUARANTY, LLC

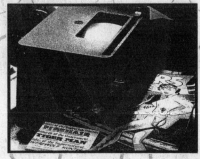

Key advantages of CGC

• CGC has created a revolutionary new protective comic book holder that is attractive, durable, and tamper-evident. It has a dessicant in each holder to protect the book from moisture and from damaging chemical reactions between paper and ink. It is slim and lightweight, making for easy storage and transportation while at the same time being remarkably strong. It is also easily and safely openable, though opening the holder voids the certification.

• Each CGC certified comic is graded using a standardized 1-10 scale matched with its equivalent nomenclature description such as "NM", "VF", "Fine", etc. This system is identical to the Overstreet Price Guide grading system also called the Overstreet Numerical Equivalent (ONE)

• CGC's commitment to the hobby is to achieve the highest possible level of consistency in grading. To establish a market standard CGC traveled across the country interviewing collectors and dealers, and having each independently grade 50 different comics. These grades were then averaged to create a consensus which represents the average industry standard in grading. CGC strives to hold to these parameters every day and with every book, grading your books consistently and accurately the first time, every time.

• CGC certified books will expand the market for comics by providing an impartial third party grading opinion, an essential criteria for many collectors not currently buying comic books.

• CGC employees are not allowed to engage in the commercial buying or selling of comics. In this way, CGC can remain completely impartial, having no vested interest other than a commitment to serving clients through accurate and consistent grading. CGC has top experts, both collectors and former dealers, as their graders.

• All restoration detected on each comic book will be clearly printed on the CGC grading label. For dealers, this will minimize returns for your mail order/internet business. For collectors, there are no unpleasant surprises when receiving an addition to your collection.

COMICS

GUARANTY, LLC

certification for
Collectors and Dealers alike

• CGC graded books have one of 4 labels. Modern label (red) is for books made after 1975. Universal labels (blue) are for books that have no qualifying defects. Restored label (purple) are for restored comics and indicate the apparent grade. Qualified labels (green) would be used for an unrestored book with a significant defect that calls for specific description. For example, a VF/NM 9.0 book with a 4-inch tear on the back cover is not a VF/NM 9.0, but it is a disservice to the seller, as well as the buyer, to grade such a book VG since it has a superior appearance to the VG grade. This book would have a qualified grade and label of "VF/NM 9.0, 4-inch tear on back cover."

• Your comics are guaranteed to be safe while at CGC, thanks to our advanced security system, multi-million dollar insurance coverage, and the assurance that your comics are touched only by trained professionals who understand the unique handling requirements of comic books.

• Comics Guaranty LLC, is the newest independent member of the Certified Collectibles Group (CCG). CCG is an umbrella organization, which also consists of the Numismatic Guaranty Corporation of America (NGC), the leading grading service in rare coins and Sportscard Guaranty LLC (SGC), the fastest growing grading service in sportscards. These certification companies, known for their commitment to integrity and impartiality in grading, are a leading force in their fields. It was this experience which impressed virtually every hobbyist, dealer, and retailer who had a chance to meet face to face with the CGC team.

• CGC will offer a population report that shows how many of what book CGC has certified and in what grades. This tool is indispensable for both dealers and collectors. Each CGC certified book is given a unique number. You will be able to know where your specific book appears in CGC's population report with respect to grade.

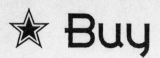

Front cover art, Painting by Alex Ross, SUB-MARINER Character: TM & © 2000 Marvel Characters, Inc. Used with permission. The painting depicts the Golden Age artist Bill Everett at his drawing board, with his creation The Sub-Mariner rising above him in the background. Artist Alex Ross used the original painting that Everett did in the 1930's as the basis of his Sub-Mariner.

THE ORIGINAL COMIC ART PRICE GUIDE, INCLUDING PRICES FOR SCIENCE FICTION ART, PULPS, MONSTER MAGS, FANZINES AND UNDERGROUND COMIX. (2nd edition) is an original publication of Arcturian Books. This work has never before appeared in book form.

ARCTURIAN BOOKS
18 Edgemoor Road
Gloucester, Massachusetts 01930
You may contact the author by E-mail at jweist@shore.net

Copyright © 2000 by Jerry N. Weist
Cover and interior design by Brian Reilly.
Editorial work by Robert Boyd and Christopher B. Boyko. Special editorial work on the Cosmos article in the SF Section by Joseph Wrzos.

Library of Congress Catalog Card Number:
ISBN: SC 0-9700922-0-2
       HC 0-9700922-1-0

Library of Congress Cataloging in Publication Data:

Weist, Jerry.
    Original Comic Art Price Guide, Including Prices for Science Fiction Art, Pulps, Monster Mags, Fanzines, and Underground Comix. / Jerry Weist.—2nd ed.
    Includes index.
    1. Comic books, strips, etc.—Collectors and collecting. 2. Comic art paraphernalia—Collectors and collecting. I. Title. II. Series.

First Arcturian Books Trade Printing: Summer, 2000
First Arcturian Books Limited Edition Hardcover Printing Fall, 2000

Printed in the U.S.A. by Ripon Printers, Inc.

OPM   10   9   8   7   6   5   4   3   2   1

Artist John Romita with his cover re-creation for THE AMAZING SPIDER-MAN No. 50, done in 1994 for Sotheby's 4th comic art auction. Photographed in the Marvel offices in New York City. © Photo by Jerry Weist

This edition is dedicated to the memory of every comic book artist who worked late into the night to meet a deadline. This book is also dedicated to the memory of Fred Cook, Ed Wood, Frank D. McSherry, and Sam Moskowitz - pioneers in the ongoing process of discovery within the field of Science Fiction.

SPECIAL ADVISORS TO THIS EDITION

ADVISORS TO THE CHAPTERS ON NEWSPAPER STRIP ARTWORK AND COMIC BOOK ARTISTS:

Russ Cochran • Roger Hill • Tom Horvitz • William Hughes • Pete Koch • Joe Mannerino
Harry Matetsky • Albert Moy • John Snyder • Robert Weinberg • Phil Weiss

ADVISORS TO THE CHAPTER ON SCIENCE FICTION ARTWORK

Forrest J Ackerman • Danton Burroughs • Jane Frank • Roger Hill • Tom Horvitz
David A. Kyle • Bob Madel • Roger Read • Jean Scrocco • Robert Weiner
Robert Weinberg • Phil Weiss • Joseph Wrzos

ADVISORS TO THE CHAPTER FOR PULP PRICES

Roger Hill • Robert Lessor • Bob Madel • James Payette • Joe Ranone • James Steranko
Mark Troost • Robert Weinberg • Phil Weiss • Joseph Wrzos

ADVISORS TO THE CHAPTER FOR SCIENCE FICTION FANZINES

Forrest J Ackerman • David Kyle • Richard Newsome • Harry Warner, Jr. • John White

ADVISORS TO THE CHAPTERS ON FANZINES; UNDERGROUND COMIX

Robert Boyd • Gary M. Carter • Michael Cohen • Tom Devlin • Dan Fleming • Roger Hill
Denis Kitchen • James Payette • Eric Sack • Billy Schelly • Jay Rogers • Robert Weiner

ADVISORS TO THE CHAPTER ON MONSTER MAGAZINES

Forrest J. Ackerman • John Ballantine • Steve Dolnick • Roger Hill • Michael Pierce

Annie Gaines (paddle no. 816) and Grant Geissman (paddle no. 832)
at Sotheby's MAD about MAD auction in October 1995.
© Photo by Jerry Weist

ACKNOWLEDGMENTS

This book could never have taken form without the original encouragement that came from Bruce Hamilton and Bob Overstreet, who in 1990 began to encourage the author to start work on an Original Comic Art Guide. Their advice and concern helped to stretch the author's reach on historical matters and brought clarity to a three-column, four-point pricing system. Bob Overstreet has allowed certain terminology from his Price Guide and paragraphs of description from his Preface to be used in this volume.

My appreciation is also be extended to Roger Hill and Tom Horvitz who originally gave me the most support when the first edition of the Original Comic Art Price Guide took form. Roger Hill contributed greatly to the format of the book, helped with specific research on comic book artists, brought the Preface into a clear focus, and wrote the key to understanding price ranges. Roger has extended the listing in the second edition for specific Golden Age and 1950's comic book artists. Tom Horvitz has done specific research for the newspaper strip listings. My appreciation to Tom also is extended for contributions of illustrations, and counsel with the content of this book. Bill Cole has written the article on restoration and preservation of original artwork for this second edition.

I am especially thankful to Denis Kitchen and the staff of Kitchen Sink Press for their initial encouragment and editorial support during the beginning phases of this second edition. Robert Boyd, was my editor at Kitchen Sink during the primary phase of this second edition, and has remained with me throughout the final stages of this books' publication, his assistance has been invaluable. Lee de Broff and Christopher Boyko have also extended considerable time toward final editing of the text of this Second Edition.

It seems like it was only yesterday that the 1994 Sotheby's Comic Art auction took place and Roger Hill was doing research on the Joe Shuster Superman Daily. This article began as an extension of his research for the catalog description, and various questions that had arisen during the consignment of this important original. The final work, I believe is one of the more informative articles ever written about comic art. My thanks go to Roger for allowing this expanded version to appear in the second edition of the Comic Art Guide.

This year the Comic Art Guide is expanding into new territory. The pulp listing could not have been as complete or as detailed without the advice and direction of several people. First on the list is Robert Weinberg who guided the author from the beginning and allowed use of his *The Hero Pulp Index* for listings and number dates. Bob Madel, James Payette, Roger Hill, Mark Trost, Robert Lessor, all reviewed the pulp prices and gave the author specific input. Jim Steranko also reviewed the list, brought in new title listings, and helped the author with introductory information.

The Monster Magazine price guide owes a primary debt of gratitude to Michael W. Pierce author of the *Monsters Among Us* price guide, and we thank him for allowing listings for fanzines and magazines to be taken directly from his guide. Fellow collectors John Ballantine, Roger Hill and especially Steve Dolnick have tightned up corrections and given the author advice on pricing for this new chapter.

Howard and Jane Frank wrote extensively on recent science fiction artists. Roger Clark provided an extensive computer listing that gave the author a wide range of price values. John Snyder laboriously went over the newspaper script and honed it toward a more accurate historical final copy.

The Fanzine and Underground Price Guide could not have been developed without the kind assistance of Jay Rogers, Eric Sack, Roger Hill, Gary M. Carter and Mark Miller. Special thanks are due to Jay Rogers, Eric Sack and Peter Flynn for opening up their own personal collections of alternate press comics for the authors inspection. Dave Kyle wrote the informative article about printing fanzines in the 1930's which appears in this chapter. My thanks is also due to Dan Fleming, long time comics fan and friend for helping me with the Fanzine section.

Special thanks are also due to Robert Weiner of Don Grant Publishing for allowing the author to use listings from his original Archival Press edition of *The Illustrated Checklist to Underground Comix*. The author also recieved a special listing of comics fanzines from Bill Schelly that was invaluable to the chapter on Comics Fanzines. Harry Warner Jr., John Newsome and Johnathon White all contributed to the Science Fiction Fanzine chapter and their efforts are greatly appreciated by the author.

Special thanks is also extended to Teresa Carducci, and Forrest J. Ackerman for use of Michael Carducci's excellent interview with Forry.

The author could never have finished this book, or ended up with the quality of design, without the continued support of his designer Brian Reilly who displayed "poise under fire," great creative intuition, and had the stamina to complete this project within the deadline.

Jim Kitchen has assisted the author with Ripon Press in Wisconsin, and his advice has been invaluable with printing decisions.

I would like to extend my thanks to Russ Cochran, whom I met for the first time at the 1966 World Science Fiction Convention during the "Dum-Dum" annual Burroughs meeting as he was showing a book of photographs from King Kong to Forrest J. Ackerman, for inspiring me to do this book in the first place.

And last but not least, the author is thankful to his wife, who kept hounding him to "Finish!" and his two sons who did not erase any of the chapters off his computer.

The author with Graham Nash, inspecting some of Graham's original work,
just before pulling a Sotheby's comic art consignment, Winter 1995.
Photo by Tom Horvitz.

CONTENTS

Golden and Silver Age Master Jack Kirby, at his drawing table in Thousand Oaks, California in 1994.
The re-creation cover Jack is working on was for Sotheby's 4th comic art auction- TALES OF SUSPENSE No. 39;
estimated at $4,000 to $5,000; selling at auction for $7,474 in June of 1994. © Photo by Jerry Weist

PREFACE

PRICE RANGE KEY

RARITY — Brackets [ ] around a price indicate that this example is very scarce and could exceed maximum estimate.

<u>Covers</u>

No work produced in this category— XXX

No price available due to lack of information— ***

CONDITION — Age, color, marks, tears, etc.

<u>Pages</u>
[400   500   600]

CHARACTER — Is the primary character featured, or is the original characteristic of a great example in the story line?

CONTENT — is the theme or story line exceptional or below average?

VALUE RANGE

Minimum   Medium   Maximum

RARITY

The [ ] Brackets indicate RARITY, if these brackets are used the reader can potentially double the price range in all three catagories.

Original art values listed in this Price Guide have been recorded from convention sales, computer filed lists from *The Comics Buyers Guide*, collectors' lists, and by correspondence with dealers and collectors from many regions of the United States. Remember as you use this guide that it is only a reference guide, not a price list with exact values. Unlike a first-edition book, a comic book, a premium ring from the 1940s, or a pulp adventure magazine from the 1930s, prices quoted in this guide reflect the complex nature of all original artwork. A five-point pricing system has been created specifically for this edition of comic book and related artwork. Throughout this volume the reader will find three price ranges. For science fiction artwork and newspaper strip artwork, these price ranges will always follow the given period of time or specific listing; within the comic book artist listings, these same three price ranges will follow either the cover or the page listing. Two other symbols will be found by the reader, the * notation and a price in brackets [$400]. These five different listings will represent the following:

1. *Character.* Character is most often universal with this book. Does the Spider-Man page by Steve Ditko feature Spider-Man in many of the panels, and does Peter Parker come up against one of his more famous villians like the Green Goblin on this page? Under secondary character, quite often the villain, or another strong character, can steal the show, so to speak. Collectors will many times want a prime example of the secondary character all by himself, or in some instances, the villain with the primary character. In other words, "charac-

ter" is usually why collectors collect. With Superman, Batman, Spider-Man, or the X-Men, and including over 75 percent of comic book artwork and especially newspaper strip artwork, character will always play the dominating role in the decision to buy artwork. With comic book artwork, where "character" is not obvious (as in an EC science fiction story from Weird Science by Wally Wood), then "character" transfers over to "characteristic." "Characteristic" stories by Wally Wood usually involve weird aliens, beautiful women, 1950s rocket ships, and exotic worlds in other solar systems. When a primary character is not obvious, look for characteristic or classic examples of a style or type. Remember, this simple rule applies to a Segar "Popeye" daily, a very expensive Alex Raymond "Flash Gordon" Sunday page, or a painting by Earle Bergey to a Thrilling Wonder Stories pulp cover from 1943.

2. *Content, story line, or theme.* This second category in determining price is very important. Has Peter Parker, alias the Spider-Man, just been bitten in the lab as a student by a spider, or is he in the death throes of an all-important fight with the Green Goblin? In other words, is a page of artwork from one of Steve Ditko's Spider-Man stories part of the origin of the superhero, or is it a classic fight page with his most famous supervillain included? This very important second factor will apply universally across the board. Is Prince Valiant (from the Hal Foster strip) in a battle or being knighted on a particular Sunday page? Is Uncle Scrooge swimming in his money bin and tossing coins over his head in joy, or is he in some dense jungle in search of gold (from a Carl Barks comic book story, "Lost in the Andes")? Are the Fantastic Four locked into battle with their greatest nemesis Doctor Doom (from the Marvel comic by Jack Kirby), with all four characters from the Fantastic Four pictured in action scenes, or has Kelly Freas illustrated one of the great Robert Heinlein covers for the Magazine Of Fantasy And Science Fiction? All are very important factors to consider. If the story line involves an important historical moment in the newspaper strip, comic book story, or science fiction illustration, its value will rise.

3. *Condition.* Condition affects the value of original artwork but does not dominate value as it does with comic books. If a Sunday page or a comic book page is torn, stained, or missing a balloon, with title lettering paste-overs, it has less value. Veteran collectors will still buy a moderately damaged original, then spend the money to restore or clean the artwork to as close to its original state as possible. Common sense dictates that severe or minimal damage will affect value by a greater or lesser degree. The worst kind of condition problem is missing artwork! Harold Foster was in the habit of cutting out panels to send to fans who wrote requesting original art, and today many "Prince Valiant" Sunday pages surface with one or more panels missing. Comic book pages and covers were also cut up during the 1940s and 1950s for various reasons (depending on the publisher) and do occasionally surface in the marketplace. Science fiction interior magazine illustrations were oftentimes cut up with such disregard as to harm the original or cause loss of part of the artist's work. When portions of the artwork itself are "missing," again, common sense will guide the collector in determining value. A word about restoration: when work has been done to any original work of art by a professional expert there is very little loss of value unless a great percentage of the original work has been replaced, reinked, or repainted.

4. *Rarity or scarcity, and "nonexistent" artwork.* This fourth and important rule can be found symbolically within the text pricing by looking for brackets around the price: [$2,000]. These brackets [ ] will signal to the reader that the fourth rule of pricing applies to this listing. Certain examples of Golden Age DC covers are extremely rare, yet the original cover art to Action Comics No. 15 (possibly the earliest surviving Superman cover) is sitting with some lucky collector. Golden Age Timely artwork is relatively "nonexistent," but a complete 12-page story from *Sub-Mariner* by Carl Pfeufer turned up for auction at the second Sotheby's

comic art auction. And since this time a classic Alex Schomburg *Human Torch* cover has surfaced. Pages of comic book artwork by Carl Barks from the 1940s are almost unheard of, yet a few have surfaced. Sunday pages of "Little Orphan Annie" by Harold Gray are rare because practically the entire estate was donated to the Boston University Library, although a few Sunday pages have come into the collector's market. Even a contemporary strip such as "Calvin and Hobbes" by Bill Watterson can present a case of rarity in the marketplace, since the artist exercises very strict control over the release of his originals; almost none are known to reside on collectors' walls. The rarity or scarcity factor can drive a particular original up 25 percent to 100 percent, or more.

Determining rarity requires years of experience in the field and a great deal of knowledge about the particular artist so that an honest assessment of value can be made. In some instances, the bracket [ ] symbol will indicate to the reader that this particular example of artwork is considered nonexistent to the author and advisors on this book. This can apply, of course, to many different examples from the Golden Age and Silver Age of comic art especially. For historical reference, we have attempted to go ahead and list as much art as possible that was known to have been produced by the artists who are listed here. The problem that arises is who determines what art is actually in existence or nonexistent? The fact of the matter is that no one specific art dealer or collector knows exactly what the other art dealers or art collectors know about what actually exists in collections spread across the United States and other countries. You can get a consensus of opinion on nonexistent art from a number of authorities in the field, but the reality is that no one can be 100 percent positive that a certain example doesn't presently exist or won't eventually turn up. Just like comics and other collectibles, with each passing year more collections of older art continue to surface from storage units, attics, basements, closets, and warehouses. A lot of this art was thought to be nonexistent for many years. In some listings of the nonexistent artwork, we have proceeded with caution in attempting to formulate a reasonable judgment/estimate of what the art's value would be, based on other similar or related examples that have entered the marketplace. Some purists may argue with this particular strategy of pricing, but our objective is to make this Price Guide as helpful and complete as possible for all collectors.

By the same token, we feel that certain nonexistent examples of truly historical importance could not be estimated at all. It would be impossible to closely estimate a value on one of Joe Shuster's early *Action Comics* covers, or on Bob Kane's early *Detective Comics* covers. Or to stretch that point a step farther, what if the cover to *Action Comics* No. 1 or *Detective Comics* No. 27 turned up? We would surmise that there is no expert in the field who could properly estimate the value of this cover—especially since a cover of such historical importance would invariably be sold at auction. So this fourth rule of rarity, scarcity, or nonexistent artwork will have the brackets [ ] as indicated around the price range listed, except when listing certain historical examples, which will be indicated by ***. Inserted throughout this book is the Price Range Key to remind the reader of these important five price variables.

In addition to the price range listing for original comic art in this second edition we have also included listing for Pulp Magazines, Monster Magazines, Underground Comics, and Fanzines and related Comic Collectibles. The grading for these catagories depends on the chapter. For Pulps, a more appropriate listing of Good, to Very Good to Fine is used. For Underground Comics, Fanzines, and Monster Magazines, the standard Good to Fine to Near Mint catagories are used.

There are now many parts to this book. Part III contains the newspaper comic strip listing. To find the strip in this part, look for the title name of the strip; do not look for the artist's name. To find Harold Foster, the reader would look up both "Tarzan" and "Prince Valiant."

To find Bill Griffith, the reader would look up "Zippy the Pinhead." Part IV, the largest listing, is for comic book artists; here the listing is alphabetical by artist name from A to Z. Each artist's career is historically listed, with more complete information for major artists such as Jack Kirby. All major eras are covered, and the reader can follow Jack Kirby through the Golden Age of comics to the Silver Age of comics. This section is followed by listings for Science Fiction and Pulp Artwork; followed closely by a chapter which introduces the first serious listing of Pulp Magazine Prices. The last part of this book contains listings of Monster Magazines, Underground Comics, and comic book fanzines.

IMPORTANT. Prices-and values listed in this book are in U.S. currency and are for reference only. The true value of any original is what you are willing to pay. Prices listed herein are an indication of what collectors (not dealers) would probably pay. For one reason or another, these collectors might want a certain original badly, or need a specific page to complete a story they own, so they are willing to pay more. Dealers are not in a position to pay the full prices listed, but work on a percentage that is largely contingent on the amount of investment required and the quality of material offered. Usually they will pay from 20 percent to 70 percent of the list price, depending on how long it will take them to sell the collection or single original after making the investment; the higher the demand and the better the rating from the five-point pricing system, the more the percentage. Most dealers are faced with expenses such as advertising, travel, telephone and mailing, rent, employee salaries, plus convention costs. These costs all go in before the originals are sold. The high-demand originals usually sell right away, but there are often many other original works that are difficult to sell due to low demand. Sometimes a dealer will have expenses tied up in this type of work for several years before finally realizing a sale. Remember, his or her position is that of handling, demand and overhead. Most dealers are victims of these economics.

PRICE RANGE KEY

RARITY — Brackets [ ] around a price indicate that this example is very scarce and could exceed maximum estimate.

	Covers
No work produced in this category—	XXX
No price available due to lack of information—	***

CONDITION — Age, color, marks, tears, etc.

	Pages		
	[400	500	600]

CHARACTER — Is the primary character featured, or is the original characteristic of a great example in the story line?

CONTENT — is the theme or story line exceptional or below average?

VALUE RANGE

Minimum	Medium	Maximum

RARITY

The [ ] Brackets indicate RARITY, if these brackets are used the reader can potentially double the price range in all three catagories.

PART I

INTRODUCTION

The author with Ray Bradbury. Mr. Bradbury has just finished signing splash pages to his original EC adaptation stories, Washington D.C., 1994. Photo by Roger Hill

UNDERSTANDING PRICE RANGES

The intricacies of pricing original comic book art among three different price ranges rely on many different factors. These factors consist of detailed criteria which ultimately control range values between the low, middle, and high ends of prices realized on any given piece of artwork. The following are a few basic elements of information to help collectors in the field understand why prices on art can vary so much.

COVERS

A cover that qualifies for the high-end category of pricing is either an excellent example of an artist's work, a strong image reflecting the contents of the characters and stories found inside the comic, or an example with extreme importance to many people—supply and demand—and condition taken into account.

Cover art produced by two different artists can present problems in the pricing ranges. This is found most often in contemporary superhero artwork produced over the past twenty-five years, but can also apply to certain examples dating back to the early 1940s. An artist who is both a good penciller and a good inker and is popular with art collectors can command a high-end range for his originals. Supply and demand will be the controlling factor, as always. But in collaborative efforts, where one artist pencils and another inks, the blending of styles can be a controlling factor in determining both the success of the comic and the price range of original art. The pairing of a strong penciller with a weak inker can demote a page of art from the high-end range to the middle- or low-end range. This same rule, to some degree, would also apply to the collaborative success of artist and writers.

Collectors should be aware that certain popular trends of collaborative or individually-produced art in the high-end price ranges today can become the unpopular trends and low-end price ranges of art tomorrow. A good rule of thumb to follow is to buy what you like, not what others like.

There are many elements that can determine a cover's strong or weak points. Such elements can and usually do play a part in the pricing and selling of original art. Some basic questions to think about: Does the cover show a larger image of the stories' main character, good guy, superhero, etc., as compared to secondary characters, bad guys, supervillains, etc.? Is the main character seen from a distance which reduces his size to that of a postage stamp, or is he in the foreground, close up, at a height near that of the art itself? Is he posed in action or standing idle? The answers will guide you to a correct decision.

Another element is correctness of the art itself. In other words, did the artist do a good job on the anatomy of characters and background perspective? Does the overall cover display a posterlike design/balance that is appealing to the eye, and most of all, appealing to you? If the answer to many of these questions is no, then a cover is more apt to fall into one of the lower categories of price ranges.

A cover original that was used for any first issue of a comic is more apt to be of importance to many different collectors. A cover which introduces a new character to comics, especially a popular character, is always going to be pricier than other cover examples for the same comic title and by the same artist. Perhaps a cover original turns up by an artist who is not popular or collected by many fans, and yet the art itself turns out to be an example cited in Dr. Frederic Wertham's *Seduction of the Innocent*, a book published during the 1950s. You can definitely expect to pay more for such a cover. People collect artwork for all kinds of reasons, and the market will try to cater to those needs, but always for a price. Price invariably returns to one major factor, supply and demand. As far as vintage original art from the 1940s through the 1960s, the demand far outweighs the supply.

Condition is always an important factor, too, and can sometimes be detrimental to covers that would normally fall into a high-end price range. Condition problems include soiling, glue stains, cuts, tears, excessive use of white-out, yellowing, tape, dirt, etc. A missing logo or word balloon is not good, but can be replaced fairly easily by a restorer who knows how. Extensive wear and tear or damage to a cover can and will easily lower its desirability and price from a high-end level to a middle- or even low-end level, except in cases of extreme historical importance. If the cover to *Action Comics* No. 1 turned up folded in half, totally coffee-stained, and missing all logo paste ups, there would still be 100 art collectors waiting in line to buy it. Restoration is always a possible solution to improve the appearance of a cover, and usually worth the time and investment.

Outside of historically important cover art, paste-over corrections do have a negative effect on cover value, especially when the paste-over has been performed in a sloppy way, or in cases where the paste-over is missing. This, of course, usually leaves an unattractive glue stain in its place, detracting from the overall beauty of the art. Marvel superhero artwork produced during the 1960s and 1970s seems to be notorious for having paste-overs. Sometimes these paste-overs are blown-up stats of characters that were drawn too small in the initial rendering of the cover; or, in some cases, the paste-over may have been another piece of original art, cut out and fitted in. A missing stat can sometimes be replaced, but a missing paste-over of original art is almost impossible to replace. Many collectors have a tendency to shy away from cover art with either sloppy or missing paste-overs.

Finally, the size change that took place in the industry in 1967-1968, when page size of original artwork went from 12½"x18½" to the smaller 10"x16" new standard, will have an effect on cover value. A strong cover from the period with the larger format will bring a higher value.

INTERIOR PAGES

In most cases, a splash page or title page of a story is the most desirable to collectors. Usually these lead pages feature a single large illustration taking up the entire page, and in other cases will have a large panel placed above a tier of two panels. Either way, splash pages are more in demand by collectors and will normally fall into the high-end category of pricing. One of the attractions/bonuses of splash pages is that in many cases they will depict central characters/sequences from the story. Another attraction is that, in more contemporary art, splash pages usually are the ones which list all credits relative to who wrote, penciled, inked, and lettered the story, and in fact are the most likely pages of a story to be signed by the artist. Pinup pages (full-page illustrations), popular in more recent times, are also referred to as splash pages.

Other pages that could qualify for the high-end price range are exceptional or outstanding panel pages that also feature a substantial amount of characters or action sequences in the story. This price range could also include certain panel pages from a story that are considered classic specimens of a particular writer's or artist's work. Remember, supply and demand will ultimately control pricing habits. Pricing history demonstrates that even if a piece of art itself isn't that attractive to one's tastes, if the story is popular or considered special for various reasons, it will be high-demand artwork to the collectors.

Panel pages that fall into the middle-end price range are usually those identified as average good pages, and this could include some splash pages that aren't considered particularly strong examples. Most regular panel pages will fall into this category as long as at least half the panels feature main characters or crucial sequences in the story. This category could also include high-end splash pages or panel pages that, due to condition problems, aren't acceptable at the higher price levels. Art condition is one of the most important factors to consider before buying art. A wide variety of condition factors are applicable to comic art, including: soiling, glue stains, cuts, tears, excessive use of white-out, yellowing, tape, dirt, etc. One or more of these condition factors—depending on severity—could easily preclude an outstanding panel page or splash page from qualifying in the high-end price range. The only exceptions to the rule which can override condition problems are the elements of scarcity/rarity and restoration possibilities. The question that arises is whether or not a severely damaged page can be restored to its former beauty, and if so, how much will it cost? How much money can you afford to put into it before you override its actual value? When extremely rare examples turn up in the marketplace, it's almost always worth the investment.

Original art that falls into the low-end category will usually be weak examples of an artist's work or panel pages with few or no characters and action sequences relative to the story. This could also include splash pages or good panel pages that suffer from condition problems as noted in the middle-end price range. Low-end panel pages are those containing one or no panels of significant characters or action sequences. While it may appear to some collectors that the low-end pages are undesirable, keep in mind that the prices are much lower and more affordable for those with limited budgets. In some cases, the reasoning is that it's better to have an example of a certain artist's work than no example at all. Also, it has been proven by the passing of time that many pages which start out at low-end price ranges can and do move up in value depending on the demand from collectors. By the same token, they can also move down.

This second edition carries new chapters with additional price guide chapters. Collecting pulp magazines is a hobby where the focus is not as direct on condition as it is with comic books. Collectors are concerned with finding copies that are sound, and many times reading copies are all that is sought out. The pulp magazines began at the turn of the century and the chances of finding them in near mint condition are almost impossible.

Collectors of fanzines are just as likely not to be concerned with condition. For science fiction fanzines, finding them is the primary objective. Very few copies of pre-1939 fanzines are found in very fine or above condition.

However, with Undergound Comics, and specific comics fanzines, condition is king. Just as many Marvel Silver Age comic books were printed on thin paper stock, so too many early Undergound comic titles were printed on cheap or unusual paper, and the goal is to find them in top condition.

With any guide there are bound to be mistakes, incorrect listings, or questions from readers. The author would encourage anyone with information-be it prices realized, historical notes, or personal biographical information-to write for inclusion in the next edition of this Price Guide. Please send all correspondence to Jerry Weist, 18 Edgemoor Road, Gloucester, Massachusetts 01930, or e-mail me at jweist@shore.net

MARKET REPORT,
RECENT TRENDS IN COLLECTING COMIC
AND SCIENCE FICTION AND PULP ART:
INCLUDING MARKET REPORTS FOR PULP MAGAZINES, FANZINES, AND UNDERGROUND COMIC BOOKS.

Since the publication of the first Comic Art Price Guide in 1992 the comic art market and related fields have seen tremendous growth and development take place. Not only have collectors pushed prices of original artwork from the Silver Age through the roof but previously unknown and known originals from the Golden Age of comic book covers have brought record prices. While the newspaper original strip market has come down to earth no one can deny that specific works of exceptional content and rarity have also brought new remarkable levels of pricing. And the science fiction and pulp art markets, while remaining quietly on the sidelines, are undergoing a revolution of their own in pricing. The common denominator within each of these fields is true "rarity" coupled with quality and public demand.

This year the market report will be broken down into specific categories. Over the past four years evidence is building that a growing number of collectors who have been in the field for years are beginning to focus on very specific and quality works when they buy. This trend is accentuated by the reality that many originals have grown past the $1,500 to $2,500 range that they enjoyed in the mid to late 1980's and have now become $7,500 originals in what would seem to be an overnight development! Or, paintings that just yesterday ranged from $2,000 to $4,000 are now $10,000 dollar works of art. This growth in price has caused many seasoned collectors to encounter the big "limp" as they struggle to pay off one original and go on to the next. While higher prices can slow down buying, the scarcity of quality works within the given markets have kept demand high. Despite the "known" collectors, however, there is also evidence that a new generation of buyers, and first time collectors from other markets are beginning to enter the comic book and science fiction markets. These new collectors are stirring the soup up just enough to keep most markets on a pattern of growth. When important originals and important collections enter any market they create new levels of excitement and record prices. Certainly the period of 1992 through 1998 has witnessed some of the most spectacular discoveries, and special collections entering the market place, and as long time pulp collector Bob Lessor likes to say, "The best is yet to come!"

SILVER AGE COMIC ARTWORK

The Silver Age of comics traditionally began either November of 1955 with *Detective Comics* No. 255, or September/October of 1956 with *Showcase* No. 4. As much as original art collectors may agree with comic collectors on dates, collectors of artwork have to satisfy themselves with very few existing examples of prime Silver Age work from the years 1955 through 1959. We owe some of the few surviving works to the foresight of such artists and editors as Murphy Anderson, Joe Kubert and Julie Schwartz. Both Murphy and Joe in their own way helped preserve artwork for future collectors by saving it and taking it home for storage. In Julie's case, he gave away specific covers, stories and pages to fans who happened to visit the offices of DC comics during the 1950's, or wrote special letters to him at the DC offices.

Some exceptional examples to surface recently have been the covers for *Showcase* No. 17 and *Detective Comics* No. 327 (first new look Batman) which were purchased by Steven Fishler of Metropolis Comics in New York. Probably the earliest and most remarkable original from the early Silver Age to surface in recent times was auctioned off at Sotheby's eighth comic book auction in June of 1998 when the cover artwork by Carmine Infantino inked by Joe Giella for *Showcase* No. 14 (the fourth Flash *Showcase* cover, and the earliest known Silver Age cover to ever surface) came to the auction block and sold for $20,700. Collectors were also recently impressed with the final hammer price of $26,000 for the cover to *Fantastic Four* No. 57 penciled by Jack Kirby and inked by Joe Sinnott which sold at Christie's East on December 18th 1997. Even though the Kirby/Sinnott *Fantastic Four* cover dates from 1966, the price of $26,000 stands as a record at auction and serves notice to collectors everywhere that the days are gone for cheap prime Silver Age covers.

Indeed, sales across the entire field reinforce the fact that Silver Age artwork is on the rise. Christie's East also realized a hammer of $13,000 for a splash page of *Captain America* (featuring the retelling of the origin of *Captain America*) by Jack Kirby/Frank Giacoia from *Tales of Suspense* No. 63. In this same sale a Steve Ditko *Spider-Man* page from No. 21 (page 15 with excellent fight scenes between The Human Torch and Spider-Man) sold for $5,000 and a six page story penciled by Kirby and inked by Ditko from *Spider-Man* No. 8 sold for $18,000. The demand for key Silver Age covers was so high at Chrisite's East that a preliminary pencil cover (twice up in size) by Jack Kirby for *Fantastic Four* No. 20 sold for an amazing $13,000. Sotheby's seventh comic art auction in June of 1997 offered a Carmine Infantino/Joe Giella cover for *Batman* No. 189 (dated February 1966) which sold for $17,250. In 1996 Sotheby's also sold covers by Murphy Anderson for *Hawkman* No. 1 at $11,500 and *Brave And The Bold* No. 61 (featuring Starman and Black Canary) for $17,250. That same Sotheby's sale also offered the only Silver Age Marvel origin story ever brought to public auction (for Iron Man, from *Tales of Suspense* No. 39, with pencil concepts by Jack Kirby and inks by Don Heck - this lot also included the original cover re-creation penciled by Jack Kirby to *Tales of Suspense* No. 39) and fetched $46,000. Other sales of note from the past few years include: Jim Steranko, cover re-creation in color for *Nick Fury Agent of S.H.I.E.L.D.* No. 6 selling for $10,350; Jack Kirby/Joe Sinnott, Splash page from *Fantastic Four* No. 51 selling for $14,950; Jack Kirby, *Fantastic Four* No. 34 Pin-Up page selling for $5,520; Curt Swan/George Klein, cover of *Superman* No. 170 selling for $5,750; Gil Kane, re-creation art in color for *Showcase* No. 24 selling at $4,025; Jack Kirby/Dick Ayers, Pre-Hero Monster splash page from *Journey Into Mystery* No. 71 which hammered for $4,300; Jack Kirby/Joe Sinnott, cover art for *Fantastic Four* No. 65 selling at $12,650; and the splash page by Jack Kirby/Dick Ayers for *Fantastic Four* No. 17 selling for $9,775.

Just as the modern era of EC comic art collecting began with the advent of Russ Cochran's EC comic art auctions in the 1970's, the modern era of Silver Age artwork was pumped up by the return of original artwork by both DC and Marvel Comics to the original artists during the mid 1970's and finally by the return of all of Jack Kirby's artwork (including large numbers of pages inked by Dick Ayers to the Ayers family) in 1984. With the existing covers and pages already in the market, and the additional high quality artwork returned by DC and Marvel, new prices and new collectors began to enter the market at a breathtaking pace.

As recently as the Winter of 1999/2000 a most remarkable private sale of one of the largest personal collections of Jack Kirby artwork has brought about even more record breaking prices for Silver Age artwork. Some prices realized from this purchase are following: *Fantastic Four* #3, minus page 1 (22 pages total), selling for $120,000; *Fantastic Four* No. 11, first story (11 pages), selling for $33,850; the complete "Thor" story from *Journey Into Mystery* No. 84 realizing $30,000; several pages from *The Avengers* No. 1 at $3,000 each; several pages from

Daredevil No. 1 at $3,500 to $5,500 each; *The Avengers* No. 5, the complete book, selling for $57,000. These are remarkable prices, but the high prices continue with: *Fantastic Four* No. 5 splash page selling for $25,000; *Fantastic Four* No. 5 splash page 6, selling for $18,000; *X-Men* No. 2 splash page selling at $25,000; *X-Men* No. 9 complete book selling at $50,000. Other highlights include: *Hulk* No. 3, the complete book, selling for $100,000; *Fantastic Four* No. 8 complete book for $80,000; *Fantastic Four* No. 59 page 6 (Doomsday page) for $8,000; *J.I.M.* No. 83 origin page #4 selling for $10,000; *Strange Tales* No. 114, a Dr. Strange 5-page story by Ditko selling at $19,000; *Daredevil* No. 6 splash page selling for $15,000. Manning Auctions also sold, from a seperate collection, Steve Ditko pages to *Spider-Man* No. 8, splash page at $30,000 and the splash page from *Spider-Man* No. 12 for $25,000.

In addition to the prime Silver Age years there is also a rise in demand for mid 1970's to late 1970's and early 1980's Marvel and DC covers. Especially the smaller (not twice up) covers by Neal Adams have seen record prices just in the past three years. Berni Wrightson, Joe Kubert, Curt Swan, Murphy Anderson, Russ Heath, Jack Kirby, Gil Kane, and John Romita all continued to perform at high standards throughout the 1970's and covers by them that were once thought to be of little worth and importance are now "hot."

Beside the interest in both DC and Marvel as the mainstay publishers of the Silver Age, collectors have not ignored other companies. Charlton artwork by Steve Ditko, and again especially covers, have seen enormous growth in the past four years. Tower Comics covers and pages (the covers are fairly scarce) have also been in constant demand, with Wally Wood artwork leading the way over Reed Crandall, Gil Kane and other Tower artists. Even the special Fanzine cover artwork from this period of time (though it might be difficult to consider this Silver Age work) that relates to the Silver Age has been sought out by collectors. Areas of little growth would include Atlas artwork, and much of the Gold Key and Dell artwork that was done during this period of time. Some excellent Gold Key *Twilight Zone, Star Trek,* and *Boris Karloff* covers have come into the public market with both private sales and at auction and demand has been lukewarm.

A sideline of the Silver Age "frenzy" are the large numbers of re-creation covers that have been done by the original Silver Age artists mostly over a ten year period between 1985 through 1995. In the best case scenarios like Jack Kirby's final efforts for Sotheby's fourth auction in June of 1994 where he penciled (and 'penciled' for Dick Ayers inks) some his most famous covers for Marvel Comics titles, the buyers have purchased near 'blue-chip' works. The problem that develops with this idea is the artists' temptation to do more than one single image of a classic cover. Seasoned collectors can remember the 1970s when L.B. Cole "classic" covers were done in editions of four or more! Most of the great Silver Age artists stick to one single redo for any famous cover or splash page - when this policy is broken prices can fall. Among some of the top performers in this area are Jack Kirby, Gil Kane, Jim Steranko, Russ Heath, who has begun to do a series of masterpiece "wash" covers from his famous period between 1956 and 1969, Dick Ayers, and Murphy Anderson, who has been commissioned by Diamond Galleries in Maryland to do a series of famous Lou Fine Golden Age covers that veteran collectors are snapping up as fast as Murphy can bring them off the drawing board! These artists have all maintained their original power to pencil or ink in their original styles, and are popular with the collecting community because the results are superior works of art. Some of the softer performers in this area are Chic Stone, Irwin Hasen, and Mike Esposito.

In summation, evidence continues to enforce the reality that there is more money being spent and at higher levels for Silver Age artwork than either Golden Age or newspaper artwork, and there is a larger number of active collectors for this still-booming market.

GOLDEN AGE ARTWORK

Since the publication of the last price guide the Golden Age market has also experienced some fantastic record-breaking prices, and some very remarkable discoveries that would prove that no matter how long anyone has been collecting there are still surprises in store for everyone. By far the two highest sales involve the origin daily that was sold in 1994 at Sotheby's for the prototype *Superman* strip (sold 24 hours after the auction to a private buyer for $77,000), and the recent trade sale involving the earliest known Superman cover from Action Comics No. 15 by Fred Guardineer which traded hands in excess of $150,000 cash and two important Frazetta originals. It should come as no surprise that *Superman* original artwork would lead the way in prices, and that the two works mentioned here represent the earliest known examples for both strip artwork and comic book covers.

Recent trends across the board with Golden Age artwork have tended to reinforce the idea that many younger collectors are acknowledging that important Golden Age covers and interior pages are the cornerstone of any important collection. Because of the obvious cross over with artists like Jack Kirby, Joe Simon, Carmine Infantino, Carl Barks, Joe Kubert and others, some Silver Age collectors have begun to push back the time table on their want list. Most important, however, is the simple fact that everyone knows that there are fewer Golden Age covers and pages to be found, and this keeps demand ahead of supply in every area of Golden Age comic art.

To give anyone an idea of how rare Golden Age covers are, consider the following comparison. If you take the published numbers given for estimated existence of the rarest comic books from The Overstreet Comic Book Price Guide 27th edition for number titles on *Action Comics* No. 1, *Detective Comics* No. 27, *Superman* No. 1, *Marvel Comics* No. 1, and *Detective Comics* No. 1, you get a number of 395. The number of 395 is plus (+), in other words the probability is that a greater number than 450 exists for the five rarest comic book titles! And these are copies that in high grade sell for hundreds of thousands of dollars each. At a current estimate agreed upon by a majority of experienced collectors and dealers there are only 170 known Golden Age covers within the market. Why should the "original" works for these rare comic books still be lingering in the four column price range when their reproduced off-spring bring five and six column price tags? This point is becoming apparent to a small number of collectors and investors who understand that real quality Golden Age covers are way undervalued.

Some recorded sales from the past few years reveal the trend toward higher prices. In 1992, at Sotheby's, the cover for *Detective Comics* (artist undetermined at time of auction) No. 59 (1942) sold for $13,200, and in the same auction the only known complete Timely story from an undetermined issue of *Sub-Mariner* sold for $4,250. In that same auction in 1992 a Win Mortimer cover for *World's Finest* No. 33 sold for $3,300 and a drawing of *Superman* holding Joe Shuster and Jerry Siegel sold for $3,750. The most remarkable sale in 1992 at Sotheby's however was when the classic cover for *Master Comics* No. 27 by Mac Rayboy (most likely the best surviving example by this artist for any Golden Age cover) only brought its $10,000 reserve price, which meant that only one person was interested enough to following the bidding up to the reserve price! In 1993 the cover for *Motion Picture Funnies* No. 1 shocked the crowd when it hammered at $20,700 and in that same auction a *Superman* Sunday page by Jack Burnley, dated January 1943, fetched $9,900 while a very important Lew Schwartz cover for *Detective Comics* No. 168 (an actual splash page that was identically used for the cover, featuring the origin of the Joker) sold for only $3,850! In 1994 a Fred Ray cover for *Action Comics* No. 50 (1942) sold at auction for $15,400, while in the same auction at Sotheby's another Fred Ray cover for *Worlds Finest* No. 5 (1942) sold for $15,400. The following year at Sotheby's, 1995, original daily introductory strips for *Batman* by Bob Kane for the second daily dated October 26, 1943 sold for $29,900, with the number five daily bringing $21,850, and the sixth daily fetching $10,350. In the same auction an Alex Schomburg cover for *Green Hornet* No. 21 sold for $4,132, and a Jack Kirby cover for *Speed Comics* No. 23 (1942) sold for $4,312. In 1996 Sotheby's again posted numbers for Harry G. Peter when an unpublished *Wonder Woman* cover brought $5,750 and two All Star covers by Arthur Peddy & Benard Sachs brought $6,900 for issue No. 50 and $8,625 for issue No. 54. However the star of that particular auction was the Lou Fine cover for *Hit Comics* No. 5 (a masterwork regarded as the finest surviving example by this artist for a Golden Age cover) sold for $16,675. And just when everyone thought that Sotheby's might run out of steam with Golden Age discoveries, along came 1997 with Fred Ray's original cover for *Batman* No. 12 (the earliest known cover to this title) selling for $21,800 and the cover for *Superman* No. 17 (August 1942, the classic cover where Superman is atop the world holding Hitler and General Tojo) hammering at $32,000. Obviously prices for Golden Age covers at Sotheby's changed from the year 1992 (when covers were going for reserve prices) to the year 1997 when new records were being broken.

Christie's East also presented Golden Age originals and some of their prices are as follows. In 1992 an Alex Schomburg *Green Hornet* No. 19 cover sold for $1,980, and a splash page from *Fighting American* No. 1 by Simon & Kirby brought $3,080. In 1993 Christie's sold a *Speed Comics* No. 43 cover by Al Avison for $805. In 1994 an Alex Schomburg re-creation for *U.S.A. Comics* No. 10 (painted re-creation cover) sold for $11,500. In 1995 a Jack Kirby *Boy's Ranch* No. 1 cover sold for $2,530 and in 1996 at Christie's East several prime golden interior pages were offered. Among the best of the interior pages were Joe Kubert's splash page from *Hawkman* No. 72 (1946) selling at $4,025; a Jack Burnley *All Star* No. 9 interior page (featuring Starman) selling at $4,025; and a Paul Reinman page from *All American* No. 55 (featuring the Green Lantern) selling at $2,530.

During this period of time some major sales occurred in the private market. A major collection of *Batman* Golden Age covers and interior pages including covers to *Batman* No. 30, 79 (unpublished version), with complete interior stories from *Batman* No. 56 and several other works traded hands for thousands of dollars. Absolutely first-rate pages from Jack Kirby and Joe Simon's *Captain America* period sold during the winter of 1997 for over $7,000 per page. The cover for *Superman* No. 16 (now the earliest known cover) has been recently discovered and is about to be sold. And as rare as Timely artwork is a very fine example of an Alex Schomburg *Human Torch* cover has been uncovered.

Though there is a limited amount of Golden Age artwork that finds it way to the public market each year in comparison to the numbers posted by Silver Age stories and covers (of which there were considerably larger numbers saved by fans and artists from the 1950's), it is apparent that there is still a small minority of collectors taking advantage of the obvious spread between Golden Age versus Silver Age in relation to "true rarity." If the majority ever catch on then prices for this period of time will explode instead of experiencing a steady rise.

1950's HORROR & SCIENCE FICTION COMIC ART, EC, AND OTHER CATEGORIES OF ARTWORK

Let it be stated clearly with this market report that when our last price guide was issued the author put collectors of EC artwork on notice that the "times they are a-changing." When the 1992 through 1995 auction seasons opened at both Christie's East and Sotheby's there were still major amounts of EC artwork turning up in force. That state of affairs was brought about by two special factors. First, one of the most important buyers of EC artwork from the original Russ Cochran auctions (a private collector) had struck a deal with Russ Cochran, whereby over 200 original stories and covers re-entered the market. Most of this work came to Sotheby's and some of it to Christie's East during the early to mid-1990's. The second factor was that Russ Cochran still retained, for the Gaines Family, important and deep holdings of EC Pre-Trend cover and story artwork, and had temporarily decided to retire and consign this artwork to Sotheby's auctions. Because of these two events, major stories and covers were offered to collectors, and eventually the very best of the Russ Cochran private purchase came to the public when Diamond International Galleries in Baltimore published a stellar catalogue offering many important covers (Kurtzman's *MAD* No. 4, Graham Ingels cover for *The Haunt of Fear* No. 14, etc.) and stories. In the words of Diamond Galleries' John Snyder, "I never saw anything like it, the phones were burning up, I never knew there were SO many EC art collectors and that they had SO much money!" Indeed, prices at auction during this period time reinforce Mr. Snyder's observation.

In 1993, along with the Gaines File copy sets of EC comics, Sotheby's auctioned Johnny Craig's Pre-Trend cover for *Crime Patrol* (the first Crypt Keeper appearance) No. 15 for $4,025. In this same auction the origin story for The Crypt Keeper from *Crime Patrol* No. 15 by Al Feldstein sold for $4,600 and the cover for *Crime Patrol* by Johnny Craig sold for $4,025. The most famous EC horror story "Foul Play!" from *Haunt of Fear* No. 19 illustrated by Jack Davis sold for $6,038 in this auction while Ray Bradbury's "Zero Hour" from *Weird Fantasy* No. 18 by Jack Kamen sold for $3,738 and the Al Williamson/Frank Frazetta "Mad Journey" from *Weird Fantasy* No. 14 sold for $10,350. The master-work story by Alex Toth for "Thunder Jet!" from *Frontline Combat* No. 8 sold for $6,325; "Atom Bomb!" by Wally Wood from *Two-Fisted Tales* No. 33 sold for a mere $2,875; Joe Orlando's "Revulsion!" from *Weird Fantasy* No. 15 sold at $1,150; and Graham Ingel's "Pickled Pints!" from *Vault of Horror* No. 29 sold for $1,380. In 1994 at Sotheby's the only science fiction EC cover ever brought to auction, *Weird Science Fantasy* No. 26 by Al Feldstein sold for $4,400. Wally Woods cover for *Shock Suspenstories* No. 14 sold at $3,750; a Jack Davis cover for *Two-Fisted Tales* No. 35 passed at a reserve of $2,500; the origin story for The Vault Keeper by Al Feldstein from *War Against Crime* No. 10 sold for $3,300; and Wally Woods SF story "Clean Start" from *Incredible Science-Fiction* sold for $3,200. In 1995, Sotheby's offered the first EC 3-D artwork (inked on mylar sheets up to 8 layers deep for some single pages!). Two stories by Wood and by Krigstein failed to sell, while Reed Crandall's "Child of Tomorrow" sold for $2,875, and Al Williamson's "Planetoid" sold for $4,600. In the same auction Harvey Kurtzman's cover for *MAD* No. 7 sold at $11,500; Kurtzman's cover for *EC 3-D Classics* No. 1 sold for $6,900; Johnny Craig's cover for *Crime Patrol* No. 8 sold at $1,265; Graham Ingel's cover for *Gunfighter* No. 12 sold at $1,610; and the powerful Al Feldstein covers for *A Moon, A Girl...Romance* No. 10 sold at $2,875 (this cover has already been re-sold in the private market in 1998 for $5,000!) and *A Moon, A Girl...Romance* No. 11 sold for $3,737(this cover has also already sold in the private market in the winter of 1998 for $4,950!). During 1996 the final consignment of Pre-Trend work from Russ Cochran before he resumed his own individual sales were offered at Sotheby's. Sales included; Al Feldstein, cover for *Modern Love* No. 11 at $1,610; Al Feldstein, cover for *War Against Crime* No. 11 selling at $4,025; Al Feldstein, cover for *3-Dimensional Tales From the Crypt of Terror*, fetching $6,325; Wally Wood, cover for *Tales From the Crypt* No. 26 selling at $8,625; Wally Wood's story "V-Vampires" (3-D version) selling at $5,750; Reed Crandall, the cover to *Terror Illustrated* No. 1 hammering at $8,025; and Reed Crandall's cover for *Crime Illustrated* No. 2 selling at $2,875. The year 1996 marked the end of a tremendous period of EC consignments with Sotheby's, and the end of much of the important Pre-Trend and Picto-Fiction artwork that was left in the Gaines estate. Smaller quantity offerings continued through future Russ Cochran auctions.

At Christie's East EC artwork was burning up the carpet and the following results took place. In 1992 Kurtzman's cover for *MAD* No. 6 somehow failed to meet its reserve price; however Wally Wood's "Under Cover" from *Shock Suspenstories* No. 6 sold at $2,860; George Evan's cover for *Aces High* No. 4 sold for $1,320; Graham Ingel's "Chatter-Boxed!" sold for $1,430; Wally Wood's "Flying Saucer Report" sold for $1,430; Johnny Craig's "Werewolf Concerto" from *Vault of Horror* No. 16 sold for $1,100; the final Jack Davis story from *Tales From the Crypt* No. 46 sold for $2,200; Joe Orlando's "Midnight Mess" from *TFTC* No. 35 sold for $1,430; these prices were realized along with the second set of Gaines File Copy comic books to be put up for public auction. In 1993 Christie's East again offered the Gaines File Copy comic book titles and the following original EC artwork. Harvey Kurtzman's "...The Man Who Raced Time" sold for $2,875; the Jack Davis story "The Light In His Life!" sold for $1,150; Jack Davis's single page ad for the new *Crypt of Terror* sold for $2,300; the cover for the first *Vault of Horror* No. 12 (1950) sold for $5,750; Wally Wood's "A Baby!" sold for $2,185; and Joe Orlando's "The Teacher From Mars" sold for $1,380. In 1994 Graham Ingle's cover for *The Haunt of Fear* No. 13 sold for $2,990; the Jack Davis story "Tin Can" sold for $805; and Will Elder's "Ganefs!" from *MAD* No. 1 sold for $9,200. Christie's East for 1995 posted Johnny Craig's cover for *The Vault of Horror* No. 34 for $2,530 and Bill Elder's "Ping Pong" from *MAD* No. 6, selling at $6,325. Christie's and Sotheby's EC consignments dwindled down coincided with the Baltimore Diamond Galleries Vault EC Catalogue and Russ Cochran resuming his EC/Strip Art auctions.

Before continuing with some of Russ Cochran's art auction results for EC artwork it can be said that the period of time from 1991 through 1995 represented a "Golden Era" of opportunity for collectors of EC artwork. With this period passed, history will not repeat itself. Since 1995 EC artwork has become more and more difficult to bring into the market place. Covers, in particular, are going to explode in price, because there will be few classic originals offered to buyers. EC Fandom experienced its first great surge of interest in artwork when Russ Cochran began his EC art auctions at the behest of William M. Gaines during the 1970's. When these first auctions took place, the relatively few EC collectors who focused their time and money came away with the bargains of the decade! Wally Wood *Weird Science* covers were selling for $2,000 each and major stories were to be had from $500 to $800 to $1,500 each. When this period passed, the second great offering took place at the major auction houses - now this era is gone. What has taken it's place?

In the private market the following examples speak for the future of EC artwork. The Frank Frazetta story from *Shock Suspenstories* No. 13 entitled "Squeeze Play" traded hands twice at $60,000 and then $75,000. The cover to *Incredible Science Fiction* No. 33 by Wally Wood (Wood's last cover for an EC SF title) sold at San Diego in the summer of 1996 for $22,500. Al Feldstein's cover for *Weird Fantasy* No. 13 traded hands at $10,000. The classic story by Al Williamson entitled "By George" from *Weird Fantasy* No. 15 traded hands at $12,000. Al Williamson's "Fish Story" from *Weird Science Fantasy* No. 23 was traded for an original Harold Foster *Prince Valiant* Sunday page from 1939 valued at $12,500. Harvey Kurtzman's original color-rough painting for *MAD* No. 1 traded hands valued at $22,500. The Kurtzman cover for *MAD* No. 4 with Graham Ingels cover for *Haunt of Fear* No. 22 and the cover for *Two-Fisted Tales* No. 22 by Kurtzman went in trade for a Frazetta Painting from a Ray Bradbury book valued at $55,000. An Al Feldstein SF painting commissioned by Bill Gaines in 1954 sold at Christie's East for $11,500. Wally Wood's masterpiece Ray Bradbury adaptations for "There Will Come Soft Rains" from *Weird Fantasy* No. 17 traded hands at $15,000; and "Mars Is Heaven" from *Weird Science* No. 18 traded hands at $25,000 - both stories from Bradbury's *The Martian Chronicles*. The cover to *Weird Fantasy* No. 21 by Al Williamson/Frank Frazetta sold in the summer of 1996 for $34,000! And finally the cover for *Weird Science* No. 20 first traded hands for a Chesley Bonestell painting, and was then sold within six months for $25,000 cash. These prices are just a small part of the action that has taken place for "key" stories and covers during the past four years - and these trends are going to continue!

In addition to the surge of interest in EC artwork during the past five years collectors have also driven up prices for all Horror and Science Fiction 1950's artwork. Recent articles in other publications have focused on the fact that next to Golden Age comic books, the second most popular and "blue-chip" comic book investment over the past twenty years (for growth in profit in dollars) has been with horror comic book titles. The same could be said for the artwork from this period of time. The problem is that beside the Harvey Warehouse Horror covers and stories, examples of art from Avon, Fiction House, Atlas, and other publishers are nearly as hard to come by as Golden Age artwork! The few examples of Russ Heath Atlas Horror covers, or Fiction House science fiction stories, or the early Murphy Anderson *Strange Adventures* and *Mystery in Space* covers and stories have all been going up and up in price. Most of the Frank Frazetta *White Indian,* and other 1950's artwork has also experienced remarkable growth. Single panels from Frazetta "Came The Dawn" have sold in the thousands of dollars, and Frazetta's cover for *Buster Crabbe* No. 5 sold for $27,500 in 1995. Other Frazetta 1950's western covers have also sold for big numbers during the past three years. In October of 1994, the Alexander Gallery in New York City mounted the most comprehensive public show of Frank Frazetta's artwork ever assembled and the Frazetta market has never been the same since. With full page ads in the New York Times, a gala opening that could complete with the most resplendent of New York's fine art galleries, and a major catalogue, the Alexander Gallery gave Frank Frazetta the respect that comic collectors always felt he was due.

Another trend that has been quietly developing over the past three years is the shift in prices for pages of artwork by Carl Barks. Since a very limited number of pages exist from the 1940's, the majority of pages traded in the late 1980's and 1990's came from the very late 1950's and 1960's. For years the page price from the 1960's remained within $3,500 to $5,000 per page. Recently however Sotheby's offered a page from *Uncle Scrooge* No. 61 (dated January 1966) and the final buyers price was $10,350. What this price signals is that the period of time is over when Barks pages were available easily within the market. And now that the price of paintings have begun to soar out of sight for the normal collector, the prices for individual Carl Barks *Donald Duck* or *Uncle Scrooge* comic book art will begin to climb. Other examples of recent sales include the cover for *Walt Disney's Comics* No. 134 for $15,000 and the cover for *Walt Disney's Comics & Stories* No. 96 for $15,000.

Americans have always idolized the popular culture of the 1950's while at the same time accusing this same period of being politically conservative, with life at home uneventful and often boring. However the "Father Knows Best" generation also brought forth the Beat Generation, an era of jazz music that is to this day unsurpassed, remarkable movies, and the ascension of action painting and the beginnings of Pop-Art - all in one decade! Unlike the period of comic art just preceding the 1950's where very little originals exist, the 1950's still provides some of the best opportunities in our market. .

NEWSPAPER STRIP ARTWORK

Over the past five years, critics and pundits alike have been declaring either an end or new beginning for the newspaper strip market. Part of the problem in analyzing just where this market is headed is the fact that several realities are going on all at the same time. Just before the entry of the major auction houses, along with Howard Lowery, Russ Cochran, Phil Weiss Auctions, and Illustration House in New York into this market rumors were flying about the higher and higher prices paid for either a prime "Tarzan" or "Flash Gordon" Sunday page. In 1988, 1989 and 1990 every time a collector turned around there was talk about the last most remarkable price paid for a particular original comic strip daily or original. While these prices were all true, what was happening was that the market was maturing, and select collectors were beginning to hunt out only the very best examples, and in doing so were offering higher and higher prices to the older collectors who owned the originals they were attempting to buy.

Once the majority of auction houses entered the market, and larger collections began to surface at auction during the early 1990's what seemed to happen was that the market slowed down. But did it? All during this time hundreds upon hundreds of originals were entering the market and bringing good to decent prices at auction, and one must remember that at public auction there is no barter. Genuine coin of the realm is spent in a public forum and the only politics involved might be the formation of a private "ring" to try and depress the price of a given original, so that a specific person can buy at the lesser price.

After about three years of Christie's East and Sotheby's auctions there appeared to be a rise in the comic strip market, powered in part by the entry of several new players, and a strong overseas international collecting community that bid for keeps at the auctions for the best quality works. Now in 1997 through 1999 this market seems to show some signs that it is sagging again. What's happening?

Basically all collectors need to remember that unlike the EC market where 100% of the original artwork was saved by Bill Gaines, and then released to the public (where a great majority of it was bought by life-long collectors of this genre), with small percentages then re-entering the secondary market later - comic strip art takes an entirely different evolutionary road. There are virtually hundreds of originals in existence in the world today that are held by either family members, or associates among the trade, or relatives and friends of the now gone or living artists, or part of institutional collections (and against the popular myth that institutional collections are "never" sold is the reality that from time to time they are sold). Many of these originals are NOT KNOWN to exist among the collecting community. In other words, it is safe to say that with the newspaper strip market there is a higher probability (much higher) for undiscovered collections, and great numbers of as of yet unknown originals entering the market place. To repeat, with Golden Age artwork there are approximately 170 known comic book covers, is it likely that another 170 will be discovered in the coming five years? Very unlikely! However, every day, every week, every month that passes brings to light another fantastic discovery about original newspaper artwork. Whether or not it's a previously unknown hand-colored "Krazy Kat" original by George Herriman, or a hoard of daily originals by Frank King of the important strip "Gasoline Alley." Herein lies the true answer regarding why this market seems so unstable to many collectors.

Given the simple formula that even if a new player comes into the newspaper strip collecting market he or she will most likely want to own only one or two "examples" of each important strip: and this formula encounters the continual progression of "new" originals flowing into the public market its easy to see why there seems to be "stops-and-starts" all across market place. Rare is the collector who says, "I love the work of Frank King, and having four or five great examples of his daily originals are not enough. I want to own in excess of 20 prime dailies!" Most serious strip collectors (even if new to the market and with deep pockets) are content with one given example by a strip artist or title. In other words there has been tremendous growth within this market and there have been many new collectors, but the demand is very balanced by supply and at the present time supply is staying just ahead of the steady and growing demand among new and old collectors for original art.

One could draw a parallel between what is going on now with newspaper strip artwork and the Golden-Age comic book market. Now that the big years of growth have taken their toll on prices for very rare comics (with years of big percentage jumps), and now that many of the new and inexperienced collectors for these comics have left the market, it has come down to earth and the collecting community is left with what was fundamental in the first place. Golden Age comic books are still selling if they are unrestored and rare. However, a great deal of what was in the market place at either overpriced or overrestored-and-overpriced levels is now languishing with dealers and store owners. Only the quality comics are selling, and they must be priced within reason. This is exactly the situation within the newspaper original art market. Only the quality originals are bringing higher prices, and the rest of the market is languishing if not priced fairly. This does NOT mean the market is in trouble, it simply means that there are enough opportunities for both new and seasoned collectors to be able to buy something somewhere at a great or reasonable price, especially if they have the patience to wait. And many collectors are waiting, thus we see normal, reasonable spending.

Recently at Christie's East last comic art auction a hand colored George Herriman "Krazy Kat" specialty work hammered at $37,000. During the winter of 1999 in a very small region-al auction forum in Portland, Maine, a rare full page "Yellow Kid" page by R.F. Outcault sold for an extraordinary price of $25,300. During this same period of time a special hand colored "Prince Valiant" Sunday page colored by Hal Foster sold for $37,500, and a special hand colored (the only one know to exist) "Tarzan" Sunday page from 1933, again colored by Hal Foster, traded hands at $50,000 in EC original artwork. In 1995, Sotheby's auctioned a Hal Foster "Prince Valiant" page dated June 25th, 1939 for $20,700. In the 1999 Spring Sotheby's auction the earliest known "Prince Valiant" page, from 1937, for the 16th Sunday page went up for auction. Quality originals, or strip artwork from very scarce periods will always be Blue Chip investments, and though the supply is continuous and vast - so, too, are the collectors devoted to this period of time in American comic art.

SCIENCE FICTION AND PULP ARTWORK

Before the adventures of Batman in *Detective Comics*, where readers could thrill to the dark avenger and his unusual villains, there was *The Shadow*, who knew what evil lurked within the hearts of men. Before *Superman* and his universe of adventures and attending characters, *Tarzan* stalked the wilds of Africa joining with nature and the environment against the forces of evil and greed. Before *Flash Gordon* went to Mars in a space ship, *John Carter* bridged the cold reaches of space; before *Spy Smasher* there was *Operator #5,* and before *Amazing Spider-Man* there was *The Spider*. All of these characters from the Pulp Magazines of the 1900's through the 1940's came before their comic book cousins by sometimes as much as a full decade. The difference was that the readership was mostly adult, and the format was the cheap pulp paper that allowed publishers to print their magazines for very little money. And instead of the bright panels of color, readers were offered interior black and white illustrations to page after page of typeset adventures.

To the generation of readers who experienced the Pulp magazines first hand the thrill can never be replaced. Writers as diverse as Isaac Asimov, Ray Bradbury, Brian Aldiss, and Frederik Pohl have all stated that they picked up their first science fiction pulp magazines because of the fantastic artwork that was on the covers of these magazines. So, because of Frank R. Paul, J. Allen St. John, Wesso, Howard V. Brown, and a host of other early pioneer

Pulp artists we have the first great generation of science fiction writers and the deep rich history that they produced during their lifetimes.

It is no wonder that collectors of science fiction, pulp magazines, the works of Edgar Rice Burroughs, or any of the other diverse genres within this field have long sought after original artwork by either their favorite artist or work involving their favorite author. It is also no wonder that the "cross-over" factor from Comic Book artists such as Roy G. Krenkel, Frank Frazetta, Al Williamson, Jim Steranko, Lou Fine, Will Eisner, and even Jack Kirby, is both wide and continuous. All of these comic artists pay the same tribute to the early Pulp artists, just as the SF authors before them did in their youth.

So while the market for this artwork during the 1960's through the 1980's was barely a ripple upon the larger collecting markets, in fact important and rare works were surfacing and entering collections all over America. Now in the 1990's Pulp Art, and Pulp Fiction (like the title of the movie) have come into vogue. But this does not look to be a brief intensity upon the part of collectors, and as prices continue to rise it is becoming apparent that Pulp art is here to stay as a collectible.

The state of this market is strong, but it is under the same pressure as Golden Age comic book artwork. There are very few pre-1939 Pulp paintings entering the market each year, so demand stays well ahead of supply. The other common lament heard from collectors is that "the numbers of opportunities are there, but the quality - is only to be found once in a blue moon!" So when important works surface, prices jump. Edd Cartier's cover painting for *UNKNOWN* for December of 1939, featuring L. Sprague de Camp's "Least Darkness Fall" sold for $35,000 in 1998. The J. Allen St. John painting for an unpublished *Tarzan* scene sold in this same year for $90,000. Frank R. Paul's cover to *Science Wonder Stories* for September of 1929 (the fourth issue) sold first in the summer of 1997 for $14,000 - and then later in 1998 for a combination cash/trade deal for $42,500. An interior black and white painting by J. Allen St. John from Edgar Rice Burroughs *Pellucidar* sold for $35,000. These prices represent just the tip of the iceberg, though prices for most pulp paintings tend to range in the $3,000 to $7,000 category. Finally the market received a shot in the arm with The Sam Moskowitz Collection which went up for auction at Sotheby's in June of 1999. The highlight of the sale was a pitched battle for the cover lot which featured the Frank R. Paul cover for *Science Wonder Quarterly* for Winter of 1930, The bidding topped out at $76,750! This is a new world record for a science fiction pulp painting sold at auction. Later in the Fall of 1999 Illustration House hosted an auction where SF paintings did extremely well. Perhaps the only factor that will hold this market down is the inability of collectors to find quality originals.

THE PULP MAGAZINE MARKET

Collectors of pulp magazines for years have enjoyed a calm market with a majority of original buyers who had as their primary goal reading and completing their sets of pulp magazines. The original science fiction collectors of the 1930's kept their magazine runs because when they were buying there were relatively few hardcover collections of their favorite authors works available. Times have changed, today only a few of the original titles survive on the newsstand in a smaller digest format, and the market that drove the original pulp magazines is gone.

The reasons for collecting pulp magazines are as diverse as the reasons for collecting comic books. The difference is age. The comic book became popular in the late 1930's, however pulps stretch as far back at the turn of the century.

It would be inappropriate to make any further comparisons between the pulp and comic books markets since there is very little that they hold in common other than some artists who crossed over during their careers such as Alex Schomburg, Wally Wood and Kelly Freas. The most expensive and rare of all pulp titles is the October 1912 *The All-Story* magazine with the complete novel for Edgar Rice Burroughs *Tarzan of the Apes*. The known copies for this pulp are estimated at a dozen or less. The collection of Sam Moskowitz went up for auction in June of 1999 at Sotheby's and a very good example with 1/2 inch restoration to the cover sold for $17,250. After this example, with the exceptions of *Weird Tales* No.1 and *The Shadow* No. 1, prices drop dramatically.

In 1999 and into the year 2000 the hot areas of pulp collecting include the Spicy Pulp titles which are selling in all grades and prices and are in extremely high demand. The Spicy titles are followed closely by the rarest of the Hero titles such as *The Spider, The Shadow, Doc Savage, Wu Fang*, and other runs. The very early Burroughs novels and short stories that appear in *All-Story, Argosy, and Blue Book* are constantly in demand, and when they turn up in higher condition the prices are always healthy. *Weird Tales* in high grades from 1937 backward are now bringing prices that three years ago would have been considered extreme. The rare bed-sheet issues, and special early Lovecraft copies demand their own level of price when they seldom turn up in the market.

Behind the Hero pulp titles, and the Burroughs market follow the traditional science fiction pulp runs. Within this market it must be understood that there is plenty of availability, and only a few titles demand higher prices. In recent years the Clayton issues of *Astounding Stories* have become extremely difficult and expensive when encountered in fine or better condition. The Gernsback titles for *Amazing Stories* are not terribly rare, however in fine to very fine they now turn up infrequently. More important for the early Gernsback titles is the *Amazing Annual*, and the first two to three issues of *Amazing Stories Quarterly* which can genuinely be described as rare. The *Amazing Annual* has now sold twice at public auction in near fine condition for over $1,500. Though not rare, *Planet Stories* in higher grades such as fine plus to very fine are bringing very strong prices. However, for the rest of the SF pulp market it must be remembered that there are many collections, and the demand from collectors wishing to complete runs such as *Thrilling Wonder, Startling Stories,* and *Unknown* is steady but slow.

Certain detective titles, with *Black Mask* leading the pack, have shown strong demand in the past two years. For the majority however, if the primary authors such as Dashiell Hammett, Raymond Chandler, and Earle Stanley Gardner are not present then demand can be flat. The rarest of the Romance titles, including the more racy cover titles have some demand, however generally demand is low. The least collected pulp magazines are the Western titles, and condition would have to be extremely high for the seller to obtain any high prices.

Jim Steranko agreed with author Jerry Weist recently at PulpCon when at a panel discussion he was asked if there were a Pulp Cover Guide (where every pulp cover were printed in color) published, would it effect the market? He said that he believed it would change the market, and more people would be drawn to certain pulps because of their cover artwork. This brought a negative reaction from the long time PulpCon audience. Yet this very fact is changing the market every year. Many younger collectors do not read their rare pulps. Just as a serious collector who might buy a first edition of Tarzan of the Apes for $25,000; or a fine inscribed copy of Bram Stoker's Dracula for $40,000 would not be expected to sit down and read from these copies, it would not be rational to believe that anyone buying near fine copies of the *Black Mask* containing the five installments for Dashiell Hammett's The Maltese

Falcon would then sit down to read the pulp magazines. These collectors have already read the classics, from paperback copies, book club editions, or other reprint variations in book form. However they collect the original first editions and first appearances for condition and rarity. Why all the fuss then in the pulp market when collectors confess to being interested in the original pulp art, or the artists who did interior artwork for these great magazine titles?

Since 95% of everything of value from the pulps has been reprinted in more permanent hardcover or paperback format it becomes more understandable with each passing year when collectors express their desire to have the original *Weird Tales* issues with Robert E. Howard *Conan* stories so that they can enjoy owning the original appearance as well as perhaps a classic Margaret Brundage cover, and they are even more thrilled if the copy is in very fine conditon! Trends such as these will continue to drive the pulp market, whether or not fans and collectors can agree on their virtue of it or not.

Lloyd Currey recently spoke to the author about the similarity of the conditions which would cause a rare first edition book to be very expensive, and how this relates directly to the way comic books are valued. Lloyd stated that an original copy, in "as new" condition, with its original dust jacket, in "as new" condition (with not a hint of cleaning or restoration!) would be the most expensive possibility for Edgar Rice Burroughs *A Princess Of Mars*. Lloyd then turned to the author and asked if this was not the basic formula for *Action Comics* No. 1? The answer is simply, Yes. Collectors want to experience the thrill of owning an original first appearance, in the condition that it appeared in when it first became available. This same basic rule can be applied to the pulp market, where condition, content and rarity will determine value.

MONSTER MAGAZINES AND FANZINE MARKET REPORT

What keeps the Monster Magazines popular with collectors 40 years after their inception? Horror comic books, horror movies, Stephen King fans, Movie paper and Posters collectors, and a host of other cross-over factors are part of the reason that Monster Magazines collected with passion by growing numbers of collectors.

Many of the baby boomers who have serious EC collections or Silver Age collections got their start in 1958 with *Famous Monsters of Filmland*. And just as this generation seeks to have their original comics in top condition, the demand for higher grades in Monster Magazines is what fuels the market.

It is also easy to see why collectors of serious Horror Movie paper who might be used to paying several thousand dollars for an important 1940's one sheet to their favorite horror movie have no trouble paying over $1,000 for a very fine copy of FM No. 1. Like the 1950's horror comics, there is also a finite number of late 1950's and mid 1960's titles to collect - so it would be possible to get to a near complete collection after expending some time and effort.

What percentage of these collectors go on to include rare Monster Fanzines in their collection? For the entire spread, the numbers would probably be small 10% at best. However, almost 95% of these collectors still treasure their early copies of *Horrors Of The Screen* , or their worn copies of *Monster Journal* or *Screen Chills* and this can sometimes lead to their seeking out other early fanzines. Will these people pay very high prices for the right fanzines? The author would gladly pay $200 for a fine copy of *Terror* No. 1, and $150 each for *Terror* #'s 2, and 3 - any takers?? - definitely not (!) - and there are a dozen other monster magazine fans who would probably break down and pay similar prices to own these rarities. Don't be fooled by a fringe market within a cult market; rare fanzines in top condition for the right titles are "hot."

FM would still lead other titles in demand followed closely by the very rare copy titles from the late 1950's such as *World Famous Creatures* and *Monsters and Things*, or *Monster Parade*. Most of these collectors however are not new to the market, and are famaliar with the original availability of titles, thus first issues of *Journal of Frankenstein* are know to have been around for quite some time in superior numbers and condition.

The foreign titles both early and mid-1960's are also showing continued demand and they bring premium prices in the higher grades.

This market may be viewed by some as a minority market within a larger group of collectibles but make no mistake: Monster Magazines and Fanzines are on the rise and they show no indication of slowing down over the next few years.

UNDERGROUND COMIC BOOKS AND FANZINES

It would seem that the Undergound comic book/comix market has been in limbo for the past twenty years. The rarest of the Underground comics highlighted by S. Clay Wilson's *Looseleaf Portfolio*, or the first printing of the Plymell *ZAP* No. 1, or the scarce color 8½" x 11" editions of *Lenny of Laredo*, or the even rarer red cover 8½" x 11" first edition of Jack Jackson's *Godnose*, to the impossibly rare loose paged first printing for Vaughn Bode's *Das Kampf:* all of these comics remain harder to find in any condition than a high grade *Amazing Fantasy* No. 15. However, despite the fact that many of the rarest of the first underground comics far outstrip any Silver Age comic book for true scarcity the market remains flat. Part of the reason for this can be attributed to a memory that the author holds of the first Sotheby's comic book auction when the committee for Grading stated flatly that they would not grade two lots of Underground Comics - "because they weren't true comic books." This very simple perception among long time comic collectors has kept Underground on the outside of the market for too long. The consultant threw a major fit, and the comittee finally graded the comix, however the startling fact is that the liberals from within this same committee were the very individuals who did not want to grade the Underground comic books. Suprisingly, it was not James Payette, who has been on every Sotheby's grading committe since and is renowned among members for his conservative political views!

The fact of the matter is that many people are starting to seek out the early 1960's fanzines with the great artwork of Berni Wrightson, Richard Corben, George Metzger, Rick Griffin, or a number of other cross-over artists. And as they begin their search, they inevitably are lead into the search for important Underground comic book titles. High grade examples of comix titles from 1965 to 1970 are now becoming harder to find. But just as it takes eclectic tastes to move into collecting Underground titles, it also takes a focus that is more diverse and widespread. Kip Forbes wrote a famous article for Sotheby's Newsletter in 1993 about the motivation for his collecting Golden Age *Flash Comics*. His fundamental statement was that collecting comic books was both easy, and fun. Easy in that they were numbered in series, therefore any collector could begin with issue No. 70 or No. 105 (in the case of the Silver Age *Flash* No. 105 was the first issue!) and work their way chronologically. Conversely, over 70% of the underground titles of the late 1960's and early 1970's were one-shot titles!

What may develop over the next several years in the Underground market is a situation that is similar to collecting 1950's science fiction and horror comic books. When collectors focus on the 1950's they sometimes stick to titles, or even certian publishers, however most often they are following the tracks of their favorite artists. Al Williamson, Jack Kirby, Joe Sinnott, Frank Frazetta, Harvey Kurtzman, and a host of other important historical figures all cut their teeth in the 1950's and the collectors know it. Collectors of 1950's comics have interests that are diverse, and this same broad focus can apply to beginning to collect Underground comic titles.

Exclusion from the traditional comic book price guides has been another factor in limiting the development of price ranges for Underground comic titles. This trend will possibly be changed with this current guide, however it will take the combined interests of newer collectors, and dealers who begin to decide that this market has a future before any fundamental changes begin to take shape.

The old adage "collect what you love," can apply directly to this market. There are many collectors of Silver Age comics who have saved high grade examples of their favorite Underground comic titles. There are obviously very serious collectors for the artwork when cover examples by Robert Crumb can break the records for individual cover prices in the comic art market. When more of these people with diverse interests step into the market and begin to demand deep runs of high grade titles, and at the same time begin to seek out the more important and early first printings of the historically important titles, the market will begin to come alive.

SCIENCE FICTION FANZINES

Though science fiction fans may deny that fanzines are collected or priced for condition or rarity, and even though they may complain that a price guide will do nothing but "drive the prices up," they cannot deny the following historical facts. Within science fiction fandom there are a number of people who collect specifically fanzines. As early as the 1960's early copies of *Slant, Science Fiction, The Acolyte, Quandry, The Nekromantikon* and *Futuria Fantasia* were already bringing high prices. Many important science fiction authors including Ray Bradbury, Harlan Ellison, Robert Silverberg, Arthur C. Clarke, Robert Bloch, Roger Zelanzy and many others, either published a fanzine of their own, or cut their teeth as young fans writing for SF fanzines. By 1949 there had been just about 1,400 Pro-Mags published in the SF field, however, the number of SF fanzines by 1949 would run into the thousands. The entire history of science fiction is contained within SF fandom and the fanzines. This guide will seek to serve as a resource for this early time, as well as a guide line (for the first time) on how to price many of these obscure and rare publications.

The author with Jerry Siegel, who is sitting with the original typewriter that produced early *Superman* stories. Photo by Tom Horvitz

PART II
COMIC ART COLLECTING

HISTORY OF COMIC ART COLLECTING
IN AMERICA
by Jerry N. Weist

> *Collecting is an addiction, a healthy, wonderful addiction. It is a diversion from the pressures of everyday life.*
>
> *The true collector is one who collects with "love." The discovery of a new item for the collection gives a feeling beyond words. There is a critical interplay between the eye of the collector and the object. A message travels from the work, to the eye, to the brain, and back to the object. The collector chooses in a moment, and the choice stands the test of time. The relationship is like that in Cinderella. "Do I love you because you are beautiful, or are you beautiful because I love you?" Comic strip art is true Americana. Its history, like America's, is short but exciting. Entertainment and mass appeal are the goals of comic strip artists. They satisfy all walks of life, regardless of age, day in and day out. This is our tribute to them for their efforts.*

George L. Sturman

(Excerpted from *Best of the Comics*
Leid Discovery Children's Museum Catalogue,
The Museums at Stony Brook, New York)

At the turn of the century, when comics began to appear with regularity in newspapers all across America, a new art form was born. It would be six decades before any kind of organized activity centered around collecting and preserving comic book art would begin to take place. Early comics fandom was for years a poor sister to the longer established and more organized science fiction fandom, which had held its first annual World Science Fiction Convention during the Labor Day weekend of 1939. Comic art was regarded in the 1920s, the 1930s, and the 1940s as something interesting but beneath serious criticism or long-term consideration. Perhaps a comics reader would stumble across a copy of *The Seven Lively Arts*, written by Gilbert Seldes in 1924, and read about the magic of George Herriman's "Krazy Kat" with its richness of language and cast of characters. Perhaps someone in a movie theater in the 1930s would see a rerun of "Steamboat Willy" with Mickey Mouse from its November 18,1928, premiere and wonder just what kind of work was behind the animated motion that was unfolding upon the silver screen. Perhaps Edgar Rice Burroughs enthusiasts attending the World Science Fiction Convention in Denver, Colorado, held in 1941, would wax romantic about the powerful brush style of Harold Foster when he illustrated "Tarzan" before beginning his other mythical tale of valor. Whatever the occasional curiosity might have been for people to focus on these newly developing arts, it would remain brief and rarely see print in any form for years to come.

By 1951, comic book publishing had already passed through the Golden Age of superhero comics, and newsstands were flooded with hundreds of crime and horror comic books. In the 1950s comic book publishers began, for the first time, to run regular letter columns in select titles. E.C. (Educational, and later Entertaining, Comics) publisher Bill Gaines ran regular letter columns in all of his science fiction and horror comics of the mid-1950s. Julie Schwartz, who was an active science fiction fan in the 1930's, became a major editor at DC Comics and started to run letters columns with printed addresses. As fans began to contact each other through the addresses in these letter columns, they also began to print and distribute fan publications—fanzines. Most of the early comic fanzines were focused on the creative genius of Harvey Kurtzman's MAD comics. With titles like *Foo, Klepto, Wild!, Blase,* and *Squire,* a new generation of comic enthusiasts began to express themselves. Many of the young artists like Robert Crumb, Denis Kitchen, Jay Lynch, and Skip Williamson who worked on these fan publications would later change the course of history forever for collectors of original artwork. Enthusiastic fans Dick and Pat Lufpoff who published the remarkable XERO, a science fiction fanzine, began a comics column entitled "All In Color For A Dime" in the early 1960's.

From the infancy of formalized comics fandom in the 1950s came the next phase in the 1960s. As the Silver Age of comics began to unfold and comic book fans became more organized, they began to hold their own conventions as science fiction fans had done in the years before. By the mid-1960s, Phil Seuling in New York City had orchestrated a remarkably successful convention, held each summer in July. Phil succeeded in getting many famous comic book artists to attend these conventions. For the first time, many longtime collectors were able to meet their favorite artists. They could now exchange ideas, inquire about purchasing original artwork, and conduct interviews directly for their fan publications. The author remembers one such summer Seuling convention in 1967. Al Williamson invited me into his home to view his artwork and admire his collection of Foster and Raymond originals. A young fan artist by the name of Berni Wrightson submitted artwork for publication in the fanzine *Squa Tront.* An entire afternoon was spent with other fans in the hotel room of Frank and Ellie Frazetta, pouring over original artwork (yours truly was one of only three fans offered the chance to purchase an original page of artwork from "White Indian" by Frazetta for $17) and then going with the Frazettas to a dinner where Harold Foster spoke and was honored by the convention attendants. It was a heady experience.

Early dealers who turned up original artwork in the 1960s contributed to the newfound interest that many people were beginning to pursue. Phil Seuling, Claude Held (who at one time between 1966 and 1968 sold numerous Sunday pages by Burne Hogarth from "Tarzan" for $75), Bill Thailing, and Howard Lowery and Malcolm Willitts of the Collectors Book Store in Hollywood, California, provided many fans with treasured original artwork. As conventions continued and fanzines became more professional in their production (many opting for color covers, typeset interior script, and totally offset interiors) and collectors began to spend more and more money on artwork, another, completely separate event took place.

The same young artists who had grown up on Harvey Kurtzman and Albert Feldstein's MAD, and who produced the early fanzines of the 1950s, were now a part of the "cultural revolution" that was beginning to evolve all over America. These artists were producing comic books of their own, filled with characters and stories that they wrote and owned, comics that were being distributed through the head shops and poster galleries all across the country. What at first appeared to be a ragtag group of rebel artists was, in fact, destined to change the course of history in the comics field forever. These artists boldly copyrighted everything in their own name, received full royalties on reprints, owned all future options for books and movies (which in Robert Crumb's case with "Fritz the Cat" became a kind of curse), and, just as importantly, retained possession of all of their original artwork separate from their publishers! This was unheard-of before in the commercial world of newspaper syndicates and comic book companies. The bitter years of artists creating and then turning over characters like *Superman* and *Scrooge McDuck* who would then make the publishing company untold profits—all for a per-page rate that guaranteed practically no rights—those days were quickly drawing to a close.

Many crossover artists like Berni Wrightson and Richard Corben, who both worked for underground and aboveground major publishers, and especially Neal Adams, who was near the height of his popularity, all began to agitate for better terms from the mainstream publishers, especially National Periodicals (DC Comics) and Marvel Comics. As the 1960s moved into the 1970s, the result of all this upheaval was change in corporate policy. Both DC. and Marvel began to return all artwork to their artists. Artists began to negotiate for better terms and future royalties. Even newspaper syndicates began to allow artists to merchandise and endorse advertising with characters that they had created and made popular. These syndicate artists began to also keep all of their original artwork. In a famous and long-drawn-out settlement, Marvel Comics returned all of comic book great Jack Kirby's original art to him. As new comic book publishers began to come into business, they offered ownership of artwork, copyright of characters, and fair royalties as the foundation for their negotiations with their artists. Today, artists such as Berke Breathed, Bill Watterson, Matt Groening, Todd McFarlane, Jim Lee, and Robert Leifeld, along with a host of others, owe their present situation, in which they alone control the marketing of their original artwork, to the "counter culture" artists of the 1960s.

As this same fundamental change began to take place in the American marketplace, other equally important and historic events began to unfold. Malcolm Willitts and Howard Lowery, who owned the famous Collectors Book Store in Hollywood, California, began Collectors Showcase, an auction of comic books and comic book artwork first held in 1977. Russ Cochran of West Plains, Missouri began to publish his lavish Graphic Gallery in 1973 (it would last 11 issues, until 1977, with a 12th issue published in conjunction with Camelot, based in Houston, Texas). Russ Cochran, along with Bruce Hamilton, was beginning to develop the market for an artist who at one time was forgotten to history - known simply as "the good duck artist" - Carl Barks. In 1972, for approximately $250, you could be put on the waiting list for an original oil painting of your favorite comic book cover or theme (from *Walt Disney's Comics and Stories* or *Uncle Scrooge*) by this veteran cartoonist. Many people signed up - so many, in fact, that it soon became apparent that it would take years for the artist to oblige his fans with original oil paintings. This situation eventually lead to the publication of signed and limited-edition lithographs of these exciting new paintings. The paintings soon began to change hands, and were also being auctioned off in the art catalogues of Russ Cochran's Graphic Gallery.

In 1979-80, another formative and historic set of events began. The one publisher with exceptional vision, the one publisher who had saved an entire era, the one publisher who would make it possible for an entire generation to again experience the very best of the 1950s in comics, Bill Gaines of EC Publications and *MAD* magazine began to release all of the EC and *MAD* original artwork. Through a series of auctions that were ongoing until the late 1990's, Russ Cochran began to offer the Gaines treasures. This set of sales did more to focus and develop the original art market than any other event. Cochran began to gather other major originals into his auction and offered prime examples by Hal Foster, Alex Raymond, and George Herriman, along with every auction's offering of classic EC covers and interior stories. A few examples of early prices realized (the first six issues of *Tales from the Crypt* and *Weird Science* were offered for sale in Cochran's regular newsletter, with no illustrations, all at one time) from catalogue No. 1 in 1980: The cover for *Tales from the Crypt* No. 23 by Al Feldstein sold for $900. The cover to *Tales from the Crypt* No. 24 by Feldstein sold for $925. The cover to *Weird Science* No. 12 by Wally Wood sold for $1,200. The cover to *Weird Science*

No. 13 by Wally Wood sold for $1,500. Later, in 1981, the cover to *Tales from the Crypt* No. 34 by Jack Davis sold for an unprecedented $1,815 (the highest price paid for a *Crypt* cover at that time), and Wally Wood's cover to *Weird Science* No. 19 sold for $1,280. It is hard to believe that it was twenty years ago that these auctions began realizing their prices, especially with today's prices!

Ted Hake, who specialized in comic-related premiums, from time to time offered comic book artwork; and by the mid-1980s, Chuck Wooley in Florida was offering original artwork in his auction catalogues. In the 1970s and 1980s, artists were willing and able to supply the ever-growing demand for original artwork to their fans. Many new and capable dealers entered the field and began to specialize in certain areas and contributed to the ever-present pressure to turn up new collections of artwork which could then be offered in the marketplace. Conventions became more numerous and grew larger; private auction prices continued to rise. Individual and private trades and purchases continued to break records. One would hear of a Wally Wood *Weird Science* cover going for $2,500, then $3,500, then $5,000 and up. Harold Foster's Prince Valiant art became more expensive with each succeeding year (despite the appearance of several Valiants sold on the market, which were the result of a theft from the Cartoon Museum of Art in Port Chester, New York) as they became harder to find and longtime collectors held fast to their own originals.

The first-of-its-kind Amateur Press Association for collectors of original artwork began in June of 1985, when Roger Hill of Wichita, Kansas, formed the C.F.A.A.P.A. (Comic and Fantasy Art Amateur Press Association) with 17 initial members. People began to spend as much for restoration and cleaning on a particular original as the work itself had sold for just five years prior. The prestigious auction houses of New York—Christie's East and Sotheby's—began to offer animation artwork on a regular basis at auction. Howard Lowery began a series of auctions for animation art and related items on December 4, 1989, with beautifully produced catalogues. These auctions became stronger each year, and with Howard's purchase of the famous collection of Murray Harris in the winter of 1991-1992, many historically important and dramatic originals by Hal Foster, George Herriman, Winsor McCay, and other comic artists began to appear in his auction catalogues.

With the advent of the 1990's both Sotheby's and Christie's East went head to head with a series of spectacular public comic book and comic art auctions. Eventually Christie's East with consultant Joe Mannerino held their auctions in the Fall around October, and Sotheby's opted for the Spring/Summer dates during June. At this same point in time Alex Acevedo of the Alexander Gallery began his annual Fall one-man-shows at his prestigious New York Gallery on Madison Avenue. Acevedo timed some of his most famous efforts, the Robert Crumb exhibit and the Frank Frazetta exhibit just before the Christie's East Comic Art Auctions. Black tie openings were held, with late night parties, and attending collectors ranged from the likes of John Kennedy Jr. to Pete Koch! Acevedo will also be remembered for producing some of the finest exhibit catalogues for comic art ever done. The 1990's will most likely eventually be remembered as the Go-Go years for the rapid growth in prices realized for comic strip and comic book artwork. Just as it was easy for Golden Age comics to move from tens to hundreds to thousands of dollars for key books from the 1960's to the 1980's, in the 1990's records continued to be broken in every level of comic art collecting. In addition to the major aucitons, and the activity of the Alexander Gallery, the owner of Diamond Comics, Steve Geppi, built a lavish gallery at his Timonium offices in Baltimore. Long time comic art historian and collector John Snyder was put in charge of Diamond Galleries and a series of important shows, openings, and catalogues began to emerge from the Diamond Galleries. Collectors now had a number of important and high profile venues with which to spend their money, the only problem was coming up with enough money to keep up with events and price changes! The annual San Diego Convention held in the late Summer of each year also reached its greatest period of growth in the 1990's. If early 1960's comic book collectors could have been transported instantly into a 1997 San Diego "Trade-Show" exhibit area (this would be two to three days before the regular Comic Convention would open) they would probably have imagined that they were in the year 2097 - and not 1997! The sheer size and expense of the exhibits were enough to stagger the imagination of any early fan.

Every bubble must burst, and every Bull Maket will eventually settle down or take a sharp dive. Just as the comic book market seemed poised to take over even larger percentages of the American economic market a series of changes were about to unravel the Go-Go 1990's. Marvel Comics announced that they were going to go it alone in the distribution game; and this single act caused more negative reactions within the direct-comic market in eight months than had happened in the previous twenty years. By the time the dust had settled around 1998 there were serious implications for a number of specialty comic book store owners, and the numbers of these stores nationally began to implode. Sales on new comics dropped dramatically. Some of the very best of the special publishers were soon headed for scaled down operations, or outright closings. The most painful loss to the market was the closing of Kitchen Sink Press in Northampton, Massachusetts run by Denis Kitchen. By the end of the 1990's even Kevin Eastman's Museum of Cartoon art, The Words And Pictures Museum, was headed for hard times.

The most interesting overall trend during the late 1990's adjustment is that the prices for Silver Age, EC, Golden Age, and other rare artwork continued to climb: this despite the gloomy predictions of the demise of the modern comic book market! Perhaps there is strength in numbers, but there is even more strength in a small, committed group of collectors who continue to pursue their lifelong interest in comic art, come Hell or high water. It is this central core of individuals who continue to confound the experts, surprise the comic book artists themselves, and renew the imagination and horizons for a younger and newer generation of collectors who will undoubtedly contribute to changing the history of collecting comic art well past the year 2000.

The author with Susan Cicconi (Restoration Expert for Sotheby's auctions)
and Denis Kitchen at the opening of the R. Crumb exhibit at the
Alexander Gallery, November 1993.

PRESERVATION AND STORAGE OF COMIC ART, UNDERGROUND COMICS, PULPS AND MAGAZINES.
by William M. Cole, P.E.

Collecting Original Comic Art, Underground Comics, Pulps and Magazines today is for both fun and profit. Yet, the paper ephemera you though was going to increase in value year after year has suddenly turned yellow after only a short period of time and is now compromised in its value. What happened? What could have been done to prevent the yellowing? This article will discuss how paper is made, what materials are best suited for long term storage and the guidelines for proper preservation.

HOW PAPER IS MADE

Paper generally has plant fibers that have been reduced to a pulp, suspended in water and then matted into sheets. The fibers in turn consist largely of cellulose, a strong, lightweight and somewhat durable material. Cotton is an example of almost pure cellulose fiber. Although cotton and other kinds of fiber have been used in paper making over the years, most paper products today are made from wood pulp.

Wood pulps come in two basic varieties: groundwood and chemical wood. In the first process, whole logs are shredded and mechanically beaten. In the second, the fibers are prepared by digesting wood chips in chemical cookers. Because groundwood is the cheaper of the two, it is the primary component in such inexpensive papers as newsprint, which is used in many newspapers, comic books and paper back books. This same cheap ground wood was the basis for most papers used in the Pulp magazines of the 1930's and 1940's. Chemically purified pulps are used in more expensive applications, such as stationery and some magazines and hardcover books. Since groundwood pulp is made from whole wood fiber, the resulting paper does not consist of pure cellulose. As much as one third of its content may consist of non-cellulose materials such as lignin, a complex woody acid. In chemical pulps, however, the lignin and other impurities are removed during the cooking process.

DETERIORATION OF PAPER

The primary causes of paper deterioration are oxidation and acid hydrolysis. Oxidation attacks cellulose molecules with oxygen from the air, causing darkening and increased acidity. In addition, the lignin in groundwood paper breaks down quickly under the influence of oxygen and ultraviolet light. Light induced oxidation of lignin is what turns newspapers yellow after a few days' exposure to sunlight. (Light can also cause some printing inks to fade.)

In acid hydrolysis, the cellulose fibers are cut by a reaction involving heat and acids, resulting in paper that turns brown and brittle. The sources of acidity include lignin itself, air pollution, and reaction by products from the oxidation of paper. Another major source is alum, which is often used with rosin to prepare the paper surface for accepting printing inks. Alum eventually releases sulfuric acid in paper.

Acidity and alkalinity are measured in units of pH, with 0 the most acidic and 14 the most alkaline (Neutral pH is 7.0). Because the scale is based on powers of 10, a pH of 4.5 is actually 200 times more acidic than a pH of 6.5. Fresh newsprint typically carries a pH of 4.5 or less, while older more deteriorated paper on the verge of crumbling, may run as low as pH

3.0. Although some modern papers are made acid free, most paper collectibles are acidic and need special treatment to lengthen their lives. Other factors that contribute to the destruction of paper include extremes of temperature and humidity, insects, rodents, mold and improper handling and storage.

GUIDELINES FOR PRESERVATION

First and foremost, keep your paper collectibles cool, dark and dry. Store books and other items in an unheated room, if possible, and regularly monitor the humidity. Excess heat and humidity should be controlled with an air conditioner and a dehumidifier. Storage materials such as envelopes, sleeves and boxes, should be of ARCHIVAL QUALITY only to prevent contamination of their contents.

MYLAR®

According to the US Library of Congress, the preferred material for preserving valuable documents is uncoated archival quality polyester film, such as Mylar® type D by Dupont Co. or equivalent material Melinex® 516 by ICI Corp. Mylar® is an exceptionally strong transparent film that resists moisture, pollutants, oils and acids. With a life expectancy of hundreds of years, Mylar® will outlast most other plastics. In addition, the brilliance and clarity of Mylar® enhances the appearance of any paper collectible.

POLYETHYLENE AND POLYPROPYLENE

For years collectors have stored their comic art, pulps, comic books, magazines and other collectibles in polyethylene bags, PVC sheets and plastic wraps. Although such products may be useful in keeping away dirt, grease and vermin, many plastic sleeves contain plasticizers and other additives which can migrate into paper an cause premature aging. Both polyethylene and polypropylene contains solvents and additives in their manufacture to assure clarity and increase the flexibility in the plastic. Polyethylene when uncoated without any solvents is a good moisture barrier but has a high gas transmission rate, and eventually shrinks and loses its shape under warmer conditions.

In recent years polypropylene bags have been sold under the guise of being archivally sound. This is far from the truth. Only uncoated and untreated material is suitable for archival protection. Currently, the only way to seal polypropylene is to add a substance called PVDC (Polyvinyl Dichloride which is a relative of PVC) to allow the material to be heat sealed. Therefore, once you add the harmful additive, the sleeve now becomes non archival and should not be used for long term storage.

ACID FREE BOARDS AND BOXES

Because ordinary cardboard is itself acidic, storage in cardboard boxes may be hazardous to your collection, and is a leading cause of premature deterioration of comic book and pulp magazine collections. For proper storage, only acid free boards that meet the US Government's MINIMUM requirements are acceptable. These requirements have been defined as boards having a 3% calcium carbonate buffer throughout and a minimum pH of 8.5. Anything less will hasten your collection's destruction. While many advertisers claim that their boards are "acid free at time of manufacture," they are in reality only spray coated with an alkaline substance making them acid free for only a very short time. Boards termed "acid free at time of manufacture" do not offer sufficient protection or storage for anything other than short term. True acid free boards have been impregnated with a calcium buffer resulting in an acid free, alkaline pH content of 8.5 throughout.

DEACIDIFICATION

Another way to extend the longevity of your collectibles is to deacidify them before storage. Deacidifying sprays and solutions are now available for home use. By impregnating the paper with an alkaline reserve, you can neutralize existing acids and inhibit oxidation, future acidity and staining due to certain fungi. However it is best left to the professionals to deacidify your pulp magazines or comic books. Deacidification with proper storage conditions will add centuries to the lifetime of paper. Recently a new acid free board that has a thin layer of activated charcoal in it, absorbs and dissipates the contaminates in the atmosphere. This product may also be a substitute to deacification.

In summary, we recommend the following guidelines for the maximum protection of your collectibles: deacidify the paper; store in Mylar® sleeves with acid free boards and cartons; and keep the collection cool, dry and dark. Periodic inspections and pH and humidity tests are also recommended. By following these simple guidelines you can be assured of a comic book, original art, or pulp magazine collection that not only will increase in value, but will also last for many years to come.

Authors note: Bill Cole is a Registered Professional Engineer and President of Bill Cole Enterprises, Inc., a company involved in the design and production of materials for archival storage of comic books and other collectibles. Questions may be addressed to him at PO Box 60, Randolph, MA, 02368 or e-mail him at bcemylar@cwbusiness.com.

A further note from the author: Many people who will read this article will, upon reflection, realize that many parts of their own collection are at risk. They may perhaps be depressed, or discouraged to realize that it really isn't a simple task to address all of the concerns expressed within Mr. Cole's article. The author personally has a large pulp magazine collection, and thousands of first edition hardcover science fiction books and a large number of originals on illustration board and paper and canvas. The authors own personal reaction, upon fully reading Mr. Cole's article is that he has a LOT of work to do for his own collection!

What most collectors should strive for is not 100% perfection, but perhaps a step by step process of improvement for protecting their collection. If you can't afford to humidify or air condition each room with your collection, then perhaps you can simply make sure that the home heat is kept down in these rooms, and that direct sunlight is not allowed to fall directly upon your exposed collectibles (such as the spines of first edition books) and that windows are kept shut during large rain storms.

We would all like to have museum conditions for every part of our collection, however, short of this a simple priority for improving what we do have that is most valuable might bring more of us peace of mind for the future. Mr. Cole's article is an excellent guideline for beginning any process of protecting "any" collection of value that is based in paper.

AUCTIONS: HOW TO BID AND WIN!
by Thomas R. Horvitz

Because of various myths that have sprung up, collectors in some fields get scared when they first hear the word AUCTION. Auctions are not an evil way to stop people from collecting what they love, but a resource to building a better collection. Auctions do not price items away from collectors. Prices are changing daily in every collecting field. Auctions are a part of every major industry, and are only a way of distributing goods. Participating in an auction gives everyone a fair chance at owning something.

It is very simple to participate in an auction. All auction houses publish a catalogue. This catalogue will list and/or picture all of the items to be sold on a certain date. Other information provided in the catalogue, includes the location and time of the sale. Most catalogues are priced between $10-30, and will be shipped to you 2-6 weeks prior to the sale date. Many of the major auction houses hold more than one sale a year, and have a subscription department where you can order the catalogues in advance.

Auction houses have a resident expert consultant who has spent several months organizing what is to be sold. This expert has spent a lot of time authenticating and inspecting all of the items in the sale, and is one of the most knowledgeable people in the world about the specific group of items to be sold. Do not blindly trust any outside source about the goods being sold in the auction. Every collector marketplace is filled with egos and chatter. The collector or dealer you call for an opinion on an item to be sold may have ulterior motives. They may want it for themselves, a client (including you), or even have a grudge with the owner. In contrast, the auction house should be your best ally. They will bend over backwards to make you a better informed buyer, they want you to be educated and to bid on the items. The auction house wants you as a return client, and will help you any way that they can. The consultant will give you more information than they were able to place in the catalogue before printing deadline. This includes more in-depth background information on the pieces, as well as getting you better pictures. Try not to be too needy. Only ask about the pieces that are important to you. There are other collectors that they have to deal with, and as the day of the sale approaches, the consultant's time gets short.

All auctions have a privacy policy. Unless it is stated in the catalogue, they are not allowed to indicate who the seller is. This carries over to after the sale. They are also not allowed to say whom the buyer is who bid on an item, or who called for information.

CATALOGUE INFORMATION

All catalogues have very important information that you must be aware of. The most vital information is that it will tell you when and where the auction is to be held. Also listed are the days you may come and personally inspect the items to be sold, the hours, and how to pay. The auction staff is also listed, along with their experts, where to contact them, the billing and credit departments and the auctioneer's name. The last bit of information at the beginning is the BUYERS PREMIUM, the percentage of the sale price that must be added to pay the house. This is common to almost all auction houses worldwide, and varies between 5%-20%. Everyone pays this, no exceptions, even auction house employees.

Author Tom Horvitz with *Comic Book Marketplace* editor Gary M. Carter, outside of Sotheby's in 1991, moments before the first Sotheby's comic book auction.

Many auction houses live with an unwritten clause "LET THE BUYER BEWARE." What this boils down to is that they want nothing to be returned. Still, property can be returned. Auctions include mistakes, and you should not suffer for them. The most common reasons are that the house miswrote the description of the lot. You must read all the fine print in the front of the catalogue discussing the houses liabilities to see if you are able to return an item. A possible example of their being wrong, and the item then being returned by you, is if the catalogue uses phrases such as "hand colored by the artist, inked by, or UN-restored." Should another person have done the coloring, you may be able to return it. If there was a different inker (or penciller) on the art other than the one specified, you may return it. If the item that you bought was restored, and they listed it as UN-restored, you could return it. Every auction house has a different policy regarding the grace period you may do the return within. Some give you one month, others have several years for you to execute this clause and get your money back.

One phrase that gives an auction house their out, and that requires you to do research is "ATTRIBUTED TO." This will translate into "we think we know who or what, but we don't know for sure, and if we are wrong, you lose." What you must do as a buyer is to know more about the item than they do before you spend your money.

Should a problem arise after you bought something, the catalogue will also indicate who to contact, and how to return an item. There will be instructions on how to have your purchases shipped to you, or where and when you may go and pick them up. Remember, if you have any questions, call the expert. They will explain all the legal paragraphs in the front of the catalogue (which their lawyers wrote in legalese for their protection), or anything else you want to know. No question is stupid. The auction house wants you to know all about what you are buying.

All auction houses have an inspection period prior to the sale. Some are the immediate hours before the auction, many are for several days prior. If you are dealing with one of the major international houses, there may be several locations for the preview. You will read in the first pages of the catalogue for where and when the previews will be. If you can travel to inspect the items, go! Your own opinion is the best one. Give yourself hours to see all the items you want to buy. The auction house will have experts on the floor to help, and sometimes it may take time for them to get free to help you. Most auction houses will supply a printed correction sheet to the sale's items available at the preview, these sheets are called the addendum. Read them. They contain additional information on the items in the sale, withdrawn lots, or last minute additions to the sale.

To make it easier for you to buy, the auction house likes to establish a credit history with you. If you are a first time buyer, you should talk to their bid department. This takes a few minutes. What they want to know is who you are, where you are from, and your bank information.

BIDDING

Before the auction starts, know what you are going after, and how much you plan to spend. It is also a good idea if you are a first time buyer to attend another auction before attending the one that has the things you want! Most Sunday newspapers have an auction listing in their business section. It does not matter if it is for art, machinery, cars, or whatever. Go to it to get a feel of how the process works. Watching people is a wonderful learning method. When the auction you plan to buy at occurs, you will be prepared.

Your first priority is to have a spending limit set before entering. If the catalogue says lot #42 is estimated at $400-600, and you are willing to spend $800, then that is your limit. If you know that this is a piece that you have waited 10 years to own, and that it may well be another 10 before whoever buys it decides to sell, factor this into what you will spend. Maybe you should spend $1,100 instead of the $800. Remember that for many collectors there is a cutoff point at an even hundred dollar, or thousand dollar increments. That one bid many times makes the difference as to the lot's next owner.

When you are at the auction and ready there are 3 common ways to do the bidding. They are: 1) in the room doing the bidding yourself, 2) on the phone, 3) allowing the auction house to do the bidding for you. The first is the easiest. You are there, you do it. For the second, you must talk to the house in advance. A place for them to call you at is established, and a time range for you to be there is arranged. If they cannot reach you, you will not be able to bid. You must keep your phone line clear during the designated times. The final choice is called absentee bidding. This entails several options also. You can fax in a bid to the bid department, leave a bid with them at the preview, or call them in advance to go over your bids. Currently, except for several Internet auctions, most auction houses do not use the Internet for onsite bidding. Every auction house will always contact you if you are the winning bidder.

The final way to bid is to have a friend or agent do it for you. An agent is normally a dealer in the field and will do this for a fee, normally 10% of the final price. Every agent has different terms. You must establish them in advance. Normally, for their 10%, an agent will bid for you, arrange delivery, and be a go-between should any problems arise once you have received your property. An agent should also inspect the item during the preview, and let you know of any surprises not listed in the catalogue. This may include rips, tears, or restoration, along with other types of defects that may not be noted in the catalogue.

If you are going to the auction, you must show up early. What you have to do is register for a bid number. The number is for their internal bookkeeping, and assigned to all the bidders at the sale. They will then give you a paddle with the same number on it. Once this is completed, find the bathroom. It does not matter if you need it, at some point you could, and you do not want to scramble just before the item you want is placed up for sale. Most auctions take 2-5 hours to conduct. Food is usually available there, but bringing your own is allowed.

There are several misconceptions about how the auctioneer takes bids. There are always rumors about how someone scratched an ear and ended up buying a stuffed moose head. At every major house, only a long time client has signals arranged in advance. So do not worry. Almost every auctioneer will only accept bids from a paddle being held in the air. So don't wave your paddle at a friend.

There is a strategy to bidding, and the odds are in your favor. The auction room is filled with collectors and dealers. Many of them are going after items different from you, and a dealer rarely will spend more than a collector. When an item comes up that you want, raise the paddle, and keep it in the air until either you have bought the item, or it has gone beyond where you limit is (and your paddle is now DOWN). Another part to strategy is where you are in the room. Some people like to stand against the back wall, others prefer to be sitting in the front row. This matters little as long as the auctioneer sees you. He will always announce where the bidding is. "I have $200 from the gentleman in the back row, now $250 from the gentleman on my right. The back row is now high bid at $300, do I have any more? SOLD to the gentleman in the last row, Bidder #486."

INTERNET AUCTIONS

Internet auctions are quickly becoming a part of the collecting world. These sales are taking the selling directly from one collector to another. No longer will an item wait in storage at the auction house for months until the sale date. The Internet sales go on daily with countless items in endless categories, with new items being added by collectors as old ones sell. Most sales will run from 3 days to 2 weeks. You have to read all the bidder info, and be willing to stick to whatever you bid. Inspection in person is next to impossible when the sellers are literally worldwide, so do not plan on seeing the item in person before buying, although the seller should be willing to supply pictures before you bid, as well as answer any question that you may have. The payment and shipping information is nearly identical to any other auction, and expect to receive what you bought in the same time frame as in a mail auction.

The biggest surprise in an Internet auction that you have to look out for is that many collectors will wait until literally the last minute to make their bid. Remember, if you want an item, don't be afraid to bid your maximum early on. Computers and computer systems do shut down unexpectedly. There is no reason to bid in little increments over the course of the sale. If you are serious about building a collection, bid seriously. The Internet auction house's computer will execute your bid as others bid against you, until the bid limit has been met. Their computers will not go to your maximum immediately, unless another persons bid is just below the limit you had chosen. Only another person's bid will increase you to your limit during the course of the sale.

Another aspect of Internet auctions is that the possibility of fraud, or theft of your money by the seller. This is not too common, but there are thieves out there. Only trust established dealers with your charge card numbers. If you mail a money order or check, and are ripped off, this is MAIL FRAUD, and the US government post office loves to prosecute the thieves.

SHIPPING

If you choose to be invoiced, or were not physically at the sale, you will be invoiced by mail. The common payment terms are NET NOW. You do not have 30 or 60 days to get the money to them. This is the key reason that you talk to the bid department in advance. If you need the extra time for payment, many times they will make arrangements with you. If you surprise them, they could cancel the sale, sue you, or refuse your right to participate in future auctions.

The timing for receiving goods by paying when you receive the invoice from the auction house in the mail is slow. It could run a week for you to receive the invoice, then a week for it to return with your check. Two weeks for a check to clear, and finally up to four weeks for an item to be shipped out to you. This is a minimum of 2 months from the sale for you to get your new property. In auctions that are strictly done by phone or mail bidding, it is a bit quicker, and usually has a maximum of five weeks for the turn around.

Other disadvantages to not taking the property with you are the costs. Should you choose to have an item shipped, be aware that shipping is not the primary function of the auctioneers. You can expect to have your property to go to an outside professional packer who will charge top dollar for their services. The auction house does this for insurance reasons. Expect a shipping bill form $75-300 for most items that you can carry under one arm. If you can have a friend or relative do the pick up for you, or if you can make arrangements to stop by later in the week, do it. Going with the professional packer will always take longer for you to receive your property.

Overall, auctions are a wonderful way for you to build your collection. Happy bidding!

COLLECTING HAND-COLORED
ORIGINAL COMIC ART
The rewards and dangers associated
with this special interest
by Jerry N. Weist

Collecting original newspaper strip artwork can be an exciting and rewarding experience. Within this unique hobby there exists an aristocracy of originals that have long challenged the veteran collectors in their desire to expand their horizons and dedication to the hunt. These unique original pages are the result of the artist hand-coloring over the original Sunday or Daily page with watercolor or gouache paint. Usually the color work was the result of a special occasion or a private gift or commission. For the purpose of the research and focus of this article for The Original Comic Art Price Guide, attention will be paid to this category for "newspaper strip" artwork though the author acknowledges that the boundaries for these originals extend from the turn of the century through the 1950's and right up to contemporary times, and can extend to other comic art categories.

"The rarest of the rare," "that most unique creature," "the impossible goal that few can attain," these are a few of the many descriptions that one might use to describe the feeling of searching for and finding a hand-colored specialty comic art original. Because most newspaper strip artists in the 1900's through the 1930's never aspired to be painters, and because of the nature of the professional process involved in producing comics for newspapers, the thought of hand-coloring their originals if they were lucky enough to retain any after publication was an almost unknown event. The author remembers speaking with one of the few legends from this era, Burne Hogarth, who likened hand-coloring "Tarzan" Sunday pages to the idea of coloration of classic Black and White movies from the 1930's. "Why would one ever want to do it, when the black and white Sunday page is complete unto itself!" In Mr. Hogarth's own words collectors might be given the other reason for the scarcity of such originals. It took a degree of patience and some special prodding from the grandson of Edgar Rice Burroughs, Danton Burroughs, to bring into the collecting world the few remaining "Tarzan" Sunday pages that were hand-colored specially by Mr. Hogarth in the final three years of his life. Robert Crumb, one of the few contemporary artists who works mostly in black and white, would never consider going back to hand color any original page - other than a cover design.

One of the most famous and highly regarded comic strip artists did, however, on occasion color his original pages. George Herriman hand-colored a very limited number of his Sunday and Daily "Krazy Kat" pages. At the time of this writing collectors and auction houses are still uncovering some of his original watercolors of "Krazy Kat." Not only did Herriman watercolor over previously existing pages for special occasions and gifts, but he produced a small body of original works that stand to this day as masterpieces within our field. Because these colored originals were always rare to begin with, collectors have witnessed the Herriman Sunday page and specialty works moving from the thousands of dollars to the tens of thousands of dollars. A current price for a "Krazy Kat" hand-colored Sunday page or specialty work could range between $20,000 to $40,000 easily. This new range of price has brought forth a problem that did not exist before in this hobby: forgery. There is a growing body of evidence that some people tempted by the prospect of making a greater profit on any given original, have turned to hand-coloring original newspaper strip artwork and marketing it as originally done by the original cartoonist.

Few people are aware of just how many objects of art that reside in major museums are in actuality fakes. A number of as yet unidentified forgeries have already fooled some of the institution's best experts and authorities in their respective fields. With the advent of new and better technologies detection and the investigative powers increase for the museums and collectors. Alas, the new technologies increase the skill of the forger to fool both the experts and experienced institutions as well. If this activity has expanded with the growth of the contemporary and modern art markets are there any lessons to be learned for the newly emerging comic art markets?

The answer is Yes. Not only have the markets for animation and comic art witnessed similar events but each of these new markets have their own particular problems. This article will explore some of these problems and inform both the experienced and inxperienced collector on how they may identify forgeries.

How can the new collector, or for that matter the seasoned veteran collector protect themselves against this new dangerous reality that has entered into the market place for hand-colored originals? In a word, any buyer or collector can protect themselves by staying focused on "provenance." Provenance, or the origin of any given colored original, can usually clear up the cloudy questions surrounding any particular work. With this article the author will provide an outline and give the reader a map that he or she may follow to insure that any decisions they make with this unique collectible will be informed decisions.

George Herriman as an artist presents one of the clearest examples for any collector to study in coming to an understanding of what is "real" and what is "false" with hand colored originals. Before the publication of the excellent book on "Krazy Kat," authored by Patrick McDonnell, Karen O'Connell, and Georgia Riley De Havenon published by Harry N. Abrams, Inc., many people had never seen reproductions of hand-colored "Krazy Kat" strips. Suddenly the reader had some of the most exquisite and more remarkable examples to pour over within the pages of that book. Of the sixteen colored originals that collectors were presented within the Abrams book, not only did each work have impeccable provenance, but also certain characteristics were prominent for the collector to study. With the study of these characteristics lies the key to understanding how best to recognize "original" hand colored works by any comic artist.

Every human being has a tell-tale way of speaking that is unique; and each person also has a different style of hand writing that is unique their own character. As people speak and write, so too will artists behave artistically in a way that is unique to their own character. With Herriman several specific "sign-posts" raise their head for the collector to study. To begin with one should always look for the background color to flow-through the balloons, in other words almost 90% of the time Herriman would color right through the word balloon with the background color where another artist would leave the color outside and the balloon with its original white on the inside. With almost every original Sunday or Daily or specialty work (with possibly the exception of one or two known examples) Herriman would personally inscribe and sign the original to the recipient. So, much like an association copy of an important first edition book inscribed by the author, every hand-colored Herriman original carries with it an inscription and second signature. In some cases the inscription would reveal the reason for the original being gifted, and in many cases the more important originals went to people who are known to have been close friends with Herriman during his lifetime. In almost 70% of the cases with these hand-colored originals there is sun-fading or a bleached out quality to the color. Because these originals were cherished by their owners, they were framed and hung upon the wall, and for years were exposed to some UV light. Because of this fading many times a given original can be taken out of its original frame, and there is a small original outline of color that was either matted over, or framed over - and the original brilliant color stands out for the eye to see. Not only did Herriman take the time to color these originals, but in some special cases he built and painted original frames. There is a unique use of primary colors (reds pushed right up to primary greens, etc.) that will usually cause the experienced observer to know immediately that this is a frame created by Herriman himself (see color example in the color section of this edition of the Price Guide for an example of Herriman's framing technique and colors.) and not the work of another artist. Earth colors, browns, muted and ochre yellows, faint blues and shades of pink, were favorite color uses by this artist. There is a quality of very delicate, deliberate and sophisticated knowledge of using watercolor for emotional lighting effects. Unlike other artists who might follow the original Sunday color scheme (and one should remember that when many of the handcolored "Krazy Kat" Sundays were done, there was NO colored Sunday sections, thus the originals were printed in black and white only.) Herriman was apt to take his own path when he colored a given Sunday. Sometimes he would rarely (one more than one occasion) use a linear bordering device within the panels that would be repeated upon the matte or frame (as with the published example in this edition).

If any collector were to view a hand-colored "Krazy Kat" Sunday page that had bright primary colors, and these colors did not intrude into the balloons, and the work was not inscribed to any specific individual, then said original should become suspect as forged. Herriman's personal style of hand-lettering each page is very, very difficult to copy. Also by using either a "known" name or faked name on the inscription the forger would allow the buyer to research the provenance, and possibly come up with an answer that is not positive for the given "original" being offered for sale.

The greatest tool however that would aid any prospective buyer is experience. If one takes the time to study the coloring techniques and style that Herriman used on the confirmed color originals, it should be fairly easy to spot a forgery. Another signal to look for would be if the price seems too low, or the original offered is given a deadline like "you have to buy this in 24 hours or the seller will change his mind!" Quite often the pressure tactic will allow a questionable seller to force the novice or anxious buyer to make a hasty and often times bad decision! Any reputable seller will allow a reasonable period of time for study and decisions, and will stand 100% behind provenance and offer the buyer a full return privilege. So the perfect example of when not to buy here might be a poorly developed photo (that is not very large) that is sent to the buyer, the original is available from another country than the USA, where the laws might not be enforceable or known to the buyer, and there is a time pressure put upon the decision making process - however its available for a great price! Indeed! Moving faked color originals from America to France, or from America to Spain and back to the USA again allows the forger to protect themselves somewhat against prosecution by the law. It's much harder for any individual or group to sue for damages from country to country. Are there known examples of George Herriman's Krazy Kat Sunday pages that are believed by experts to be forged? Sadly, the answer is Yes. In one specific case the buyer took in a given original for over $20,000 and is now faced with owning a "marked" and "known" forgery.

Some other examples of known information for other famous strips are following. In the case of Harold Foster, with the exception of two originals, there are no known "Price Valiant" or "Tarzan" Sunday pages colored by Mr. Foster himself. Many of the examples surviving of "Price Valiant" Sunday pages were colored by Syndicate artists for the engravers at the printing plant, or as special gifts. While beautiful in their coloration they are not by Foster. The two known examples have the following provenance and history. The Tarzan page for January 1, 1933 (pictured in the color section of this edition) was requested from Harold Foster by none other than Edgar Rice Burroughs himself. This original hung in Mr. Burroughs private offices (and thus suffered fairly serious UV damage) for years, and then was gifted to his son John Colman Burroughs. It is the only known "Tarzan" colored by the artist himself. The only "Prince Valiant" known to have been colored by Foster carries a personal inscription to an individual who was in the hospital at the time of the gifting, and carries all of the tell-tale stylistic uses of watercolor that Foster was known to use in other non-strip original watercolor works.

So what's the positive side to all of these problems connected with forgeries in hand colored comic strip pages? The answer is simple. Don't let a few rotten apples spoil what has become one of the most rewarding parts of strip collecting. The author himself considers George Herriman one of the premier American cartoonists, and owns a hand colored "Krazy Kat" Sunday page that remains one of the most prized of any originals within his entire collection. Not only do these originals represent blue-chip investments, they are thrilling to track down and own and can become works of art that are enjoyed for a lifetime.

Beside the problems inherent with hand colored newspaper Sunday pages that might be forged, another area of great abuse over the past few years has been with animation cels. For further logical instructional guidelines the author has included information about animation cels even though this guide has dropped the animation section listing from this present volume. To the degree that lower prices within the comic market have kept the forgers hand to a minimum, however a $60,000 dollar price tag for a single animation cel original or a $7,000 dollar price for a simple ink original by Frank Frazetta will tempt the hand of any skilled forger. Historically there is very little if any activity within the science fiction and pulp art markets of forged originals, however there is an abundance of restored paintings and re-created classic works, most are properly identified. Within the animation market the range of abuse is very possibly wider and across the board. With animation the collector runs the risk of encountering faked pencil sketches to falsely rendered or improperly placed backgrounds to cel originals, to even improperly or unidentified re-paints to the cel overlay colors themselves! The sheer range of possibility for mistreatment to any cel original is as complex and broad as the artform itself. In the case of the recently released special Disney auctions at Sotheby's one need only consult the catalogue to compare backgrounds for the one-of-a-kind cels prepared by Disney artists for these special auctions, which include the highly successful *Lion King* and *Who Framed Roger Rabbit* auctions. The salient point here is that Disney only made the special one-of-a-kind cels for their more recent computer generated films and the auction releases represent the only originals. The films that are included on their list include *The Hunchback of Notre Dame, Beauty & the Beast* (the first film to use this new technology), *The Lion King* and recently *Hercules*.

For older cel originals the possible problems are the following. One should first look to the background for possible abuses. Is the scene itself a proper match with the foreground figure? By using a VCR to view the original film, anyone with some patience and the remote-stop auction button can check for accuracy. A simple example would be any cel from *Snow White*. By using a video tape, TV, and stop motion the collector can come to the exact moment of the cel being considered for purchase. Is the figure a proper match to the background when the evil witch hands the poisoned apple to Snow White? With older and more scarce cartoon cels, or cels to shorts that no longer are known to exist, it is harder to verify positioning. Remember that the rarer the cel, or the older and more obscure and thus more expensive, the greater the temptation for anyone wanting to make a profit on matching parts that did not originally belong together. Sometimes a simple request for provenance from the seller, or questions raised with a knowledgeable dealer or collector will reveal possible problems with an older or more expensive cel. Another simple test is taking any cel in question and putting it under inspection in a dark room with a black light. This test method often reveals surface touch ups or changes of color and replaced color to the figure.

Collectors should always question specially signed cels by Walt Disney, since studio artists are known through the years to have signed his name with personal notes upon hundreds of black and white and cel originals. In most cases "studio signatures" do not retard any originals value, and are an excepted reality to the animation market - but only experienced Disney staff, auction consultants, and long time dealers and experienced collectors know how to identify the real Walt Disney signature versus the studio signature.

There are additionally new technologies and advances in photo-copiers that add to the possible list of problems in collecting animation art originals. Beware of simple black and white or monochrome cel overlays to complex or deeply developed backgrounds. Photo-copiers can now duplicate black and white and color images on clear mylar. This acetate or mylar can then be "yellowed" or "painted" and "cut-and punched-out" to look like original cels. Again, close inspection or black light observations can reveal a forgery.

There is verification within collectors circles that large amounts of original studio animation paper were released within the market from 1970 through the 1980's. Have these blank pages been expertly filled with pencil drawings? It is entirely possible, and if the forger were well versed in pencil work, and utilized a good light table along with a source of original drawings it would be extremely hard to spot forgeries. This probable problem within animation art collecting is controlled only by having the best provenance possible from the buyer.

Though the possibility for tampering and forgeries exist within the animation market and comics market new collectors should keep these problems within a proper perspective. Both the Baseball Card market, and the Rock & Roll collectors markets have had their share of forged signatures, and improper presentation. At this stage of any advanced collectibles market the high prices bring with them people who are willing to take advantage of newer and inexperienced collectors.

To review the fundamental theme of this article, any new collector is advised to take the time to study throroughly any new area where they may begin to want to collect and spend serious money. By reading all possible sources of historical information, by familiarizing themselves with the artwork involved from paitent observation, and by taking the time to talk with as great a number of professional people within the business, the novice protects themself against serious mistakes.

THE SUPERMAN DAILY STRIP No. 1:
The Complete Story
by Roger Hill

One of the most interesting things about serving as art-advisor to the Sotheby's Comic Book and Art auctions is that it allows me to come into contact with a lot of tremendous artwork. Just the visual experience of it alone is usually enough to satisfy most people's collecting curiosities. Not so in my case. Fortunately or unfortunately (however you look at it) I have always been "stricken" with an attitude of over-curiosity about certain pieces of comic book or comic strip art that I have come into contact with, that I determine have great historical significance attached to them. I have always enjoyed researching artwork and the artists themselves very much. During the cataloging for Sotheby's 1994 auction, it was my good fortune to inspect what truly can be called one of the most important pieces of comic art I have ever encountered, or had the opportunity to research and write about: the three-panel remnants of a Superman daily newspaper strip, written by Jerry Siegel and drawn by Joe Shuster.

For many years the "myths" or "misconceptions" about this particular work of art have run rampant through the community of Fandom and have become distorted beyond belief. When I first heard about these three Superman panels in the late 1970's (at the time the art changed hands from Joe Shuster to a private collector) I was told the art - depicting the origin of Superman - included the actual panels used in *Action Comics* No. 1, dated June, 1938. I remember being quite surprised at the time, but had no real reason to doubt the validity of such information since it came directly from one of the top dealers of original comic art in the U.S. The dealer, I might add, had actually seen the original, and held it in his hands.

Over the next fifteen years many rumors emerged surrounding this daily. It has, at one time or another, been referred to as:

1) The Superman origin panels that were printed in *Action Comics* No. 1 (June 1938).
2) The Superman origin panels from *Action Comics* No. 1, reworked/revised and published in *Superman* No. 1 (Summer 1939).
3) The Superman origin panels from the first published daily newspaper strip (January 1939).
4) The Superman origin panels from an unpublished version of the first daily newspaper strip (date unknown).

No doubt there are probably a few other rumored descriptions that I've forgotten about.

My research on this very early Superman daily began when the art was consigned for the 1994 Sotheby's auction. During that period of time I spent well over a hundred hours studying every piece of published reference or documentation written about the creation of Superman and this daily that I could get my hands on. I also traveled to New York City twice and on both occasions spent at least an hour closely examining the actual original art panels. The three panels are very interesting, and revealed to me information not previously realized. It was a great learning experience, to say the least, and during that period of research I formulated some opinions or theories about that historic daily that should now be shared with the public.

Superman Daily No. 1, as it appeared at Sotheby's 1994 comic art auction. The missing panel with question mark design. Superman and all characters related are TM and © DC Comics, National Periodical Publications and Time Warner Enterprises, Worldwide.

The two best sources I found in doing research was Superman historian Tom Andrea's in-depth interview with Siegel and Shuster, first published in *Nemo* magazine in August, 1983; then later reprinted in the 1988 *Overstreet Comic Book Price Guide*. Also, Harry Matetsky's 1988 book titled *The Adventures of Superman Collecting* was very helpful, as was the article titled "Up, Up and Awa-a-y!" by John Kobler that appeared in the *Saturday Evening Post* magazine on June 21, 1941.

Carefully considering the four different rumors that I listed which have circulated about this daily strip art, are any of them correct? In my opinion, No - none of the above! My conclusion is that the true answer, or proper description should be a combination of rumors No. 1 and No. 4. It would read as follows:

"The unused origin panels from the first Superman daily newspaper strip, missing two panels that were cut-out and possibly used in the pasted-up, printed version in *Action Comics* No. 1 (June, 1938). Date of the art: 1934."

Let's look at some of the simple and logical facts that have been there to recognize and decipher for some time now. Then you be the judge. I do believe the one main problem that has continued to create confusion and varying opinions about this daily is that the many different sources of published evidence have never been brought together in a single presentation or article. Along with the comics, the art itself, and quotes from Siegel and Shuster, there is also supportive evidence from notarized documents, written and signed by Joe Shuster, that accompanied this daily, when it came to Sotheby's auction in June of 1994.

Superman Daily No. 1, again with the missing panel. Superman and all characters related are TM and © DC Comics, National Periodical Publications and Time Warner Enterprises, © Worldwide.

Most fans, collectors and historians realize that Superman made his official comic book debut in *Action Comics* No. 1, dated June, 1938, and eventually became one of the most successful creations in comic book history. What many people don't yet realize is that the initial creation of this colorfully-clad American Icon actually dates back to early 1933. At that time, writer Jerry Siegel and artist Joe Shuster produced a story called "The Reign of Superman" and published it in Siegel's mimeographed fanzine titled *Science-Fiction*. Although this early effort is crude and depicts Superman as a villain, it didn't take long for the two teenagers from Cleveland, Ohio to realize that Superman (as a hero rather than a villain) might make a better comic character. A few months later, Siegel and Shuster prepared a comic book version of the new character called "The Superman." This version featured a strong-man action hero, wearing a T-shirt and pants, and acclaimed to be "A genius in intellect," "A Hercules in strength," and "A nemesis to wrongdoers." It was submitted to a publishing company who had agreed to publish it, but then changed their mind. This caused Joe Shuster - in a fit of disappointment - to destroy the originals. Later on, Siegel decided he'd like to do Superman as a newspaper strip.

Siegel: "That occurred to me in late 1934, when I decided that I'd like to do Superman as a newspaper strip. I approached Joe about it, and he was enthusiastic about the possibility. I was up late one night, and more and more ideas kept coming to me, and I kept writing out several weeks of syndicate scripts for the proposed newspaper strip. When morning came, I had written several weeks of material, and I dashed over to Joe's place and showed it to him."

Shuster: "That was one very important day in our lives. We just sat down, and I worked straight through. I think I had brought in some sandwiches to eat, and we worked all day long."

Siegel: "That night when all the thoughts were coming to me, the concept came to me that Superman could have a duel identity, and that in one of his identities he could be meek and mild, as I was, and wear glasses, the way I do."

Shuster: "In the third version Superman wore sandals laced halfway up the calf. You can still see this on the cover of *Action Comics* No. 1, though they were covered over in red to look like boots when the comic was printed."

Little did Siegel and Shuster realize that over the next few years, Superman would be rejected by practically every newspaper syndicate in the country; in some cases two or three times by the same syndicate. Even in the face of continuing criticism and rejection, the boys from Cleveland struggled along, hoping for acceptance of their "Dr. Occult" feature, first published in *New Fun Comics* No. 6, dated October, 1935. This was followed by "Federal Men" in *New Comics* No. 2, dated January, 1936. In late 1936, they sold two more features to National (DC) Publications called "Slam Bradley" and "Spy," both of which showed up in *Detective Comics* No. 1, dated March 1937.

Siegel: "Slam Bradley was a dry run for Superman. Superman had already been created, and we didn't want to give away the Superman idea; but we just couldn't resist putting into Slam Bradley some of the slambang stuff which we knew would be in Superman if and when we got Superman launched."

The history books have already documented various viewpoints and stories related to the roles played by Sheldon Mayer, Max C. Gaines, and Harry Donenfeld and Vincent Sullivan in the series of events that led to the acceptance of Superman for *Action Comics* No. 1. Their involvement is of equal importance.

Here's the way I believe it happened: Sheldon Mayer was an editor and production chief working at the McClure Syndicate in New York City. His boss was Max Gaines, an interpreter of the early four-color comic book, a man recognized today as the "originator of American comic books," having packaged and published the first newspaper strip reprint comic in 1934 titled *Famous Funnies*. As a production and advertising executive, Gaines' job was to keep the presses rolling at the McClure Syndicate, usually with contracts from the Dell Publishing Company. The Superman daily strips by Siegel and Shuster were sitting in the McClure offices in late 1937, had already been rejected twice by company officials (including Gaines) and were about to go down for the third and final count.

Harry Donenfeld was the co-owner of a printing plant who had only recently taken up the role of "comic book publisher." Donenfeld had successfully launched *Detective Comics* in March of 1937, giving him a total of three successful comic titles now being produced out of his DC (Detective Comics) offices located at 480 Lexington Avenue. Based on the well-known pulp publishing theory of those times that it was almost as cheap to print four comics as it was to do three, Donenfeld had decided to bring out a new ten cent monthly - to be called *Action Comics* - and was having trouble finding new material for the first issue. Vincent Sullivan had been named as editor for *Action*, working under Donenfeld, and was responsible for overseeing the material that would make-up that first issue. Unbeknown to these four gentlemen, they were all about to play an intricate part in the series of events that would lead to the debut of Superman.

Due to an enthusiastic nudging from Sheldon Mayer (who liked the Superman feature) Gaines took a closer look at the already rejected Superman strips and sent them over to DC for consideration. The McClure Syndicate was already handling the printing of *Detective Comics* for Donenfeld and Gaines knew that if the new *Action Comics* title was successful, he'd probably land a new contract for printing it. Gaines didn't realize until much later that he had let the hottest property in comic book history slip through his hands. Meanwhile, over at the DC offices, *Action Comics* editor Vincent Sullivan was busy putting together the first issue and was shown the Superman samples. He liked what he saw in the character, but knew the daily strip format wouldn't work in the restricted comic book size. Donenfeld was somewhat apprehensive about such a fantastic character and reportedly, later on, upon seeing the cover art for *Action Comics* No. 1 (depicting Superman lifting a car up in the air) became worried that nobody would believe it; that it was ridiculous. Without great enthusiasm, Donenfeld told Siegel and Shuster to proceed and create a thirteen page Superman story since the daily strips were not the correct size. The boys from Cleveland set to work immediately. Joe Shuster was a very meticulous artist, and with a pressing deadline looking over their shoulders, he and Jerry decided to cut the strips into panels and paste them up on a board the size of the required comic book page dimensions.

Shuster: "*Action* No. 1 was taken directly from the newspaper strip: It was pasted up. They were in a rush to meet the deadline on the first issue. Everything happened very fast: they made the decision to publish it and said to us, 'Just go out and turn out thirteen pages based on your strip.' It was a rush job and one of the things I like least to do is to rush my artwork. I'm too much of a perfectionist to do anything which is mediocre. This only solution Jerry and I could come up with was to cut up the strips into panels and paste the panels on a sheet the size of the page. If some panels were too long, we would shorten them - cut them off - if they were too short, we would extend them. You see, some of the panels were extended to fit the size of the page; it was quite an art job."

As history has recorded, three issues of *Action Comics* came out before the first signs of success were seen. Sales began to climb with issue No. 4 and - after a newsstand survey was conducted by DC - the results showed that "The Man of Tomorrow," Superman, was a smash hit with the kids. Succeeding issues began to sell out and within a year *Action Comics* leaped to a circulation of 900,000 copies a month. Predictably, Gaines got the contract to print the new comic title, and within a few months the McClure Syndicate negotiated with Donenfeld, to handle the newspaper rights. On January 16, 1939 the daily *Superman* strip debuted in four newspapers, followed by the Sunday page feature on November 5, and within two years over 300 daily and 90 Sunday newspapers were carrying the feature, with a combined circulation of over twenty million. Donenfeld followed up quickly to reader demand by issuing a new comic title filled with Superman stories. *Superman* No. 1 hit the stands during the Summer of 1939, and by 1941 enjoyed a bimonthly circulation of 1,300,000 copies.

Now lets take a close look at the Superman daily that was consigned to Sotheby's 1994 Comic Art auction. By its markings, and contents, many people feel this to be the first Superman daily ever created by Siegel and Shuster. It was never published and until recently the daily was thought to be missing only one panel. Further research now shows positive evidence that the daily is missing two panels. What's humorous about all this is that the proof of two missing panels has for some time now been right there in front of us; we just didn't see it. But more about that later. The three panels remaining in the daily consist of panels Nos. 1, 4, and 5. When put together, they measure a combined length of 14¼ inches by a height of 5 inches. The border areas remaining around the existing pieces measure between 1 inch to 1¼ inch wide on all sides, except on the right side of panel 1, and the left side of panel 4, where the art was trimmed closely during the removal of panels 2 and 3. In the border, just above panel 1 is neatly lettered in pencil "*Superman* No. 1." In the bottom right-hand corner of panel 4 is letter in ink "No. 1." Just above panel 5, lettered in pencil is "by Jerome Siegel and Joe Shuster." On the back side of panel 1, neatly printed in pencil is "Jerome Siegel, 10622 Kimberly Ave., Cleveland, Ohio." The art is rendered with pen and ink on "Uni-shade" art paper. Uni-shade paper was actually developed and produced by the Craftint Company, located in Siegel and Shuster's hometown of Cleveland, Ohio during the early 1930's. It involved a process where by the artist applied a chemical/developer to the paper which would bring out, or highlight, a dot-pattern embedded in the paper itself. This dot-pattern added a shading effect to the final art, allowing the artist to create "painted" panels of soft tonal shades in contrast to the usual restriction of black and white.

In order to fully understand the history behind the creation of this paper and the Superman daily, I contacted the Grafix Art Systems Company of Cleveland, Ohio, who today are the only manufacturers of the paper now called "Duo-shade." I spoke with Mr. Larry Katz who is president, CEO and owner of the company, and who (after hearing my request for information) was most helpful. In fact, Mr. Katz informed me that his uncle had known Siegel and Shuster at Glenville High School during the early 1930's. He also told me that the original company called Craftint had started in business around 1932 as a supplier of many different art supplies. The dot-pattern paper was originally conceived by a chemist whose wife worked as an illustrator for one of the newspapers there in Cleveland. This chemist (whose name appears to be lost to history) worked at the Craftint Company and the first dot-pattern paper he created was called "Uni-shade." Sometime during the 1940's, Craftint introduced another, more sophisticated version which offered a double dot-pattern effect that came with two different chemicals/developers. This new paper became known as "Duo-tone." Duo-tone actually allowed the artist to capture three different dot-patterns of shade in his work. One chemical brought out a light shade pattern. Another chemical brought out a dark shade pattern. The combination of both chemicals brought out both shade patterns creating a darker shade yet. Sometime during the 1950's, after Craftint had shifted directions and became more of a manufacturer of "paint-by-number" art kits and other merchandise, they went out of business and were bought-out by another company. The chemist who had invented Uni-shade and Duo-Tone paper apparently held the original patents and in 1963 started his own art supply business under the name of Ohio Graphic Arts Inc. Then later, the company changed hands and is known today as Grafix Art Systems. After sifting through some old papers, Mr. Katz informed me that he has a reference or document in his files referring to a patent application for Uni-shade being filed in 1935. This brings up a good question that must be asked: How could Jerry Siegel say that the first Superman daily newspaper strips were created in 1934, when Uni-shade didn't get patented until sometime in 1935?

Further research indicates that even though Uni-shade may not have been patented until 1935, several well known newspaper strip artists had tested the new paper before then. Even the great Noel Sickles, who took over the "Scorchy Smith" syndicated strip in late 1934 from John Terry, experimented with "Ben-day" (another form of shaded paper) and "Uni-shade" during his first two weeks of dailies. Sickles' first strip appeared on January 14, 1935, and since the normal syndicate flow-time between the time the art is created and being published usually runs a few months, they must have been drawn in late 1934. There are early examples by other artists who experimented with the new process as well. So whether or not Uni-shade was patented in 1935, it was available in 1934.

The Superman No. 1 daily is accompanied by three notarized statements of authenticity prepared by Joe Shuster, including one document where Shuster stated "these three drawings, the original artwork, are the first daily strips created by Joseph Shuster and Jerry Siegel of the character known as Superman," duly witnessed and notarized in Los Angeles County, California, on August 29, 1978, at the time the art changed hands from Shuster to a private collector. Some questions have been raised about these documents and about Joe Shuster's memory of this daily. It has even been suggested that perhaps Joe was coerced into signing a document (prepared by others) that he couldn't even read due to his failing eyesight. While it is true that Joe's eyes were pretty bad during the latter part of his life, that question doesn't hold water, since after all, this document I quoted from was hand-written by Shuster. Also, the artist's eyes couldn't have been *that* bad since he was still able to do comic cover recreations and specialty drawings of Superman as late as 1978.

I have already presented the quote from Jerry Siegel stating that in late 1934 he conceived the idea of the daily newspaper strips which Shuster then produced. One opinion recently aired said the daily could not have been produced in 1934 because Joe Shuster was very poor in those "early" days, was known to use cheap paper to work on, and couldn't have afforded to buy the more expensive Uni-shade paper. Based on this assumption, the conclusion was that Joe Shuster couldn't have afforded the Uni-shade paper until sometime after the success of *Action Comics* No. 1 in 1938. This seems to be one of the most far-fetched assumptions I have ever heard concerning this daily, but let's consider it anyway. It is known that when Shuster was a young teenager during the late 1920's, he was apt to draw and sketch on whatever paper he could get his hands on, including the backs of wallpaper and calendars. But let's not forget that by the time Joe entered high-school, he had already held several jobs and later on *was* able to afford night classes at the John Huntington Art School in Cleveland, at a cost of ten cents a lesson. Now if art classes could be had for ten cents a lesson before the Wall Street crash of 1929, just how expensive could a sheet of Uni-shade paper have been during the depths of the depression in 1934? Perhaps a nickel a sheet? Maybe even ten cents? How do we know Shuster didn't pick up a remnant of Uni-shade out of a scrap-bin in one of the art supply stores? Or for that matter, who's to say Shuster didn't personally know the chemist who developed the paper for Craftint. There are a lot of other possibilities as well.

But the other important point to remember here is that by 1934 Siegel and Shuster had already been submitting various other strips to different syndicates since 1933. Even though these strips were also rejected, wouldn't it seem logical that by 1934, they had gained considerable knowledge about the importance of presentation to a syndicate? I think it is reasonable to assume that by 1934 they knew that if they were going to be taken seriously, in a competitive market, they could not submit strip samples drawn on the backside of wall-paper. It is commonly believed, however, that most of the early daily strips created by Siegel and Shuster during this period were actually drawn on regular art paper with straight "pen and ink" technique. After all, we already know for a fact that those daily strips were cut-up and used in *Action Comics* No. 1, and none of them show any traces of Uni-shade dot-patterns.

Perhaps the most reasonable explanation as to why Joe Shuster prepared this first daily on Uni-shade is that he wanted to demonstrate an advanced degree of versatility to the syndicates when submissions were made. One other small note of importance should be made about this daily. When Tom Andrea's interview with Siegel and Shuster was reprinted in the 1988 *Overstreet Comic Book Price Guide*, this daily was reproduced with a caption that was partially incorrect. A portion of that descriptive caption stated: "Because he could not afford Craftint paper, Shuster simulated the effect by using a toothbrush to flick ink dots on the figures of Superman and the buildings of Krypton." Let's set the record straight once and for all. This daily was executed on "legitimate" Uni-shade/Craftint paper, having now been closely examined and verified by several knowledgeable people in the field. I do know that Shuster occasionally used the "toothbrush" method to create a shaded/stipple effect in his work, as did many other artists in those days; however, that technique was not used on this daily.

Finally, here is one of the most important statements that Jerry Siegel ever made concerning the No. 1 Superman daily, and the cut and paste-up of dailies that went into *Action Comics* No. 1 in late 1937. I should also mention that it wasn't until I read this statement for the third time, that I fully understood what Siegel was saying. Up to that moment of realization, I still thought (as the rumors had always said) that the daily was only missing one panel. This Siegel quote comes from Harry Matetsky's Superman book, and was printed just opposite a reproduction of the daily.

> Siegel: "I rewrote what had been the fourth panel in Superman daily strip No. 1 and extended it into panels 4, 5, and 6 on the first page of "Superman" in *Action* No. 1. This made it necessary for Joe to create three new drawings to replace that deleted panel 4. Joe had previously drawn a scene of Superman in costume, out racing a train, in that strip No. 1. At my instruction, he redrew the scene so that Superman was, in the newly drawn panels, attired in his civilian garments instead of his costume...because I did not want to have him seen in his colorful action costume until after he had adopted the alter ego of Superman. We inserted two new panels on the first page of the comic book, panels 8 and 9, in order to fill in the remaining space on the page. Also, on page one of *Action Comics*, Joe did not use the similar first panel he had previously drawn in strip No. 1. Instead, he redrew the panel, lowering the caption from the top down to the bottom of the redrawn panel. Panel 7 on page one was also redrawn, and we created the final promotional ad panel to fill in the space left on the page after the material from the transposed four weeks of daily strips ran out. Joe also designed and drew the now world-famous Superman logo and added our byline."

Granted, you might need a road map to fully understand what Siegel had explained, but if you happen to own a copy of *Action Comics* No. 1, or the oversized reprint edition issued by D.C in 1974, it's simple to understand. What I had failed to realize during my first two readings of this statement was that Siegel clearly refers to the Superman daily panel (depicting Superman out racing the train) as "panel 4." I, along with apparently many others had known exactly what panel Siegel was describing, but had missed the significance of him referring to it as panel 4. Obviously, this told us that the No. 1 Superman "origin" daily was a "five" panel strip to begin with. Aside from explaining why panel 4 wasn't used, he also clearly tells us why the daily panel 1 could not be used; Joe had to redraw it to lower the caption from top to bottom, leaving room for him to design and letter the new Superman logo, plus ad the Siegel and Shuster byline at the top. He also tells us that panel 5 of the daily (depicting Superman standing over the cityscape) was redrawn for *Action* No. 1, but doesn't explain why. One logical reason might be because in the Uni-shade daily panel version, Superman looks a bit too old to have just reached maturity (age 18 to 21?) and started a career of leaping buildings and fighting criminals. The depiction of Superman in panel 7 of *Action* No. 1 appears to make him look about ten years younger. In the redrawing of this panel it's interesting to note that Shuster eliminated Superman's feet from extending down into the lower narration portion, and also removed the sandals that were laced half way up the calf. Perhaps all these elements combined led to the redrawing of this panel. Siegel didn't mention anything about the "Uni-shade" dot-pattern being a problem. We may never know the true answer.

Siegel's statement also told me something that I have not found documented in any other source of historical reference to *Action Comics* No. 1 or Superman. He reveals that "four weeks" (one month) of daily newspaper strips existed, and were transposed into the thirteen pages in *Action* No. 1. Another fascinating "historical" anecdote that can be clearly understood from this statement is that Siegel reveals to us exactly which panels in *Action Comics* No. 1 were entirely new drawings. In this case, he notes panels 1, 4, 5, 6, 7, 8, 9 and the final promotional ad panel located at the bottom of page 13; the last page of the story. By Siegel identifying these panels as being new drawings in *Action* No. 1, he has inadvertently told us exactly which panels were not redrawn, thus, taken directly from the cut-up dailies.

I now draw your attention to panels 2 and 3 of the page one origin depicted in *Action* No. 1. If you have not yet read all the text on this page, or on the three existing panels from Superman No. 1 daily, you might want to do that now. Before our readers start counting panels and comparing things, I should point out that all panels on the first page of *Action* No. 1 are numbered, except for the slender panel of text located right after panel 6. While Siegel didn't identify this panel as being re-lettered, a comparison to the Superman daily No. 1 reveals assuredly that it was re-lettered, and widened slightly. Upon finishing *your* comparison of panels between the No. 1 daily and *Action Comics* No. 1, plus reading the origin text similarities between the two, would it not make perfect sense to conclude that panels 2 and 3 of the comic are perhaps the same panels 2 and 3 missing from the daily?

When I first theorized this possibility I decided to reconstruct the No. 1 Superman daily as it might have looked when first created by Joe Shuster. It was not as simple a process as some might think. It wasn't just a matter of slipping panels 2 and 3 from *Action Comics* No. 1 into the space between panels 1 and 4 of the daily. I knew first I would have to determine the "space" factor between these daily panels, assuming they originally had spaces between them. Based on panels 4 and 5 of the daily, there had been no space left between the two, other than the slender panel of text that separated them. And that's not really a space. I prematurely concluded that there had been no spaces between any of the panels; that they had just been butted-up next to each other. Later, when I thought to re-examine the Xerox copies

Action Comics No. 1 (June 1938, origin page). Superman and all characters related are TM and © DC Comics, National Periodical Publications and Time Warner Enterprises, © Worldwide.

I had of the No. 1 daily, I noticed something of great importance. As previously mentioned in my description of the daily, I had noted the border areas on the right side of panel 1 and the left side of panel 4 as being trimmed closely. While that is a true statement, there is still ⅟₁₆ of an inch of excess paper located just beyond the black vertical inked border line on the left side of panel 4. There is half as much excess located beyond the vertical border line on the right side of panel 1. But there *was* just enough to determine that the top and bottom horizontal border lines had not extended past these two panels, and therefore, had never connected with the missing two panels. That told me there was originally spaces between panels 1 and 2 and between panels 3 and 4, but I still had no idea of what that space measurement had been between panels 2 and 3, if indeed there even was one. Since panel 2 was another one of the slender panels, with mostly text in it, I figured it had probably butted-up next to panel 3.

So I spent more time studying the origin page in *Action Comics* No. 1 concentrating on the space between panels 2 and 3, looking for any kind of evidence that would tell me whether or not those two panels had originally been butted-up next to each other. While concentrating so hard on that aspect of it, I was failing to see the overall picture of differential spacing that is so apparent on this page. It finally dawned on me that the vertical spaces between all panels on this first page in *Action* No. 1 were of equal proportions with approximately ⅛ of an inch between them, except for the space between panels 2 and 3 which measured only ¹⁄₁₆ of an inch. When you think about it, it makes perfect logical sense that Shuster would not have gone to the trouble of separating panels 2 and 3 if there was already a small space between them. My conclusion is that with the deadline pressure he was under at the time, he didn't want to bother with it, so he just cut both panels out as one complete piece and pasted them down. Furthermore, if the Uni-shade dot-pattern presented a problem to reproduction, I believe Shuster could have dealt with that problem quickly. There is not a lot shading in these two panels and it would have been easier and faster for him to have used white-out over the shaded areas and replaced it with black ink lines, rather than redrawing both panels entirely. Also, we should consider this: if panels 2 and 3 were new drawings in *Action* No. 1, why would Shuster not have drawn them to a more correct size that would have allowed the spacing between them to be the same as all the other spacing on this page?

Based on this hypothesis, I proceeded to do a Xerox blow-up of panels 2 and 3 from the comic to a height of 5 inches, matching the size of the daily original art. Naturally, during the blow-up, the space between panels 2 and 3 increased to a measurement of ⅛ of an inch. Based on that measurement, I was able to properly space the other panels and complete the reconstruction of the entire daily. Assuming my theory was correct about this daily, I was not able to take it a step further, and blow-up the entire origin page from *Action* No. 1, to the same size configuration. Theoretically this gave me the exact dimensions of the comic formatted pages that Siegel and Shuster worked on during the cut and paste-up process used on *Action Comics* No. 1. This dimension measured 11 x 15 and ⅜ inches; not quite twice-up (13 x 18).

One final element to consider here is the first twelve published Superman daily newspaper strips. The first strip appeared on January 16, 1939, beginning the first expanded version of the origin of Superman, and concluding with the twelfth daily. As we already learned from Siegel's statement, the early version of the dailies (created in late 1934) consisting of four

Reconstructed "Superman Daily" No. 1. Superman and all characters related are TM and © DC Comics, National Periodical Publications and Time Warner Enterprises, © Worldwide.

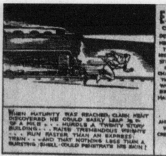

"Superman" Daily No. 12. Superman and all characters related are TM and © DC Comics, National Periodical Publications, and Time Warner Enterprises, © Worldwide.

weeks worth, were cut-up and pasted-up for *Action* No. 1. Looking at the twelfth daily from this second series of dailies, it's suspiciously similar to panels seen in *Action* No. 1; only using a straight pen and ink technique, how do we know this isn't the first true Superman origin daily, created as part of that first four weeks worth back in 1934? The answer is simple. If that were true, then why wouldn't Shuster have cut up and used the panels from this daily in *Action* No. 1? The fact is... he didn't. Close inspection reveals panels 2, 3 and 4 are all new drawings, based on panels 3, 6 and 7 from *Action Comics* No. 1. Obviously, this daily didn't exist in late 1934, nor in late 1937. If there was a straight pen and ink version of the first Superman origin daily, why wasn't it ever used in *Action* No. 1 or the daily strips that followed?

My final conclusion is that this daily is the first one created by Joe Shuster for various reasons I have pointed out:

1.) It depicts the origin of the character.

2.) It is lettered on the daily - "No. 1."

3.) The art belonged originally to Joe Shuster.

4.) The notarized statement from Joe Shuster says it is the first.

5.) Jerry Siegel has referred to it as the first one and has stated why two out of three panels weren't used in *Action Comics* No. 1.

As far as my theories go relating to the use of two panels from this daily in *Action Comics* No. 1: That's exactly what it is, just a theory. I don't think at this point, that anyone could prove either way what actually happened back in late 1937. Joe Shuster and Jerry Siegel have passed away. So ask yourself the same question that I did at this point: if panels 2 and 3 didn't go into *Action Comics* No. 1, then why were they cut out of the daily to begin with, and where did they go?

Superman No. 1 (Summer 1939), page 2. Superman and all characters are TM and © DC Comics, National Periodical Publications and Time Warner Enterprises, © Worldwide.

Advance Preview-Introductory "Superman" Sunday Page (October 1939). Superman and all characters related are TM and © DC Comics, Nationall Periodical Publications and Time Warner Enterprises, © Worldwide.

Postscript:

In light of additional rumors and confusion about panels being reused or redrawn between the comics, dailies and Sunday pages, the following facts have been verified through close examination and comparison of *Action Comics* No. 1, *Superman* No. 1, the first twelve published *Superman* dailies, the advance-preview-introductory Sunday newspaper strip and the first Sunday newspaper strip. These facts are listed in the correct order of the arts' first appearance.

1.) *Action Comics* No. 1 (June, 1938) - panels 8 and 9 were later cut-out or statted and used in the advance-preview-introductory Sunday newspaper page as panels 5.

2.) TWELFTH "SUPERMAN" DAILY STRIP (January 1939) - All four panels in this daily are new drawings, with panels 2, 3 and 4 closely resembling panels in *Action* No. 1. Panels 1, 2 and 3 in this daily were later cut-out or statted and used in the advance-preview- introductory Sunday newspaper page as panels 2, 3 and 4.

3.) *Superman* No. 1 (Summer 1939) - This issue retells the origin of Superman in an expanded two-page version which is all new art. None of these panels were used later on in the comics, dailies or Sunday pages.

4.) ADVANCE-PREVIEW-INTRODUCTORY "SUPERMAN" SUNDAY PAGE (October 1939) - This is the Sunday page that appeared in newspapers one week in advance of the actual first Sunday page that debuted on November 5, 1939. Panels 2, 3 and 4 were cut-out or statted from panels 1, 2 and 3 of the twelfth Superman daily strip. Panels 5 and 6 were cut-out or statted from panels 8 and 9 in *Action Comics* No. 1.

Each Season Sotheby's offers the most comprehensive selection of Comic Books and original Comic Art at auction. This spring Sotheby's will celebrate the seventh Comic Book and Comic Art auction with a stunning catalogue packed with extraordinary comic books and comic art. Two years ago Sotheby's topped over two million dollars with a single sale, last year was just over $1,700,000, and this seventh year promises remarkable opportunities for collectors.

Highlights from our spring 1997 sale include:

• *Complete runs of nearly all the DC Golden Age titles, including, ACTION, ADVENTURE, ALL STAR, ALL-AMERICAN, BATMAN, DETECTIVE, FLASH, GREEN LANTERN, SUPERMAN, and WORLDS FINEST.*

• A near complete offering of FICTION HOUSE comics, with near complete runs of JUNGLE COMICS, JUMBO COMICS, and PLANET COMICS.

• One of the most remarkable offerings of Newspaper Strip originals ever brought to market including the earliest POPEYE Sunday page ever discovered with a topper from 1930. Other masterworks include a full Sunday size FLASH GORDON from 1935 from the renowned Tournament sequence, a 1941 PRICE VALIANT Sunday page, a POGO Sunday with an original "origin" sequence finished on the reverse side, and other early rare daily and Sunday pages.

• Never before seen premiums including the proto-type SUPERMAN hood ornament cast in bronze and a rare SUPERMAN badge that was not even listed in the new Hake Premium Guide!

• File copy VF and NM runs of Silver Age comics including both DC and Marvel, with some scarce Charlton and Gold Key titles.

• The complete inventory from Blue Goose Records/Yazoo Records of original artwork by famed comic book artist Robert Crumb. This collection includes completely colored original Covers to some of Crumb 's most famous Record Albums. Originals from ZAP No. 1 and other important works are also consigned.

High grade unrestored Golden Age keys highlighted by ADVENTURE COMICS No. 40, ALL STAR COMICS

Nos. 1-8, FLASH COMICS No. 1, ALL FLASH No. 1, and other important titles. The "Mile High" Golden Age comics, and "White Mountain " Silver Age comics are also returning.

(1) E.C. Seagar, Theaton Thimble Popeye 12-21-1930   Estimate $10,000-15,000

For more information, please call Jerry Weist at (212) 606-7862, or Dana Hawkes at (212) 606-7910, Sotheby's, 1334 York Avenue, New York, New York, 10021. To order catalogues in advance by credit card you may call toll free (800) 444-3709. To inquire about consigning important property call Jerry Weist at either (212) 606-7862, or   (978)-283-1419

PART III

NEWSPAPER STRIP ART

DICK TRACY, Chester Gould, original introductory daily strip, circa mid-1930's, offered at Sotheby's June 17, 2000 auction. Estimate: $2,000/4,000. © The Chicago Tribune Syndicate

TERRY AND THE PIRATES, Milton Caniff, original introductory daily strip, circa mid-1930's, offered at Sotheby's June 17, 2000 auction. Estimate: $2,000-4,000. © The Chicago Tribune Syndicate

HOW TO USE THE NEWSPAPER STRIP SECTION

Remember that the standard comic strip results in some 313 Daily strips and 52 Sunday pages a year, which is part of the reason "in some cases" there has been such a high survival rate for the original art. However many originals did not survive Syndicate abuse.

Most often an artist-writer would create a strip like "Dick Tracy," a syndicate would buy the strip and, if it was popular, run the title for years. Remember that the character, Dick Tracy, is what was important to the syndicate and the public, not the artist.

After a period of time the author/artist might farm out the job of illustration to various ghost artists. The illustrations created by these artists might later have as much or more value than the work of the original author of the strip. While this section will list the artists' names, it is important to note that the names do not actually appear on the original art work.

All original art from either a Daily or Sunday strip will have the strip name in the top left corner. If this name is not on the top middle, sometimes if will appear on the backside in handwritten form along with the title of the Daily or Sunday strip. The day or month it was created in is always inked in by the artist on the corner of some panel in the strip. The original will also have the syndicate copyright paste-over with the year, although sometimes this strip will have fallen off with age.

Originals are then identified by the strip title, day-month-year of creation. For easy identification, this section is organized alphabetically by strip name. Each strip is described and broken down chronologically by year as the strip evolved, with Daily strips listed first and Sunday strips second.

This guide is also listing specific sales results for some of the more important strip titles. The purpose of these listings is to give the new collectors or uninformed individuals a better range of prices for comparison on range of value. It must be stressed, however, that if high prices are listed (without printed examples) the reader should remember that a higher priced original is most likely the result of an outstanding example, therefore the formula for pricing used in this guide is confirmed - quality will always engage with the higher sale.

ABBIE AN' SLATS

Created in 1937 by Al Capp (writer) and magazine illustrator Raeburn Van Buren. Eliot Caplin continued the writing in 1946 until the end of the strip's run In 1971. "Abbie An' Slats" centered around Crabtree Comers, yet because it was an adventure strip, the whole world was its stage. Syndicated by United Features.

Daily Strips

1937-50	R. Van Buren	$15	$30	$45
1950-71	R. Van Buren	10	25	35

Sunday Strips

1939-50	R. Van Buren	30	80	180
1951-71	R. Van Buren	40	60	80

ABIE THE AGENT

Beginning in 1914 by Harry Hirshfield, "Abe" lasted until 1940. Syndicated by King Features.

Daily Strips

1914-40	H. Hirshfield	$100	$150	$200

Sunday Strips

1924-40	H. Hirshfield	225	350	[450]

ALLEY OOP, V.T. Hamlin and David Graue, artwork for 3 Sunday pages and 8 dailies, dated 1940's and 1950's. Estimate: $1,000/2,000; sold for $1,380 in 6/96 (Sotheby's 6th comic art auction). © The N.E.A. Syndicate

ADAM

A humor strip centered on the baby. Developed by Brian Basset.

Daily Strips

1984-				
Present	B. Basset	$50	$100	$150

Sunday Strips

1984-				
Present	B. Basset	150	200	400

AGATHA CRUMM

Created by Bill Hoest in 1977, the strip was continued by assistant John Reiner and Bunny Hoest in 1987. Syndicated by King Features.

Daily Strips

1977-87	B. Hoest	$25	$75	$150
1987-97	J. Reiner	20	35	60

Sunday Strips

1977-87	B. Hoest	50	150	250
1987-97	J. Reiner	25	50	100

ALLEY OOP

"Oop" was created in 1933 by Vincent T. Hamlin. The story takes place in prehistoric times, focusing on the title character, Alley Oop. In 1939, Professor Wonmug entered the strip, and his time machine sent Oop and various other characters throughout history. In 1971, Hamlin retired and long-time assistant David Graue took over. It should be noted that pre-1945 originals exist, but the Sundays are extremely scarce. The most interesting artwork was drawn before 1950. Syndicated by the N.E.A.

Daily Strips

1933-40	V. T. Hamlin	$350	$650	[$900]
1941-50	V. T. Hamlin	100	250	450
1950-60	V. T. Hamlin	100	150	250
1960-68	V. T. Hamlin	25	75	100
1969-90	D. Graue	15	30	45
1991-				
Present	Jack Bender/			
	Graue	15	35	45

ALLEY OOP, V.T. Hamlin, daily, dated 8/6/38. Estimate: $500/700; sold for $460 in 10/93 (Christie's East Comic Art Auctions). © N.E.A. Syndicate

ALLEY OOP, V.T. Hamlin, daily, circa 1933. Estimate: $1,500/2,000; sold for $2,587 in 1997 (Sotheby's 7th comic art auction)© N.E.A. Service Inc.

Note: examples from 1933-1940 have been offered at public auction within the listed range and have twice failed to meet reserve prices, other examples have sold.

Sunday Strips

1934-45				
(rare)	V. T. Hamlin	900	1,800	[2,750]
1946-50	V. T. Hamlin	400	500	[900]
1950-60	V. T. Hamlin	300	400	[650]
1960-73				
(April)	V. T. Hamlin	150	300	450
1973-90	D. Graue	35	75	150
1991-				
Present	Jack Bender/			
	Graue	30	65	150

Note: existing examples from 1934 through 1945 are extremely rare, or not known to exist.

THE AMAZING SPIDER-MAN

Spider-Man was created as a comic book hero in 1962 by Stan Lee and Steve Ditko. The syndicated feature began in 1977, with creator Stan Lee writing and John Romita drawing. Syndicated by King Features.

Daily Strips

1977-88	J. Romita	$50	$85	$125
1988-				
Present	L. Lieber	20	30	50

Note: a large percentage of the early Romita daily strips are in permanent collections, however adequate numbers of the Lieber dailys are available and still entering the market.

Sunday Strips

1977-88	J. Romita	100	150	200
1988-				
Present	F. Dery	50	75	100
	L. Lieber	50	75	100

AND HER NAME WAS MAUD

Debuted by cartooning pioneer Fred Opper in 1926 as a topper to his "Happy Hooligan" strip, "Maud" ran until 1932. Earlier incarnations of "Maud" were drawn by Opper in the early 1900s appearing occasionally for several years. Syndicated by King Features.

Sunday Strips

1903-10	F. Opper	$500	$800	$1,200
1926-32	F. Opper	250	425	600
1914-18	F Opper	500	750	1000

ANDY CAPP

An American distribution since 1957 it's syndicated by North American Syndicate. A humor strip about a working-class Englishman. Common gags are avoiding the landlord, drinking, and playing rugby

THE AMAZING SPIDER MAN, Larry Leiber, 3 daily strips (two shown), dated from 1988 to 1991. Estimate: $700/900; sold for $748 in 6/93 (Sotheby's 3rd comic art auction). © Marvel Comics Group/ King Features Syndicate

or soccer.

Daily Strips

| 1957-1998 | R. Smythe | $50 | $75 | $100 |

Sunday Strips

| 1960-1998 | R. Smythe | 100 | 150 | 200 |

ANIMAL CRACKERS

A humor strip by Rog Bollen about jungle animals syndicated by Tribune Media. There are a number of originals for this strip done with magic marker on vellum.

Daily Strips

| 1968-1994 | R. Bollen | $25 | $45 | $65 |

Sunday Strips

| 1968-1994 | R. Bollen | 50 | 75 | 125 |

APARTMENT 3-G

"Apartment 3-G" began as both a Daily and a Sunday strip first appearing in 1961. Drawn by Al Kotsky and written by Nick Dallis ("Rex Morgan" and "Judge Parker"). Syndicated by North American Syndicate .

Daily Strips

| 1961- Present | A. Kotsky/ N. Dallis | $30 | $40 | $50 |

Sunday Strips

| 1961-Present | A. Kotsky/ N. Dallis | 50 | 100 | 150 |

APPLE MARY- MARY WORTH

Created in 1932 by Martha Orr, "Apple Mary" was renamed "Mary Worth" after Orr left the strip. The Depression Era adventure strip has metamorphosed over the years into the leading "soap opera" comic strip today. Syndicated by North American Syndicate.   Of the estimated 15,695 Mary Worth Dailies and Sundays the current studio artists estimate that only 1,000 survived the trashcan.

Daily Strips

1932-40	M. Orr	$150	$300	$500
1940 42	D. Connor	100	200	300
1942-91	K. Ernst	50	100	150
1991-Present	J. Giella	25	50	75

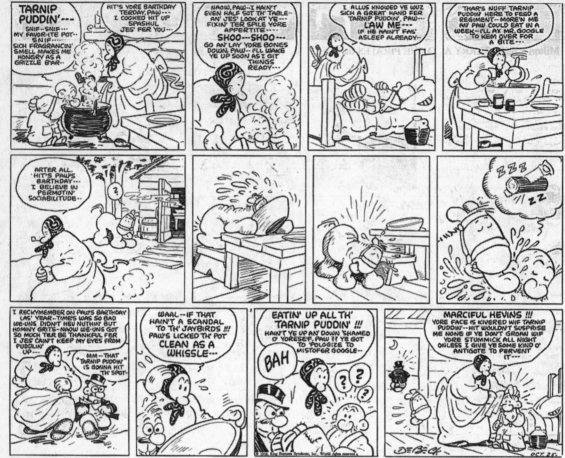

BARNEY GOOGLE AND SNUFFY SMITY, Billy DeBeck, Sunday page, dated 10/25/36. Estimate: $1,000/2,000; sold for $1,512 in 6/97 (Russ Cochran's comic art auction). © King Features Syndicate

Sunday Strips

1940-50	K. Ernst	75	150	300
1951-91	K. Ernst	50	75	150
1991-present	J. Giella	50	100	150

ARCHIE

Created in 1941 as a comic book, America's most popular teenager starred in his own comic strip beginning in 1947. Creator Bob Montana worked until the early 1970s on "Archie." Syndicated by King Features.

Daily Strips

1946-1947	B. Montana	$400	$800	$1,500
1948-50s	B. Montana	150	350	800
1951-Present	D. De Carlo	15	30	45
1951-Present	S. Goldberg	15	30	45

(Note: recent private sale of three 1946 Daily strips, for $1,200 each.)

Sunday Strips

1947-48	B. Montana	[1,000	2,000	3,000]
1948-50	B. Montana	150	300	550
1952-70s	B. Montana	100	200	350
1970-Present	S. Goldberg	25	50	75
1970-Present	D. De Carlo	25	50	75

BABY BLUES

A humor strip about parents coping with a six-month-old baby and how their lives have shifted to its concerns. Distributed by Creators Syndicate.

Daily Strips

1988- Present	R. Kirkman/ J. Scott	$50	$75	$100

Sunday Strips

1988- Present	R. Kirkman/ J. Scott	100	125	150

BACK HOME AGAIN

Ed Dodd's first strip was the panel "Back Home Again." This ran from 1930 through 1945. In 1946, he created his classic "Mark Trail." Syndicated by United Features.

Daily Strips

1930-45	E. Dodd	$25	$75	$150

BARNABY

"Barnaby" was a wonderful strip about a boy's imagination. Creator Crockett Johnson may well be best known for his "children's books" on "Harold and His Purple Crayon." Chicago Sun Times Syndicate.

Daily Strips

1942-46	C. Johnson	$250	$550	$750
1946-52	J. Morley	100	200	300

BARNEY BAXTER

First appearing as a daily (December 17,1936), "Barney Baxter" was about a pilot barn stormer. The outbreak of World War II put Barney and friends in the Air Force. "Barney Baxter" adventures became a classic war strip, highlighted by Miller's intricate penwork. Syndicated by King Features.

Daily Strips

1936-43	F. Miller	$50	$100	$200
1948-50	F. Miller	50	75	100
1943-48	B. Naylor	45	100	175

Sunday Strips

1937-43	F. Miller	100	300	450
1948-50	F. Miller	100	200	300
1943-48	B. Naylor	45	100	200

BARNEY GOOGLE

"Married Life," Billy DeBeck's first comic strip started in 1916, shifted in 1919 to the minor character, Barney Google. In 1935, DeBeck hired Fred Lasswell as his assistant. Upon DeBeck's death in 1942, Lasswell took over the strip, and the focus shifted almost exclusively to Snuffy Smith from Barney Google and his horse racing. Lasswell continued for over 50 years, drawing without assistance. The bulk of Lasswell's work now resides at the Ohio State University Library. Both DeBeck's work and Lasswell's work are around, but getting tougher to find. Syndicated by King Features.

Daily Strips

1919-30	B. DeBeck	$400	$1000	[$1800]
1931-42	B. DeBeck	250	400	800
1942- Present	F. Lasswell	75	150	225

Note: an extremely strong daily dated 8/20/31 with Barney Google dreaming of the races with Spark Plug sold at Sotheby's for $7,475. Two dailies together dated 11/26/31, and 11/27/31 (with lots of black inking) sold for $5,175.

Sunday Strips

1919-31 (very rare)	B. DeBeck	[700	1200	2,500]
1932-42	B. DeBeck	300	600	900
1942-45	F. Lasswell	150	250	450
1946- Present	F. Lasswell	100	200	300

Note: an extremely strong example of an early DeBeck Sunday page from an early period sold at Illustration House in 1997 for $8,800. For very strong examples of Barney Google it is obvious that serious collectors are willing to go the distance.

BARON BEAN

George Herriman created his second most popular strip where the Nobel British character of Mr. Bean is accompanied by the ever present Grimes.

Daily Strips

1916-1919	George Herriman	[$700	$900	$1,800]

Note: though this strip is considered scarce in the market place, only a few key examples have brought high prices, as it seems the primary focus of collectors remains true to the "Krazy Kat" strip.

BATMAN, Bob Kane and Charles Paris, 3 daily strips, dated 7/23/45, 7/24/45 and 7/25/45. Estimate: $6,000/8,000; sold for $9,775 in 1995 (Sotheby's 5th comic art auction). © National Periodical Publications

BATMAN

In 1939, "Batman" premiered in Detective Comics No. 27, created by Bob Kane and Bill Finger. The comic strip itself reflects concerns from Hollywood. Each time a project appeared on film or TV, the comic strip was in the papers. It should also be noted that the top artists of the "Batman" comic book stories were called upon to do the comic strips. It is unfortunate that much of this art does not exist. Dick Sprang's work was limited to one story

from February 11,1946, to March 23,1946. Of these 32 dailies, only three (3) are known at this time to exist.

The author is leaving the top paragraph intact from the fist guide to illustrate a classic example of how history can be changed on a single strips pricing. In June of 1995 Sotheby's offered the only known Bob Kane daily strips ever bought to auction. As luck would have it these three dailies were from the introductory first week and were the second, the fifth, and

BATMAN, Carmine Infantino, daily, dated 3/29/67. Sold in group lot for $125.
© National Periodical Publications

the sixth dailies and featured "first appearance" content (i.e.' the fifth daily featured the first appearance in strip form of the "Bat-Cave") along with the original Bob Kane signatures that were originally whited-out by the syndicate.   Since there were no known examples of Kane's work in the market the first guide column pricing listing for Bob Kane was $1,500-$2,000-to [$2,500] - indeed! What happened at auction was the No. 2 daily sold for an amazing $29,900 under fierce bidding, the No. 5 daily brought another remarkable price of $21,850, and the No. 6 daily sold for $10,350. Not only do these three examples offer an excellent example to collectors everywhere that when the "right" rare original artwork turns up for a "famous" strip, even though previous projected prices may be conservative the market will find its own true level. But these three examples also reinforce that even though a larger number of originals may enter the market than previously known if they are for the right artist and strip the price will not be depressed - it will rise.

Daily Strips

1943-44				
(rare)	B. Kane	[$5,000	$8,000	$12,000]
1945	B. Kane/			
	Charles Paris	1,000	2,000	3,000
1945	J. Burnley	500	1,000	1,800
1946	D. Sprang			
	(only three			
	known)	2,500	3,500	5,500
1966-72				
/90-91	C. Infantino			
	or A. Plastino	100	150	250
1989-90	M. Rodgers	50	100	150

Note: three Kane/Paris daily strips dated July 23, 24, 25, 1945 sold at Sotheby's in 1995 for $9,775.

Note: one more Bob Kane Batman daily has been discovered from the early period and has not entered the market, opening the possibly that other early rare dailies will turn up in the coming years.

BATMAN, Bob Kane, daily, dated 10/30/43 (the 6th daily). Estimate: $3,000/5,000; sold for $10,350 in 1995 (Sotheby's 5th comic art auction).© National Periodical Publications

BATMAN, Bob Kane, daily, dated 10/26/43 (the 2nd daily). Estimate: $5,000/10,000; sold for $29,9000 in 1995 (Sotheby's 5th comic art auction). © National Periodical Publications/DC Comics

BATMAN, Bob Kane, daily, dated 10/29/43 (the 5th daily). Estimate: $3,000/5,000; sold for $10,350 in 1995 (Sotheby's 5th comic art auction).© National Periodical Publications

Sunday Strips

1943-44	B. Kane	[4,000	4,000	7,000]
1966-72	Infantino/Giella			
	or A. Plastino	200	400	600
1989-90	M. Rodgers	100	200	300
1990-92	C. Infantino	160	225	300

B. C.

Created in 1955 by Johnny Hart, this pre-historic humor comic strip has been popular over the years. Field Syndicate.

Daily Strips

1955-Present	J. Hart	$75	$95	$200

Sunday Strips

1955-present	J. Hart	150	225	500

BEETLE BAILEY

Mort Walker began his comic strip about Beetle's life in the Army in 1950. Syndicated by King Features.

Daily Strips

1950-Present	M. Walker	$75	$150	$200

Sunday Strips

1952-60	M. Walker	150	250	450
1961-Present	M. Walker	125	225	300

BATMAN, Joe Giella, daily, circa 1970's. Estimate: $300/500; sold for $235 in 1994 (Christie's East art auctions).© National Periodical Publications

BELVEDERE

A standard "dog" strip created by artist George Crenshaw.

Daily Strips
1974-Present G. Crenshaw $30 $40 $55

Sunday Strips
1975-Present G. Crenshaw 50 70 90

BEN CASEY

Although "Ben Casey" ran only three and a half years from November 26,1962, to July 31, 1966, it was instrumental for introducing a relatively unknown artist, Neal Adams. Adams has gone on to be one of the most popular cartoonists in the last 30 years. N.E.A. Syndicate.

Daily Strips
1962-66 N. Adams $40 $80 $160

Sunday Strips
1962-66 N. Adams 200 250 400

B.C.   by johnny hart

B.C., Johnny Hart, daily, dated 1/11/86. Sold privately in 1996 for $80. © The Field Sydicate

BERRY'S WORLD
Feature by Jim Berry for N.E.A. Syndicate.

Daily Strips

1963-Present	J. Berry	$15	$30	$60

Sunday Strips

1963-present	J. Berry	50	75	100

BETTY
One of the early glamour girl strips drawn by Charles Voight for the New York Tribune syndicate.

Daily Strips

1920-43	C. Voight	$40	$55	$70

Sunday Strips

1920-43	C. Voight	50	75	125

BETTY BOOP
The "Betty Boop" comic strip reflects the Fleischer cartoon heroine's life as a budding actress in Hollywood. There are less than ten dailies known and few Sundays known to exist. Created by Bud Counihan for King Features Syndicate.

Daily Strips

1934-38	B. Counihan	[$800	$1600	$3600]

Note: a private sale was recorded for a daily at $5,000 in 1997

Sunday Strips

1934-38	B. Counihan	[800	1,600	2,900]

Note: existing Sundays for this strip are either extremely rare, or not known to exist.

BEYOND MARS
A short lived science fiction strip illustrated by comic book artist Lee Elias. The legendary SF author Jack Williamson contributed to the original story line.

Sunday Strips

1952-1955	L. Elias	$65	$85	$125

BIG BEN BOLT
An adventure strip about a boxer. Started by John Cullen Murphy. Syndicated by King Features.

Daily Strips

1950-71	J. C. Murphy	$50	$100	$150

Sunday Strips

1950-71	J. C. Murphy	100	200	300

BIG GEORGE
Daily Strips

1960-Present	V. Parch	$20	$40	$60

Sunday Strips

1960-Present	V. Parch	30	60	90

THE BLACK HOLE
Popular comic book artist Jack Kirby devoted one year to this strip. Syndicated by King Features, serializing the Disney movie.

Sunday Strips

1979-80	J. Kirby	$400	$650	$1,000

BLONDIE
"Blondie," by Chic Young, debuted September 15,1930. Over the years, "Blondie" has become one of the world's most enduring and loved comic strips. Syndicated by King Features. Alex Raymond assisted Chic Young from 1931 to 1933. In January of 1933, Dagwood went on his famous hunger strike. This lasted 28 days and, in the end, his parents allowed him to marry his girlfriend, Blondie. Dagwood was disinherited by his filthy-rich parents at the wedding. This changed the direction of the comic strip to its present theme of a fumbling, white-collar family man. Dagwood and Blondie's son, Alexander, was named for former assistant and good friend, Alex Raymond. It should also be noted that "Blondie" was one of the first strips produced by a studio of talent, not just one man (Chic Young). Although Young's signature appeared on all strips until his death in the 1970s, he did not draw it all. People like Jim Raymond (Alex's brother) and Paul Fung, Jr. spent years unaccredited. Today, Stan Drake (artist) shares the byline with Chic Young's son, Dean (writer).

Note: Both "The Family Foursome" and "Colonel Potterby and the Duchess" are top strips to "Blondie" from 1930 to 1963. These add a value of $200 to $350 to the value of the "Blondie" strips when found in matched pairs.

BLONDIE, Chic Young, daily, dated 1/17/33 (from the hunger strike sequence). Estimate: $1,200/1,500; sold for $1,100 in 1991 (Sotheby's 1st comic art auction). © King Features Sydicate

Daily Strips

1930 (rare)	C. Young	[$250	$550	$900]
1931-36	C. Young	[200	400	700]
1936-73	C. Young	[100	200	300]
1931-34	A. Raymond	[200	500	800]
1960-72	P. Fung, Jr.	40	90	180
19440-80	J. Raymond	40	80	120
1980-86	J. Gersher	50	75	100
1986-Present	S. Drake	50	75	100

Sunday Strips

1930-40	C. Young	[300	600	1,200]
1940-73	C. Young	[150	300	450]
1931-34	A. Raymond	[200	400	600]
1960-72	P. Fung, Jr.	75	150	225
1940-80	J. Raymond	75	150	225
1980-86	J. Gersher	75	150	225
1986-Present	S . Drake	50	125	200

BLOOM COUNTY

"Bloom County" has proved itself to be one of the more creative and popular contemporary comic strips. Opus and a cast of unique characters have been collected into softcover books in which people can review Berke Breathed's remarkable sense of humor. Washington Post Syndicate.

Daily Strips

1980-88	B. Breathed	$300	$400	$500

Sunday Strips

1980-88	B. Breathed	[500	750	1,000]

BOOB MCNUTT

A unique character strip created by Rube Goldberg.

Sunday Strips

	R. Goldberg	$450	$700	$950

BOBBY SOX

A teen strip created by Martha Links, popular in the early 1940's which began to loose its focus by the 1950's.

Daily Strips

1944-1974	M. Links	30	45	60
1975-1979	T. Martine	15	25	35

Sunday Strips

1945-1979	M.Links/ T. Martine late 70's	35	55	75

BONERS ARK

Created by Mort Walker in 1968. Syndicated by King Features. Humor strip about a mildly competent Noah (Boner) and the animals which seem to rule his ark.

Daily Strips

1968-71	M. Walker	$50	$75	$100
1971-Present	F. Johnson	20	40	60

Sunday Strips

1966-71	M. Walker	100	150	200
1971-present	F. Johnson	50	75	100

BRENDA STARR

Dale Messick created the first major female-main-character adventure comic strip in 1940 as a Sunday feature. In 1945, a daily strip followed. Syndicated by Tribune Media Syndicate.

Daily Strips

1945-80	D. Messick	$30	$60	$90
1980-95	R. Fradon	20	40	60
1995-Present	J. Brigman	20	40	60

Sunday Strips

1940-45	D. Messick	100	250	500
1946-50	D. Messick	90	150	350
1950-80	D. Messick	60	125	200
1995-Present	J. Brigman	30	60	90

BRINGING UP FATHER, George McManus, daily, dated 5/15/39. Estimate: $400/600; sold for $880 in 10/92 (Christie's East comic art auctions). © King Features Sydicate

BRINGING UP FATHER, George McManus, daily, circa 1918. Estimate: $500/700; sold for $467 in 6/97 (Russ Cochran auctions). © King Features Sydicate

BRICK BRADFORD

Created by Clarence Gray for King Features Syndicate. A science fiction/adventure strip focusing on Earth more than other worlds. Unlike "Flash Gordon," Brick centered on the science aspect of adventure with journeys into other eras using his time top.

Daily Strips

| 1933-52 | C. Gray | $100 | $200 | $300 |
| 1952-86 | P. Norris | 50 | 75 | 100 |

Sunday Strips

| 1933-52 | C. Gray | 300 | 600 | 900 |
| 1952-86 | P. Norris | 75 | 125 | 150 |

BRINGING UP FATHER

"Bringing Up Father" by George McManus began in 1912 as a Sunday feature. This would alternate weeks with "Rosie's Beau" and "The Newlyweds" until approximately 1918, when it became the dominant feature. Syndicated by King Features. Please note that many dailies from the 1930s and 1940s have glue stains. In 1939 and 1940, McManus took his characters on a tour of the United States. These originals of famous cities and landmarks are the pinnacle of the strip's run. It should also be noted that McManus hand-colored a number of pages in the 1920s. These have no greater value over the uncolored originals. It should however also be noted that collectors should not confuse a colored page done roughly as a guide to the engravers with a specially colored presentation original. The specially colored presentation originals would carry more value.

Daily Strips

1918-24	G. McManus	$125	$250	$450
1925-54	G. McManus	100	200	400
1954-				
Present	All others	15	30	50
1939	U.S. tour			
	sequence	250	350	450

Sunday Strips

1912-24	G. McManus	1,000	1,500	2,500
1925-54	G. McManus	600	1,200	1,700
1954-				
Present	All Others	500	750	1,000
1930	U.S. Tour			
	Sequence			
	(N.Y.C. page)	[3,000	6,000	9,000]

Note: any hand-colored originals are color-guided for the engraver (usually pre-1920), and as a result are only partially colored. However specially colored presentation works can be more complete.

BROOM-HILDA, Russell Myers, daily, dated 9/27/71, 6"x21". Estimate: $250/350; sold for $200 in 3/91 (Russ Cochran auctions). © The Chicago Tribune

BROOM-HILDA

Created by Russ Myers. Syndicated by Chicago Tribune. A humor strip focusing on a fifteen hundred-year-old witch. Myers shows an influence of Herriman with his wonderful backgrounds.

Daily Strips

1970-Present	R. Myers	$75	$150	$225

Sunday Strips

1970-Present	R. Myers	100	200	300

BRUCE GENTRY

Created by Ray Bailey for the Post Syndicate. Like "Steve Canyon," "Scorchy Smith," and "Johnny Hazzard," "Bruce Gentry" is another well-drawn adventure strip focusing on a freelance pilot.

Daily Strips

1945-52	R. Bailey	$75	$125	$175

Sunday Strips

1945-52	R. Bailey	150	300	450

BUCK ROGERS

Buck Rogers was the first major character developed for a science fiction comic strip. Read by millions and supported as a classic for its influence on the expansion of science fiction stories. Ray Bradbury and other notable writers hailed Calkins as the creator of a new type of super story telling.

PRICE RANGE KEY

RARITY — Brackets [ ] around a price indicate that this example is very scarce and could exceed maximum estimate.

	Covers
No work produced in this category—	XXX
No price available due to lack of information—	***

CONDITION — Age, color, marks, tears, etc.

	Pages		
	[400	500	600]

CHARACTER — Is the primary character featured, or is the original characteristic of a great example in the story line?

CONTENT — is the theme or story line exceptional or below average?

VALUE RANGE

Minimum	Medium	Maximum

RARITY

The [ ] Brackets indicate RARITY, if these brackets are used the reader can potentially double the price range in all three catagories.

BUCK ROGERS, Rick Yager, Sunday page, dated 1952. Estimate: $800/1,200; sold for $863 in 6/93 (Sotheby's 3rd comic art auction). © The John F. Dille Co.

BUCK ROGERS, Dick Calkins, daily, dated 1935. Estimate: $1,000/2,000; sold for $920 in 6/96 (Sotheby's 6th comic art auction). © The John F. Dille Co.

From the N.E.A. Syndicate. Very few Sunday examples exist by Dick Calkins and the great majority were known to be destroyed in the 1940's.

Daily Strips

1929-35	D. Calkins	[$1,000	$2.000	$3,500]
1936-40	D. Calkins	800	1,600	2,400
1940-47	D . Calkins/			
	R. Yager	500	1,000	1,500
1947-49	Murphy			
	Anderson	150	300	500
1951-58	Rick Yager	150	300	450
1959-67	G. Tuska	40	80	120

Note: a Rick Yager Sunday from 1951 sold in 1995 at Sotheby's for $1,092. Also a Dick Calkins daily dated 1937 - No. 511 sold at Sotheby's in 1994 for $2,600.

Sunday Strips

1930-33	Calkins/			
(*very, very*	Keaton			
rare)	(one known)	[3,000	6,000	9,500]
1933-40	Calkins/Yager	1,000	2,000	3,000
1940-58	Rick Yager	300	600	950
1959-65	George Tuska	75	150	225
1958-59	Murphy			
	Anderson	300	600	900

Note: the family of Rick Yager owns a number of specialty hand-colored Buck Rogers works that the artist did in the 1940's, most are approximately 12" x 12" in format.

Probable range of price if any enter the market.

[1,000   1,800   2,500]

Note: a number of very early Sunday proof sheets are known to exist in excellent condition. Probable range of price.

[150   250   350]

BUGS BUNNY

"Bugs Bunny" was first syndicated (N.E.A. Syndicate) under the Leon Schlesinger/ Warner Brothers copyright, but was drawn by various staff artists, including Ralph Heimdall, Roger Ammstrong (1941-1944, Sundays), and Charles McKimson.

Daily Strips

1948-55	Staff Artists	$75	$150	$300
1956-72	Staff Artists	75	100	125

Sunday Strips

1941-44	Staff Artists	500	750	1,200
1945-72	Staff Artists	200	300	450

THE BUNGLE FAMILY

Created by Harry Tuthill for McNaught Syndicate this strip was called "Home Sweet Home" until 1924.

Daily Strips

1918-24	H. Tuthill	$100	$200	$300
1925-45	H. Tuthill	60	100	150

Sunday Strips

1925-30	H. Tuthill	200	400	500
1931-45	H. Tuthill	100	150	200

BUSTER BROWN, R.F. Outcault, Sunday page, dated 8/15/10. Estimate: $2,000/3,000; sold for $1,150 in 6/94 (Sotheby's 4th comic art auction). © United Feature Syndicate

BUSTER BROWN

Begun by R. F. Outcault, this is the second feature by the man who is considered the father of the comic strip. Many pages appear with "color-guides" for the printer. In its later reprint (late teens, early twenties), Sundays would be "silver printed" (an early reproduction method) and a "staff artist" added outside panel borders in ink and signed Outcault's signature. These are hard to distinguish from "originals." New York Herald Tribune Syndicate.

Sunday Strips

1902-10	R. F. Outcault	[$2,000 $3,500 $4,500]
1910-20	R. F. Outcault	[1,000 1,500 2,000]

BUZ SAWYER

"Buz Sawyer' is one of the all-time great comic strips, noted for Crane's crisp style and use of blacks and craftone, as well as top-notch writing. Syndicated by King Features.

Daily Strips

1943-50	R. Crane	$125	$250	$375
1951-70	R. Crane	125	160	200
1970-Present	H. Schlensker and Others	20	40	60

Sunday Strips

1943-55	R Crane	300	550	300
1956-70	R. Crane	100	200	300
1970-Present	H. Schlensker and Others	60	120	180

CALVIN AND HOBBES

Bill Watterson produced a remarkably strong comic strip from the simple relationship between an imaginary tiger named Hobbes and his childhood friend, Calvin. Hobbes exhibits quite a similarity to the original A.A. Milne "tigger," and just as Winnie the Poo had a best friend, so did Calvin for the run of this very popular strip. No other contemporary American newspaper strip has enjoyed such a favorable and intense following among readers. Watterson managed to prove during the run of this very original and strongly drawn story line that "new" strip ideas need not be watered down or thoughtless in their content to be successful with the public. The last page for this strip appeared on December 31, 1995.

Though the artist has tightly controlled the release of any original artwork, to the extent of even keeping original works out of benefit auctions, two original hand-colored examples surfaced at Sotheby's.

Daily Strips

1984-1995	B. Watterson	[$400	$700	$900]

Note: a hand colored daily dated 1984 sold at Sotheby's 1996 auction for $4,025.

Sunday Strips

1984-1995	B. Watterson	[500	950	2,500]

Note: a hand colored Sunday dated 1984 sold at Sotheby's 1996 auction for $7,475.

THE CAPTAIN AND THE KIDS

Rudolph Dirks created an early comic strip called "The Katzenjammer Kids." When he switched publishers, he had to rename it; thus, "The Captain and the Kids" was born. Syndicated by United Features.

Daily Strips

1932-37	B. Dibble	$100	$200	$300

Sunday Strips

1914 (rare)	R. Dirks	400	800	1200
1915-32	R. Dirks	300	600	900
1932-37	B Dibble	150	300	450
1946-present	J. Dirks	75	150	225

CAPTAIN EASY

N.E.A. Syndicate. Formerly titled "Wash Tubbs." This strip was originally a daily gag strip. In the early 1930s, Roy Crane introduced Captain Easy, and one of the world's best adventure strips began. Captain Easy and Wash Tubbs showed that being a soldier of fortune was glamorous as they toured the world. Eventually, the Easy character took over the strip entirely and Wash Tubbs got married and left the strip.

Daily Strips

1924-44	R. Crane	$150	$300	$750
1944-60s	L. Turner/ M. Graff	50	100	150
1960-Present	Others	10	20	30

Sunday Strips

1933-43	R. Crane	600	900	1,500
1943-60s	L Turner/ M. Graff	100	200	300
1960-Present	Others	25	50	75

CAPTAIN STUBBS AND TIPPIE

A warm, friendly, well-drawn strip about a boy and his dog.

Daily Strips

1921-40	E. Dumm	$75	$150	$225
1941-67	E. Dumm	50	75	100

Sunday Strips

1934-45	E. Dumm	100	200	300
1946-67	E. Dumm	100	150	200

CASEY RUGGLES, Warren Tufts, daily, dated 12/31/51. Estimate: $800/1,000; sold for $1,495 in 1991 (Sotheby's 8th comic art auction). © United Feature Syndicate

CASEY RUGGLES

One of the great Western adventure strips by Warren Tufts. Syndicated by United Features.

Daily Strips

1949-54	W. Tufts	$75	$150	$225

Sunday Strips

1949-54	W. Tufts	100	300	400

CATFISH

A Western humor strip by Rog Bollen. Tribune Media Syndicate.

Daily Strips

1971-86	R. Bollen	$25	$50	$100
1986-				
Present	Various Artists	20	40	60

Sunday Strips

1971-86	R. Bollen	60	100	150
1986-				
Present	Various Artists	40	80	100

CATHY

The working single girl in America today. Cathy is the product of artist Cathy Guisewite. Universal Press Syndicate.

Daily Strips

1977-				
Present	C. Guisewite	$125	$250	$375

Sunday Strips

1977-				
Present	C. Guisewite	225	450	675

CHARLIE CHAN

McNaught Syndicate. The infamous Chinese detective starred briefly in his own comic strip. "Charlie Chan" is Milton Caniff's assistant, Alfred Andriola's, first major outing with his own strip. "Kerry Drake," Andriola's next strip, would put him into comics history. "Charlie Chan" is very well drawn (heavily Caniff and Sickles influence) and originals are almost nonexistent.

Daily Strips

1938-42	A. Andriola	[$300	$600	$950]

Sunday Strips

1938-42	A. Andriola	[$600	1,200	2,000]

CHARLIE CHAPLIN'S COMIC CAPERS

This is the first work by "Popeye" creator E.C. Segar. No examples are known to exist. Syndicated by The Chicago Herald.

Daily Strips

1915-17	E. C. Segar	[$500	$1,000	$1,500]

Sunday Strips

1915-17	E. C. Segar	[1,000	2,000	3,000]

CICERO'S CAT

"Cicero's Cat" was the top strip to "Mutt and Jeff." King Features.

Sunday Strips

1933-62	A. Smith	$40	$80	$120

CISCO KID

First appealing as a daily in 1951, this well-drawn Western strip was illustrated by the commercially successful Argentine artist Jose Luis Salinas. A significant number of originals have surfaced in the past few years. Syndicated by King Features.

Daily Strips

1951-59	J. L. Salinas	$125	$225	$325
1960-68	J. L. Salinas	75	150	225

CICERO'S CAT, Bud Fisher, daily, dated 2/9/47. Estimate: $100/200; sold for $110 in 1998 (Russ Cochran auctions). © King Features Syndicate

COLONEL POTTERBY AND THE DUCHESS

The top strip to "Blondie" which ran intermittently with other strips from approximately 1935 to 1965. Usually drawn by Young's assistants. Syndicated by King Features.

Sunday Strips

1935-65	Artist's Assistants	$40	$80	$120

CONAN THE BARBARIAN

Based on the Marvel Comics' version of the Robert E. Howard pulp character. Syndicated by King Features.

Daily Strips

1978-79	J. Buscema	$20	$40	$60
1979-88	E. Chan	20	40	60

Sunday Strips

1978-79	J. Buscema	40	80	120
1979-88	E. Chan	40	80	120

CONNIE

Ledger Syndicate. Frank Godwin was one of the top illustrators in comic strip history. His heroine adventure strip "Connie" exemplifies his genius.

Daily Strips

1927-37 (rare)	F. Godwin	[$250	$375	$750]
1938-44	F. Godwin	[150	200	350]

Sunday Strips

1927-44	F. Godwin	[400	800	1,600]

Note: very few known to exist.

CONRAD

Syndicated by Tribune Media. A frog, his princess, and Bill Schorr's wonderful imagination .

Daily Strips

1982-86	B. Schorr	$100	$150	$200

Sunday Strips

1982-86	B. Schorr	150	225	300

COUNT SCREWLOOSE

Created by Milt Gross for syndication by King Features. Topper to "Dave's Delicatessen."

Sunday Strips

1929-48	M. Gross	$100	$200	$300

CRANKSHAFT

Universal Press Syndicate. A humorous daily strip about a senior-citizen school bus driver and his bleak attitudes.

Daily Strips

1987-Present	T. Batiuk	$20	$30	$40

Sunday Strips

1987-Present	T. Batiuk	30	55	80

CROCK

North American Syndicate. Foreign Legion-focused humor strip.

Daily Strips

1971-present	B. Rechin	$40	$80	$120

Sunday Strips

1971-Present	B. Rechin	100	250	400

CURTIS

King Features Syndicate. One of the few comic strips about African-American domestic life in the 1990s.

Daily Strips

1988-Present	R. Billingsley	$75	$150	$225

Sunday Strips

1988-present	R. Billingsley	100	200	300

DAN DARE (PILOT OF THE FUTURE)

Created, written, and drawn by Frank Hampson. Produced in a Sunday page format and appearing in Eagle magazine. One of the top British strips ever done. Considered by many to be equivalent to "Buck Rogers" and "Flash Gordon" in importance of science fiction strips.

Sunday Strips

1950-59	F. Hampson	[$400	$600	$850]
1959-60	F. Bellamy	[500	750	1,000]

DAN DUNN

Average detective comic strip. Typically weak "Dick Tracy" clone without interesting villains .

Daily Strips

1933-42	N. Marsh	$50	$100	[$150]
1942-43	A. Andriola	100	200	300

Sunday Strips

1933	N. Marsh	150	350	550
1934-42	N. Marsh	150	300	450
1942-43	A. Andriola	200	400	600

DANY DINGLE

Syndicated by King Features and United Features.

Daily Strips

1927-38	B. Dibble	$150	$225	$300

Sunday Strips

1927-48	B. Dibble	200	300	400

DARK SHADOWS

A very short lived strip by artist Ken Bald(who signed his name on the strip K. Bruce) based on the popular Vampire TV series of the same name, for Dan Curtis Productions Inc.

Daily Strips

1971	K. Bald(K.Bruce)	$50	$60	$90

Sunday Strips

1971	K. Bald(K.Bruce)	200	250	350

(many of the Sunday pages have xerox panels used from the daily strip, if more than one are used - price falls.)

DATELINE DANGER

Published by Hall Syndicate. A well-crafted adventure strip by Alden McWilliams.

Daily Strips

1968-74	A. McWilliams	$20	$40	$60

Sunday Strips

1968-74	A. McWilliams	50	100	150

DAVEY JONES

Syndicated by United Features. A shortlived adventure strip focusing on scuba diver Davey Jones.

Daily Strips

1961-65	A. McWilliams	$20	$40	$60
1961-65	W. Boring	15	30	45

DENNIS THE MENACE

The lovable "Brat Next Door" was created by Hank Ketcham. Syndicated by Hall Syndicate and later North American Syndicate.

Daily Strips

1951-present	H. Ketcham	$75	$150	$300

Sunday Strips

1951-Present	H. Ketcham	125	250	500

DICK'S ADVENTURES IN DREAMLAND

Written by Max Trell and illustrated by Neil O'Keefe this adventure strip incorporated American history directly into its weekly format.

Sunday Strips

1947-1956	N. O'Keefe	$75	$150	$300

DICK TRACY, Chester Gould, daily, dated 2/7/36. Estimate: $500/1,000; sold for $797 in 4/97 (Russ Cochran's art auctions). © The Chicago Tribune

DICK TRACY, Chester Gould, daily, dated 10/20/44. Estimate: $600/900; sold for $605 in 10/92 (Christie's East comic art auction). © The Chicago Tribune

DICK TRACY

Tough cops and robbers initially set the tone for the first decade of America's greatest crime-stopping comic strip. In the early 1940s, villains took on personas as intriguing as their names. Flattop, Fly Face, The Brow, Prune Face, and a host of other aptly titled villains became the stars, and Dick Tracy capably hunted them down. The 1940s produced Tracy's greatest villains. Chester Gould's story telling, art, and imagination have placed "Dick Tracy" above all other detective comic strips. Upon Gould's retirement in 1977, he hand-picked top mystery writer Max Allan Collins and former art assistant Rick Fletcher to carry on. Upon Fletcher's death, another former Gould assistant and Pulitzer Prize winner, Dick Locher, assumed the art chores. The pre-1955 time-period examples are scarce.

Daily Strips

1931	Chester Gould	[$1,200	$2,100	$4,000]
1932-33	C. Gould	[900	1,800	2,900]
1934-40	C. Gould	[500	900	1,600]
1941-48	C. Gould	[400	750	950]
1949-58	C. Gould	[250	450	550]
1958-77	C. Gould	150	300	450
1977-83	R. Fletcher	25	50	75
1983-present	D. Locher	25	50	75

* use 100% to 300% more for apperances of villains in daily strips.

Note: villains are a key to dailies going up in price! The more unique and special for the villains appearance in any daily the more probable the price will be more expensive. There are recorded prices for private sales on select Flattop and Mrs. Pruneface dailies for up to $5,000. Some examples are 1/25/1945 with Flattop appearance selling at Sotheby's in 1995 for $2,300; a Breathless Mahoney dated 6/12/1945 sold for $805; a Flattop daily dated 2/22/1944 sold at Christie's East in 1992 for $1,540; and a daily featuring Tess Trueheart, Junior and Tracy from 5/10/1934 sold at Christie's East in 1992 for $2,640.

DICK TRACY, Chester Gould, Sunday page, dated 7/14/40. Estimate: $2,000/3,000; sold for $2,640 in 6/97 (Russ Cochran's comic art auction). © The Chicago Tribune

DICK TRACY, Chester Gould, daily, dated 1/19/35. Estimate: $4,000/5,000; sold for $3,450 in 1995 (Sotheby's 5th comic art auction). © The Chicago Tribune

DICK TRACY, Chester Gould, daily, dated 7/22/43. Estimate: $2,000/3,000; did not meet reserve in 1995 (Sotheby's 5th comic art auction). © The Chicago Tribune

DICK TRACY, Chester Gould, daily, dated 1/25/44. Estimate: $2,000/3,000; sold for $2,300 in 1995 (Sotheby's 5th comic art auction). © The Chicago Tribune

DICK TRACY, Chester Gould, daily, dated 5/5/44. Estimate: $2,000/3,000; sold for $805 in 1995 (Sotheby's 5th comic art auction). © The Chicago Tribune

DICK TRACY, Chester Gould, daily, dated 6/12/45. Estimate: $500/700; sold for $575 in 1995 (Sotheby's 5th comic art auction). © The Chicago Tribune

DICK TRACY, Chester Gould, two daily strips, dated 12/25/60 and 12/25/74. Estimate: $600/800; sold for $575 in 1995 (Sotheby's 5th comic art auction).© The Chicago Tribune

Note: there are only three to four known dailies within the years of 1934 through 1936.

Sunday Strips

1931	(not known to exist)			
	C. Gould	[10,000	12,5000	15,000]
1932-40	C. Gould	[1,000	2,000	3,000]
1941-48	C. Gould	[400	800	1,200]
1948-60	C. Gould	[250	500	600]

1960-76	C. Gould	[200	400	600]
1977-83	R. Fletcher	60	120	180
1983-present	D. Locher	60	120	180

Note: 1941-1944, no known Sundays. Did Flattop steal them?

THE DINGBAT FAMILY, George Herriman, daily, dated January 1912. Estimate: $10,000/15,000; sold for $6,900 in 1997 (Sotheby's 7th comic art auction). © The New York Journal

DICKEY DARE

Syndicated by A.P. News Services.
Adventure strip of a boy who imagines himself with historical and fictional characters.

Daily Strips

1933-34	M. Caniff	$250	$500	$750
1934-44	C. Waugh	75	150	225
1944-58	O. Waugh	75	150	225

DINGBAT FAMILY
(THE FAMILY UPSTAIRS)

The first major strip to be developed by George Herriman for the Hearst newspapers. This strip hosted a domestic family story line, however its real historical and collectible value lies in the fact that beneath the Dinbat Family in a slim four to five panel format Herriman first developed the character Krazy Kat. Appearing in the main strip at first as the family kat, Krazy soon introduced "the mouse" Ignatz, and the bricks soon came into play.

Daily Strips

1910-1916	George Herriman	[$1,500	$3,000	$7,500]

DIXIE DUGAN

NcNaught Syndicate. A long-lasting strip about its title character, working girl Dixie Dugan.

Daily Strips

1929-65	J. Striebel	$100	$200	$300

Sunday Strips

1929-65	J. Striebel	200	300	400

DR. KILDARE

Syndicated by King Features. Comic strip based on the TV show.

Daily Strips

1962-68	K. Bald	$15	$30	$45

Sunday Strips

1964-68	K. Bald	40	80	120

DONALD DUCK, Al Taliaferro, daily, dated 1/15/58. Estimate: $150-300; sold for $495 in 6/97 (Sotheby's 5th comic art auction). © The Walt Disney Company

DONALD DUCK, Al Taliaferro, daily, dated 1938. Estimate: $2,000/3,000; sold for $3,450 in 1995 (Sotheby's 5th comic art auction). © The Walt Disney Company

DONALD DUCK, Al Taliaferro, daily, dated 7/11/41. Estimate: $800/1,200; sold for $935 in 1995 (Christie's East comic art auctions). © The Walt Disney Company

DONALD DUCK

Walt Disney's second most popular character debuted in 1934 in the "Wise Little Hen" Silly Symphony. After his debut in the "Silly Symphonies" comic strip, he quickly took it over and started until his own "Donald Duck" strip debuted in 1939. Al Taliaferro is the best-known artist on this strip and his work is scarce and prized, along with other Disney greats Floyd Gottfredson ("Mickey Mouse") and Carl Barks (*Donald Duck* comic books). Syndicated by King Features.

Daily Strips (note: in 1938 less than 5 known)

1938	A. Taliaferro			
(very rare)		[$2,000	$3,500	$4,500]
1939-40	A. Taliaferro (less than 15 known)			
(rare)		[1,500	2,500	3,750]
1941-49	A. Taliaferro	500	900	1,400
1950-60	A. Taliaferro	400	800	1,000
1961-70	A. Taliaferro	200	400	700
1970-				
Present	Studio Artists	100	200	300

Sunday Strips

"Silly Symphonies"

1936-37 (note: less than 10 known to exist)				
(very rare)	A. Taliaferro	[6,000	9,500	15,000]
1938-40				
(rare)	A. Taliaferro	3,000	5,500	6,000
1941-70	A. Taliaferro	200	600	1,200
1970-				
Present	Studio Artists	100	200	300

Note: Diamond Galleries in Baltimore sold a 1940 "Silly Symphonies" in 1997 for $7,500.

Note: The second page to a "Silly Symphonies" Sunday from 1936 sold in 1997 for $15,000.

DONDI

Chicago Tribune Syndicate. Story strip about a World War II child refugee and his life in the United States.

Daily Strips

1955-86	I. Hasen	$25	$50	$75

Sunday Strips

1955-86	I. Hasen	75	150	225

DON WINSLOW OF THE NAVY

Adventure strip of Navy Intelligence Officer Don Winslow.

Daily Strips

1934-42	L. Beroth/			
(very rare)	C. Hammond	[$500	$600	$700]
1942-44	L. Beroth/			
	K. Ernst	[200	300	400]

DOONESBURY   by Garry Trudeau

DOONESBURY, Gary Trudeau, daily, dated 9/24/71. Estimate: $1,200/1,500; sold for $1,150 in 1994 (Christie's East comic art auctions). © Universal Press Syndicate

DOONESBURY, Gary Trudeau, Sunday page, dated 3/31/74. Estimate: $1,500/2,000; sold for $2,300 in 1995 (Sotheby's 5th comic art auction). © Universal Press Syndicate

1945-55	E. Moore/ A. Levin/ Berola	20	40	60

Sunday Strips

1934-42	L. Beroth/ C. Hammond	[600	700	800]
1942-44	L. Beroth/ K. Ernst	[100	200	300]
1944-55	E. Moore/ A. Levin/Berola	75	150	225

DOONESBURY

This controversial political strip is considered the contemporary successor to Walt Kelly's "Pogo." Universal Press Syndicate.

Daily Strips

1970-Present	G. Trudeau	$250	$400	$700

Sunday Strips

1970-Present	G. Trudeau	500	800	1,400

DREAM OF THE RAREBIT FIEND, Winsor McCay, Sunday page, dated 4/22/09. Estimate: $2,000/3,000; sold for $1,035 in 6/93 (Sotheby's 3rd comic art auction). © Universal Press Syndicate

DRABBLE

United Features Syndicate. Contemporary daily gag strip.

Daily Strips

1979-Present	K. Fagan	$75	$140	$225

Sunday Strips

1979-Present	K. Fagan	200	300	400

DRAGO

Syndicated by King Features. "Drago" is an exciting adventure strip focusing on a South American gaucho. Drago's short life is the result of Burne Hogarth's return to "Tarzan" in early 1948.

Sunday Strips

1946-47	B. Hogarth	$800	$1,200	$1,600

DREAM OF THE RAREBIT FIEND

This strip predates McCay's classic, "Little Nemo in Slumberland" by a year. Like Nemo, McCay takes the reader into the imaginary world of dreams. Surreal settings, contorted faces and people, and anthropomorphic animals dominate McCay's drawings. New York Herald Syndicate.

Sunday Strips

1904-19	W. McCay	$1,500	$2,500	[$4,000]

Note: some individual sales include Christie's East 1996, "Rarebit Fiend" dated 1908 selling for $2,875; and another "Rarebit Fiend" dated 1906 selling at $2,875, with a third dated 1908 hammering at $3,220 with buyers premium.

DROPOUTS

Two men, alone on an island, in this daily gag strip. Syndicated by N.E.A.

Daily Strips

1968-Present	H. Post	$30	$60	$90

Sunday Strips

1968-Present	H. Post	75	100	125

DUMB DORA

This comic strip helped Chic Young mold the "Blondie" comic strip, which he introduced to the world in 1930. Syndicated by King Features.

Daily Strips

1924-30	C. Young	$150	$250	$375
1930-32	P. Fung, Sr.	75	100	125
1932-35	B. Dwyer	50	75	100

Sunday Strips

1930-32	P. Fung, Sr.	200	300	400
1932-35	B Dwyer	100	150	200

EEK AND MEEK

Daily gag strip about two mice. The Tribune Media Syndicate.

Daily Strips

1965-Present	H. Schneider	$20	$40	$60

Sunday Strips

1965-Present	H. Schneider	75	100	150

ELLA CINDERS

Syndicated by United Features. A working-girl-in-Hollywood story strip.

Daily Strips

1927-50	C. Plumb	[$50	$100	$150]
1950-61	R. Armstrong	50	100	150

Sunday Strips

1927-50	C. Plumb	100	200	300
1950-61	R Armstrong	75	55	150

ELMER

Originally called "Just Boy" it changed to "Elmer" in 1925. Syndicated by King Features.

Daily Strips

1916-25	A. C. Fera	$200	$800	$400
1925-56	D. Winner	50	75	100

Sunday Strips

1916-25	A. C. Fera	300	400	500
1925-56	D. Winner	75	150	225

ERNIE

King Features Syndicate. A blue-collar-worker daily gag strip.

Daily Strips

1988-present	B. Grace	$100	$125	$150

Sunday Strips

1988-present	B. Grace	200	250	300

ETTA KETT

Syndicated by King Features. Cute daily gag strip about a working girl.

Daily Strips

1925-53	P. Robinson	$50	$100	$200

Sunday Strips

1925-58	P. Robinson	100	200	350

FAMILY CIRCUS - THE

This one panel (circle panel) family gag strip has been popular since it was first introduced by Bil Keane in 1960.

Daily Panels

1960-Present	B. Keane	$45	75	95

FAMILY FOURSOME

See "Blondie."

THE FAR SIDE   By GARY LARSON

"Just a minute, young man!.. What are
you taking from the jungle?"

THE FAR SIDE, Gary Larsen, daily, dated 4/16/83.
Estimate: $1,000/1,500; sold for $2,070 in 6/96 (Sotheby's
6th comic art auction).
© Chronicle Features Syndicate

THE FAR SIDE   By GARY LARSON

THE FAR SIDE, Gary Larsen, daily, dated 2/28/83.
Estimate: $1,500/3,000; sold for $1,853 in 3/98
(Russ Cochran Auctions).
© Chronicle Features Syndicate

FAMILY UPSTAIRS
See "The Dingbat Family"

FAR SIDE
Universal Press Syndication. Outrageous
daily gag strip about people, bugs, animals,
anything Gary Larson thinks of. Almost all
originals are unavailable.

Daily Strips
l980-95   G. Larson   [$500 $700 $1,500]

Note: a "Far Side" panel from 4/16/1983
sold at Sotheby's in 1996 for $2,070.

Sunday Strips
l980-95   G. Larson   [600   800   1,250]

FEARLESS FOSDICK
See "Li'l Abner."

FEIFFER
Syndicated by Publishers Hall Syndicate.
Jules Feiffer stands almost alone as an
artist and writer. His weekly strip for the
Village Voice has been the standard-bearer
for social commentary for more than four
decades. While he is still doing Feiffer, the
strip has been dropped by the Village
Voice.

Weekly Strips
l956-1959   J. Feiffer   [$300 $450 $600]
1959-Present   J. Feiffer   250   300   400

FELIX THE CAT
Syndicated by King Features. Created by
Pat Sullivan, of whose art almost none
exists. Otto Messmer, the longtime assistant
to Sullivan, drew "Felix" for many years
before signing his own name from the late
1930s on. All artwork before 1930 is
extremely scarce, and from 1930 to 1936, it
is a bit more common but still tough to
find.

Daily Strips
1927-36   O. Messmer $300 $700 $1,400
1935-54   O. Messmer   100   200   300
1954-1967 J. Oriolo/
          Studio Artists   25   50   75

FELIX THE CAT, Otto Mesmer, Sunday page, dated 3/20/1932. Sold for $1,452 in 10/96 (Russ Cochran's art auctions). © King Features Syndicate

Note: a daily dated 8/26/1929 sold at Sotheby's 1997 auction for $1,610.

Sunday Strips

1923-30	O. Messmer	[$900	$1,400	$2,000]
1931-36	O. Messmer	800	1,200	1,800
1937-54	O. Messmer	150	400	900
1954-1967	J. Oriolo/			
	Studio Artists	50	75	100
1984-1987	Studio Artists	35	60	75

Note: two Felix Sunday pages dated 10/20/1935 and 9/21/1941 sold at Sotheby's in 1995 for $2,875.

FERD'NAND

Pantomime strip. It is one of a few strips without any dialogue. Syndicated by United Features.

Daily Strips

1947-70	H. D. Mikkelson	$100	$200	$300
1970-93	A. Plastino	20	40	60
1993-Present	H. Rehr	20	40	60

Sunday Strips

1948-70	H. D. Mikkelson	200	300	400
1970-93	A. Plastino	50	75	100
1993-Present	H. Rehr	50	75	100

FLAMINGO

Syndicated by Phoenix Features. "Flamingo" is a beautifully crafted strip about a gypsy girl by one of America's best "good-girl" cartoonists, Matt Baker.

Daily Strips

1952	M. Baker	$150	$200	$350
1952-53	J. Thornton	50	75	100

FLASH GORDON, Mac Rayboy, Sunday page, dated 3/13/66. Estimate: $600/800; sold for $750 in 6/98 (Sotheby's 8th comic art auction). © King Features Syndicate

FLASH GORDON

Considered by many to be the finest-ever science fiction comic strip. Alex Raymond's art from 1935-1940 is some of the most impressive drawing ever to appear in the newspapers. His assistant, then successor, was noted American illustrator Austin Briggs. All the Raymond prices are without the matching "Jungle Jim" topper. Syndicated by King Features. Size format appreciably affects value. From 1934-1936's are the largest Sundays; certain late 1938's through 1939's are the next largest. The 1937, 1938, 1940 are similarly sized, and for 1941 the page-size shrinks. The 1942 on the page is smallest. Austin Briggs ghosted the strip in 1938. Unsigned pages by Raymond are known to exist. The year 1935-1936 is considered the artistic peak of Alex Raymond.

Daily Strips

1940-44	A. Briggs	$100	$225	$300
1951-53	D. Barry*	100	200	300
1953-89	D. Barry	40	80	120

Sunday Strips

1934	A. Raymond	[9,000	14,000	20,000]
1935	(full page format)			
	A. Raymond			
	(rare)	[10,000	25,000	35,000]
1936-38	A. Raymond	8,000	12,000	16,000
1939-41	A. Raymond	4,000	6,500	9,500
1942-44	A. Raymond	2,000	3,000	5,500
1944-48	A. Briggs	400	600	800
1948-53	M. Rayboy	400	500	600
1954-67	M. Rayboy	150	200	300
1967-89	D. Barry &			
	B. Fugtaine	75	150	225

*In 1952-53, Dan Barry had assistance with story and art from Harvey Kurtzman, Frank Frazetta, and Jack Davis. These strips are two to three times the higher value.

*Collectors should consider that the high column prices for years 1934-41 include the "Jungle Jim" topper strips with the "Flash Gordon" Sunday page.

Note: an Austin Briggs "Flash" Sunday dated 7/24/38 sold for $4,887 at Sotheby's in 1996.

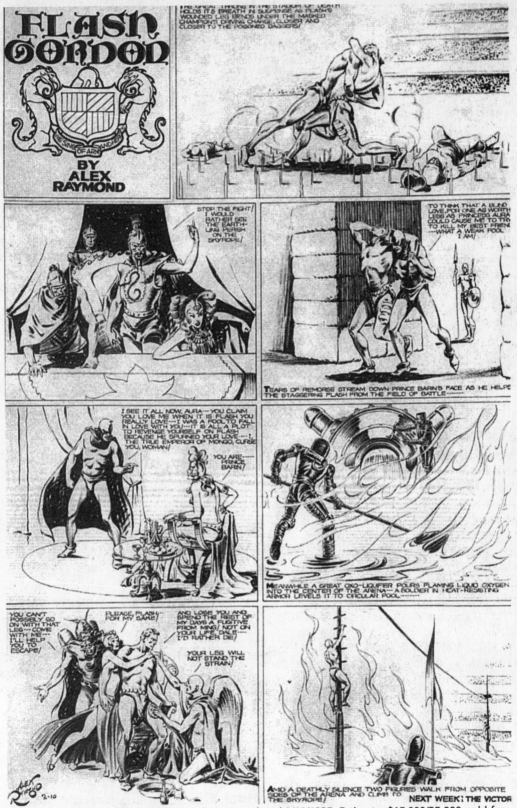

FLASH GORDON, Alex Raymond, Sunday page, dated 2/10/1935. Estimate: $15,000/25,000; sold for
$27,600 in 1997 (Sotheby's 7th comic art auction). © King Features Syndicate

FLASH GORDON, Mac Rayboy, Sunday page, dated 2/1/59. Estimate: $200/300; sold for $460 in 1993 (Sotheby's 3rd comic art auction). © King Features Syndicate

FLASH GORDON, Alex Raymond, Sunday page, dated 2/10/38. Estimate: $9,000/12,000; sold for $9,500 in 6/98 (Sotheby's 8th comic art auction). © King Features Syndicate

FLASH GORDON, Alex Raymond, Sunday page, dated 2/28/43. Estimate: $3,000/5,000; sold for $5,462 in 6/96 (Sotheby's 6th comic art auction). © King Features Syndicate

FLASH GORDON, Austin Briggs, from a lot of 6 dailys in sequence, dated 1944. Estimate: $1,000/1,200; sold for $770 in 1995 (Sotheby's 2nd comic art auction). © King Features Syndicate

In 1997 Sotheby's offered one of the few Flash Gordon Sunday pages in full format without the Jungle Jim across the top tier, dated 2/10/1935; the sale price was $27,600. In 1992 another full vertical Sunday Flash page dated 5/12/1935 failed to reach its reserve price with a low estimate of $30,000 at Christie's East. In 1994 a Sunday dated 9/24/1939 sold for $9,775 at Sotheby's.

FLASH GORDON, Harvey Kurtzman, pencil preliminary for a daily, circa 1950's. sold privately at $250 in 1994. © King Features Syndicate

THE FLINTSTONES

Drawn by Hanna-Barbera staff artists, including Gene Hazelton, based on the cartoon series.

Daily Strips

1961-80s	G. Hazelton	$50	$75	$150

Sunday Strips

1961-80s	G. Hazelton	100	200	350

FLYIN - JENNY

Created by "Buck Rogers" assistant Russell Keaton for the Bell Syndicate. Another airplane adventure strip.

Daily Strips

1938-45	R. Keaton	$200	$250	$300
1945-46	M. Swayze	100	150	200

Sunday Strips

1939-43	R. Keaton	400	500	600
1943-46	M. Swayze	200	300	400

FOR BETTER OR FOR WORSE

By Lynne Johnston. Not to be confused with the Sunday humor strip in the mid-1920s by Tom Dorgan, this "For Better or Worse" is about the daily life of a dentist and his wife and three children. Like predecessor "Gasoline Alley," everyone ages daily. "For Better or Worse" may appear as a standard gag-a-day format at first, but when it is taken in segments of a week, a month, or a year, you see the characters' lives evolve. "For Better or Worse" is truly one of the best-drawn and best-written story strips produced today.

Daily Strips

1979-present	L. Johnston	$100	$125	$150

Sunday Strips

1979-present	L. Johnston	200	250	300

FOR BETTER OR WORSE

Syndicated by King Features.

Sunday Strips

1920s	T. Dorgan	$75	$150	$225

FOX TROT

Gag strip focusing on family life and the kids' antics. Originals from this strip are not available in the market at this time.

Daily Strips

1987-Present	B. Ahmed	[$100	$150	$200]

Sunday Strips

1987-Present	B. Ahmed	[300	400	500]

FOXY COUSIN

Syndicated by Midwestern Syndicate. Created and written by Alfred D. Hayward, this popular "flapper" female strip character brought praise during its short run.

Daily Strips

1924-28	A.D. Hayward	$100	$200	$300

Sunday Strips

1924-28	A.D. Hayward	200	300	400

FOXY GRANDPA

Syndicated by King Features.

Daily Strips

1920-30	C.E.Schultze	[$75	$150	$250]

Sunday Strips

1900-18	C.E.Schultze	[200	400	900]
1920-30	C.E.Schultze	150	300	450

FLYIN' JENNY, Russell Keaton, Sunday page, dated 4/28/40. Sold privately for $225 in 1996.
© The Bell Syndicate

FRECKLES AND HIS FRIENDS

Syndicated by N.E.A. Syndicate. Cute-kid gag strip, better in its early days.

Daily Strips

1915-65	M. Blosser	$75	$100	$150
1965-71	H. Formhals	75	100	150

Sunday Strips

1924-65	M. Blosser	150	200	300
1965-73	H. Formhals	75	100	150

FRIDAY FOSTER

One of the first comic strips to focus on an African-American working girl. News Tribune Syndicate.

Daily Strips

1970-74	J. Longaran	$20	$40	$60
1974	G. Morrow	20	30	40

Sunday Strips

1970-74	J. Longaran	30	60	90
1974	G . Morrow	30	60	90

FRITZI RITZ

Syndicated by United Features. Ernie Bushmiller's humor strip that introduced

Nancy. The strip eventually changed its name to "Nancy."

Daily Strips

1925-35	E. Bushmiller	$200	$300	$400
1936-82	E. Bushmiller	75	150	225
1982-83	M. Lasky	50	75	100
1983-94	J. Scott	100	150	200
1994-Present	G. Gilchrist	100	150	200

Sunday Strips

1928-35	E. Bushmiller	200	350	600
1936-82	E. Bushmiller	100	200	250
1982-83	M. Lasky	100	150	200
1983-94	J. Scott	100	200	300
1994-Present	G. Gilchrist	100	200	300

FU MANCHU

Sax Rohner's famous pulp character debuted for a short run with a daily strip only with remarkable artwork by artist Leo O'Mealia.

Daily Strips

1931-1933	L. O'Mealia	[$900	$1,800	$3,500]

Note: there are almost no known examples of this strip in collections today.

FUNKY WINKERBEAN

Syndicated by Publishers Hall/North American Syndicate. Daily gag strip about a teenager and his friends.

Daily Strips

1972-Present	T. Batiuk	$30	$60	$90

Sunday Strips

1972-Present	T. Batiuk	40	80	120

FUNNY BUSINESS

N.E.A. Syndicate.

Daily Strips

1966-79	R. Bollen	$25	$45	$80

GAMIN AND PATCHES

Syndicated by King Features. Short-run gag strip of a boy and his dog.

Daily Strips

1987-88	M. Walker	$50	$75	$100

Sunday Strips

1987-88	M. Walker	100	150	200

GARFIELD

Syndicated by Universal Press. Enormously successful and popular strip about a boy and his cat. Garfield is fat and lazy, and eats a steady diet of lasagna. He lives to make an utter fool out of his master.

Daily Strips

1977-Present	J. Davis	$300	$500	$650

Sunday Strips

1977-Present	J. Davis	600	700	900

GARTH

British fantasy strip noted mostly for Frank Bellamy's work.

Daily Strips

1943-57	S. Dowling	$100	$175	$250
1957-71	J. Allard	100	150	200
1971-mid-1970s	F. Bellamy	75	100	125

GASOLINE ALLEY

One of America's most important strips. Frank King transformed the focus of Walt Wallet and his garage co-workers in 1921 to the rearing of the baby he found on his doorstep. From that day on, the characters aged daily with the readers. Baby Skeezix grew up, went to war, married his childhood sweetheart, and fathered a new generation of characters. Like a Norman Rockwell painting, King's contribution to the comics is Americana at its best. Note that Frank King's dates on the strip cross over the assistants'. The work by him for the years that assistants are listed is very limited in the drawings. He was mostly writing in the later years. Syndicated by The Chicago Tribune. In the 1940s, Frank King went on a lecture tour. For this, he hand-colored several pages from each decade of the strip. These are worth about double the uncolored pages.

Since publication of the first Comic Art Price Guide a large number of "Gasoline Alley" daily strips have entered the market from a single estate collection. Much to the surprise of veteran collectors this estate caused prices on the dailies to dip. It is not known at this time whether or not early daily prices will bounce back after this situation. Prices on Sunday pages have not been affected.

Daily Strips

1919-20	F. King	[$750	$1,120	$1,500]
1919-28	F. King	400	700	1,000
1929-69	F. King	100	300	500
1953-86	D. Moores	40	80	100
1986-Present	J. Scancarelli	10	20	30

Note: individual sales include three King Gasoline Alley dailies dated 1933, 1934, and 1936 selling at Sotheby's in 1995 for $920; two more groups of three dailies sold for the same price level in the same auction. A single daily dated 6/3/1921 sold for $690 in the same Sotheby's auction.

Note: over the first four years, the daily strip alternated from a single panel to a multiple panel.

Sunday Strips

1918-23	F. King	[1,500	2,500	4,500]
1924-45	F. King	[1,200	2,000	3,000]
1946-69	F. King	[800	1,200	1,600]
1940s-50s	B. Perry	400	600	800
1953-66	D. Moores	150	225	300
1986-Present	J. Scancarelli	50	75	125

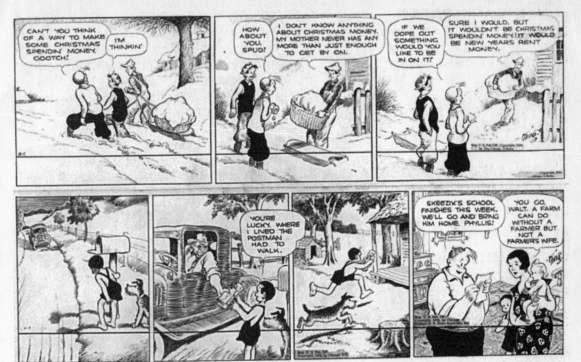

GASOLINE ALLEY, Frank King, artwork to 4 dailies (two shown), from 1934 and 1938. Estimate: $2,000/3,000; sold for $1,150 in 6/96 (Sotheby's 6th comic art auction). © N.Y. New Syndicate, Inc.

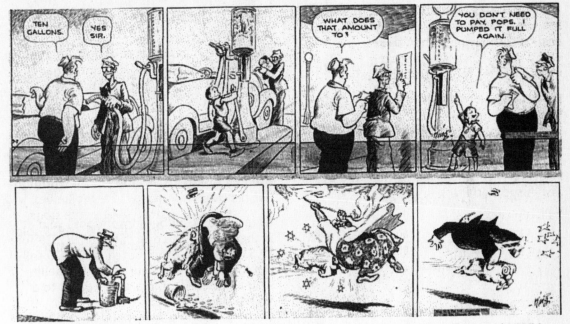

GASOLINE ALLEY, Frank King, artwork for 3 daily strips (two shown), dated 11/2/33, 7/7/34 and 3/23/36. Estimate: $1,000/2,000; sold for $920 in 1995 (Sotheby's 5th comic art auction). © The Chicago Tribune

Note: Frank King personally hand colored a limited number of "Gasoline Alley" Sunday pages in the early 1960's for the purpose of either a series of college lectures, or a special exhibition. These originals were uncovered in the Bill Perry estate by Jim Ivy and bought into the market. There were only about 15 to 20 done, they

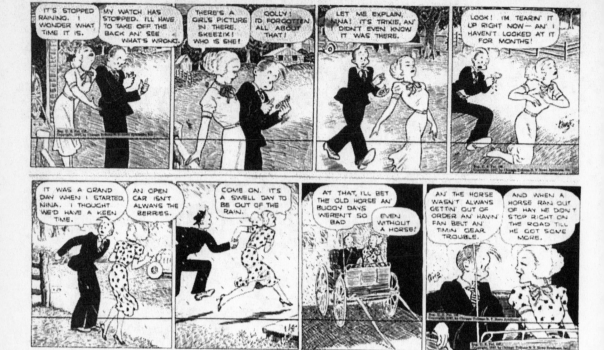

GASOLINE ALLEY, Frank King, artwork for 3 daily strips (two shown), dated 4/30/37, 10/8/37 and 4/29/37. Estimate: $1,000/2,000; sold for $920 in 1995 (Sotheby's 5th comic art auction). © The Chicago Tribune

carry no special signature or inscription and are not colored to the guidelines of the original Sunday published pages.

The first Sunday is dated 1921, and there examples through 1945. Prices for these special pages are exceptions to the normal market

.   [2,500   3,500   7,000]

GAY THIRTIES
Aka "Colonel Gilfeather." Syndicated by The Associated Press.

Daily Strips

1927-33	A. Capp	$200	$300	$400
	M. Caniff	200	300	400
	Miscellaneous			
	Others	20	40	60

GIRL FRIENDS
Unpublished comic strip done prior to "Dick Tracy," not syndicated.

Daily Strips

1931	C. Gould	$400	$500	$600

RUBE GOLDBERG INVENTIONS
These special works were almost unique among American strips in that the gag functioned entirely without the use of word balloons.

Daily Strips

1920's-30s	R. Goldberg	[$800	$1,000	$1,650]
1940's-50s	R. Goldberg	400	750	900

Used by Goldberg in various strips throughout his career.

Note: Two "Goldberg Inventions" sold at Sotheby's in 1996, one dated 6/29/1929 for $2,530 and the other dated 3/30/1929 selling for $2,530.

GORDO
Gordo is one of a few comic strips done with Mexican lead characters. Syndicated by United Features.

Daily Strips

1946-85	G. Arriola	$50	$100	$150

Sunday Strips

1943-85	G. Arriola	100	175	250

THE GUMPS, Gus Edson, Sunday page, dated 1/5/year unknown. Sold privately for $400 in 1997.
© The New York New Syndicate

GRIN AND BEAR IT

Created by George Lichtenstein for the Chicago Daily Times, this gag cartoon has remained popular since its inception.

Daily Panel Strips

1932-1974	G. Lichtenstein	$30	$40	$60
1974-Present	F. Wagner	10	20	30

GROSSLY EXAGGERATED

Syndicated by the New York Mirror.

Daily Strips

1930s-40s	M. Gross	$100	$150	$200

Sunday Strips

1930s-40s	M. Gross	300	350	400

THE GUMPS

Sidney Smith's middle-class family from Chicago, "The Gumps," was one of America's most widely read strips. Syndicated by The New York News Syndicate. Stanley Link did adventure Sundays in the 1920s.

Daily Strips

1917-23	S. Smith	$100	$150	$300
1924-34	S.Smith	90	125	250
1935-59	G. Edson	50	100	150

Sunday Strips

1919-23	S. Smith	300	400	700
1924-34	S. Smith	250	300	550
1935-41	G. Edson	200	250	[300]
1942-59	G. Edson	75	150	200

HAGAR THE HORRIBLE, Dik Browne, Sunday strip, dated 9/12/82. Sold in a group lot for $75 in 1994. © King Features Syndicate

HAGAR THE HORRIBLE

Syndicated by King Features. One of the wittiest comic strips around. Dik Browne was a genius, and his work and gags on "Hagar" continually showed his comic talents. His son, Chris, is keeping up the standards his father created.

Daily Strips

1973-89	D. Browne	$100	$150	$250
1989-Present	C. Browne	50	75	100

Sunday Strips

1973-89	D. Browne	200	250	400
1989-Present	C. Browne	100	150	200

HAIRBREADTH HARRY

Philadelphia Ledger Syndicate. Melodramatic hero-vs.-villain story strip. Well drawn and scarce.   Many comic historians consider Hairbreadth Harry to be the first adventure strip.

Daily Strips

1923-31 (note: only 10 known to exist)

(very rare)	C. W. Kahles	[$200	$300	$500]
1931-39	F. O. Alexander	75	100	125

Sunday Strips

1906-31	C. W. Kahles	300	400	500
1931-39	F. O. Alexander	200	300	400

HALF HITCH

Syndicated by King Features.

Daily Strips

1970-75	H. Ketcham/			
	D. Hodgins, Jr.	$50	$75	$100

Sunday Strips

1970-75	H. Ketcham/			
	D. Hodgins, Jr.	100	150	200

HAPPY HOOLOGAN (THE DOINGS OF HAPPY HOOLIGAN)

Syndicated by King Features. Popular early strip by noted cartoonist Fred Opper.

Daily Strips

1930-32	F. Opper	$200	$250	$300

Sunday Strips

1900-15	F. Opper	500	800	1,400
1916-32	F. Opper	475	700	900

HAROLD TEEN

Before Archie Andrews, the hip teenager was Harold Teen. Syndicated by The Chicago Tribune.

Daily Strips

1926-30	C. Ed	$60	$80	$150
1931-59	C. Ed	30	60	90

Sunday Strips

1926-30	C. Ed	200	300	500

HAGAR THE HORRIBLE, Dik Browne, daily, dated 9/10/79. Sold in a group lot for $300 in 1994.

| 1931-59 | C. Ed | 125 | 200 | 400 |

THE HAWK
Short-lived swashbuckler strip syndicated by noted comic book publisher Jerry Iger for the Phoenix Syndicate.

Daily Strips

| 1953 | R. H. Webb | $50 | $75 | $100 |

HAWKSHAW THE DETECTIVE
Syndicated by United Features. Originally based on Sherlock Holmes. This strip initially was a page unto itself, then returned in 1931 as a top strip to "The Captain and The Kids."

Sunday Strips

| 1913-22 | G. Mager | $200 | $350 | $500 |
| 1931-64 | G. Mager | 50 | 125 | 200 |

HAZEL
Panel strip centering on the maid.

Daily Strips

| 1969-Present | T. Key | $200 | $300 | $400 |

THE HEART OF JULIET JONES
Syndicated by King Features. "The Heart of Juliet Jones" has always been a well-drawn comic strip. Drake's style has influenced countless artists. Cartoonists, most notably Neal Adams, still draw in the Stan Drake style.

Daily Strips

| 1953-89 | S. Drake | $50 | $75 | $150 |

Sunday Strips

| 1954-89 | S. Drake | 125 | 200 | 275 |

HEATHCLIFF
Daily gag panel about a cat.

PRICE RANGE KEY

RARITY — Brackets [ ] around a price indicate that this example is very scarce and could exceed maximum estimate.

Covers
No work produced in this category— XXX
No price available due to lack of information— ***

CONDITION — Age, color, marks, tears, etc.

Pages
[400   500   600]

CHARACTER — Is the primary character featured, or is the original characteristic of a great example in the story line?

CONTENT — is the theme or story line exceptional or below average?

VALUE RANGE

| Minimum | Medium | Maximum |

RARITY
The [ ] Brackets indicate RARITY, if these brackets are used the reader can potentially double the price range in all three catagories.

Daily Strips

1980-Present	G. Gatley	$100	$150	$200

Sunday Strips

1980-Present	G. Gatley	200	300	400

HENRY

"Henry" started as a Saturday Evening Post Cartoon, then graduated to newspaper syndication in 1934. Syndicated by King Features.

Daily Strips

1932	C. Anderson	[$200	$300	$600]
1933-39	C. Anderson	200	300	500
1940-42	C. Anderson	150	200	300
1943	C. Anderson	100	150	200
1942-70s	J. Cinley	50	75	100

Sunday Strips (1935-36 are rare)

1935-36	C. Anderson	[400	600	900]
1937-42	C. Anderson	250	350	500
1942-70s	D. Tracte	100	150	200

HERMAN

Classic humor panel by Jim Unger. Syndicated by Universal Press Syndicate.

Daily Strips

1977-present	J. Unger	$100	$150	$200

Sunday Strips

1977-Present	J. Unger	200	300	400

HEROS THE SPARTAN

A weekly British color adventure cartoon in a Sunday page format by one of the top British artists, Frank Bellamy.

Sunday Strips

1962-66	F. Bellamy	$500	$650	[$800]

HI AND LOIS

Syndicated by King Features. Suburban-couple daily gag strip by one of the top creative teams in comic strip history. Chris Browne, longtime assistant to his father, Dik, took over the drawing upon his father's death in 1989.

Daily Strips

1954-89	M. Walker/			
	D. Browne	$100	$150	$200
1989-Present	M. Walker/			
	C. Browne	100	150	200

Sunday Strips

1954-89	M . Walker/			
	D. Browne	200	300	500
1989-Present	M. Walker/			
	C. Browne	200	300	400

HOPALONG CASSIDY

The popular movie cowboy became a regular feature in the funny pages with artwork by Dan Spiegle.

Daily Strips

1949-1955	D. Spiegle	$50	$75	$150

Sunday Strips

1949-1955	D. Spiegle	75	150	250

HOWDY DOODY

Comic strip takeoff of the popular TV show. United Features Syndicate.

Daily Strips

1950-52	Chad	$50	$100	$200

Sunday Strips

1950-52	Chad	150	300	600

INVISIBLE SCARLET O'NEILL

Adventure strip about a woman who turns invisible. Chicago Times Syndicate. Became "Stainless Steel" in 1953.

Daily Strips

1940-44	R. Stamm	$300	$400	$500
1944-46	Studio			
	Assistants	100	150	200
1946-56	R. Stamm	100	150	200

Sunday Strips

1942-56	R. Stamm	700	900	1,100

JANE ARDEN

Story strip about a female reporter. Register and Tribune Syndicate.

Daily Strips

1928-1935	F. Ellis	$100	$150	$200
1935-1955	R. Ross	60	80	100
1956-1963	J. Speed/			
	W. Hargis	20	40	60
1964-1968	B. Schoenkye	20	40	60

Sunday Strips

1933-1950	Russell Ross/			
	Studio artists	50	70	90
1935-1968	Russell Ross/			
	Studio artists	40	60	80

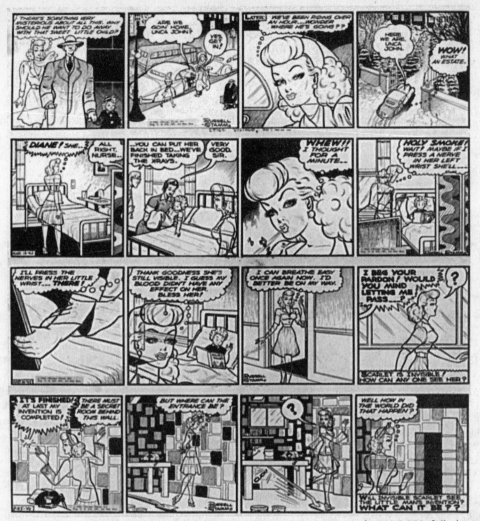

INVISIBLE SCARLET O'NEIL, Russell Stamm, daily strips, dated 1942. Estimate: $1,500/2,000; failed to meet reserve price (Sotheby's 6th comic art auction). © Chicago Times Tribune

JERRY ON THE JOB

Well-drawn gag strip about a working teenager. Syndicated by King Features.

Daily Strips

1913-35	W. Hoban	$50	$75	$100

Sunday Strips

1921-35	W. Hoban	100	150	200

JIM HARDEY (BECOMES WINDY AND PADDLES)

Syndicated by United Features. "Jim Hardy" is a detective strip in the "Dick Tracy" vein by Gould's former assistant, Dick Moores. This format quickly changed to a gag strip focusing on two background characters, Windy & Paddles.

Daily Strips

1935-42	D. Moores	$60	$90	$200

JOE JINKS (CURLY KAYOE - POST 1945)

Long-running story strip started by Vic Forsythe. Syndicated by United Features.

Daily Strips

1918-33	V. Forsythe	$50	$75	$100
1933-36	P. Llanuza	40	60	80
1936-44	M.Leff, M. Weiss, and Studio Assistants	30	40	50

Sunday Strips

1918-33	V. Forsythe	100	150	200
1933-44	H. Formhals	50	75	100

JOE PALOOKA

The boxing strip that made Al Capp famous. Capp, an early Fisher assistant, wrote several stories, including one about a hillbilly family. Fisher ignored the popularity of these characters and Capp went on to fame with them as "Li'l Abner." From the McNaught Syndicate.

Daily Strips

1928-35	H. Fisher	$200	$300	$400

1936-55	H. Fisher	60	120	180
1955-84	M. Leff	20	40	60

Sunday Strips

1928-35	H. Fisher	500	750	1,000
1936-55	H. Fisher	200	350	600
1955-84	M. Leff	100	150	200

JOHN DARLING

Daily gag strip about a talk-show host. North American Syndicate.

JOHNNY HAZARD, Frank Robbins, Sunday Page, dated 1/8/67. Estimate: $250/350; sold for $368 in 1995 (Christie's East Comic Art Auctions). © King Features Syndicate

JOHNNY HAZARD, Frank Robbins, Sunday Page, dated 1/8/67. Estimate: $1,000/1,500; sold for $633 in 1993 (Sotheby's 3rd comic art auction). © King Features Syndicate

JOHNNY COMET, Frank Frazetta, daily, dated 3/11/52. Estimate: $1,000/2,000; sold for $1,100 in 6/95 (Sotheby's 8th comic art auction). © The McNaught Syndicate

JOHNNY COMET, Frank Frazetta, daily, dated 6/7/52. Estimate: $1,000/2,000; sold for $1,430 in 6/97 (Russ Cochran Auctions). © The McNaught Syndicate

Daily Strips

1979-80	T. Batiuk	$30	$40	$50

Sunday Strips

1979-80	T. Batiuk	75	100	125

JOHNNY HAZARD

Syndicated by King Features. Frank Robbins' style was greatly influenced by Milton Caniff; a top-notch aviation adventure strip.

Daily Strips

1944-77	F. Robbins	$50	$100	$150

Sunday Strips

1944-77	F. Robbins	200	400	600

JOHNNY COMET (BECOMES ACE MCCOY)

While short-lived, this racing-car strip features some of the finer artwork of Frank Frazetta. The strip is remarkable for its unevenness in artistic quality. At its best in early 1952 in Sunday and daily formats, and in late 1952 and early 1953 in daily format. The first tour months were larger-format dailies. The strip's final months found it renamed "Ace McCoy." From the McNaught Syndicate.

Daily Strips

1952-53	F. Frazetta	$600	$1,200	$2,400

Sunday Strips

1952-53	F. Frazetta	2,000	3,000	4,000

JUDGE PARKER

Well-drawn "soap opera" strips. Syndicated by the Field Syndicate.

Daily Strips

1952-65	D. Heilman	$100	$150	$200
1965-80s	H. LeRoux	50	75	100
1980s-Present	T. Di Preta	50	75	100

JUMP START

A family strip by artist Robb Armstrong for United Feature Syndicate

Daily Strips

1990-Present	R. Armstrong	$50	$75	$100

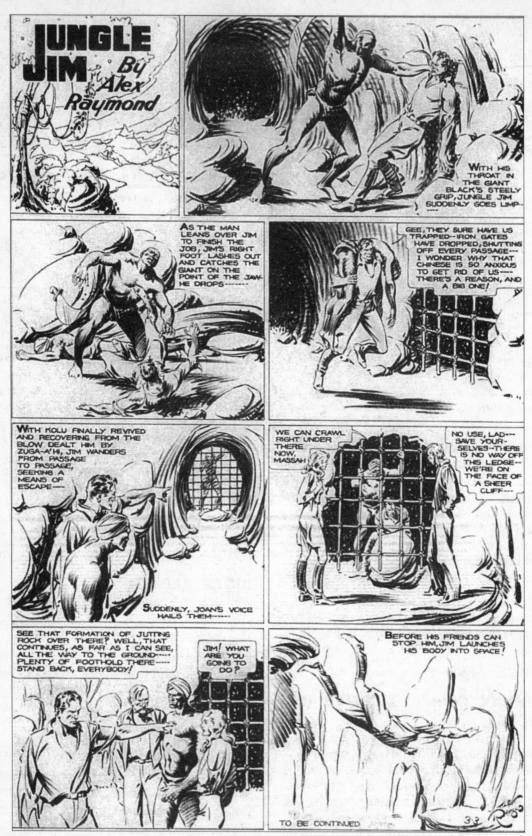

JUNGLE JIM, Alex Raymond, Sunday Page, dated 3/3/1935. Estimate: $7,000/10,000; sold for $6,325 in 6/97 (Sotheby's 7th comic art auction). © King Features Syndicate

JUNGLE JIM, Alex Raymond, Sunday Page, dated 1/1/1938. Estimate: $1,200/1,500; sold for $1,495 in 1994 (Sotheby's 4th comic art auction). © King Features Syndicate

JUNGLE JIM

"Jungle Jim" ran as a top strip to "Flash Gordon." The pairing of these strips adds about 20 percent to their individual prices. Syndicated by King Features.

Sunday Strips

1934	A. Raymond	[$2500	$3,500	$4500]
1935	A. Raymond			
	(Full pages)	5,000	7,500	11,000
1935-36	A. Raymond	2,000	2,500	3,500
1937-41	A. Raymond	1,000	1,500	2,000
1942-44	A. Raymond	800	1,200	1,600
1944-48	A. Briggs	300	400	500
1948-54	P. Norris	200	300	400

Note: individual sales include a Full Sunday page dated 3/3/1935 selling for $6,275 at Sotheby's 1997 comic art auction; another Full Page Sunday format page dated 5/26/35 sold at Christie's East in 1992 for $9,350.

JUST KIDS

Daily gag strip about kids. Syndicated by King Features.

Daily Strips

1923-57	A. Carter	$50	$100	$150

Sunday Strips

1923-57	A. Caner	100	200	250

THE KATZENJAMMER KIDS

The oldest United States comic strip in existence. Creator Rudolph Dirks lost control of his title in a legal suit when he changed publishers. Dirks continued his characters under the name "The Captain and the Kids" in 1914. Syndicated by King Features. It should be noted that the early Katzenjammer Sunday pages are extremely rare, and only a handful are known to exist.

Sunday Strips

1897-1912	R. Dirks	[$1,500	$3,000	$4,500]
1914-49	H. Knerr	250	500	750
1949-	D. Winner,			
Present	J. Musial,			
	H. Eisman,			
	Studio Artists	100	200	300

KERRY DRAKE

Alfred Andriola created this detective strip after being an assistant to Milton Caniff. Like "Dick Tracy," the villains usually reflected their offbeat names. The Field Syndicate.

Daily Strips

1943-50	A Andriola	$100	$150	$200
1950-83	A. Andriola	35	70	105

Sunday Strips

1943-50	A. Andriola	300	400	500
1950-83	A. Andriola	100	150	200

KRAZY KAT, George Herriman, Sunday Page, dated 9/22/35. Estimate: $4,000/7,000; sold for $4,510 in 6/97 (Russ Cochran's Art Auctions). © King Features Syndicate

KRAZY KAT, George Herriman, daily, dated 10/15/31. Estimate: $1,500/2,500; sold for $2,875 in 6/99 (Sotheby's 9th comic art auction). © King Features Syndicate

KEVIN THE BOLD
(FORMELY MITZI MCCOY)

An adventure strip for the NEA Service Syndicate by artist Kreigh Collins.

Sunday Strips

1948-72	K. Collins	$50	$75	$150

THE KEWPIES

Early American strip centering around babies by Rose O'Neill for King Features Syndicate.

Daily Strips

1917-18	R. O'Neill	$75	100	175
1935-37	R. O'Neill	50	75	125

Sunday Strips

1917-18	R. O'Neill	100	150	250
1935-37	R. O'Neill	75	100	175

KING AROO

Syndicated by the McClure Syndicate. Outlandishly funny and inventive humor strip by Jack Kent.

Daily Strips

1950-65	J. Kent	$100	$125	$150

Sunday Strips

1950-65	J. Kent	200	250	300

KRAZY KAT

George Herriman's "Krazy Kat" stands alone in a creative world of artists making him/her one of the outstanding comic strip characters in American history. "Krazy" made her/his first appearance as a bottom strip under the "Dingbat Family" and then "The Family Upstairs," two of Herriman's earlier strips. From the simple motif of the Kat and the Mouse and the "brick," Herriman would later develop a third character, Officer Pup, and bring Kokonino County into being. For those who read "Krazy Kat" daily, it was a beloved strip. With the artist's use of language as poetry, and the tremendous visual invention that took place constantly within the space of the panels, "Krazy Kat" remains a strip with worldwide popularity and respect fifty years after its last appearance. Herriman's art remained consistent from 1916 on. For the true fan, any original will do, but many people look for a strip of Ignatz throwing a brick at Krazy Kat. These "brick" dailies will always be higher-priced. Herriman also hand-colored a number of originals. These sell at a value of about two (to three) times what is listed. Herriman watercolored various Sundays (see the special article at the beginning of this book about collecting hand colored originals) and a few dailies. His watercoloring was especially well executed, and these were usually personally endorsed to a fan or a friend. Provenance is all-important on these pieces. Watercolored pieces were either in light and primary colors or in the Southwestern colors for which Herriman was so justly famous.

Daily Strips

1910-13	G. Herriman	[$1,500	$2,250	$3,000]
1918-20	G. Herriman	1,000	1,700	[2,500]
1920-30	G. Herriman	700	1,400	[1,800]
1930-44	G. Herriman	750	1,200	[1,750]

Note: unlike specialty watercolors, or hand colored Sunday pages which are known to exist in higher numbers, there are most likely only two or three known hand colored watercolor "Krazy Kat" dailies.

Note: some individual prices for dailies include 4/4/1932 selling for $2,875; 8/31/1933 selling for $1,610; 3/1/1935 sell-

KRAZY KAT, George Herriman, Sunday Page, dated 10/3/20. Estimate: $6,000/9,000; sold for $7,700 in 10/96 (Russ Cochran's comic art auctions). © King Features Syndicate

ing for $1,380; an upright daily dated 11/6/circa 1916 selling for $3,450; 1/26/1938 selling for $1,610; 1/14/1941 selling for $2,415; all sales at Christie's East and Sotheby's.

Sunday Strips

1916-17	G. Herriman	[7,000	9,000	12,000]
1918-20	G. Herriman	6,000	7,000	8,000
1920-36	G. Herriman	4,000	5,000	6,000
1936-44	G Herriman	2,500	3,250	4,000

Note: 1943 Sunday pages that are unsigned should sell for less.

Note: individual sales on Sunday pages include 3/11/1934 selling for $5,750; 7/4/1943 selling for $5,520; 9/28/1941 selling for $5,060; 9/4/1941 (with Walt Disney letter sent to Herriman family) selling for $8,050; 10/3/1920 selling for $5,462; August/1920 selling for $5,750; all sales from Christie's East and Sotheby's.

Note: specialty originals that have sold publicly within the past four years include the following examples: a small watercolor (bound within a book) measuring 8" x 5 1/2" circa 1920's or 1930's selling at $5,750; possibly the finest of the desert scenes dated 9/9/1933 measuring 14" x 20" watercolor on board selling for $40,250; Sunday hand-colored page from the estate of Murray Harris, dated 11/17/1918 with special inscription by Herriman selling for $29,250; two very early Sunday pages both inscribed and hand colored dating from 1916 being the No. 2 and No. 4 pages selling for $80,000; these prices are from Christie's East, Sotheby's, Howard Lowery and private sales.

LADY LUCK
Backup feature to the weekly "Spirit" section Syndicated for the Register and Tribune.

Sunday Strips
1940-46   K. Nordling $200 $250 $300

LANCE
Like "Johnny Comet" by Frank Frazetta, Warren Tufts' "Lance" was not popular when it came out. It was a Western adventure strip with exceptional artwork and strong writing. Today, collectors respect and admire Tufts' work, and it is highly prized. Syndicated by United Features.

Sunday Strips
1955-57   W. Tufts $200 $300 $400

LIFE IN HELL
Artist Matt Groening cut his teeth with this provocative strip years before developing the popular TV series "The Simpsons." Originally presented in the *Los Angeles Reader* this unique strip was quickly picked up and syndicated. Very few originals have found their way into the market place.

Weekly Format Strip
1980-
Present   M. Groening   [$600 $1,200 $2,500]

LIFE'S LIKE THAT
Artist Fred Neher was responsible for this single panel and strip format cartoon for the United Feature Syndicate. The majority of this artists originals were donated by the family to the University of Colorado.

Single Panel Strips
1934-77   F. Neher $25 $30 $40
Sunday Format Strips
1950's-77   F. Neher   30   45   75

LI'L ABNER
Al Capp created the classic hillbilly strip in 1934 with his "Li'l Abner." With solid art and writing, "Li'l Abner" quickly became one of the best humor strips ever done. Capp's political views entered into the story

LI'L ABNER, Al Capp, daily featuring FEARLESS FOSDICK, dated 12/1/51. Estimate: $1,500/2,000; sold for $1,380 in 6/99 (Sotheby's 9th comic art auction). © United Features Syndicate

LI'L ABNER, Al Capp, Sunday page, dated 1/6/52. Estimate: $1,200/1,500; sold for $2,070 in 6/93 (Sotheby's 3rd comic art auction). © United Features Syndicate

line over the last few years, but so did a multitude of zany characters. Capp ran a studio and there were various assistants always working with him. The 1954-1959 range reflects the work of Frank Frazetta, who worked on a large portion, but not all, of the comic strips. Characters such as Fearless Fosdick (1943) and the Shmoos (1948) will cause strip value to be higher with their appearances. Syndicated by United Features.

It must be noted that since the publication of the first Comic Art Price Guide prices have gone flat for low quality "Li'l Abner"

strips. Part of the problem is a plentiful supply of daily and Sunday originals within the market at the moment. Prices for the coveted Fosdick and Shmoo appearances on quality examples are rising.

Daily Strips

1934-35	A. Capp	$250	$550	$850
1936-52	A. Capp/			
	Studio Artists	150	225	300
1944-52	(Fosdick			
	appearances)	800	1,600	2,400
1948-	(First Shmoo			
(rare)	story.)	[2,500	4,500	6,500]

LI'L ABNER, Al Capp, 3 consecutive dailies, dated 2/29/40, 3/1/40 and 3/2/40. Estimate: $800/1,000; sold for $660 in 3/98 (Russ Cochran auctions). © United Features Syndicate

LI'L ABNER, Al Capp, daily featuring FEARLESS FOSDICK, dated 11/30/51. Estimate: $1,500/2,000; sold for $1,380 in 6/99 (Sotheby's 9th comic art auction). © United Features Syndicate

1949-54	(Shmoos appearances)	[1,500	2,500	4,000]
1953-59	A. Capp/ Studio Artists	100	150	300
1960-76	A. Capp/ Studio Artists	40	60	90

Note: a private sale took place in 1997 for what is considered one of the very best existing example of a Shmoo daily for the entire sequence at $15,000.

LI'L ABNER, Al Capp, daily, dated 3/11/49. Estimate: $400/600; sold for $715 in 10/92 (Christie's East comic art auctions). © United Features Syndicate

Sunday Strips

1935-42	A. Capp/			
	Studio Artists	800	1,400	3,000
1942-50	(Fosdick			
	appearances)	1,000	1,800	2,800
1949-	(First Shmoo			
(rare)	Story)	2,500	3,500	5,000
1950-52	(Shmoos			
	appearances)	1,000	1,800	3,000
1943-52	A. Capp/			
	Studio Artists	400	600	800
1953-59	A. Capp/			
	Studio Artists	350	550	900
1960-76	A. Capp/			
	Studio Artists	150	350	500

Note: individual sales include: eight dailies from 1940 selling for $2,070; eleven dailies from 1945-50 selling for $1,840; nine dailies from 1944-48 selling for $2,530; a daily dated 10/15/1934 selling for $690; all sales from Christie's East. From Sotheby's a "Fearless Fosdick" daily dated 6/30/1944 sold for $3,162; sixteen daily strips from June 24 - July 26/1944 sold for $4,312; two dailies dated 7/14-15/1944 with "Fosdick" reference sold for $3,450.

Sunday page sales include 12/17/1939 selling for $1,380; two consecutive Sunday pages dated 12/11/1949 & 12/18/1949 selling for $1,495.

Note: a series of lithographic prints were published with Al Capp's signature in limited edition numbers; these sets are very soft in the market place. A small number of acrylic paintings on canvas have also been offered from the 1970's onward as being original Al Capp paintings, buyers however

should be aware that many long time Capp associates confirm that studio artists "may" have been involved in the production of these paintings on some level.

LITTLE ANNIE FANNY

"Little Annie Fanny" is the brainchild of Harvey Kurtzman, one of the most important comic artists of the last 40 years. The two to six-page adventures were published in *Playboy* magazine over a 23- year period. Usually coproduced with Bill Elder, with a host of who's who in comics who lent their hand in rendering, including Jack Davis, Russ Heath, Al Jaffee, Paul Coker, and Frank Frazetta.

Monthly Strips

1962-85	H . Kurtzman/			
	B. Elder			
	(Full-Page			
	Strips)	[$750	$1,250	$1,500]

LITTLE ANNIE ROONEY

Adventure strip starring a twelve-year-old girl. Syndicated by King Features.

Daily Strips

1929-30	E. Verdier	$30	$60	$90
1930-66	D. McClure	20	40	60

Sunday Strips

1930-32	D. McClure	50	75	100
1932-65	N. Afosky	30	60	90
1932-52	M. Fu (Adventure			
	Bottom Strip)	75	100	125

LITTLE IODINE

Syndicated by King Features.

LITTLE LULU, Margiorie Henderson Buell, circa 1930's. Estimate: $500/600; sold for $690 in 1993 (Sotheby's 3rd comic art auction). © United Features Syndicate

Sunday Strips

1943-67	J. Hatlo	$80	$120	$160
1967-70's	B. Dunn	50	75	100
1970's-86	H. Eisman	20	40	60

LITTLE JIMMY

Syndicated by King Features. Swinnerton's kid strip is noted mostly for the mid-1930s sequences taking place in the Southwest. This strip is starting to get attention as one of the true pioneers of early cartoon art along with such artists as Palmer Cox, Richard Outcault, Fred Opper and Winsor McCay. Syndicated by The Chicago Tribune.

Daily Strips

1900-07	J. Swinnerton	$150	$350	$450

Sunday Strips *(rare-less than 20 known)*

1904-ll	J. Swinnerton ("Jimmy," not "Little Jimmy")	[750	1,200	2,000]
1920-58	J. Swinnerton	300	650	1,000

THE LITTLE KING

Pantomime strip. "Sentinel Louie" was the topper. Syndicated by King Features.

Sunday Strips

1934-40s	0. Soglow	$300	$375	$450
1940s-75	Studio Artist	100	150	200

LITTLE LULU

"Little Lulu" was originally a Saturday Evening Post panel by Marge Henderson Buell, then later a comic book and comic strip.

1935-*Panels* M. H. Buell/ Saturday Evening Post Panels (*Single Panels*)

	$800	$1,200	$1,500

Daily Strips

1955-67	R. Armstrong/ Various Artists	50	75	125

LITTLE NEMO IN SLUMBERLAND

Windsor McCay created a spectacular comic strip with "Little Nemo in Slumberland." With a flair for dramatic content, imaginary landscapes, and architectural vistas, Mr. McCay brought forth Nemo's dreams and adventures week after week in one of America's most remembered strips. Syndicated by New York Herald. Color-guided watercolored Nemos are known to exist, however absolute provenance does not exist for this colored originals and they may be the result of studio or syndicate artists who were finishing color guides for engravers and printers as was the case with the "Prince Vailant" strip. Many times up until the early 1930's these colored pages had one or two figures colored, and the remainder of the page was left black and white. Little Nemo occasionally appeared with "In the Land of Wonderful Dreams," a secondary strip with color-guided pieces of art known to exist.

Sunday Strips

1905-11	W. McCay	$6,000	$12,000	$21,000
1924-27	W. McCay	[3,000	5,000	8,000]

Note: a nearly fully colored Little Nemo came to auction in 1995, dated 6/15/1913 with catalogue estimate of $50,000-$60,000, this original failed to meet its reserve price at Christie's East comic art auction.

Note: individual sales include 2/6/1910 selling for $21,850; 6/17/1906 selling for $9,775; 4/9/1906 selling for $12,650; 6/21/1908 selling for $8,575; 10/11/1908 selling for 8,575.

LITTLE NEMO IN SLUMBERLAND, Winsor McCay, Sunday page, dated 2/6/10. Estimate: $18,000/22,000; sold for $21,850 in 11/96 (Christie's East comic art auctions). © New York Herald Co.

A watercolor with excellent provenance of Little Nemo in a ship with other characters from the strip sold for $8,050.

Note: the estate of the family of Windsor McCay still holds many original Sunday pages of Little Nemo, along with other McCay strips and many of the editorial cartoons. The quality and condition is high,

and they allow very few sales during any given year.

LITTLE MISS MUFFET

A child orphan strip created by Fanny Cory for King Features Syndicate.

Daily Strips

1935-56	F. Cory	$50	$75	$125

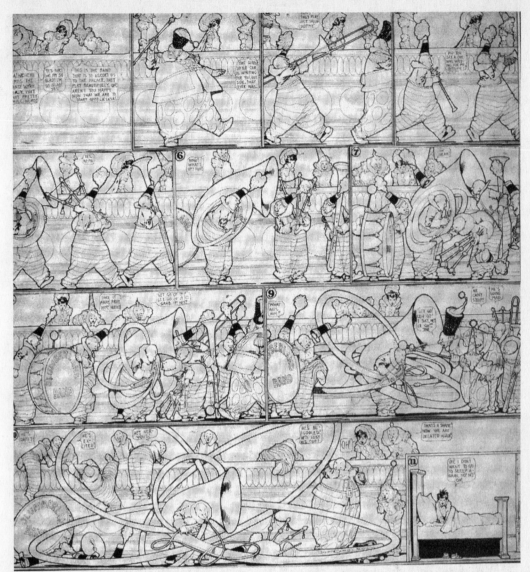

LITTLE NEMO IN SLUMBERLAND, Winsor McCay, Sunday page, dated 4/9/06. Estimate: $10,000/12,000; sold for $12,650 in 1995 (Sotheby's 5th comic art auction). © New York Herald Co.

LITTLE ORPHAN ANNIE

A major story strip, famous for its art and political statements (ultraconservative). "Little Orphan Annie" is an important slice of cartoon history. It should be noted that almost every existing original resides in the Boston University Library. Of those not in the library, almost all of the early strips are trimmed to the panel borders. Syndicated for The Chicago Tribune. A large number of originals were directly donated to the permanent collection of Boston University after the artists death by the family and estate, so for certain periods of time original Annie's are impossible to find.

Daily Strips

1924-30	H. Gray	$1,500	$2,250	$3,500
1931-50	H. Gray	[400	800	1,400]
1950-62	H. Gray	[200	300	400]
1962-67	H. Gray	[100	200	300]
1967-80	Studio Artists	20	30	60
1980-Present	L. Starr	60	60	120

Sunday Strips

1924-30	H. Gray	[6,000	7,000	8,000]
1931-50	H. Gray	[1,000	2,000	3,000]
1950-67	H Gray	[300	600	900]
1967-80	Studio Artists	50	75	100

LITTLE ORPHAN ANNIE, Harold Gray, set of six unpublished daily strips, turned in by the artist just before his death, and unused by the Syndicate. For sale at Sotheby's June 17, 2000 comic art auction. Estimate: $2,000/4,000. © The Chicago Tribune

ARCHIE, Bob Montana, original set of the first six daily strips, kept by the Montana family. Auctioned at Sotheby's June 17, 2000 comic art auction. Estimate: $6,000/9,000. © King Features Syndicate

Note: individual sales include: daily dated 4/24/1935 selling for $950; daily from 6/23/1967 selling for $250; four dailies from 1957-1964 selling for $575; sales from Howard Lowery and Sotheby's.

THE LITTLE PEOPLE
Humor strip about a valley of elf-sized people. Syndicated by N.E.A. Syndicate.

Sunday Strips

1952-80	W. Scott	$75	$100	$125

LITTLE SAMMY SNEEZE
Winsor McCay drew this strip about a little boy who could sneeze his way through countless adventures and situations for the Telegram and Evening Telegram in New York.

Sunday Strips

1904-06	W. McCay	[$1,250	$2,250	$3,500]

Note: individual sales include, a 1907 selling for $1,800 at Howard Lowery Auctions; two Sammy Sneeze Sundays dated 1905 selling for $4,025 at Sotheby's.

The estate and family of Winsor McCay hold a number of originals to this strip; they are rarely offered into the market.

LOCKHORNS
Contemporary daily gag panel. Syndicated by King Features.

Daily Strips

1968-88	B. Hoest	$50	$75	$100
1988-present	J. Reiner	35	60	100

Sunday Strips

1968-88	B. Hoest	100	200	300
1988-Present	J. Reiner	50	75	100

LONG SAM
A strip created by Al Capp and illustrated by veteran great Bob Lubbers for United Feature Syndicate. A female creature from the inventive mind of Al Capp, this strip was eventually written as well by Lubbers.

Sunday Strips

1954-62	B. Lubbers	$75	$100	$125

THE LONE RANGER
Syndicated by King Features. This classic Western hero, along with his trusty side-kick, Tonto, kept the West safe from outlaws. Russ Heath's work is considered by many to be the best done on this comic strip.

Daily Strips

1938-39	E. Kressy	$150	$200	$250
1939-50	C. Flanders	150	200	250
1950-71	C. Flanders	25	50	75
1979-81	R. Heath	75	100	125

Sunday Strips

1979-81		50	75	100

LYTTLE WOMEN
Syndicated by King Features. Bright contemporary gag strip focusing on a little girl and her doll.

Daily Strips

1991-Present	K. LeMieux	$100	$150	$200

Sunday Strips

1991-present	K. LeMieux	200	300	400

MALE CALL
"Male Call" is a daily strip focusing on soldiers or sailors with pinup girl Miss Lace. Distributed exclusively for the armed forces during World War II. The first few strips originally featured "Terry and the Pirates" femme fatale Burma. Almost all originals are at Ohio State University.

Daily Strips

1943-46	M. Caniff	[$400	$800	$1,200]

Note: though some of Caniff's work has become leveled out in the recent market place "Male Call" would be an exception to the rule, these originals are truly rare and sought out by veteran collectors.

MANDRAKE THE MAGICIAN
Syndicated by King Features. With a hypnotic gesture, you will agree that "Mandrake" is a wonderful adventure strip. It is still written today by its creator, Lee Falk.

Daily Strips

1934-40	P. Davis	[$400	$600	$1,200]
1940-42	P. Davis	400	600	1,000
1943-64	P. Davis	100	200	300
1964-Present	F. Fredericks	20	40	60

MANDRAKE THE MAGICIAN, Lee Falk and Phil Davis, Sunday page, dated 12/7/47. Estimate: $900/1,200; failed to meet reserve in 1995 (Christie's East Comic Art Auctions). © King Features Syndicate

MANDRAKE THE MAGICIAN, Phil Davis, daily, dated 10/6/47. Estimate: $500/700; sold for $588 in 3/98 (Russ Cochran art auctions). © King Features Syndicate

MANDRAKE THE MAGICIAN, Phil Davis, daily, dated 10/3/36. Estimate: $600/1,000; sold for $920 in 1996 (Sotheby's 6th comic art auction). © King Features Syndicate

Sunday Strips (1935-38 are very rare)

1935-38	P. Davis	[900	1,900	4,800]
1939-42	P. Davis	[600	1,200	1,800]
1954-64	P. Davis	200	250	300
1964-Present	F. Fredericks	25	50	75

Note: individual sales include, a Sunday dated 7/24/1938 selling for $2,200; and a daily dated 8/1/1940 from Howard Lowery Auctions; a daily dated 10/3/1936 selling for $920 at Sotheby's.

MARK TRAIL
Long before Greenpeace, Ed Dodd taught us to respect the beauty of our planet Earth. Syndicated by the Field Syndicate.

Daily Strips

1946-80s	E. Dodd	$25	$50	$75

Sunday Strips

1946-90s	E. Dodd	50	125	200

MARMADUKE
A Great Dane is the focus of this daily gag panel created by Brad Anderson for United Features Syndicate.

Daily Strips

1954-Present	B. Anderson	$50	$75	$100

Sunday Strips

1954-Present	B. Anderson	100	200	300

MARRIED LIFE
Syndicated by King Features. A domestic comic strip that was bland until it introduced a racetrack "tout" later named Barney Google, who eventually (1919) took over the focus in the strip and made Billy DeBeck very famous. Almost no "Married Life" originals exist.

Daily Strips

1916-19	B. DeBeck	[$600	$800	$1,000]

Sunday Strips

1916-19	B. DeBeck	xxx	xxx	xxx

MARY WORTH
See "Apple Mary" listing.

MARVIN
A baby (Marvin) stars in this daily gag strip. Syndicated by North American Syndicate.

Daily Strips

1980s-Present	T Armstrong	$25	$50	$75

MANDRAKE THE MAGICIAN, Phil Davis, sunday page. © King Features Syndicate

MICKEY MOUSE, Floyd Gottfredson, daily, dated 4/19/35. Estimate: $6,000/10,000; sold for $6,050 in 6/97 (Russ Cochran auctions). © The Walt Disney Company

MICKEY MOUSE, Floyd Gottfredson, daily, dated 5/27/38. Estimate: $1,500/2,500; sold for $1,947 in 6/97 (Russ Cochran auctions). © The Walt Disney Company

Sunday Strips

1980-Present	T. Armstrong	75	100	125

THE MEDIEVAL CASTLE

Syndicated by King Features. Bottom strip which ran with "Prince Valiant" for 20 months. Very few known examples of originals from this strip exist today in the collectors market.

Sunday Strips

1944-45	H. R. Foster	[$500	$1,000	$1,500]

MICKEY FINN

A slice of Irish life, stereotyped in the 1930s and 1940s. Mickey Finn is a cop and his hangout is the local bar. For the McNaught Syndicate. A large number of daily originals to this strip have been discovered recently to no great demand in the market place.

Daily Strips

1936-70	L. Leonard	$50	$75	$125
1971-75	M. Weiss	20	30	40

Sunday Strips

1938-70	L. Leonard	100	250	350
1970-75	M. Weiss	35	50	75

MICKEY MOUSE

Quite probably the universe's best-known mouse. Created in 1928 by a theater cartoon. In January of 1930, Ub Iwerks and Win Smith began drawing the comic strip with Walt Disney doing the writing. Within a year, Floyd Gottfredson began a 40-year stint as the daily strip artist (the writing went to various studio personnel), and Sundays up until the early 60s, then intermittently into the 1970s. Almost all of the early strips do not exist. The most-sought-after are the pie-eyed Mickeys, which ran prior to 1938. In 1955, the strip changed format from an adventure strip to a gag-a-day strip. Since Gottfredson's retirement, the strip has changed hands several times amongst studio personnel. Syndicated by King Features.

Daily Strips

1930-	U. Iwerks /W.Smith	1st story - Plane Crazy (rare) [$15,000	$50,000	$90,000]
1930-31	U. Iwerks/ W. Smith	[8,000	20,000	40,000]
1931-33	F. Gottfredson	[5,000	10,000	15,000]
1934-38	F. Gottfredson	[1,500	2,800	6,500]
1938-55	F. Gottfredson	[300	600	2,000]
1955-75	F. Gottfredson	[100	300	500]

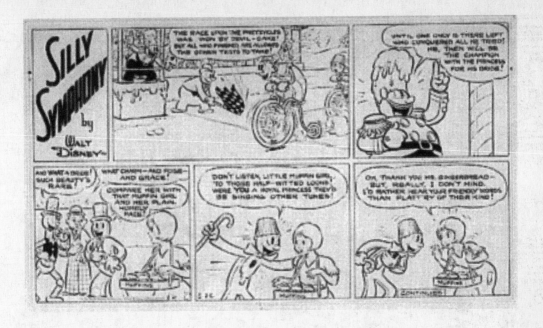

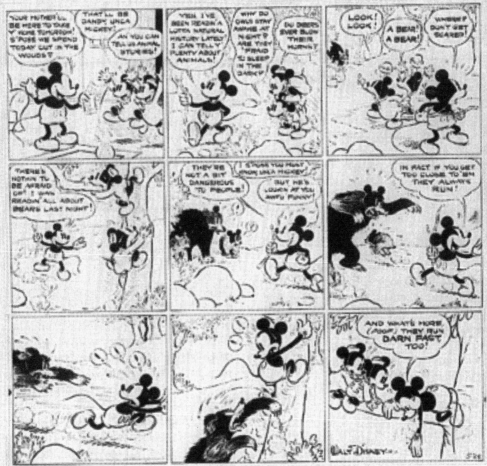

MICKEY MOUSE/ SILLY SYMPHONIES, Floyd Gottfredson, Sunday page (one of the few ever found with top-per intact), dated 5/26/35. Estimate: $18,000/24,000; sold for $30,800 in 10/92 (Christie's East comic art auctions). © The Walt Disney Company

MICKEY MOUSE, Disney Studio, Sunday page, dated 4/19/42. Estimate: $1,500/2,500; sold for $1,650 in 6/97 (Russ Cochran's comic art auctions). © The Walt Disney Company

MICKEY MOUSE, Disney Studio, daily, dated 6/15/38. Estimate: $1,500/3,000; sold for $3,190 in 4/97 (Russ Cochran's comic art auctions). © The Walt Disney Company

| 1975-Present | Studio Artists | 50 | 100 | 250 |

Note that "Silly Symphonies" ran as a topper strip to "Mickey Mouse" from 1932 to 1939. These are priced below, as well as the "Donald Duck" feature, which replaced "Silly Symphonies." The "Donald Duck" feature brings higher prices, and the exact character featured in the "Silly Symphonies" topper will also determine price.

Sunday Strips (1932-38 are rare)

1932-38	F. Gottfredson	[6,000	9,500	14,000]
1939-45	F. Gottfredson	[600	1,500	3,000]
1946-75	Others/ F Gottfredson	250	500	1,000
1975-Present	Studio Artists	100	200	300

Note: some individual sales include: daily dated 9/13/34 selling for $6,200; daily dated 12/8/1934 selling for $4,800; daily dated 1/14/36 selling for $3,700; daily dated 11/25/1936 selling for $5,200; daily dated 1/8/1937 selling for $1,900; all from Howard Lowery Auctions. A daily dated 4/19/1935 failed at its reserve with low estimate of $6,000 at Sotheby's in 1996. Other sales include Sunday with "S. Symphonies" topper dated 5/26/1935 selling for $30,800 at Christie's East in 1992; Sunday dated 1/3/1937 selling for $8,800; daily dated 9/12/1936 selling for $8,250; daily dated 12/24/1934 selling for $4,887; daily dated 1939 selling for $1,265; four dailies dated 1957-62 selling for $2,587; all sales from Christie's East and Sotheby's auctions.

MICKEY MOUSE, Floyd Gottfredson, Sunday page, dated 1/3/1937. Estimate: $8,000/12,000; sold for $8,800 in 10/92 (Christie's East comic art auctions). © The Walt Disney Company

MICKEY MOUSE, Floyd Gottfredson, daily, dated 4/25/32. Estimate: $10,000/12,000; sold for $9,200 in 10/93 (Christie's East comic art auctions). © The Walt Disney Company

MICKEY MOUSE, Floyd Gottfredson, daily, dated 4/25/32. Estimate: $500/1,000; sold for $1,463 in 6/97 (Russ Cochran auctions). © The Walt Disney Company

MINUTE MOVIES

"Minute Movies" was one of the first comic strips to have an ongoing story. From the George Matthew Adams Syndicate.

Daily Strips

1921-36	E. Wheelan	$200	$250	$300

MIRACLE JONES

Syndicated by United Features. During his hiatus from "Tarzan," Burne Hogarth created two comic strips. "Drago," a South American-based adventure strip, and "Miracle Jones." "Miracle Jones" is about a daydreamer and his daydreams. Noted EC artist Bernard Krigstein assisted in drawing the strip.

Sunday Strip

1947-48	B. Hogarth	$600	$800	$1,000

MISS FURY

This action-adventure strip was fashioned by one of the famous women cartoonists of the 1940s, for the Bell Syndicate.

Daily Strips

1941-49	T. Mills	$200	$400	$700

Sunday Strips

1941-49	T. Mills	900	1,200	1,600

MISS PEACH

"Miss Peach"'s story line evolves around a teacher and her class at the Kelly School.

Daily Strips

1957-present	M. Lazarus	$50	$75	$100

Sunday Strips

1957-present	M. Lazarus	75	125	150

MISTER BOFFO

Joe Martin rivals Gary Larson in twisted brilliance. Tribune Media Syndicate.

Daily Strips

1986-present	J. Martin	$50	$75	$100

Sunday Strips

1986-present	J. Martin	200	250	300

MR. JACK

One of the better-known strips by Jimmy Swinnerton. The 1926-1935 run was paired with the "Little Jimmy" strip. Syndicated by King Features.

Daily Strips

1904-11	J. Swinnerton	$200	$250	$400

Sunday Strips

1902-04	J. Swinnerton	[800	1,000	1,400]
1912-19	J. Swinnerton	400	500	[650]
1926-35	J. Swinnerton	200	250	[400]

MR. MYSTIC

A backup feature in the weekly "Spirit" section about a magician. Syndicated by Register and Tribune.

Sunday Strips

1940-46	B. Powell	$200	$300	$400

MODESTY BLAISE

A British action-adventure-spy comic strip, started during the James Bond craze. "Modesty Blaise" is noted for its good writing by creator Peter O'Donnell and solid art by Holdaway and then Romero. Syndicated by London Times Mirror.

Daily Strips

1966-70	J. Holdaway	[$75	$125	$175]
1970-present	E. Romero	50	75	100

MOMMA

Field Enterprises Syndicate/Creators Syndicate. Humor strip about a nagging mother and her grown-up kids who can't seem to please her.

Daily Strips

1970-Present	M. Lazarus	$40	$80	$120

Sunday Strips

1970-Present	M. Lazarus	60	120	160

MOON MULLINS

Syndicated for the Chicago Tribune. This strip has experienced a flattening out in the market over the past five years.

Daily Strips

1923-45	F. Willard	$75	$150	$250
1946-58	F. Willard	50	100	175
1958-93	F. Johnson	25	50	75

Sunday Strips

1923-30	F. Willard	300	450	[850]
1931-40	F. Willard	150	250	350
1941-58	F. Willard	100	150	200
1958-93	F. Johnson	40	60	80

MISTER JACK AND CANYON KIDDIE, James Swinnerton, Sunday Page, dated 1/16/30. Estimate: $1,000/2,000; sold for $517 in 1997 (Sotheby's 7th comic art auction). © International Feature Service Inc.

MOTHER GOOSE AND GRIMM

Tribune Media Syndicate.

Daily Strips

1984-Present	M. Peters	$100	$200	$275

Sunday Strips

1984-Present	M. Peters	400	500	600

MUGS MCGINNIS -(LATER MUGGS AND SKEETER)

Syndicated by King Features. A kid strip in the vein of "Skippy" and "Peanuts."

Daily Strips

1927-74	W. Bishop	$20	$40	$60

MUPPETS

Syndicated by King Features. Based on the Jim Henson characters.

Daily Strips

1980s	G.and B. Gilcrest	$25	$40	$60

Sunday Strips

1980s	G. and B. Gilcrest	50	75	100

MUTT AND JEFF

Syndicated by King Features. The first daily strip to run continuously. The original "Odd Couple," "Mutt and Jeff" set the pace for humor strips to come.

Daily Strips

1907-12	B. Fisher/Studio (very rare)	$500	$750	$1,000
1912-33	B. Fisher/Studio	100	300	600
1933-82	A . Smith	25	50	100

Sunday Strips

1918-25	B. Fisher (very rare)	[750	875	1,500]
1925-33	B. Fisher	200	400	600
1934-82	A . Smith	50	75	100

MYRA NORTH - SPECIAL NURSE

Adventure strip about a nurse, for the N.E.A. Syndicate.

Daily Strips

1936-39	C. Coll	$100	$200	$300

Sunday Strips

1936-41	C. Coll	200	300	400

MUTT AND JEFF, Bud Fisher, daily, dated 11/24/24. Estimate: $300/500; sold for $220 in 1998 (Russ Cochran auctions). © King Features Syndicate

NANCY

United Features Syndicate. One of the top daily gag strips ever done. Ernie Bushmiller's genius lasted 42 years, until his death in 1982. Successor Jerry Scott, though not "Nancy"'s creator, has shown his mastery of the characters and has proved to be an extremely worthy successor to Bushmiller with his art and gags. (Also, see "Fritzi Ritz.")

Daily Strips

1940-50	E. Bushmiller	$100	$250	$400
1951-60	E. Bushmiller	100	200	300
1961-81	E. Bushbiller	75	150	225
1982-83	M. Lasky	50	75	100
1983-94	J. Scott	100	150	200
1994-Present	G. Gilchrist	20	40	60

Note: individual sales include eight dailies from 1949 selling for $1,265 at Christie's East in 1996.

Sunday Strips

1940-50	E. Bushmiller	300	450	650
1951-82	E. Bushmiller	200	300	400
1982-83	M. Lasky	100	150	200
1983-94	J. Scott	100	200	300
1994-Present	G. Gilchrist	40	60	100

NAPOLEON

Dailies began in 1931, Sundays in 1933. This quintessential dog-as-man's-best-friend strip began as an elaborately drawn adventure strip. Its gentle humor eventually captivated a huge international audience. Syndicated by La Fave.

Daily Strips

1931-50	C. McBride	$100	$150	$200
1950-61	R Armstrong	30	60	90

Sunday Strips

1933-50	C. McBride	400	500	600
1950-61	R Armstrong	50	100	150

NAVY BOB STEELE

Written by Wilson Starbuck, and illustrated by Erwin Greenwood, this real life adventure strip of life at sea was done for the McClure Syndicate.

Sunday Strips

1939-45	E. Greenwood	$100	$200	$350

THE NEBBS

Quirky, humorous family daily comic strip. Syndicated by Bell.

Daily Strips

1923-33	W.A. Carlson	$75	$125	$175
1934-46	W.A. Carlson	35	55	125

THE NEIGHBORHOOD

Offbeat humor panel strip. Creators Syndicate.

Daily Strips

1982-90	J. Van Amerogen	$25	$50	$75

THE NEWLYWEDS

One of several strips done by George McManus prior to his "Bringing Up Father." Pulitzer Syndicate/King Features Syndicate.

Daily Strips

1906-07	G. McManus	[$200	$300	$400]

Sunday Strips

1904-12	G. McManus	[500	1,000	1,500]
1912-18	A. Carmichael	400	600	800

PRICE RANGE KEY

RARITY — Brackets [ ] around a price indicate that this example is very scarce and could exceed maximum estimate.

	Covers
No work produced in this category—	XXX
No price available due to lack of information—	***

CONDITION — Age, color, marks, tears, etc.

Pages

[400 500 600]

CHARACTER — Is the primary character featured, or is the original characteristic of a great example in the story line?

CONTENT — is the theme or story line exceptional or below average?

VALUE RANGE

Minimum Medium Maximum

RARITY

The [ ] Brackets indicate RARITY, if these brackets are used the reader can potentially double the price range in all three catagories.

NORBERT (BEGUN AS SNIFFY)

A dog character strip created by George Fett .

Daily Strips

1964-82	G. Fett	$30	$50	$70
1982-83	D. Cavalli	20	30	40

OAKY DOAKS

Associated Press/N.E.A. Syndicate. Medieval times are the setting for R.B. Fuller's humorous knights-in-ammor adventures.

Daily Strips

1935-61	R. B. Fuller	[$100	$150	$200]

Sunday Strips

1939-61	R. B. Fuller	[300	400	500]

OLD DOC YAK

"Old Doc Yak" preceded Smith's famous feature, "The Gumps," then was later brought back as a bottom strip for "The Gumps." Syndicated by Chicago Tribune.

Daily Strips

1914-15	S. Smith	$100	$150	$200

Sunday Strips

1912-19	S. Smith	300	400	500
1930-35	S. Smith	150	200	250

ON STAGE

"On Stage" is an interesting, well-drawn strip about actress Mary Perkins (hence the title "On Stage"). Creator/artist Leonard Starr can now be seen drawing "Little Orphan Annie." Syndicated by Chicago Tribune.

Daily Strips

1957-67	L. Starr	$50	$75	$150
1968-79	L. Starr	35	50	125

Sunday Strips

1957-67	L. Starr	100	200	300
1968-79	L. Starr	50	100	250

OUR BOARDING HOUSE

Humorous strip following the life inside a rooming house with Major Hoople and his wife, Star. Syndicated by N.E.A.

Daily Strips

1923-36	G. Ahern	$150	$225	$300
1936-69	B Freyse	50	75	100
1969-80s	Studio Artists	20	30	40

PEANUTS, Charles Schultz, daily, dated 7/30/70. Estimate: $1,800/2,500; sold for $4,950 in 1992 (Sotheby's 2nd comic art auction). © King Features Syndicate

Sunday Strips

1923-36	G. Ahern	400	500	600
1936-39	B. Freyse	100	175	250
1969-80s	Studio Artists	40	50	60

OUT OUR WAY (ALSO KNOWN AS WHY MOTHERS GET GRAY)

N.E.A. Syndicate. Panel strip showing the lighter side of family life.

Daily Strips

1921-57	J. R. Williams	$150	$200	$250

Sunday Strips

1920s-80s	N Cochran	100	150	200

OZARK IKE

Syndicated by King Features. Beautifully drawn baseball-theme strip.

Daily Strips

1945-54	R. Gotto	$100	$200	$300
1954-58	B. Lignante	40	50	60

Sunday Strips

1945-54	R. Gotto	150	250	400
1954-58	B. Lignante	75	100	125

PATSY

Noted cartoonist Noel Sickles assisted Mel Graff in 1939-40 and did not sign the strip. Syndicated by A.P. News Features. "Patsy" was a blend of fantasy adventures and real life, focusing on a ten-year-old girl (Patsy).

Daily Strips

1934-40	M. Graff	$100	$150	$200
1939-41	N. Sickles/ C. Raab	400	500	600
1942-44	G. Storm	200	300	450
1943-55	Studio Artists	50	75	100

PEANUTS

Syndicated by United Features. Charles Schulz has dissolved the generation gap with his strip, "Peanuts." By creating characters who have both "adult" and "child-like" sensibilities within the same moment, Schulz has crafted a story line rich in human nature. Charlie Brown, Lucy, Linus, and a dog with a mind of his own, Snoopy, have all become part of one of America's most popular strips. This beloved strip has become "hot" within the last five years and shows no signs of slowing down. The only area where Peanuts strips have leveled off are within the mid 1980's to the present dates. A special note should be made to the proto-type strip for Peanuts which was entitled "Li'l Folks" and ran only in the St. Paul Pioneer Press Newspaper. The retirement and subequent death of Schulz in 2000 should cause prices to rise even further.

Daily Strips

1950-52	C. Schulz	[$700	$1,700	$3,500]
1953-62	C. Schulz	500	1,500	2,500
1962-72	C. Schulz	700	1,200	1,800
1972-82	C. Schulz	500	700	1,000
1983-00	C. Schulz	400	500	600

Note: dailies that feature appearances of Snoopy as the Red Baron, or Charlie Brown in the Pumpkin Patch around Halloween sell for considerably more.

Note: individual sales of daily strips include: daily dated 11/24/1950 (from second month of the strip) selling at $6,900; daily dated 7/23/1958 selling for $1,840; daily dated 10/3/1951 selling for $3,450; daily dated 1/27/1967 (Snoopy as Red Baron) selling for $2,750; all sales from Sotheby's comic art auctions. It should also be noted that

PEANUTS, Charles Schulz, 2 daily strips, dated 6/8/53 and 3/2/53. Estimate: $1,000/2,000; sold for $4,312 in 1995 (Sotheby's 5th comic art auction). © King Features Syndicate

PEANUTS, Charles Schulz, daily, dated 1/27/67. Estimate: $600/800; sold for $3,025 in 10/92 (Sotheby's 2nd comic art auction). © King Features Syndicate

PEANUTS, Charles Schulz, daily, dated 7/23/58. Estimate: $1,500/2,000; sold for $1,840 in 6/96 (Sotheby's 6th comic art auction). © King Features Syndicate

"Peanuts" originals exhibit within the selling market what might be called "The Jack Kirby Effect." By this the author means that very large numbers of collectors from all walks of life are in the buying field. It seems at this point in time as if any "Peanuts," from any period of time can bring a healthy price, and very few remain unsold, or fail to meet their reserve price in any auction setting.

Sunday Strips

1948-49				
("Li'l Folks")	C. Schulz	[7,000	9,000	14,000]
1952-54	C.Schulz	[1,500	3,000	5,500]
1955-62	C. Schulz	1,000	1,800	4,000
1262-72	C. Schulz	1,500	2,000	3,250
1972-82	C. Schulz	800	1,200	1,600
1983-00	C. Schulz	700	900	1,200

Note: Sunday pages that feature Snoopy as the Red Baron or have Charlie Brown in the Pumpkin Patch during Halloween or Charlie Brown on the pitcher's mound will sell for more money.

Note: a very special early proto-type strip to "Peanuts" entitled "Li'l Folks" dated 7/24/1949 in an upright Sunday format, was brought to Sotheby's in 1996 and set a

THE PHANTOM, Lee Falk, Sunday page, dated 6/6/43. Estimate: $800/1,200; sold for $1,320 in 10/92 (Christie's East comic art auctions). © King Features Syndicate

world record for any Schulz original selling at $17,250. Other sales include: daily dated 5/76/1975 selling at $2,400; a daily dated 5/78/1977 selling at $2,600 at Howard Lowery Auctions. Additional sales include: Sunday dated 12/5/1965 selling at $5,750; daily dated 7/23/1958 selling for $1,840; daily (from second month of strip) dated 11/24/1950 selling for $6,900; Sunday dated 12/29/1957 selling at $5,175; Sunday for 5/1983 selling at $4,025; daily dated 1/27/1967 (Red Baron) selling at $2,750, all sales at Sotheby's.

Sales at Christies East include: Sunday dated 1/15/1978 selling at $5,175; Sunday dated 12/18/1955 selling at $4,600; daily for 1/1/1970 selling at $3,680; Sunday dated 2/9/1997 selling at $1,270.

PENNY
A girl strip created by Harry Haenigsen for the New York Herald Tribune.

Daily Strips

1943-64	H. Haenigsen	$30	$60	$90
1965-70	B. Hoest	20	40	60

PETE THE TRAMP
Syndicated by King Features. At the height of the Depression, being homeless was humorous.

Daily Strips

1934-37	C. D. Russel	$50	$75	$100

Sunday Strips

1932-63	C. D. Russel	100	200	800

PETER RABBIT
N.Y. Tribune Syndicate. The classic children's-book character was expertly adapted to the comics by Cady and Fago.

Sunday Strips

1920-48	H. Cady	$200	$250	$300
1948-53	V. Fago	100	125	150

THE PHANTOM
"The Ghost Who Walks" (The Phantom's nickname) made this a great adventure strip in the '30s and '40s. He dealt out justice in his own style, and those who crossed him met an appropriate demise. He ruled in a mythical region of Africa. Written by Lee Falk, who created "Mandrake the Magician." Syndicated by King Features.

While the "Phantom" does not enjoy the popularity of "Tarzan" or "Prince Valiant" with collectors, the scarcity of quality originals keep prices very healthy for this strip.

Daily Strips

1936-41	R. Moore	[$700	$1,200	$1,800]
1942-61	W. McCoy	100	200	400
1962-94	S. Barry	20	60	100

Sunday Strips

1939-41	R. Moore	[2,000	2,500	4,500]
1942-61	W. McCoy	250	500	750
1961-94	S. Barry	50	100	150

Note: individual sales include a Sunday dated 6/6/1943 selling at $1,320.

PHOEBE'S PLACE
Daily gag strip about anthropomorphic animals at a boardinghouse run by a cat. L.A. Times Syndicate.

Daily Strips

1990-91	B. Schorr	$50	$100	$150

Sunday Strips

1990-91	B. Schorr	100	200	250

A PILGRIMS PROGRESS BY MISTER BUNION
One of the most unusual strips that Winsor McCay ever created, for The Evening Telegraph.

Sunday Strips

1905-10	W. McCay	[$2,000	$4,000	$6,000]

Note: while the family estate collection might contain some artwork to this strip, otherwise known examples are very rare.

POGO
Walt Kelly used his history of drawing "funny animal" characters for *Animal Comics* and *Walt Disney's Comics and Stories* in the 1940s as a springboard for the greatest strip of his career, "Pogo." "We have seen the enemy and he is us." No more penetrating or political comic strip has ever appeared before or after Kelly's "Pogo." Oftentimes the whimsy and charm of Kelly's drawing made his craft for writing even more powerful in its reading. For Publishers Hall syndicate.

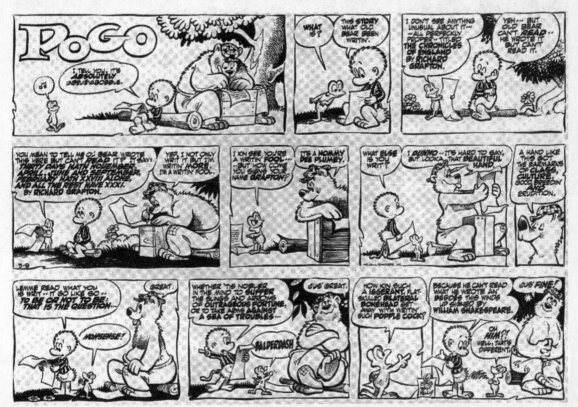

POGO, Walt Kelly, Sunday page, dated 3/8/58. Estimate: $2,000/2,500; sold for $1,840 in 1995 (Christie's East comic art auctions). © The Hall Syndicate

POGO, Walt Kelly, Sunday Page, dated 12/24/67, personally inscribed and dated by the artist. Estimate: $12,000/16,000; sold for $11,500 in 1995 (Sotheby's 5th comic art auction). © The Hall Syndicate

POGO, Walt Kelly, daily, dated 12/25/69. Estimate: $1,500/3,000; sold for $3,630 in 4/97
(Russ Cochran art auction). © The Hall Syndicate

Daily Strips

1948-50	W. Kelly	$800	$1,000	$1,200
1950-73	W. Kelly	300	400	700
1974-75	S. Kelly	75	100	150
1987-91	N. Stemacky	75	125	175
1991-93	C. Kelly	40	75	100

Note: certain daily originals will sell for more, especially Christmas dailies. Some individual sales include: daily dated 12/20/52 selling for $690; three dailies from 1955/1957/1971 selling for $1,150; daily dated 7/28/1951 selling at $650; sales from Howard Lowery, Sotheby's and Christie's East.

Sunday Strips

1950-73	W. Kelly	800	1,800	2800
1973-75	S. Kelly	200	300	450
1987-91	N. Stemacky	50	100	150
1991-93	C. Kelly	40	80	125

POLLY AND HER PALS, Cliff Sterrett, Sunday Page, dated 12/1/29. Estimate: $2,500/4,500; sold for $2,300 in 1997 (Sotheby's 7th comic art auction). © King Features Syndicate

Note: individual sales include: special Sunday with original pencil and inked story development on backside dated 10/26/1952 selling at $2,300; Sunday dated 3/22/1970 selling at $1,100; a special hand-colored and inscribed Pogo dated 12/24/1967 (a Christmas Sunday), selling for $11,500; at Sotheby's comic art auctions.

POLLY AND HER PALS

Cliff Sterrett is often seen as the "other" great creative comic strip artist alongside George Herriman. There are certainly similar characteristics with these two artists; however, Sterrett from the beginning took his own separate artistic path. Evolving his strip from a simple "family" format,

POLLY AND HER PALS, Cliff Sterrett, daily, dated 9/20/33. Estimate: $1,000/2,000; sold for $805 in 1997 (Sotheby's 7th comic art auction). © King Features Syndicate

Sterrett began to improvise with his drawing style and was soon producing story lines that were visually years ahead of their time. "Polly" was both a topical and a timeless strip that will be remembered for years. Syndicated by King Features.

As strip art collecting continues to grow, "Polly" artwork sales have shown a renewed interest. This strip will show growth during the next few years as collectors realize the strength of Sterrett's style, and its close association to the complex style of George Herrimans "Krazy Kat" strip. Syndicated by King Features.

Daily Strips

1912-26	C. Sterrett	$300	$450	$600
1926-34	C. Sterrett	200	400	600
1935-58	P. Fung, Jr.	100	250	350

Sunday Strips

1913-25	C. Sterrett	[1,000	1,400	1,800]
1935	C. Sterrett	*27 1/2" x 21"* (larger size)		
(rare)		[2,000	3,000	5,000]
1927-40	C. Sterrett	1,500	2,000	[3,000]
1940-58	C. Sterrett	250	600	850

Note: a special hand colored Sunday page by Sterrett turned up in the summer of 1997 from a famed "cubist" story line, dated 9/26/1926; it traded hands at the San Diego Comic Convention for $15,000 in trade. To date this is the only known hand-colored Polly to surface. Other individual sales of Sunday pages include: a Sunday dated 11/28/1948 selling for $1,610 at Christie's East.

POPEYE (ORIGINALLY TITLED THIMBLE THEATRE)

E. C. Segar created one of those "eternal" characters with Popeye, the spinach-eating, good-natured sailor who remained faithful to his one true love, Olive Oyl, throughout the run of this widely popular comic strip. Sunday pages by Segar are rare; only fifty are known to exist. Syndicated by King Features.

Daily Strips

1919-29	E. C. Segar	[$500	$750	$1,000]
1929-38	E. C. Segar	600	900	1,600
1938-39	D. Winner	200	250	300
1939-58	B. Zaboly	100	150	200
1959-86	B. Sagendorf	100	150	200
1986-94	B. London	100	150	200

Note: individual sales include, daily dated 3/30/1937 selling at $1,610; daily dated 9/1/1932 selling at $1,495; daily dated 12/28/1937 selling at $1,320; from sales at Christie's East and Sotheby's.

Sunday Strips

1919-29	E. C. Segar	2,000	3,500	6,500
1929-30	E. C. Segar	[2,000	3,500	7,500]
1931-37	E. C. Segar	1,750	3,000	6,000
1938-39	D. Winner	400	600	800
1939-58	B. Zaboly	300	400	500
1959-86	B. Sagendorf	200	250	300
1994-Present	H. Eisman	200	250	300

Note: individual sales of Sunday pages include: 1/26/1964 selling at $300 at Howard Lowery Auctions; Sunday with top-

POPEYE, E.C. Segar, Sunday page, dated 8/25/35. Estimate: $5,000/7,000; sold for $4,840 in 12/96
(Russ Cochran's comic art auction). © King Features Syndicate

POPEYE, Bill Zaboly, Sunday page, one of four pages offered in a lot. Estimate: $800/1,200; sold for $403 in 1993 (Sotheby's 3rd comic art auction). © King Features Syndicate

per dated 12/21/1930 selling at $9,775; Sunday dated 9/10/1933 selling for $4,600; Sunday dated 10/1/1933 selling at $8,625 at Sotheby's Auctions.

PRINCE VALIANT

Considered by many to be the quintessential adventure strip. The story-telling skills of Hal Foster combined with superb draftsmanship created an unparalleled accomplishment in the Sunday strip format. The early years (1937-1940), and the banner years (when the "Valiant" logo ran the width of the top of the page), through mid-1944, are among the finest work in the comics. While the '40s and early '50s saw the strip slow in pace, it maintained its beauty well into the last Foster years (1970s). Syndicated by King Features.

It should be stated that up until 1996 there was no known hand-colored Sunday page of "Prince Vailiant" that was confirmed to be colored by Foster's own hand.

Published for the first time in the color section of this edition is the only known example. A 1939 Prince Valiant Sunday Page sold for $29,700 at Howard Lowery's (1993) auction from the collection of Murray Harris. This is a great example of the kind of price that can be realized for a colored Sunday.

Sunday Strips

1937-38	H. Foster	[$10,000	$12,500	$20,000]
1939-45	H. Foster	4,000	6,000	8,000
1946-49	H. Foster	3,000	5,000	6,000
1950-61	H. Foster	1,500	3,000	4,500
1962-71	H. Foster	1,000	1,750	2,500
1972-Present	J.C. Murphy	200	300	400

Note: individual sales include: Sunday dated 4/7/1940 (with large panel depicting Val before a crowd of knights after battle) selling for $21,700; Sunday dated 3/19/1939 (with static romantic scenes) selling for $9,775; Sunday dated 5/31/1942 selling at $8,625; Sunday dated 7/22/1962 selling at

PRINCE VALIANT, Hal Foster, Sunday page, dated 11/20/60. Estimate: $3,000/5,000; sold for $5,750 in 10/97 (Russ Cochran's comic art auctions). © King Features Syndicate

Our Story: REYNOLDE, USUALLY SO GENTLE, FLIES INTO A RAGE WHEN ONE OF THE YOUNG SQUIRES IS CRUEL TO HIS MOUNT. WORDS ARE SPOKEN IN ANGER, TEMPERS FLARE.

THOUGH EACH IS ARMED WITH WOODEN PRACTICE WEAPONS, ANGER LENDS POWER TO THEIR STROKES. REYNOLDE'S FINE HORSEMANSHIP GIVES HIM A GREAT ADVANTAGE. ONLY HIS CLUMSINESS WITH WEAPONS PREVENTS QUICK VICTORY.

THEN HIS ADVERSARY PUTS CRUEL SPURS TO HIS MOUNT AND IT FLINCHES AWAY, LEAVING AN OPENING THAT EVEN REYNOLDE CANNOT MISS. IT IS HIS FIRST VICTORY.

"DO YOU WISH TO BREAK THE SPIRIT OF THIS FINE HORSE? ARE YOU SO MEAN OF SOUL THAT YOU WOULD MASTER IT THROUGH CRUELTY? LOOK AT THAT BRIDLE, DRAWN SO TIGHT THE BIT HAS DRAWN BLOOD. THE SPURS YOU WEAR ARE MORE LIKE WEAPONS!"

THEN, HIS LECTURE ENDED, REYNOLDE ADJUSTS THE HARNESS AND MOUNTS. WITH FIRM BUT GENTLE HANDS HE SOON CALMS THE HORSE AND THEREAFTER PUTS IT THROUGH ITS PACES. "BRING YOUR YOUNG FRIEND TO ME, VAL," SAYS THE KING. "WE HAVE NEED OF SUCH A MAN."

THE KING TELLS OF THEIR NEED FOR HORSES, HORSES AND MORE HORSES, AND REYNOLDE, HIS FACE ALIGHT WITH ENTHUSIASM, TELLS OF HIS SUCCESS IN BREEDING STRONG, SWIFT MOUNTS, AND HOW THE SAME COULD BE DONE HERE IN CAMELOT. THE SUN SINKS ERE HE IS FINISHED.

5-28

© King Features Syndicate, Inc. 1967. World rights reserved.

1581

"WILL HE GIVE UP HIS DREAM OF BECOMING A GREAT WARRIOR AND BE CONTENT TO IMPROVE OUR STOCK?" ASKS THE KING. "NO, SIRE," ANSWERS VAL. "A PRETTY GIRL IS INVOLVED." ARTHUR NODS SADLY. THERE IS ALWAYS A GIRL SOMEWHERE TO UPSET ONE'S PLANS.

NEXT WEEK—Despair

PRINCE VALIANT, Hal Foster, Sunday page, dated 5/28/67. Estimate: $4,000/6,000; sold for $4,675 in 1996 (Russ Cochran's comic art auctions). © King Features Syndicate

$3,450; Sunday dated 8/7/1960 selling at $2,875 from Sotheby's Comic Art Auctions. Other examples include a Sunday dated 8/14/1949 selling at $9,200; a Sunday dated 5/25/1947 selling at $4,025; a Sunday dated 9/29/1968 selling at $2,070 from Christie's East.

PUSSYCAT PRINCESS

Grace Drayton's second most famous creation for King Features Syndicate.

Sunday Strips

1935-36	G. Drayton	$300	$500	$700
1936-46	R. Carroll	100	150	200

QUINCY

Created by King Features Syndicate by artist Ted Shearer.

Daily Strips

1970-86	T. Shearer	$40	$60	$80

RADIO PATROL

A police comic strip whose gimmick was using a radio to contact patrol cars. Syndicated for King features.

Daily Strips

1933-46	C. Schmidt	$100	$200	$300

Sunday Strips

1934-50	C. Schmidt	400	500	600

REAL FOLKS AT HOME

This strip used continuing situations, and not regular characters, created by artist Clare Briggs for the New York Tribune.

Daily Strips

	C. Briggs	$80	$120	$225

THE RED KNIGHT

A strip more closely related to the superhero characters of the 1940's comic books, written by John Welch and drawn by artist Jack McGuier.

Daily Strips

1940-43	J. McGuier	$50	$125	$250

RED BARRY

Styled after the broader-caricature feature, "Dick Tracy." Will Gould created an artistically superior stylized strip crafted around an undercover cop. Originals are somewhat rare. Syndicated by King Features.

Daily Strips

1934-38	W. Gould	[$300	$400	$500]

Sunday Strips

1935-39	W. Gould	[400	600	800]

REDEYE

Syndicated by King Features. A Western humor strip focusing on Native Americans.

Daily Strips

1957-91	G. Bess	$40	$60	$80
1991-Present	M. Casson	40	60	80

Sunday Strips

1957-91	G. Bess	75	100	150
1991-Present	M. Casson	40	60	80

RED RYDER

A well-drawn Western adventure strip for United Features Syndicate.

Daily Strips

1939-49	F. Harmon	$200	$400	$600
1950-59	Harmon/			
	E. Good/J.Gray	100	200	300
1960-64	B. McLeod	40	60	80

Sunday Strips

1939-49	F. Harmon	300	600	1,200
1950-59	Harmon/			
	E.Good/J.Gray	150	300	700
1960-64	Assistants	100	150	200

REGULAR FELLAS

Popular kids' gag strip. Syndicated by New York Herald.

Daily Strips

1917-30	G. Byrnes	$50	$100	$150
1931-49	G. Byrnes	40	60	100

Sunday Strips

1917-30	G. Byrnes	100	200	300
1931-49	G. Byrnes	75	125	200

REX MORGAN

"Rex Morgan" and "Judge Parker" were both created by Nick Dallis. For Publishers Hall Syndicate.

Daily Strips

1948-58	F. Edgington/			
	M. Bradley	$50	$100	$150

RED RYDER, Fred Harman, Sunday page, dated 3/10/46. Estimate: $600/900; sold for $605 in 1992 (Christie's East comic art auctions). © United Features Syndicate

1959-80	F. Edgington/			
	M. Bradley	35	70	100
1987-Present	T. DiPreta	35	70	100

Sunday Strips

1948-58	F. Edgington/			
	M. Bradley	100	200	300
1959-80	F. Edington/			
	M. Bradley	50	75	150
1987-Present	T. DiPreta	50	75	150

RICK O'SHAY

Stan Lynde created a humorous Western strip about the sheriff and the characters in his town. In 1991, Stan Lynde had a fire and the bulk of all "Rick O'Shay"s no longer exist. Syndicated for The Chicago Tribune .

Daily Strips

1958-81	S. Lynde	$25	$50	$75

Sunday Strips

1958-81	S. Lynde	50	100	150

RIGHT AROUND HOME

A single-panel Sunday page in a Columbus, Ohio, paper in 1933, this "American neighborhood" humor strip was memorably drawn and written by Dudley Fisher. Syndicated in 1938 by King Features.

Sunday Strips

1938-54	D. Fisher	$200	$350	[$650]

RIP KIRBY

Written around a marine-turned-detective (imitating in part the wartime experience of Alex Raymond). In the initial years, the cramped-panel style appeared elegant, while cluttered. The initiation of a writer and fewer panels in the strip's daily format in 1952 helped Raymond create memorable sequences in the latter years of the strip. Raymond died in a tragic car accident in 1956 while still working on "Rip Kirby." Al Williamson assisted John Prentice from 1962 to 1966. Syndicated by King Features.

Daily Strips

1945-56	A. Raymond	$150	$300	[$400]
1956-Present	J. Prentice/			
	Al Williamson			
		50	75	[150]

RIPLEY'S BELIEVE IT OR NOT!

Syndicated by King Features, then syndicated by United Features. The odd facts of the world posed a fresh concept for comics. Robert Ripley gathered the obscure trivia of the world.

Daily Strips

1918-49	R. Ripley	$100	$200	$300
1949-89	W. Frehm	50	75	100
1989-Present	Various Artists	20	30	40

Sunday Strips

1918-49	R. Ripley	200	400	600
1949-89	W. Frehm	100	150	200
1989-Present	Various Artists	40	50	60

ROBIN MALONE

Short-lived story strip by former "Tarzan" artist. Syndicated by N.E.A.

Daily Strips

1969-70	B. Lubbers	$20	$30	$40

Sunday Strips

1969-70	B. Lubbers	50	75	100

ROCKY AND BULWINKLE

Jay Ward's TV characters had a brief newspaper syndication. Bell McClure Syndicate.

Daily Strips

1965-68	A. Kilgore	[$50	70	90]

Sunday Strips

1965-68	A. Kilgore	[80	120	240]

ROSIE'S BEAU

Originally one of several revolving Sunday features, before "Bringing Up Father" became dominant, it eventually became the top strip for most of the "Bringing Up Father" run. It is rarely found separate from "Bringing Up Father" in the later years. King Features.

Sunday Strips

1916-18	G. McManus	[$600	$800	$1,100]
1926-54	G. McManus			
	(topper)	100	150	200

ROY ROGERS

From the movies to the newspapers Roy Rogers was illustrated by Chuck and Tom (signed name on strip is Al) McKimson for King Features Syndicate.

Daily Strips

1949-53	C. & T. McKimson	$40	$60	$80
1953-61	C.&T./Mike Arens	30	40	60

Sunday Strips

1949-53	C.&T. McKimson	50	75	125
1953-61	C.&T./ Mike Arens	40	60	100

RUSTY RILEY

Written and illustrated by the well-established commercial artist Frank Godwin, this Americana tale of a boy's love for dogs and horses was constructed around Godwin's son's adventures on their Florida farm. Syndicated by King Features.

Daily Strips

1948-59	F. Godwin	$150	$225	$300

Sunday Strips

1948-59	F. Godwin	150	300	450

S'MATTER POP

An early strip featuring the domestic doings of father, mother, and child. Drawn by Charles M. Payne for the New York World and the New York Sun.

Daily Strips

1910-40	C. Payne	$25	$50	$75

SECRET AGENT X-9, Alex Raymond, Sunday page, dated 10/9/34. Estimate: $1,000/2,000; sold for $920 in 1996 (Sotheby's 6th comic art auction). © King Features Syndicate

Sunday Strips				
1920's-40	C. Payne	40	60	90

THE SAD SACK

Drawn at first for Yank magazine by artist George Baker and eventually distributed by The Bell Syndicate.

Daily Strips				
1946-58	G. Baker	$30	$50	$75

SALESMAN SAM

Unusual strip by artist George O. Swanson for the NEA Service.

Daily Strips				
1921-27	G. Swanson	$40	$60	$120
1927-36	C. D. Small	30	50	75

Sunday Strips				
1922-27	G. Swanson	50	75	150
1927-36	C. D. Small	35	45	100

SAM'S STRIP

One of the great "unknown" humor strips. This starred Sam and retired King Features characters. Syndicated by King Features.

Daily Strips				
1961-63	M. Walker/			
	J Dumas	$100	$125	$150
1977-Present	Studio Artists	25	40	55

SAPPO

Originally known as the "5:15" as a daily, this domestic gag strip shifted over in 1926 to the top strip on Segar's strip, "Thimble Theater." Syndicated by King Features.

Sunday Strips				
1926-38	E. C. Segar	$400	$500	$700

SCAMP

Syndicated by King Features. "Scamp," the son of Lady and the Tramp, was given his own comic strip by the Disney Company. Syndicated by King Features.

Daily Strips				
1955-56	Dick Moores	***	***	***
1956-59	Bob Grant	$100	$150	$250
1960-77	Grant/Fuson/			
	Schmitz	75	100	150
1978-88	Roger Armstrong	75	100	125

Sunday Strips				
1955-56	Dick Moores	400	500	600
1956-59	Bob Grant	350	400	500
1960-77	Grant/Fuson/			
	Schmitz	250	300	350
1978-88	Roger Armstrong	150	200	300

SCORCHY SMITH

Syndicated for The Associated Press. Adventurer and aviator "Scorchy Smith" is best remembered for the work of Noel Sickles and Frank Robbins.

Daily Strips				
1930-33	J. Terry	$200	$300	$400
1933-36	N. Sickles	[400	700	900]
1936-38	B. Christman	100	150	200
1939-44	F. Robbins	100	150	200
1944-61	Studio Artists	50	75	100

Sunday Strips				
1939-44	F. Robbins	300	400	500
1944-61	Studio Artists	150	200	300

SECRET AGENT X-9

"Secret Agent X-9" (no name initially, though later renamed Phil Corrigan) was written in the beginning by Dashiel

SHADOW, Vernon V. Greene, 2 dailies, dated 10/9/34. Estimate: $300/500; sold for $330 in 3/98 (Russ Cochran Auctions). © The Ledger Syndicate

Hammett, then Leslie Charteris. Later, in the 1967-1976 period, noted comic book writer Archie Goodwin paired up with artist Al Williamson (longtime Alex Raymond fan) to establish a second peak to this classic adventure strip. Syndicated by King Features.

Daily Strips

1934-35	A. Raymond	$800	$1,200	$1,500
1935-38	C. Flanders	200	250	300
1939	N. Afosky	75	125	175
1939-40	A Briggs	75	125	175
1940-60	M. Graff	50	75	100
1960-67	B. Lubbers	40	60	80
1967-76	A. Williamson	100	150	300
1977-96	G. Evans	35	50	75

Note: individual sales include a daily dated 10/9/1934 selling for $920; a 3/29/1935 daily selling for $935; both sales at Sotheby's and Christie's East.

SENTINEL LOUIE
Syndicated by King Features. Top strip to "The Little King."

Sunday Strips

1934-50s	O. Soglow	$100	$150	$200

THE SHADOW
The pulp character had a brief four-year run in the comic strips. The Ledger Syndicate. Artist Vernon Green would later photo-stat or cut up some of his daily strips for use in the comic book stories. About 75 of these originals have entered the market in 1994 and 1995 from an estate collection at Sotheby's comic art auction. About 1/2 of these did not have The Shadow in them. The originals with Shadow are selling at higher prices.

Daily Strips

1938-42	V. Green	$250	$500	$700

SHOE
Pulitzer Prize-winning political cartoonist Jeff McNeily's strip about birds in humanesque guise. Syndicated by Chicago Tribune.

Daily Strips

1977-Present	J. McNeily	$200	$275	$350
1977-Present	J. McNelly	400	550	700

SHORT RIBS
Daily gag strip for the N.E.A. Syndicate.

Daily Strips

1958-Present	F. O'Neal	$25	$50	$75

145

SHADOW, Vernon Greene, artwork for 9 dailies, dated 1940-1941. Estimate: $1,000/1,500; sold for $2,415 in 6/94 (Sotheby's 4th comic art auction). © Street & Smith Publications/ The Ledger Syndicate

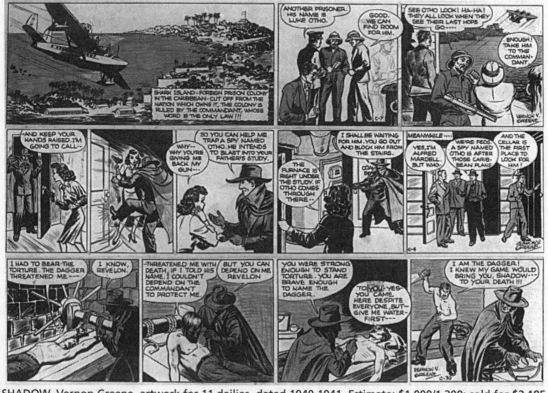

SHADOW, Vernon Greene, artwork for 11 dailies, dated 1940-1941. Estimate: $1,000/1,200; sold for $2,185 in 6/94 (Sotheby's 4th comic art auction). © Street & Smith Publications/ The Ledger Syndicate

SKY MASTERS, Jack Kirby and Wally Wood, artwork for 5 consecutive dailies, from 10/20 to 10/24/58. Estimate: $3,000/5,000; sold for $3,162 in 9/99 (Sotheby's 9th comic art auction). © George Matthew Adams Service

SKY MASTERS, Jack Kirby and Wally Wood, a daily and two drawings, dated 1950's. Estimate: $700/900; sold for $1,035 in 6/99 (Sotheby's 9th comic art auction). © George Matthew Adams Service

Sunday Strips

1959-Present	F. O'Neal	50	100	150

SILLY SYMPHONIES (SEE LISTING UNDER DONALD DUCK)

The years 1932-1939 contained adaptations of the Disney cartoons and the feature film *Snow White and the Seven Dwarfs*. From September 1936 through October 1937, Donald Duck starred as the featured character. In 1939, when Donald Duck got his own strip "Silly Symphonies" ceased and the "Donald Duck" strip ran over the "Mickey Mouse" feature. Various artists did the work. Al Taliaferro predominated on "Donald." King Features Syndicate.

Sunday Strips

1932-39	"Silly Symphonies"			
		[$6 000	$8,000	$10 000]
1939-45	"Donald Duck"			
	A. Taliaferro	2,000	3,000	4,000
1945-70	A. Taliaferro	100	300	1,000
1970-Present	Various Artists	100	200	400

Note: individual sales include two strips from 4/1 and 4/22/1943 selling together for $5,175 at Christie's East in 1966.

SKIPPY

Syndicated by King Features. Percy Crosby's classic kid strip. In initial years, it appeared in a magazine panel, then became nationally syndicated in 1927.

Daily Strips/Panels

1919-43	P. Crosby	[$200	$300	$400]

Sunday Strips

1927-43	P. Crosby	[600	1,200	1,500]

SKY MASTERS

"Sky Masters" was written by Dick and Dave Wood, both veteran comic book writers. The art was by Jack Kirby, the greatest comic book penciller of all time, and Wally Wood, who had established himself at EC as the top outer-space artist in comics. Syndicated by George Matthew Adams Syndicate.

Daily Strips

1958-59	J. Kirby/			
	W. Wood	$400	$600	$800

Sunday Strips

1958-59	J Kirby/			
	W. Wood	1,000	1,250	2.000

Note: individual sales include a Sunday page dated 6/21/1959 selling for $2,185; a daily dated 1/15/1959 selling for $805; both selling at Christie's East.

SKY ROADS

A well-done aviator strip by former "Buck Rogers" assistants, syndicated by John Dille.

Daily Strips

1929	D. Calkins	$500	$750	$1,000
1930-33	Z. Mosley			
	/R. Keaton	300	400	500
1933-42	R. Keaton	250	300	350

SMILIN' JACK

After a brier stint on "Sky Roads," Zack Mosley created his own aviator, Smilin' Jack. Syndicated by The Chicago Tribune.

Daily Strips

1936-73	Z. Mosley	$75	$150	$300

SMOKEY STOVER, Bill Holman, daily, dated 3/11/56. Estimate: $600/900; sold for $550 in 1992 (Sotheby's 2nd comic art auction). © The Chicago Tribune

SMITTY

Humor strip about a newspaper office boy. Syndicated for The Chicago Tribune.

Daily Strips

1922-43	W. Berndt	$50	$100	$250
1944-74	W. Berndt	25	75	150

SMOKEY STOVER/SPOOKY

Humor artist Bill Hollman had a drawing style unto himself. His "zany" and "busy" humorous adventure of Fireman Smokey Stover was full of crashes, explosions, and other sight-oriented gags. Syndicated for The Chicago Tribune. "Nuts and Jolts" was his accompanying daily strip.

Daily Strips

1935-55	B. Hollman/			
	"Nuls & Jolts"	$75	$100	$150
1956-73	B. Hollman/			
	"Nuls & Jolts"	50	75	100

Sunday Strips

1933-55	B. Hollman	200	300	400
1956-73	B. Hollman	150	200	300
	"Spooky"			
	toppers	50	75	100

SONG OF BERNADETTE

Hal Foster's adaptation of the classic story. Syndicated by King Features.

Daily Strips

1943	H. Foster	[$500	$600	$700]

THE SPIRIT

Will Eisner's "Spirit" was an original undertaking. His Sunday comic strip was, in reality, a souvenir eight-page comic book in the Sunday "Comics" section. The Spirit was another crime fighter operating outside normal law channels. He lived under a mausoleum in the local cemetery and continually had some of the most incredible women infatuated with him or wanting him dead. The art was a smooth blend of shading and long angles, reminiscent of film noir cinematography. The Sunday prices reflect per-page, not complete, story prices. Des Moines Register and Tribune Syndicate.

Daily Strips

1942-43	W. Eisner	[$500	$750	$1,000]
1943-44	W. Eisner/L. Fine/			
	J. Cole/J. Belfi	400	800	1,000

Sunday Sections

1940-42	W. Eisner	[600	800	900]

SPIRIT, Jack Cole, daily, dated 11/11/43. Estimate: $800/1,200; sold for $880 in 6/98 (Sotheby's 8th comic art auction). © The Des Moines Register & Tribune Syndicate

1942-46	W. Eisner/			
	L. Fine/ J. Cole/			
	J. Belfi/R. King	400	500	600
1946-52	W. Eisner/			
	J. Grandenetti/			
	Feiffer/Kotsky/			
	Perlin	500	600	700
1952	Feiffer/Eisner/			
	W. Wood	[400	700	900]

Note: Splash pages for The Spirit can go up to $2,500.

STAR HAWKS

"Star Hawks" was possibly the only strip drawn in a vertical double-size panel. N.E.A. Syndicate. Note that Gil Kane inked many of these in marker and they have faded. Those are basically worthless.

Daily Strips

| 1977-79 | G. Kane | $20 | $30 | $40 |

Sunday Strips

| 1977-79 | G. Kane | 75 | 100 | 150 |

STAR WARS

George Lucas' space epic graced comic pages with art by two of the masters. Unfortunately, almost all are unavailable to collectors. L.A. Times Syndicate.

Daily Strips

| 1979-81 | R. Manning | [$100 | $200 | $800] |
| 1981-84 | A. Williamson | [250 | 500 | 750] |

Sunday Strips

| 1979-81 | R. Manning | 500 | 750 | 1,000 |
| 1981-84 | A. Williamson | 500 | 750 | 1,000 |

STEVE CANYON

After a long feud with The Chicago Tribune over ownership of "Terry and the Pirates," Milton Caniff left in 1947 to start "Steve Canyon." An Air Force officer, Steve was instrumental in helping to win the Cold War in the funny papers. Naturally, being a Caniff creation, "Steve Canyon" was filled with action, adventure, and femmes fatales who made young men drool! Syndicated by Field Syndicate.

Daily Strips

| 1947-67 | M. Caniff | $100 | $200 | [$300] |
| 1967-88 | M. Caniff | 150 | 200 | 250 |

Sunday Strips

| 1947-67 | M. Caniff | 300 | 500 | [800] |
| 1967-88 | M. Caniff | 200 | 400 | 600 |

STEVE ROPER
(FORMERLY BIG CHIEF WAHOO)

A private-detective-story strip. Syndicated for the Field Syndicate.

Daily Strips

| 1936-53 | E. Woggon | $100 | $175 | $250 |
| 1953-Present | B. Overgard | 50 | 75 | 100 |

Sunday Strips

| 1936-53 | E. Woggon | 150 | 225 | 300 |
| 1953-Present | B. Overgard | 100 | 150 | 200 |

STUMBLE INN

One of the most charming strips George Herriman ever drew, for King Features Syndicate.

Specialty drawing for SUPERMAN, Waying Boring, daily, dated 1965. Estimate: $400/600; sold for $660 in 1998 (Sotheby's 8th comic art auction). © National Periodical Publications

SUPERMAN, Joel Shuster Studio, daily, dated 1940's. Estimate: $1,500/2,000; sold for $2,415 in 1994 (Sotheby's 4th comic art auction). © National Periodical Publications

Daily Strips

1922-23 G. Herriman [$700 $1,000 $1,500]

Sunday Strips

1922-26 G. Herriman [800 1,600 3,250]

Note: individual sales include a Sunday dated 3/3/1932 selling for $3,162 at Sotheby's in 1996.

Note: daily strips are almost unknown in the market, and Sunday pages are extremely rare as well.

SUBURBAN COWGIRLS

Tribune Media Syndicate. Well-written and -drawn strip focusing on radio disc jockey and her family. The charm of the strip is the last panel, where her T-shirt has the poignant punch line (a la The Yellow Kid's shirt).

Daily Strips

1991- 97	J. Alfieri and			
	E. Colley	$20	$40	$60

SUPERMAN

For the McClure Syndicate. "Superman" as a comic strip came out in January of 1939. It was drawn initially by creator Joe Shuster and assistants Jack Burnley and Wayne Boring were soon added. Shuster, by the mid-'40s, was drawing few of the "Superman" features. Wayne Boring almost exclusively would draw the comic strip until its demise. Brief stints by Al Plastino and Curt Swan in the mid-1950s broke up the Wayne Boring run.

Daily Strips

circa 1930's	J.Shuster (prototype daily No. 1) recorded sale			$77,000
1939	J. Shuster (*no known pages*)	[***	***	***]
1940-43	J. Shuster/ W. Boring/ J. Burnley	[900	1,800	3,800]
1944-46	Shuster/Boring/ Burnley	[800	1,400	2,800]

AS A DISTANT PLANET WAS DESTROYED BY OLD AGE, A SCIENTIST PLACED HIS INFANT SON WITHIN A HASTILY DEVISED SPACE-SHIP, LAUNCHING IT TOWARD EARTH.

SUPERMAN, Joel Shuster, artwork for an incomplete daily strip, circa 1930's. Depicting the origin of SUPERMAN, estimated at $80,000/90,000 and failing to sell at auction in 1994. It sold privately 24 hours after Sotheby's 4th comic art auction for $77,000. © National Periodical Publications/DC Comics

1946-52	W. Boring	[400	600	800]
1952-67	W. Boring/			
	C. Swan	[200	250	300]

Sunday Strips

1939	J. Shuster			
	(no known			
	pages)	[***	***	***]
1940-43	J. Shuster/W. Boring/			
	J. Burnley	[5,000	7,000	9,000]
1944-46	Shuster/W. Boring/			
	Burnley	[4,000	6,000	8,000]
1946-67	W. Boring	[300	600	900]

Note: comic history was made in 1994 when the proto-type No. 1 daily was brought to public auction at Sotheby's, this daily failed to meet its reserve price on the day of the auction - and then 24 hours later sold for $77,000, breaking a record for any daily strip at auction and setting a new record for any Golden Age comic book artwork at that time. Please see special feature article at beginning of this guide for more information.

Note: individual sales include: Shuster Studio circa 1940's strip selling for $2,100;

two dailies from 1942 selling for $2,300; a Sunday dated January 1943 selling for $9,900; all sales from Sotheby's auctions.

TAILSPIN TOMMY
One of the first and most interesting aviator strips. Distributed by the Bell Syndicate.

Daily Strips

1928-30	H. Forrest	$100	$150	$200
1931-50	H. Forrest	20	60	100

Sunday Strips

1929-34	H. Forrest	300	500	700
1935-50	H. Forrest	50	150	250

Colored Pages

1929-32	H. Forrest	300	450	600

Note: Only the first 150 Sunday pages are hand-colored by creator Hal Forrest.

TALES OF THE GREEN BERETS
During the height of the Vietnam War, veteran cartoonist Joe Kubert was called up to draw this classic war strip.

Daily Strips

1965-68	J. Kubert	$75	$100	$150

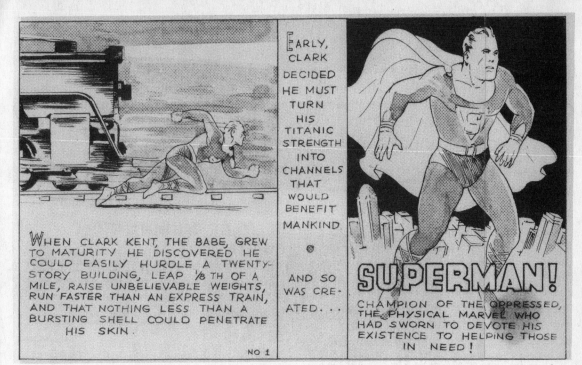

SUPERMAN, Joel Shuster, artwork for an incompleate daily strip, circa 1930's. Depicting the origin of SUPERMAN, estimated at $80,000/90,000 and failing to sell at auction in 1994. It sold privately 24 hours after Sotheby's 4th comic art auction for $77,000. © National Periodical Publications/DC Comiccs

Sunday Strips

| 1965-68 | J. Kubert | 100 | 150 | 200 |

TANK MCNAMARA

A fumble-mouthed sportscaster/ex-jock is the lead character. Syndicated for the Universal Press.

Daily Strips

| 1974 | Millar [writer] | | | |
| -Present | and Hinds | $25 | $50 | $75 |

Sunday Strips

| 1974 | Millar | | | |
| -Present | and Hinds | 50 | 75 | 100 |

TARZAN

From the enormous popularity of Edgar Rice Burroughs' *Tarzan* books, and a fortuitous meeting between Hal Foster and Burroughs (arranged when the commercial illustrator was weathering an inactive period), the daily "Tarzan" strip that Foster illustrated created history. In 1931, the combination of the naturalistic style of Foster and the interest in the strip by the public boosted both into prominence. Foster worked on "Tarzan" until 1937 when he debuted "Prince Valiant." The detailed decorative style of Burne Hogarth who followed Foster became synonymous with the most popular period of the strip for many fans. Syndicated by United Features.

Daily Strips

1929	(not known to exist)			
	H. Foster	[$3,000	$4,000	$5,000]
1930-35	R. Maxon	100	200	500
1936-47	R. Maxon	100	200	300
1947	B. Hogarth	200	250	300
1947-49	D. Barry	100	150	200
1949	J. Lehti	100	150	200
1949-50	P. Reinman	50	100	150
1950	N. Viskardy	50	100	150
1950-54	B. Lubbers	50	100	150
1954-67	J. Celardo	50	100	150
1968-72	R. Manning	100	150	200

Sunday Strips

1931				
(March)	R. Maxon	[1,000	1,750	2.500]
1931				
(Sept)-32	H. Foster	[12,500	15,000	17,500]
1933-34	H. Foster	[3,000	6,000	9,000]
1935-37	H. Foster	[1500	3,500	7000]
1937-45	B. Hogarth	1500	3500	[6,000]

1945-47	R. Moreira	500	650	800
1948-50	B. Hogarth	2,000	3,000	4,000
195C-54	B. Lubbers	300	350	400
1954-68	J. Celardo	300	350	400
1968-78	R. Manning	500	650	800
1979-80	G. Kane	300	450	500
1981-83	M. Grell	300	400	500
1983-Present	G. Morrow	150	200	250

Note: there are no known 1931 Foster Sunday pages, and there are only two or three known to exist from the year 1932.

Note: individual sales include: Sunday dated 5/5/1935 selling for $5,720; Sunday dated 5/29/1949 selling for $5,280; Sunday dated 12/15/1935 selling for $4,950; Sunday dated 5/26/1940 selling for $5,252; from Russ Cochran Comic Art Auctions. Other examples include: 1/30/1944 selling for $3,680; and 7/2/1944 Sunday selling for $4,140 at Christie's East. Also, Sunday's dated 7/31/1949 (Ononoes) selling at $7,150; 10/10/1949 selling for $7,150; 5/22/1949 selling for $4,125; Sunday dated 8/20/1933 selling for $4,313; Sunday dated 3/19/1959 (the first public offering of a hand colored Hogarth) selling for $14,950; 8/1/1949 selling for $3,162; 5/10/1942 (hand colored Hogarth Sunday) selling for $8,625; 4/21/1935 selling for $5,750; all sales from Sotheby's Comic Art Auctions.

Note: Burne Hogarth did a limited number of hand-colored Sunday pages at the request of Danton Burroughs from the years 1992 to the time of his death. The total number of Sunday pages colored by Mr. Hogarth was seventeen. Within the first year five private sales were made at $10,000 each and the first Sunday to appear at auction sold for $14,950. Since this time one Sunday has failed to meet its reserve at auction. Though Mr. Hogarth at first declined requests for hand-colored originals, feeling that they were not true to the original form of the strip, he later put some of this best work into these originals.

Note: There is only one known hand-colored Harold Foster Tarzan Sunday. This Sunday is pictured in the color section of this book. The original was the result of a direct request in the 1930's from none other than Edgar Rice Burroughs himself who, through his agent, requested an original to hang on his office wall from Mr. Foster. Harold Foster replied with the hand colored original reproduced in this book. It is now in the collection of Russ Cochran who traded $40,000 worth of prime EC original artwork to obtain this original. No other Foster Tarzan hand-colored originals are known to exist and none are likely to surface.

TEENAGE MUTANT NINJA TURTLES

"Teenage Mutant Ninja Turtles" stars the pizza-loving terrapins of Saturday morning TV comic book and feature-film fame. Syndicated by King Features.

Daily Strips

1990-Present	Mirage Studio	$20	$40	$60

TERRY AND THE PIRATES

For its writing and art, "Terry and The Pirates" stands alone. The consummate adventure strip from the top storyteller in comics. The greatest rogues and femmes fatales ever created flowed from Caniff's brush. Burma, Dragon Lady, Captain Blaze, and the ill-fated Raven Sherman are just a few who crossed the path of Terry Lee and Pat Ryan in this China-based strip. At the outbreak of World War II Caniff, like most cartoonists, put his heroes in uniform. The dogfights by Flip Corkin and Terry Lee are superb. If the syndicate had given ownership to Caniff as requested in 1945, he would have stayed. The year 1946 showed the return of every major villain in Caniff's swan song year. George Wunder took over in 1947 and continued the strip admirably until its demise in 1973. Caniff's style of art and cinematographic story telling laid such an impression on future cartoonists that today's most respected artists, such as Frank Robbins, Joe Kubert, Alex Toth, Al Williamson, and Steve Rude, consider Milton Caniff to be a major influence on their own styles. Syndicated by The Chicago Tribune.

Daily Strips

1934	M. Caniff	$500	$750[$1,000]	

TARZAN, Burne Hogarth, Sunday page, dated 7/31/49. Estimate: $7,500/8,500; sold for $7,150 in 10/92
(Sotheby's 2nd comic art auction). © ERB Inc. Resold at Russ Cochran auctions in 1998 for $10,450.

TARZAN, Burne Hogarth, Sunday page, dated 5/29/49. Estimate: $5,000/7,000; sold for $5,280 in 10/96 (Russ Cochran's comic art auctions). © ERB Inc.

1935-46	M. Caniff	300	550	[850]
1947-57	G. Wunder/			
	Wood/Evans	50	125	150
1958-73	G. Wunder	35	75	100

Note: Individual sales include: daily dated 12/30/1943 selling for $550; a 3/9/1946 selling for $800; from Howard Lowery Auctions. Daily dated 7/20/1944 selling at $302.50; daily dated 5/19/1939 selling at $3,190; both at Russ Cochran's Comic Art Auctions.

Sunday Strips

1934-36	M. Caniff	[2,000	3,000	4,000]

		(none known to exist)		
1937-41	M. Caniff	1,000	1,750	2,750
1942-46	M. Caniff	600	1,200	1,500
1947-57	G. Wunder/			
	Wood/Evans	100	150	200
1958-73	G. Wunder	75	100	150

Note: Individual sales include a Sunday dated 2/25/1945 selling for $2,500 at Sotheby's.

Note: an acrylic on canvas painting done by Caniff for an Overstreet Guide cover that was never used sold for $3,450 at Chrisite's East.

Tarzan
by Edgar Rice Burroughs

DARTS OF DEATH

AS THE ARROWS PIERCED THE HIDE OF BULGA, THE SHE-APE, SHE CRIED OUT IN TERROR.

THE OTHER APES RUSHED ABOUT IN PANIC AT THE UNEXPECTED ATTACK.

THE DRUNKEN SOLDIERS, SHOOTING THE ARROWS, LAUGHED MADLY AT THE QUEER ANTICS OF THE APES.

BUT SUDDENLY THEIR LAUGHTER STOPPED AS THEY HEARD THE BLOOD-CURDLING CRY OF THE BULL-APE. IT WAS TARZAN WHO UTTERED THE CRY.

LEAPING UPON TWO OF THE SOLDIERS, THE APE-MAN LIFTED THEM AND SMASHED THEIR HEADS TOGETHER

ONE BY ONE, HE HURLED THEM, UNCONSCIOUS, INTO THE PIT WHERE THE SACRED APES WERE KEPT.

BUT THE THIRD SOLDIER FLED.

TARZAN DASHED DOWN INTO THE MIDST OF THE APES AND DISARMED ONE OF THE SOLDIERS.

"FOLLOW ME!" THE APE-MAN COMMANDED.

UP THE STAIRCASE RACED THE APE HORDE.

MEANWHILE THE SOLDIER WHO HAD FLED SOUGHT THE AID OF HIS COMRADES.

AS TARZAN LED THE APES TO THE PALACE WALL, THE SOLDIERS SHOT A FUSILLADE OF ARROWS.

NEXT WEEK: THE VENGEANCE OF THOTH

TARZAN, Hal Foster, Sunday page, dated 2/26/33. Estimate: $7,000/10,000; sold for $6,600 in 10/97 (Russ Cochran's comic art auction). © ERB Inc.

Tarzan
by EDGAR RICE BURROUGHS

WITH A CRASH MAN AND BEAST CAME TO EARTH. NUMA SNARLED AND ROARED SAVAGELY, BUT THE MAN-THING CLUNG TENACIOUSLY TO HIS BACK.

THE WARNING CRY OF THE GREAT APES MINGLED WITH THE ROAR OF THE LION AS A NAKED WHITE GIANT DIVED HEADLONG OUT OF THE TREES.

REMORSELESSLY HE DROVE THE KNIFE THROUGH THE TAWNY HIDE UNTIL, WITH AN AGONIZED ROAR, NUMA ROLLED OVER ON HIS SIDE.

THEN THE APE-MAN RAISED HIS HEAD AND THE SAVAGE VICTORY CRY OF THE GREAT APES RANG THROUGH THE FOREST.

STEPPING INTO THE "TANGLE OF BRANCHES BESIDE THE TREE-MAN," TARZAN PUT A SHOULDER BENEATH THE TREE AND SLOWLY STRAIGHTENED. THE WEIGHT SLOWLY LIFTED, AND THE TREE-MAN CRAWLED OUT.

TARZAN LET THE TREE FALL AND TURNED TO FACE HIM. "I AM WOLLO, CHIEF OF WALOKS, THE TREE-MEN," GROWLED THE CREATURE, "WHO ARE YOU?"

"I AM TARZAN," THE APE-MAN REPLIED. "I SAVED YOU SO THAT YOU MIGHT GUIDE ME TO THE COUNTRY OF THE ONONOES."

HOGARTH

TARZAN, Burne Hogarth, Sunday page, dated 7/10/49. Estimate: $7,000/8,000; sold for $6,600 in 10/92 (Sotheby's 2nd comic art auction). © ERB Inc./United Feature Syndicate

TERRY AND THE PIRATES, Milton Caniff, daily, dated 7/20/44. Estimate: $250/350; sold for $302 in 10/97 (Russ Cochran's comic art auction). © The Chicago Tribune

TERRY AND THE PIRATES, Milton Caniff, daily, dated 7/20/44. Estimate: $300/400; sold for $330 in 1996 (Russ Cochran's comic art auction). © The Chicago Tribune

Note: appearances by The Dragon Lady, and Burma can cause a strip to sell for more.

THIMBLE THEATRE
See "Popeye."

TIGER
Humorous contemporary kid strip. Syndicated by King Features.

Daily Strips

1965-Present	B. Blake	$20	$40	$60

Sunday Strips

1965-Present	B. Blake	100	150	250

TILLIE THE TOILER
One of the first working-girl story strips. Syndicated by King Features.

Daily Strips

1921-54	R. Westover	[$75	$100	$150]
1954-59	B. Gustafson	25	50	75

Sunday Strips

1921-54	R. Westover	100	250	400
1954-59	B. Gustafson	50	75	125

TIM TYLERS LUCK
Syndicated by King Features. Adventure strip of teenage Tim Tyler. "Tim Tyler's Luck" was created by the brother of "Blondie" creator, Chic Young. Lyman Young, like Chic, used a studio to produce his work from early on. Amongst the artists Lyman employed were Jim and Alex Raymond, and Burne Hogarth.

Daily Strips

1928-32	L. Young	$150	$225	$300
1932-34	A. Raymond	100	150	200
1934-38	B Hogarth	100	150	200
1952-72	T. Massey	25	50	75

Sunday Strips

1931	L. Young	300	350	400
1932-33	A. Raymond	500	550	600
1934-37	B. Hogarth	200	250	300
1952-72	T. Massey	50	75	100

TINY TIM
Stanley Link created this very imaginative strip during the 1930's for the New York News Syndicate.

TERRY AND THE PIRATES, Milton Caniff, Sunday page, dated 2/25/45. Estimate: $1,000/2,000; sold for $2,500 in 1992 (Sotheby's 2nd comic art auction). © The Chicago Tribune

Sunday Strips

1931-38	S. Link	350	500	[750]
1939-58	S. Link	250	400	550

Note: a Sunday page dated 10/20/1935 sold at Sotheby's in 1993 for $825.

TOM CORBETT - SPACE CADET
Based on Robert Heinlein's juvenile series for Schribners, *Space Cadet*, drawn by Ray Bailey, and written by Paul Newman.

Daily Strips

1951-53	R. Bailey	$30	$60	$90

Sunday Strips

1951-52	R. Bailey	50	75	125

TOONERVILLE FOLKS
Classic offbeat humor strip focusing around a trolley car. Syndicated by the McNaught Syndicate.

Daily Strips

1915-55	F. Fox	$200	$350	$500

Sunday Strips

1922-56	F. Fox	300	500	700

TOOTS AND CASPER
A domestic gag strip. Syndicated by King Features.

TERRY AND THE PIRATES, Milton Caniff, daily, dated 6/27/36. Estimate: $500/800; sold for $1,870 in 6/97 (Russ Cochran auctions). © The Chicago Tribune

TERRY AND THE PIRATES, Milton Caniff, daily, dated 11/23/39. Estimate: $300/500; sold for $385 in 4/97 (Russ Cochran's comic art auctions). © The Chicago Tribune

TERRY AND THE PIRATES, Milton Caniff, daily, dated 5/19/39. Estimate: $2,000/3,000; sold for $3,190 in 1997 (Russ Cochran's comic art auctions). © The Chicago Tribune

Daily Strips				
1919-51	J. Murphy	$25	$75	$150
Sunday Strips				
1922-56	J. Murphy	100	200	300

TUMBLEWEEDS
Contemporary Western gag strip.
Syndicated by King Features.

Daily Strips				
1965-Present	T. Ryan	$50	$75	$100
Sunday Strips				
1965-Present	T. Ryan	75	100	125

TWIN EARTHS
Well-drawn science fiction outer-space story strip. Syndicated by United Features.

Daily Strips				
1953-55	A. McWilliams	$50	$75	$100
1956-63	A. McWilliams	35	65	90
Sunday Strips				
1953-55	A. McWilliams	200	300	400
1956-63	A. McWilliams	175	250	350

THIMBLE THEATER, E.C. Segar, Sunday page, dated 5/19/39. Estimate: $10,000/15,000; sold for $9,775 in 1997 (Sotheby's 7th comic art auction). © King Features Syndicate

THIMBLE THEATER, E.C. Segar, daily, dated 8/20/38. This is one of Segar's last dailies; he drew only six more after this one. Estimate: $2,000/3,000; sold for $2,200 in 6/97 (Russ Cochran auctions). © King Features Syndicate

UPSIDE DOWNS OF LITTLE LADY LOVEKINS AND OLD MAN MUFFARO

Syndicated by the New York Herald. No art is known to exist, but this is as unique a concept as could be. This comic was meant to be turned upside down, and the strip continues! There is a reprint book out there. Find it and you will be very happy to have discovered this lost gem.

Sunday Strips
1903-05   G. Verbeek   ***   ***   ***

UP FRONT

Syndicated by United Features. The adventures of Willie and Joe during World War II. Bill Maudlin enlisted in the Army from his home state of Texas, went on to World War II, and drew cartoons based on real-life experiences. His courage, insight and humor lifted the spirits of service men and women throughout the war effort.

Daily Strips
1940-45   B. Maudlin   [$300 $450 $950]

Note; individual sale includes single panel cartoon featuring Willie sold at Sotheby's for $1,320.

WALNUT COVE

Contemporary humor strip. King Features Syndicate.

Daily Strips
1991-Present   M. Callum $25 $45 $65
Sunday Strips
1991 -Present   M. Callum   45   75   125

WASH TUBBS

See "Captain Easy."

WEE PALS

Innovative, multiracial kid gag strip. Syndicated by King Features.

Daily Strips
1965-present   M. Turner $25 $50 $75
Sunday Strips
1965-present   M. Turner   200   250   300

WHEN I WAS SHORT......

Fun, contemporary gag strip. King Features Syndicate.

Daily Strips
1989-Present   G. Vasizovich $30 $60 $70

WHITE BOY

Syndicated by The Chicago Tribune. A "white boy" is captured and raised by Native Americans.

Sunday Strips
1938-36   G. Price   [$500 $600 $700]

WINNIE WINKLE

Well-done working-girl-story strip. Syndicated by The Chicago Tribune.

Daily Strips
1920-62   M. Branner $30 $50 $70
1962-80   M. Von Bibber   20   30   40
1980-97   F. Bolle   15   25   30
Sunday Strips
1922-30   M. Branner   100   200   250
1931-62   M. Branner   50   75   150
1962-80   M. Von Bibber   40   50   60
1980-97   F. Bolle   20   30   40

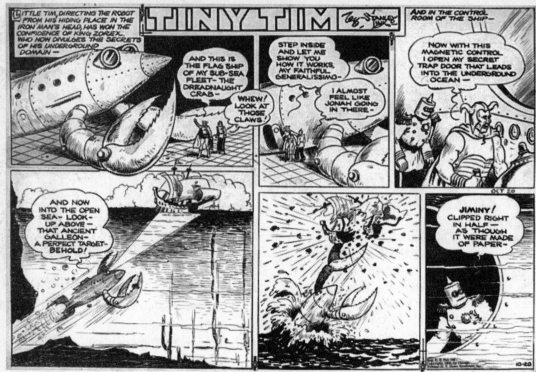

TINY TIM, Stanley Link, Sunday page, dated 10/20/35. Estimate: $1,000/1,500; sold for $863 in 6/93 (Sotheby's 3rd comic art auction). © The Chicago Tribune

WIZARD OF ID

Popular strip featuring the Wizard, the King, Sir Rodney, and the Spook in the dungeon. Syndicated by the Field Syndicate.

Daily Strips

1964-present	B. Parker	$100	$200	$300

Sunday Strips

1964-present	B. Parker	200	300	400

THE YELLOW KID

Considered to be the first comic strip. Unfortunately, only several examples are known to exist, and almost all are in museums and institutions. His shirt always bore the theme or message of Outcault's humor. Syndicated by New York World.

Daily Strips

1895	R. F. Outcault	
-96	Weekly Panels	[$10,000 $15,000 $30,000]

Note: Hard to price, never found, extremely rare, priceless.

Note: A full page example, dated July 12th 1896 from the New York World turned up at Cheney Auctions in Portland Maine, in the winter of 1999, and sold for $25,300.

ZIGGY

Daily gag panel. Universal Press Syndicate.

Daily Strips

1966-Present	T. Wilson	$50	$75	$100

Sunday Strips

1970-Present	T. Wilson	150	200	250

ZIPPY THE PINHEAD

Bill Griffith's underground comic character displays his insight into today's events in this well-written and -drawn comic strip. Syndicated by King Features.

Daily Strips

1974-79 (College Syn.)	B. Griffith	$275	$375	$500
1980-1990	B. Griffith	250	325	400
1991-Present	B. Griffith	150	200	300

Sunday Strips

1980-1990	B. Griffith	400	500	600
1991-Present	B. Griffith	300	400	500

ZIPPY THE PINHEAD, Bill Griffith, daily strip, dated 4/27/91, entitled "Hi Art, Lois Art," sold privately in 1994.
© King Features Syndicate

PRICE RANGE KEY

RARITY — Brackets [ ] around a price indicate that this example is very scarce and could exceed maximum estimate.

	Covers
No work produced in this category—	XXX
No price available due to lack of information—	***

CONDITION — Age, color, marks, tears, etc.

Pages

[400   500   600]

CHARACTER — Is the primary character featured, or is the original characteristic of a great example in the story line?

CONTENT — is the theme or story line exceptional or below average?

VALUE RANGE

Minimum	Medium	Maximum

RARITY

The [ ] Brackets indicate RARITY, if these brackets are used the reader can potentially double the price range in all three catagories.

COLLECTOR PAYING COLLECTOR PRICES!

Looking for...

FRANK MILLER
- DARK KNIGHT
- SPIDER-MAN ANNUAL #15
- DAREDEVIL (ESPECIALLY ISSUES 175, 176, 179 & 181)
- RONIN
- SIN CITY
- 300
- ANY MARVEL COVERS

STEVE DITKO
- SPIDER-MAN
- COMPLETE MARVEL PRE-HEROES STORIES

GEORGE PEREZ
- TITANS
- JLA
- AVENGERS (FIRST RUN)

MICHAEL GOLDEN
- MICRONAUTS, DEFENDERS & DR. STRANGE COVERS
- AVENGERS ANNUAL #10

BRIAN BOLLAND
- KILLING JOKE
- JUDGE DREDD/2000 AD

JOHN BYRNE
- X-MEN
- X-MEN
- FANTASTIC FOUR
- MARVEL TEAM-UP
- OH YEAH, ALSO ANY X-MEN

CURT SWAN
- 60's SUPERMAN ART
- BIZZARO ART

NEAL ADAMS
- ANY MARVEL OR DC
- PREFERABLY NOT STOLEN

DAVE GIBBONS
- WATCHMAN

ANY MARVEL OR DC ART...
- ANY TWICE-UP COVERS
- ART ADAMS
- MIKE MIGNOLA
- JIM STERANKO
- AND SOME GUY NAMED... KIRBY?
- IF YOUR NOT SURE IF I WANT IT, I PROBABLY DO. LET ME KNOW WHAT YOU HAVE! IF YOUR SELLING, I'M BUYING..

DAVID MANDEL
DavidM6785@aol.com (Best Contact)
(323) 851-9014 FAX
(818) 560-7818

SELL ME YOUR, YOUR, ART, AND YOU'LL GET TO MEET THE GIRLS!*

No guarantee that you will get to meet any actual women.

PART IV

ORIGINAL COMIC ART

Wally Wood, page 11 from WEIRD-SCIENCE FANTASY No. 26,
12/54, offered at Sotheby's June 17, 2000 auction. Estimated:
$1,000/1,400. © William M. Gaines, EC Publications

ADAMS-ART

Year	Publisher & Descriptive Information

1984 Pacific: *Alien Worlds 3-D*

Covers ($):	xxx		
Pages ($):	40	80	100

Marvel: *Classic X-Man, Cloak and Dagger, Excalibur, Fantastic Four, Heroes For Hope, Longshot, New Mutants, Spider-Man, X-Factor, X-Men*

Covers ($):	400	800	[1,200]
Pages ($):	xxx		

Black Widow, Conan, Daredevil, Defenders, Double Dragon

Covers ($):	200	475	750
Pages ($):	75	150	300

1986-91 DC: *Batman, Challengers of the Unknown, Spectre, Superman, Wonder Woman*

Covers ($):	250	350	450
Pages ($):	100	200	300

1987-88 Comico: *Gumby*

Covers ($):	xxx		
Pages ($):	60	100	150

1989 Eclipse: *Appleseed*

Covers ($):	300	400	500
Pages ($)	xxx		

1989 Genesis West: *Last of the Viking Heroes*

Covers ($):	200	350	300
Pages ($)	xxx		

1990's Dark Horse and Legend Comics: various projects

Pages ($):	60	100	150

ADAMS-NEAL

Year	Publisher & Descriptive Information

1959-62 Archie: Teenage humor— "Jughead," etc.

Covers ($):	xxx		
Pages ($):	[75	100	125]

1967-74 National/DC: *Batman, Deadman, Green Lantern, Green Arrow, Spectre, Superman*

Covers ($):	2,000	3,500	[5,500]
Pages ($):	350	600	900

Adam Strange, Aquaman, Challengers of the Unknown, Creeper, Flash, Hot Wheels, Justice League, Lois Lane, Manbat, Phantom Stranger, Teen Titans, Tomahawk, others

Covers ($):	1,000	1,500	2,500
Pages ($):	300	500	800

Misc. horror, mystery, sci-fi, Western, war

Covers ($):	500	900	1,400
Pages ($):	200	300	400

Bob Hope, Jerry Lewis, romance

Covers ($):	500	800	1,000
Pages ($):	75	100	150

1969-74 Marvel: *Avengers, Conan, Inhumans, Thor, X-Men*, horror

Covers ($):	900	1,800	[2,500]
Pages ($):	250	500	800

1975 Atlas/Seaboard: *Ironjaw, Planet of the Vampires*

Covers ($):	400	600	900
Pages ($):	xxx		

1976-77 National/DC: *Flash, Justice League, Superman*, etc.

Covers ($):	900	1,500	2,000
Pages ($):	xxx		

1983 Pacific: *Ms. Mystic*, etc. as Adams Studios

Covers ($):	600	900	1,600
Pages ($):	50	75	100

Note: individual sales would include cover for Superman No. 233 selling for $4,888; from Sotheby's comic art auctions.

Note: very little of Neal Adams art has surfaced at public auction, considering the amounts of Kirby, Ditko, and other silver age artwork by other artists to surface in the past ten years, it is evident that Adams artwork is either held by original owners, or much more scarce to the maket than previously thought.

ALLAN-DOUG

Year	Publisher & Descriptive Information

1990's *Steven, Blab, Snake-Eye,* other titles

Covers ($):	200	300	400
Pages ($):	50	75	125

Neal Adams, cover artwork for SUPERMAN #233, 1970's. Estimate: $1,000/1,500; sold for $4888 in 6/92 (Sotheby's 3rd comic art auction). © National Periodical Publications/DC Comics

Neal Adams, preliminary pencil cover design for STRANGE ADVENTURES, 1968. Sold privately for $5,000 in 1996. © National Periodical Publications/DC Comics

ALLRED-MIKE

Year	Publisher & Descriptive Information		
1990's	Madman, Red Rocket, various projects		
	Pages ($): 100	200	300

ANDERSON-MURPHY

Year	Publisher & Descriptive Information		
1944-47	Fiction House: Star Pirate, misc. sci-fi		
	Covers ($): xxx		
	Pages ($): 200	400	600
1950-52	Standard: Horror, sci-fl		
	Covers ($): xxx		
	Pages ($): 200	250	300
1950-52	Ziff-Davis: Lars of Mars, misc. sci-fi		
	Covers ($): xxx		
	Pages ($): [300	400	500]
1950-88	National/DC: Hawkman, Hawkgirl,		

Spectre, Starman & Black Canary, Dr. Fate & Hourman, Justice League, *Adam Strange and *Batman

Covers ($):	5,000	8,000	12,000
Pages ($):	400	800	900

Atomic Knights, Black Condor, Captain Comet, Dollman, Space Ranger, Superboy, Superman, Uncle Sam, and others

Covers ($):	1,500	2,500	3,500
Pages ($):	250	400	800

Fantasy, horror, sci-fi, Mystery in Space, Strange Adventures

Covers ($):	1,250	2,500	[3,000]
Pages ($):	200	400	600

War

Covers ($):	xxx		
Pages ($):	75	100	150

*For prices on Adam Strange and Batman art "penciled" by Carmine Infantino and inked by Murphy Anderson, see listing under "Infantino." Also, see strip art section for "Buck Rogers" listing. These prices apply to covers and pages penciled by Carmine Infantino and inked by Murphy Anderson.

Note: individual sales include: Flash No. 123 Cover $17,600; Mystery in Space No. 90 Cover $9,900; Showcase No. 56(Dr. Fate & Hourman) $4,950; Mystery in Space No. 21 Cover $4,025; Hawkman No. 4 Cover $5,175; Justice League of America No. 17 Cover $5,463; Cover art to Hawkman No. 2 $7,700; Cover art to Hawkman No. 1 $11,500; cover art for Showcase No. 61 selling at $17,250; all sales from Sotheby's comic art auctions.

Note: some of Murphy Andersons silver age covers have sold for more than golden age covers in the past few years as collectors have been willing to pay more and more money for the few remaining covers in Mr. Anderson's private collection. It is also of note to mention the classic re-creation golden age covers that Murphy has done for Diamond International Galleries in Baltimore. These covers are based on some of Mr. Anderson's most admired Lou Fine classic covers and are selling out at a

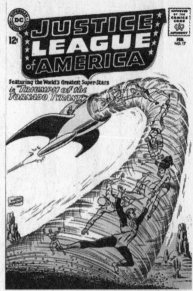

Neal Adams & Dick Giordiano, splash page artwork for GREEN LANTERN #266. Estimate: $750/1,000; sold for $1,035 in 1993 (Christie's East comic art auctions). © National Periodical Publications/DC Comics

Murphy Anderson, cover artwork for HAWKMAN #8, 1964. Estimate: $3,000/4,000; sold for $5,750 in 1993 (Christie's East comic art auctions). © National Periodical Publications/DC Comics

Murphy Anderson, cover artwork for JUSTICE LEAGUE OF AMERICA #17, 1962. Estimate: $3,000/4,000; sold for $5,750 in 1993 (Christie's East comic art auctions). © National Periodical Publications/DC Comics

Murphy Anderson, artwork for two page pin-up for JUSTICE SOCIETY OF AMERICA, 1969. Estimate: $2,000/3,000; sold for $9,200 in 1993 (Sotheby's 3rd comic art auction). © National Periodical Publications/DC Comics

Murphy Anderson, cover artwork for HAWKMAN #1, 5/64. First offered at Sotheby's in 1992 with an estimate of $8,500/9,500 and failed to sell at $7,500 bid; offered again at Sotheby's in 1996 estimated at $12,000/18,000 and selling for $11,500. © National Periodical Publications/DC Comics

Murphy Anderson, cover artwork for THE BRAVE AND THE BOLD #61, 1965. Estimate: $12,000/15,000; sold for $17,250 in 1996 (Sotheby's 6th comic art auction). © National Periodical Publications/DC Comics

Murphy Anderson, cover artwork for STRANGE ADVENTURES #138, 1962. Estimate: $1,000/2,000; sold for $2,760 in 6/93 (Sotheby's 3rd comic art auction). © National Periodical Publications/DC Comics

Murphy Anderson, interior page from HAWKMAN #1, 1964. Private sale at $500 in 1995 (T.R.H. Galleries). © National Periodical Publications/DC Comics

Murphy Anderson, splash page to two page lot from STRANGE ADVENTURES and SENSATION MYSTERY, 1952-53. Estimate: $1,500/2,000; sold for $1,495 in 1994 (Sotheby's 4th comic art auction). © National Periodical Publications/DC Comics

retail price of $5,000 each! These covers are done in the twice up cover format, and are fully hand-colored by the artist.

Note: a final observation about the Murphy Anderson market that would be obvious to anyone comparing notes from prices on the first Comic Guide and this present edition is that covers have exploded, however the prices paid for pages and stories have remained stable. Therefore, for anyone loving this artist's work who cannot afford to keep up with the cover madness, advice is given to collect the interior pages, stories, or splash pages.

ANDRU-ROSS

Year	Publisher & Descriptive Information		
1957	DC War titles, Twice-Up size art		
-70's	Covers ($):	800	2,000	3,500
	Pages ($):	50	100	150
	Metal Men, Twice-Up size art		
	Covers ($):	1,500	2,200	4,000
	Pages ($):	100	200	400

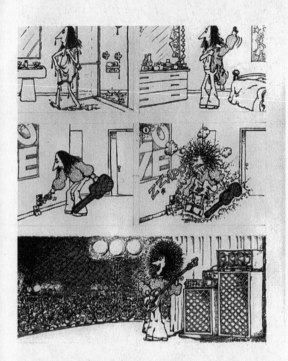

Sergio Aragones, original page from MAD #200, 7/78. Estimate: $600/800; sold for $385 in 6/98 (Sotheby's MADsterpieces Auction). © William M. Gaines/ EC Publications/ National Periodical Publications

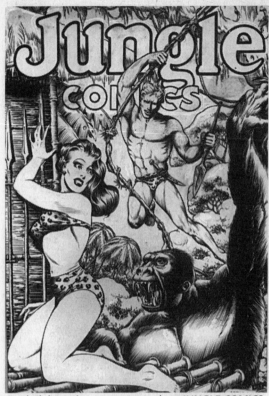

Raphalel Asarita, cover artwork to JUNGLE COMICS #46, 1943. Estimate: $1,000/2,000; sold for $3,495 in 6/93 (Sotheby's 3rd comic art auction). © Fiction House Publications

Spiderman;

Covers ($):	100	200	400
Pages ($):	25	50	100

APARO-JIM

Year	Publisher & Descriptive Information
1960--80's	*Batman, Phantom Stranger, Spectre,* DC & Charlton Projects

Covers ($):	75	200	450
Pages ($):	25	50	100

AVISON-AL

Year	Publisher & Descriptive Information
1940-42	Timely: *Captain America*

Covers ($):	[10,000	20,000	30,000]
Pages ($):	[2,000	4,000	6,000]

Vision, Wizzer

Pages ($):	[1,000	2,000	3,000]

1941-42	Fawcett: *Captain Marvel*

Pages ($):	[500	700	900]

1941-42	Harvey: *Captain Freedom, Red Blazer, Shock Gibson*

Covers ($):	800	1,000	1,200
Pages ($):	200	300	400

1945-50	Harvey: *Casper the Ghost, Humphrey, Joe Palooka, Kerry Drake, Little Dot*

Covers ($):	200	400	600

1951-54	Harvey: horror titles, *Witches Tales, Tomb of Terror,* etc

Covers ($):	800	1,000	1,200
Pages ($):	100	200	300

Harvey: Crime, War, and Misc. titles

Covers ($):	300	400	500
Pages	50	75	100

AYERS-DICK

Dick Ayers experienced a return of much of his Marvel Artwork at the same time that Jack Kirby settled with Marvel. Because Dick had inked much of the important silver age work that Jack Kirby penciled, and because of the Marvel settlement, 50% of the stories inked by Ayers on Kirby pencils were returned to him. The artist sold most

Dick Ayers, complete 13 page story from STRANGE TALES #112, 1963. Estimate: $2,000/3,000; sold for $1,898 in 6/93 (Sotheby's 3rd comic art auction). © Marvel Comics Group

Dick Ayers & John Severin, cover artwork for SGT. FURY #52, 1968. Estimate: $500/600; sold for $748 in 6/93 (Sotheby's 3rd comic art auction). © Marvel Comics Group

of this early work within the first two years of receiving back his pages - so most of it entered fandom. Ayers early work for the western titles for Marvel was also returned to him, consequently he still holds early 1950's work which is 100% Ayers pencils and inks.

The artist has also begun to do a series of very tightly inked re-creations covers from his classic Pre-Hero and Super-Hero days at Marvel that have been very popular with fans.

Year	Publisher & Descriptive Information		
1947	Studio work with Oscar LeBeck, penciling for *Funnyman*		
	xxx		
1948	Work for *Jimmy Durante* Book		
	Pages ($): xxx		
1951-56	Atlas, Horror Comic title stories, Covers and stories for *Black Rider, Kid Colt,* & Westerns		
	Covers ($):	600	800	1,600
	Pages ($):	75	125	150
	For Atlas Horror stories		
	Pages ($):	100	125	200
1953-55	*EH!* satire comic title, Horror stories for Charlton		
	Covers ($): xxx		
	Pages ($):	75	100	150
1950-56	*Ghost Rider, Bobby Benson,* & other M.E. titles		
	Covers ($):	250	400	[800]
	Pages ($):	50	75	125
1954-59	Marvel, *Rawhide Kid, Kid Colt, Gunsmoke.* Individual stories with his own inks, and begins to work inking Jack Kirby stories in later 1950's.		
	Covers ($):	250	300	400
	Pages ($):	35	50	125
	Western covers with Kirby pencils.		
	Covers ($):	350	600	[850]

Dick Ayers, cover re-creation artwork for STRANGE TALES #101, 1994. Estimate: $2,500/3,500; sold for $3,737 in 6/94 (Sotheby's 4th comic art auction). © Marvel Comics Group

Western stories with Kirby pencils.

Pages ($): 50 100 150

1958-63 Marvel/Atlas, the Pre-Hero period, individual fantasy stories, and stories and covers with Kirby Pencils.

Covers - Kirby Pencils

($): 4,000 6,000 [9,000]

Note: only two Pre-hero Marvel fantasy covers are known to exist, and they exist as Splash pages that were then used verbatim for the cover design. If any previously unknown original covers were to be discovered for this period, prices would be explosive.

Pages ($): pure Ayers pencils

and inks. 50 75 150

Pages ($): with Kirby pencils

Splash Pgs [1,000 2,500 5,000}

Pages ($): 250 500 800

1960-65 Marvel Super-hero period, work with Kirby is found in Jack Kirby listing. *Human Torch* stories, pure Ayers pencils and inks in *Strange Tales*.

Splash pgs ($):350 500 [750]

Pages ($): 75 125 250

1962-78 Marvel comics, *Sgt. Fury & His Howling Commandos*, War titles

Covers ($): 400 600 [800]

Pages ($): 50 125 150

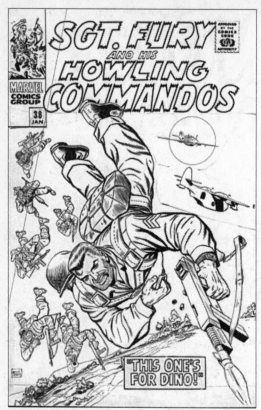

Dick Ayers, cover artwok for SGT. FURY AND HIS HOWLING COMMANDOS #38, 1966. Estimate: $600/800; sold for $575 in 6/93 (Sotheby's 3rd comic art auction). © Marvel Comics Group

Dick Ayers & John Severin, example from 32 interior pages from various issues of SGT. FURY. Estimate: $2,000/2,500; sold for $1,955 in 6/93 (Sotheby's 3rd comic art auction). © Marvel Comics Group

Pages - with Ditko pencils
($):   100   125   200
Pages - with Kirby pencils
($):   100   150   250

1990's   Cover re-creations for classic Marvel pre-hero and super-hero titles, *Fantastic Four, X-Men, Avengers, Journey into Mystery,* etc.
Covers ($): black and white - super-hero titles
1,000 2,000   3,000
Covers ($): black and white - pre-hero fantasy titles
800 1,250   1,750
Covers ($): colored, super-hero titles
1,000 1,500   2,250

Note: individual prices would include: Kirby/Ayers re-creation cover for *Strange Tales* No. 89 (Fing Fang Foom) selling at

$7,125; re-creation cover for *Strange Tales* No. 101 selling at $3,250; re-creation cover for *Fantastic Four* Annual No. 1 selling at $3,250; cover re-creation for *Hulk* No. 3 selling at $1,750; cover for *Ghost Rider* No. 5 selling at $715; thirteen page *Torch* story from *Strange Tales* No. 107 selling for $1,870; cover for *Sgt. Fury* No. 40 selling for $700; pencil cover concept for *Sgt. Fury* selling at $460; thirteen page *Torch* story from *Strange Tales* No. 112 selling at $1,898; Kirby/Ayers page from *Rawhide Kid* No. 18 selling for $460; all price from Sotheby's comic art auctions.

BAGGE-PETER

Year	Publisher & Descriptive Information
1981-92	Fantagraphics Books: *Neat Stuff, HATE!*

Covers ($):   300   400   600
Pages ($):   100   150   250

1992-98 *Real Stuff, Hate!*, record album
         covers, various projects
         Covers ($): 250   400   500
         Pages ($):   75   125   200
         A/Cvrs ($): 300   400   700

BAILY-BERNARD

Year	Publisher & Descriptive Information

1938-45 National/DC: *Spectre*
         Covers ($):[15,000 20,000 25,000]
         Pages ($): [2,000   3,000   4,000]

         Hourman
         Covers ($):[12,000 18,000 24,000]
         Pages ($): [1,000   1,500   2,000]

         *Buccaneer, Mr. America, Tex
         Thompson*
         Pages ($): [300   600   900]

1948-51 Prize: horror titles
         Pages ($): [200   400   600]

         Romance, War, & Western titles
         Pages ($): [100   200   300]

1951-52 Fawcett: horror titles
         Covers ($): [1,000   1,500   2,000]
         Pages ($): [200   400   600]

1956-58 Atlas/Marvel: Fantasy comic titles
         Pages ($): [200   400   600]

1952-67 National/DC: *Prince Ra-Man, Cave
         Carson*
         Pages ($): [250   500   750]

         Fantasy, mystery, & science-fiction
         titles
         Pages ($): 200   400   600

1961   Archie: *The Fly, Jaguar*
         Pages ($): 100   200   300

1973   DC Comics; horror titles
         Pages ($): 100   200   300

Individual sales would include: original art
to specialty drawing of The Hourman and
Jimmy Martin, 1940, selling for $1,870 at
Sotheby's in 1994.

BAKER-MATT

Year	Publisher & Descriptive Information

1944-52 Fiction House: *Camilla, Mysta,
         Sheena, Tiger Girl*
         Covers ($): [2,000   4,000   6,000]

         Pages ($): 300   600   900

         Clipper Kirk, Skull Squad
         Covers ($):   xxx
         Pages ($): 300   500   700

         Romance
         Covers ($):   xxx
         Pages ($): 100   300   450

1945-47 McCombs Publs.: *Jungle—
         "Vooda"*
         Covers ($): [2,000   3,000   4,000]
         Pages ($): 200   400   600

         Ace of the Newsreels, misc.
         adventure, mystery
         Covers ($): [2,000   2,500   3,000]
         Pages ($): 200   400   600

1946   Gilberton: *Classics Illustrated:
         Lorna Doone*
         Covers ($): [2,000   3,000   4,000]
         Pages ($): 200   400   600

1946-47 Universal Phoenix Features: *South
         Sea Girl*
         Covers ($): 2,500   4,000   5,500
         Pages ($): 300   600   900

1947   Pentagon Publs.: *Flyin' Jenny*
         Covers ($): 1,500   2,000   2,500
         Pages ($):   xxx

1949   Timely/Marvel: horror titles
         Pages ($): [300   600   900]

1947-49 Fox: **Phantom Lady*
         Covers ($): [***]
         Pages ($): [***]

         Jojo, Rulah, Tegra, Zegra
         Covers ($): [3,000   4,000   6,000]
         Pages ($): 300   600   900

1948-55 St. John: *Canteen Kate*, misc.
         romance
         Covers ($): [1,500   2,500   3,500]
         Pages ($): [200   400   600]

         Horror, jungle—*"Wild Boy"*
         Covers ($): [1,500   3,000   4,000]
         Pages ($):   xxx

         Crime, Western—*"The Hawk,"
         "The Texan"*
         Covers ($): [2,000   2,500   3,000]
         Pages ($): [200   400   600]

1950-56 Quality: *Romance, Robin Hood*

Covers ($): [2,000   2,500   3,000]
Pages ($): [200   400   600]

1954-55 Western/Dell: *Lassie*
Covers ($): xxx
Pages ($): 100   150   200

1951 Superior: Horror
Covers ($): xxx
Pages ($): 300   600   900

1952-55 Farrell Publs./Ajax: *Vooda*
Covers ($): [2,000   3,000   4,000]
Pages ($): 200   400   600

Horror, *Wonder Boy*
Covers ($): xxx
Pages ($): 300   600   900

1954 Dynamic Publs.: Horror/mystery
Covers ($): [2,000   3,000   4,000]
Pages ($): 300   600   900

1954 National/DC: romance titles
Pages ($): [200   400   600]

1956-59 **Atlas: Mystery, Western
Covers ($): xxx
Pages ($): 100   200   300

1958 Harvey Publications; horror titles
Pages ($): 100   200   300

1959 **Charlton: fantasy titles
Pages ($): 100   200   300

*Although Matt Baker did several *Phantom Lady* covers during the 1940s, the cover to issue No. 17, dated April 1948, is considered one of the most classic "bondage" covers of that period. The cover was also cited as an example in Dr. Fredric Wertham's book *Seduction of the Innocent*, which dealt specifically with comic books and juvenile delinquency. Any of the *Phantom Lady* original art is considered quite rare and to date, no known examples have surfaced.

** Some of this later work for both Marvel and Charlton was inked by Vince Colletta since Baker was working in Colletta's studio at this time. Baker used several different inkers on his comic work during his long career in the comics, and of course, inked a lot of his work himself.

BALENT-JIM

Year	Publisher & Descriptive Information		
1990's	DC Comics: *Catwoman* (very little work in the market at present)		
	Covers ($): 200	300	450
	Pages ($): 50	100	150

BARKS-CARL

Year	Publisher & Descriptive Information		
1942-67	Western/Dell/Gold Key: *Donald Duck (and nephews), Mickey Mouse, Scrooge McDuck (Uncle Scrooge)		
	Covers ($): [5,000	10,000	15,000]
	Pages ($): [1,500	4,750	8,000]

Includes such famous Donald Duck and Uncle Scrooge story classics as:

"Pirate Gold, Mummy's Ring, Frozen Gold, Ghost of the Grotto, Christmas on Bear Mountain, Sheriff of Bullet Valley, Lost in the Andes, Voodo Hoodo, Ancient Persia, Old California, A Christmas for Shacktown, Golden Helmet, Only a Poor Man, Back to the Klondike"

Covers ($): [7,000 15,000 25,000]
Pages ($): [1,500   2,500 4,000]

Andy Panda, Barney Bear, Beagle Boys, Benny Burro, Daisy Duck, Gladstone Gander, Granma Duck, Gyro Gearloose, Junior Woodchucks, Magica deSpell, Porky Pig

Covers ($): [2,000 4,000 6,000]
Pages ($): [800   1,200 1,600]

*Carl Barks' very first Donald Duck story, titled "Pirate Gold," was actually a shared venture with artist Jack Hannah while both men were employed at the Walt Disney Studios. The artists did not "cross-work' on each others art, but simply split the book in half, with each man doing his own portion.

CHRONOLOGY
A Complete Chronological Index to All of Carl Barks's Walt Disney Oils, 1971-1976

	Chronological number	Title (or subject, if untitled)	Height X Width (inches)	Barks's Identification Number on the Painting	Current Market Value
c	1	A Tall Ship and a Star to Steer Her By	18X24	13-71	
c	2	Money Lake	20X16	14-71	
c	3	Bullet Valley	20X16	15-71	$45,000
c	4	Bullet Valley (Red Sky)	18X14	16-71	$40,000
c	5	Golden Helmet	20X16	17-71	
c	6	Ancient Persia	20X16	18-71	
c	7	Money Lake	20X16	19-71	
c	8	Wishing Well	20X16	20-71	$60,000
c	9	Blue Composition of Ducks	20X16	21-71	
c	10	Bullet Valley	18X14	22-71	$35,000
c	11	Money Lake	20X16	23-71	
c	12	Old Castle	20X16	24-71	
m	13	Truant Officer	20X16	25-71	
m	14	Money Lake	20X16	26-71	
m	15	Ancient Persia	20X16	27-71	$55,000
m	16	Christmas Composition	20X16	1-72	$100,000
m	17	Pleasure in the Treasure (first Money Bin)	16X20	2-72	$125,000
m	18	Golden Helmet	20X16	3-72	
m	19	Sailboat	18X24	4-72	$60,000
m	20	Christmas Carolers (intended comic book cover)	17X12	5-72	$35,000
m	21	The Wadfather	16X20	6-72	
m	22	Bullet Valley (Red Sky)	18X14	7-72	$55,000
m	23	Golden Fleece	12X24	8-72	$80,000
m	24	Treasure Island	20X16	9-72	
m	25	Bombie the Zombie	20X16	10-72	$20,000
m	26	Scrooge #2 Cover	20X16	11-72	
m	27	Money Bin Memories	16X20	12-72	$125,000
m	28	Fair Wind Off Bora Bora	16X20	13-72	$45,000
m	29	Reading the Scandal Sheet	16X20	14-72	
m	30	Klondike Kaper	20X16	15-72	$75,000
m	31	Sea Cruise	18X14	16-72	$60,000
m	32	Truant Officer	20X16	17-72	$50,000
m	33	Money Lake	20X16	18-72	$75,000
m	34	Flubbity Dubbity Duffer	20X16	19-72	$90,000
m	35	Golden Helmet	20X16	20-72	
m	36	Old Castle With Scrooge	20X16	21-72	$85,000
m	37	Vacation Panel	24X18	22-72	$80,000
m	38	Flying Dutchman	18X24	23-72	$65,000

Note: works notated with "c" are on canvas; works notated with "m" are on masonite.

CHRONOLOGY
A Complete Chronological Index to All of Carl Barks's Walt Disney Oils, 1971-1976

Chronological number	Title (or subject, if untitled)	Height X Width (inches)	Barks's Identification Number on the Painting	Current Market Value
m 39	Flying Dutchman	18X24	25-72	
m 40	Blue Persia	20X16	1-73	
m 41	Bullet Valley	18X14	2-73	
m 42	Treasure Island	20X16	3-73	
m 43	Blizzard Tonight	20X16	4-73	$65,000
m 44	Secret Safe	16X20	5-73	$150,000
m 45	Green Persia	20X16	6-73	$65,000
m 46	What's In There?	16X20	5-73	
m 47	Another Long Day's Work	20X16	6-73	
m 48	Eight-Cornered Eggs	20X16	9-73	$60,000
m 49	Isle of Golden Dreams	20X16	10-73	
m 50	Menace Out of the Myths	18X24	11-73	$100,000
m 51	Visitor From Underground (Money Bin—lithograph)	16X20	12-73	$150,000
m 52	Square Eggs	20X16	13-73	
m 53	Sheriff Donald's Last Stand	18X14	14-73	$60,000
m 54	Family Portrait	20X16	13-73	$110,000
m 55	Sea Fever	18X14	16-73	
m 56	Time Out For Fun	16X20	17-73	$115,000
m 57	Much Ado About a Dime	16X20	18-73	$120,000
m 58	Time Out For Therapy	16X20	19-73	$100,000
m 59	Who's Out There?	16X20	20-73	$120,000
m 60	In Voodoo Land	20X16	21-73	$75,000
m 61	Luck of the North	16X20	22-73	$150,000
m 62	Webfoot Tenderfoot	18X14	23-73	$40,000
m 63	This Dollar Saved My Life at Whitehorse	16X20	24-73	$125,000
m 64	Cave of Ali Baba	16X20	25-73	$80,000
m 65	Spoiling the Concert	16X20	27-73	$125,000
m 66	Lavender and Old Lace	16X20	28-73	$85,000
m 67	Sheriff Donald at Gory Gap	18X14	29-73	$75,000
m 68	The Goose Egg Nugget	20X16	30-73	$100,000
m 69	Duck in the Iron Pants	16X20	31-73	$75,000
m 70	Halloween in Duckburg	18X24	33-73	$125,000
m 71	Snow Fun	18X24	1-74	$80,000
m 72	El Dorado, Gilded Man	16X20	2-74	$75,000
m 73	Slow Boat to Duckburg	18X14	4-74	
m 74	Trick or Treat	14X18	5-74	$75,000
m 75	Only a Poor Old Duck	20X16	6-74	
m 76	A Hot Defense (produced as a lithograph)	16X20	7-74	$75,000
m 77	Sport of Tycoons	14X18	9-74	$90,000
m 78	Danger Tycoon at Play	16X20	10-74	$135,000
m 79	Dangerous Discovery	16X20	11-74	$75,000

Note: works notated with "c" are on canvas; works notated with "m" are on masonite.

CHRONOLOGY
A Complete Chronological Index to All of Carl Barks's Walt Disney Oils, 1971-1976

Chronological number	Title (or subject, if untitled)	Height X Width (inches)	Barks's Identification Number on the Painting	Current Market Value
m 80	A Binful of Fun	14X16	12-74	$90,000
m 81	Nobody's Spending Fool (quintessential Scrooge)	16X20	13-74	$150,000
m 82	Rude Awakening	20X16	14-74	$65,000
m 83	McDuck of Duckburg	18X14	15-74	$120,000
m 84	Season To Be Jolly	16X20	16-74	$135,000
m 85	Voodoo Hoodooed	18X14	17-74	$75,000
m 86	Terror of the River	20X16	18 74	$75,000
m 87	Red Sails in the Sunset	18X14	19-74	$75,000
m 88	Where Ducks and Antelope Play	10X8	20-74	$35,000
m 89	Pick and Shovel Laborer	10X8	21-74	$50,000
m 90	Make Your Move, Podner	10X8	22-74	$25,000
m 91	Always Another Rainbow	10X8	23-74	$50,000
m 92	Compleat Golfer	16X12	1-75	$45,000
m 93	Dude For a Day	10X8	2-75	$35,000
m 94	I Found It, I Keep It	10X8	3-75	$50,000
m 95	Miser's Hangup	8X6	4-75	$55,000
m 96	The Old Money Magician	10X8	5-75	$35,000
m 97	Rug Riders Last Flight	16X12	6-75	$55,000
m 98	Far Out Safari	12X16	7-75	$60,000
m 99	Banker's Salad	10X8	8-75	$30,000
m 100	Time Wasters	16X20	9-75	$140,000
m 101	Hi, I'm Donald Duck	8X6	10 75	$35,000
m 102	Mayday on the Prairie	16X12	1175	
m 103	Unsafe Vehicle	16X12	13-75	
m 104	Cave of the Miniature	16X20	14-75	
m 105	Business Long Overdue	9X12	15-75	$45,000
m 106	Hands Off My Playthings	16X20	16-75	$140,000
m 107	Oh, Oh!	10X8	17 75	
m 108	Buyer Beware	12X9	18 75	
m 109	She Was Spangled and Flashy	16X20	19-75	$95,000
m 110	Menace From the Grotto	16X12	20-75	$75,000
m 111	The Expert	10X8	21-75	$40,000
m 112	Lake of Gold	20X16	22-75	$50,000
m 113	Golden Cities of Cibola	16X20	23-75	$85,000
m 114	Rumble Seat Roadster	10X8	24-75	$35,000
m 115	Gifts For Shacktown	10X8	25-75	$65,000
m 116	Golden Christmas Tree	16X12	26-75	$70,000
m 117	Pirate Gold	16X12	1-76	$60,000
m 118	Business As Usual	16X20	2-76	$160,000
m 119	July Fourth in Duckburg	18X24	3-76	$150,000
m 120	Disputed Claim	20X16	4-76	$75,000
m 121	Live It Up, Kid!	16X12	6-76	$110,000
c 122	Over the Bounding Main	18X14	7-76	

Note: works notated with "c" are on canvas; works notated with "m" are on masonite.

Carl Banks, artwork for preliminary drawing for "The Last Money Bin," 1970's. Estimate: $1,500/2,000; sold for $2,587 in 1994 (Sotheby's 4th comic art auction). © The Walt Disney Company

Carl Barks remained anonymous as a comic writer and artist for nearly 25 years while at Western Publishing. To the many comic readers and fans who grew up exposed to his genius, he has always been considered "the good duck artist." A legion of fans and collectors continues to follow his creative output today, which includes original paintings, lithographs, and numerous reprint editions of his comic book work.

* Barks's missing identification numbers represent paintings that were abandoned or never finished and a few non-Disney oils

Note: a word of caution about Carl Barks prices for paintings. Never at any other point in this book is the work "guide" more appropriate, the author has chosen

to deviate from the standard three column price range for Barks paintings in an attempt to be more accurate in pricing these paintings. Buyers and sellers should keep in mind that the above prices are based on actual sales, and comparables to similar paintings. Unlike the Frazetta market where many times paintings are over-priced (and there are only a handful of serious buyers) the Barks painting market has shown very healthy results (with active competative bidding) at public auctions at both Christie's East and Sotheby's. Not only are there numerous collectors in the United States but there is a growing and well-healed European and International group of collectors who play on the major Barks paintings.

PRELIMINARY PENCIL WORKS FOR PAINTINGS

Banks did sometimes as many as a half dozen preliminary pencil works, many to full scale for the major paintings. These pencil works have become very collectible in the past five years as prices for paintings continue to esclate.

Preliminary Works on Velum up to 10 x 14"
| Pencil Works ($): | 500 | 750 | 1,750 |

Preliminary Works on Velum above 10 x 14" in scale
| Pencil Works ($): | 750 | 1,500 | 2,750 |

MARKET UPDATE ON CARL BARKS LITHOGRAPHS (winter 1998)

Title		Size (inches)	Market Value of Painting
1. Sailing the Spanish Main	$10,000	25X20	$175,000
2. An Embarrassment of Riches	4,200	20X25	$175,000
3. Till Death Do Us Part		25X20	$125,000
Gold Plate	3,000		
Regular	2,000		
4. "A 1934 Belchfire Runabout!"		24X30	$200,000
Gold Plate	3,150		
Regular	2,100		
5. In Uncle Walt's Collectery		25X20	$150,000
Gold Plate	3,750		
Regular	2,500		
6. Return to Morgan's Island		24X30	$155,000
Gold Plate	2,550		
Regular	1,700		
7. Afoul of the Flying Dutchman		25X30	$175,000
Gold Plate	3,750		
Regular	2,500		
8. Dam Disaster at Money Lake		20X25	$125,000
Gold Plate	2,400		
Regular	1,600		
9. Dubious Doings at Dismal Downs		20X25	$160,000
Gold Plate	2,550		
Regular	1,700		
Progressives	6,000		
10. First National Bank of Cibola		25X20	$150,000
Gold Plate	1,800		
Regular	1,200		
Progressives	4,250		
11. Trespassers Will Be Ventilated		20X25	$135,000
Gold Plate	1,800		
Regular	1,200		
Progressives	4,000		
12. The Makings of a Fish Story		25X20	$150,000
Gold Plate	2,250		
Regular	1,500		
Progressives	5,000		

MARKET UPDATE ON CARL BARKS LITHOGRAPHS *(winter 1998)*

Title		Size (inches)	Market Value of Painting
13. Return to Plain Awful		24X30	$125,000
Gold Plate	1,800		
Regular	1,300		
Progressives	3,750		
14. Holiday in Duckburg		24X30	$175,000
Gold Plate	2,250		
Regular	1,500		
Progressives	4,500		
15. An Astronomical Predicament		26X20	$160,000
Gold Plate	1,650		
Regular	1,100		
Progressives	3,500		
16. Snow Fun		18X24	$100,000
Gold Plate	1,950		
Regular	1,300		
Progressives	4,000		
17. The Stone That Turns All Metals Gold		25X20	$175,000
Gold Plate	1,800		
Friends of the Ducks	1,500		
Regular	1,200		
Progressives	4,000		
18. Mardi Gras Before the Thaw		24X30	$200,000
Gold Plate	2,100		
Golden Anniversary	1,750		
Regular	1,400		
Progressives	4,500		
19. Halloween In Duckburg		18x24	$125,000
Gold Plate	2,100		
50 Years of Ducks	1,750		
Regular	1,400		
Progressives	4,500		
20. Dangerous Discovery		16x20	$75,000
Gold Plate	1,440		
Piece of the Roc:	1,200		
Regular	960		
Progressives	3,500		
21. This Dollar Saved My Life at Whitehorse		16x20	$125,000
Gold Plate	2,700		
Silver Dollars	2,250		
Regular	1,800		
Progressive Folio Book	3,500		
22. Leaving Their Cares Behind			
Gold Plate	1,200		
Vacation Edition	1,000		
Regular	800		
Progressives	3,250		

Title		Size (inches)	Market Value of Painting
23 In the Cave of Ali Baba		16x20	$80,000
Gold Plate	1,140		
Jeweled McDuck	950		
Regular	760		
Progressives	3,250		
24 Nobody's Spending Fool		16x20	$150,000
Gold Plage	1,650		
Regular	1,100		
Progressives	3,750		
Special Stone Lithograph: The Money Lender			
Japon	1,475		
Commemorative	1,225		
D'Arches	980		

MINIATURE LITHOGRAPHS

Title		Size (inches)	Market Value of Painting
1. A Hot Defense		16x20	$75,000
Gold Plate	960		
10th Anniversary	800		
Regular	640		
Progressives	2,500		
2. Visitor From Underground		16x20	$150,000
Gold Plate	2,250		
Regular	1,600		
Progressives	3,500		
3. Gifts For Shacktown		8x10	$65,000
Gold Plate	660		
Regular	440		
Progressives	2,000		
4. Always Another Rainbow		8x10	$50,000
Gold Plate	1,950		
Regular	1,300		
Progressives	3,500		
5. Blizzard Tonight		20x16	$65,000
Gold Plate	1,800		
H.D.& Louie	1,500		
Regular	1,200		
Progressives	3,250		
6. Pick & Shovel Laborer		10x8	$50,000
White Sculpture	1,500		
Gold Plate	960		
Top Pick	800		
Regular	640		
Progressives	2,500		

Carl Banks, original illustration for OVERSTREET PRICE GUIDE, 1976. Estimate: $2,500/3,000; sold for $5,463 in 6/93 (Sotheby's 3rd comic art auction). © The Walt Disney Company

MARKET UPDATE ON CARL BARKS LITHOGRAPHS (winter 1998)

Title		Title	
7. Sixty Years Quacking		11. Lavender and Old Lace	
Gold Plate	660	Gold Plate	660
Birthday Cake	550	Family Portrait	550
Regular	440	Regular	440
Progressives	2,000	Progressives	2,000
8. Menace Out of the Myths		12. Menace From the Grotto	
Gold Plate	750	Gold Plate	660
Maniacal Cackle	625	Ghost	550
Regular	500	Regular	400
Progressives	2,000	Progressives	1,750
9. Far Out Safari		13. The Expert	
Gold Plate	660	Gold Plate	1,140
So Far & No Safari	550	96th Birthday	950
Regular	440	Golden Anniv.	950
Progressives	2,000	Regular	760
10. Goose Egg Nugget		Progressives	3,000
Gold Plate	600	14. Dude for a Day	
Klondike	500	Gold Plate	660
Klondike Special	500	Regular	440
Regular	400	Progressives	2,000
Progressives	2,000		

Collectors should also keep in mind that as recently as the last year and a half prices of $200,000 and $250,000 have been realized for specific larger Barks oil paintings, and in a few cases lesser works have been selling for remakably higher levels. Thus some of the above quoted prices could easily move up $20,000 or more on any given day at auction or to a specific buyer.

(Prices for all Lithographs are based on Another Rainbow research to current market values for "mint" lithos - with their original Certificates of Authenticity. Some prints have one or two accompanying comic books that may have matching numbers (shown by asterisk[*]. Missing comics reduce resale values. Low numbers (2-10) command an additional 15% or more, depending on various factors. The values of #1's vary widely.)

Note: individual prices would include: page 13 from *Uncle Scrooge* selling at $3,250; preliminary pencil to "The Gilded Man" selling at $1,600; four pages from *Uncle Scrooge* No. 63 selling at $13,200; cover art for *Four Color* No. 1140 selling at $2,875; splash page from *Uncle Scrooge* No. 62 selling at $4,313; specialty illustration printed in *Overstreet Guide* No. 7 selling at $5,463; watercolor illustration for "Witches of Salem" selling for $4,888; Oil painting for "Hands off My Playthings" selling at $112,000; preliminary painting for "Return to Plain Awful" selling at $6,500; preliminary pencil drawing for "Dam Disaster at Money Lake" selling at $2,500; page from *Uncle Scrooge* No. 63 selling at $8,000; group of four original watercolor paintings to variations on "An Embarrassment of Riches" selling for $16,100; all sales from Sotheby's comic art auctions.

BARRY-DAN

Year	Publisher & Descriptive Information		
1940-42	Pines Publications: *Doc Strange*		
	Pages ($): [xxx	xxx	xxx]
1942-43	Lev Gleason: *Thirteen, Young Robin Hood*		
	Pages ($): [xxx	xxx	xxx]
1942-44	Hillman: *Airboy, Boy King, Nightmare, Skywolf*		
	Pages ($): [xxx	xxx	xxx]
1943	Holyoke: *Blue Beetle*		
	Pages ($): [xxx	xxx	xxx]
1943-44	Novelty: *Blue Bolt*		
	Pages ($): [xxx	xxx	xxx]
1944-47	Fawcett: *Captain Midnight, Commando Yank*		
	Pages ($): [200	300	400]
1947-48	Brown Shoe Co.: *Adventure*		
	Covers ($): [800	1,200	1,600]
	Pages ($): [150	200	250]
1947-48	Hillman: *Airboy, The Heap*		
	Covers ($): [2,000	3,000	4,000]
	Pages ($): [300	500	700]
	Hillman: *Gunmaster,* Western		

titles
	Covers ($): [1,000	1,500	2,000]
	Pages ($): [100	150	200]
1947-49	Lev Gleason: *Daredevil*		
	Pages ($): [400	600	800]
	Lev Gleason: *Crime Buster, Crime;*		
	Pages ($): [200	300	400]
1948-53	National/DC: *Johnny Quick, Vigilante*		
	Pages ($): [400	600	800]
	DC: *Alan Ladd, Bigtown, Gang Busters, Crime*		
	Covers ($): [1,000	2,000	3,000]
	Pages ($): [200	300	400]
1951-52	Ziff-Davis: science fiction titles		
	Pages ($): [200	300	400]

BARRY-LYNDA

Year	Publisher & Descriptive Information		
1980-92	*Girls & Boys, Breaking Up!, Real Comet Press, Esquire, Village Voice*		
	Covers ($): ***		
	Pages ($): [500	750	1,000]
1992-98	New books and various projects		
	Covers ($): xxx		
	Pages ($): [500	750	1,000]

BECK-CHARLES-CLARENCE

Year	Publisher & Descriptive Information		
1939-53	Fawcett: *Captain Marvel, Captain Marvel Jr., Ibis, Mary Marvel, Spy Smasher*		
	Covers ($): [4,000	6,000	8,000]
	Pages ($): 300	900	1,200

*Captain Marvel (originally created as Captain Thunder) was conceived by Fawcett editor Bill Parker and visualized by artist C. C. Beck in the fall of 1939. Later on, under Beck's watchful eye as chief artist, he oversaw the entire flow of scripts and art produced by two different art shops between 1941 and 1953. The shop responsible for producing most of the *Captain Marvel* art was located in New Jersey and was run under the direction of artist Pete Costanza. Costanza produced a significant amount of art himself and employed dozens of other artists to work in the consistent simplistic style which Beck had originally created for the character. Specific identification of Beck's art on any given original after 1941 can be difficult to determine. C. C. Beck is considered to be the founding father and principal driving force that made Captain Marvel one of the most successful characters in the history of comic books.

Year	Publisher & Descriptive Information		
1959	A.C.G.: mystery/fantasy titles, (Beck pencils only, with Pete Constanza inks.)		
	Pages ($): [100	200	300]
1967	Milson Publs.: *Fatman, Tinman*		
	Covers ($): 400	600	800
	Pages ($): 100	125	150
1973-74	National/DC: *Captain Marvel, Captain Marvel Jr., Mary Marvel*		
	Covers ($): 600	900	1,200
	Pages ($): 150	200	250
1974-78	Paintings done on commission, most of classic Golden Age covers, *Special Edition Comics, Whiz,* etc.		
	Covers ($): 600	800	1,000
	Pages ($): xxx		

BEYER-MARK

Some people might describe Beyer as a protégé of Rory Hayes; others would claim that he is the Paul Klee of comics. His expressive, tightly rendered, and emotional stories have appeared in *RAW*, *Arcade*, and *Kaktus*. His strip, "Amy and Jordan," appears in weekly alternative newspapers around the country. Recently Beyer's studio was broken into and all of his original artwork was stolen along with his handmade dolls. Throughout Europe and America, collectors and dealers are asked to contact Mr. Beyer with any information regarding his missing original artwork.

Mark Beyer, 1518 Union Boulevard, Allentown, PA 18103

BIRO-CHARLES

Year	Publisher & Descriptive Information		
1940-42	MLJ Publications: *Black Hood, Mr. Justice, Steel Sterling*		
	Covers ($): [xxx	xxx	xxx]
	Pages ($): [xxx	xxx	xxx]
1942	Hillman: *Airboy*		
	Covers ($): [xxx	xxx	xxx]
	Pages ($): [400	600	800]
1941-56	Lev Gleason: *Daredevil*		
	Covers ($):[10,000	15,000	20,000]
	Pages ($): [800	1,200	1,600]
	Crimebuster		
	Covers ($): [8,000	12,000	16,000]
	Pages ($): [400	600	800]
	Crime Does Not Pay		
	Covers ($): [1,000	2,000	3,000]
	Pages ($): [200	300	400]
	Little Wise Guys		
	Covers ($): [800	1,200	1,600]
	Pages ($): [75	150	225]
	Tops		
	Covers ($): [1,000	2,000	3,000]

BISLEY-SIMON

Year	Publisher & Descriptive Information		
1987-91	Fleetway: *Slaine, Judge Dredd*		
	Covers ($): 800	1,000	1,200
	Pages ($): 300	550	800
1990-92	DC: *Batman/Judge Dredd*		
	Covers ($): ***		
	Pages ($): ***		
	Doom Patrol, Demon, Swamp Thing		
	Covers ($): 900	1,200	[1,500]
	Pages ($): xxx		
	Lobo		
	Covers ($): 900	1,200	[2,000]
	Pages ($): 400	800	1,200
1991-92	Dark Horse: *Terminator*		
	Covers ($): 1,000	1,250	1,500
	Pages ($): xxx		
	Aliens		
	Covers ($): xxx		
	Pages ($): 400	600	800
1991	John Brown: *Mr. Monster*		
	Covers ($): 1,000	1,250	1,500
	Pages ($): 600	800	1,000
1992-98	Various Projects		
	Covers ($): 900	1,000	1,400
	Pages ($): 500	700	900

BODE-VAUGHN

Vaughn Bode used his experiences from the Army and military life to alter the tone of his work after being one of the first counterculture cartoonists to publish a comic with *Das Kampf* in May of 1963. Bode drew visually cute cartoon characters in oftentimes tragic and real-life exaggerations and his stories tended to have a dramatic effect on the reader. Vaughn was the first editor of the historic *Gothic Blimp Works*, and later developed the multimedia presentation of the cartoon concert. The original pencil works by this artist can be as exotic as the colored paintings done for *Deadbone Erotica* or *Cheech Wizard*.

Year	Publisher & Descriptive Information
1963-69	*Das Kampf, Gothic Blimp Works, The Man, Cheech Wizard, Gosh Wow*

    Covers ($):   2,000   2,500   [3,000]
    Pages ($):   500   625   [750]

1970-80	*Deadbone Erotica, Squa Tront, Junkwaffel, Fantasy Illustrated*

    Covers ($):   2,000   2,500   3,000
    Pages ($):   500   675   850

Vaughn Bode, cover artwork for THE EAST VILLAGE OTHER, 10/68. Private sale at $1,500 in 1992 (T.R.H. Galleries). © the Vaughn Bode Estate

---

PRICE RANGE KEY

RARITY — Brackets [ ] around a price indicate that this example is very scarce and could exceed maximum estimate.

	Covers
No work produced in this category—	XXX
No price available due to lack of information—	***

CONDITION — Age, color, marks, tears, etc.

	Pages		
	[400	500	600]

CHARACTER — Is the primary character featured, or is the original characteristic of a great example in the story line?

CONTENT — is the theme or story line exceptional or below average?

VALUE RANGE

Minimum   Medium   Maximum

RARITY

The [ ] Brackets indicate RARITY, if these brackets are used the reader can potentially double the price range in all three catagories.

Brian Bolland, Portfolio Illustration, 1970's. Private sale at $2,500 in 1996 (T.R.H. Galleries) © Brian Bolland

BOLLAND-BRIAN

Year	Publisher & Descriptive Information		
1978-89	*Fleetway, Eagle, Titian, Quality, Judge Dredd*		
	Covers ($): 800	1,200	[1,600]
	Pages ($): 150	375	[600]
1980-92	DC: *Batman: The Killing Joke*		
	Covers ($): ***		
	Pages ($): 400	600	[800]
	Camelot 3000		
	Covers ($): 800	1,200	1,500
	Pages ($): 125	250	375

Animal Man, Black Canary, Challengers of the Unknown, Green Lantern, Prince, Robin, Superman, Justice League, Vigilante, Wonder Woman

Covers ($): 800	1,200	[1,600]
Pages ($): xxx		

Aquaman, Swamp Thing, misc. sci-fi and mystery stories

Covers ($): 400	600	800
Pages ($): 60	120	180

Eclipse: *Axel Pressbutton, Valkyrie*

Covers ($): 300	400	500
Pages ($): xxx		

Real War Stories

Covers ($):	xxx		
Pages ($):	75	150	225

1986-90 Marvel: *She-Hulk, Howard the Duck*

Covers ($):	300	400	500
Pages ($):	xxx		

1986 Harrier: *Redfox*

Covers ($):	***		
Pages ($):	xxx		

1986 First: *Mundens Bar*

Covers ($):	xxx		
Pages ($):	75	150	225

1989-91 Atomeka: *Actress & The Bishop*

Covers ($):	***		
Pages ($):	300	400	[500]

1989-94 *Wonder Woman*

Covers ($):	400	700	1,000

BOLTON-JOHN

Year	Publisher & Descriptive Information

1966-80's *Classic X-Men, Bizarre Adventures, Kull, ManBat,* etc.

B&W/Cvs ($):	100	200	300
Pages ($):	50	150	300
C/Covers	500	1,200	3,000
C/Pages ($):	200	500	1,200

BORING-WAYNE

Year	Publisher & Descriptive Information

1938-67 National/DC: *Superboy, Superman*

Covers ($):	[2,500	3,500	5,000]
Pages ($):	[300	900	1,500]

Federal Men, Slam Bradley

Covers ($):	xxx		
Pages ($):	[300	450	600]

1946-48 Novelty Press: *Blue Bolt, Dick Cole, Tony Gayle*

Covers ($):	[600	800	1,000]
Pages ($):	[150	200	250]

1972-73 Marvel: *Captain Marvel, Gulliver on Mars*

Covers ($):	xxx		
Pages ($):	75	100	125

BRERTON-DAN

Year	Publisher & Descriptive Information

1990's Painted works & recent projects

C/Covers ($):	300	450	600
C/Pages ($):	75	150	250

BRIEFER-RICHARD(DICK)

Year	Publisher & Descriptive Information

1936 *Henle,* Misc.

Pages ($):	[200	400	600]

1938-41 Fiction House: *Hunchback of Notre Dame*

Pages ($):	[800	1,200	1,600]

Flint Baker, Crash Barker

Pages ($):	[200	400	600]

1940-54 Prize Comics: *Frankenstein*

Covers ($):	[2,000	3,000	4,000]
Pages ($):	200	400	600

1950 *Fawcett, Andy Devine*

Pages ($):	[50	75	100]

1950-52 Hillman: *Roisie Romance, Tossout Terry*

Pages ($):	[50	75	100]

1952 Atlas/Marvel: horror titles

Pages ($):	[200	400	600]

BROWN-BOB

Year	Publisher & Descriptive Information

1960's DC titles, *Challengers of the Unknown, Doom Patrol, Superboy*

Covers-Twice-Up in size

($):	500	800	1,400
Pages ($):	75	125	200

Covers, smaller size works

($):	100	250	400
Pages ($):	25	50	75

BROWN-CHESTER

Year	Publisher & Descriptive Information

1989-92 *Yummy Fur*

Covers ($):	***		
Pages ($):	200	400	[600]

1993-98 *Underwater;* also re-drawn panels and pages;

Covers ($):	***		
Pages ($):	***		

BRUNNER-FRANK

Year	Publisher & Descriptive Information

1970's *Howard the Duck, Dr. Strange*

Covers ($):	300	600	[900]
Pages ($):	100	200	300

Carl Burgos, artwork for splash page from YOUNG MEN #26, 1954. Estimate: $3,000/4,000; sold for $2,300 in 1996 (Sotheby's 6th comic art auction). © The Marvel Comics Group/Atlas Comics

BURGOS-CARL

Year	Publisher & Descriptive Information
1939-41	Centaur: *Iron Skull*
	Covers ($): xxx
	Pages ($): [200 300 400]
1939-41	Timely: *Human Torch & Toro, Thunderer*
	Covers ($): [***]
	Pages ($): [***]
1940-41	Funnies Inc./Novelty Pubs.: *White Streak*
	Covers ($): xxx
	Pages ($): [200 400 600]
1945	Timely: *Human Torch & Toro*
	Covers ($): xxx
	Pages ($): [***]

Year	Publisher & Descriptive Information
1954	Atlas/Marvel: *Human Torch & Toro*
	Covers ($): [2,000 4,000 6,000]
	Pages ($): [400 800 1,200]
1954	Atlas/Marvel: humor/satire titles;
	Covers ($): [1,000 1,500 2,000]
	Pages ($): [200 300 400]
1958	Farrell Publs. (magazine): Humor/satire
	Covers ($): xxx
	Pages ($): 50 75 100
1958-59	Major Magazines (magazine): Humor/satire
	Covers ($): xxx
	Pages ($): 50 75 100
1959	Satire Publs. (magazine): Humor/satire

Jack Burnley, original artwork for SUPERMAN Sunday Page, 1/43. Estimate: $10,000/12,000; sold for $16,000 in 6/93 (Sotheby's 3rd comic art auction). © The McClure Syndicate/National Periodical Publications/DC Comics

| Covers ($): | xxx | | |
| Pages ($): | 50 | 75 | 100 |

1964-65 Marvel: *Giant Man & The Wasp, Human Torch, Thing*

| Covers ($): | xxx | | |
| Pages ($): | 200 | 400 | 600 |

1969-71 Eerie Publs (magazine): Horror

| Covers ($): | xxx | | |
| Pages ($): | 50 | 75 | 100 |

BRUNETTI-IVAN

Year	Publisher & Descriptive Information

1993-98 *Antarctic, Fantagraphics, Schizo;*

Covers ($):	300	400	500
Pages ($):	100	150	200
Strips ($):	50	75	100

Note: Burnetti's originals are large, often measuring 20" x 30."

BURNLEY-JACK

Year	Publisher & Descriptive Information

1939-47 National/DC: *Superman, Batman, Justice Society, Starman, Superboy, Action*

| Covers ($): | [4,000 | 7,500 | 9,500] |
| Pages ($): | [900 | 1,600 | 2,200] |

Note: individual sales would include an interior page to "Starman" from *All Star* No. 9 (1942) selling for $4,025 at Christie's East in 1996.

BURNS-CHARLES

Year	Publisher & Descriptive Information
1980-92	Raw Books, Big Baby, RAW, Pixie Meat

Covers ($): 1,000   2,000   [3,000]
Pages ($):   750   1,500   [2,250]

1992-98	Black Hole; New Yorker advertising work

Covers ($): 1,000   2,000   3,000
Illos ($):   500   750   1,500

BUSCEMA-JOHN

Year	Publisher & Descriptive Information
1948-50	Atlas misc. crime, horror, mystery, romance, sci-fi

Covers ($): xxx
Pages ($): [100   200   300]

1954-60	Western/Dell: Western—Roy Rogers

Covers ($): xxx
Pages ($): [50   100   150]
Movie Adaptations: *Alexander the Great, Helen of Troy, Hercules, Seventh Voyage of Sinbad, Sharkfighters, Sir Lancelot, Spartacus, The Vikings.* TV series: *The Deputy*

1956-57	Charlton: *Nature Boy*

Covers ($): [400   800   1,200]
Pages ($): [100   200   300]

1966-91	Marvel: *Avengers, Captain America, Conan, Daredevil, Defenders, Dr. Strange, Fantastic Four, Hulk, Iron Man, Nick Fury, Spider-Man, Sub-Mariner, Tarzan, Thor, Wolverine, X-Men, Ghost Rider, Human Fly, Human Torch, Kazar, Kull, Magik, Man-Thing, Master of Kung Fu, Ms. Marvel, Nova, Peter Parker, ROM, She-Hulk, Team-Up, Warlock, Weird Worlds, What If?,* misc. jungle and romance, etc.

Covers ($): 150   300   450
Pages ($):   30   60   150
Above Prices for smaller size, prices below for Twice-Up size art.
Covers ($): 1,000   2,000   3,500
Pages ($): 100   200   300

1960's	Silver Surfer, and Avengers

Covers ($) [1,500   3,000   6,000]
Pages ($)   125   250   500

Note: individual sales would include: entire interior thirty-nine page story from Silver Surfer No. 4 selling at $11,000 at Sotheby's in 1992. In 1998 the cover art for Silver Surfer No. 1 sold for $17,000 privately.

BUSCEMA-SAL

Year	Publisher & Descriptive Information
1970-90's	Captain America, Defenders, & Marvel projects

Covers ($): 100   200   400
Pages ($):   25   50   75

BYRNE-JOHN

Year	Publisher & Descriptive Information
1975-76	Charlton: *ROG 2000 Space 1999*

Covers ($): 150   200   250
Pages ($): 150   100   150

1975-92	Marvel: *X-Men*

Covers ($): 4,500   5,500   [7,500]
Pages ($):   250   550   [800]

Alpha Flight, Captain America, Fantastic Four, Namor, Silver Surfer, She-Hulk, Wolverine, X-Factor,

Covers ($): 200   300   500
Pages ($): 100   175   250

Avengers, Daredevil, Dr. Strange, Ghost Rider, Hulk, Iron Man, New Mutants, Secret Wars, Spider-Man, Starlord, Thing, West Coast Avengers

Covers ($): 150   300   500
Pages ($):   75   100   250

Champions, Indiana Jones, Iron Fist, Machine Man, Mighty Mouse, Powerman, ROM, Spiderwoman, Star Brand, Star Wars, misc. horror, humor, sci-fi

Covers ($): 150   200   250
Pages ($):   60   120   180

1980-92	DC: *Batman, Legends, OMAC, Superman*

Covers ($): 200   400   470
Pages ($): 100   175   250

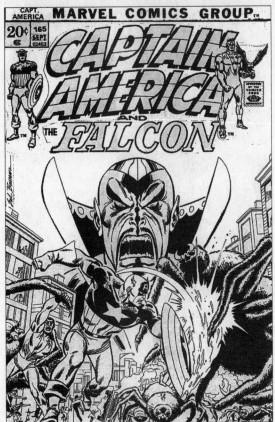

Sal Buscema, cover artwork for CAPTAIN AMERICA #165, 9/77. Sold privately for $300 in 1998 (T.R.H.Galleries). © The Marvel Comics Group

John Byrne, cover artwork for SUPERMAN #3. Sold privately for $1,500 in 1999 (T.R.H. Galleries). © National Periodical Publications/DC Comics

Atom, Doom Patrol, Green Lantern , Hawkman, Legion, Teen Titans

Covers ($):	150	200	250
Pages ($):	60	120	180

1985 *Eagle: Judge Dredd*

Covers ($):	xxx		
Pages ($):	150	200	250

1987 Genesis West: *Last of the Viking Heroes*

Covers ($):	200	250	300
Pages ($):	xxx		

1990 Archie: *To Riverdale & Back Again*

Covers ($):	200	250	300
Pages ($):	xxx		

1991-92 Dark Horse: *Next Men*

Covers ($):	250	300	350
Pages ($):	100	175	250

1992-98 Various Projects:

Covers ($):	200	300	400
Pages ($):	100	200	300

CAMPBELL-EDDIE

Campbell's career started with handmade limited run comics in the 70's and has progressed to more high profile projects like the critically acclaimed *From Hell* series.

At the current time, only pages from his *From Hell* series are for sale to the public, and some of the color and B&W covers.

Year	Publisher & Descriptive Information
1977-98	Kitchen Sink, Dark Horse: *Fantagraphics, Eddie Campbell Comics, Acme/Eclipse, Tundra, Harrier, Deadface, Bacchus, The Complete Alec, Grafitti Kitchen, From Hell, Dead Muse, Eyeball Kid,* etc

Covers ($):	100	150	200
Clr. Cvs.($):	300	150	450
Pages ($):	75	100	125

Nick Cardy, cover artwork for THE WITCHING HOUR!
#4, 9/69. Estimate: $300/500; sold for $360 in 1998
(Phil Weiss Auctions).
© National Periodical Publications/DC Comics

Nick Cardy, artwork for AQUAMAN #1,splash page,
1962. Estimate: $800/1,200; sold for $1,380 in 1995
(Christie's East comic art auctions).
© National Periodical Publications/DC Comics

CAMPBELL-JEFF-SCOTT

Year	Publisher & Descriptive Information		
1990's	*Veil 13;* other projects		
	Covers ($): 500	750	1,000
	Pages ($): 100	200	300

CAPULO-GREG

Year	Publisher & Descriptive Information		
1990's	*Angela, Spawn, X-Force,* various Marvel projects		
	Covers ($): 200	300	500
	Pages ($): 100	200	300

CARDY-NICK

Year	Publisher & Descriptive Information		
1940's	*Fiction House, Jumbo, Jungle, etc*		
	Covers ($): 1,500	2,500	4,000
	Pages ($): 100	200	300
1960's	*Aquaman, Teen Titans, Batlash;* Covers Twice-Up		
	in size ($): 2,000	3,000	4,000
	Pages/T-Up 100	200	300

Covers (smaller size silver age pages) ($): 400	600	800
Pages ($): 50	100	150
1970's	DC covers, for misc. titles		
	Covers ($): 200	300	400

CARTIER-EDD

Year	Publisher & Descriptive Information		
1943	Street & Smith: *The Shadow*		
	Covers ($): [3,000	5,000	7,000]
1946-47	Street & Smith: *Red Dragon, Herrman The Great*		
	Covers ($): [2,000	3,000	4,000]
	Pages ($): [400	600	800]
1952	Harvey: horror titles		
	Pages ($): [300	500	700

CHADWICK-PAUL

Year	Publisher & Descriptive Information		
1985-86	Marvel: *Dazzler*		
	Covers ($): 100	150	200
	Pages ($): 50	75	100

Gene Colan, cover artwork for DOCTOR STRANGE #172, 9/68. Sold privately for $2,000 in 1997 (T.R.H. Galleries). © The Marvel Comics Group

1986-92	Dark Horse: *Concrete*			
	Covers ($):	150	300	450
	Pages ($):	100	175	250
	Cheval Noir			
	Covers ($):	***		
	Pages ($):	xxx		
1990	DC: *Superman*			
	Covers ($):	xxx		
	Pages ($):	75	100	125

CHAREST-TRAVIS

Year	Publisher & Descriptive Information			
1990's	DC: *Darkstars, Flash, Batman, Wildcats*			
	Covers ($):	500	1,000	1,500
	Pages ($):	100	200	400

CHAYKIN-HOWARD

Year	Publisher & Descriptive Information
1973-88	DC: *Blackhawk, Shadow, Batman, Enemy Ace, Fafhrd & the Grey Mouser, Star Trek, Superman, Vigilante,* misc. mystery and sci-fi

	Covers ($):	75	150	225
	Pages ($):	25	50	100
1975	Atlas/Seaboard: *Scorpion*			
	Covers ($):	75	150	225
	Pages ($):	25	50	100
1976	Star Reach: *Cody Starbuck*			
	Covers ($):	100	200	300
	Pages ($):	50	100	150
1976-89	Marvel: *Nick Fury/Wolverine, Dominic Fortune, Micronauts, Star Wars, Conan, Indiana Jones, Monark Starstalker, Red Sonja, Solomon Kane*			
	Covers ($):	75	150	225
	Pages ($):	30	60	100
1983-89	First: *American Flagg*			
	Covers ($):	200	300	400
	Pages ($):	75	100	125
1988-90	Vortex: *Black Kiss, Badlands*			
	Covers ($):	75	150	225
	Pages ($):	75	150	225

CLOWES-DANIEL

Clowes started his career with a highly stylized minimalist mock-50's art style for *Lloyd Llewellyn* and matured into a more detailed Crumbesque style for *Eightball*. The artist offeres a catalogue of his pages with pricing information.

Year	Publisher & Descriptive Information	
1980-97	Fantagraphics: *Lloyd Llewellyn, Eightball*	
	Covers ($):	xxx
	Pages ($):	xxx

COLAN-GENE

Year	Publisher & Descriptive Information			
1953	EC: War Pages			
	Covers ($):	xxx		
	Pages ($):	100	200	300
1950-57	Atlas: Horror, mystery, war, Western			
	Covers ($):	400	800	1,200
	Pages ($):	50	100	150
1958	Charlton: western titles			
	Pages ($):	[50	100	150]
1965-68	Warren: Horror			
	Covers ($):	xxx		

Pages ($): 100 200 300

1965-80 Marvel: *Iron Man, Sub-Mariner, Daredevil, Dr. Strange, Dracula, Captain America, Avengers, Captain Marvel*

    Covers ($): 800 1,200 1,600
    Pages ($) 100 200 300

Above prices for smaller art-
Below prices for Twice-Up size art
    Covers ($): 1,000 2,000 3,000
    Pages ($): 50 100 150

Howard The Duck
    Covers ($): 300 600 900
    Pages ($): 50 100 150

1979-84 DC: *Batman, Wonder Woman, Phantom Zone*
    Covers ($): 100 200 500
    Pages ($): 50 75 100

1970-90 Eclipse: Graphic Novel work on *Stuart The Rat*
    Pages ($): 25 40 90

COLLETTA-VINCE

Year	Publisher & Descriptive Information		
1954-62	Atlas/Marvel: Romance		
	Covers ($): 300	450	600
	Pages ($): 40	80	120

Note: From 1962 to 1990, Vince Colletta was exclusively an inker at both Marvel and DC His talent and speed had him working on virtually all characters at both companies.

COLE-JACK

Year	Publisher & Descriptive Information		
1938-40	Centaur: Crime, humor, "Mantoka"		
	Covers ($): xxx		
	Pages ($): [200	400	600]
1938	Globe: Humor		
	Covers ($): xxx		
	Pages ($): [200	400	600]
1939-40	MLJ: *Comet*		
	Covers ($): xxx		
	Pages ($): [400	800	1,200]
1939-41	Lev Gleason: *Claw, Daredevil, Silver Streak*		
	Covers ($): [***]		
	Pages ($): [1,000	2,000	3,000]

1940-54 Quality: **Plastic Man*
    Covers ($): [***]
    Pages ($): [1,000 2,000 3,000]

* Cole's "Plastic Man" artwork from the late 1940s to the mid-1950s can be difficult to identify. At that time other talented artists were brought in on the feature and could imitate his style almost to perfection, although his story-telling ability was unmatched.

Death Patrol, Midnight, Quicksilver
    Covers ($): [3,000 4,000 5,000]
    Pages ($): [600 1,000 1,400]

Misc. crime, horror
    Covers ($): [2,000 2,500 3,000]
    Pages ($): [400 800 1,200]

Misc. humor—*Blimpy, Burp and Twerp, Carnie Carnahan, Dan Tootin, Ike An Dooit, Inkie, Odd Jobs, Pvt. Dogtag, Slap Happy Pappy, Windy Breeze, Wun Cloo,* and others
    Covers ($): xxx
    Pages ($): [200 400 600]

1947-48 Magazine Village: *Misc. crime
    Covers ($): [***]
    Pages ($): [***]

* Includes the classic "drug" story from True Crime Vol. 2, No. 1, titled "Murder, Morphine and Me," later cited in Dr. Fredric Wertham's book *Seduction of the Innocent*, which dealt specifically with comic books and juvenile delinquency.

COLE-LEONARD-B.

Year	Publisher & Descriptive Information		
1943-44	Ace Publications: *Magno & Davey*		
	Pages ($): [300	400	500]
1943-46	Continental Magazines: *Catman*		
	Covers ($): [3,000	6,000	9,000]
	Pages ($): [1,000	1500	2,000]

Continental: *The Tracker, Crime, Suspense, The Boomerang, Miss Victory*
    Pages ($): [400 800 1,200]

Continental: *Mr. Nobody, Satan*
    Covers ($): [4,000 8,000 12,000]

1944-46 *Holyoke/Four Star Publications, Black Cobra, Captain Aero, Captain Flight*

    Covers ($): [2,000   3,000   4,000]
    Pages ($): [300   400   500]

    Holyoke/Four Star: *Funny Animals;*
    Covers ($): [1,000 1,500, 2,000]

1947-50 Novelty Publications: *Dick Cole;* Adventure titles;
    Covers ($): [1,000   1,500 2,000]

1948-54 Star Publications: horror and science fiction titles
    Covers ($): [3,000   5,000 7,000]

    Star Pub.: *Jungle*
    Covers ($): [2,000   4,000 6,000]

    Star Pub.: War, Crime, humor titles
    Covers ($): [1,500   2,500 3,500]

1958-61 Gilberton Publications: *Classics Comics* titles
    Cover Paintings
        ($): [2,000   3,000 4,000]

1980-85 *Cover Re-Creations: horror, jungle, science fiction titles
    RC/Cvrs ($): 1,000   2,000 3,000

* From 1980 to 1985 L.B.Cole produced a number of special full color cover recreations of many of his famous comic book covers from the 1940's and 1950's. These were usually rendered with brush, india ink and watercolors on illustration board. These recreations were flawlessly reproduced in matching almost line for line from the original covers. There were three different sizes available including the same size as the comic - 7¼" x 10¼," or one and a half times up - 10⅞" x 15¾," or twice up - 14½"x 21". In the 1996 Sothebys comic book and art auction, twice-up cover recreations fot *Mask Comics* Nos. 1 and 2 sold for $1,840 and $1,495 respectively.

(note: collectors should realize that Mr. Cole, unlike the majority of other golden age artists who executed recreation covers, sometimes did multiple numbers for the same comic book title. If he was commissioned over a period of three years to do the cover for *Mask Comics* No. 1 by three different fans, he would have done three covers, each with a slightly different range of color - or possibly with identical color schemes. The existance of multiple numbers on the same covers will have some effect on value over time.)

COLEMAN-JOE

Year	Publisher & Descriptive Information		
1965-79	Early one shot comics for Underground Publishers		
	Covers ($): 500	800	1,600
	Pages ($): 100	200	350
1974-90's	Paintings		
	($): 1,000	1,500	[2,500]

COOPER-DAVE

Year	Publisher & Descriptive Information		
1987-97	Fantagraphics, Dark Horse: *Deadline U.S.A, Dark Horse Presents, Synthia Petal's Sex Frenzy, Pressed Tongue, Suckle, Crumple,* etc.		
	Covers (painted) ($): 600	1,000	1,500
	Pages (painted) ($): 150	250	350
	Pages ($): 150	200	300

CORBEN-RICHARD

Year	Publisher & Descriptive Information		
1970-78	Misc. Underground Pub: fantasy, horror, sci-fi		
	Covers ($): 500	750	1,800
	Pages ($): 150	225	300
1972-81	Warren: fantasy, horror, sci-fi		
	Covers ($): 1,000	1,500	2,250
	Pages ($): 150	225	300
1975	Marvel: sci-fi		
	Covers ($): xxx		
	Pages ($): 150	225	300
1977-92	HM Communications: *Den, Rowlf, Sinbad,* misc. sci-fi		
	Covers ($): 1,000	1,500	2,000
	Pages ($): 100	200	300
1990-91	Fantasy Press: fantasy, horror, sci-fi		
	Covers ($): 400	600	900
	Pages ($): 100	200	300
1991	Mirage Studios: *Teenage Mutant Ninja Turtles*		

Johnny Craig, cover artwork for THE VAULT OF HORROR #32, 1953. Private sale at $6,000 in 1995. The original artwork for this cover featured the "uncensored" version of Craig's design. © William M. Gaines, EC Publications

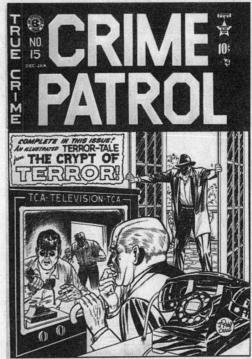

Johnny Craig, cover artwork for CRIME PATROL #16, 1950. Estimate: $600/900; sold for $4,025 in 1993 (Sotheby's 3rd comic art auction). © William M. Gaines, EC Publications

Johnny Craig, cover artwork for CRIME PATROL #15, 1949. Estimate: $750/1,000; sold for $4,025 in 1993 (Sotheby's 3rd comic art auction). © William M. Gaines, EC Publications

Johnny Craig, cover artwork for THE VAULT OF HORROR #28, 1953. Estimate: $3,500/4,500; sold for $2,750 in 1992 (Sotheby's 2nd comic art auction). © William M. Gaines, EC Publications

Johnny Craig, original artwork to ad page from THREE-DIMENSIONAL TALES FROM THE CRYPT, Spring 1954. Estimate: $1,500/2,500 (Sotheby's 2nd comic art auction). © William M. Gaines, EC Publications

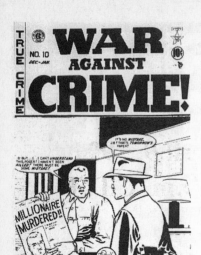

Johnny Craig, cover artwork for
WAR AGAINST CRIME #10, 1949.
Estimate: $400/800; sold for $3,850
in 4/9/97 (Russ Cochran's comic art
auctions). © William M. Gaines,
Agent, Inc.

Johnny Craig, cover artwork for
WAR AGAINST CRIME #5, 1949.
Minimum Bid: $400; sold for $1,452
in 10/9/96 (Russ Cochran's comic art
auctions). © William M. Gaines,
Agent, Inc.

Johnny Craig, cover artwork for
WAR AGAINST CRIME #6, 1949.
MINIMUM BID: $400; sold for
$1,177 in 10/9/96 (Russ Cochran's
comic art auctions). © William M.
Gaines, Agent, Inc.

Johnny Craig, cover artwork for
WAR AGAINST CRIME #7, 1949.
Minimum Bid: $400; sold for $660
in 12/11/96 (Russ Cochran's comic
art auctions). © William M. Gaines,
Agent, Inc.

Johnny Craig, cover artwork for
WAR AGAINST CRIME #8, 1949.
Minimum Bid: $400; sold for $880
in 12/11/96 (Russ Cochran's comic
art auctions). © William M. Gaines,
Agent, Inc.

Johnny Craig, cover artwork for
WAR AGAINST CRIME #9, 1949.
Minimum Bid: $400; sold for $1,17
in 12/11/96 (Russ Cochran's comic
art auctions). © William M. Gaines
Agent, Inc.

| Covers ($): | 800 | 1,200 | 1,600 |
| Pages ($): | xxx | | |

CRAIG-JOHNNY

Year	Publisher & Descriptive Information		
1948	M.E.: Western		
	Covers ($):	xxx		
	Pages ($):	[75	100	125]
1948	Lev Gleason: Crime		

| Covers ($): | xxx | | |
| Pages ($): | [75 | 100 | 125] |

1949	Fox Features: Crime/Western		
	Covers ($):	xxx		
	Pages ($):	[75	100	125]

1947-56 EC: *Horror—'The Vault Keeper"

* Johnny Craig started at EC around 1947,
working on the crime and Western "pre-
trend" titles. When the company made the

Johnny Craig, cover artwork for THE VAULT OF HORROR #34, 1949. Estimate: $2,000/3,000; sold for 2,530 in 1995 (Christie's East comic art auctions). © William M. Gaines/EC Publications

Johnny Craig, cover artwork for SADDLE JUSTICE #4, 1948. Estimate: $400/800; sold for $588.50 in 10/15/97 (Russ Cochran's comic art auctions). © William M. Gaines, Agent, Inc.

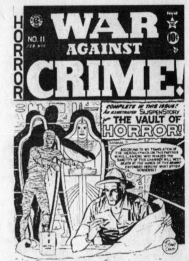

Johnny Craig, cover artwork for WAR AGAINST CRIME #11, 1950. Estimate: $1,000/2,000; sold for $4,025 in 1996 (Sotheby's 6th comic art auction). © William M. Gaines/EC Publications

conversion to horror in 1950, he went on to produce some of his most memorable work. Because he is noted for his clean approach to linework and "Eisnerish" story-telling abilities, his art enjoys a favorable demand from collectors. He is known especially for his *Vault of Horror* stories as introduced by the EC "ghoulunatic" horror-host, The Vault Keeper. In 1971, Johnny started doing oil painting commissions of "The Vault Keeper" and certain EC cover re-creations. Thanks to EC's publisher, Bill Gaines, and the EC art auctions that began in 1980, most of Johnny's art is now in private collections. It should be noted that one complete horror story, a few crime pages, and four covers from his EC New Trend and New Direction output are missing.

| | Covers ($): | 1,750 | 2,500 | [4,000] |
| | Pages ($): | 100 | 250 | 500 |

Captain Crime, crime

| | Covers ($): | 800 | 1,000 | 1,200 |
| | Pages ($): | 75 | 150 | 225 |

Moon Girl, New Direction titles, Western

| | Covers ($): | 400 | 600 | 1,000 |
| | Pages ($): | 50 | 100 | 150 |

1964-66 ACG: Horror, mystery

| | Covers ($): | xxx | | |
| | Pages ($): | 50 | 75 | 100 |

1965-67 Warren (magazine): Horror

| | Covers ($): | xxx | | |
| | Pages ($): | 100 | 275 | 450 |

1968-70 Marvel: *Iron Man, Sub-Mariner*

| | Covers ($): | 400 | 800 | 1,200 |
| | Pages ($): | 75 | 150 | 225 |

1975 Marvel: horror titles

| | Pages ($): | 75 | 100 | 150 |

1971-92 EC-related & EC cover recreation oil paintings, most 20"x26", some larger.

| | Covers ($): | 700 | 900 | 1,500 |

Note: individual sales would include: oil painting for Vault Keeper (done in early 1970's) $2,250; cover for *Crime Patrol* No. 10 selling at $1,495; cover for *War Against Crime* No. 11 selling for $4,025; cover for *Crime Patrol* No. 13 selling for $1,610; cover for *Extra* No. 2 (B&W painting) selling for $2,300; cover for *Crime Patrol* No. 16 (the P cover) selling for $4,025 (and selling again in 1996 for $7,500); cover for *The Vault of Horror* No. 32 selling for $7,500; cover for *Crime Suspenstories* No. 7 selling for $2,300; all sales private or from Sotheby's comic art auctions.

Reed Crandall, artwork for 5 page story, 1956.
Estimate: $1,000/1,500; sold for $920 in 1994
(Sotheby's 4th Comic Art Auction). © William M.
Gaines, Agent, Inc.

CRANDALL-REED

Year	Publisher & Descriptive Information		
1940-43	Quality: *Blackhawk, Doll-Man, Firebrand, Hercules, Paul Bunyan, Ray Stormy Foster, Uncle Sam*, etc.		
	Covers ($): [2,500	4,500	6,500]
	Pages ($): [400	800	1,200l
1941	Champ Publs. Co.: *The Human Meteor*		
	Covers ($): [***]		
	Pages ($): xxx		
1943	Fiction House. *Jungle—"Kaanga"*		
	Covers ($): xxx		
	Pages ($): [300	600	900]
1946-53	Quality: *Blackhawk, Captain Triumph, Doll Man, Ken Shannon, Plastic Man, T Man*		
	Covers ($): [2,000	3,000	4,000]
	Pages ($): 250	500	750
	Adventure, crime, Western		
	Covers ($): 1,000	2,000	3,000
	Pages ($): 200	400	600

1953-56	EC: *Crime, horror, sci-fi, adventure, war*		

(Note: Crandall covers - *Piracy* and the few other EC covers almost never enter the market)

	Covers ($): [2,000	3,000	4,500]
	Pages ($): 200	400	600
1956-59	Atlas: Fantasy, mystery war, Western		
	Covers ($): xxx		
	Pages ($): 200	400	600
1957-58	Brown Shoe Co.: Jungle, sci-fi		
	Covers ($): xxx		
	Pages ($): [150	350	450]
1960-72	George A. Pflaum Co.: Adventure, historical, war, Western, science		
	Covers ($): 900	1,500	2,000
	Pages ($): 100	200	300
1961-64	Western/Dell/Gold Key: Mystery, movie adapt.		
	Covers ($): xxx		
	Pages ($): 100	200	300
1961-62	Gilberton: Classics Illustrated: *Oliver Twist, Hunchback of Notre Dame*		
	Covers ($): xxx		
	Pages ($): 100	200	300
1964-70	Warren (magazine): Horror, war		
	Covers ($): xxx		
	Pages ($): 150	350	550
1965-66	Tower: *Dynamo, Thunder Agents, Noman*, etc.		
	Covers ($): xxx		
	Pages ($): 300	500	800
1967-68	King/Charlton: *Flash Gordon*		
	Covers ($): 1,000	2,000	3,000
	Pages ($): 250	450	550

Note: individual sales would include: 3-D art for story entitled "Child Of Tomorrow" selling at $2,875; cover for *Terror Illustrated* No. 1 (picto-fiction) selling at $8,025; cover for *Crime Illustrated* No. 2 selling at $2,875; ten pg story from *Terror Illustrated* No. 1 selling for $2,300; all sales from Sotheby's comic art auctions.

Year	Publisher & Descriptive Information

1955-60 *Crumb Brothers Almanac, FOO,* early stories and sketches

Covers ($): [500   1,250   2,500]
Pages ($):   100   200   300

Single Crumb Brothers Almanac
Covers ($):   650   1,250   2,250

1961-67 American Greeting Cards Illustrations
Pages ($):   500   600   700

Early pages from *Cavalier* ("*Fritz*")
Pages ($): [750   1,250   2,000]

East Village Other, HELP!
Covers ($): [3,000   4,000   9,000]
Pages ($):   550   750   [950]

Yarrowstalks
Covers ($):   3,000   3,500   [4000]
Pages ($):   500   650   800

The Yum Yum Book, 152 p., color
Covers ($):   ***
Pages ($):   5,000   10,000   [20,000]

1968-70 *Cover to Cheap Thrills, Joplin* $21,000 sale, Sotheby's

ZAP 1 *and ZAP* 0
Covers ($):[20,000   30,000   50,000]
Pages ($): 1,000   2,500   [5,000]

East Village Other, Gothic Blimp Works, Yellow Dog
Covers ($): 2,000   3,500   [6,000]
Pages ($):   500   1,250   2,000

1969 *Snatch, Creem, Motor City 1, ZAP 4, Big Ass 1, Ozone 1, R. Crumb's Comics & Stories, Meatball 1, JIZ, Bijou*
Covers ($): [4,000   6,500   8,000]
Pages ($):   500   1,000   1,500

1970 *Despair, Motor City 2, ZAP 5, Bijou 4, Mr. Natural 1, Uneeda*
Covers ($): [4,000   6,500   8,000]
Pages ($):   500   750   1,000

1971-75 *Home Grown, Hytone, Big Ass 2, Mr. Natural 2, Bijou 6*
Covers ($): [4,000   6,500   8,000]
Pages ($):   500   750   1,000

1972 *Funny Aminals, ZAP 7, XYZ Comics, People's Comics, Melotoons 1*

Robert Crumb, artwork for interior page entitled "Remember Keep On Truckin?" from XYZ COMICS, 1972. Estimate: $4,000/6,000; sold for $4,600 in 1996 (Sotheby's 6th comic art auction). © Kitchen Sink Press/Robert Crumb

Covers ($): [3,000   5,500   7,000]
Pages ($):   500   625   750

1973 *Artistic Comics, El Perfecto, ZAP 6, S.F. Comic Book, Bijou*
Covers ($): [3,000   5,000   7,000]
Pages ($):   350   550   750

1974 *ZAP 7, Dirty Laundry 1, ZAM, Young Lust 4, Mendocino Grapevine*
Covers ($): 1,000   1,750   3,250
Pages ($):   350   550   750

1975 *Funny Papers 1-3, Arcade 1-4, Felch, Snarf 6, Bizarre Sex 8, ZAP 8*
Covers ($): 2,000   4,000   7,000
Pages ($):   350   550   750

1976-80 *Esquire, Village Voice, Arcade, American Splendor, Melotoons 2*
Covers ($): 1,250   2,500   3,500
Pages ($):   250   375   500

1977 *Mr. Natural 3, Dirty Laundry 2, High Times, American Splendor*

Robert Crumb, cover artwork for R. CRUMB'S FRITZ THE CAT, The Ballantine large format paperback book, 10/69. Estimate: $35,000/45,000; sold for $56,350 in 1996 (Sotheby's 6th comic art auction). © Ballantine Books/Robert Crumb

Robert Crumb, artwork for original (lost) version of the cover for ZAP COMICS #1, 1967. Estimate: $20,000/30,000; sold for $46,000 in 1996 (Sotheby's 6th comic art auction). © The Print Mint/Robert Crumb

Robert Crumb, cover artwork for THE EAST VILLAGE OTHER, Vol. 5, #10, 1970. Estimate: $10,000/15,000; sold for $9,775 in 1998 (Sotheby's 8th comic art auction). © The East Village Other/Robert Crumb

Robert Crumb, 3 page story from "Ducks Yas Yas" from ZAP COMICS #0, 1967. Estimate: $15,000/17,000; sold for $16,675 in 6/93 (Sotheby's 3rd comic art auction). © Robert Crumb & The Print Mint

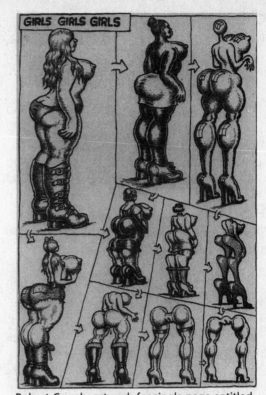

Robert Crumb, artwork for single page entitled "Girls, Girls, Girls" from XYZ COMICS, 1972. Estimate: $4,000/6,000; sold for $8,625 in 1996 (Sotheby's 6th comic art auction). © Kitchen Sink Press/Robert Crumb

	Covers ($):	1,500	3,000	5,000
	Pages ($):	250	375	500

1978 *American Splendor 3, Mondo Snarfo, CoEvolution Quarterly, ZAP 9*

	Pages ($):	250	375	500

1979 *Best Buy Comics, American Splendor 4, Fox River Patriot, CoEvolution Quarterly*

	Covers ($):	1,500	3,000	4,500
	Pages ($):	250	375	500

1980 *Village Voice, Snoid Comics, CoEvolution Quarterly, TELETimes, High Times, Energy Comics*

	Covers ($):	1,500	3,000	5,500
	Pages ($):	250	375	500

1981-92 *ZAP, RAW,* covers for *The Complete R. Crumb, ID Comics, Hup Comics, Meet the Beats Portfolio*

	Covers ($):	1,500	3,000	4,500
	Pages ($):	250	375	500

Note: individual sales would include; story entitled "MeatBall" from *ZAP* No. 0 selling for $32,000; painted wooden Figure of Honey Bunch Kominsky (1974) selling for $11,500; cover for *ZAP* No. 0 (original version) selling for $46,000; cover for Ballantine paperback book to *Fritz The Cat* (1969) selling for $56,350; five page story entitled "Mr. Natural In Death Valley from *ZAP* No. 0 selling for $14,950; single page entitled "Schuman Human's Night of Terror" from *Motor City* no. 2 selling for $3,162; ten page *Fritz the Cat* story from *Head Comix* selling for $36,800; cover for *Big Ass* No. 2 selling for $11,500; single page entitled "How Snoids are Born" selling for $3,162; single page entitled "Girls,Girls,Girls," from *XYZ* selling for $8,625; single long panel entitled "The Family That Lays Together, Stays Together" from *Snatch Comics* No. 2 selling for $8,050; all sales from Sotheby's comic art auctions.

CRUSE-HOWARD

Year	Publisher & Descriptive Information		
1973-92	Snarf, Barefootz, Dope Comix, Bizarre Sex, Gay Comix, Comix Book		
	Covers ($): 250	350	450
	Pages ($): 75	125	200
1990 -present	Stuck Rubber Baby & others.		
	Covers ($): 250	350	500
	Pages ($): 75	175	200

DAVIS-ALAN

Year	Publisher & Descriptive Information		
1982-85	Marvel U.K.: Captain Britain		
	Covers ($): 150	250	350
	Pages ($): 75	150	225
1982-84	Quality: Marvelman*		
	Covers ($): xxx		
	Pages ($): 75	150	225
1984-86	Fleetway: D.R. & Quinch		
	Covers ($): 175	250	375
	Pages ($): 75	150	250
1986-91	DC: Batman		
	Covers ($): 150	200	300
	Pages ($): 75	125	175
	Outsiders		
	Covers ($): [250]	300	400
	Pages ($): 50	100	150
1987-92	Marvel: Wolverine		
	Covers ($): 200	400	600
	Pages ($): 75	150	225
	Excalibur, Knights of Pendragon, X-Men		
	Covers ($): 200	250	300
	Pages ($): 60	120	175

* Reprinted in U.S. as Miracle Man after threatened lawsuit by Marvel Comics

DAVIS-JACK

Year	Publisher & Descriptive Information		
1950-51	Nation Wide Publs.: Lucky Star		
	Covers ($): [800	1,200	1,600]
	Pages ($): [100	200	300]
1951-56	EC: Horror—"The Crypt Keeper" (now extremely scarce in the market)		
	Covers ($): [4,000	6,000	9,000]
	Pages ($): 100	300	550
	Humor/satire MAD (prices will vary from early EC comic covers which would include No. 2 only, to very early MAD Magazine covers (few) and Mad Special covers - to post 1980's covers.)		
	Covers ($): 1,750	3,500	7,000
	Pages ($): 200	400	700
	Crime, sci-fi, war		
	Covers ($): 1,000	2,500	4,500
	Pages ($): 150	250	450
1956-62	Atlas: Mystery, sci-fi		
	Covers ($): [1,000	2,000	3,000]
	Pages ($): [100	200	350]
	War, Western		
	Covers ($): [800	1,200	1,600]
	Pages ($): [100	150	200]
1957	HMH Publishing Co.: Humor/satire		
	Covers ($): xxx		
	Pages ($): [250	350	450]
1957-58	Humbug Publishing Co.: Humor/satire		
	Covers ($): [1,500	2,000	2,500]
	Pages ($): [250	350	450]
1959	Harvey: The Fly, w/Joe Simon assist.		
	Covers ($): xxx		
	Pages ($): 150	250	350
1959-62	Major Magazines Inc.: Humor/satire		
	Covers ($): 1,000	1,500	2,000
	Pages ($): 150	250	350
1962-66	Headline Publs.: Humor (watercolor covers)		
	Covers ($): 1,000	1,500	2,000
	Pages ($): [150	250	350]
1961-62	Western/Dell: Humor—YAK YAK (watercolor covers)		
	Covers ($): [1,000	1,500	2,000]
	Pages ($): [100	200	300]
1988	Triad Publs.: Honeymooners, horror (watercolor covers)		
	Covers ($): 1,000	1,500	2,000
	Pages ($): xxx		
1960-70	Record Album covers, a few Horror & Weird titles (very scarce to the market).		
	Paintings ($): [900	1,800	3,500]

THE CRYPT OF TERROR

HEH, HEH! AH... *SPRING* IS HERE, EH, FIENDS? IT'S *BASEBALL TIME* AGAIN. WELL, I'VE GOT A *BASEBALL HORROR YARN* THAT WILL DRIVE YOU *BATTY*. SO CREEP INTO THE *CRYPT OF TERROR*, SETTLE DOWN ON THAT *SACK*, AND YOUR *CRYPT-KEEPER* WILL *PITCH* YOU THE *BLOOD-CURDLING, SPINE-TINGLING, FEARFUL FUNGO-FABLE* I CALL...

FOUL PLAY!

IT IS MIDNIGHT... THE EVE OF OPENING DAY. CENTRAL CITY'S BUSH-LEAGUE BALL PARK LIES IN DARKNESS. THERE IS A SMELL OF FRESHLY PAINTED SEATS AND RAILS AND HOT-DOG STANDS HANGING IN THE COOL NIGHT AIR. THE CHAMPIONSHIP PENNANT SAGS LIMPLY FROM THE NEW-WHITENED FLAGPOLE IN THE OUTFIELD, LIFTING SADLY NOW AND THEN TO FLAP IN THE SOFT BREEZE THAT SWEEPS IN AND ACROSS THE SILENT DESERTED GRANDSTANDS. BUT DOWN ON THE GREEN PLAYING FIELD, ILLUMINATED BY THE COLD MOONLIGHT, ARE FIGURES... FIGURES IN BASEBALL UNIFORMS... EACH IN ITS POSITION... WAITING... WAITING FOR THE WORDS...

PLAY BALL!

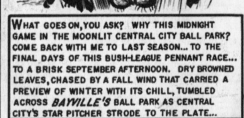

WHAT GOES ON, YOU ASK? WHY THIS MIDNIGHT GAME IN THE MOONLIT CENTRAL CITY BALL PARK? COME BACK WITH ME TO LAST SEASON... TO THE FINAL DAYS OF THIS BUSH-LEAGUE PENNANT RACE... TO A BRISK SEPTEMBER AFTERNOON. DRY BROWNED LEAVES, CHASED BY A FALL WIND THAT CARRIED A PREVIEW OF WINTER WITH ITS CHILL, TUMBLED ACROSS *BAYVILLE'S* BALL PARK AS CENTRAL CITY'S STAR PITCHER STRODE TO THE PLATE...

C'MON, HERBIE! LET'S GET SOME *RUN-INSURANCE!*

GET ON *BASE*, HERBIE BOY!

Jack Davis, 7 page story entitled "Foul Play" (perhaps EC's most famous horror story) from HAUNT OF FEAR #19, 1953. Estimate: $4,000/5,000; sold for $6,038 in 1993 (Sotheby's 3rd comic art auction). © William M. Gaines/EC Publications

Jack Davis, splash page from 7 page story from HAUNT OF FEAR #18 (this story was a Ray Bradbury adaptation), 1953. Estimate: $3,500/4,000; sold for $4,125 in 1992 (Sotheby's 2nd comic art auction). © William M. Gaines/EC Publications

Steve Ditko, artwork to page 6 of AMAZING SPIDER-MAN #6, 1963. Estimate: $1,500/2,000; sold for $3,105 in 6/93 (Sotheby's 3rd comic art auction). © MARVEL COMICS GROUP

1960-90's *Time Magazine,* Advertising work, Poster paintings, and other mainstream work

Paintings($)	1,500	2,500	5,500

DAY-GENE

Year	**Publisher & Descriptive Information**		
1970-80's	*Master of Kung Fu, Stars Wars*		
Covers ($):	75	150	250
Pages ($):	25	50	75

DEITCH-KIM

Year	**Publisher & Descriptive Information**		
1964-70	Individual Pages, single cartoon, and pages for *The East Village Other,* and other UG papers. "The Sunshine Girl"was one of the first UG comix characters in the 1960's		
Pages ($):	100	200	300
Cartoons ($):	50	75	150
Sunshine Girl Pages from EVO			
($):	200	350	[700]

1967-82 Individual UG Corn Fed, other titles;

Covers ($):	350	500	800
Pages ($):	100	150	250

1983-98 Fantagraphics: *Beyond the Pale, Hollywoodland, All Waldo Comics, A Shround for Waldo, No Business Like Show Buisness!, Boulevard of Broken Dreams, Mishkin File, Waldoworld, RAW, Banzia!, Eating Raoul.*

Covers ($):	250	400	700
Pages ($):	75	150	175

DEODATO-MIKE

Year	**Publisher & Descriptive Information**		
1990's	*Wonderman, Elektra, Thor, Avengers, Glory*		
Covers ($):	100	200	400
Pages ($):	30	75	150

Steve Ditko, splash page artwork for CAPTAIN ATOM #89 (with complete 17 page story), 1967. Estimate: $3,000/4,000; sold for $4,025 in 1995 (Christie's East comic art auctions). © The Charlton Comics Group

Steve Ditko, artwork from EERIE #10, 1967. Estimate: $1,200/1,500 (wash pages by Ditko are rare in the market); sold for $1,150 in 1994 (Sotheby's 4th comic art auction). © Warren Publications

DITKO-STEVE

Year	Publisher & Descriptive Information
1953	Ajax: Horror

Covers ($):   xxx
Pages ($):   [400   600   800]

1953	Prize: Horror

Covers ($):   xxx
Pages ($):   [400   600   800]

1954-62	Capitol/Charlton: *Captain Atom*

Covers ($):   xxx
Pages ($):   [***]

Gorgo, Konga, Mysterious Traveler, misc. fantasy, horror, sci-fi

Covers ($): [2,000   3,000   4,500]
Pages ($): [600   900   1,000]

Crime, humor, war, Western

Covers ($): [1,200   1,600   2,000]
Pages ($): [250   350   450]

1956-66	Atlas/Marvel: *Amazing Spider-Man* (evidence is beginning to surface that there are a few sur-

viving Spider-Man covers within collectors circles; with individual pages the price can vary widly based on the villian/action/character appearances.)

Covers ($):[10,000 16,000 24,000]
Pages ($): [800   1,800   3,500]

Antman and Wasp, Dr. Strange, Hulk, Iron Man, Thor

Covers ($):   [***]
Pages ($):   [800   900   1,200]

Fantasy, horror, war, Western, sci-fi

Covers ($):   [xxx]
Pages ($):   400   600   800

1966	ACG: Horror

Covers ($):   xxx
Pages ($):   200   300   400

1966	Western/Dell: *Nukla,* TV Series: *Get Smart, Hogan's Heroes*

Covers ($):   1,000   1,500   2,000
Pages ($):   150   200   250

1966-67	Tower: *Dynamo, Thunder Agents*

WHERE LURKS THE GHOST!

Steve Ditko, splash page from 5 page story from TALES TO ASTONISH #25, 1961. Estimate: $1,000/1,500; sold for $1,540 in 10/92 (Sotheby's 2nd comic art auction). © Marvel Comics Group

Covers ($):   xxx   xxx   xxx
Pages ($):   300   600   900

1966-69 Warren: (magazine) Fantasy, horror (it should be noted that the later Warren work by Ditko where he was experimentingwith "wash" brush work pages are in higher demand.)

Covers ($):   xxx
Pages ($):   350   800   1,200
Wash
Pages ($):   300   550   850

1965-85 Charlton: *Blue Beetle, Captain Atom*

Covers ($): [3,250   5,500   7,500]
Pages ($):   250   350   550

Dan Flagg, E-Man, Jungle Jim, The Question, Static, others

Covers ($): 1,000   1,500   2,000
Pages ($):   150   250   350

Horror, sci-fi
Covers ($): 1,000   1,500   2,000
Pages ($):   150   250   350

1968-69 DC: *Creeper, Hawk and Dove*
        Covers ($): 1,750   3,250   [4,500]
        Pages ($):   300   600   900

1969, Wood: *Heroes Inc.*
1976   Covers ($): [2,000   3,000   4,000]
        Pages ($):   [300   600   900]

1975 Atlas/Seaboard: *The Destructor,*
     sci-fi
        Covers ($):   xxx
        Pages ($):   150   250   350

1975-81 DC: *Man-Bat, Shade, Stalker,*
        Covers ($): [1,000   1,500   2,000]
        Pages ($):   [200   500   750]

1979-80 Marvel: *Machine Man, Micronauts*
        Covers ($): 1,000   1,500   2,000
        Pages ($):   200   300   400

1983 Eclipse: *Static*
        Covers ($):   xxx
        Pages ($):   [200   300   400]

1983 First: *Warp*
        Covers ($):   xxx
        Pages ($):   [200   300   400]

1983 John C. Prods: *Thunder Agents*
        Covers ($):   600   800   1,000
        Pages ($):   xxx

1984 Archie/Red Circle: *The Fly, The Jaguar, Noman*
        Covers ($): [600   800   1,000]
        Pages ($):   [200   300   400]

1984-89 Marvel: *Indiana Jones, ROM, Speedball*
        Covers ($): [600   800   1,000]
        Pages ($):   [200   300   400]

The demand for "vintage" Ditko comic art is constantly on the rise. Unfortunately, there is very little of it surfacing these days. Steve Ditko remains one of the most popular artists to have worked on a number of Marvel's earliest Silver Age characters, including The Amazing Spider-Man, Dr. Strange, and The Hulk. His tenure during the "superhero" development-years lasted only three and a half years. He continues to work in the field today off and on for various publishers and for many years has maintained a personal policy to keep all of his original art.

Some of the scarcest Ditko art seems to be his Charlton work, done between 1954 and 1962 on such characters as Captain Atom, Gorgo, Konga, Mysterious Traveler, etc. This "vintage" material is virtually nonexistent. Even art from his later Charlton period (1965-1975) of Blue Beetle and Captain Atom is very scarce, with only a small amount of material accounted for. It has been reported that Charlton instituted a policy of destroying original art and saving only stats sometime in the late 1960s or early 1970s. Unfortunately, at least two of their storage facilities suffered from leaky roofs and New England flooding.

Ditko's Marvel artwork from 1956 to 1966 has had much better luck than the Charlton material, but only in certain areas. Complete books of interior Spider-Man pages have surfaced over the years, but almost no covers. Dr. Strange pages, including two or three complete stories, have been accounted for also, as have a few Hulk pages. Several of Ditko's "pre-hero" fantasy and 'big-foot' monster stories have turned up over the years as well, but again, no covers. In all cases of "vintage" Marvel art turning up, the demand has far outweighed the supply.

Note: some individual sales would include; splash page to "Living Brain!" from *Spider-Man* No. 8 selling at $12,650; four pages (4,5,11,12) from *Spider-Man* No. 8 selling at $6,325; four pages (8,15,16,17) from *Spider-Man* No. 8 selling at $6,210; page 20 from *Spider-Man* No. 21 selling at $3,680; six page second story from *Spider-Man* No. 8 where Ditko inked Kirby's pencils entitled "Spider-Man Tackles The Torch!" selling for $20,700; sales from Christie's East 1996-1997.

DOUCET-JULIE
The most highly regarded woman cartoonist working in the alternative press today. At this time none of her black and white work is available for purchase (other than the occasional spot illustrations), but she does sell her color covers.

Mort Drucker, Artwork for MAD Subway poster,
1988. Estimate: $2,000/3,000; sold for $1,380 in
1993 (Christie's East comic art auctions). © William
M. Gaines/Time Warner/National Periodicals
Publications/DC Comics

Year	Publisher & Descriptive Information		
1988-98	*Drawn & Quarterly, Dirty Plotte*		
	Illos. ($):	40	50	60
	Clr/Cvrs($):	700	800	1,000

DRESCHLER-DEBBIE

Year	Publisher & Descriptive Information		
	Fantagraphics, *Drawn & Quarterly, Daddy's Girl, Nowhere*		
	Covers ($):	xxx		
	Pages ($):	75	150	250

DRUCKER-MORT

Drucker began his career in comics during
the 1950's illustrating for War, Romance,
and Western titles at DC comics. He first
began to work for MAD in 1957, and soon
began to draw with regularity the feature
'satire' story for each issue of MAD.

Year	Publisher & Descriptive Information		
1952-55	DC, War, Romance, and Western Titles. No covers.		
	Pages ($):	[75	150	225]
1957 -90's	MAD, feature stories, and occasional covers.		
	Covers ($):	[2,000	3,000	5,000]
	Pages ($):	250	325	[500]

Note: individual sales include: five pg
"Adnauseam Family" from MAD No. 311
selling for $1,840; seven pg "Battyman"
story from MAD No. 289 selling at $4,312;
seven pg "Buttman Returns" from MAD
No. 314 selling at $1,955; five pg "Teen-
Rage Moola Nit Wit Turtles II" from MAD
No. 306 selling at $690; cover art for MAD
Super Special No. 80 selling at $3,450;
cover for MAD No. 297 selling at $4,887;
cover for MAD Super Special No. 83 (Star
Trek satire) selling at $6,325; all sales from
MAD About MAD auction at Sotheby's
1995.

EASTMAN-KEVIN-AND-LAIRD-PETER

Year	Publisher & Descriptive Information		
1978-92	*The Teenage Mutant Ninja Turtles*		
	Covers ($):	[***]		
	Pages ($):	150	400	[600]

EISNER-WILL

Year	Publisher & Descriptive Information		
1936	Henle: *Flame, Hawk*		
	Covers ($):	xxx		
	Pages ($):	[1,000	1,200	1,400]
1938-40	Fiction House: *Hawks of the Sea, Kaanga, Shark Brodie, Sheena*		
	Covers ($):	[***]		
	Pages ($):	[***]		
1939	Fox: *Flame, Wonderman, Yarko the Great*		
	Covers ($):	[***]		
	Pages ($):	[***]		
1937-42	Quality: *Black Condor, Blackhawk, Dollman, Espionage, Hawk, Uncle Sam*		
	Covers ($):	[4,000	6,000	8,000]
	Pages ($):	[800	1,200	1,600]

Will Eisner, cover artwork to THE SPIRIT #15, 1949. Estimate: $3,500/4,500; sold for $3,300 in 1992 (Sotheby's 2nd comic art auction). © Quality Comics Group

Will Eisner (ghosted by Wally Wood), page from THE SPIRIT, 8/17/52. Estimate: $2,500/3,500; sold for $3,025 on 6/11/97 (Russ Cochran's comic art auctions).

Will Eisner Studio, splash page from THE SPIRIT, 3/2/52. Estimate: $1,200/1,500; sold for $1,375 on 10/97 (Russ Cochran's comic art auctions).

1944-50 Quality: *Spirit

    Covers ($): [2,500   3,500   4,500]

    Pages ($):   xxx

* Will Eisner created The Spirit character originally for newspaper syndication in 1940 while working for the Quality Comics Group. Unlike other syndicated strips at that time, "The Spirit" feature was produced in a standard comic book format. In 1942, many of these strips were reprinted in *Police Comics* and eventually in *The Spirit* comic title itself between the years of 1948 and 1950, Eisner created comic covers for the reprints of comics produced by Quality. For prices on "The Spirit" syndicated strip art, refer to the Newspaper Strips section of this guide.

1949   Will Eisner Prods.: *Fireball Bambino, Rube Rookie*

    Covers ($): [1,000   1,500   2,000]

    Pages ($): [300   450   600]

1952-54 Fiction House: *Spirit*, w/assist by Jerry Grandenetti on covers

    Covers ($): [1,500   2,000   2,500]

    Pages ($):   xxx

1966-67 Harvey: *Spirit*

    Covers ($): [1,200   1,400   1,600]

    Pages ($): [300   500   700]

1973   Kitchen Sink: *Spirit*

    Covers ($): [800   1,000   1,200]

    Pages ($): [250   350   450]

1974-76 Warren Publs.: (magazine) *Spirit*

    Covers ($): [900   1,200   1,800]

    Pages ($): [250   350   450]

1977-85 Kitchen Sink: (magazine) *Spirit* (painted covers)

    Covers ($): [1,000   1,500   2,000]

    Pages ($): [250   350   450]

1983-92 Kitchen Sink: *Spirit*

    Covers ($):   800   1,000   1,200

    Pages ($):   xxx

ELDER-BILL (WILLIAM)

Year   Publisher & Descriptive Information

1952-56 EC: *Humor/satire—*MAD

*Bill Elder came to EC Publications in 1951 with artist collaborator John Severin. Between 1951 and 1954, the team of Severin and Elder turned out numerous

Bill Elder, example from 5 panels from GOODMAN BEAVER, published originally in HELP!, 1962. Estimate: $1,200/1,700; sold for $1,000 on 6/93 (Sotheby's 3rd comic art auction). © Warren Publications Inc.

stories and one cover- *Frontline Combat* No. 10, dated Jan.-Feb. 1953. Since the price listings in this book are based first on the primary pencilier, John Severin receives the initial listing for much of the EC, and pre-EC, work that these artists jointly produced. Although this well respected team of artists didn't actually split up for good until 1954, Bill Elder began producing entire stories on his own in late 1952 with the premier issue of MAD. His one and only solo cover appeared on MAD No. 5, dated June-July 1953.

	Covers ($):	[3,000	4,000	7,500]
	Pages ($):	300	600	900

Crime, horror, sci-fi

	Covers ($):	xxx		
	Pages ($):	250	350	450

1957	HMH Publishing Co.: Humor/satire			
	Covers ($):	xxx		
	Pages ($):	[250	350	450]

1957-58	Humbug Publishing Co.: Humor/satire			
	Covers ($):	[***]		
	Pages ($):	[250	350	450]

1958-59	Major Magazines Inc.: Humor/ satire

	Covers ($):	xxx		
	Pages ($):	[250	350	450]

1974-92	Special color consignment paintings of EC-related or *Annie Fanny* related art.			
	Covers ($):	600	800	1,000
	Pages ($):	xxx		

1962-75 *Playboy* magazine appearances of "Little Annie Fanny" (note: Elder's work for this feature was more consistant than any other artist who worked with Harvey Kurtzman on this famous and elaborate comic strip. Many consider the labor extended over each page of Annie Fanny by Kurtzman/ Elder to be among the finest within comics.

	Pages ($) (after Kurtzman's roughs)		
	700	900	1,500

1985, 1989	Work with Harvey Kurtzman for *MAD* magazine, signed "WEHK"		
Covers ($):	1,250	1,750	2,250

Back

Covers ($):	600	800	1,200
Pages ($):	300	400	500

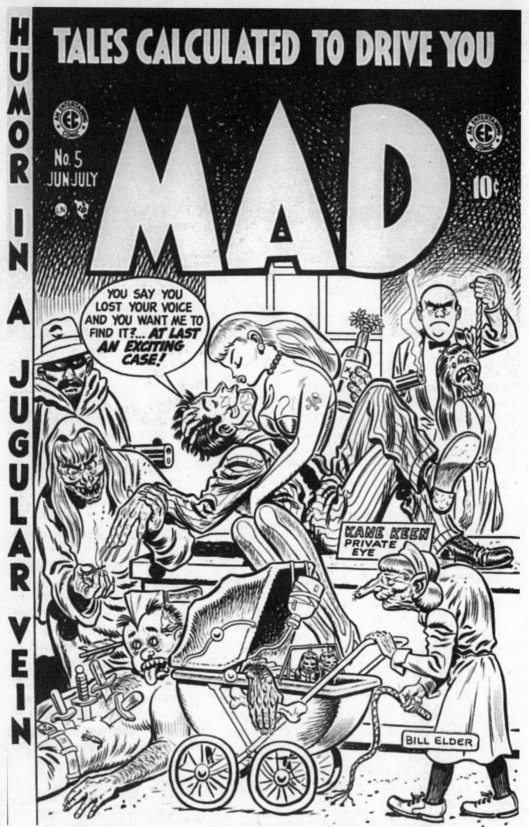

Bill Elder, cover artwork to MAD #5, 1953. Estimate: $5,000/6,000; sold for $4,950 on 10/92 (Sotheby's 2nd comic art auction). © William M. Gaines/EC Publications

Bill Elder, artwork for story entitled "Ganefs!" from MAD #1, 1952. Estimate: $6,000/8,000; sold for $9,200 on 1994 (Christie's East comic art auctions). © Willam M. Gaines/EC Publications

Bill Elder, artwork for 7 page story entitled "Ping Pong!" from MAD #6, 1953. Estimate: $6,000/7,000; sold for $6,325 on 1995 (Christie's East comic art auctions). © Willam M. Gaines/EC Publications

ELIAS-LEE

Year	Publisher & Descriptive Information

1943-46 Fiction House: Sci-fi- *Flint Baker, Space Rangers*

Covers ($):	xxx		
Pages ($):	100	200	300

Captain Wings, Firehair, Phantom Falcon, Suicide Smith

Covers ($):	[1,000	1,500	2,000]
Pages ($):	100	200	300

1946-56 Harvey: *Black Cat, Terry and the Pirates*

Covers ($):	600	900	[1,200]
Pages ($):	100	200	250

Horror, sci-fi

Covers ($):	600	900	[1,400]
Pages ($):	75	100	125

Romance, war, Western

Covers ($):	200	300	400
Pages ($):	25	50	75

1947 National/DC: **Flash*

* During the late 1940s, DC would occasionally utilize a splash page from an interior story for the cover of the comic. In such instances, a splash page (used also as a cover) would qualify and fall into the higher cover price range as listed. At least one Lee Elias *Flash* cover was created this way, and possibly more.

Covers ($):	[2,000	3,000	4,000]
Pages ($):	[200	500	800]

1947 Timely/Marvel: *Sub-Mariner*

Covers ($):	xxx		
Pages ($):	[250	350	450]

1958-76 National/DC: *Automan, Cave Carson, Eclipso, Green Arrow, Tommy Tomorrow*

Covers ($):	[1,000	1,500	2,000]
Pages ($):	[200	400	600]

Fantasy, mystery, sci-fi

Covers ($):	xxx		
Pages ($):	100	200	300

1966-67 Tower: *Undersea Agent*
       Covers ($): [400   600   800]
       Pages ($): [50   75   125]

1977-79 Marvel: *Human Fly*
       Covers ($): 400   600   800
       Pages ($): 75   125   175

1979-82 Warren: (magazine) Sci-fi—
       Goblin, Kronos, Rook
       Covers ($): xxx
       Pages ($): 100   200   300

EVANS-GEORGE

Year   **Publisher & Descriptive Information**

1947-50 Fiction House: *Jane Martin, Lost World, Senorita Rio, Tigerman, Werewolf Hunter*
       Covers ($): xxx
       Pages ($): 150   300   450

1949-52 Fawcett: *Captain Video* w/Al Williamson. Movie adaptation—*When Worlds Collide*, w/Al Williamson
       Covers ($): xxx
       Pages ($): [300   600   900]
       Horror
       Covers ($): [800   1,000   1,200]
       Pages ($): 100   200   300
       Romance, war, Western
       Covers ($): xxx
       Pages ($): 75   150   225

1952-56 EC: Crime, horror, sci-fi, war/aviation, and others
       Covers ($): 2,000   3,000   4,000
       Pages ($): 200   350   550
       Picto-Fiction—crime, horror
       Covers ($): xxx
       Pages ($): 150   350   550

1956-62 Gilberton: *Classics illustrated*
       Covers ($): xxx
       Pages ($): 100   150   250

"The Buccaneer, The Crisis, In Freedom's Cause (w/Crandall), Julius Ceasar (w/Crandall), The Little Savage, Lord Jim, Reign of Terror, Romeo and Juliet, The Three Musketeers, *The Hunchback of Notre Dame, *Oliver Twist."

* See Reed Crandall listing for prices on this art.

1961-62 Western/Dell/Gold Key: *Frogmen*
       Covers ($): xxx
       Pages ($): [75   150   225]
       Frogmen, w/Frazetta
       Covers ($): xxx
       Pages ($): [400   600   800]
       Mystery—*Boris Karloff, Twilight Zone*, and others
       Covers ($): xxx
       Pages ($): 75   150   225
       Adventure—movie adaptations
       Covers ($): xxx
       Pages ($): 75   150   225

1969-80 National/DC: *Blackhawk, Losers, Scalp-hunter, Sgt. Rock*
       Covers ($): 300   600   900
       Pages ($): 50   75   100
       Mystery, weird war, misc. war, and others
       Covers ($): 200   400   600
       Pages ($): 40   80   120

EVERETT-BILL

Year   **Publisher & Descriptive Information**

1938-40 Centaur: *Amazing Man, Dirk the Demon, Skyrocket Steele*
       Covers ($): [***]
       Pages ($): [***]

1940-41 Novelty: *Bull's-eye Bill, Chameleon, Dick Cole, Sub-Zero, White Streak*
       Covers ($): [***]
       Pages ($): [***]

1939-42 Timely: *Fin, Human Torch, Patriot, Sub-Manner*
       Covers ($): [***]
       Pages ($): [2,500   5,000   7,500]

(note: one spash page recently discovered.)

1940-51 Eastern Color: *Dickie Dare, Hydroman, Mud Master*
       Covers ($): [4,000   6,000   8,000]
       Pages ($): [800   1,200   1,600]

1946-57 Timely/Atlas: *Sub-Mariner*
       Covers ($): [4,000   6,000   8,000]
       Pages ($): [1,000   2,000   3,000]

PRICE RANGE KEY

RARITY — Brackets [ ] around a price indicate that this example is very scarce and could exceed maximum estimate.

	Covers
No work produced in this category—	XXX
No price available due to lack of information—	***

CONDITION — Age, color, marks, tears, etc.

	Pages		
	[400	500	600]

CHARACTER — Is the primary character featured, or is the original characteristic of a great example in the story line?

CONTENT — is the theme or story line exceptional or below average?

VALUE RANGE

Minimum	Medium	Maximum

RARITY

The [ ] Brackets indicate RARITY, if these brackets are used the reader can potentially double the price range in all three catagories.

Jann of the Jungle, Lorna the Jungle Girl, Marvel Boy, Namora, Venus, misc. horror, humor, sci-fi

Covers ($):	[3,000	4,000	5,000]
Pages ($):	[800	1,200	1,600]

Two Gun Kid, misc. Western, *Combat Casey,* misc. war, crime, and others

Covers ($):	[1,200	2,400	3,600]
Pages ($):	[400	800	1,200]

1963-72 Marvel: *Daredevil

Covers ($):	[***]
Pages ($):	[***]

* Bill Everett had a long career in the comics and made a lasting impression on many fans and collectors during that time period. His original art is very much in demand in the marketplace. Everett did the cover and interior art for the Silver Age revival of Daredevil appearing in the premier comic of the same title from Marvel Comics in April 1964. To date, none of this art is known to have surfaced.

Captain America, Dr. Strange, Hulk, Kazar, Spider-Man, Sub-Mariner and others,

Covers ($):	2,000	3,000	[4,000]
Pages ($):	400	800	1,200

Captain America, Dr. Strange, Hulk, Kazar, Spider-Man, and others

Covers ($):	800	1,200	1,600
Pages ($):	200	400	600

1970-72 Skywald Publs.: Horror (pinup Illus)

Covers ($):	xxx		
Pages ($):	400	800	1,200

Al Feldstein, original MAD insert from THE 8TH ANNUAL EDITION OF MORE TRASH FROM MAD, Summer, 1965. Estimate: $1,500/2,500; sold for $1,900 in 6/98 (Sotheby's MADsterpieces auction). © National Periodical Publications/DC Comics

FELDSTEIN-AL (ALBERT)

Year	Publisher & Descriptive Information		
1946	Aviation Press: *Golden Eagle*		
	Covers ($): xxx		
	Pages ($): 75	100	125
1946	Humor Pubs./Ace: Adventure/science		
	Covers ($): xxx		
	Pages ($): 75	100	125
1947-48	Fox: *Corliss Archer, Junior, Sunny*		
	Covers ($): [1,000	2,000	3,000]
	Pages ($): [150	250	350]
1948	Prize Publications: crime titles		
	Pages ($): [200	400	600]
1949	ACG: Misc. horror		
	Covers ($): xxx		
	Pages ($): [100	175	250]
1948-55	EC: *Horror, science fiction		
	Covers ($): [3,500	5,500	10,000]
	Pages ($): 250	500	750

*Al Feldstein was a major force behind the EC line during the 1950s, producing both stories and art successfully. As editor of EC's horror, science fiction, crime, shock, and New Direction titles, he generally wrote a story each day for several years running and, as an artist, produced many memorable stories and covers for such titles as *Tales from the Crypt* and *Weird Fantasy*. He also edited *MAD* magazine for over 30 years before retiring from the business. In 1991, Al Feldstein produced his first EC cover re-creation in oils- *Weird Fantasy* No. 15- which was then sold through a Sotheby's auction in New York for $4,500

Crime, suspense		
Covers ($): 2,000	3,000	4,000
Pages ($): xxx		
Humor/ satire		
Covers ($): 1,000	1,500	2,500
Pages ($): xxx		
Pre-trend—crime, educational, romance, Western		
Covers ($): 800	1,200	[3,500]
Pages ($): 50	100	150
EC: re-creation covers in oil		
Covers ($): 3,500	4,500	5,500

Al Feldstein, cover artwork for THREE DIMENSIONAL TALES FROM THE CRYPT OF TERROR, 1954. Estimate: $4,000/6,000; sold for $6,235 in 1996 (Sotheby's 6th comic art auction). © William M. Gaines/ EC Publications

Al Feldstein, cover artwork for PANIC #1, 3/54. Estimate: $1,500/2,000; sold for $1,100 in 1992 (Sotheby's 2nd comic art auction). © William M. Gaines/ EC Publications

Al Feldstein, artwork entitled "The Last City," from WEIRD FANTASY #4, eight page story, 1951. Estimate: $2,000/2,500; sold for $1,689 in 1998 (Phil Weiss auctions). © William M. Gaines/ EC Publications

Al Feldstein, cover artwork for MODERN LOVE #1. Minimum bid: $400; sold for $2,750 on 10/9/96 (Russ Cochran's comic art auctions). © William M. Gaines, Agent, Inc.

Al Feldstein, cover artwork for MODERN LOVE #2. Minimum bid: $400; sold for $2,310 on 10/9/96 (Russ Cochran's comic art auctions). © William M. Gaines, Agent, Inc.

Al Feldstein, 8 page story from TALES FROM THE CRYPT, 1951. Estimate: $1,000/1,200; sold for $1,955 in 1993 (Sotheby's 3rd comic art auction). © William M. Gaines/ EC Publications

Al Feldstein, 7 page story from CRIME PATROL #15 (first appearance of the Crypt Keeper) #4, 1949. Estimate: $2,000/3,000; sold for $4,600 in 6/93 (Sotheby's 3rd comic art auction). © William M. Gaines/ EC Publications

Note: individual sales would include; cover for *Weird Fantasy* No. 13 (1952) at $10,000, cover for *Weird Science Fantasy Annual* No. 1 at $12,500; cover painting for *SQUA TRONT* No. 3 (executed in 1954 for Bill Gaines) at $11,500; cover for *Tales From the Crypt* No. 24 at $10,000; cover to *3-D Tales FromThe Crypt of Terror* selling at $6,325; re-creation cover painting for *Weird Fantasy* No. 17 selling for $4,025; re-creation cover painting for *Weird Fantasy* No. 11 selling at $4,500; painting of Bill Gaines with three Ghoul Lunatics selling for $8,000; cover for *War Against Crime* No. 11 selling at $4,025; cover for *Modern Love* no. 8 selling at $1,265; cover for *A Moon, A Girl...Romance* No. 10 selling at $2,875; all sales private, Sotheby's and Christie's East.

FINE-LOUIS-K.

Year	Publisher & Descriptive Information
1938-40	Fiction House: *Count of Monte Cristo, Diary of Dr. Hayward, Wilton of the West*

Covers ($):	xxx		
Pages ($):	900	1,200	1,600

Flint Baker, Kaanga, Shark Brodie, Sheena, Stuart Taylor, ZX-5

Covers ($):	[6,000	8,500	12,000]
Pages ($):	[900	1,500	2,000]

1939-40 Fox Features: *Blue Beetle, Electro, Flame, Green Mask, Lt. Drake, Rex Dexter, Samson, Yarko the Great,* others

Covers ($):	[***]		
Pages ($):	[900	1,500	2,000]

1939-43 Quality: *Black Condor, Defender, Dollman, Hack O'Hara, Hercules, Neon the Unknown, Quicksilver, Ray, Red Bee, Stormy Foster, Spirit, Uncle Sam*

Covers ($):	[6,000	9,000	12,000]
Pages ($):	[900	1,500	2,000]

Note: individual sales would include: cover to *HIT* Comics No. 6 (cover logo missing) selling for $11,000; cover for *HIT* Comics No. 5 selling at $16,675; both sales from Sotheby's comic art auctions.

Louis K. Fine, cover artwork for HIT COMICS #5, 1940. Estimate: $15,000/20,000; sold for $16,675 in 1996 (Sotheby's 6th comic art auction). © Quality Comics Group

Frank Frazetta, artwork for preliminary concept of CONAN THE BARBARIAN, 1996. Estimate: $5,000/7,000; sold for $6,325 in 1996 (Christie's East comic art auctions). © Lancer Books/The Frazetta Estate

FINGERMAN-BOB

Year	Publisher & Descriptive Information		
1970 -80's	Mens Magazines, *Cracked* Magazine		
	Pages ($): 75	100	150
1985-98	Fantagaphics, Eros, Dark Horse: *Skinheads in Love, Minimum Wage, White Like She, Otis Goes to Hollywood*		
	Covers ($): xxx		
	Pages ($): 150	200	250

FLEENER-MARY

Year	Publisher & Descriptive Information	
1980-97	*Drawn and Quarterly, Fantagraphics, Slutburger, Fleener*	
	Covers ($): xxx	
	Pages ($): xxx	

FOX-MATT

Year	Publisher & Descriptive Information		
1952-53	Youthful Publications: horror and fantasy titles		
	Covers ($): [4,000	5,000	6,000]
	Pages ($): [300	500	700]
1952-56	Atlas/Marvel: horror and fantasy and science fiction titles		
	Covers ($): [2,000	3,000	4,000]
	Pages ($): [200	500	700]
1962-63	Marvel: fantasy, science fiction-Pre-Hero titles; (some stories with pencil work by Larry Leiber)		
	Pages ($): 100	200	300

FRANK-GARY

Year	Publisher & Descriptive Information		
1990's	*Supergirl, Hulk, Black Canary*		
	Covers ($): 150	250	350
	Pages ($): 40	75	150

Year	Publisher & Descriptive Information

1944 Baily Pubs. Co.: *Snowman*

Covers ($): xxx
Pages ($): [***]

1947-51 Standard: Text illustrations, funny animal

Covers ($): xxx
Pages ($): [1,000 1,200 1,400]

Stories: funny animal, *"Judy of the Jungle," "Looie Lazybones," "Trail Colt"*

Covers ($): xxx
Pages ($): [800 1,000 1,200]

1948-52 M.E.: *Dan Brand and Tipi ("White Indian"), Bobby Benson, Ghost Rider, Straight Arrow, Tim Holt*

Covers ($): [6,000 7,500 10,000]
Pages ($): 900 1,200 1,400

Thunda

Covers ($): [***]
Pages ($): [***]

1950-51 National: *Sci-fi, Shining Knight*

Covers ($): xxx
Pages ($): [1,000 1,500 1,800]

Crime, Western, *Jimmy Wakely, Tomahawk*

Covers ($): xxx
Pages ($): [900 1,400 1,600]

1951-55 Eastern Color/Famous Funnies: *Buck Rogers*

Covers ($): [25,000 40,000 75,000]
Pages ($): xxx

* Frazetta's legendary "Buck Rogers-" covers for *Famous Funnies* Nos. 209 through 216, and the cover for *Weird Science-Fantasy* No. 29 pub- lished by EC (a rejected "Buck Rogers" cover), are revered among the art collecting world as possibly his finest contribution to the science fiction genre. Although all of the original cover art is known to exist, at this point in time three have been sold.

Buster Crabbe

Covers ($): 6,000 8,000[14,000]
Pages ($): xxx

Romance

Covers ($): xxx
Pages ($): [2,500 3,500 5,500]

Heroic adventure, war, etc.

Covers ($): xxx
Pages ($): 900 1,400 1,600

1954-55 EC: Sci-fi (rejected "Buck Rogers" cover)

Covers ($):[25,000 30,000 70,000]
Pages ($): xxx

Crime/shock

Covers ($): xxx
Pages ($): 1,750 2,500 3,000

1964 Warren: *Vampirella, fantasy, horror

Covers ($):25,000 35,000 60,000
Pages ($): 2,000 3,000 4,000

* See Fantasy and Science Fiction section of this book for prices on Frazetta paintings.

1988 Genesis West: *Viking Heroes*

Covers ($): 4,000 5,000 6,000
Pages ($): xxx

Prints

Frank Frazetta Portfolio 1—sword & sorcery prints published by Middle Earth; 7 plates (1971) (500 printed). $100

Burroughs Portfolio—Opar Press 1968; 16 B&W prints on 8 pages (some prints previously published in Erb-Dom & in Burroughs hardback) $150

Burroughs Portfolio—Opar Press 1973 same as first portfolio except printed on separate pages. Five extra plated Included & one color plate. The only new art is on the back of plate 16 $150

Famous Funnies prints—Russ Cochran Pubs. (8 prints colored by Frazetta). $50

Buster Crabbe No. 5—17½ X 22 B&W print from original (Ed April Jr.) [xxx]

Tarzan & Bolgani—Vem Coriell Pub. (8½ x 11). $10

Beauty and the Beast (signed copies exist) (7x22). $25

Weird Science Fantasy No. 29½x11 from original (signed copies exist). $75-$125

Tarzan and the Antmen—same as the back cover to *Burroughs Bulletin* No. 29. $10

La of Opar-Attezarl pubs. (color print of FF No. 1 centerfold). $25

Lost Continent print (8/xtP/f300 print nun. Watercolor sketch of paperback (1st Worldbeaters poster). $25

Uncle Creepy print (8½x11) obtained by joining fan club. $25

Monster Mania print—reprint, but nice (11x17) $25

Sparkle of Quicksilver—Frodo's Press reprint. Includes interview (signed copies exist). $50

Southwestern Con Poster 1970—Conan sketch (number of 250). $25

Efficiency Expert—House of Greystoke 1966) (only 4 signed copies exist). $200

Conan Print—color print in ed. of 350 (7x9). $25

Cat Girl—advertising the Frazetta Art Museum. Poster size 16x24; image area 15x15. $20

The Executioner—later published In Frazetta Book I (8x8). $25

Reign of Wizardry—revised version of paper back (8x8). $25

Barbarian with Axe—pencil (11x11). $25
Golfing Nymphs—edition of 3 prints (11x14) pub. by Frank Frazetta. $30

Signed & Numbered Editions

SIGNED & NUMBERED PORTFOLIOS

Lord of the Rings; 5 plates—1st plate S&N of 1,000 $200

Women of the Ages; 6 plates—1st plate S&N of 1,500 $100

Kubla Khan; 5 plates—1st plate S&N of 1,500 $125

SIGNED & NUMBERED PRINTS

Nude Watercolor—S&N of 100 (16x20 matted) $350

Golden Girl—S&N of 2,000 (17x18) $550

Death Dealer—S&N of 345 (1-100 are gold ed.) (27 / x20) $675

Weird Science Fantasy No. 29—Hand-colored print; S&N of 50 but only 40 were done. Additional sketch on bottom of print. (This one borders on being an original as each one is different in color combinations.) (14x18 1/2) $2,500

Frazetta Photoprint(llxl4):photocopy of Warner paperback Night Winds $350

Cat Girl S&N of 350; original ink illus. added at bottom (15x16) $900-$2,200

Egyptian Queen—edition of 500, S&N with an additional remarque of a cat in pencil $5,500

Author Services has Issued a series of high-quality continuous tone lithographs in a S&N edition of 500. Currently available.

1. Battlefield Earth $5,000
2. Dreamflight $5,000
3. Moonrider $5,000
4. The Countess $5,000
5. The Encounter $5,000
6. Lieutenant $5,000
7. Leaping Lizards $5,000

Note: individual sales would include: seven page "White Indian" story from *Durango Kid* No. 4 selling for $13,200; eight pg "White Indian" story from *Durango Kid* No. 4 selling for $8,800; story entitled "Squeeze Play" from *Shock Suspenstories* No. 13 selling for $60,000; cover for *Buster Crabbe* No. 5 selling for $27,500.

Frank Frazetta, artwork for cover to TIM HOLT No. 17, 1950. Estimate: $20,000/$30,000; failed to meet reserve price in 1996. (Sotheby's 6th comic art auction) ©M.E. Publications/Frank Frazetta Estate.

Kelly Freas, artwork for re-creation painting to MAD No. 30, executed in 1994. Estimate: $3,000/$4,000; sold at $4,312 in 1994 (Sotheby's 4th comic art auction). ©William M. Gaines/EC Publications.

FREAS-KELLY

The great SF artist had a limited career in comics, occasionally doing covers for Avon Horror titles, and the remarkable string of MAD covers that have forever made him famous with EC and MAD collectors.

Year	Publisher & Descriptive Information
1952-54	Avon, Horror covers as paintings (none are known to exist)
	Covers ($): [1,500 3,000 4,500]
1958-62	*MAD Magazine*, front covers, Annuals and Specials
	Covers ($):[2,500 4,500 9,500]

Note: it should be noted with Freas MAD covers that they almost never re-enter the market place once they were sold at Russ Cochran's EC auctions, Christie's East MAD auction and Sotheby's MAD About MAD auctions. Because of this fact, if any early 1950's or 1960's MAD Freas covers were to come to public auction they would be fiercely bid upon.

1957-62	Pages ($):	[175 350 750]	
1957-62	Pages (color interior and back cover pages)		
		($): [1,000 2,000 3,000]	

Note: individual sales include: cover to *More Trash from MAD* No. 1 selling at $4,312; cover for Fourth Annual Edition of *More Trash from MAD* selling at $4,132; back cover from MAD No. 41 (1958) selling at $1,840; all sales from Sotheby's MAD About MAD auction in 1995.

FRIEDMAN-DREW

Year	Publisher & Descriptive Information
1982-92	Fantagraphics Books, *Warts and All, Any Similarity Between Persons Living or Dead Is Purely Coincidental*
	Covers ($): 500 700 900
	Pages ($): 300 400 500
1980's -90's	*MAD Magazine* features and covers.
	Covers ($)800 1,400 2,800
	Pages ($)150 250 400

GAINEY-RON

Year	Publisher & Descriptive Information
1990's	Marvel Projects: *Captain America, Silver Surfer*
	Covers ($): 150 200 300
	Pages ($): 40 75 125

GARCIA-LOPES-JOSE-LUIS

Year	Publisher & Descriptive Information
1975-91	DC: *Atari Force, Batman, Cinder & Ashe, Deadman, Superman, Twilight*
	Covers ($): 100 175 250
	Pages ($): 50 100 150
	Flash, Jonah Hex, Phantom Stranger, Teen Titans
	Covers ($): 75 125 175
	Pages ($): 35 70 100
	Hercules, Joker, Tarzan
	Covers ($): 75 100 125
	Pages ($): 25 50 150
1977	DC/ Marvel: *Batman/Hulk*
	Covers ($): 150 200 250

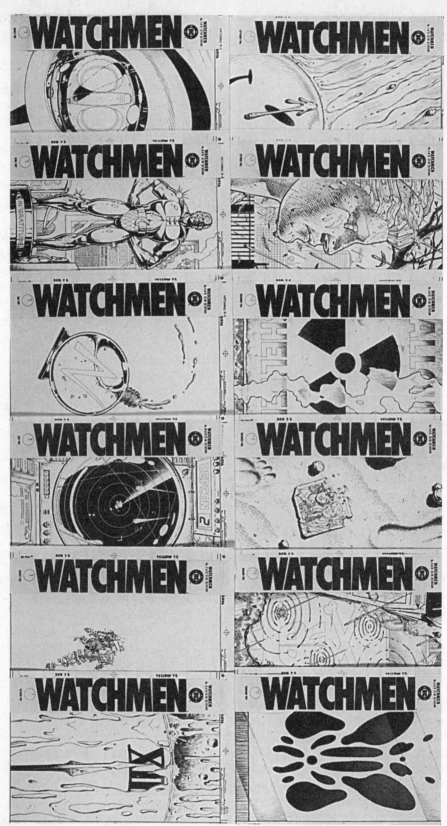

Dave Gibbons, artwork for covers Nos. 1 through 12 to WATCHMEN, 1986. Estimate: $20,000/$30,000; sold for $17,250 in 1993. (Sotheby's 3rd comic art auction). © National Periodical Publications/DC Comics.

Pages ($): 50 100 150
First: *Nexus*
Covers ($): 100 125 150
Pages ($): 50 75 100

GIBBONS-DAVE

Year	Publisher & Descriptive Information

1983-87 DC: *Watchmen*
Covers ($): 1,000 1,250 [1,500]
Pages ($): 250 400 [750]

Batman, Superman
Covers ($): 150 200 250
Pages ($): 60 120 175

Green Lantern
Covers ($): 100 150 200
Pages ($): 35 70 100

1984-85 Marvel: *Dr. Who*
Covers ($): 100 125 150
Pages ($): 25 50 75

1988 *Dr. Strange*
Covers ($): 200 250 300
Pages ($): 75 150 225

1990-91 Dark Horse: *Give Me Liberty*
Covers ($): ***
Pages ($): 200 275 350

1991-98 *Martha Washington*
Pages ($)175 250 325

Note: individual sales would include the covers for Watchman No. 1-through 12 sold as one lot at Sotheby's in 1993 for $17,250.

GIFFEN-KEITH

Year	Publisher & Descriptive Information

1976-92 DC: *Ambush Bug, Dr. Fate, Legion*
Covers ($): 60 120 185
Pages ($): 60 90 120

All Star, Batman, Hell on Earth, Invasion, Omega Men, Superman
Covers ($): 50 100 170
Pages ($): 50 75 100

Atari Force, Blue Devil, Challengers of the Unknown, Claw, Firestorm, Hex, Kobra, misc. mystery, sci-fi, war
Covers ($): 50 75 100
Pages ($): 25 50 75

1976-87 Marvel: *Defenders, Jack of Hearts, Micronauts, Nightmask, Spider-Man*
Covers ($): 75 100 150
Pages ($): 50 75 100

1984 Deluxe: *Thunder Agents*
Covers ($): xxx
Pages ($): 25 50 75

GIORDANO-DICK

Year	Publisher & Descriptive Information

1960's *Batman* Projects (penciller),
-70's Charlton Projects
Covers ($): 100 200 350
Pages ($): 25 50 75

GLANZMAN-SAM

Year	Publisher & Descriptive Information

1980 DC & Dell War titles; etc
-90's Covers ($): 75 125 200
Pages ($): 25 50 75

GOLDMAN-MICHAEL

Year	Publisher & Descriptive Information

1977-91 DC: *Batman, Batmite, Demon, Man-Bat, Mr. Miracle, Superman*
Covers ($): xxx
Pages ($): 120 200 300

Misc. mystery
Covers ($): xxx
Pages ($): 60 90 120

1977-92 Marvel: *Avengers, Sub-Mariner, Defenders, Dr. Strange, Hulk, Micronauts, Nam, Punisher, ROM, She-Hulk, Spider-Man, Star Wars, X-Men*
Covers ($): 300 700 [900]
Pages ($): 100 200 300

Battlestar Galactica, Conan, Cops, Crystar, G.I. Joe, Howard the Duck, Indiana Jones, Kull, Man-Thing, Starlord, U.S. 1
Covers ($): 200 300 400
Pages ($): 75 150 250

1984-90 Continuity: *Bucky O Hare*
Covers ($): ***
Pages ($): ***

Rick Griffin, artwork from the song "Why Don't We Do It In The Road," 1970's. Estimate: $1,500/$2,000; sold for $1,980 in 1992. (Sotheby's 2nd comic art auction) ©The Rick Griffin Estate

Bill Griffith, cover artwork for YOW COMICS No. 1, 1978. Estimate: $3,500/$4,500; sold for $3,300 in 1992. (Sotheby's 2nd comic art auction.
© Last Gasp Publications

GONZALEZ-JOSE

Year	Publisher & Descriptive Information		
1964-70's *Vampirella*, Warren Projects			
Covers ($):	xxx		
Pages ($):	50	150	300
Illos. ($):	200	400	700

GONZALO-MAYO

Year	Publisher & Descriptive Information		
1964-70's *Vampirella*, assorted Warren Projects			
Covers ($):	xxx		
Pages ($):	35	75	150

GRELL-MIKE

Year	Publisher & Descriptive Information		
1974-92 DC: *Batman, Green Arrow, Green Lantern, Legion, Warlord*			
Covers ($):	150	250	350
Pages ($):	75	150	225
Deadman, Flash, Justice League, Karate Kid, Spectre, Superman, Vigilante, Wonder Woman			
Covers ($):	100	150	200

Pages ($):	50	75	100
1982-83 Pacific First: *Starslayer*			
Covers ($):	100	150	200
Pages ($):	75	100	125
1983-87 First: *Jon Sable*			
Covers ($):	150	200	350
Pages ($):	75	125	175

GRIFFIN-RICK(1944-1991)

The untimely loss of Rick Griffin as he rode his motorcycle to a Grateful Dead concert has left the art world in comics with both sorrow and fond memories. Griffin grew up in California and worked at his early cartoon style with *Surfer, Car-Toons, Hot Rod Cartoons, Surf-toon,* and *Big Daddy Roth*. These car magazines of the early and mid-1960s encouraged other artists to become part of the underground comics movement. Griffin was a leader with many dance posters for Avalon and Fillmore concerts, and did some of his most remarkable work for the album covers of the Grateful Dead. Rick became one of the ZAP "regulars" with the second issue, designed the logo for Rolling Stone magazine, and was included in many of the most important underground comics. Later in his career, Griffin became very spiritual, and his work reflected the change from within this most gifted artist.

Year	Publisher & Descriptive Information		
1965-67	Surfer, Car-Toons, Hot Rod Cartoons		
	Pages ($): 200	300	400
	Avalon & Fillmore Concert Posters		
	Covers ($): [2,500	5,000	9,000]
	Pages ($): 2,000	3,000	[4,000]
1968-78	ZAP 2, 3, 4, 5, 6, Yellow Dog, Snatch		
	Covers ($): [3,000	6,000	10,000]
	Pages ($): 750	1,625	[2,500]

Tales from the Tube, Underground cover - $5,000 Sale at Sotheby's

	San Francisco Comic Book All Stars, Promethean Enterprises, King Bee		
	Covers ($): 750	1,625	[3,500]
	Pages ($): 400	600	[800]

GRIFFITH-BILL

From his beginnings in the mid-1960s with early "Toad" comics for *Screw* magazine, *East Village Other*, and *The Gothic Blimp Works*, Bill Griffith has improved to become one of the major voices in comics with "Zippy the Pinhead." The editor of the early taboo buster, *Young Lust*, Griffith has always had a special flair for digging beneath the surface of American culture. One of Griffith's favorite early comics is "Lemme Outa Here!," a U.G. comic about life in the suburbs. Griffith's work has remained topical throughout his career. The artist closely guards his original artwork, and most of the early and important originals are not in the marketplace.

Year	Publisher & Descriptive Information		
1967-99	East Village Other, Gothic Blimp Works, Tales of Toad, Yellow Dog, Young Lust		
	Covers ($): 750	1,625	[2,750]
	Pages ($): 250	325	400

Zippy Stones, YOW, Young Lust,

Arcade (co-editor with Spiegelman)

Covers ($): 1,500	2,500	[4,500]
Pages ($): 350	550	750

Note: individual sales would include: cover for YOW No. 1 selling at $3,300; cover for ZIPPY No. 3 selling at $3,850; two page spread entitled "Pertinent Points About Pinheads" selling for $4,400; from Sotheby's comic art auctions.

Note: listings for "Zippy The Pinhead," the newspaper strip, are to be found in the Newspaper strip listing under "Z."

GULACY-PAUL

Year	Publisher & Descriptive Information		
1975-91	Marvel Epic: *Master of Kung Fu, Six From Sirius, Shanna the She-Devil*		
	Covers ($): 300	550	800
	Pages ($): 60	120	175
1978-88	Eclipse: *Sabre*		
	Covers ($): 200	275	350
	Pages ($): 75	150	225
	Air Boy, Miracle Man, Phaze		
	Covers ($): 150	200	250
	Pages ($): xxx		
1990-91	DC: *Batman*		
	Covers ($): 200	400	600
	Pages ($): 75	150	225
1991	Dark Horse: *Terminator*		
	Covers ($): 200	250	300
	Pages ($): 75	125	175

HART-TOM

Year	Publisher & Descriptive Information		
1980-97	Black Eye, Top Shelf, Spit and a Half; Alternative Press: Hutch Owen't Working Hard, New Hat, The Sands, Ramadan, Triple Dare		
	Covers ($): 100	150	200
	Pages ($): 60	80	100
	Clr/Pages($): 250	350	400

HEATH-RUSS

Year	Publisher & Descriptive Information		
1943-44	Holyoke: *Hammerhead Hawley* (first comic work)		
	Covers ($): xxx		

Russ Heath, interior page from ALL-AMERICAN MEN OF WAR, Private sale at $250 in 1996. (TRH Galleries) © National Periodical Publications/DC Comics

Russ Heath, cover artowrk for MEN'S ADVENTURES No. 26, 1952. Private sale at $1,250 in 1997. (TRH Galleries) Atlas Comics/The Marvel Comics Group

Don Heck, 5 page story entitled "I Saw The Serpent..." from TALES OF SUSPENSE, 1960. Private sale at $850 in 1997. (TRH Galleries) ©Marvel Comics Group

		Pages ($):	200	400	600

1948-59 *Atlas: Human Torch, Marvel Boy*

	Covers ($):	xxx		
	Pages ($):	[300	600	900]

Horror, sci-fi

Covers ($):	1,500	2,500	3,500
Pages ($):	[200	500	750]

Apache Kid, Arizona Kid, Arrowhead, Black Rider, Kid Colt Outlaw, Matt Slade Gunfighter, Rawhide Kid, Two Gun Kid, misc. western, *Combat Casey, Combat Kelly, Kent Blake, Spy Fighter,* misc. war, *Lorna the Jungle Girl,* misc. jungle, and others

Covers ($):	1,000	1,500	2,500
Pages ($):	[150	250	350]

Humor/satire, romance

Covers ($):	[800	1,200	1,600]
Pages ($):	[100	150	250]

1951, 1954 EC: War, satire

Covers ($):	xxx		
Pages ($):	[200	300	400]

1953 *St. John: Tor* (filler pages)

Covers ($):	xxx		
Pages ($):	[200	300	400]

1953-78 National/DC *Golden Gladiator, Robin Hood, Silent Knight, Sea*

Devils

Covers ($):	[2,000	3,000	4,000]
Pages ($):	[300	600	900]

Balloon Buster, Frogmen, Haunted Tank, Hunters Hellcats, Sgt. Rock, misc. war

Covers ($):	2,000	2,500	3,000
Pages ($):	250	450	650

Mystery, *Jonah Hex, Wonder Woman*

Covers ($):	xxx		
Pages ($):	150	200	250

1960-62 Western/Dell: TV Series: *Tales of Wells Fargo, Laramie* w/Gil Kane

Covers ($):	xxx		
Pages ($):	[100	125	150]

1966 Warren (magazine): War

Covers ($):	xxx		
Pages ($):	300	500	700

1972-88 Marvel: Misc. horror, *G.I. Joe, Kazar, Son of Satan, X-Men*

Covers ($):	400	600	800
Pages ($):	100	150	200

1975 Atlas/Seaboard: *Grim Ghost,* others

Covers ($):	400	600	800
Pages ($):	100	150	200

Don Heck (with Jack Kirby concept pencils), included with cover re-creation for cover - the 13 page original story from TALES OF SUSPENSE No. 39 featuring the origin of Iron Man, 1963. Estimate: $40,000/$50,000; sold for $46,000 in 1996. (Sotheby's 6th comic art auction) © Marvel Comics Group

1976-77	Warren (magazine): Horror		
	Covers ($):	xxx	
	Pages ($):	300	500	700
1984	Eclipse: *Rocketeer* (pinup)		
	Covers ($):	xxx	
	Pages ($):	400	600	800
1991	W.D. Pubs: *Rocketeer* movie adaptation		
	Covers ($):	xxx	
	Pages ($):	250	350	450
1991-99	Dark Horse: *James Bond,* other recent work		
	Covers ($):	200	450	600
	Pages ($):	125	250	350

HECK-DON

Year	Publisher & Descriptive Information		
1952-54	Comic Media: Horror		
	Covers ($):	[800	1,000	1,200]
	Pages ($):	[100	200	300]
	Duke Douglas, Johnny Dynamite, misc. war		
	Covers ($):	[600	800	1,000]
	Pages ($):	[75	100	125]
	Romance titles		
	Covers ($):	[300	400	500]
	Pages ($):	25	50	75
	Charlton: *Captain Gallant*		
	Covers ($):	xxx	
	Pages ($):	[50	75	100]

1954-75	Atlas/Marvel: *Avengers, Antman, Giantman, *Iron Man,* others		
	Covers ($): 1,250	2,500	3,500
	Pages ($): 125	325	525

Amazing Spider-Man, Captain Marvel, Daredevil, Kazar, Sub-Mariner, X-Men, others

Covers ($):	500	700	900
Pages ($):	75	150	225

Crime, fantasy, horror, jungle, etc.

Covers ($):	xxx		
Pages ($):	75	150	225

Misc. Western—*Rawhide Kid* and others

Covers ($):	xxx		
Pages ($):	50	75	100

1966　Gold Key: *The Man from U.N.C.L.E.*

Pages ($):	[50	75	100]

1971-72　DC: *Batgirl, Jason Bard,* and others

Covers ($):	xxx		
Pages ($):	75	100	125

"Don Heck penciled and inked the first story of "Iron Man" appearing in Marvel's *Tales of Suspense* No 39, dated March 1963. These original 13 pages of art have survived the past 29 years and could easily exceed this price range." The following statement is left in from the first guide to illustrate a point: in 1996 at Sotheby's, the thirteen page story inked by Don Heck from *Tales of Suspense* No. 39 sold (with the Kirby pencil cover re-creation for *Suspense* No. 39) at auction for $46,000 - breaking any previous public record for a silver age origin story.

HERNANDEZ-GILBERT

Year	Publisher & Descriptive Information		
1980-82	Fantagraphics: *Love & Rockets, Birdland*		
	Covers ($): [500	900	1,500]
	Pages ($): [400	600	800]
1990's	Dark Horse Series: *Girl Crazy*		
	Covers ($): 450	650	900
	Pages ($): 300	500	650
1990's	Fantagraphics projects		
	Covers ($): 450	650	900
	Pages ($): 300	500	650

HERNANDEZ-JAIME

Year	Publisher & Descriptive Information		
1980-92	Fantagraphics: *Love & Rockets, Mr. X*		
	Covers ($): 500	1,000	1,500
	Pages ($): 500	750	1,000

HUGHES-ADAM

Year	Publisher & Descriptive Information		
1989-91	Innovation: *Legends of the Star Grazers*		
	Covers ($): 150	275	400
	Pages (x):xxx		
	Maze Agency		
	Covers ($): 100	150	200
	Pages ($): 40	80	120
1989-91	DC: *Justice League*		
	Covers ($): 200	300	500
	Pages ($): 60	120	175
	Star Trek		
	Covers ($): 100	150	200
	Pages ($): 100	200	300
1991	Atomeka: *Betty Page*		
	Covers ($): xxx		
	Pages ($): 200	250	300
1991-92	Marvel: *X-Men*		
	Covers ($): 250	400	550
	Pages ($): 60	120	175
1992-98	*Gen-13; Ricochet & Rapture; Vampirella; Penthouse Comics*		
	Covers ($): 400	1,000	1,500
	Pages ($): 75	150	300
	Sketches($) 75	150	250
	Painted Cvs 500	1,000	2,000

HUMBERTO-RAMOS

Year	Publisher & Descriptive Information		
1990's	*Impulse, X-Men*		
	Covers ($): 100	200	300
	Pages ($): 35	65	100

IMMOMEN-STUART

Year	Publisher & Desciptive Information		
1990's	*Legion, Superman,* various DC Projects		
	Covers ($): 100	150	225
	Pages ($): 25	50	100

INFANTINO-CARMINE

Year	Publisher & Descriptive Information		
1943-48	Timely: *Captain Wonder, Human Torch, Jack Frost, others*		
	Covers ($): xxx		
	Pages ($): [300	400	550]
1947	Lev Gleason: *Daredevil, others*		
	Covers ($): xxx		
	Pages ($): [300	400	500]
1946-48	Hillman: *Airboy, Flying Dutchman, Gunmaster, Heap, Rackman*		
	Covers ($): xxx		
	Pages ($): [300	400	500]
1947-67	National/DC: *Adam Strange, Atom, Batman, Flash, Green Lantern, Justice Society, Superman*		
	Covers ($): 5,500	9,000	12,000
	Pages ($): 400	800	1,200
1968-78	Covers ($): 1,500	3,000	4,500
	Pages ($): 100	150	300

Carmine Infantino, cover artwork for British Weekly STAR WARS No. 115, 1970's. Estimate: $150/$250; sold for $41 in 1998. (Phil Weiss auctions) ©Lucas Productions/National Periodical Publications

* Throughout his prolific and respected career in the comics, much of Carmine Infantino's art was inked by other artists. Many of the characters he worked on for DC Comics during the Silver Age and later were inked by such noted artists as Murphy Anderson, Sy Barry, Frank Giacoia, Joe Giella, Dick Giordano, Sid Greene, Joe Kubert, and others. Inker identification is important and will cause price fluctuation.

Fantasy, science fiction, horror, mystery
Covers ($): [1,500   3,000   4,500]
Pages ($): 200   400   600

Black Canary, Charlie Chan, Dan Foley, Detective Chimp, Elongated Man, Ghost Patrol, Human Target, Jimmy Wakely, Johnny Thunder, King Farraday, Pow Wow Smith, Rex The Wonder Dog, Secret Six, Silent Knight, Super-Chief, Trigger Twins, and others
Covers ($): 1,200   2,400   3,600
Pages ($): 150   300   450

Crime, romance, war
Covers ($): 1,000   2,000   3,000
Pages ($): 150   200   250

Carmine Infantino & Murphy Anderson, cover art to DETECTIVE COMICS No. 364, 1967. Estimate: $800/$1,200 and sold for $1,600 in 1992 - then sold again in 1996 for $9,775. (Sotheby's 2nd and 6th auctions). ©National Periodical Publications.

Carmine Infantino & Joe Giella, cover artwork for SHOWCASE No. 14 (Presenting THE FLASH), 1958.
Estimate: $15,000/$25,000; sold for $20,700 in 1998. (Sotheby's 8th comic art auction)
© National Periodical Publications/DC Comics

Carmine Infantino and Murphy Anderson, cover artwork for MYSTERY IN SPACE No. 73, 1962. Estimate: $5,000/$6,000; sold for $4,600 in 1994. (Sotheby's 4th comic art auction) © National Periodical Publications

1977-80	Marvel: *Spider-Woman, Star Wars,* others		
Covers ($):	400	600	800
Pages ($):	75	125	175
1979-82	Warren: (magazine) *Horror/ fantasy		
Covers ($):	xxx		
Pages ($):	150	250	350

1990's	Re-creation covers for silver age super-hero titles		
Covers ($):	1,250	1,500	1,750

* All of Infantino's art for Warren Publishing was inked by other artists, including Alfredo Alcala, George Benny, Wayne Howard, Steve Leialoha, Pablo Marcus, Alex Toth, and Berni Wrightson. Prices will fluctuate with inker identification.

Graham Ingels, cover artwork for SADDLE JUSTICE
No. 8, 1949. Estimate: $400/$800; sold for $786.50
in 1997. (Russ Cochrans comic art auctions)
© William M. Gaines/EC Publications

INGELS-GRAHAM

Year	Publisher & Descriptive Information		
1943-44	Fiction House: Sci-fi—*The Lost World*		
	Covers ($):	xxx		
	Pages ($):	150	250	350
	Clipper Kirk, Commando Rangers, Sea Devil, Suicide Smith		
	Covers ($):	xxx		
	Pages ($):	100	125	150
1946-47	Eastern Color: *Adventure heroics		
	Covers ($):	[1,000	1,500	2,000]
	Pages ($):	[100	125	150]

* Painted cover art

1947-48	Standard: *Lance Lewis, Space Detective, Tygra, Wonderman,* misc.		
	Covers ($):	[2,000	3,000	4,000]
	Pages ($):	[150	250	350]

1948-49	Fiction House: Sci-fi, *Auro, Lord of Jupiter*		
	Covers ($):	xxx		
	Pages ($):	150	250	350
1948-49	M.E.: Crime—*The Duke* Western—*Trail Colt*		
	Covers ($):	[800	1,000	1,200]
	Pages ($):	[100	150	200]
1948	D.S. Publishing: *Crime*		
	Covers ($):	xxx		
	Pages ($):	[100	150	200]
1949	Avon: *Western*		
	Covers ($):	[800	1,000	1,200]
	Pages ($):	xxx		
1949-50	Youthful Magazines: Western		
	Covers ($):	[800	1,000	1,200]
	Pages ($):	[100	150	200]
1950	Kirby Publishing: Crime/mystery		
	Covers ($):	xxx		
	Pages ($):	[150	300	450]
1948-56	EC: *Horror—"The Old Witch" *Haunt of Fear* covers		
	Covers ($):	[3,000	6,000	10,000]
	Pages ($):	200	350	600

Crime, romance, sci-fi, *Shock suspenstories, Crime suspen stories*		
Covers ($):	xxx		
Pages ($):	150	200	250

New Direction and Picto-Fiction titles		
Covers ($):	xxx		
Pages ($):	200	400	600

Pre-Trend EC western covers and stories		
Covers ($):	1,000	2,000	3,000
Pages ($):	75	100	150

* Graham Ingels is considered by many to be among the most popular horror artists who ever worked in the comics field. From 1950 to 1954 he drew most of the "Old Witch's Cauldron" features that ran regularly in EC's three horror comic titles: *The Haunt of Fear, Tales from the Crypt*, and *The Vault of Horror*. Each of these books had their own horror hosts introducing the stories, and through Graham's talents, "The Old Witch" became one of the favorites. In 1989, after a long absence from any comic-

related art activity, Graham Ingels returned to do a number of "Old Witch" paintings in oil, for inclusion in Russ Cochran's quarterly art auctions. Before Graham's death in April of 1991, he produced a total of four finished paintings and ten preliminary concept paintings.

1956   Gilbertson: *Classics Illustrated:* "Waterloo," other misc. pages
        Covers ($):   xxx
        Pages ($):   50   75   100

1957   George A. Pfaum: Western, adventure, war, historical
        Covers ($):   xxx
        Pages ($):   50   75   100

1989-91   EC: *"The Old Witch"* (oil paintings)
        Finished Paintings
        Covers ($): 5,000   6,250   7,500
        Pages ($):   xxx
        Preliminary paintings
        Covers ($): 1,000   1,550   2,100
        Pages ($):   xxx

Note: individual sales would include: cover for *The Haunt of Fear* No. 13 (1952) selling for $2,990 at Christie's East. From Sotheby's the cover for *Gunfighter* No. 12 selling at $1,610; cover for Gunfighter No. 10 selling at $1,380; art to twelve page story from *Terror Illustrated* selling at $920. Diamond Galleries sold the cover to *Haunt of Fear* No. 14 for $12,000 in 1996. Private sales include the story "The Handler" at $2,000, and "Warts So Horrible" at $3,000.

IRONS-GREG

Year	Publisher & Descriptive Information
1966-69	*Family Dog,* Fillmore and Avalon posters

        Pages ($): 1,000   1,500   2,000

1967-79   *Light Comics, Heavy Tragic-Comics, Slow Death, Deviant Slice*
        Covers ($):   500   1,000   1,500
        Pages ($):   250   300   350

JAFFEE-AL

Al Jaffe was close friends with Harvey Kurtzman and Bill Elder when all three attended the High School of Music and Art. Jaffe remained faithful to Kurtzman during the *Humbug* era, and eventually established his real notarity with the now famous MAD fold-ins.

Year	Publisher & Descriptive Information
1955-57	*Mad Magazine,* two to three page features

        Pages ($):   150   250   350

1957-58   *Humbug,* interior features
        Pages ($):   150   225   300

1958-63   *Mad Magazine* interior features, B&W
        Pages ($):   125   250   275

1964-74   *Mad Magazine,* the fold-ins, inside Back Covers
        B&W Fold-Ins ($): 150   250   400
        Color Fold-Ins($): 650   1,250   [2,500]

1975-85   *Mad Magazine,* fold-ins, and occasional covers
        Color
        Fold-Ins ($):   600   1,000   [1,750]
        Covers ($): 2,500   3,000   3,750

1985-90's   *Mad Magazine,* Fold-Ins, covers
        Color
        Fold-Ins ($):   500   850   1,500
        Covers ($): 1,500   2,000   3,000

Note: individual sales would include: cover to MAD No. 199 selling at $3,737; cover for Mad No. 224 (1991) selling at $1,955; cover for MAD No. 258 (1985) selling at $3,162; fold-in from MAD No. 296 selling at $1,610; fold-in from MAD No. 141 (1971) selling at $1,150; two fold-ins B&W (1967) from MAD Nos. 110, 113, selling at $632; all sales from Sotheby's MAD About MAD auction in 1995.

JACKSON-JACK (JAXON)

Year	Publisher & Descriptive Information
1964-66	*Godnose, Texas Ranger, Austin Iconoclastic Magazine*

        Covers ($):   400   600   [800]
        Pages ($):   200   250   300

1967-74   *Godnose, Skull, Slow Death, Hydrogen Bomb, Up From the Depths*
        Covers ($):   500   625   750
        Pages ($):   250   375   500

Jeff Jones, 7 page story entitled QUEST, 1968. Estimate: $1,500/2,000; sold for $2,530 in 6/93 (Sotheby's 3rd comic art auction). © Warren publications

Dan Jurgens and Brett Breeding, cover artwork for SUPERMAN #70, 1992. Estimate: $750/1,000; sold for $690 in 6/93 (Sotheby's 3rd comic art auction). © National Periodical Publications/DC Comics

Mike Kaluta, cover artwork for DETECTIVE COMICS #424, 1972. Estimate: $500/800; sold for $575 in 1993 (Christie's East comic art auctions). © National Periodical Publications/DC Comics

1975-90	White Comanche, Red Raider, Blood on the Moon, Death Rattle		
Covers ($):	800	900	1,000
Pages ($):	250	375	500
1990-Present	Dead In The West, Last of The Mohicans, John Wesley Harding		
Covers ($):	750	800	900
Pages ($):	225	350	500

JONES-KELLEY

Year	Publisher & Descriptive Information		
1985-90	Marvel: Comet Man, Micronauts, Thor		
Covers ($):	75	100	125
Pages ($):	25	50	75
1987	DC: Batman, Deadman, Sandman		
Covers ($):	150	225	300
Pages ($):	75	150	250
1989-92	Doom Patrol, Robin, Swamp Thing		
Covers ($):	150	200	250
Pages ($):	60	100	150
	Archie: Bayou Billy		
Covers ($):	150	175	200
Pages ($):	xxx		

1990	First: Badger, Grim Jack		
Covers ($):	150	200	250
Pages ($):	60	80	100
1990-91	Atomeka: Betty Page		
Covers ($):	xxx		
Pages ($):	50	75	100
1991	Dark Horse: Aliens		
Covers ($):	300	400	500
Pages ($):	100	200	300

JURGENS-DAN

Year	Publisher & Descriptive Information		
1980's-90's	DC Projects, Death of Superman story-line		
Covers ($):	100	200	400
Pages ($):	35	50	75
	Superman vs. Aliens limited series (Kevin Nowlan inks)		
Covers ($):	300	400	500
Pages ($):	50	125	175

KALUTA-MICHAEL-WILLIAM

Year	Publisher & Descriptive Information		
1969	Charlton: Romance, war, Western		
Covers ($):	xxx		
Pages ($):	75	100	125

Mike Kaluta, cover artwork for MADAME XANADU #1, 1981. Estimate: $1,500/2,000; sold for $2,530 in 6/93 (Sotheby's 3rd comic art auction). © National Periodical Publications/DC Comics

Mike Kaluta, cover artwork for DETECTIVE COMICS #428, 1972. Private sale at $500 in 1996 (TRH Galleries). © National Periodical Publications/DC Comics

Gil Kane, cover artwork for GREEN LANTERN, 1966. Private sale at $6,000 in 1996 (TRH Galleries). © National Periodical Publications/DC Comics

1969-70 Major Magazines: (magazine) Horror

Covers ($):	xxx		
Pages ($):	100	200	300

1971,1973 Skywald: Sci-fi

Covers ($):	xxx		
Pages ($):	100	200	300

1972-81 DC: *Shadow*

Covers ($):	[2,500	4,000	5,000]
Pages ($):	300	500	700

Carson of Venus, David Innes

Covers ($):	xxx		
Pages ($):	[200	400	600]

***Batman, Batman Family, Ironwolf, Vampire, Madame Xanadu,* misc. horror/mystery, sci-fi, sword and sorcery, war, and others**

Covers ($):	800	1,200	1,600
Pages ($):	200	400	600

1982-83 H.M. Communications: (magazine) *Starstruck*

Covers ($):	xxx		
Pages ($):	200	400	600

1984-89 Marvel: *Conan* (B&W art)

Covers ($):	400	600	800
Pages ($):	xxx		

(water colored art)

Covers ($):	800	900	1,200
Pages ($):	xxx		

***Shadow,* with Russ Heath inks. (cover not inked by Heath)**

Covers ($):	2,000	2,500	3,000
Pages ($):	200	400	600

Starstruck

Covers ($):	400	600	800
Pages ($):	200	350	500

1984 Eclipse: *Rocketeer* (pinup)

Covers ($):	xxx		
Pages ($):	500	700	900

1986-91 DC: *Batman, DragonLance, Nightwing, Shadow, Spectre,* and others

Covers ($):	500	800	1,100
Pages ($):	xxx		

1991 Dark Horse: *Vampirella*

Covers ($):	1,000	1,200	1,400
Pages ($):	xxx		

1991 A.C. Comics: Sci-fi

Covers ($):	600	700	800
Pages ($):	xxx		

Bob Kane, artwork for page from BATMAN #11 with two unpublished partially finished try-out pages by an unknown artist 1942. Estimate: $2,000/4,000; sold for $4,025 in 1996 (Sotheby's 6th comic art auction).
© National Periodical Publications/DC Comics

KANE-BOB

Year	Publisher & Descriptive Information
1936	Henie: *Hiram Hick*

Covers ($):   xxx
Pages ($):   [400   500   600]

1937   Comics Magazine Co.: Adventure, crime

Covers ($):   xxx
Pages ($):   [400   500   600]

Fiction House: *Jest Laffs, Peter Pupp, Pluto*

Covers ($):   xxx
Pages ($):   [400   500   600]

Globe: *Sidestreets of New York, Van Bragger*

Covers ($):   xxx
Pages ($):   [400   600   800]

1937-47   National/DC: *Batman & Robin*

Covers ($):[10,000   15,000   20,000]
Pages ($): [2,500   4,000   6,000]

* Note: Batman original art produced by Bob Kane between 1939 and the late 1940s is extremely rare and recognized for its historical importance. Kane artwork produced during the first two or three years is almost non-existent and could exceed estimated values. From about 1947 on, Kane utilized "ghost" artists to emulate his style, including Sheldon Moldoff and Lew Schwartz.

Clip Carson, Rusty and His Pals

Covers ($):   xxx
Pages ($):   [400   600   800]

Ginger Snap, Oscar the Gumshoe

Covers ($):   xxx
Pages ($):   [300   450   600]

KANE-GIL

Year	Publisher & Descriptive Information		
1943- 1947,64	National/DC: *Atom, Green Lantern*		
	Covers ($): [2,500	4,500	7,500]
	Pages ($): 400	600	900
1965-72	Covers ($): 1,500	3,000	4,500
	Pages ($): 150	350	600
1957-72	*Adam Strange, Batman, Captain Action, Captain Comet, Flash,* misc. horror/mystery, misc. sci-fi and others		
	Covers ($): 2,000	3,000	4,000
	Pages ($): 300	600	900
	Don Caballero, Hopalong Cassidy, Johnny Thunder, Nighthawk, Trigger Twins. Wildcat, misc. Western, *Rex The Wondor Dog,* crime, other titles		
	Covers ($): [800	1,600	2,400]
	Pages ($): 150	300	450
1960-63	Western/Dell: *Brain Boy, Hennessey* and misc. TV Western		
	Covers ($): xxx		
	Pages ($): [100	150	200]
1965-67	Tower: *Menthor, Noman, Raven, Thunder Agents, Undersea Agent*		
	Covers ($): 1,000	1,500	2,000
	Pages ($): 200	350	500
1967	King: *Flash Gordon*		
	Covers ($): 2,000	2,500	3,000
	Pages ($): xxx		
1968	Adventure House Press: *Savage*		
	Covers ($): 400	800	1,200
	Pages ($): 75	150	225
1971-81	Marvel: *Avengers, Captain America, Captain Marvel, Conan, Daredevil, Dr. Strange, Fantastic Four, Gulliver of Mars, Human Torch, Iron Man, John Carter, Spider-Man, Sub-Mariner, Thor, X-Men,* others		
	Covers ($): 400	800	[1,200]
	Pages ($): 75	150	225
	Champions, Defenders, Ghost Rider, Human Fly, Iron Fist, Kazar, Kung-Fu, Man-Thing, Skull, Warlock, misc. horror, others		

Gil Kane & Bill Everett, cover artwork for SUB-MARINER #48, 4/72. Private sale at $700 in 1996 (TRH Galleries).
© Marvel Comics Group

Covers ($):	300	600	900
Pages ($):	50	100	150
Misc. war and Western			
Covers ($):	300	450	600
Pages ($):	xxx		
1983-88 DC: *Atom, Captain Marvel, Green Lantern Corps, Superman,* others			
Covers ($):	300	400	500
Pages ($):	50	100	150
1990's Re-creation covers for silver age titles, usually hand lettered with watercolor finishes by the artist.			
Covers ($)	2,500	3,500	4,500

KATCHOR-BEN

Year	Publisher & Descriptive Information		
1984-97	*RAW, Penguin, Little Brown, Cheap Novelties, Julius Knipl, Real Estate Photographer*		
	Covers ($): xxx		
	Pages ($): xxx		

Sam Kieth, cover artwork for MARVEL COMICS PRESENTS #101, 1992. Sold privately for $750 in 1997 (TRH Galleries). © Marvel Comics Group

KAYANAN-RAFAEL

Year	Publisher & Descriptive Information		
1980-90's	Conan, Turok, Magic		
	Covers ($): 250	325	400
	Pages ($): 50	75	150

KAZ

Year	Publisher & Descriptive Information	
1985-97	Fantagraphics: Buzzbomb, Sidetrack City, Underworld	
	Covers ($): xxx	
	Pages ($): xxx	

KELLY-WALT

Year	Publisher & Descriptive Information		
1935-36	Humor		
	Covers ($): ***		
	Pages ($): ***		
1940s	Humor pages		
	Covers ($): xxx		
	Pages ($): ***		
1941-49	"Our Gang," "Elmer Bugs," "Golly Goose," " X-Mas with Mother Goose," "Pogo," "Oswald the Rabbit," "Albert"		
	Covers ($): 2,000	4,000	6,000
	Pages ($): 500	1,000	1,500
	Walt Disney's Comics and Stories		
	Covers ($): [4,000	6,000	8,500]
	Pages ($): xxx		

KEOWN-DALE

Year	Publisher f Descriptive Information		
1990-92	Marvel: Hulk		
	Covers ($): 200	400	600
	Pages ($): 60	125	200
	She-Hulk		
	Covers ($): 125	175	225
	Pages ($): xxx		

KIETH-SAM

Year	Publisher & Descriptive Information		
1988-90	DC: Epicurus, Sandman		
	Covers ($): 150	200	325
	Pages ($): 75	150	225
	Batman, Man-Hunter		
	Covers ($): xxx		
	Pages ($): 50	100	175
1988	Eclipse: AirBoy		
	Covers ($): 75	100	125
	Pages ($): 50	75	100
	Adolescent Radioactive Black Belt Hamsters		
	Covers ($): 75	125	175
	Pages ($): 25	50	75
1989-90	Quality: Nemesis		
	Covers ($): 150	250	400
	Pages ($): xxx		
1989-92	Marvel: Cable, Ghost Rider, Wolverine		
	Covers ($): 400	600	[900]
	Pages ($): 100	250	[450]
	Hulk, Spider-Man		
	Covers ($): 200	275	350
	Pages ($): 75	125	175
1990	Dark Horse: Aliens		
	Covers ($): xxx		
	Pages ($): 50	150	250

KINNEY-JAY

Year	Publisher & Descriptive Inform		
1967-70	Young Lust, Company & Sons, Ace, Rat, Gothic Blimp Works		
	Pages ($): 150	200	250
1971-81	Anarchy, Young Lust, Bijou Funnies, El Perfecto, Print Mint Publications		
	Covers ($): 300	400	500
	Pages ($): 150	225	300

Jack Kirby, artwork for Marvel poster entitled "Galactus and the SILVER SURFER" measuring 24"X"16. Estimate: $10,000/12,000; sold for $10,925 in 1993 (Christie's East comic art auctions). © Marvel Comics Group

Jack Kirby & Dick Ayers, artwork for THE INCREDIBLE HULK #4, page 6, 1962. Estimate: $1,000/2,000; sold for $1,840 in 1995 (Christie's East comic art auctions). © Marvel Comics Group

Jack Kirby & Joe Sinnott, artwork for THE FANTASTIC FOUR #63, page 13, 1967. Estimate: $1,000/1,500; sold for $1,380 in 1995 (Christie's East comic art auctions). © Marvel Comics Group

KIRBY-JACK (JACK KURTZBERG) (1917-1994)

Jack Kirby proved to be one of the most prolific and creative comic artists for over 50 years in the comics field. Kirby and his partner, Joe Simon, created numerous comic books and characters during the Golden Age of comics, including such popular heroes as Captain America and The Boy Commandoes. While Jack Kirby is considered the principal penciller on most of this great body of work, it should be noted that Joe Simon also penciled and inked some of this art during those collaborative years, as well as writing and scripting a least part of the early stories. At the same time, it should be pointed out that a wide array of other artists and inkers were employed to assist, many of whom remain uncredited even today. Since these employed artists were required to work in the Simon and Kirby style, identification of who exactly worked on which pages during the 1940s is sometimes difficult to determine. In most instances, due to the scarcity of original art from this period, this fact would not necessarily affect the value.

The following is a listing of just some of

the artists who assisted or inked Jack Kirby's art: Jack Kirby, Matt Baker, Gil Kane, Wally Wood, Joe Simon, Dick Ayers, Al Avison, Bill Everett, Mort Meskin, Joe Sinnott, George Klein, Don Heck, Mike Sekowski, Chic Stone, Reed Crandall, Vince Colletta, Syd Shores, John Giunta, Carl Burgos, Gene Colan, Herb Trimpe, Mike Esposito, George Tuska, Frank Giacoia, Al Gabriel, Marie Severin, George Roussos, John Severin, Charles Nicholas, John Verpoorten, John Prentice, Tom Palmer, Marvin Stein, Sol Brodsky, Al Williamson, Paul Reinman, Steve Ditko, John Romita, Bob Powell, Dan Adkins, Werner Roth, Greg Theakston and Mike Royer.

Year	Publisher & Descriptive Information
1938	Fiction House: *The Count of Monte Cristo*

Covers ($):   xxx
Pages ($):   [800   1,000   1,200]

Wilton of the West

Covers ($):   xxx
Pages ($):   [700   900   1,000]

1940	Crestwood: *The Black Owl*

Covers ($):   [***]
Pages ($):   [***]

Fox: *Blue Bolt, Wing Turner,*

Jack Kirby, unpublished pencil portrait of SILVER SURFER, 1970's. First estimate: $1,500/2,000; sold for $3,575 in 1992; second estimate: $3,500/4,500; sold for $9,200 in 1998 (Sotheby's 2nd and 8th comic art auctions). © Marvel Comics Group

Jack Kirby, pencil artwork for cover re-creation of AMAZING FANTASY #15, 1970's. Estimate: $5,000/7,000; sold for $10,925 in 1994 (Sotheby's 4th comic art auction). © Marvel Comics Group

Jack Kirby, unpublished original pencil cover artwork for CAPTAIN AMERICA #105, 1968. Estimate: $750/1,000; sold for $1,725 in 1993 (Sotheby's 3rd comic art auction). © Marvel Comics Group

Jack Kirby & Chic Stone, artwork for FANTASTIC FOUR #34, pin-up page, 1964. Estimate: $4,000/5,000; sold for $5,520 in 1995 (Christie's East comic art auctions). © Marvel Comics Group

Jack Kirby, THE MIGHTY THOR #164 splash page, signed middle left, 1969, 14"X10". Estimate: $600/900; sold for $935 in 10/97 (Russ Cochran's comic art auction). © Marvel Comics Group

Jack Kirby & Dick Ayers, splash page from "SSERPO!" from AMAZING ADVENTURES, 1961. Private sale at $3,750 in 1997 (TRH Galleries). © Marvel Comics Group

Jack Kirby & Dick Ayers, from a 3 page lot featuring PRE-HERO Marvel artwork, 1961. Estimate: $2,000/2,500; sold for $1,870 in 1992 (Sotheby's 2nd comic art auction). © Marvel Comics Group

Jack Kirby & Dick Ayers, splash page from SGT. FURY #2, 1963. Estimate: $2,500/3,000; sold for $3,300 in 1992 (Sotheby's 2nd comic art auction). © Marvel Comics Group

Jack Kirby & Dick Ayers, cover artwork for re-creation of X-MEN #1, 1994. Estimate: $5,000/7,000; sold for $4,887 in 6/94 (Sotheby's 4th comic art auction). © Marvel Comics Group

Jack Kirby & Dick Ayers, 6 page story from STRANGE TALES #84, 1961. Estimate: $1,000/1,500; sold for $1,093 in 6/93 (Sotheby's 3rd comic art auction).
© Marvel Comics Group

Jack Kirby & Vince Colletta, splash page from complete story from JOURNEY INTO MYSTERY #124, 1966. Estimate: $4,500/5,500; sold for $4,950 in 1992 (Sotheby's 2nd comic art auction).
© Marvel Comics Group

Cosmic Carson
Covers ($): [***]
Pages ($): [***]

Timely: *Red Raven, Mercury, Comet Pierce*
Covers ($): [***]
Pages ($): [***]

Harvey: *Champion*
Covers ($): [xxx]
Pages ($): xxx

1941-42 Timely: *Captain America, Young Allies*
Covers ($): [***]
Pages ($): [2,000   3,500   6,000]

Fawcett: *Captain Marvel*
Covers ($): [***]
Pages ($): [***]

1942-46 National: *Boy Commandoes, Manhunter, News Boy Legion, Sandman*
Covers ($): [4,000   5,500   7,500]
Pages ($): [800   900   1,400]

1946-56 Harvey: *Boy Explorers, Boy's Ranch, Fighting*
Covers ($): 1,500   3,000   4,000
Pages ($): 300   600   900

Stuntman
Covers ($): 3,000   4,500   6,500
Pages ($): 500   900   1,400

Fighting American
Covers ($): 5,000   7,000   10,000
Pages ($): 500   1,000   1,500

Mystery, romance, Sci-fi, war
Covers ($): 800   1,000   1,200
Pages ($): 200   300   400

1947-49 Hillman: *Airboy*, crime, *Flying Fool*
Covers ($): [1,000   2,000   3,000]
Pages ($): [300   400   450]

1947-59 Crestwood: *Black Magic—* horror/fantasy
Covers ($): [2,000   3,000   4,000]
Pages ($): [300   500   700]

Crime, romance
Covers ($): [900   1,800   2,800]
Pages ($): [200   300   400]

Jack Kirby & Dick Ayers, artwork for re-creation cover to STRANGE TALES #89, 1994. Estimate: $3,000/4,000; sold for $5,750 in 6/94 (Sotheby's 4th comic art auction). © Marvel Comics Group

1954-55	Mainline: *Bullseye*—Western		
	Covers ($): 1,200	1,800	2,500
	Pages ($): 200	350	550
	Crime, romance, war		
	Covers ($): 800	1,200	1,600
	Pages ($): 200	300	400
1955	Charlton: Sci-fi, humor		
	Covers ($): [800	1,200	1,600]
	Pages ($): [300	400	500]

1956-59	National: Adventure, mystery		
	Covers ($): [2,000	4,000	6,000]
	Pages ($): [200	400	600]
	Challengers of the Unknown, artwork with Wally Wood		
	Covers ($): [***]		
	Pages ($): 800	1,600	2,800
	Green Arrow		
	Covers ($): xxx		
	Pages ($): [700	900	1,400]

Jack Kirby, artwork for re-creation cover to AMAZING SPIDER-MAN #1, 1994. Estimate: $5,000/7,000; sold for $14,950 in 1994 (Sotheby's 4th comic art auction). © Marvel Comics Group

1957	Gilberton: *Classics Illustrated*: ("The Last Days of Pompeii") (misc.- "World Around Us")		
	Covers ($):	xxx	
	Pages ($):	[200	300	400]

1959	MLJ: *Double Life of Private Strong, The Fly*		
	Covers ($):	[2,000	4,000	6,000]
	Pages ($):	[300	500	700]

1956-62	Atlas/Marvel: Fantasy, horror, Si-fi, "big foot" monster era		
	Covers ($):	[3,500	5,500	8,500]
	Splash Pgs:	[1,500	3,000	5,500]
	Pages ($):	300	600	800

Yellow Claw

	Covers ($):	xxx	
	Pages ($):	[300	500	700]

Romance, war, Western

	Covers ($):	[800	1,200	1,600]
	Pages ($):	200	300	400

Jack Kirby & Dick Ayers, artwork for cover re-creation to FANTASTIC FOUR #1, 1994. Estimate: $6,000/8,000; sold for $7,475 in 1994 (Sotheby's 4th comic art auction). © Marvel Comics Group

Jack Kirby, artwork for CAPTAIN AMERICA Pin-Up, 1964. Estimate: $8,000/10,000; sold for $9,200 in 1993 (Christie's East comic art auctions). © Marvel Comics Group

Jack Kirby & Joe Sinnott, artwork for cover to FANTASTIC FOUR #65, 1964. Estimate: $12,000/16,000; sold for $12,650 in 1996 (Sotheby's 6th comic art auction). © Marvel Comics Group

Jack Kirby & Dick Ayers, artwork for splash page from FANTASTIC FOUR #17, 1963. Estimate: $4,000/5,000; sold for $9,775 in 1996 (Sotheby's 6th comic art auction). © Marvel Comics Group

Jack Kirby & Joe Sinnott, artwork for page 6 from FANTASTIC FOUR #59, 1966. Estimate: $2,000/2,500; sold for $10,350 in 1994 (Christie's East comic art auctions). © Marvel Comics Group

Jack Kirby & Frank Giacoia, artwork for page 18 from FANTASTIC FOUR #39, 1965. Estimate: $2,000/3,000; sold for $2,070 in 1996 (Sotheby's 6th comic art auction). © Marvel Comics Group

Jack Kirby & Dick Ayers, artwork for re-creation cover to THE AVENGERS #1, 1994. Estimate: $3,000/4,000; sold for $8,050 in 6/94 (Sotheby's 4th comic art auction). © Marvel Comics Group

Note: Technically speaking, no known covers exist for the Pre-Hero fantasy Marvel titles with a Kirby/Ayers cover, however there are a few examples (such as *Tales to Astonish* No. 34) where the actual splash page was used for the cover and in this case, the cover artwork would be in existence. Prices can vary widly for Kirby's Big-Foot monster and fantasy work for Marvel from 1952 through 1960 Splash Pages dominate the higher brackets, with proto-type super-hero characters at the top of the list.

Marvel Silver Age

Jack Kirby's contributions to the creation and popularity of Marvel's explosive Silver Age of comics between the years of 1961 and 1970 are unparalleled. Although artwork from this time period is more readily available than artwork from the Golden Age years, the demand has far outweighed the supply. Due to Kirby's consistent ability to turn out dramatic pencils or layouts at an incredible rate of speed and Marvel's awareness of his popularity with their readers, once again other artists were assigned the inking chores so as to "speed" things along as fast as possible. Unlike the art produced during the 1940s and 1950s, most of Kirby's-interior art produced for Marvel from 1959 on is usually credited on the splash page of each story. Unfortunately most of his covers went unsigned but in all cases are still easily recognized as Kirby's pencils and someone else's inks. For further detail and documentation on Jack Kirby's prolific contribution to comics, there are numerous Jack Kirby treasuries and Marvel indexes available in the marketplace.

Marvel: *Antman, Avengers, Captain America, Daredevil, Fantastic Four, Giantman, Hulk, Human Torch, Inhumans, Nick Fury, Silver Surfer, Spider-Man, Thor, Wasp, X-Men,* and others

1961-65			
Covers ($):	[4,000	8,000	15,000]
Splash Pgs	[2,500	5,000	8,000]
Pages ($):	[400	900	1,500]

1966-70			
Covers ($):	[2,500	4,500	10,000]
Splash Pgs	1,500	3,000	5,500
Pages ($):	350	650	1,500

1971-76 National/DC: *Challengers of the Unknown, Demon, Forever People, Jimmy Olsen, Kamandi, Mister Miracle, New Gods, Omac, Sandman,* and others

Covers ($):	1,500	2,500	[3,500]
Splash Pgs	200	350	550
Pages ($):	100	200	350

1975-76 Marvel: *Devil Dinosaur, Skull the Slayer, Thor,* and others

Covers ($):	900	1,500	[2,500]
Splash Pgs	100	250	400
Pages ($):	75	125	175

1961-84 Pacific: *Captain Victory, Silver Star*

Covers ($):	700	900	1,400
Pages ($):	75	125	200

1984-86 National/DC: *Justice League of America*

Covers ($):	700	900	1,400
Pages ($):	75	125	175

1987-88 Genesis West: *Last of the Viking Heroes*

Covers ($):	600	900	1,200
Pages ($):	xxx		

1990-94 Re-creation covers for Marvel titles Pencil Cover re-creations

Covers ($):	2,500	4,500	7,500

Within the past three years the market for Jack Kirby original artwork has reached an astounding level of collector demand especially for Golden Age and Silver Age examples produced for DC and Marvel. Much of Kirby's Golden Age output is unaccounted for, as is a large amount of his pre-1965 Silver Age art; the scarcest examples being the DC material produced between 1956 and 1959. This scarcity results partly from DC's adoption d a policy to destroy most of its old inventory during the early 1960s, unfortunately eliminating thousands of pages by Kirby and many other artists. In comparison, more of Kirby's Marvel art has surfaced- over the years including complete stories from the "big foot" monster era and even a fair amount of superhero pages from as far back as *Fantastic Four* No. 1, dated

RARITY — Brackets [ ] around a price indicate that this example is very scarce and could exceed maximum estimate.

Covers
No work produced in this category—   XXX

No price available due to lack of information—   ***

CONDITION — Age, color, marks, tears, etc.

Pages
[400   500   600]

CHARACTER — Is the primary character featured, or is the original characteristic of a great example in the story line?

CONTENT — is the theme or story line exceptional or below average?

VALUE RANGE

Minimum   Medium   Maximum

RARITY

The [ ] Brackets indicate RARITY, if these brackets are used the reader can potentially double the price range in all three catagories.

November 1961. On the other hand, and for reasons still unclear, pre-1965 Kirby Marvel covers are quite scarce and rarely surface.

Note: individual sales would include: splash page from Big-Foot fantasy story from *Journey into Mystery* No. 71 selling at $4,312; splash page from *Fantastic Four* No. 17 selling at $9,775; cover for *Fantastic Four* No. 65 (with Sinnott inks) selling at $12,650; cover for *Marvel's Greatest Comics* No. 27 (1970) selling at $3,162; cover for Thor No. 167 (1969) selling at $2,300; page 21 from *Avengers* No. 1 selling at $4,132; art to *Fantastic Four* house ad (1961 single panel) selling at $8,626; cover re-creation (pencils only) for *Amazing Spider-Man* No. 1 selling at $14,300; cover re-creation to *Fantastic Four* No. 1 (with Ayers inks) selling for $7,250; cover re-creation for *Amazing Fantasy* No. 15 selling at $10,500 (and later selling at Diamond Galleries for $15,000); all sales from Sotheby's comic art auctions.

Sales at Christie's East include: splash page from *Fantastic Four* No. 35 selling at $5,750; splash page from *Journey Into Mystery* No. 112 for $2,530; page no. 6 from *Fantastic Four* No. 59 (inks by Sinnott) selling at $10,350; splash page to *Fantastic Four* No. 51 selling at $14,950; cover for *Mr. Miracle* No. 6 selling at $2,530; cover for *Fantastic Four* No. 57 (1966 with Sinnott inks) selling at $29,900; splash page (featuring origin of Captain America) from *Tales of Suspense* No. 63 selling for $14,975.

KRIGSTEIN-BERNARD (BERNIE)

Year	Publisher & Descriptive Information		
1947-49	Fawcett: *Golden Arrow, Nyoka*		
	Covers ($): xxx		
	Pages ($): 100	150	200
1948-53	National: *Atom, Wildcat*		
	Covers ($): xxx		
	Pages ($): [300	600	900]
	Sci-fi, war		
	Covers ($): [800	1,200	1,600]

Joe Kubert, artwork for TARZAN #220, 1973.
Estimate: $3,000/5,000; sold for $2,875 in 1995
(Christie's East comic art auctions). © National
Periodical Publications/DC Comics

Joe Kubert, interior page from OUR ARMY AT WAR
#109, 1961. private sale at $400 (TRH galleries).
© National Periodical Publications/DC Comics

	Pages ($):	100	200	300

1948-53 Hillman: Crime, romance, sports,
war, Western

	Covers ($):	xxx		
	Pages ($):	[100	150	200]

1950-57 Atlas: Crime, romance, sports, war

	Covers ($):	xxx		
	Pages ($):	[100	150	200]

Fantasy, horror, mystery, sci-fi

	Covers ($):	xxx		
	Pages ($):	[200	300	400]

1951-52 Ziff Davis: *Explorer Joe*, horror,
Space Busters, Space Patrol

	Covers ($):	xxx		
	Pages ($):	[150	250	350]

1953-55 EC: crime, horror, humor, sci-fi

	Covers ($):	xxx		
	Pages ($):	200	250	400

New Direction titles

	Covers ($):	[1,000	1,500	3,000]
	Pages ($):	75	125	175

1954 St. John: Horror, war

	Covers ($):	xxx		
	Pages ($):	[75	125	175]

1955 Charlton: sci-fi

	Covers ($):	xxx		

	Pages ($):	[75	125	175]

Note: individual sales would include: the
current owners of "The Master Race" have
refused cash offers of $25,000 to $30,000;
the six page story "The Flying Machine"
(Bradbury adaptation) from *Weird Science
Fantasy* No. 23 for $15,000; story "Monster
From the 4th Dimension" from 3-D
unpublished EC selling at $1,610.

KITCHEN-DENIS

Year	Publisher & Descriptive Information

1968-74 *Moms Homemade Comics, Snarf,
Deep 3-D, Bugle-American, Pro-
Junior, Bijou 6, Comix Book*
(Marvel)

	Covers ($):	550	950	[1,250]
	Pages ($):	150	200	250

1975-91 *Mondo Snarfo, Snarf, Bizarre Sex,
Fox River Patriot* (many covers)
Arcade, Energy Comics

	Covers ($):	500	1,000	[1,700]
	Pages ($):	150	200	250

Joe Kubert, splash page from BRAVE & THE BOLD #24, 1959. Estimate: $2,000/2,500; sold for $1,980 in 1992 (Sotheby's 2nd comic art auction). © National Periodical Publications/DC Comics

KUBERT-ADAM

Year	Publisher & Descriptive Information		
1980's -90s	Marvel Projects, *Ka-zar, Hulk, Wolverine*		
	Covers ($): 175	400	600
	Pages ($): 75	175	250

KUBERT-ANDY

Year	Publisher & Descriptive Information		
1980's -90s	Marvel Projects & *X-Men*		
	Covers ($): 150	300	450
	Pages ($): 75	150	225

KUBERT-JOE

Year	Publisher & Descriptive Information		
1942-43	Holyoke: *Alias X, Flag-Man, Spark Stevens, Volton*		
	Covers ($): xxx		
	Pages ($): [150	200	250]

Year	Publisher & Descriptive Information		
1942-43	MLJ: *Black Witch, Boy Buddies, Zoom O Day*		
	Covers ($): xxx		
	Pages ($): [150	200	250]
1942-43	Quality: *Espionage, Phantom Lady*		
	Covers ($): xxx		
	Pages ($): [150	250	350]
1943-48	Harvey: *Black Cat, Robin Hood, Scarlet Phantom, Shock Gibson, Zebra*		
	Covers ($): xxx		
	Pages ($): 200	300	400
1943-51	National: *Crimson Avenger, Dr. Fate, Flash, Hawkman, Johnny Quick, Newsboy Legion, Star Spangled Kid, Vigilante, Wildcat, Justice Society,* others		
	Covers ($): [***]		
	Splash Pgs: [1,000	2,000	3,500]
	Pages ($): [400	800	1,200]

1949-54   St. John: *Tor*
           Covers ($): [2,000   3,000   4,000]
           Pages ($): [***]
           Adventure, Horror
           Covers ($): [2,000   2,750   4,500]
           Pages ($): [200   400   600]
           Humor, *Three Stooges*
           Covers ($): [1,000   1,500   2,000]
           Pages ($): [150   300   450]
1955   Atlas: horror titles
           Pages ($): [250   350   450]
1947-52   Avon: Horror, sci-fi *Kenton of the Star Patrol*
           Covers ($):   xxx
           Pages ($): [300   600   900]
1953   EC: *War*
           Covers ($):   xxx
           Pages ($):   250   350   450
1961-62   *The Brave & The Bold, Hawkman*
           Covers ($): [7,000   9,000 14,000]
           Splash Pgs [2,000   4,000   6,500]
           Pages ($):   500   800   1,500
1953-78   National/DC: *Hawkman, Viking Prince*
           Covers ($):[3,000   6,000   9,000]
           Pages ($):   600   800   1,500
           Atom, Adam Strange, All Star Squadron, Avenger, Batman, Cave Carson, Challengers, Enemy Ace, Firehair, Flash, John Carter, Justice League, Korak, Nightmaster, Ragman, Rip Hunter, Robin Hood, Shadow, Superman, Tarzan, Tomahawk, Tor, others
           Covers ($):   1,400   2,400   [3,400]
           Pages ($):   200   500   900
           G.I. Joe, Haunted Tank, Johnny Cloud, Losers, Unknown Soldier, misc. war
           Covers - twice up size
              ($):   1,500   3,000   4,000
           Covers ($):   600   1,200   2,000
           Pages - twice up size
              ($):   200   400   600
           Pages ($):   100   200   350
           Misc. horror, sci-fi
           Covers ($):   900   1,500   [2,000]
           Pages ($):   150   300   450

           Atomeka Press: *Tor*
           Covers ($):   xxx
           Pages ($): [200   400   600]

Note: individual prices would include: splash page for *Brave & Bold* No. 36 (Hawkman) selling for $7,763 (at auction in 1993) at Sotheby's.

KURTZMAN-HARVEY (1924-1993)

Year	Publisher & Descriptive Information
1943	Ace: *Buckskin, Lash Lightning, Magno and Davey, Mr. Risk, Paul Revere, Jr.*

           Covers ($): [1,000   2,000   3,000]
           Pages ($): [300   500   700]

1943-44   Quality: *Bill the Magnificent, Flatfoot Bums*
           Covers ($):   xxx
           Pages ($): [400   600   800]
1945   Aviation Press: *Black Venus*
           Covers ($):   xxx
           Pages ($): [300   400   500]
1946-51   Timely: *Egghead Doodle, Giggles N Grins, Little Aspirin, Mister Nexdoor, Muscles Malone, Pigtails, Rusty*
           Covers ($):   xxx
           Pages ($): [600   900   1,400]
           Hey Look
           Covers ($):   xxx
           Pages ($): [1,000   1,500   2,500]
           (only a few *Hey Look* pages are known to exist)
1950-52   Toby: *Genius*
           Covers ($):   xxx
           Pages ($): [900   1,500   1,800]
           Prize: Western
           Covers ($):   xxx
           Pages ($):   250   450   650
1952   National/DC: *Pot Shot Pete*
           Pages ($):   1,000   1,500   2,000
1949-55   EC: Humor/satire—*MAD*
           Covers ($): [5,000   7,500 11,000]
           Pages ($):   xxx
           Pencil concept 8 1/2 x 11" sheets to *MAD* stories
              ($):   100   200   300
           Watercolor on board preliminary

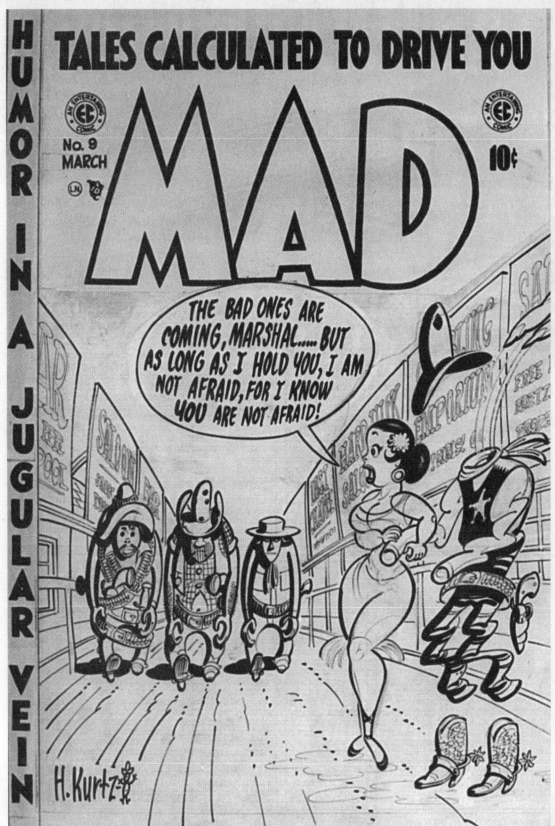

Harvey Kurtzman, cover artwork for MAD #9, 3/53. Sold privately for $6,000 in 1993 (Russ Cochran auctions).
© William M. Gaines/EC Publications

Harvey Kurtzman, original preliminary watercolor for HELP! Vol. 2, #4, 1962. Estimate: $2,000/3,000; sold for $2,013 in 1993 (Sotheby's 3rd comic art auction). © Warren Publications Inc.

Harvey Kurtzman, artwork for sample page submitted to Stan Lee between 1949-1950. Estimate: $1,000/1,500; sold for $2,990 in 1993 (Christie's East comic art auctions). © The Harvey Kurtzman Estate

concept paintings for *MAD* comic book covers

Covers ($) for issue No. 1 [15,000 17,000 20,000]

Covers ($) for issues above No. 3 [4,500 6,500 8,500]

Sci-fi, war

Covers ($):	[1,750	3,000	6,000]
Pages ($):	300	600	900

Crime, horror

Covers ($):	xxx		
Pages ($):	300	500	700

1957-58 *Humbug,* interior stories and concept work

Covers ($):	[800	1,600	3,400]
Pages ($):	200	250	300

Pencil Preliminary pages to stories

($):	100	125	150

1959 *The Jungle Book, Ballantine Books*

Pages ($):	200	250	[350]

1960-63 *Help Magazine,* covers, concept work, features

Covers (most were destroyed in the Warren warehouse days, only a few survive in their final form)

($):	[300	350	500]

Note: These covers were photo montage, or photo layout finals, and in many cases did not represent direct inking by the artist.

Covers (preliminary watercolor concept works where Kurtzman would work out the photograph to be shot for the final cover, many of these original survive.)

($):	[800	1,600	2,500]

1962-75 Hugh Hefner: *Little Annie Fanny*

Covers ($):	xxx		
Pages ($):	[900	1,500	1,800]

Note: This comic feature, although always written and laid out in pencil by Harvey Kurtzman, was usually assisted on by other artists, including Jack Davis, Will Elder, Frank Frazetta, and others.

1973-74 Kitchen Sink: Humor

Covers ($):	700	1,000	[1,600]
Pages ($):	xxx		

1985-89 *MAD Magazine,* individual pages, as well as work with Will Elder bearing signature "WEHK" where most work was done by Elder, However individual pages are 100% Kurtzman

Pages ($): 150 200 300

Note: individual sales include: preliminary cover watercolor for HELP! No. 6 selling at auction for $2,200; preliminary watercolor painting for HELP! No. 2/4 selling for $2,013; cover for EC 3-D Classics No. 1 selling at $6,900; cover for MAD No. 7 selling at $11,500; all sales at Sotheby's comic art auctions. Private sales include MAD No. 1 cover at Russ Cochran auction in 1970's for $15,000; the concept painting for MAD No. 1 (which preceeds any MAD artwork of any kind) at $22,500; concept painting for MAD No. 8 at $8,500; cover for MAD No. 4 at $12,500 (from Diamond Galleries EC Vault sale); cover for *Two-Fisted Tales* No. 22 at $2,250; cover for *Frontline Combat* No. 3 at $6,000.

LARSON-ERIK

Year	Publisher & Descriptive Information		
1988-89	DC: *Doom Patrol, Superman*		
	Covers ($): 100	150	250
	Pages ($): 75	100	125
1989-92	Marvel: *Spider-Man, Wolverine*		
	Covers ($): 200	350	[500]
	Pages ($): 100	175	[250]
	Hulk, Punisher, Thing		
	Covers ($): 150	225	300
	Pages ($): 75	125	175

LEE-JIM

Year	Publisher & Descriptive Information		
1987-92	Marvel: *X-Men*		
	Covers ($): 400	1,400	[2,400]
	Pages ($): 200	500	[800]
	Ghost Rider, Punisher, Wolverine, X-Factor		
	Covers ($): 300	500	[750]
	Pages ($): 100	250	[400]
	Alpha Flight, Captain America, Cloak and Dagger, Conan, Moon Knight, Nam, Quasar,		

Jim Lee & Scott Williams, artwork for cover to X-MEN #270, 1990. Estimate: $800/1,000; sold for $1,265 in 1996 (Sotheby's 6th comic art auction). © Marvel Comics Group

Sub-Mariner, Transformers

Covers ($):	150	300	450
Pages ($):	75	150	225

* Low-to-middle price range refers to Mr. Lee's work on "Uncanny X-Men." Higher-range prices apply to "X-Men." The Sotheby's auction at which Mr. Lee's *X-Men* No. 1 sold for $40,000 has opened a new door for contemporary artists.

LEE-JOE

Year	Publisher & Descriptive Information		
1990's	*Namor, Vampy, X-Men, Hellshock*		
	Covers ($): 250	500	850
	Pages ($): 50	150	300

LEIFELD-ROBERT

Year	Publisher & Descriptive Information		
1988-89	DC: *Hawk and Dove, Warlord*		
	Covers ($): 150	200	250
	Pages ($): 60	100	150
1989-92	Marvel: *X-Force*		
	Covers ($): 300	500	[650]
	Pages ($): 100	125	[200]
	New Mutants, Wolverine, X-Factor, X-Men, Cable		

Jim Lee, cover artwork for WOLVERINE #27, 7/91. Estimate: $500/700; sold for $1,400 in 6/93
(Sotheby's 3rd comic art auction). © Marvel Comics Group

Beast, Ghost Rider

Covers ($):	200	400	[600]
Pages ($):	100	150	[200]

1992 Image: *Young Blood*

Covers ($):	***		
Pages ($):	150	175	250

LIBERATORE

Year	Publisher & Descriptive Information
1970's -90's	*Rauxenox, Savage Sword*, various titles

B&W Pages	400	600	800
C/Pages ($):	800	1,200	2,000
C/Covers ($):	1,500	2,500	5,500
B&W Illo ($):	500	1,500	2,500

LIGHTLE-STEVE

Year	Publisher & Descriptive Information
1984-91	DC: *Cosmic Boy, Doom Patrol, Legion, Teen Titans*

Covers ($):	100	150	200
Pages ($):	50	100	150

Year	Publisher & Descriptive Information
1989-91	Marvel: *Avengers, Daredevil, Excalibur, Spider-Man, X-Men*

Covers ($):	100	150	200
Pages ($):	50	100	150

LIM-RON

Year	Publisher & Descriptive Information
1988-92	Marvel: *Captain America, Fantastic Four, Infinity Gauntlet, Silver Surfer, Thanos*

Covers ($):	100	200	300
Pages ($):	50	100	150

Conan, Excaliber, West Coast Avengers

Covers ($):	100	125	150
Pages ($):	50	100	150

1988-90 First: *Badger*

Covers ($):	100	125	150
Pages ($):	25	50	75

1989 Innovation: *Hero Alliance*

Covers ($):	75	100	125
Pages ($):	25	50	75

Lopez, artwork for style art guide from BATMAN RETURNS, 1991. Estimate: $150/250; sold for $182 in 1998 (Phil Weiss auctions). © National Periodical Publications/DC Comics

LISNER-JOE

Year	Publisher & Descriptive Information
1990's	*Cry For Dawn;* etc

Pages ($):	xxx (N.F.S.)		
Sketches ($):	50	150	300
Commission Paintings			
($):	500	1,000	1,500

LOPEZ-JOSE-GARCIA

Year	Publisher & Descriptive Information
1980-90's	DC various projects

Covers ($):	100	200	300
Pages ($):	25	50	75

LUTES-JASON

Year	Publisher & Descriptive Information
1993-97	*Penny Dreadful, Black Eye, Jar of Fools, Berlin,* stories in *Drawn & Quarterly, Real Stuff*

Covers ($):	200	250	300
Pages ($):	150	175	200

LYNCH-JAY

Year	Publisher & Descriptive Information
1962-66	*WILD!* (Don Dohler), *HELP!,* Warren Pub.

Covers ($):	300	400	500
Pages ($):	100	175	250

Joe Maneely, artwork for 2-GUN WESTERN #4, 1956. Estimate: $1,200/1,500; sold for $1,840 in 1994 (Christie's East comic art auctions). © Atlas Comics/ The Marvel comics Group

Joe Maneely, artwork for NAVY COMBAT #7, 1956. Estimate: $600/800; sold for $1,093 in 1994 (Christie's East comic art auctions). © Atlas Comics/ The Marvel comics Group

Joe Maneely, artwork for cover to BLACK KNIGHT #5, 1956. Estimate: $600/800; sold for $3,910 in 1993 (Christie's East comic art auctions). © Atlas Comics/ The Marvel comics Group

1967-74	Bijou, East Village Other, Gothic Blimp Works, The Realist, Yellow Dog, Dope Comix, Snarf		
Covers ($):	400	600	[800]
Pages ($):	150	200	[250]

MANEELY-JOE

Year	Publisher & Descriptive Information
1947-48	Street & Smith: Nick Carter, Red Dragon, Supersnipe, Tao Anwar, etc.

covers ($):	xxx		
Pages ($):	[xxx]		

1949-58	Atlas/Marvel: Human Torch, Sub-Mariner

covers ($):	[***]		
Pages ($):	[300	600	900]

Misc. horror, mystery, sci-fi—Spider Carter, Black Knight, Yellow Claw

Covers ($):	[1,000	2,000	3,000]
Pages ($):	[150	300	450]

Misc. Western—Arizona Kid, Arrowhead, Apache Kid, Black Rider, Gunhawk, Kid Colt Outlaw, Man Slade, Outlaw Kid, Rawhide Kid, Ringo Kid, Texas Kid, Two-Gun Kid, Whip Wilson, Wyatt Earp, and others

Covers ($):	[800	1,200	1,600]
Pages ($):	[100	150	200]

Misc. war—Battleship Burke, Combat Kelly, and others

Misc. jungle—Jann of the Jungle, Lorna—The Jungle Girl, and others

Misc. crime, funny animal humor, spy, sports, etc.

Covers ($):	[800	1,000	1,200]
Pages ($):	100	150	200

1958	National/DC: mystery titles

Pages ($):	[150	300	450]

MANNARA-MILO

Year	Publisher & Descriptive Information
1960-80's	Click, Indian Summer, Butterscotch, European Publications released in the U.S. by Catalan;

Covers ($):	xxx		
Pages (sold as single 1/3rd page strips)($):	500	1,000	1,500

Specialty Paintings

($):	2,000	4,000	8,000

Russ Manning, single illustration, MAGNUS ROBOT FIGHTER, concept in 1962. Private sale at $1,500 in 1996 (TRH Galleries). © Western Publishing Company

MANNING-RUSS

Year	Publisher & Descriptive Information
1953-67	Western/Dell/Gold Key: *Magnus—Robot Fighter, Tarzan*

Covers ($):	1,000	1,500	2,000
Pages ($):	250	400	550
Pin-Ups ($):	900	1,400	[2,000]

Aliens, Brothers of the Spear, Korak

Covers ($):	xxx		
Pages ($):	150	250	350

TV Characters: *Danny Thomas Show, Rawhide, Ricky Nelson, Sea Hunt, 77 Sunset Strip, Wyatt Earp;* Movie adapt: *Ben Hur, Rob Roy;* Western stars: *Dale Evans, Gene Autry, Johnny Mack Brown, Rex Allen* and others

Covers ($):	xxx		
Pages ($):	100	150	200

MARSH-JESSE

Year	Publisher & Descriptive Information
1946-65	Western/Dell: *John Carter of Mars, Tarzan*

Covers ($):	[800	1,200	1,600]
Pages ($):	50	175	300

Misc. Western—*Gene Autry, Johnny Mack Brown, Rex Allen,* others; Movie & TV series—*Annie Oakley, Range Rider,* and others

Covers ($):	[400	600	800]
Pages ($):	25	50	75

MARTIN-DON

One of the two or three all time most favorite MAD artists, beginning his career with MAD in 1957 and leaving after a fight with Bill Gaines over ownership of original artwork to work for *Cracked Magazine*.

Year	Publisher & Descriptive Information

MAD Magazine, interior pages and color pages and covers.

1957-67	Pages ($):	200	400	600
1968-70's	Pages ($):	150	300	500
1957-70's	Covers ($):	1,250	2,000	2,750
1957-70's	Color Pgs ($):	1,000	1,500	2,250

Cracked Magazine, covers and interior pages.

1970's -present	Pages ($):	100	200	350
	Covers ($):	1,000	2,000	3,000

Note: individual sales include: interior page from MAD No. 149 selling at $373; four pg feature from MAD No. 176 selling at

Don Martin, example from 6 pages from MAD #231 & 242, 1983. Estimate: $1,200/1,800; sold for $1000 in 6/98 (Sotheby's MADsterpieces auction). © William M. Gaines/ EC Publications/ National Periodical Publications

$1,265; three page feature "One Fine Day With King Kong" from MAD No. 262 selling at $1,380; back cover to MAD No. 242 selling at $1,725; poster fold out from *MAD Super Special* No. 25 (The Beatles) selling at $7,475; cover for MAD No. 229 selling at $2,875; all from Sotheby's MAD About MAD auction in 1995.

MCCARTHY-BRENDAN

Year	Publisher & Descriptive Information		
1980's -90's	*Freakwave, Paradax, Judge Dredd, Shade*		
	Covers ($): 200	400	800
	B&W ill($): 60	120	200
	Paintings($): 100	200	400

MAZZUCCHELLI-DAVID

Year	Publisher & Descriptive Information		
1983-86	Marvel: *Daredevil*		
	Covers ($): 200	400	[600]
	Pages ($): 75	200	[350]
	Angel, X-Factor		
	Covers ($): 250	300	350
	Pages ($): 75	150	225
1986-87	DC: *Batman*		
	Covers ($): ***		
	Pages ($): ***		

George Metzger, artwork for wraparound cover to MOONDOG #1, 1969. Estimate: $1,200/1,500; sold for $1,650 in 1992 (Sotheby's 2nd comic art auction). © The Print Mint

MCFARLANE-TODD

Year	Publisher & Descriptive Information		
1985-91	Marvel: *Spider-Man*		
	Covers ($): 600	1,400	[2,800]
	Pages ($): 250	500	[800]
	Hulk, Wolverine		
	Covers ($): 300	450	[800]
	Pages ($): 200	300	500
	Conan, Daredevil		
	Covers ($): 150	200	[250]
	Pages ($): xxx		
	Coyote, G.I. Joe, Spitfire		
	Covers ($): 100	150	200
	Pages ($): 50	75	100
1985-89	DC: *Batman*		
	Covers ($): 300	400	[500]
	Pages ($): 150	250	350
	Invasion		
	Covers ($): 150	200	250
	Pages ($): 75	125	175
	All Star Squadron, Infinity Inc.		
	Covers ($): 100	150	200
	Pages ($): 50	75	100
1990	Dark Horse: *Flaming Carrot*		
	Covers ($): 250	300	350
	Pages ($): xxx		
1990's	*Spawn*		
	Covers: (early covers are penciled with concept work only and painted by other artists.)		
	Pages ($): 300	500	[750]

MESKIN-MORT

Year	Publisher & Descriptive Information		
1940's	*Golden Lad,* various titles		
	Covers ($): 1,000	2,000	3,000
	Pages ($): 200	450	700
1950's	Romance titles, *Tom Corbett Space Cadet,* etc		
	Covers ($): 600	800	1,200
	Pages ($): 50	75	100
1960's	*Tales of the Unexpected,* various DC titles		
	Covers ($): 1,000	2,000	3,000
	Pages ($): 100	200	300

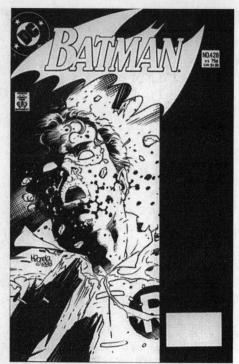

Jim Aparo, Mike Mignola & Dan DeCarlo, cover example from group of artwork for BATMAN Nos. 426-429, complete excepting two covers. Estimate: $5,000/7,000; sold for $4,400 (Sotheby's 2nd comic art auction). © National Periodical Publications/DC Comics

MIGNOLA-MIKE

Year	Publisher & Descriptive Information		
1983-91	Marvel: *Captain America, Daredevil, Defenders, Hulk, Wolverine, X-Factor, X-Force, X-Men*		
	Covers ($): 150	250	[350]
	Pages ($): 60	125	200
	Alpha Flight, Cloak and Dagger, Dr. Strange, Eddy Current, Fafhrd & the Gray Mouser, Rocket Raccoon, Soloman Kane, Sub-Mariner, Thor, Wild Cards		
	Covers ($): 100	200	300
	Pages ($): 50	100	150
1987-92	DC: *Batman, Cosmic Odyssey*		
	Covers ($): 150	250	350
	Pages ($): 50	100	150
	Blue Beetle, Phantom Stranger, Robin, Shadow, Spectre, Starman, Superman, Swamp Thing		
	Covers ($): 100	200	300
	Pages ($): 50	75	100

1990-91	Dark Horse: *Aliens, Cheval Noir*			
	Covers ($):	300	400	500
	Pages ($):	xxx		
1990's	*Hellboy Comics;*			
	Covers ($):	500	700	900
	Pages ($):	100	200	400

MILLER-FRANK

Year	Publisher & Descriptive Information		
1978-86	DC: *Dark Knight (Batman)*		
	Covers ($): ***		
	Pages ($): 400	900	[1,500]
	Ronin		
	Covers ($): ***		
	Pages ($): ***		
	Superman		
	Covers ($): 300	600	1,000
	Pages ($): xxx		
	*Batman**		
	Covers ($): xxx		
	Pages ($): 75	150	300

*Miller's first artistic turn on *Batman DC Special* No. 21 predates *Dark Knight* by six years and is a separate entity from *Dark Knight.*

	Misc. mystery, sci-fi, war			
	Covers ($):	xxx		
	Pages ($):	25	50	75
1979-90	Marvel: *Elektra*			
	Covers ($):	xxx		
	Pages ($):	***		
	Daredevil, Wolverine			
	Covers ($):	1,000	2,000	[3,000]
	Pages ($):	200	300	[600]
	Avengers, Captain America, Dr. Strange, Dr. Zero, Fantastic Four, Hulk, Moon Knight, Powerline, ROM, Spider-Man, Thing, X-Men			
	Covers ($):	300	600	1,200
	Pages ($):	100	175	250
	Captain Marvel, *John Carter, Machine Man, Meteor, Micronauts, Power Man, Spiderwoman, Star Wars*			
	Covers ($):	100	300	500
	Pages ($):	50	75	100
1984	Eclipse: *Destroyer Duck*			

Norman Mingo, artwork for preliminary pencil work to the cover of MAD #174, mid 1970's. Estimate: $400/800; sold for $633 in 1993 (Christie's East comic art auctions). © William M. Gaines/ EC publications

Norman Mingo, artwork for preliminary MAD cover #174, mid 1970's. Estimate: $800/1,000; sold for $690 in 1994 (Christie's East comic art auctions). © William M. Gaines/ EC publications

Covers ($):	250	300	350
Pages ($):	xxx		

First: *Lone Wolf and Cub*

Covers ($):	***
Pages ($):	xxx

Dark Horse: *Sin City*

Covers ($):	***
Pages ($):	***

Note: despite the popularity of Frank Miller's work, there is a similiar trend that is equal to Neal Adams originals: with both artists there is very little turning over in the public market. Both artists are known to hold privately large percentages of their work, and they are not motivated to sell at the present time - therefore prices could continue to climb.

MINGO-NORMAN (1896-1980)

A commercial artist who produced movie poster art and advertising art until he answered an ad from the New York Times and was hired in 1956 to produce his first Alfred E. Neuman cover for MAD No. 30. He went on to become the favorite cover artist for MAD and continued to work for Bill Gaines until near the end of his career.

Year	Publisher & Descriptive Information		
	Mad Magazine covers featuring Alfred E. Neuman		
1956-59	Covers ($): 3,000	6,000	9,000
1960-70	Covers ($): 2,500	5,000	7,500
1970-80	Covers ($): 2,000	4,000	6,000
1970-80	Covers(PB)		
	($): 1,500	2,500	4,000

Note: individual sales would include: cover to PB Book "World,World,Mad" (1973) selling for $2,875; book cv to "Mad Frontier" selling for $3,450; cover *More Trash From MAD* No. 3 (1960) selling at $4,600; cover to Fifth Annual Edition *More Trash MAD* (1962) selling at $6,325; cover to the Ninth Annual Edition of Works of *MAD* (1966, cover features Alfie with many pop stars including Dylan, Beatles, Elvis, Sinatra, etc.) selling for $19,550; cover to "Burning Mad" PB title(1975) sellin gat $2,875; cover to MAD No. 206 (1979) selling at $6,900; all sales from Sotheby's MAD About MAD auction in 1995.

MOEBIUS-JEAN-GIREAUD

Year	Publisher & Descriptive Information		
1970's	Arzach, Incal, Assorted European Publications		
	Covers ($): 1,500	2,500	5,500
	Pages ($): 400	800	1,200
1980's	*Lt. Blueberry*		
	Covers ($)xxx		
	Pages ($): 400	700	1,000
	Finished B&W illustrations		
	($): 500	700	1,500
	Finished Color illustrations		
	($): 800	1,600	2,500
	Silver Surfer		
	Covers ($): 800	1,200	1,500
	Pages ($): 200	400	600

MORROW-GRAY

Year	Publisher & Descriptive Information		
1956-58	Atlas: Mystery, sci-fi, fantasy, Western		
	Covers ($): [550	900	1,200]
	Pages ($): [100	150	200]
1959-61	Gilberton: *Classics Illustrated*		
	Covers ($): xxx		
	Pages ($): 50	75	125
1965-68	Warren: War, horror, *Creepy*		
	Covers ($): 500	800	1,100
	Pages ($): 150	250	350
	Marvel: Science fiction, horror		
	Covers ($): 400	600	800
	Pages ($): 50	100	150
1974-75	Red Circle: Horror		
	Covers ($): 200	300	400
	Pages ($): 25	50	75
	Wonder Woman, Madame Xanadu, etc		
	Covers ($): 200	300	400
1970-80s	DC:		
	Pages ($): 35	50	75
1983	Pacific Comics		
	Covers ($): xxx		
	Pages ($): 35	50	75

MOSCOSO-VICTOR

Year	Publisher & Descriptive Information		
1964-70	Fillmore West/East, Avalon Ballroom, The Family Dog poster designs (very few known to exist in the market.)		
	Poster Designs ($):[5,000	7,000	10,000]
1965-70	*ZAP Comix*, interior stories, *Jams*, covers		
	Covers ($): 3,000	5,000	[7,000]
	Pages ($): 350	650	[950]
1971-91	*ZAP, Color, Yellow Dog, Radical America, The Print Mint, Rip Off Press*		
	Covers ($): 2,000	2,500	3,000
	Pages ($): 350	550	750

1966-69 ZAP - the JAM pages. In tribute to the spirit of Victor Moscoso it is only appropriate that the JAM pages done for the interior front or back covers of ZAP comix be listed under his name. These very scarce pages were worked on by Robert Crumb, Gilbert Shelton, Rick Griffin, Spain, S. Clay Wilson, Victor, and Robert Williams. It was Victor who got the original crew of seven ZAP artists to think more as a group, to think about copyright laws, and to encourage the JAM pages. Because of Moscoso's senior age to the other six artists, and his experience as a professor at the San Francisco Institute of Art, he was able to encourage and develope a large part of the creative drive that lead ZAP Comix to become the most important comic book since Harvey Kurtzman's MAD.

(Note: these pages were held in trust by the artists themselves, and in only a very few cases have ever entered the public market; they are extremely rare.)

1966-69	JAM Pages-Crumb/Griffin/Moscoso/Shelton/Spain/Williams/Wilson		
	Pages ($): [8,000	14,000	20,000]
1970-90's	JAM Pages-Crumb/Griffin/Moscoso/Shelton/Spain/Williams/Wilson		
	Pages ($): [5,000	9,000	14,000]

Note: the last few in late 90's will be without Griffin.

NINO-ALEX

Year	Publisher & Descriptive Information			
1964-80's	DC Mystery titles			
	Covers ($):	xxx		
	Pages ($):	35	75	150
	Warren & Marvel magazine projects			
	Covers ($):	xxx		
	Pages ($):	35	75	175
	Illos. ($):	200	400	600

NOVIK-IRVING

Year	Publisher & Descriptive Information			
1940-42	MLJ: *Black Hood, Black Jack, Hangman, Scarlet Avenger, Shield, Steel Sterling, Web, Wizzard*			
	Covers ($):	[xxx	xxx	xxx]
	Pages ($):	[600	800	1,200]
	MLJ: *Bob Phantom, Boy Buddies, Capt. Commando, Kalthar*			
	Pages ($):	[300	400	500]
1943-46	MLJ:(pencils only) *Black Hood, Shield, Steel Sterling*			
	Covers ($):	[3,000	4,000	5,000]
	Pages ($):	[400	500	600]
1951-53	Ziff-Davis Publications: war titles			
	Pages ($):	[50	100	150]
1952-53	Ziff-Davis Publications: *G.I. Joe*			
	Pages ($):	[50	100	150]
1952-53	Stanmore Publications: war titles			
	Covers ($):	400	600	800
	Pages ($):	50	100	150
1955-67	National/DC: *Robin Hood, Sea Devils, Silent Knight, Space Ranger,* science fiction, mystery, sports-fantasy titles			
	Covers ($):	[2,000	4,000	6,000]
	Pages ($):	100	300	500
	DC: *Captian Storm, Gunner & Sarge, Haunted Tank, Johnny Cloud,* war titles			
	Covers ($):	1,200	1,600	2,000
	Pages ($):	75	150	225
1967-69	DC: *Batman & Robin*			
	Covers ($):	1,200	1,600	2,000
	Pages ($):	75	150	225

DC: *Captain Storm, Flash, Joker, Lois Lane, Wonder Woman,* war titles

Covers ($):	800	1,000	1,200
Pages ($):	50	100	150

NOWLAN-KEVIN

Year	Publisher & Descriptive Information			
1983-90	Marvel: *Critical Mass, Defenders, Dr. Strange, Dr. Zero, Hulk, Moon Knight, New Mutants, St. George, Wolverine*			
	Covers ($):	200	300	[450]
	Pages ($):	75	150	225
1984	Fantagraphics: *Grimwoods Daughter*			
	Covers ($):	xxx		
	Pages ($):	75	125	175
1985-91	DC: *Batman, Green Lantern, Man-Bat, Outsiders, Wonder Woman*			
	Covers ($):	200	300	[450]
	Pages ($):	75	150	225
	Plastic Man			
	Covers ($):	xxx		
	Pages ($):	50	75	125
1991	Atomeka: *Dalgoda*			
	Covers ($):	xxx		
	Pages ($):	100	150	200
1992	Continuity: *Armor*			
	Covers ($):	150	200	250
	Pages ($):	xxx		

ORDWAY-JERRY

Year	Publisher & Descriptive Information			
1981-92	DC: *Superman*			
	Covers ($):	***		
	Pages ($):	***		
	Batman			
	Covers ($):	***		
	Pages ($):	***		
	All Star Squadron, Batman, Infinity Inc.			
	Covers ($):	150	200	500
	Pages ($):	50	100	150

Joe Orlando, splash page from 7 page story entitled "I, Robot," from WEIRD SCIENCE FANTASY #27. Estimate: $1,200/1,500; sold for $1,100 in 1992 (Sotheby's 2nd comic art auction). © William M. Gaines/ EC Publications

Joe Orlando, splash page from DAREDEVIL #4, 10/64. Private sale at $1,000 in 1995 (TRH Galleries). © Marvel Comics Group

ORLANDO-JOE

Year	Publisher & Descriptive Information		
1950-51	Avon: Sci-fi, horror, mystery		
	Covers ($): [1,000	1,500	2,000]
	Pages ($): [200	400	600]
1951-58	EC: Sci-fi, humor, horror, crime and war stories		
	Covers ($): [2,000	2,500	4,000]
	Covers SF		
	($): [3,000	4,500	6,000]
	Pages ($): 200	300	400
1955-58	Atlas: Fantasy, mystery, war, science fiction		
	Covers ($): [800	1,200	1,600]
	Pages ($): 100	150	200
1959-60	Gilberton: *Classics Illustrated*		
	Covers ($): xxx		
	Pages ($): 50	100	150
1958-61	Prize: Mystery, romance, fantasy, crime		
	Covers ($): [300	600	900]
	Pages ($): 100	125	150
1964	Marvel: *Daredevil*		
	Covers ($): xxx		
	Pages ($): 200	300	400

1965-67	Warren: Horror		
	Covers ($): xxx		
	Pages ($): 100	150	200
1965	Gold Key: *Twilight Zone*, mystery titles;		
	Pages ($): 50	75	100
1967-99	DC: War, horror, humor		
	Covers ($): 125	200	250
	Pages ($): 40	80	120

Note: individual sales would include; "Judgment Day" from *Weird Fantasy* No. 18 (7 pgs) valued at $7,500; seven pg "Mistake in Miltiplication" from *Weird Fantasy* No. 9 selling at $1,380; six pg story "The Meddlers" from *Shock suspenstories* No. 9 selling at $690; four pg story from MAD No. 128 selling at $770; results from private sales, Sotheby's comic art, and MAD About MAD sales.

PACHECO-CARLOS

Year	Publisher & Descriptive Information		
1990's	*Bishop, Classic X-Men, Fantastic Four,* Marvel Projects		
	Covers ($): 100	200	300
	Pages ($): 50	75	125

PALAIS-RUDOLPH (RUDY)

Year	Publisher & Descriptive Information		
1941-42	Fiction House: *Captain Wings, Captain Flight, Kaanga, Kayo Kirby, Lost World, Red Comet, Rip Carson*		
	Pages ($): [200	400	600]
1942	Great Publications: *Futuro*		
	Pages ($): [400	600	800]
1942-44	Quality Publications: *Black Condor, Dollman, Phantom Lady, The Ray, Stormy Foster, The Unknown*		
	Pages ($): [600	800	1,000]
1944-46	Holyoke/Continental: *Catman*		
	Covers ($): [2,000	3,000	4,000]
	Pages ($): [600	800	1,000]
	Holyoke: *Captain Aero, The Deacon, Mr. Nobody, Sky Scouts,* war titles		
	Covers ($): [1,500	2,500	3,500]
	Pages ($): [300	500	700]
1944-47	Lev Gleason: *The Claw*		
	Pages ($): [400	600	800]
	Lev Gleason: *Hero of the Month,* Crime titles		
	Pages ($): [200	300	400]
1944-49	Hillman: *Black Angel, Boy King,* crime, sports, western titles		
	Pages ($): [200	300	400]
1945	Rural Home: *Lucky Aces,* crime titles		
	Pages ($): [200	300	400]
1945-49	Ace: *Captain Courageous, Magno and Davey*		
	Covers ($): [1,000	1,500	2,000]
	Pages ($): [200	300	400]
	Ace: *Mr. Risk, Unknown Soldier,* western, crime titles		
	Pages ($): [100	200	300]
1947	Dynamic: *Torpedoman*		
	Pages ($): [200	300	400]
1947	Prize: western titles		
	Pages ($): [50	100	150]
1945-54	Harvey Publications: *Black Cat, Captain Freedom*		
	Covers ($): 800	1,000	1,200

	Harvey: horror titles		
	Pages ($): 100	200	300
	Harvey: war titles		
	Pages ($): 75	100	125
1947-49	Avon Publications: crime, western titles		
	Pages ($): [100	150	200]
1947-54	Gilberton Publications: *Classics Illustrated* ("Crime & Punishment," "David Balfour," "The Gold Bug," "Men Against The Sea," "The Pioneers," "The Prarie," "Rob Roy")		
	Covers ($): [600	800	1,000]
	Pages ($): [50	100	150]
1948	National/DC: *Dr. Midnight*		
	Pages ($): [600	800	1,000]
1949-50	EC Publications: crime titles		
	Pages ($): 100	150	200
	EC: romance titles		
	Pages ($): 50	75	100
1950	Fawcett: romance titles		
	Pages ($): [50	75	100]
1962	A.C.G.: Fantasy and horror titles		
	Pages ($): [50	100	150]
1967-68	Charlton: horror titles		
	Pages ($): [50	100	150]

PAISIER-GARY

Year	Publisher & Descriptive Information		
1984-92	*Raw Books, RAW, WEIRDO, Jimbo*		
	Covers ($): 900	2,500	[4,000]
	Pages ($): 750	1,500	[2,250]
1992-98	Facetasm, & other recent works		
	Covers ($): 800	2,000	4,000
	Pages ($): 650	1,000	1,500
1980's -90's	Paintings ($): 3,000	5,000	9,000

PEARSON-JASON

Year	Publisher & Descriptive Information		
1990's	DC: *Starman, Legion*		
	Pages ($): 25	35	75
	Penthouse, Image projects		
	Covers ($): 100	150	250
	Pages ($): 50	100	150

Arthur Peddy & Bernard Sachs, artwork for cover to ALL STAR COMICS #54, 1950. Estimate: $8,000/12,000; sold for $8,625 in 1996 (Sotheby's 6th comic art auction). © National Periodical Publications/DC Comics

Arthur Peddy & Bernard Sachs, artwork for cover to ALL STAR COMICS #50, 1950. Estimate: $7,000/10,000; sold for $6,900 in 1996 (Sotheby's 6th comic art auction). © National Periodical Publications/DC Comics

PEREZ-JOE

Year	Publisher & Descriptive Information		
1974-91	Marvel: *Infinity Gauntlet, Avengers, Fantastic Four*		
	Covers ($): 150	300	500
	Pages ($): 75	150	225
	Black Widow, Captain America, Defenders, Ghost Rider, Inhumans, Iron Man, Powerman, Thing		
	Covers ($): 150	300	600
	Pages ($): 50	100	150
	Beatles, John Carter, Mighty Mouse		
	Covers ($): 100	125	150
	Pages ($): 40	60	80
1980-91	DC: *Batman, Crisis, History of the DC Universe, Justice League, Superman, Teen Titans, Wonder Woman.*		
	Covers ($): 300	500	750
	Pages ($): 75	150	225
	Flash, Outsiders, Green Lantern		
	Covers ($): 150	200	275
	Pages ($): 40	80	125

All Star Squadron, Amethyst, Firestorm

Covers ($):	100	150	225
Pages ($):	35	70	100

Misc. mystery, war

Covers ($):	xxx		
Pages ($):	25	50	75

Note: the entire *Crisis* cover series sold privately in 1999 for over $1,500 per cover.

PETER-H.G.

Year	Publisher & Descriptive Information		
1941-44	Eastern Color/Famous Funnies:		
	Pages ($): xxx		
1950-52	*Fearless Flint*		
	Covers ($): xxx		
	Pages ($): [150	250	350]
	Heroic adventure		
	Covers ($): xxx		
	Pages ($): [100	200	300]
1942-58	National/DC: *Wonder Woman*		
	Covers ($): [2,500	3,000	5,000]
	Pages ($): 300	450	600

George Perez & Terry Austin, cover artwork for THE AVENGERS #171, 7/80. Estimate: $1,000/1,400; sold for $1,210 in 1992 (Sotheby's 2nd comic art auction). © Marvel Comics Group

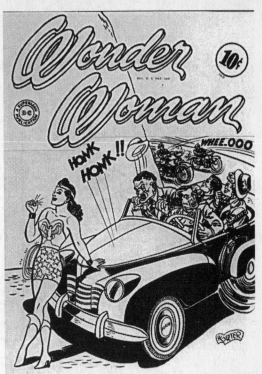

Harry G. Peter, unpublished cover artwork for WONDER WOMAN, 1940's. Estimate: $6,000/8,000; sold for $5,750 in 1996 (Sotheby's 6th comic art auction). © National Periodical Publications/DC Comics

Note: individual sales would include; unpublished cover for Wonder Woman (circa 1940's) selling for $5,750.

PINI-WENDY

Year	Publisher & Descriptive Information		
1978-91	*Elfquest, WARP Graphics, Elfquest Portfolios, Beauty and the Beast*		
	Covers ($): 500	1,000	[1,700]
	Pages ($): 500	750	1,000

Note Wendy Pini has had close connections to science fiction fandom, and over the years has done a number of special color originals for fans. These originals range in size from 8½" x 11" and larger.

($):	500	750	[1,200]

PLATT-STEVEN

Year	Publisher & Descriptive Information		
1990's	*Prophet, Moonknight,* etc.		
	Covers ($): 200	300	500
	Pages ($): 50	125	200

PLOOG-MIKE

Year	Publisher & Descriptive Information		
1973-79	Marvel: *Ghost Rider*		
	Covers ($): 400	800	1,200
	Pages ($): 100	200	300
	Conan, Frankenstein, Kull, Manthing, Weird Worlds, Werewolf by Night		
	Covers ($): 400	600	800
	Pages ($): 100	150	300
1989-90	First: *Tom Sawyer*		
	Covers ($): 300	600	800
	Pages ($): 100	200	300
	Illos. ($): 400	800	1,200

PLUNKETT-KILIAN

Year	Publisher & Descriptive Information		
1990's	*Star Wars* and Dark Horse projects		
	Covers ($): 400	650	800
	Pages ($): 150	175	225

SUPERMAN

THIS STORY, PREPARED IN CLOSE COOPERATION WITH THE LATE *PRESIDENT KENNEDY*, WAS SCHEDULED FOR PUBLICATION IN *SUPERMAN* NO. 168, WHEN WORD OF HIS TRAGIC ASSASSINATION REACHED US. WE IMMEDIATELY TOOK IT OFF THE PRESS AND SUBSTITUTED OTHER MATERIAL. HOWEVER, WHITE HOUSE OFFICIALS HAVE SINCE INFORMED US THAT *PRESIDENT JOHNSON* WANTED IT PUBLISHED, AS A TRIBUTE TO HIS GREAT PREDECESSOR. AND SO WE DEDICATE TO THE MEMORY OF OUR LATE, BELOVED PRESIDENT THIS PLEA FOR HIS PHYSICAL FITNESS PROGRAM, TO WHICH HE WAS WHOLEHEARTEDLY DEVOTED DURING HIS LIFE...

"SUPERMAN'S MISSION for PRESIDENT KENNEDY!"

Al Plastino, 10 page story from SUPERMAN #170, 2/64. Estimate: $5,000/6,000; sold for $5,175 in 6/93 (Sotheby's 3rd comic art auction). © National Periodical Publications/DC Comics

POPE-PAUL

Year	Publisher & Descriptive Information
1992-97	Horse Press, Dark Horse, Oni Press, DC: *Sin Titulo, Ballad of Doctor Richardson, THB, One Trick Rip-Off, Batman Chronicles*

Covers ($):	xxx		
Pages ($):	xxx		

POPLASKI-PETER

Year	Publisher & Descriptive Information
1969-89	*Corporate Crime, Comic Book*

Covers ($):	200	400	650
Pages ($):	100	200	300

1989-92	*Batman,* and related covers/pages

Pages ($):	600	700	800

Oil paintings on current themes

($):	700	950	1,200

PORTACIO-WHILCE

Year	Publisher & Descriptive Information
1990's	*X-Factor, Iron Man, X-Men, Punisher,* etc

Covers ($):	200	400	800
Pages ($):	75	150	300

POWELL-BOB

Year	Publisher & Descriptive Information
1939-41	Fiction House: *Auro, Carnilla, Captain Nelson, Cob, Flint Baker, Gab Allen, Power Man, Inspector Dayton, Sheena,* and others

Covers ($):	[***]		
Pages ($):	[100	200	300]

1939-41	Fox: *Blue Beetle, D-13, Dr. Fung, Flame, Green Mask*

Covers ($):	xxx		
Pages ($):	[100	200	300]

1940-44	Quality: *Mr. Mystic*

Covers ($):	xxx		
Pages ($):	[200	400	600]

Abdul the Arab, Lee Preston, Loops N Banks, Spin Shaw

Covers ($):	xxx		
Pages ($):	[100	200	300]

1942-66	Harvey: *Man In Black*

Covers ($):	400	650	[950]
Pages ($):	100	150	200

Bob Powell, splash page from 8 page story from JET POWERS #3, 1951. Estimate: $700/900; sold for $9901 in 1992 (Sotheby's 2nd comic art auction). © M.E. Publications

Black Cat, Flying Fool, Green Hornet, Scarlet Arrow, Spirit of '76

Covers ($):	300	450	[900]
Pages ($):	75	100	125

Horror, sci-fi

Covers ($):	[500	900	1,400]
Pages ($):	75	100	125

Humor, *Ripley's,* romance, war

Covers ($):	xxx		
Pages ($):	50	75	100

1948-51	Hillman: Crime, sports

Covers ($):	xxx		
Pages ($):	50	75	100

1946-49	Street & Smith: *The Shadow*

Covers ($):	[***]		
Pages ($):	[150	300	450]

Doc Savage, Nick Carter, Red Dragon

Covers ($):	[***]		
Pages ($):	[100	150	250]

Air Ace, Bill Barnes, Buffalo Bill, Ghost Breakers, Tim McCoy, crime, sports

Covers ($):	[300	500	700]

PRICE RANGE KEY

RARITY — Brackets [ ] around a price indicate that this example is very scarce and could exceed maximum estimate.

	Covers
No work produced in this category—	XXX
No price available due to lack of information—	***

CONDITION — Age, color, marks, tears, etc.

Pages
[400 500 600]

CHARACTER — Is the primary character featured, or is the original characteristic of a great example in the story line?

CONTENT — is the theme or story line exceptional or below average?

VALUE RANGE

Minimum Medium Maximum

RARITY

The [ ] Brackets indicate RARITY, if these brackets are used the reader can potentially double the price range in all three catagories.

		Pages ($):	[75	100	125]
1948-53	Fawcett: Horror, sci-fi-n				
		Covers ($):	xxx		
		Pages ($):	100	150	200
	Crime, romance, war, Western, and others				
		Covers ($):	xxx		
		Pages ($):	50	75	100
1949-57	Marvel/Atlas: *Sub-Mariner*				
		Covers ($):	xxx		
		Pages ($):	250	450	650
	Fantasy, horror, sci-fi				
		Covers ($):	xxx		
		Pages ($):	[100	125	150]
	Crime, war, Western				
		Covers ($):	xxx		
		Pages ($):	50	75	100
1950-57	M.E.: *Jet Powers, Major Inapak*				
		Covers ($):	[800	1,200	1,600]
		Pages ($):	100	200	300
	Avenger, Cave Girl, Thunda				
		Covers ($):	600	1,200	[1,800]
		Pages ($):	100	125	150
	Bobby Benson, Lemonade Kid, Red Hawk, Robin Hood, Straight Arrow, Strong Man, Undercover Girl, misc. crime, romance, war, Western, and others				
		Covers ($):	300	500	[700]
		Pages ($):	50	75	100
1951-52	Ziff-Davis: Horror				
		Covers ($):	xxx		
		Pages ($):	75	100	125
	Sports, war				
		Covers ($):	xxx		
		Pages ($):	25	50	75
1954-55	St. John: Horror				
		Covers ($):	xxx		
		Pages ($):	75	100	125
	Crime				
		Covers ($):	xxx		
		Pages ($):	50	75	100
1959	Archie: *Fly*				
		Covers ($):	xxx		
		Pages ($):	75	100	125
1965	Marvel: *Daredevil, Giantman, Hulk, Human Torch*				

Covers ($):   xxx
Pages ($):   200   400   600

Note: individual sales would include: *The Avenger* cover No. 1 (1955) selling for $660; five page story entitled "Colorama" from *Black Cat Mystery* No. 45 selling at $1,035; six pg story from *Cave Girl* No. 11 selling for $518; all sales at Sotheby's.

PROHIAS-ANTONIO

A Cuban artist who became very important as a political cartoonist in Cuba. Because of some anti-Fidel cartoons Prohias fled Cuba, and in 1961 began to work for Bill Gaines doing the famous "Spy VS Spy" feature for MAD.

Year	Publisher & Descriptive Information
1961-80's	*Mad Magazine, Spy VS Spy* one and two page features.

Pages ($):   175   225   325

Note: individual sales would include; 3 pgs from MAD Nos. 138-139, 143 selling for $920; three pgs from MAD Nos. 126,134,126, selling at $1,092; three pgs from MAD Nos. 124, 145,147, fetching $1,150; all sales from Sotheby's MAD About MAD auction in 1995.

QUESADA-JOE

Year	Publisher & Descriptive Information
1990's	*X-Men, Asrael, Ash*

Covers ($):   300   500   900
Pages ($):   80   150   250

RAYBOY-MAC

Year	Publisher & Descriptive Information
1940	Prize Publ.: *Green Lama*

Covers ($):   xxx
Pages ($):   [400   600   800]

1940-46   Fawcett: *Captain Marvel, Captain Marvel Jr, Captain Midnight, Mary Marvel*

Covers ($):   [4,000   8,000 12,000]
Pages ($):   [800   1,600   2,400]

Dynamic Publ.: *Dynamic Man*

Covers ($): [2,500   5,000   8,500]
Pages ($):   [600   900   1,400]

Spark Publ.: *Green Lama*

Covers ($): [4,000   6,000   7,500]
Pages ($):   [500   900   1,200]

Note: it should be noted that Raboy and assistants to him while working at Fawcett often employed the use of photostats of Captain Marvel Jr. figures previously drawn over and over again in order to save time. Rayboy was a very slow artist. So popular was Rayboy's work on Captain Marvel Jr. that even after he left Fawcett Publications in 1944, other artists who took over after he left continued to emulate Rayboy's inking style, both on covers and with interior pages for stories.

Note: individual sales would include the cover to Master Comics No. 27 (1942-considered one of the finest surviving Rayboy super hero covers) selling at $11,000 at Sotheby's in 1992.

REDONDO-NESTOR

Year	Publisher & Descriptive Information
	Swamp Thing;Black Orchid, & various DC Projects;

Covers ($):   100   200   300
Pages ($):   30   50   75

REINMAN-PAUL

Year	Publisher & Descriptive Information
1944-49	DC: Golden Age *Green Lantern*

Covers ($):   xxx
Pages ($):   200   400   600

1957-66   Marvel: Pre-Hero Fantasy work

Covers ($):   xxx
Pages ($):   30   50   80

1960's-70's   *Archie Comics, Red Circle*

Covers ($):   100   200   300
Pages ($):   35   75   100

ROBBINS-TRINA

Year	Publisher & Descriptive Information
1966-82	*East Village Other, Gothic Blimp Works, All Gin' Thrills!, It Ain't Me Babe, Girl Fight, Yellow Dog, Wimmens Comix*

Covers ($):   200   300   350
Pages ($):   75   150   250

Mac Rayboy, original cover artwork for MASTER COMICS #27, 1942. Estimate: $11,000/15,000; sold for $11,000 in 1992 (Sotheby's 2nd comic art auction). © Fawcett publications

Fred Ray, original cover artwork for SUPERMAN #17, 7/42. Estimate: $20,000/40,000; sold for $32,000 in 6/97 (Sotheby's 7th comic art auction). © National Periodical Publications/DC Comics

Fred Ray & Jerry Robinson, cover artwork for BATMAN #12, 1942. Estimate: $15,000/25,000; sold for $21,850 in 6/97 (Sotheby's 7th comic art auction). © National Periodical Publications/DC Comics

Joe Shuster, 2 pages from Shuster's sketchbook depicting how Superman could be merchandised in 1936. The 2 pages are laminated, sold with the origin artwork SUPERMAN Daily Strip at Sotheby's, June 19, 1994. © National Periodiacal Publications/DC Comics

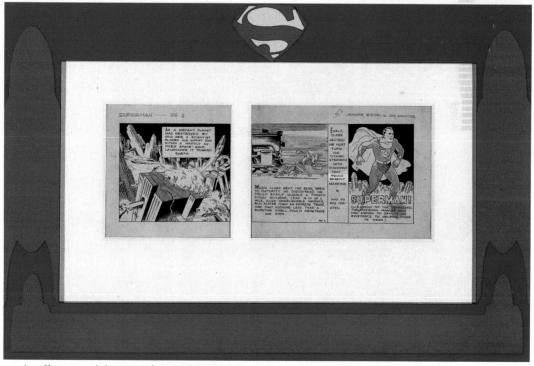

Joe Shuster, origin artwork to SUPERMAN Daily No. 1, circa 1930's, pen and ink on Craftint paper, offered at Sotheby's 4th comic art auction, June 18, 1994, selling one day after the auction for $77,000. © National Periodical Publications/DC Comics.

Note: Refer to "The Superman Daily Strip No. 1: The Complete Story" by Roger Hill on page 40.

Hal Foster, original hand watercolored PRINCE VALIANT Sunday Page dated 8/7/38, No. 78 in this series. This Sunday page is the only PRINCE VALIANT confirmed as colored by Hal Foster. Sold in 1996 by the Alexander Gallery, New York City. © King Features Syndicate

Note: Refer to "Hand-Colored Original Comic Art" by Jerry Weist on page 35.

George Herriman, original hand watercolored KRAZY KAT Sunday Page dated 8/29/36. The matt is watercolored by the artist as is the hand painted wood frame. © King Features Syndicate.

Note: Refer to "Hand-Colored Original Comic Art" by Jerry Weist on page 35.

Hal Foster, original artwork for hand-colored Sunday Page for TARZAN, dated 1/1/33. This original was presented by Foster to Edgar Rice Burroughs as a gift at the authors request in 1933. The tan lines on the panels are the result of shadows from the deep cut matt. © United Features Syndicate.
Note: Refer to "Hand-Colored Original Comic Art" by Jerry Weist on page 35.

Lawrence Herndon, original artwork for BlueBook "Tarzan" cover, circa 1930's, oil on canvas, sold privately in 1998 for $15,000. © Edgar Rice Burroughs Inc.

Burne Hogarth, original artwork for TARZAN
Sunday Page dated 5/16/43, hand-colored by the
artist in 1994 and inscribed to Danton Burroughs.
© United Features Syndicate/ERB Inc.

Burne Hogarth, original artwork for TARZAN
Sunday Page dated 12/13/42, hand-colored by the
artist in 1994 and inscribed to Danton Burroughs.
© United Features Syndicate/ERB Inc.

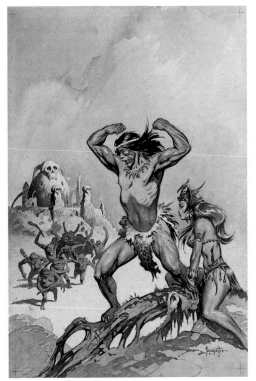

Frank Frazetta, original artwork for Ace Paperback
Burroughs cover entitled "Tarzan the Invincible."
© Edgar Rice Burroughs Inc.

Burne Hogarth, original artwork for TARZAN
Sunday Page dated 6/7/42, hand-colored by the
artist in 1994 and inscribed to Danton Burroughs.
© United Features Syndicate/ERB Inc.

Virgil Finlay, original artwork for cover painting to *Fantastic Universe* for January, 1959; sold at Sotheby's 1995 auction for $4,600.
© King Size Publications

Virgil Finlay, original artwork for SF BookClub Advertisement for Arthur C. Clarke's *The Lion of Comarre & Against the Fall of Night*, 1972.
© The SF Book Club inc.

Ed Emshwiller, original artwork for the cover painting to *The Magazine of Science and Fiction*, illustrating "Soft Landing," for June 1960.
© The Mercury Press Inc.

Chesley Bonestell, original artwork for "The Binary Beta Lyrae," from *Beyond the Solar System*, The Viking Press, 1964.
© The Viking Press/Bonestell Estate.

RODRIGUEZ-SPAIN-(SPAIN)

Year	Publisher & Descriptive Information
1966-70	*East Village Other, Zodiac Mindwarp, Trashman, Gothic Blimp Works, Insect Fear*

Covers ($):	700	950	[2,000]
Pages ($):	150	225	[300]

Young Lust, ZAP, Print Mint, Tales of the Leather Nun

Covers ($):	750	1,500	2,500
Pages ($):	250	300	350

Year	Publisher & Descriptive Information
1971-90's	*Trashman, ZAP* & other titles

Covers ($):	600	1,400	2,000
Pages ($):	200	250	300

ROGERS-MARSHALL

Year	Publisher & Descriptive Information
1976-91	DC: *Batman*

Covers ($):	600	1,200	1,800
Pages ($):	300	450	700

Madame Xanadu, Man-Bat, Mr. Miracle

Covers ($):	400	800	1,200
Pages ($):	150	250	350

Atari Force, Justice League, Shadow, Superman, Vigilante

Covers ($):	200	400	600
Pages ($):	100	150	200

Misc. mystery, sci-fi

Covers ($):	xxx		
Pages ($):	50	100	150

Year	Publisher & Descriptive Information
1979-91	Marvel: *Dr. Strange, Spider-Man*

Covers ($):	600	900	1,200
Pages ($):	150	250	350

Daredevil, Defenders, "Demon With a Glass Hand," Excalibur, Fantastic Four, G.I. Joe, Hulk, Silver Surfer, Spitfire, Wild Cards

Covers ($):	200	400	600
Pages ($):	75	100	125

Year	Publisher & Descriptive Information
1980-85	Eclipse: *Cap'n Quick & A Foozle, Coyote, Detective, Inc., Scorpio Rose*

Covers ($):	200	400	600
Pages ($):	75	100	150

John Romita, artwork for cover re-creation to AMAZING SPIDER-MAN #39, 1994. Estimate: $3,000/5,000; sold for $2,300 in 1994 (Sotheby's 4th comic art auction). © Marvel Comics Group

ROMITA-JOHN

Year	Publisher & Descriptive Information
1949	Eastern Color/Famous Funnies: Misc. romance

Covers ($):	xxx		
Pages ($):	[***]		

Year	Publisher & Descriptive Information
1950-56	Atlas/Marvel: *Captain America*

Covers ($):	[2,000	4,000	6,000]
Pages ($):	[400	600	800]

Horror, sci-fi

Covers ($):	[800	1,200	1,600]
Pages ($):	[100	200	300]

Misc. crime, jungle, war, Western—*Ringo Kid, Western Kid,* others

Covers ($):	[600	800	1,000]
Pages ($):	[75	150	225]

Romance

Covers ($):	[500	700	900]
Pages ($):	[50	75	100]

1953-66 National/DC: *Romance*

Covers ($): [xxx]

1966-77 Marvel: *Captain America, Daredevil*

Covers ($):	1,000	2,000	3,000
Covers - twice up size			
($):	2,000	3,000	4,000

The Amazing Spider-Man

Covers - twice up size			
($):	5,000	10,000	15,000
Covers - regular size			
($):	3,000	6,000	9,000
Pages - Twice Up in size			
($):	400	800	1,200
Pages ($):	300	600	900

Avengers, Conan, Dr. Strange, Fantastic Four, Ghost Rider, Hulk, Iron Man, Kazar, Shanna the She-Devil, Sub-Mariner, Team-Up, X-Men, Ms.Marvel, etc.

Covers ($):	600	1,200	1,800
Pages ($):	100	200	300

1990's Cover re-creations for Marvel Spider-Man classic covers

Covers ($):	1,500	2,000	2,500

Note: individual prices would include: splash page for *Spider-Man* No. 39 (the first Romita issue) selling at $5,750; the cover for *Spider-Man* No. 40 selling at $18,975; cover re-creation for *Spider-Man* No. 39 selling at $2,200; cover re-creation for *Spider-Man* No. 50 selling at $3,300; cover re-creation for *Spider-Man* No. 100 selling for $3,575; cover for *Spider-Man* No. 53 selling for $14,950; all sales at Sotheby's comic art auctions.

ROMITA-JR.-JOHN

Year	Publisher & Descriptive Information
1980's-90's	Marvel: *X-Men, Ironman, Spider-Man, Daredevil, Punisher,* other Marvel Projects

Covers ($):	75	200	450
Pages ($):	25	75	150

ROSENBERG-JOHN

Year	Publisher & Descriptive Information
1960's	DC Romance titles

Pages ($):	30	50	75

Archie Comics Group: *Jaguar, The Fly*

Covers ($):	400	800	1,200
Pages ($):	50	100	150

ROSS-ALEX

Year	Publisher & Descriptive Information
1990's	Marvel Comics: *Kingdom Come,* including promotional illustrations

Covers ($):	2,000	3,000	4,500
Pages ($):	300	700	1,400

Astro City

Covers ($):	1,250	1,750	2,250

Superman, Peace on Earth

Cover ($):	2,000	3,000	4,500
Pages ($):	1,000	2,000	3,000

Batman, War on Crime

Cover ($):	4,000	6,000	8,000
Pages ($):	1,500	2,500	3,500

Note: pages for *Superman, Peace on Earth* and *Batman, War on Crime* are double-page spreads existing on one sheet. Prices realized on *Superman, Peace on Earth* include: cover selling for $6,325; inside front cover for $6,325; double page spread to pages 26-27 selling at $13,800; double page spread to pages 20-21 selling for $6,325.

RUDE-STEVE

Year	Publisher & Descriptive Information
1981-91	Capitol/First: *Nexus*

Covers ($):	***		
Pages ($):	75	200	325

Badger

Covers ($):	***		
Pages ($):	xxx		

1984-91 DC: *Superman, Batman*

Covers ($):	***		
Pages ($):	100	250	450

Mr. Miracle

Covers ($):	200	250	350
Pages ($):	50	100	150

Kurt Schaffenberger, sample tryout page for LOIS LANE AND SUPERMAN, 9/57. Estimate: $1,000/1,500; sold for $3,575 in 1992 (Sotheby's 2nd comic art auction). © National Periodical Publications/DC Comics

Teen Titans

Covers ($):	100	150	200
Pages ($):	50	100	150

1986-87 Comico: *Space Ghost*

Covers ($):	***		
Pages ($):	150	250	350

Johnny Quest

Covers ($):	xxx		
Pages ($):	50	100	150

1990 Kitchen Sink: *Kings in Disguise*

Covers ($):	***	
Pages ($):	xxx	

RUSSELL-P.-CRAIG

Year	Publisher & Descriptive Information
1970-80's	*Dr. Strange, Killraven*, other titles

Covers ($):	150	300	450
Pages ($):	40	80	150

SACCO-JOE

Year	Publisher & Descriptive Information
1986-97	Fantagraphics, Dark Horse, Drawn

& Quarterly: *Yahoo, Palestine, American Splendor, Stories from Bosnia*

Covers ($):	300	400	500
Pages ($):	200	200	250

Pages (with different author)

($):	100	125	150

SALE-JIM

Year	Publisher & Descriptive Information
1990's	*Batman, Deathblow*

Covers ($):	150	225	350
Pages ($):	50	75	125

SALMONS-TONY

Year	Publisher & Descriptive Information
1990's	Marvel One-Shot Projects; *Dakota North, Penthouse Comics, Vigilante*

Covers ($):	100	200	300
Pages ($):	40	80	150

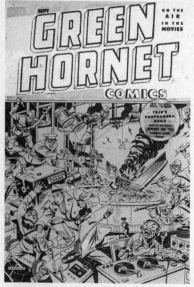

Alex Schomburg, artwork for cover to GREEN HORNET #20, 1944. Estimate: $4,000/6,000; sold for $4,312 in 1996 (Sotheby's 6th comic art auction).
© Harvey Publications Inc.

Alex Schomburg, artwork for cover to ALL-NEW COMICS #10, 1944. Estimate: $4,000/6,000; sold for $4,025 in 1996 (Sotheby's 6th comic art auction).
© Harvey Publications Inc.

Alex Schomburg, artwork for cover to ALL-NEW COMICS #9, 1944. Estimate: $2,500/3,500; sold for $1,750 in 6/93 (Sotheby's 3rd comic art auction).
© Harvey Publications Inc.

SCHOMBURG-ALEX

Year	Publisher & Descriptive Information
1940-48	*Timely: Angel, Captain America, Human Torch, Sub-Mariner

Covers ($): [4,000   8,000 14,000]

(*Note: no previously known covers exist, however in 1998 a prime Human Torch cover was discovered.)

Pages ($): [800   1,000   1,500]

Blue Blaze, Blue Diamond, Captain Daring, Captain Wonder, Challenger, Dynamic Man, Fin, Young Allies, and others

Covers ($): [***]
Pages ($): xxx

1940-51   Standard: Black Terror, Dr. Strange, Fighting Yank

Covers ($): [***]
Pages ($): xxx

(Airbrushed covers): Judy of the Jungle, Princess Pantha, Tara, Tygra

Covers ($):[4,000   8,000 12,000]
Pages ($): xxx

Group;   Brick Bradford, Commando Cubs, Grim Reaper, Wonderman

Covers ($): [3,000   6,000   9,000]
Pages ($):   xxx

Bronco Bill, Captain Easy, misc. romance, teenage, Western

Covers ($): [800   1,200   1,600]
Pages ($):   xxx

1944   Holyoke: Captain Aero

Covers ($): [2,000   4,000   6,000]
Pages ($):   xxx

1944-45   Harvey: Black Cat, Boy Heroes, Captain Freedom, Green Hornet, Red Blazer, Shock Gibson, Young Commandoes

Covers ($): 3,000   4,000   5,000
Pages ($)xxx

1950   Ziff-Davis: Sci-fi

Covers ($):   xxx
Pages ($): [800   1,200   1,600]

1970's-   Classic Timely cover-re-creation
1980   paintings, done originally for Howard Lowery's auctions, at the encouragment of Mr. Lowery for Mr. Schomburg.

(note: these paintings remained stable during the 1980's, however as the 1990's have moved on they have begun to explode in both demand and price.)

Paintings for Timely
Covers ($): [4,000   6,000   9,000]

Alex Schomburg is one of the most respected artists who worked during the Golden Age of Comics. His crisp, clean drawing style, coupled with a well-balanced poster-like design, gave him an edge in producing some of the finest and most popular comic covers during the 1940s. His figure work was always anatomically correct and precise. He became known for his great attention to detail and "action-packed" covers created for Timely's *Marvel Mystery Comics*, *Captain America*, and other titles. Unfortunately, most of Schomburg's art for Timely is unaccounted for at this time. Nine years ago approximately a dozen vintage Golden Age covers by Schomburg produced for the Harvey Publishing Company for such titles as *All New Comics*, *Green Hornet Comics*, and *Speed Comics*, surfaced from a New York City warehouse and were sold into the market-place.

Note: individual prices would include: cover for *Green Hornet* No. 22 selling at $2,750; cover for *Green Hornet* No. 21 selling at $4,132; cover for *All-New Comics* No. 10 selling for $4,025; cover for *Green Hornet* No. 20 selling for $4,312; all sales at Sotheby's comic art auctions. At Christie's East a painting re-creation for *U.S.A. Comics* No. 10 sold for $11,500 in 1994, and in 1996 a re-creation painting for *Captain America* No. 28 sold for $11,500.

SCHULTZ-MARK

Mark Schultz is a very popular contemporary artist who occassionally trades his artwork to fans in the market place. Some of these covers and pages have been sold between collectors and prices are now established.

Year	Publisher & Descriptive Information
1987-92	Kitchen Sink: *Xenozoic Tales*

Covers ($): [1,500   2,000   2,500]

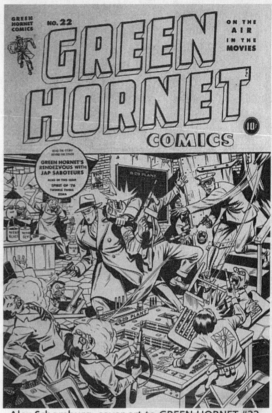
Alex Schomburg, cover art to GREEN HORNET #22, 1945. Estimate: $3,500/4,500; sold for $3,025 in 1992 (Sotheby's 3rd comic art auction).
© Harvey Publications Inc.

Alex Schomburg, cover recreation to U.S.A. COMICS #10, 1943. © Timely Publications

Pages ($): 400 600 800

1990-91 Epic: *Cadillacs & Dinosaurs* (Same as above with new covers)
    Covers ($): 1,500 2,000 2,500
    Pages ($): 400 600 800

1990's Recent Projects
    Covers ($): 900 1,400 2,500
    Pages ($): 400 550 800

SEKOWSKI-MIKE

Year	Publisher & Descriptive Information

1941-50 Marvel: *Human Torch, Sub-Mariner, Captain America, Young Allies, Whizzer, Super Rabbit*
    Covers ($): xxx
    Pages ($): 400 800 1,200

1951-56 Crime, Western, horror
    Covers ($): ***
    Pages ($): 100 200 300

1952-70 DC: Western sci-fi war, *Supergirl, Jimmy Olsen, Justice League of America, Adam Strange*

Note: Only *Justice League* artwork will hit top price ranges.

    Covers -twice up size
    for *Justice League*
        ($): 3,500 7,000 11,000
    Pages - twice up size
    for *Justice League*
        ($): 200 400 600
    Pgs/Rglr($): 150 250 400

1953 Pines: War pages and covers
    Covers ($): [300 600 900]
    Pages ($): 75 125 175

1954 Fiction House: Sci-fi, War
    Covers ($): [400 700 1,000]
    Pages ($): 75 150 225

1954-55 Sterling: *Captain Flash*
    Covers ($): [600 1,200 1,800]
    Pages ($): 150 250 350

1960 Gilberton: *Classics Illustrated, Jr.*
    Covers ($): xxx
    Pages ($): 50 75 100

1965 Archie: *Mighty Crusaders*
    Covers ($): 400 800 1,200
    Pages ($): 75 125 175

1965-68 Tower: *Nomad, Dynamo*
    Covers ($): xxx
    Pages ($): 75 100 125

1971 Marvel: *Dr. Doom*
    Covers ($): xxx
    Pages ($): 50 75 100

1974-75 Atlas/Seaboard: *IronJaw, Lomax*
    Covers ($): xxx
    Pages ($): 50 60 70

Note: individual prices would include: the splash page to *Justice League of America* No. 1 (possibly the most important JLA Sekowsky page that could ever surface) selling at Sotheby's in 1993 at $8,050.

SEVERIN-JOHN

Year	Publisher & Descriptive Information

1947-58 Crestwood: **American Eagle, Black Bull, Fargo Kid, Lazo Kid*
    Covers ($): [800 1,200 1,600]
    Pages ($): 100 200 300

Crime, romance
    Covers ($): xxx
    Pages ($): [100 150 200]

1948-51 Standard: **Western*
    Covers ($): [600 1,000 1,400]
    Pages ($): [100 150 200]

Romance
    Covers ($): xxx
    Pages ($): [50 75 100]

1948-60 Marvel/Atlas: Fantasy, horror, sci-fi, *Yellow Claw*
    Covers ($): [2,000 3,000 4,000]
    Pages ($): [150 300 450]

Apache Kid, Black Rider, Combat Casey, Devil-Dog Dugan, Kid Colt, Rawhide Kid, Ringo Kid, Sgt. Barney Parker, Two-Gun Kid, Western Kid, Wyatt Earp, misc. war and Western
    Covers ($): [800 1,200 1,600]
    Pages ($): [100 175 250]

Adventure, crime, humor
    Covers ($): [800 900 1,200]
    Pages ($): [75 125 150]

1951-55 EC: Humor- *MAD,* *sci-fi
    Covers ($): xxx
    Pages ($): 200 350 550

Mike Sekowski, artwork for interior page
to JUSTICE LEAGUE OF AMERICA #17, 1963.
Estimate: $300/500; sold for $173 in 1993
(Sotheby's 3rd comic art auction).
© National Periodical Publications/DC Comics

Gilbert Shelton, example from 8 page story to
WONDER WART-HOG, 1967. Estimate: $1,500/2,000;
sold for $2,475 in 1992 (Sotheby's 2nd comic art
auction). © The Print Mint

Gilbert Shelton, interior page for FREAK BROTHERS.
Private sale at $1,000 in 1998 (T.R.H. Galleries).
© Gilbert Shelton

Joe Shuster, artwork to profile drawing of
SUPERMAN, circa 1940-41. Estimate: $1,000/1,500;
sold for $1,540 in 1992 (Sotheby's 2nd comic art
auction). © National Periodical Publications/
DC Comics

War, Western
    covers ($): 1,000   2,000   3,000
    Pages ($): 200   300   400

* Some of this art was inked by assistant Bill Elder. The two artists worked together as a team for several years.

1956	Gilberton: *Classics Illustrated:* "Last of the Mohicans"

Covers ($):   xxx
Pages ($):   [75   150   225]

1956-59 National/DC: War
    Covers ($):   xxx
    Pages ($):   [200   300   400]

1958-61 Charlton: *Billy the Kid, Cheyenne Kid*
    Covers ($): [600 1,000 1,400]
    Pages ($):   [100   150   200]

1958-63 Harvey: Fantasy, mystery
    Covers ($):   400   600 [800]
    Pages ($):   xxx

1963-64 I.W.: Fantasy, Western
    Covers ($):   [600   800 1,000]
    Pages ($):   xxx

1965-68 Marvel: *Hulk, Sgt. Fury, Nick Fury,* and others
    Covers ($):   400   800 1,200
    Pages ($):   200   300   400

1970-74 DC: *Losers, Sgt. Rock,* misc. war
    Covers ($):   [500   700   900]
    Pages ($):   [200   300   400]

1971-73 Marvel: *Conan, Dracula, Kull, Sub-Mariner,* war, others
    Covers ($):   [800 1,200 1,600]
    Pages ($):   [200   400   600]

SHELTON-GILBERT

Year	Publisher & Descriptive Information
1967-70	*Wonder-Wart Hog,* (Pete Miller Pub .), *HELP!,* Warren Publications

Covers ($): 1,500 2,500 [4,500]
Covers - painted covers for magazine *Wonder-Wart Hog*
    ($): 2,500 3,500 [7,500]
Pages ($): 200   400   800

Feds n' Heads, Freak Brothers, Gothic Blimp Works, Yellow Dog, ZAP

Covers ($): [2,500 3,500 5,000]
Pages ($): 450   600   750

Freak Brothers, ZAP (by *Freak Brothers* No. 4, Shelton began with inks by artist Dave Sheridan)
    Covers ($): 2,000 2,500 [3,500]
    Pages ($): 600   800 1,000

1978 -90's	*Freak Brothers,* Shelton and artist Paul Mavrides working together

Covers - by Mavrides/ Shelton are in full color
    ($): 1,500 2,500 3,750

1977-92 *ZAP, Fat Freddy's Cat,* etc.
    Covers ($): 2,000 2,500 4,000
    Pages ($): 400   550   700

SHERIDAN-DAVE

Year	Publisher & Descriptive Information
1965-79	*Meef, Mother's Oats, Skull, Slow Death*

Covers ($):   500   750 [1,500]
Pages ($):   200   400   600

SHUSTER-JOE

Year	Publisher & Descriptive Information
1936	Comics Magazine Co.: *Dr. Mystic The Occult Detective, Federal Agent*

Covers ($):   xxx
Pages ($):   [***]

1935-48 National DC: **Superman*
    Covers ($):   [***]
    Pages ($): [2,000 4,000 5,500]

* Superman, created initially in 1933 by Jerry Siegel and Joe Shuster, struggled for acceptance for five years before finally making his comic book debut in *Action Comics* No. 1, dated June 1938. The "purest" form of Joe Shuster's art is considered the work he produced during the first year or two of the character. From 1939 to about 1944, Shuster ran a studio out of Cleveland, Ohio, with other artists assisting. Shuster's art contribution to the "Man of Steel" ended around 1948. Most of Shuster's early "Superman" artwork produced during 1938 and 1939 appears to be lost or destroyed. Recognized for their historical importance in comics history, any surviving examples could easily exceed

Joe Shuster, artwork for SUPERMAN specialty piece, signed and inscribed by both Jerry Siegal and Joe Shuster, circa 1940's. Estimate: $4,000/6,000; sold for $5,730 in 1998 (Phil Weiss Auctions).
© National Periodical Publications/DC Comics

these estimated values.

Calling All Cars, Dr. Occult, Federal Men, Henri Duval, Slam Bradley, Spy
Covers ($):   xxx
Pages ($): [***]

1948   M.E.: Funnyman
Covers ($): [***]
Pages ($): [300   500   700]

1954   Charlton: horror titles (pencils only)
Pages ($): [200   300   400]

Note: see Newspaper listing for "Superman" for information on artwork selling by Joe Shuster.

SIENKIEWICZ-BILL

Year	Publisher & Descriptive Information
1979-92	Marvel/Epic: *Elektra, Daredevil, Alf, Conan, Critical Mass, Dazzler, Defenders, Dr. Zero, Dune, Hulk, Kull, Moon Knight, New Mutants, Nick Fury, Power Line, ROM, St. George, Spider-Man, Star Wars, Stray Toasters, U.S. 1*

Covers ($): (painted)	400	800	1,200
Pages ($):	50	100	200
Covers ($): (black & white)	100	200	300
Pages ($):	xxx		

1986-91	DC: *Shadow, Batman, Elvira, Question, Star Trek, Superman, Teen Titans*		
	Covers ($):	40	80	160
	Pages ($):	40	80	160

1987	Comico: *Johnny Quest*		
	Covers ($):	400	600	800
	Pages ($):	xxx

1988	First: *Brought to Light, Lone Wolf and Cub, Moby Dick*		
	Covers ($):	400	600	800
	Pages ($):	xxx

1990-91	Mad Love: *Big Numbers*		
	Covers ($):	400	600	800
	Pages ($):	50	100	200

1991	Now: *Twilight Zone*		
	Covers ($):	400	600	800
	Pages ($):	50	100	200

SILKE-JIM

Year	Publisher & Descriptive Information
1990's	*Rascals in Paradise, Xena, Betty Page Comics*

	C/Covers ($):	600	1,000	3,000
	C/Pages ($):	200	400	600
	C/Pin-Ups($):	500	1,000	2,000
	B&W			
	Pages ($):	100	200	300

SIM-DAVE

Year	Publisher & Descriptive Information
1974-92	*Aardvark Vanaheim, Cerebus the Aardvark*

	Covers ($):	1,000	1,500	[2,500]
	Pages ($):	250	500	750

SIMONSON-WALT

Year	Publisher & Descriptive Information
1973-86	DC: *Man-Hunter*

	Covers ($):	***
	Pages ($):	***

Dr. Fate, Metal Men

	Covers ($):	***
	Pages ($):	***

Batman

	Covers ($):	150	200	250
	Pages ($):	50	100	150

Captain Fear, Hercules, misc. mystery, sci-fi, war

	Covers ($):	100	125	150
	Pages ($):	35	70	100

1977-91	Marvel: *Star Slammers*		
	Covers ($):	***
	Pages ($):	***

Fantastic Four, Thor, X-Factor

	Covers ($):	200	300	[750]
	Pages ($):	75	150	300

Avengers, Balder, Battlestar Galactica, Conan, Daredevil, Deaths Head, Hulk, Iron Man, Lawnmower Man, New Mutants, Spider-Man

	Covers ($):	125	175	300
	Pages ($):	50	100	150

Marvel/DC: *Close Encounters of the Third Kind, Indiana Jones, John Carter, Kiss, Machine Man, Star Wars*

	Covers ($):	100	125	150
	Pages ($):	40	60	80

X-Men & Teen Titans Team-Up

	Covers ($):	***
	Pages ($):	100	200	300

SMITH-BARRY-WINDSOR

Year	Publisher & Descriptive Information
1968-75	Marvel: *Conan*

	Covers ($):	[3,000	5,000	8,000]
	Pages ($):	400	800	1,200

*"Kull of Atlantis"

	covers (s):xxx
	Pages ($):	300	600	900

*"Kull of Atlantis" was an Idea developed by Roy Thomas and Barry Smith in 1970-1971 for a proposed paperback comic book that never got off the ground. Exact size and format of this original art is not known, but is definitely not of usual comic art measurements. This story was eventually published in *The Savage Sword* or *Conan* No. 3 In 1974.

Avengers, Captain Marvel, Daredevil, Dr. Strange, Kazar, X-Man, misc. horror

	Covers ($):	1,500	2,000	2,500
	Pages ($):	250	400	550

Barry Smith & Sal Buscema, example splash page from group of CONAN THE BARBARIAN #6 complete 20 page story, 1971. Estimate: $6,500/7,500; sold for $6,600 in 1992 (Sotheby's 2nd comic art auction). © Marvel Comics Group

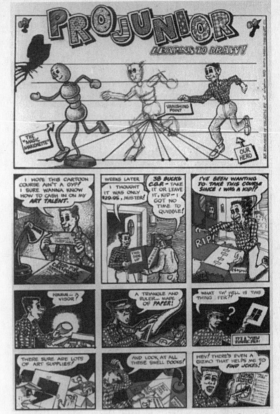

Art Spiegelman & Justin Green, splash page from 3 page story from PRO-JUNIOR #1, 1971. Estimate: $1,000/1,500; sold for $1,100 in 1992 (Sotheby's 2nd comic art auction). © Kitchen Sink Enterprises

1984	Pacific: Fantasy		
	Covers ($): 3,000	4,000	5,000
	Pages ($): 300	450	600

1984-91 Marvel: *Conan* (magazine with new "watercolor-painted" covers)

Covers ($): 4,000	5,000	6,000
Pages ($): xxx		

Machine Man, New Mutants, Weapon X

Covers ($): 800	1,200	1,600
Pages ($): 300	500	700

1980's-90's Specialty watercolor originals of *Conan,* for calendars etc.

Watercolor Paintings ($): 2,500	3,500	6,000

Note: individual sales would include; cover to *Conan* No. 1 selling at $13,200; interior twenty pages from *Conan* No. 1 selling for $11,000; both sales at Sotheby's in 1994.

SMITH-PAUL

Year	Publisher & Descriptive Information		
1981-91	Marvel: *Alpha Flight, Dr. Strange, X-Factor, X-Men*		
	Covers ($): 300	400	600
	Pages ($): 100	175	250
	Daredevil, Falcon, Iron Man, Howard the Duck		
	Covers ($): 150	200	250
	Pages ($): 50	100	150
	Conan, ROM		
	Covers ($): xxx		
	Pages ($): 75	125	175
1985	DC: *Batman*		
	Covers ($): xxx		
	Pages ($): 75	125	200
1987-89	First: *Nexus*		
	Covers ($): 150	200	275
	Pages ($): 50	100	150

SPIEGELMAN-ART

Year	Publisher & Descriptive Information
1967-78	*East Village Other, Swift?, Premium Comics, Pro-Junior, Young Lust, Snarf, Bijou Funnies, Arcade*

Covers ($):	1,000	1,500	[3,000]
Pages ($):	[300	600	900]

Year	Publisher & Descriptive Information
1979-92	*RAW, "Maus"*

Covers ($):	***
Pages ($):	***

SPRANG-DICK

Year	Publisher & Descriptive Information
1941-47	National/DC: *Batman and Robin, Superman*

Covers ($):	[7,000	12,000	14,000]
Pages ($):	[600	1,200	1,800]
1948-58 Covers ($):	[3,500	4,500	7,500]
Pages ($):	[500	800	1,000]
1959-61 Covers ($):	3,000	4,000	5,000
Pages ($):	350	500	650

* Dick Sprang's contribution to the popularity of Batman and Robin during the Golden Age period is immeasurable. Although he was never allowed to sign his work during those years, his incredible style of art earned him a reputation among comic readers as "the good Batman artist." His return to DC in 1987 doing special assignments was met with great enthusiasm. Since 1984 Dick has enjoyed great success by recreating many his Golden Age comic covers and splash pages in full-color. These recreations generally-range in price from $3,000 to $5,000.

Jimmy Olsen, Lois Lane, Supergirl, misc. adventure, Western

Covers ($):	xxx		
Pages ($):	[300	600	900]

Year	Publisher & Descriptive Information
1987-91	DC: *Batman*

Covers ($):	700	850	[1000]
Pin-UpPgs ($):	2,000	3,000	4,000

1980's-90's	Cover re-creation watercolor paintings, with inking in old style

Covers ($):	2,000	3,000	6,000

Specialty one-of-a-kind works & private commissions

($):	1,500	2,500	5,500

Black and White wash specialty works.

($):	1,000	1,500	2,500

SPROUSE-CHRIS

Year	Publisher & Descriptive Information
1990's	*Legionaires, Spiderman, Mantra, Young Blood*

Covers ($):	50	125	200
Pages ($):	20	50	90

STANLEY-JOHN

Year	Publisher & Descriptive Information
1945-60	Dell: *Little Lulu, Tubby*

Covers ($):	[200	400	800]
Pages ($):	[100	200	300]
1942-47 Western, humor			
Covers ($):	200	400	800
Pages ($):	100	200	300

STARLIN-JIM

Year	Publisher & Descriptive Information
1972-91	Marvel: *Avengers, Captain* Marvel, *Thanos, Thing, Warlock*

Covers ($):	500	800	1,100
Pages ($):	100	225	350

Captain America, Daredevil, Defenders, Dreadstar, Dr. Strange, Ghost Rider, Iron Man, Master of Kung Fu, Spider-Man, Sub-Mariner, Thor, Hulk, etc.

Covers ($):	200	350	[550]
Pages ($):	75	125	175

1987-89	*Cat, Conan, Kull, Ms.* Marvel, *Planet of the Apes, Power Man, ROM*

Covers ($):	300	500	700
Pages ($):	75	125	175

1985-86	DC: *Batman, Justice League, Legion, Superman*

Covers ($):	250	450	650
Pages ($):	50	100	125

Gilgamesh, Green Lantern

Covers ($):	200	300	400
Pages ($):	50	75	100

Jonah Hex, Kamandi, New Gods, OMAC, Star Trek, misc. mystery

Covers ($):	150	250	350
Pages ($):	50	100	150

John Stanley, artwork for re-creation cover to LITTLE LULU #61, 1989. Estimate: $5,000/6,000; sold for $4,600 in 1995 (Christie's East comic art auctions). © Western Publishing Company/Dell Comics

Jim Steranko, cover artwork for STRANGE TALES #161, 10/67. Private sale at $10,000 in 1996 (T.R.H. Galleries). © Marvel Comics Group

STEPHANS-JAY

Year	Publisher & Descriptive Information		
1988-97	Tragedy Strikes, Black Eye, Kitchen Sink, Dark Horse: *Sin Comics, Land of Nod, Atomic City Tales*		
	Covers ($): 200	225	250
	Clr/Cvrs($): 300	400	500
	Pages ($): 100	150	200

STERANKO-JIM

Year	Publisher & Descriptive Information		
1966-73	Marvel: *Captain America, Doc Savage, Fantastic Four, Hulk, Nick Fury Agent of SHIELD, X-Men*		
	Covers ($): [5,000	7,000	9,500]
	Pages ($): [700	1,200	2,400]
	Gulliver Jones, Shanna the She-Devil, Thongor		
	Covers ($): [1,400	3,400	5,400]
	Pages ($): xxx		

	Misc. horror, romance, Western— *Tex Dawson, Gunslinger*		
	Covers ($): 900	1,600	2,400
	Pages ($): 400	700	900
1983	Archie: *The Fly*		
	Covers ($): 1,600	2,400	3,600
	Pages ($): xxx		
1988	Marvel: *Nick Fury* (painted covers)		
	Covers ($): 4,000	5,500	7,500
	Pages ($): xxx		
1989	Now Comics: *Green Hornet* (painted cover)		
	Covers ($): 2,000	2,500	3,500
	Pages ($): xxx		
	Re-Creation classic Marvel covers in ink and watercolors		
	Covers ($): 4,000	5,000	6,500

Note: individual sales would include a re-creation cover for *NICK FURY, AGENT OF SHIELD* No. 6 selling at $10,350 at Christie's East.

Jim Steranko, cover artwork for DOC SAVAGE #3, 1973. Estimate: $2,000/3,000; sold after auction for $1,750 in 1992 (Sotheby's 2nd comic art auction). © Marvel Comics Group

STEVENS-DAVE

Year	Publisher & Descriptive Information		
1980-85	Pacific Comics: *Starslayer, Rocketeer*		
	Covers ($): 3,000	4,000	5,500
	Pages ($): 600	900	1,400
1980-85	Pacific Comics: Jungle, sci-fi, Good Girl		
	Covers ($): 2,000	3,000	4,500

	Pages ($): xxx		
1985-90	First: *Rocketeer*		
	Covers ($): 3,000	4,000	5,000
	Pages ($): 600	900	1,400
1985	Eclipse: *Rocketeer* covers		
	Covers ($): 3,000	4,000	5,000
	Pages ($): xxx		
1991	Disney: *Rocketeer* covers		
	Covers ($): ***		
	Pages ($): ***		

Year	Publisher & Descriptive Information

1980-84 Pacific: *Rocketeer*

Covers ($): ***
Pages ($): ***

Alien Worlds

Covers ($):	1,000	1,500	2,000
Pages ($):	400	600	800

1985-86 Eclipse: *Rocketeer*

Covers ($): ***
Pages ($): ***

Airboy, Crossfire, DNAGENTS, Mr. Monster, Rainbow, Sheena, True Love, World of Wood

Covers ($):	2,500	3,500	4,500
Pages ($):	350	400	600

1985 Comico: *Johnny Quest*

Covers ($): ***
Pages ($): xxx

1987 DC: *Elvira*

Covers ($):	2,000	3,000	4,000
Pages ($):	400	600	800

1988 Blackthorne: *Jungle, Planet*

Covers ($):	1,000	1,500	2,000
Pages ($):	350	500	600

* The scarcity and immense popularity of Stevens' work make any attempt at pricing difficult.

1988-91 Comico: *Rocketeer Christmas Special*

Covers ($):	***		
Pages ($):	350	500	600

1989-90 Dark Horse: *Cheval Noir*

Covers ($):	***		
Pages ($):	350	500	600

1990 Eclipse: *Orbit*

Covers ($):	***		
Pages ($):	350	500	600

1990 Fantagraphics: *King Kong*

Covers ($): ***
Pages ($): xxx

1994 *Madman magazine*

Covers ($):	1,500	2,000	3,000
Pages ($):	400	500	750

Note: individual sales would include: original Betty Page watercolor for trading card set selling at $4,600; back cover for *Madman* selling at $2,990; cover for *Crossfire* No. 12 with low estimate of $5,000 failed to sell at auction; cover for Eclipse's 3-D horror anthology with low estimate of $5,000 failed to sell at auction; prices from Christie's East.

SULTAN-CHARLES

Charles Sultan was a golden age artist who worked for the Chesler Shop. He produced some great art and covers for Fawcett during the early 1940's and later for Chesler Publications and Fiction House. Only a handful of pages and originals are known to exist. It appears the Sultan did a variety of work for Fawcett during the period from 1940 to 1942, which has not been catalogued or documented. It also appears that his disappperance from 1942 until 1947 suggests that he was drafted into the war.

Year	Publisher & Descriptive Information

1940-42 Fiction House: *Wings, Jumbo, Jungle, Planet, Rangers, Wings,* covers and interior work

Covers- *Planet*, none known to exist

($): [2,000   4,000   6,000]

Covers- other Fiction house titles

($):	[1,500	3,000	4,500]
Pages ($):	200	300	500

1947-48 Covers ($):

Planet, none known to exist

($): [1,000   2,000   3,000

Covers other Fiction House titles

($):	[800	1,200	1,500]
Pages ($):	50	125	200

1940-42 Fawcett: *Master, Nickel, Whiz* and *Wow Comics*, covers and interiors.

Covers ($):	[1,500	2,500	5,000]
Pages ($):	200	300	400

1947-48

Covers ($):	900	1,800	2,400
Pages ($):	50	125	200

Curt Swan, original cover artwork for ACTION COMICS #275, 1960. Estimate: $2,500/3,500; sold for $3,910 in 1993 (Christie's East comic art auctions). © National Periodical Publications/DC Comics

Curt Swan & George Klein, original cover artwork for SUPERMAN #170, 1964. Estimate: $5,000/7,000; sold for $5,750 in 1996 (Sotheby's 6th comic art auction). © National Periodical Publications/DC Comics

SUTTON-THOMAS

Year	Publisher & Descriptive Information		
1966-80's	Warren Publications: *Creepy, Eerie*, other titles		
	Pages ($): 50	75	100
1978-84	DC: *House of Secrets, House of Mystery*, suspense titles		
	Pages ($): 40	60	80
1984-88	DC: *Star Trek* - interior pages		
	Pages ($): 35	50	85

SUYDAM-ARTHUR

Year	Publisher & Descriptive Information		
1970's-80's	Horror & Fantasy; DC Mystery pages		
	Pages ($): 50	75	150
	B&W *Heavy Metal, Cholly & Flytrap*		
	Pages ($): 150	200	300
	Painted *Heavy Metal* pages, *Echo of Futurepast*		

	Pages ($): 400	1,000	1,500
1990's	*Batman vs. Predator, Tarzan*		
	Covers ($): 1,000	2,000	4,000

SWAN-CURT

Year	Publisher & Descriptive Information		
1945-91	National/DC: *Batman, Boy Commandoes, Gang Busters, Jimmy Olsen, Legion, Lois Lane, Superboy, Supergirl, *Superman, Teen Titans, Tommy Tomorrow, Wonder Woman* and others		
	Covers - twice up size		
	($): [2,500	5,000	7,500]
	Covers ($): [800	1,500	2,500]
	Pages ($): 100	300	500
	Mystery, science fiction		
	Covers ($): xxx		
	Pages ($): 100	150	225
1990's	Pencil re-creation covers and special splash pages.		

Curt Swan, original cover artwork for ADVENTURE COMICS #302, 1961. Estimate: $2,000/2,500; sold for $4,888 in 6/93 (Sotheby's 3rd comic art auction). © National Periodical Publications/DC Comics

Curt Swan & Joe Klein, original cover artwork for SUPERMAN #151, 1962. Estimate: $3,000/4,000; sold for $5,175 in 6/93 (Sotheby's 3rd comic art auction). © National Periodical Publications/DC Comics

Covers ($):	500	700	1,200
Splash Pgs	300	450	800

* Since 1955 Curt Swan has probably drawn the character of Superman (and related characters) more times than any artist in DC Comics' history. He is recognized mostly for penciling the art, while other artists usually do the inking. Prices do vary widely on his art, since a great deal of it produced between 1945 and 1967 remains missing, while most of his art from the past 20 years is known to exist. Notations of rarity are applicable to Swan's pre-1967 work only.

Note: individual sales would include; cover by Swan/Klein for *Adventure Comics* No. 302 selling at $4,888; cover for *Action* No. 301 by Swan/Klein selling at $4,888; cover for *Superman* No. 151 selling for $5,175; cover for *Superman* No. 170 selling in 1994 for $4,400 and again in 1996 for $5,750; all sales at Sotheby's comic art auctions.

TEXEIRA-MARK

Year	Publisher & Descriptive Information
1985-1990's	Marvel: *Ghost Rider, Moonknight, Wolverine;* including *Penthouse Comics*

Covers ($):	150	250	400
Pages ($):	50	90	200

Vampy, Spider-Man (painted art)

C/Covers($):	300	400	750
C/Pages ($):	100	250	500

TIBODEAUX-MIKE

Year	Publisher & Descriptive Information
1980's-90's	Pencilwork for *Last of The Viking Heroes*

Covers ($):	xxx		
Pages ($):	50	100	150

TIMM-BRUCE

Year	Publisher & Descriptive Information		
1990's	Highly regarded artist who designed the *Batman Animated Series* Batman		
	Covers ($):	300	450	600
	Pages ($):	75	150	250
	Color Specialty Drawings		
	Color ($):	200	300	500
	Black & White Specialty Drawings		
	B&W ($):	50	100	225

TOMINE-ADRIAN

Tomine's depressed romance tales for disaffected post-teens have struck a chord with the thrift shop set across that nation. Tight, simple lines informed by an old time graphic design sense combine for a stark grace.

Year	Publisher & Descriptive Information		
1993-97	Drawn & Quarterly: *Optic Nerve*		
	Covers ($):	300	350	400
	Pages ($):	150	175	200

TORRES-ANGELO

Torres attended the School of Visual Arts (Cartoonists and Illustrators School in the 1950's), and began to break into comics in the 1950's. Beside important early work with Al Williamson at EC and Atlas, Angelo eventually worked for Classics Illustrated, Dell, Charlton, Warren Publications and eventually a long tenure with MAD magazine.

Year	Publisher & Descriptive Information		
1955-57	Atlas/Marvel: Various Horror titles, *Mystic, Journey into Mystery, Strange Tales,* usually four to five page interior stories		
	Pages ($):	[100	175	250]
1958-60's	Charlton, Classics Illustrated, Dell historical titles		
	Pages ($):	75	125	150
1968-72	Sunday Pages for *Big Ben Bolt,* signed for Jack Murphy		
	S Pages ($):	80	120	160
1950-60's	*Sick Magazine,* work for Joe Simon, interior pages		

	Pages ($):	50	75	125
1969-90's	*Mad Magazine,* satire stories, features, no covers		
	Pages ($):	75	125	225
1965-70's	*Creepy, Eerie,* warren magazine interior stories		
	Pages ($):	75	150	200

Note: individual sales include: Seven pg story *MAD* No. 176 selling for $575; six pg story for *MAD* No. 145 selling at $517; four features from *MAD* Nos. 133, 149, 168 (16 pages) selling for $1,150; seven pg story from *MAD* No. 221 selling at $747; five pg feature from *MAD* No. 249 selling at $1,610; all sales from *MAD about MAD* Sotheby's auction in 1995.

TOTH-ALEX

Year	Publisher & Descriptive Information		
1947-52	National: *Atom, Dr. Mid-Nite, Flash, Green Lantern, Justice Society, Wonder Woman*		
	Covers ($):	[2,500	3,500	7,000]
	Pages ($):	400	800	1,200
	Dale Evans, Johnny Wakely, Johnny Peril, Johnny Thunder, Rex, Sierra Smith, misc. crime, fantasy, mystery romance, and others		
	Covers ($):	[1,500	2,500	3,500]
	Pages ($):	250	400	550
1952-54	Standard: Fantasy, horror, sci-fi		
	Covers ($):	[2,000	3,000	4,000]
	Pages ($):	125	225	325
1952-53	EC: *War		
	Covers ($):	xxx		
	Pages ($):	300	450	600

* Includes the eight-page story "Thunder Jet," considered by EC fan-addicts and Alex Toth fans alike to be one of the artist's finest artistic achievements in the comics.

1954-55	Lev Gleason: *Buster Crabbe,* misc. crime (some of this work utilized a "duotone" shading process—considered some of Toth's finest work)		
	Covers ($):	[2,000	3,000	4,000]
	Pages ($):	[150	300	450]

PRICE RANGE KEY

RARITY — Brackets [ ] around a price indicate that this example is very scarce and could exceed maximum estimate.

No work produced in this category—

No price available due to lack of information—

Covers
XXX
***

CONDITION — Age, color, marks, tears, etc.

Pages
[400   500   600]

CHARACTER — Is the primary character featured, or is the original characteristic of a great example in the story line?

CONTENT — is the theme or story line exceptional or below average?

VALUE RANGE

Minimum   Medium   Maximum

RARITY

The [ ] Brackets indicate RARITY, if these brackets are used the reader can potentially double the price range in all three catagories.

1956-64 Western/Dell: Movie adaptations: *Darby O'Gill and the Little People, FBI Story, Journey to the Center of the Earth, Land Unknown, No Time For Sergeants, Rio Bravo, Time Machine, Wings of Eagles,* others. TV Series adaptations: *Danny Thomas Show, Lawman, Lennon Sisters, Oh Susanna, Real McCoys, Sea-Hunt, 77 Sunset Strip, Sugarfoot, Twilight Zone, Zorro,* others

Covers ($):	1,000	1,500	2,000
Pages ($):	100	200	300

1965-77 National/DC: *Batman, Black Canary, Eclipso, Rip Hunter, Super Friends,* others

Covers ($):	xxx		
Pages ($):	200	300	400

Adventure, fantasy, mystery, sci-fi, romance, war

Covers ($):	xxx		
Pages ($):	125	200	275

1965-67 Warren (magazine): Horror, war

Covers ($):	xxx		
Pages ($):	250	350	450

1974 Archie: Mystery

Covers ($):	xxx		
Pages ($):	100	175	250

1975 Seaboard: *War*

Covers ($):	xxx		
Pages ($):	100	175	250

1975-76, 1980 Warren (magazine): "Bravo for Adventure" (written by Toth)

Covers ($):	xxx		
Pages ($):	200	300	400

Fantasy, horror—(most stories written by Toth)

Covers ($):	xxx		
Pages ($):	150	250	350

1983-84 Archie/Red Circle: *The Fox, Black Hood*

Covers ($): ·	800	1,200	1,600
Pages ($):	150	250	350

1985-86	Pacific: Misc. sci-fi			
	Covers ($):	xxx		
	Pages ($):	125	175	225
1989	Eclipse: *Zorro* (Graphic Album)			
	Covers ($):	600	800	1,000
	Pages ($):	150	250	350
1991	Marvel: *Zorro*			
	Covers ($):	600	800	1,000
	Pages ($):	xxx		

Note: the classic story "Thunder Jet!" from *Frontline Combat* No. 8 appeared at auction at Sotheby's in 1993 and sold for $6,325.

TRIMPE-HERB

Year	Publisher & Descriptive Information			
1965-1979	Marvel Comics: *Machine Man,* (inked by Barry Smith), *Hulk, Nick Fury Agent of S.H.I.E.L.D.*(inked by Severin)			
	Covers ($):	350	450	600
	Pages ($):	30	75	150

WAGNER-MATT

Year	Publisher & Descriptive Information			
1982-91	Comico: *Grendell, Mage*			
	Covers ($):	200	350	500
	Pages ($):	100	200	300
1987-92	DC: *Batman*			
	Covers ($):	600	700	800
	Pages ($):	75	150	250
	Demon, Griffin, Robin, Swamp Thing			
	Covers ($):	150	250	350
	Pages ($):	50	100	150
1989-90	First: *Lone Wolf Cub*			
	Covers ($):	300	400	500
	Pages ($):	xxx		
1989-90	Dark Horse: *Terminator*			
	Covers ($):	400	500	600
	Pages ($):	100	200	300
	Aerialist			
	Covers ($):	250	300	350
	Pages ($):	50	100	150

WARE-CHRIS

Bursting onto the alternative comics scene, Ware has taken his love of turn-of-the-century ad type and graphic experimentation and created one of the most visually stunning comic strips ever made. Craftily turning a cold, dead line into a series of challenging iconic images has provided a much needed shot in the arm for a complacent comicdom as well as a computer numbered graphic design industry. Ware's comics at times read like road maps or instructional posters infused with a soul-crushing existential depression.

Year	Publisher & Descriptive Information		
1991-97	*Fantagraphics, Acme Novelty Library;*		
	Covers ($):	xxx	
	Pages ($):	xxx	

WILLIAMS-RICHARD

A commercial artist who began to be featured as a MAD cover artist during the 1980's and 1990's.

Year	Publisher & Descriptive Information		
1983-90's	*MAD Magazine,* covers and BC color works		
	Covers ($): 3,000	5,000	7,000

Note: individual sales would include: cover to MAD No. 307 selling at $7,475; cover for MAD No. 270 selling at $5,750; cover for MAD No. 262 selling at $3,162; cover to MAD No. 248 selling for $5,725; cover for MAD No. 271 hammering at $2,587; cover for *MAD Super Special* No. 64 fetching $4,312; all sales from Sotheby's MAD About MAD 1995 auction.

WILLIAMS-ROBERT

Year	Publisher & Descriptive Information		
1966-71	*ZAP, Yellow Dog, Gothic Blimp Works*		
	Covers ($): 800	1,150	[1,500]
	Pages ($): 250	375	[500]

Al Williamson & Frank Frazetta, original art to SF sample page circa 1951. Estimate: $1,500/2,000; sold for $2,875 in 6/93 (Sotheby's 3rd comic art auction). © Williamson/Frazetta Studios

1972-91	ZAP, Tuff Shit, San Francisco Comic Book, Tasty, Illuminations, Robert Williams, Felch		
Covers ($):	800	1,650	2,500
Pages ($):	250	375	500

1967-89	Large oil paintings		
Covers ($):	10,000	20,000	[30,000]

1985-92	"Zombie Mystery Paintings", approx. 14" x 20" oil paintings offered through Tamara Bane Gallery		
Pages ($):	4,000	4.500	[5,000]

WILLIAMSON-AL

Year	Publisher & Descriptive Information		
1950-53	Toby: Sci-fi w/Frazetta		
Covers ($):	xxx		
Pages ($):	1,200	2,400	3,600

	Western—"Billy the Kid," John Wayne		
Covers ($):	xxx		
Pages ($):	200	400	500

1951-52	ACG: Fantasy/horror		
Covers ($):	xxx		
Pages ($):	[800	1,200	1,600]

1951	M.E.: Space Ace w/Wood		
Covers ($):	xxx		
Pages ($):	[800	1,200	1,600]

1952	Eastern Color: Buster Crabbe w/George Evans and Roy Krenkel		
Covers ($):	[2,500	3,500	4,500]
Pages ($):	300	600	900

	Romance w/Frazetta		
Covers ($):	xxx		
Pages ($):	[800	1,100	1,400]

1952-56 EC Science fiction with occasional
assists from Frazetta
Covers ($): [9,000   18,000 36,000]
Pages ($):   800   1,400 [1,800]

EC science fiction covers with
occasional assists from Krenkel &
Torres
Covers ($): [5,000   7,000   9,000]
Pages ($):   700   900   1,200

Crime, horror
Covers ($):   xxx
Pages ($):   400   700   900

New Directions titles: *Valor*
w/Torres
Covers ($): 3.000   4,500 [5,500]
Pages ($): [400   500   800]

1955   Crestwood: *American Eagle,* with
some assists from Krenkel,
Severin, & Torres
Covers ($):   xxx
Pages ($): [400   700   900]

1955-59 Atlas: Fantasy, mystery, sci-fi
Covers ($):   xxx
Pages ($): [400   800   1,200]

Misc. Western "Annie Oakley,"
"Jann of the Jungle," "Kid Colt,"
"Matt Slade," Outlaw Kid,"
"Rawhide Kid," "Ringo Kid," "Tex
Dawson," "Two-Gun Kid,"
"Western Kid," "Wyatt Earp" and
others
Covers ($):   xxx
Pages ($):   150   300   450

Romance, war
Covers ($): xxx
Pages ($): [150   250   350]

1957-58 Charlton: Misc. Western, most
with assist by Angelo Torres "Billy
the Kid," "Black Jack," "Cheyenne
Kid," "Kid Montana," "Tex
Ritter," "Wild Bill Hickock,"
"Wyatt Earp," and others
Covers ($):   xxx
Pages ($): [150   225   325]

1957-60 ACG: Fantasy, mystery
Covers ($):   xxx
Pages ($): [350   550   850]

1958,   Harvey: Science fiction
62, 63 w/Crandall
Covers ($):   xxx
Pages ($): [300   600   800]

1959   Archie: *The Fly*
Covers ($):   xxx
Pages ($): [250   350   450]

1958,   Western/Dell Gold Key: *Boris
1965   Karloff, Ripley's,* Mystery, Western
Covers ($):   xxx
Pages ($):   150   250   350

1964-65 Warren (magazine): Horror, war
Covers ($):   xxx
Pages ($): [400   700   1,000]

1966-67 King: *Flash Gordon, Secret
Agent X-9*
Covers ($): [2,500   4,500   6,500]
Pages ($): [600   900   1,200]

1980-82 Marvel: Sci-fi: movie adaptation
w/Garzon, *The Empire Strikes
Back*
Covers ($): [950   1,800   2,500]
Pages ($): [250   350   450]

Movie adaptation: *Blade Runner*
Covers ($): [900   1,500   2,000]
Pages ($): [150   250   350]

1984   Eclipse: *Rocketeer* (pinup)
Covers ($):   xxx
Pages ($): [600   800   1,000]

Note: individual sales would include: story
entitled "Captivity" from *Weird Science*
No. 15 selling at $880; 3-D story entitled
"Planetoid" (with George Evans) selling at
$4,600; story entitled "Brainchild" from
Weird Fantasy No. 19 selling at $2,185;
original used for Limited Edition Portfolio
of Fine Comic Art (1978-featuring Flash
Gordon in panorama space SF scene) selling
for $12,650; all sales from Sotheby's comic
art auctions. Private sales include; story
entitled "By George!" from *Weird Fantasy*
No. 15 at $12,500; cover to *Weird Fantasy*
No. 18 selling at $7,500. Sales from
Christie's East include: two pages from
Flash Gordon No. 1 (King-1967) selling at
$3,080; story entitled "The Arrival" from
Shock Suspenstories No. 8 selling at $3,080.

Al Williamson, artwork for LIMITED EDITION PORTFOLIO of FLASH GORDON, 1978. Estimate: $7,000/10,000; sold for $12,650 in 1996 (Sotheby's 6th comic art auction). © National Cartoonists Society

WILLIAMSON-SKIP

Year	Publisher & Descriptive Information		
1965-70	*Conspiracy Capers, Yellow Dog, Bijou, The Realist, HELP!, Chicago Seed, East Village Other*		
	Covers ($): 500	750	[1,500]
	Pages ($): 250	375	500
1971-92	*Bijou Funnies, Mom's Homemade, Pro-Junior, Hungry Chuck Biscuits, BLAB*		
	Covers ($): 500	625	[800]
	Pages ($): 200	300	350

WILSON.-S.-CLAY

Year	Publisher & Descriptive Information		
1965-66	Oil paintings done in comic style		
	($): [4,000	5,000	7,000]
1967	*Twenty Drawings*, Portfolio		
	Pages ($): 600	800	[2,000]
1968-69	*ZAP, East Village Other, Gothic Blimp Works, S.C. Wilson Comic*		
	Covers ($): 1,750	2,500	[5,000]
	Pages ($): 300	450	[600]

1970-76	*ZAP², Insect Fear, Arcade, Checkered Demon*		
	Covers ($): 1,000	1,500	[2,500]
	Pages ($): 200	350	[500]
1977-92	*Taboo, ZAP, Ugly Head,* Illustrations to William Burroughs editions		
	Covers ($): 1,000	1,500	[2,000]
	Pages ($): 250	375	500
1978-98	Wilson has done a number of personal commission watercolors, usually 8.5" x 11" in scale, some quite detailed.		
	Pages ($): 300	650	[1,250]

WOODRING-JIM

Year	Publisher & Descriptive Information		
1984-98	Fantagraphics: *Thudra, Kitchen Sink, Jim's Tantalizing Stories, Frank*		
	Covers ($): 1,000	2,000	3,000
	Pages ($): 300	350	400
	Clr/Pgs ($): 300	600	900

Basil Wolverton, CULTURE QUICKIE, 1970's. Estimate: $1,200/2,000; sold for $3,360 (Russ Cochran comic art auctions).

WOLVERTON-BASIL

Year	Publisher & Descriptive Information
1938	Globe Syndicate: *Disk-Eyes the Detective*
	Covers ($): xxx
	Pages ($): [***]

Spacehawk
Covers ($): xxx
Pages ($): [800   1,200   1,600]

1939-42 Centaur: *Meteor Martin, Space Patrol*
Covers ($): xxx
Pages ($): [800   1,200   1,400]

Basil Wolverton, artwork for 4 CULTURE CORNER pages from WHIZ COMICS #118 &123, 1949-50. Estimate: $1,000/2,000; sold for $4,312 in 1996 (Sotheby's 6th comic art auction). © Fawcett Publications

Wallace Wood, cover for VALOR #5. Estimate: $2,500/4,000; sold for $4,400 in 10/5/97 (Russ Cochran's comic art auctions).

Wallace Wood, cover artwork to TALES FROM THE CRYPT #26, 1951. Estimate: $8,000/12,000; sold for $8,625 in 1996 (Sotheby's 6th comic art auction). © William M. Gaines/EC Publications

1940-43 Novelty Press: *Spacehawk*
Covers ($): [***]
Pages ($): [800   1,600   2,400]

Targetoons
Covers ($): xxx
Pages ($): [400   800   1,200]

1942-44 Lev Gleason: *Scoop Scuttle*
Covers ($): xxx
Pages ($): [400   800   1,200]

1941-53 Timely/Atlas: Fantasy, horror, sci-fi, *Rockman*
Covers ($): xxx
Pages ($): [800   1,200   1,600]

Powerhouse Pepper
Covers ($): [***]
Pages ($): [600   900   1,200]
Misc. humor stories and filler pages: "Dauntless Dawson," "Dr. Dimwit," "Dr. Whackyhack," "Flap Flip Flop the Flying Flash," "Foolish Faces," "Funny Boners," "Hash House Hank," "Hothead Hotel," "Inspector Hector," "Parade of Peculiar People," "Piston Pete," "Professor Joggs," "Professor Ploop," "Salesman Sid," "Splash Morgan," others

Covers ($): xxx
Pages ($): [400   600   800]

1945-48 Fawcett: *Culture Corner, Mystic Moot and his Magic Snoot*
Covers ($): xxx
Pages ($): [400   600   800]

1949-51 Lev Gleason: *Bing Bang Buster*
Covers ($): xxx
Pages ($): [400   600   800]

1952-53 SPM Publ./Aragon Publ.: Fantasy, sci-fi
Covers ($): [900   1,200   1,600]
Pages ($): [300   600   900]

Jumpin' Jupiter
Covers ($): xxx
Pages ($): [400   600   800]

1952-53 Gillmor: Fantasy, sci-fi
Covers ($): xxx
Pages ($): [800   1,200   1,600]

1954 EC: Humor/satire
Covers ($): [4,000   6,000   8,000]
Pages ($): [400   700   1,000]

1973-75 DC: Humor—*Popular Person of the Month, Doc Rockblock*
Covers ($): 800   1,000   1,200
Pages ($): 300   500   700

WOOD-WALLACE (WALLY) (1927-1981)

With a unique talent and great deal of determination, Wally Wood became recognized as one of the finest artists to have worked in the field of comics. He is best remembered for his science fiction contributions to the EC comic titles *Weird Fantasy, Weird Science, Weird Science Fantasy,* and *Incredible Science-Fiction,* published between 1950 and 1956. Most of the artist's work produced for EC has survived. thanks in part to EC publisher William M. Gaines and through a series of auctions has been sold over the past12 years. It should be noted that the only EC cover art not accounted for is Wood's cover for EC's New Direction title *Valor* No. 1, dated March/April 1955. It should also be noted that while most of the EC art has survived, not a single page of Wood's Avon comic art has surfaced. It is known that several of his Avon cover preliminaries do exist.

(See Science Fiction and Fantasy section also)

Year	Publisher & Descriptive Information		
1948	D.S. Publishing: Crime		
	Covers ($): xxx		
	Pages ($): [100	150	200]
1949	Magazine Village: Crime		
	Covers ($): xxx		
	Pages ($): [150	200	250]
1949-50	Fox: *Dorothy Lamour, Frank Buck, Hoot Gibson, Martin Kane, Moby Dick, Sabu,* misc. adventure, crime, horror, Western		
	Covers ($): [2,000	4,000	6,000]
	Pages ($): [200	400	600]
	Judy Canova, misc. romance		
	Covers ($): [1,500	2,000	2,500]
	Pages ($): [100	150	200]
1949-51	ACG: Fantasy/horror (with Williamson)		
	Covers ($): xxx		
	Pages ($): [500	800	1,100]
1950	Ziff-Davis: Science fiction		
	Covers ($): xxx		
	Pages ($): [600	800	1,000]

1950	Fawcett: *Romance*		
	Covers ($): xxx		
	Pages ($): [100	150	200]
1950-51	Youthful: *Captain Science* (with Orlando)		
	Covers ($): [4,000	5,500	8,000]
	Pages ($): [500	700	1,000]
1950-53	Avon: Science fiction with occasional assists from Check, Frazetta, Krenkel, Orlando, and Williamson; *Kenton of the Star Patrol, Space Detective,* and others		
	Covers ($): [5,000	7,000	9,000]
	Pages ($): [600	800	1,000]
	Crime, Dr. Fu Manchu, horror, war Western, etc.		
	Covers ($): [3,000	4,000	5,000]
	Pages ($): [300	600	900]
1951-52	Trojan: Western, crime, misc.		
	Covers ($): xxx		
	Pages ($): [200	400	600]
1951	Master/Merit: Horror (with Orlando)		
	Covers ($): [2,500	4,000	5,000]
	Pages ($): [200	400	600]
1951	ME: *Space Ace* (with Williamson)		
	Covers ($): xxx		
	Pages ($): [500	800	1,100]
1952	Eisner: *Spirit* (newspaper comic insert)		
	Covers ($): xxx		
	Pages ($): 600	1,200	1,800
1952-54	Star: Horror, romance		
	Covers ($): xxx		
	Pages ($): [200	300	400]
1949-56	EC: Misc. science fiction		
	Covers ($): [7,000	10,000	20,000]
	Pages ($): 500	800	1,500
	Humor/satire		
	Covers ($): xxx		
	Pages ($): 500	800	1,100
	Pages (Superduperman story)		
	($): 1,500	2,000	3,500
	Crime, horror, war, Frontline Combat, Shock Suspenstories, etc.		
	Covers ($): [2,500	4,000	8,500]
	Pages ($): 300	500	700

Wallace Wood, 7 page story from TWO-FISTED TALES #33, 1953. Estimate:
$800/1,000; sold for $2,875 in 6/93 (Sotheby's 3rd comic art auction).

Western (with Harrison)			
Covers ($):	xxx		
Pages ($):	150	250	350

New Direction titles			
Covers ($):	2,000	3,000	4,000
Pages ($):	200	300	400

Picto Fiction magazines—romance			
Covers ($):	xxx		
Pages ($):	200	300	400

1955-59 National: War

Covers ($):	xxx		
Pages ($):	[200	300	400]

1956-59 Atlas: Mystery, Western

Covers ($):	xxx		
Pages ($):	[200	350	500]

1964 Charlton: War

Covers ($):	xxx		
Pages ($):	[150	250	350]

1964-65 Marvel: *Daredevil*

Covers ($):	[3,500	6,000	7,500]
Pages ($):	400	800	1,200

1965-66 Gold Key: *Boris Karloff*, mystery, movie, science fiction, war

Covers ($):	xxx		
Pages ($):	200	300	400

1965-69	Tower: *Agent Weed, Dynamo, Menthor, Noman, Thunderbolt, Thunder Agents, Undersea Agent,* war		
	Covers ($): [2,000	3,000	4,000]
	Pages ($): 300	500	700

1966-67	Harvey: Science fiction, war		
	Covers ($): xxx		
	Pages ($): 150	250	350

1966	King: *Flash Gordon*		
	Covers ($): xxx		
	Pages ($): [200	400	600]

1968-72	Marvel: *Captain America, Cat, King Kull*		
	Covers ($): 600	1,000	[1,400]
	Pages ($): 200	300	400

horror, sword and sorcery

	Covers ($): xxx		
	Pages ($): 250	350	450

1968-78	National/DC: *Angel and the Ape, Anthro, Captain Action, Flash, Green Lantern, Hercules, Justice Society, Kung-Fu Fighter, Sandman, Superboy, Teen Titans,* and others (most of the above in collaboration with other artists)		
	Covers ($): 600	800	[1,200]
	Pages ($): 200	300	400

Horror, humor, romance, war

	Covers ($): 400	600	[800]
	Pages ($): 150	200	250

1975	Atlas/Seaboard: *Destructor, Wulf the Barbarian*		
	Covers ($): 400	500	[650]
	Pages ($): 100	150	200

1969, 76	Wood/CPL: *Heroes Inc.*		
	Covers ($): [800	900	1,200]
	Pages ($): [250	350	450]

1970's	*Cannon, Sally Forth,* Sex comic titles.		
	Covers ($): 400	550	650
	Pages ($): 450	550	750

1968-78	*Witzend,* individual stories, *The Wizard King*		
	Covers ($): 500	700	[900]
	Pages ($): 300	350	400

1970's	Re-creation *Weird Science* covers, done with ink and watercolor - only a handful done.		

($): [3,000	4,000	6,000]

Note: individual sales would include: cover for *Incredible Science Fiction* No. 33 selling at San Diego in 1996 for $22,500; seven pg story "There Will Come Soft Rains'"(Bradbury-The Martian Chronicles) from *Weird Fantasy* No. 17 valued at $15,000; eight pg story entitled "Mars is Heaven" (Bradbury-M.C.) from *Weird Science* No. 18 selling at $25,000; from private sales. From Sotheby's sales: seven pg story "You Rocket" from *Incredible SF* No. 31 selling at $3,450; seven pg story "Atom Bomb!" from *Two-Fisted Tales* No. 33 selling at $2,875; seven pg story "Desert Fox!" from *Frontline Combat* No. 3 selling at $3,450; eight pg story "Clean Start" from *Incredible SF* No. 30 selling at $3,200; Harrison/Wood 14 pages of romance from EC pretrend title selling at $690; cover for *Tales From The Crypt* No. 26 selling at $8,625; EC 3-D story "V-Vampires," eight pages selling for $5,750.

WOODBRIDGE-GEORGE

Woodbridge began his first work on the *Masked Ranger* comic and quickly became a regular at Atlas and Dell comics during the 1950's. He began his work with MAD in 1957 and has been a regular contributor with them since.

Year	Publisher & Descriptive Information		
1954-57	Atlas, Dell: interior stories		
	Pages ($): 125	150	175
1957-90's	*MAD Magazine,* color features and stories		
	Color		
	Pages ($): 300	450	700
	B&W		
	Pages ($): 40	60	100
	Covers ($): 1000	2000	3000

Note: individual sales include: two features (15 pgs) from MAD Nos. 146 & 169 selling at $920; cover for MAD No. 241 selling at $3,737; cover *Super Special Worst from MAD* No. 49 selling at $805; all sales from MAD About MAD Sotheby's 1995 auction.

Berni Wrightson, artwork to FRANKENSTEIN Plate 1978. Estimate: $4,000/5,000; sold for $7,475 in 1995 (Christie's East comic art auctions). © Marvel Comics Group

Berni Wrightson, cover artwork to SWAMP THING, #9, 4/74. Private sale at $6,500 in 1996 (T.R.H. Galleries). © National Periodical Publication/ DC Comics

WRIGHTSON-BERNI

Year	Publisher & Descriptive Information		
1969-70	Major Magazines: " *Web of Horror*" (painting)		
	Covers ($): 2,000	3,000	4,000
	Pages ($): 400	500	600
1969-80	National/DC: *Swamp Thing*		
	Covers ($): 3,000	4,000	5,000
	Pages ($): 600	900	1,200
	Misc. horror		
	Covers ($): 2,000	3,000	4,000
	Pages ($): 300	600	900
	Nightmaster, Spectre		
	Covers ($): xxx		
	Pages ($): 200	300	400
	Jonah Hex, Kong, Sorcery, Batman, etc.		
	Covers ($): 1,500	2,000	2,500
	Pages ($): xxx		

Year	Publisher & Descriptive Information		
1970-76	Marvel: Misc. horror		
	Covers ($): 1,000	1,500	2,000
	Pages ($): 250	350	450
	King Kull		
	Covers ($): xxx		
	Pages ($): 300	500	700
	Misc. covers—*Hulk, Tomb of Dracula,* etc.		
	Covers ($): 1,500	2,000	2,500
	Pages ($): xxx		
1974-77	Warren: (magazine) Misc. horror stories		
	Insd/Cvs ($):1,000	2,000	3,000
	Pages ($): 400	800	1,200
	Illustrations; paperback books, fanzines, HC books		
	Pages ($): 800	1,400	2,400
	Frankenstein Plate illustrations (many collectors consider Wrightson's work on the		

Berni Wrightson, artwork to FRANKENSTEIN Plate 1978. Estimate: $6,000/8,000; sold for $6,900 in 1993 (Christie's East comic art auctions). © Marvel Comics Group

Frankenstein plates to be his
finest to date)

Plates ($): 3,500   5,500   [8,000]

1983-85   Marvel Misc. covers—*Dr. Strange*

Covers ($):   800   1,000   1,200
Pages ($):   xxx

Gargoyle (painted)

Covers ($): 1,000   2,000   3,000
Pages ($):   xxx

1984   National/DC: Pinups and covers—
Superman, Batman

Covers ($): 1,000   1,500   2,000
Pages ($):   xxx

1986   Marvel: *Amazing Spider-Man* (full
color painted) (cover and Interior
pages)

Covers ($): 1,000   2,000   3,000
Pages ($):   400   800   1,200

1988   National/DC: *Batman, The Cult*

Covers ($): 1,000   1,500   2,000
Pages ($):   200   400   600

1991   Marvel: *Punisher*

Covers ($): 1,000   1,500   [2,000]
Pages ($):   200   400   600

ZECK-MIKE

Year	Publisher & Descriptive Information		
1977-91	Marvel: *Punisher, Spider-Man*		
	Covers ($): 400	600	800
	Pages ($): 100	250	400

*Captain America, Daredevil, Hulk,
Master of Kung Fu, Secret Wars,
She-Hulk*

Covers ($):   150   200   250
Pages ($):   75   125   175

*Iron Fist, Man From Atlantis,
Powerman, Thanos*

Covers ($):   xxx
Pages ($):   25   50   75

1987-92   DC: *Batman, Deathstroke the
Terminator*

Covers ($):   400   500   600
Pages ($):   xxx

1989   First: *Badger*

Covers ($):   200   800   400
Pages ($):   xxx

PRICE RANGE KEY

RARITY — Brackets [ ] around a price indicate that this example is very scarce and could exceed maximum estimate.

No work produced in this category—

No price available due to lack of information—

Covers
XXX
***

CONDITION — Age, color, marks, tears, etc.

Pages
[400   500   600]

CHARACTER — Is the primary character featured, or is the original characteristic of a great example in the story line?

CONTENT — is the theme or story line exceptional or below average?

VALUE RANGE

Minimum   Medium   Maximum

RARITY

The [ ] Brackets indicate RARITY, if these brackets are used the reader can potentially double the price range in all three catagories.

PART V

SCIENCE FICTION ART

Frank Kelly Freas, original interior illustration for Robert Heinlein's DOUBLE STAR, appearing in three installments in ASTOUNDING in 1956, pen and ink on scratch-board. Sold privately in 1999 for $650.
© Street & Smith Publications

FORREST J. ACKERMAN AND THE WORLD OF SCIENCE FICTION ART
Interview conducted by
Marc Patrick Carducci

Author's Note:

The following interview was conducted with Forrest J Ackerman by long time friend Marc Carducci in 1997. We include this interview as a signpost to how the times have changed since SF fans began to collect original artwork in the 1930s. The first fandom members had no idea that a market would develop in the ensuing years where originals by their favorite artists would bring thousands of dollars. In the beginning they were simply saving what they valued and loved, the original artwork to their favorite magazines or authors by their favorite artists.

Q: Why do you think it was that the first science fiction fanzines were such a crucial link between early fans even more than the pulps themselves in a way?

A: Well, the pulps, in critiquing them, you could only talk about their artists and their stories. But you were free in the fanzines to compare prozines and authors and artists, and to discuss the whole wide field, even motion pictures, which, by and large, were not discussed in science fiction magazines. Basically, a broadening of the ability to discuss one's interests.

Q: Can you describe the differences between hectographically produced zines and mimeographed zines?

A: In hectograph, you took a pan like you were going to bake a cake, poured in a solution which, when it jelled, you then typed out your text and drew your pictures on a sheet of paper, using a special typing ribbon. Then you laid this paper on top of this gelatinous material, took it off and now you could lay sheets of paper on this and pull them off. You got about 50 legible reproductions this way.

Q: Sounds like a messy business.

A: And you'd get purple fingers! With mimeography, you'd cut a stencil and put it on a drum roll, which had been inked, and the ink came through where you had typed on it. That way you could get hundreds of reproductions. A few fanzine creators were able to, somehow or other, get hold of printing presses. There were some hand-set fanzines, too (there were no linotypes in those days), a long arduous process of setting type by hand, but getting some very nice results.

Q: During the meetings of the Los Angeles Science Fantasy Society, were there visits from other artists? Did any artwork trade hands?

Photo by John L. Coker III.

A: No, I don't think so. The only artist who ever came along was Hannes Bok. It seems to me that he moved here for a short period, perhaps a year. Ray Bradbury used him in his fanzine, *Futuria Fantasia*. And then, when Bradbury took Bok's work in 1939 to the first World Science Fiction Convention and showed it to the editor of *Weird Tales*, Farnsworth Wright, Wright was immediately impressed. So then, I believe, Bok moved to New York.

Q: **Explain to newer fans what Esperanto is, and tell us if it ever visually inspired the artwork of early sci-fi artists?**

A: Well, there are 6016 languages in the world. 2000 people from time to time have thought, "Couldn't we start all over and make up a language without all kinds of exceptions?" And Esperanto is the one language that has any success at all. It's been in several movies, including Chaplin's *The Great Dictator*. William Shatner did an entire film in Esperanto called *Succubus*. Esperanto appears in one of the Bing Crosby/Bob Hope pictures, *The Road to Bali*, I believe there's a long song sung in Esperanto. In any event, Esperanto is the only new language created to be an international language that has had any success. 1987 was the 100th anniversary of the creation of the language and I personally went to Poland, where it all began, and was amongst 7000 people from 60 countries for 10 days, and when we met we could all talk to each other. We could sit at one banquet table, with a Frenchman and a Japanese and a Russian and an Israeli and a Hindu and so on, and all carry on a conversation.

Q: **Did Esperanto's spirit affect any of the artists of the pulp era?**

A: No, I don't think it really had any impressions on the artists. But its influence turned up in science fiction stories occasionally, referred to as the "language of the 21st century." And occasionally, a story was translated into and published in Esperanto.

Q: What were the first auctions of artwork at the first science fiction conventions like?

A: Well, at the first World Science Fiction Convention, where the Guest of Honor was Frank R. Paul, I believe that top dollar paid for one of his cover paintings was a gasping ten dollars! Artwork was selling, normally, for three dollars or five dollars at the time. At the next convention, in 1940, which was held in Chicago (the publishing headquarters of *Amazing Stories),* the editor very generously donated a huge number of black and whites and paintings to be auctioned. Well, the auction just went on and on, and it finally came down to, "Who will give me ten cents for this piece?," and finally they flung the artwork into the air for grabs! There was just so much of it!

Q: What sort of prices was the artwork by, say, Ed Emsh, Kelly Freas, and Edd Cartier selling for in the 1950's?

A: Oh, I believe around $50 would get you a goodie.

Q: On your visits to the sets of various science fiction films, what artists have you met?

A: I was on the set in 1949 of Robert Heinlein's *Destination Moon,* for which the classic artist Chesley Bonestell had designed the lunar background. He toured my wife and myself around, showing us his magnificent lunar landscapes. In modern times, artist Ron Cobb, who had done covers for *Famous Monsters of Filmland* and *Spacemen,* was responsible for the outre landscape of the planet in *Alien.*

Q: What is your opinion of Chesley Bonestell's work?

A: In a word: wonderful! The next best thing to going out there with a camera. The eyeballs of the science fiction world were really knocked out when *Conquest of Space* came out, for which Bonestell did the art. It was so far and away from what most artists were doing in the field. There was such a great sense of reality to Bonestell's work. Mr. Bonestell himself gave three of his cover paintings freely to an early science fiction convention here in Los Angeles, the Westercon. They were auctioned off.

Q: I wonder where they wound up...? Did you get one?

A: Yes. (Laughs.)

Q: In your opinion, who is the most important science fiction artist of the 20's? And would you please answer the same question for the 30's, 40's, 50's and 60's?

A: I've no doubt in the 20's it was Frank R. Paul. In the 30s, it was Paul again. He was still going great guns; about his nearest rival was Wesso. In the 40's, Virgil Finlay began coming in strong. Let's see, in the 50's, Hubert Rogers did terrific work on the Doc Smith *Gray Lensman Astounding* covers. Rogers isn't remembered today as well as some others. In the '60s, I guess it would be the great Frank Kelly Freas.

Q: Some would say science fiction is merely illustration, not an art form with creative principles at its foundation. What do you think?

A: No, I think it goes beyond just illustration. On occasion, there are even fine art galleries displaying science fiction art.

Q: What artists have you personally represented via the Ackerman Agency?

A: There was Morris Scott Dollens, Neil Austin (who drew a series of portraits of writers for *Famous Fantastic Mystery*), Ron Cobb, Mel Hunter, Albert Nuetzell, Osman Astin and Roy Hunt. I have a feeling that there may have been others.

Q: What can you tell us about Ray Bradbury, painter?

A: As far as I'm aware, he's only done about a dozen paintings.

Q: What inspired him to paint?

A: I haven't the foggiest idea. I believe he mainly paints for his own amusement. I have one of his paintings in my livingroom.

Q: What are some of your fondest memories of actually meeting your favorite science fiction artists?

A: Well, I've met Paul, Finlay, Margaret Brundage...She was in Chicago, kind of past her prime I suppose, no longer drawing for *Weird Tales*. She'd changed her style.

Q: Tell us about your meetings with Frank R. Paul.

A: Well, Paul was the Guest of Honor at the first World Science Fiction convention and he gave an acceptance speech that it is a shame was never recorded. It was Paul's artwork on the cover for the October 1926 *Amazing Stories* that really sparked my interest in science fiction and got me going.

Q: Did you and Paul have any contact between 1939 and the time you commissioned two pieces of art from him? How did these commissions come about?

A: No, no contact other than a very unsatisfactory lunch I had with my two great inspirations, Hugo Gernsback and Frank R. Paul. I say unsatisfactory because, rather than talking about the golden days of science fiction and artwork and the like, the entire time was taken up with gourmet talk of meat and wines and cigars! A total loss to me.

As far as commissioning Paul, this came about by my being in the position to afford them, I suppose. Since my whole life began with his 1926 *Amazing Stories* cover, I asked him to re-draw it for me and, while he was at it, to call it Amazing Forries and place a figure of myself in it. Then I asked him to create a second painting, a Martian science fiction cover, as if they had a sci-fi magazine on Mars. (Author's note: This cover was based on an early issue of *Science & Invention*, dated August 1924, on which a Martian is pictured. Ironically the cover was by another artist, though Frank R. Paul did the interior illustrations for the article entitled "Evolution on Mars" by Hugo Gernsback.)

Q: What did Paul charge you for the work?

A: I think about $200.

Q: How did you first meet Virgil Finlay?

A: Finlay didn't show up at the first science fiction convention. But a group of us fans went over to the editorial offices of the *American Weekly*, where A. Merritt edited, to see Merritt. While we were waiting in his outer offices, this very impressive young individual with a leonine head came in with a portfolio. And he lets us see all the original stipple artwork he had with him. It's a wonder that we ever pulled away from Finlay's incredible originals to see Merritt at all!

Q: You knew Hannes Bok more intimately than either Paul or Finlay, I believe.

A: Yes, that's right. Wendy and I went to see Bok in Harlem. He had signs all over the place, GO AWAY!, LEAVE ME ALONE!, CAN'T YOU SEE I'M BUSY!, all over the door and every place. He had one fabulous great oil painting; I think it was called "The Green Woman." Both Wendy and I envied that but it was beyond my pocketbook at the time. I had to pass on it but I bought a few smaller works.

Q: Did you ever represent Bok?

A: No. But I do recall that, as my days of being a fanzine editor were coming to an end, for the 50th issue of *The Imagi-Nation (VOM)*, I wanted something special. Now a favorite science fiction novel of mine was called *The World Below* by S. Fowler Wright. And it had a page that describes the characters an amphibian woman, a man of the present who finds himself 500,000 years in the future, a bat man, a gigantic firefly and a frog man. Well, here was this one page, and I thought, if I were an artist, I'd know exactly what to draw. And I decided to, as I say, go out in this blaze of glory with my fanzine and asked Bok to draw the final cover for me.

Now, in all 49 issues the artwork for *VOM* had been contributed free. I didn't make any money from the fanzine, and it was an opportunity for artists to display their work. However, Bok wanted to be paid. Even though it went against my practice, I agreed, under the condition that I could keep the original on my wall.

Well, you cannot imagine with what excitement I opened the package I eventually received from Hannes, I did a kind of striptease with myself, opening a bit of it at a time. But if someone had been videotaping as I opened it, they would have seen my face gradually falling as I saw more and more of the art. Now, it was a great drawing per se. I often have wished I still had it and wonder what became of it. But it was certainly not photographic. I don't know whether you'd call it cubist or Dali-esque but it did not satisfy me as far as depicting these creatures. Before speaking to Bok about it, I took it to the Los Angeles Science Fantasy Society and said, "I'm going to read a description and then show you a drawing. And if you feel it's a good likeness of the description, vote yes, if you feel it's some kind of interpretation, vote no." Neither vote was to be any kind of value judgment, you understand, it was merely asking if the art followed the description. Well, everybody voted no. So armed with that I said to Hannes that I'd buy the artwork for my collection but that I didn't want to use it for the cover after all. Well, he was just incensed. He said I can't buy it, I can't have it. And, as far as I know, he never forgave me.

Q: Science fiction authors often predicted the future in their writings. Could the same be said of the artists?

A: Yes, I think so. The artists went in two directions, either fantastic machinery that was thrilling to the eye, or into depicting the world of space, rockets, life on other worlds, futuristic alien cities and so on.

Q: Who, In your opinion, was the most visionary science fiction artist?

A: (Without a moment's hesitation) Frank... Rudolph... Paul. (Smile).

Q: Do you think the artists of today are being left behind in their ability to depict the future, due to all the other future-predictive media that surrounds us?

A: It seems to me so, yes. It's all pretty much technical polish without much advancement from where we were decades ago, for the reasons you describe.

Q: Did your experiences with artwork in early science fiction fandom in any way effect the visual aspects of *Famous Monsters of Filmland?*

A: No, alas, because that was totally the province of the publisher, Jim Warren, who considered himself something of an artist.

Q: If you could choose one artist and give him or her the assignment to create a 100 page version of *METROPOLIS* in either comic book or book form, who would it be today?

A: Today? Well, possibly Anton Brezezinski, who's done over 60 recreations of Frank R. Paul artwork for me. He's beginning to think he *is* Frank R. Paul. He's done a grand job for me.

Q: If a vintage artist were given the same assignments, who would it have been?

A: Frank R. Paul, of course. You know, I'm still wishing that Disney or another creator of theme parks would create some of Paul's visions in three dimensions, two storeys high.

Q: In a way, Disney already has. Have you seen the new Disney animation building in Burbank? It's actually very Frank R. Paul, very art deco futura.

A: Really! I'll have to take a look at that!

The author with 4-S-J, in the Ackermansion, Spring 1997. Photo by Tom Horvitz.

SCIENCE FICTION AND PULP ART LISTING

The Science Fiction and Pulp artist listing for the 2000 Comic Art and SF Price Guide has been greatly enlarged for this edition. While this market does not have the wide spread numbers of collectors or deep pockets of the Comic Art Market there is growing evidence of both the Pulp art market and Science Fiction art market getting ready for new growth. The publication recently of serious books about Pulp and SF art, from Robert Lessor's excellent *Pulp Art* from Gramercy Books, which is the first book to exclusively feature artwork shot from original paintings; to the sophisticated and glamorous *Pulp Culture* by Frank M. Robinson from Collectors Press; to the very best visual history of Science Fiction artwork by artist/author Vincent DiFate entitled *Infinite Worlds* from The Wonderland Press, collectors are offered historical analysis and a wide variety of visual examples on the depth and diversity of artwork from these genres. Each of these books are highly recommended for anyone considering collecting in these fields. These books, by their publication alone, signal a new interest in the art of the science fiction world.

Just as the majority of Comic Book artwork from the 1930's and 1940's through the 1950's was destroyed, so too with the 1910's, 1920's and 1930's where most of the Pulp and Science Fiction original artwork ended up in the dumpster.. The famous and legendary story of collector and historian Sam Moskowitz coming across an assistant in the hallway during his tenure as Managing Editor for Hugo Gernsback's *Science Fiction* + during the 1950's only to discover that said assistant was about to dispose into the dumpster twelve original paintings by Frank R. Paul is both incredible and true. Mr. Moskowitz paid the very high fee in the 1950's to have these paintings taken by cab from New York City to his home in New Jersey, after receiving permission from Hugo Gernsback, otherwise they would have gone the way of 95% of all Pulp art! The dividing line for most serious pulp art collectors is 1939, anything from before this time is considered genuinely rare, and from the 1940's upward more common. Within the 1950's the entire situation changes for Science Fiction originals (and the Pulp magazines began to encounter their demise); very high percentages of both magazine, paperback, and book original paintings and black and white illustrations are now known to exist from this period onward. The common practice of publishers giving paintings to local SF Conventions and the larger Annual WorldCon provided a venue for the common fan to buy, and buy they did. Even today, small collections of originals surface from people who made their purchases at SF conventions over thirty years ago.

The final word is not in by any means, however current trends suggest that the really great original paintings by major artists for important magazine titles and author stories that are yet to surface on the market (i.e. not known to yet exist for sale) will be as few and scarce as original Golden Age Comic Book covers. Less than 150? As many as 300? The long time collectors and new-to-the-market enthusiasts can only ponder, and hope that the number will be kind to the future generations of collectors.

Many will view this guide and say that a three tier pricing system, involving CONDITION, CONTENT , and CHARACTER, cannot apply in the same way to a Pulp Painting, or Science Fiction painting the way it does to a comic book page. However, common sense dictates that just such a system does indeed work. Robert Heinlein himself would appreciate and possibly defend the logic herein. Condition will affect any original, from an Old Master painting, to a Matisse, to an original Emshwiller. The content, in the case of Pulp or Science Fiction artwork, is also critical. Does the scene show the standard

PRICE RANGE KEY

RARITY — Brackets [ ] around a price indicate that this example is very scarce and could exceed maximum estimate.

<u>Covers</u>

No work produced in this category— XXX

No price available due to lack of information— ***

CONDITION — Age, color, marks, tears, etc.

<u>Pages</u>

[400   500   600]

CHARACTER — Is the primary character featured, or is the original characteristic of a great example in the story line?

CONTENT — is the theme or story line exceptional or below average?

VALUE RANGE

Minimum   Medium   Maximum

RARITY

The [ ] Brackets indicate RARITY, if these brackets are used the reader can potentially double the price range in all three catagories.

---

sexy-girl scenario for an Earle Bergey SF painting for *Startling Stories* or *Thrilling Wonder* from the 1940's? Or would the cover happen to be the November 1948 cover for *Startling Stories* in which artist Earle Bergey did an exceptional painting for Arthur C. Clarke's "Against The Fall of Night," an early masterpiece by one of the central SF authors of our time? This painting would engage both the CONTENT and CHARACTER columns in this books listing. Remember that when the CHARACTER column does not refer to a specific character (Superman, Operator #5, Doc Savage, The Shadow, etc.) then Character would mean an exceptional example from an important authors work, or a classic example from a particular genre, or artist, western, detective, etc. By using the criteria for these four areas: 1) Condition; 2) Content; 3) Character; and 4) Brackets [ ] for Rarity you can break down almost any Pulp or Science Fiction painting or black and white illustration, and arrive at a fundamental range of value.

Future editions of this guide will expand the listings for more Pulp artists, and continue to expand the regular contemporary and foreign artist listings for Science Fiction artwork. As with any growing compendium or listing of this kind, mistakes can be made by the author or come in through erroneous sources. Readers, artists, and collectors are encouraged to write to the author with corrections and any additional information that they may feel is important to this guide. Please refer to the market report in the beginning of this book for information about sales and trends in the Science Fiction and Pulp art market.

Charles Addams, original watercolor cartoon for the
New Yorker, watercolor on paper.
© The New Yorker Magazine

ACHILLEOS, CHRIS (1947-)

An English science fiction artist who is
known for movie poster design, book
covers (Burroughs' Pellucidar, Norman's
Gor, Dr. Who, etc.) and erotic pin-up
"Amazons." Using airbrush, acrylics, dyes,
watercolors, and a wide range of media,
this artist develops a highly original style.

Paintings (prelims/sketches)			
	$600	$800	$1,200
Paintings (final works)	$4,500	$6,000	$8,000
Paintings (pin-ups, major paintings)			
	$7,500	$9,000	$20,000

ADAMS, NEAL

The famed comic book artist did a series of
paperback covers for E. R. Burroughs
Tarzan series that were excellent.

Tarzan Paintings	$2,500	$3,500	$4,500

ADDAMS, CHARLES SAMUEL (1912-)

Famed as the author of the "Addam's
Family," this off-beat and authentic
American cartoonist did many SF theme
works that had a lasting effect on later
artists such as Gahan Wilson and Arnold
Roth. Since the artist's death, and the
major exhibition at the New York Public
Library, along with the fact that the artist's
family is not putting any work on the
market, Addams' prices have escalated
strongly in the past three years.

Paintings (*New Yorker* magazine covers)			
	[$7,000	$12,000	$18,000]
Paintings (*New Yorker* "Addams Family" cartoons, Black & White)			
	[$2,000	$5,000	$10,000]
Paintings (*New Yorker* Macabre cartoons 1940's -1950's, B&W)	$1,200	$1,800	$2,800
Preliminary Paintings (for *New Yorker* magazine cartoons)	$600	$1,500	$3,500
Paintings (non-NY cartoons)			
	$1,500	$2,800	$4,000
Paintings (colored cartoons 1970's-80's)			
	$1,500	$2,500	$3,500
Souvenir Drawings	$200	$400	$1,200

ADKINS, DAN L. (1937-)

Dan Adkins is an accomplished illustrator
and veteran comic book artist who started
out in 1955 doing pen and ink illustrations
for various science-fiction digests and
eventually worked as an assistant to Wally
Wood on the *Thunder Agents* comic series
and other assignments during the mid
1960's.

Pen & Ink illustrations	$50	$100	$150

ADRANGA, ROBERT (?)

Robert Adranga appeared during the
1960's doing covers for *Amazing Stories*
and *Fantastic Adventures*, he later returned
in the 1970's to SF to do a number of Ace
paperback covers.

Paintings (1960's)	$150	$350	$500
Paintings (1970's paperback)			
	$150	$250	$400

ALEXANDER, PAUL R. (1937-)

A science fiction illustrator who did a
limited number of paperback covers in the
late 1970's and 1980's.

Paintings	$175	$325	$475

ANDERSON, ALLEN

Anderson was a prolific pulp cover artist for the Fiction House Publishing Group during the 1940's to the 1950's. He became the chief cover artist for *Planet Stories* during the later years of its run. Only a handful of his originals are known to exist.

Paintings   [$3,000 $4,000 $5,000]

ANDERSON, MURPHY (1926-)

This legendary artist has always had a soft spot in his heart for science fiction. Besides a long and successful career working in the comics, Murphy also drew the syndicated "Buck Rogers" daily newspaper strip for two years. He began working for Fiction House's *Planet Comics* during the early 1940's and eventually contributed illustrations to *Planet Stories*, the pulp magazine. He also did illos for *Amazing Stories* and *Fantastic Adventures* up through the early 1950's. To date none of his pulp original drawings have surfaced in the marketplace.

Pen & Ink Illustrations
  (no originals known to exist)
                      [$600 $800 $1,000]

ARFSTROM, JON D. (1928-)

A science fiction fan who became a professional artist for *Weird Tales* during the 1950's. From the 1980's onward this artist is mainly creating and selling personal works in the fantasy genre.

Paintings $800 $1,200 $2,000
Paintings (major paintings)
                   $1,000 $2,000 $3,500
Pen & Ink Illustrations $50 $100 $150

ARNOLD, HERB

An artist who spent time with Richard Corben, and illustrated for many fanzines during the 1960's. He also did covers for Arkham House Books.

Black & White Wash paintings
              $250 $500 $1,500

Black & White Illustrations
                  $25 $50 $100
Arkham Covers $500 $1,000 $2,000

ARTZYBASHEFF, BORIS (1899-1965)

A highly regarded artist who did more than 200 covers for *Time* magazine. His personal style included many elements of the fantastic and he has done book covers for some classic Fantasy titles such as L. Sprague de Camp and Fletcher Pratt's *Land of Unreason* and T*he Incomplete Enchanter*. Since the great majority of the artist's works are in institutional collections, notably Syracuse University, most of these prices are speculative. His anthropomorphized machine imagery is a unique brand of surrealism and is his most sought after work.

Paintings (*Time* Magazine covers)
                   [$1,500 $3,000 $7,000]
Paintings (advertisements-color)
                   [$900 $1,800 $3,500]
Pen & Ink Illustrations (Editorial Illustrations)
                   [$1,000 $4,000 $9,000]
  (Fantasy book illustrations)
                   [$300 $750 $2,000]

'ATOM'
- (see ARTHUR THOMPSON)

AUSTIN, ALICIA (1942-)

Austin is a Hugo winner for the best fan artist and has produced a body of work, much of which has seen print with Donald Grant publications. Since the mid-late 1980's primarily known for southwest/native American-folkloric themed works, and children's book illustrations.

Paintings (major paintings)
                   $3,000 $3,500 $4,000
Paintings (regular works)
                   $1,000 $1,500 $2,000
Paintings (preliminary watercolor or ink
  studies) $400 $500 $650
Preliminary Ink Studies $200 $300 $400

George Barr, cover illustration for DeCamp's THE CONAN SWORDBOOK, pen and ink with brush on paper, 1969. © The Mirage Press

Rudolph Belarski, cover painting for THRILLING WONDER STORIES for 12/42, oil on canvas, from the collection of Robert Lessor. © Standard Magazines Inc.

BAMA, JAMES ELLIOT (1926-)

An American artist who began doing commercial work for men's magazines during the 1950's and eventually went on to become one of the most "realistic" paperback covers painters of the genre. During the 1960's he became most recognized as the cover artist for the Bantam paperback *Doc Savage* series and painted 62 cover paintings all total. Since then he has become one of the most successful western painters in America and his following today is phenomenal.

Paintings (1950's SF, etc.)
$1,500 $2,500 $4,000
Paintings (for the Bantam *Doc Savage* Series)
$3,000 $6,000 $9,000

BARR, GEORGE (1937-)

Barr's first artwork was published in fanzines and he soon became a polished professional, producing gem-like covers for paperback and hardcover books.

Paintings $1,000 $1,500 $2,000
Interior Black & White Illustrations
$200 $300 $400

BARR, KENNETH J. (1933-)

This Scottish artist is known for comic art work for Marvel and DC before moving into literary illustration, and RPG cards.

Paintings (major works)$2,500 $3,500 $4,500
Paintings (normal final works)
$500 $800 $1,200
Pen & Ink Illustrations
$200 $250 $300

BAUMAN, JILL (1942-)

An American artist known for horror, mysteries, and fantasy who rarely sells her original artwork.

Paintings (major works)
$2,500 $3,500 $5,000
Paintings (final normal works)
$1,000 $1,500 $2,000
Pen & Ink Illustrations
$150 $250 $300

BEECHAM, THOMAS (?)

An artist who did numerous interior illustration for the digest SF titles of the 1950's, he had a sharp developed style that was above average for most interior artists of this time.

Black & White Illustrations

$20 $35 $50

BEEKMAN, DOUGLAS

This artist works very slowly and has very limited production output in the SF field, and has a reticence to sell originals.

Paintings (major works)

$3,000 $4,500 $6,000

Paintings (regular finals)

$2,000 $2,500 $3,500

Paintings (preliminary works)

$300 $400 $600

BELARSKI, RUDOLPH (1900-83)

Belarski was a prolific illustrator who started out in the pulp field during the late 1920's. He eventually painted covers for many of the different pulp titles including some of the earliest and most important fantasy and SF stories for *Argosy*. Some of his finest covers were for Edgar Rice Burroughs stories, however he also excelled at aviation and detective themes. When the pulps passed on, he continued working in the digest and paperback field until the late 1950's. His pulp covers, although rare, do occassionally surface in the market.

Paintings (1930's Argosy Burroughs and A. Merritt magazine.covers)

[$5,000 $8,000 $11,000]

Paintings (other Argosy covers)

$2,000 $4,000 $6,000

BENETT, LEON (1839-1917)

A french artist who became involved with illustrating twenty five of Jules Verne's *Voyages Extraordinaires*, in which he executed over two thousand engravings and drawings to the series. The artist signed his name "L. Benett." He is listed in this guide for historical reasons as his original artwork is almost unknown in the SF market.

Earle Bergey, original cover painting for STARTLING STORIES for 9/50, sold at Illustration House in the 1980's for $5,000. © Standard Magazines Inc.

Pen & Ink Illustrations and Drawings

(prices would form rough estimate only)

[$2,000 $5,000 $7,000]

BERGEY, EARLE KULP (1901-52)

Earle Bergey was a prolific illustrator and cover artist who excelled at painting beautiful pin-up girls and later on brought sexy women and brass brassieres to the covers of *Thrilling Wonder Stories* and *Startling Stories*.

During the 1940's it was Bergey who envisioned some of the wildest bug-eyed alien creatures, along with perfectly developed handsome spacemen and women to fight them, than had ever been created before. Few of his covers seem to have survived. Bergey usually did a preliminary rough for his final paintings. Several of these are known to exist.

John Berkey, cover painting entitled
"Exit and Entering," to JOHN BERKEY PAINTED
SPACE, 1991, casein and acrylic paint.
© Freidlander Publishing Group.

Paintings (*Startling Stories, Thrilling Wonder*
etc.) SF covers with women in peril
[$4,000 $6,000 $8,000]
Paintings, science fiction covers without
women in peril   [$2,000 $3,000 $4,000]
Paintings that are non-science fiction in subject
matter. $1,000 $2,000 $3,000

Note: a current market activity for this
artist would include one trade of a Bergey
Startling Stories cover from the 1940's
straight up for a Frank R. Paul *Fantastic
Adventures* back cover painting; another
Bergey was bought privately just before
the FJA Gurnesy's auction for $5,000. A
Startling Stories cover painting (a classic
scene with a woman in peril) was sold in
the winter of 1998 for $10,000 cash.

BERKEY, JOHN C. (1932-)
A science fiction artist who can walk the
line between the contemporary and the
traditional. A very accomplished and
skilled painter, who with just a few brush
strokes can bring to the viewer new worlds

of imagination.   This artists work is
becoming more popular within the past
five years with collectors. Publications
would include *The Art of John Berkey* (FPG
Pub, 1991) and two series of fantasy art
trading cards in 1994 & 1996.

Paintings mid 1960's to 1970's
$1,000 $1,500 $2,000
price can vary with both content and size, as
some paintings by this artist are quite large.
Paintings (advertising and non-genre work)
$800 $2,000 $3,500
Paintings (unpublished SF and non-genre
works) $250 $2,000 $3,500

note: recent sales would include "Valis"
cover for P. K. Dick paperback title for
$2,500; "Spartan Planet," by Chandler,
paperback cover selling for $1,500.

BERRY, D. BRUCE (1924-)
Another fan artist who ended up doing
some professional work, this artist was
primarly active in the comic field, however,
he did do some interior illustrations for
Other Worlds and *Imagination*, etc.

Pen & Ink Illustrations $50 $75 $125

BERRY, RICK (1954-)
Rick Berry stands almost alone as an artist
who truly intends to push Science Fiction
illustration beyond its traditional boundries
and prejudices toward the 21st and 22nd
centuries. Using the latest technologies of
digital art available he has fashioned
working methods that bring forth startling
and new images. Collecting his original
artwork can however become a bit of a
problem for the physcially bound
earthperson in that some of his best
paintings exist as finished works of art only
in the electronic world of cyberspace.
However, enough finished oils exist for
most of the enlightened few to be able to
enjoy the simple pleasures of retinal
observation and possession.

Paintings $1,500 $2,500 $5,500
Pen & Ink & Wash & Mixed Media Works
(some fed through computer images, and
then reworked) $150 $300 $500

Images struck from finished computer generated works, (in this case works that are painted first, then finished by working within computer graphics, and then signed). $100 $200 $300

Note: Berry is beginning work with the most advanced computer Jet-printer. This system is the first truly UV and long time permanent printing system that will strike color prints that will last for years, and not fade out in a short period of time. The limited edition prints, and/or combination paintings that will come from this process will be new to the market. However, their value will be the same as buying fine edition lithograph or color prints.

note: recent sales include "Mabelline" selling for $5,000; "Bug City" for $3,000; "Partners," selling for $4,000; editions of the digital lithos are selling from $200 to $400 each and sales are expanding.

BINDER, JACK (JOHN) R. (1902-)

The elder brother of science fiction writers Otto and Earl Binder, Jack did a number of black and white interior SF illustrations for *Startling Stories* and *Thrilling Wonder* before launching his own comic book art studio in 1940. Few if any of his original pulp illustrations are known to exist.

Pen & Ink Illustrations $100 $200 $300

BINKLEY, RIC

An artist known for his cover designs for Fantasy Press, Gnome Press and Avalon Books.

Paintings (can be mono or duo-tone as well as full color) $350 $700 $900
Pen & Ink Illustrations $50 $100 $250

BLAINE, MAHLON (1894-1970)

A very well known artist during the 1920's and 1930's who occasionally worked within the fantasy and science fiction field. His more recent work was seen in the Canaveral editions for some of Edgar Rice Burroughs titles during the 1970's. A fair number of Blaine's privately printed book illustrations are available, however his

Rick Berry, painting entitled "The Marriagable Woman," from DOUBLE MEMORY, oil on board with mixed media. © Donald Grant Publications.

work is an aquired taste, both of which contribute to low numbers on sales.

Color Ink Illustrations (from 1930's, 1940's)
          $400 $800 $1,200
Pen & Ink Illustrations (book)
          $300 $600 $900
Burroughs Illustrations (in ink from 1960's)
          $200 $300 $400

BOBER, RICHARD (?)

An American artist who has worked in many different genres of paperback cover painting including mystery, SF and fantasy, and usually never signs his work. He also does private commissions for collectors of fantasy. During the 1970's he produced a number of wonderful horror/mystery cover paintings for the *Alfred Hitchcock* paperback series.

Hannes Bok, cover illustration for THE GNOME PRESS FANTASY CALENDER for 1949, pen and ink with brush on illustration board, created in 1946. © Gnome press Inc.

Hannes Bok, pencil preliminary for unpublished book jacket design, circa 1950's pencil on paper, private sale at $500 in 1996. © The Hannes Bok Estate

Paintings (major works)

$4,000	$9,000	$13,000

Paintings (regular finals)

$2,000	$4,500	$7,000

Preliminary Studies $300 $500 $700

Paintings (published fantasy, mystery in late 70's to mid 80's)

$1,500	$3,000	$4,000

Paintings (published fantasy works in the late 1980's to 1990's) $3,000 $5,000 $9,000

BODE, VAUGHN

The popular Underground comic book artist did many beautiful black and white interior illustrations, and some covers for science fiction fanzines. He also did a few finished paintings for *Galaxy*, and other digest magazines in the 1960's.

Black & White interiors $125 $250 $500

Covers, in Black & White

$200	$400	$750

Covers, paintings $350 $550 $850

BOK, HANNES (1914-64)

Paintings
(the few estate large 40" x 30" fantasy paintings)   [$8,000 $12,000 $16,000]
(early & mid 1940's *Weird Tales*, & hardcover Arkham House and Shasta covers)
$8,000 $10,000 $15,000
(1950's Magazine Fantasy covers, Imagination, Fantasy Fiction etc.) $2,500 $5,000 $8,000
(unpublished works, smaller fantasy paintings, and miscellaneous late 1950's and 1960's works) $800 $1,600 $2,500

Prints (signed limited, and artist proof's, late 1940's and 1950's) $100 $200 $350

Pencil Works, and Preliminary Drawings
(preliminary cover and dust jacket designs, private commissions, etc.)
$200 $300 $600

Pencil Works, & smaller Preliminary Sketches $35 $75 $150

Masks & Three Dimensional Works
(wall masks, cut-out-fantasy sculptures, etc.) Size will determine price here as well as quality. $800 $1,200 $1,600

Pen & Ink
(early *Weird Tales*, Arkham House, Fantasy Press, Shasta, for the 1930's & 1940's)
[$1,000 $2,000 $3,000]
(1950's works, and minor 1940's, unpublished and fanzine works) $600 $800 $1,200
(Black and White originals for Lovecraft, Bloch, and other major fantasy authors, especially 1930's)   [$1,200 $2,400 $3,600]

Hannes Bok, artwork for Pulp Illustration to "Door at the Opera" by Ray Cummings, for ASTONISHING STORIES, 12/40; estimate; $1,700/2,250; sold for $1,375 in 10/92. Sotheby's 2nd comic art auction. © Astonishing Stories Inc.

Hannes Bok & Boris Dolgov, illustration from SF QUARTERLY, 1940's; estimate; $400/600; sold for $690 in 6/96. Sotheby's 6th comic art auction. © Double Action Magazines

Hannes Bok, interior illustration for "Half Haunted" by Gans T. Field (M.W. Wellman) From WEIRD TALES, pen and ink on heavy paper, sold privately in 1996 for $800. © Popular Fiction Publishing Company

Chesley Bonestell, original painting entitled " Surface of Mercury," from the CONQUEST OF SPACE, oil on board, in a private collection. © Viking Press/ The Chesley Bonestall Estate.

BONESTELL, CHESLEY K. (1888-1986)

(Note: Unlike many other science fiction and fantasy artists, Chesley Bonestell's original artwork is almost unknown within the confines of the traditional science fiction and fantasy fan markets. Many of the more important paintings are locked into institutional collections, and a great many of the other early works reside within private collections outside fandom. There are no records of important paintings selling within the U.S. or Great Britain at public auction. Because of the lack of any quality works in the market, if just four or five exceptional paintings were to surface in any given year the market could be turned upside down).

Paintings

(early 1940's works, Moon landscapes and Rocket themes)   [$7,000 $14,000 $28,000]

(early to mid 1950's Space Exploration, Conquest of Mars, Conquest of Space works, and other paintings) [$5,000 $10,000 $25,000]

(mid 1950's Space Station, Earth Orbit, larger paintings that function as twice normal size or larger examples)   [$8,000 $16,000 $34,000]

(lesser works from above categories, Viking Press Publications, and the same time period)
          $3,000 $9,000 $14,000

(paintings connected with the film *Destination Moon*, finished background works)   [$6,000 $12,000 $20,000]

(preliminary works, pencil, painted used for the film *Destination Moon*)
          [$1,000 $3,000 $5,000]

(works for NASA and later periods)
          $1,500 $2,500 $4,000

Chesley Bonestell, original painting for Zero Hour Minus Five, oil on board, from the collection of Forrest J. Ackerman, sold at Guernsey's in 1987. © The Chesley Bonestall Estate.

Black and White Preliminary works to paintings.

(almost unknown to the market)

[$1,000 $2,500 $4,000]

Note: The estate of Chesley Bonestell sold seven original paintings in a single sale for $80,000 in the winter of 1999. Most of these works were planetary landscapes. Other private sales include a small lunar landscape measuring 8½ x 18½ inches for $7,500, and a Martain lunar landscape for $17,500. There have also been a few private sales of individual paintings for $25,000 and above.

BOWMAN, WILLIAM R. (?)

This artist worked for a very short period of time between 1956 through 1958 doing interior illustrations for *Amazing, Galaxy, Saturn*, etc.

Pen & Ink Illustrations

$50 $75 $175

BRAUTIGAM, DONALD P. (1946-)

American artist who had designed important HC and paperback SF covers, including Del Rey's *Nerves*, and King's *The Stand*.

Paintings $800 $1,600 $3,500

BRILLHART, RALPH (?)

An artist who ended up illustrating what would almost now be called "cult" paperback titles, in that he did covers for Monarch, Belmonts Books and Pyramid.

Paintings	$250	$375	$750

BROSNATCH, ANDREW (1896-?)

A pulp artist, known for his work on the early issues of *Weird Tales* magazine.

Paintings (none are known to exist at this time)	[$3,000	$3,500	$4,000]
Pen and ink	[$100	$250	$400]

Note: higher priced items would depend on the author, as Brosnatch did do early illustrations for Lovecraft and other famous *Weird Tales* authors. Many illustrations have the lettering for the story directly on the board.

BROWN, HOWARD V. (1878-?)

This artist would perhaps be unknown to the present generation, however his place in history is secured alongside Frank R. Paul, J. Allen St. John, and other early great masters within the field. Half-way through life when given the first assignments for *Astounding Stories* during the 1930's, he had previously cut his teeth as a pulp artist in the 1920's for *Argosy*. Many of the early classic *Astounding* covers come from this artist's brush. His work is extremely rare and only a handful of paintings for the SF field are known to exist.

Paintings (from *Argosy* Magazine late 1920's)	[$4,000	$6,000	$8,500]
Paintings (from *Astounding Stories* 1930's up)	[$5,000	$7,000	$10,000]

Note: a painting for *Astounding Stories* October 1937 (Galactic Patrol cover for E. E. Smith story) failed to meet its reserve at Sotheby's first SF auction in 1995, the low estimate price was $7,000, this painting later sold privately for $5,000. Another Brown painting sold in 1998 from a Galactic Patrol cover for *Astounding* from 1934 for $10,000 in a private sale. In 1999 the cover for *Thrilling Wonder Stories* for February 1938 turned up, an offer of $20,000 was turned down and this painting was traded for another Pulp painting.

BROWN, REYNOLD (1917-91)

Brown became a prolific illustrator during the 1940's doing covers and interior illustrations for technical-scientific magazines such as *Mechanics Illustrated* and *Popular Mechanics*. Few of these examples seem to have survived over the years. From the 1950's to 1960's he became one of the best movie poster painters working in Hollywood and consequently provided wonderful fantasy images for several noted science fiction or fantasy film posters. Fortunately Brown and his family managed to save much of his movie poster art from the studios he worked for and have released some originals through a New York auction house over the past few years.

*Paintings (movie posters 1950's)	[$5,000	$10,000	$15,000]

(*prices vary widely depending on the Movie Genre/title/star etc.)

Paintings (magazine cover works)	[$1,000	$2,000	$3,000]
Pen & Ink Illustrations (for magazine interior illustrations 1940's-50's)	[$400	$900	$1,600]

BRUNDAGE, MARGARET (1900-76)

An artist whose reputation rests on her sensuous covers for *Weird Tales* magazine. Brundage worked in pastel chalks and very few of her paintings survived over the years. A very high percentage of these original *Weird Tales* covers are now in one private collection locked away from the market and other collectors. The most famous find of Brundage paintings came from Chuck Wooley in the early 1970's. While living in Peoria, Illinois, he made arrangements to buy a number of pristine condition original *Weird Tales* covers. Over the years Mr. Wooley allowed a number of these originals to come into the market. The collection of Forrest J. Ackerman held a few important Brundage originals for a number of years. They are rarely if ever offered on the market.

Paintings (*Weird Tales* covers) for R. E. Howard, or special Vampire, or other special subject matter)   [$15,000 $25,000 $35,000]
Paintings (*Weird Tales* covers non-Howard, or average covers)
     [$10,000 $15,000 $20,000]

Note: Most Brundage pastel original *Weird Tales* covers are now in permanent collections. Only one has changed hands in the last two years.

BULL, R. M.
British artist associated with cover paintings for *Science-Fantasy* and other digest magazine titles.

Paintings (1950's) $200 $400 $600

BUNCH, JOHN
An artist who did cover and interior illustrations for *Galaxy Science Fiction* magazine in the 1950's.

Paintings $100 $200 $350
Black & White Illustrations
     $10 $20 $40

BURNS, JIM (1948-)
An English artist who has won the 1985 and 1995 best artist Hugo awards, along with British Fantasy, British SF, and Chesley awards. Using an almost photo-realist technique, this artist has become one of the leading contemporary illustrators in the SF field. Reference works are *Mechanismo*, *Flights of Icarus* (P. Tiger Press), & *Heroic Dreams*.

Paintings (major paintings)
     $3,500 $5,000 $8,000
Paintings (regular finals)
     $2,000 $2,500 $3,500
Prints (Abandon Art (UK) early 1990's)
     ***   ***   ***

BURROUGHS, JOHN COLEMAN (1913-79)
(note: at least 80%, if not 90%, of John Coleman Burroughs originals for his fathers works remain with the ERB Inc. collection. For this reason originals are scarce and there are few comparable prices)

Paintings
(Edgar Rice Burroughs cover paintings for books)   [$4,000 $8,000 $20,000]
Black and White Illustrations.
(Edgar Rice Burroughs interior illustrations)
     [$1,500 $2,500 $3,500]
"John Carter of Mars," Comic Book pages. Beginning with *The Funnies* #30, May 1939 running through until issue #56, June of 1941.
     [$1,000 $2,000 $4,000]
"John Carter of Mars," Sunday Newspaper Strip pages. December 7, 1941, through March 28, 1943. Pages are rare.
     [$350 $750 $1,250]

CALDWELL, CLYDE (1948-)
Clyde Caldwell has based his original career doing illustrations for both Fantasy and SF magazines, work for *Heavy Metal* magazine, and TSR Hobbies. Reference work can be found in *The Art of Dragon Magazine, Art of Dragonlance Saga, & Art of Dungeons & Dragons* (TSR).

Paintings (major works) $5,000 $6,500 $8,000
Paintings (finals for regular works)
     $1,500 $2,000 $2,500
Paintings (preliminary works)
     $400 $500 $600
Pen & Ink Illustrations
     $500 $650 $850

CALLE, PAUL (1928-)
A pulp artist who eventually did work for hardcover books and magazines in the SF field in the 1940's and 1950's. Mr. Calle is now a famous illustrator in the mainstream, and is primarily known for his B&W reportage art for NASA these days. His early *Galaxy* interiors are done in scratchboard style derived from the work of Rockwell Kent and are quite unlike what he is known for presently.

Paintings	$400	$600	[$900]
Pen & Ink Illustrations on Scratchboard			
	$300	$400	$500

CANEDO, ALEJANDRO (?)

An artist who contributed a number of surrealistic and unique covers to *Astounding Science Fiction* in the late 1940's. He signed his name "Alejandro."

Paintings	$500	$800	$1,500

CANTY, THOMAS (?)

Part of the original "Studio" group of artists which included Jeff Jones and Barry Winsor Smith this artist developed a highly refined style.

Paintings	$2,500	$4,000	$7,500
Watercolor original works			
	$500	$1,000	$1,500
Pen & Ink Illustrations	$250	$500	$1,500

CARTER, ALICE "BUNNY" (1947-)

A contemporary SF artist who has been closely associated with Lucasfilm productions.

Paintings	***	***	***

CARTIER, EDD (1914-)

(Note: There are examples of Cartier's originals turning up from most periods within traditional fan markets, however two realities should be kept in mind. Most of these originals have surfaced and gone into permanent collections from the late 1950's through early 1970's, after this period of time it is a rare treat to be able to purchase Cartier work from any period. The number of originals within the market originally released, compared to an artist like Virgil Finlay, would be equal to about 4% of the Finlay total. This reality is reinforced by the family retaining a very

Ed Cartier, interior plate for GNOME PRESS FANTASY CALENDER for 1949, penand ink with brush on paper.
© The Gnome Press Inc.

Ed Cartier, interior plate for GNOME PRESS FANTASY CALENDER for 1950, pen and ink with brush on paper. © The Gnome Press Inc.

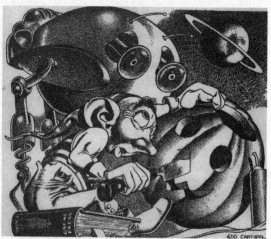

Ed Cartier, interior plate for GNOME PRESS FANTASY CALENDER for 1950, pen and ink with brush on paper. © The Gnome Press Inc.

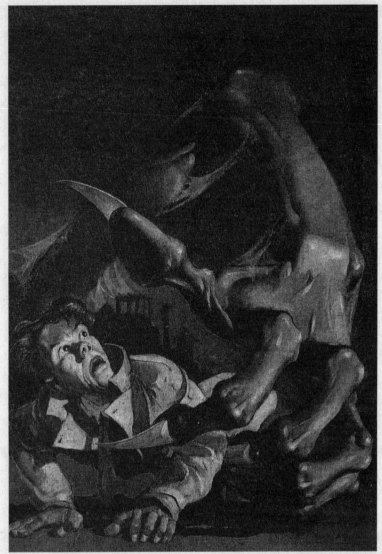

Ed Cartier, cover painting for UNKNOWN for 12/39 (one of only two fantasy paintings by this artist known to exist), oil on canvas. Sold privately in 1999 for $25,000. © Street & Smith Publications Inc.

large number of the original *Unknown* and *Astounding* originals. In addition to the scarcity of the B&W originals there have only been two recorded sales of paintings within the past twenty-five years. The only exception to this would be the release of a number (over 80) of the smaller mystery B&W illustrations in the early 1990's).

Paintings, full color.
(almost unknown to market in prior 25 years, only two to three charted in private collections)
[$4,000 $8,000 $16,000]
(monochrome, or duo-colored)
[$3,000 $6,000 $9,000]

Pen & Ink Illustrations.
(a number of 5" x 5" to 7" x 7" Mystery magazine illustrations surfaced in the 1990's)
$200 $300 $400
(1930's through 1943, *Unknown, Astounding,* Fantasy Press, Gnome Press)
[$800 $1,600 $2,400]
(1930's through 1943, *Unknown, Astounding,* larger format B&W illustrations, usually aprox. 20" x 14" in size)
[$1,500 $3,000 $4,500]
(B&W from 1944-53)
$600 $1,200 $2,000

Note: In the winter of 1998/99 a private sale of a select small number of Black and

Ed Cartier, interior illustration for Eric Frank Russell's SINISTER BARRIER, from the collection of Forrest J. Ackerman, sold in 1997 for $1,500. © Fantasy Press

White illustrations was made by the Cartier family, details of pricing and content are confidential to the family. Also in the Summer of 1998 the original oil painting for *Unknown* for December 1939, the cover featuring L. Sprague de Camp's "Lest Darkness Fall," sold for $35,000. This is one of only two known *Unknown* cover paintings by Cartier. Also at the LA Alternate World Con in August of 1999 a calendar original by Cartier was sold for $600.00

CLARKE, HARRY (1889-1931)

A gifted illustrator for children's books and classic works of literature, including the masterpiece black and white illustrations for Edgar Allan Poe's 1931 Tudor edition of *Tales of Mystery and Imagination*.

Paintings (unknown to the market, extremely rare)   [$7,500 $10,000 $20,000]

Pen & Ink Illustrations (also extremely rare)
    [$2,500 $5,000 $7,500]

Size would play a defining role in price, some Clarke originals are quite small.

Note: buyers should check Christie's and Sotheby's London book auctions, as occasional originals by Clarke are known to turn up at English auctions.

CLYNE, RONALD (1925-)

An artist who lept from fandom and fanzines to professional magazines and then on to a successful career in commercial art.

Pen & Ink Illustrations (for pulp magazines)
                $175 $225 $350

Arkham House Covers (most done as black and white designs) $250 $350 $800

COBB, RON (1937-)

An artist who began his career as an animator for Disney, later doing cover paintings for *Famous Monsters of Filmland* and *Spacemen* magazine for Forrest J. Ackerman. During the 1960's Cobb did political cartoons and was picked in 1982 to become one of the ten official artists chosen by NASA to document the launch and landing of STS4. Today he is a successful art director in Hollywood and has contributed his insightful imaginative ideas to numerous fantasy films.

Famous Monsters and Spacemen
    cover paintings $600 $800 $1,400
Political on Panel Cartoons
    Black and White $350 $500 $700
Movie preliminary and finished design and concept originals
                $400 $600 $1,200

COGGINS, JACK (1911-)

Coggins got in on the tail end of providing cover paintings for the pulp magazines during the early 1950's before converting to the new digest-sized magazine format. He continued doing covers for *Galaxy* and *The Magazine of F & SF* and worked with Fletcher Pratt on several books about space travel.

Paintings $400 $800 $1,200

COLL, JOSEPH CLEMENT (1881-1921)

Coll was a turn of the century illustrator who is considered one of the top four pen and ink artists of all time and who got his start early on doing newspaper illustrations. He was second to few in his great powers of imagination and is most fondly remembered by fantasy collectors for his detailed illustrations for Merritt's *The Moon Pool* and Doyle's *The Lost World*. A number of his originals have survived over the years but are usually snapped up immediately by collectors when they become available.

Pen & Ink Illustrations (scarce pre-1910 non science fiction themes)
                [$2,500 $4,500 $6,500]
Pen & Ink Illustrations (science fiction)
                [$3,000 $6,000 $9,000]

CORBEN, RICHARD L. (1940-)

One of the early pioneering fantasy artists who utilized and mastered the technique of airbrush in mixed media illustration. A very proflific and popular artist who has worked in all genres of professional expression including comic books, magazine, paperback and book illustration. Richard Corben has one of the largest fan followings in the fantasy market today with most of his works already locked into permanent museum collections. He has done memorable work for various ERB projects, plus created numerous science fiction, fantasy and horror works.

Lee Brown Coye, interior illustration for WEIRDISMS, from an unidentified issue of WEIRD TALES, circa late 1940's early 1950's, pen and ink with brush on illustration board. © Weird Tales Limited.

Lee Brown Coye, interior plate from GOTHICS, pen and ink on paper, 1967. © Weird Tales Limited.

Paintings

(Warren publication covers, *Creepy, Eerie*, etc.)
$1,500	$2,500	$3,500

(magazines, fanzines, paperback covers, and ERB covers 1960's through the 1980's)
$2,500	$3,500	$4,500

Pen & Ink Illustrations
(line work)	$400	$600	$900
(airbrush)	$600	$800	$1,200

COYE, LEE BROWN (1907-81)

Lee Brown Coye is remembered for his unique style, an earlier forerunner for Graham Ingles (of EC comics *Haunt of Fear* fame) and Gahan Wilson. This artist did some of his best work for *Weird Tales* magazine and Arkham House Books.

Paintings

(*Weird Tales* or *Fantastic* covers from the late 1930's through the early 1950's. These are very scarce to the market)
[$2,000	$4,000	$6,000]

Pen & Ink Illustrations.

(Lovecraft, Bloch, C. A. Smith, special author & large Splash page illustrations, especially *Weird Tales* Poetry pages)

	[$500	$1,000	$1,500]
(1944-52)	$350	$450	$550
(1953-61)	$200	$300	$400
(1962-81)	$100	$250	$325

Pencil Preliminaries (to covers and other illustrations)
	$50	$100	$150

Reed Crandall, interior illustration for E.R. Burroughs' JOHN CARTER OF MARS, pen and ink on illustration paper, in a private collection. © E.R. Burroughs Inc./ Canaveral Press

Reed Crandall, interior title page illustration for Richard Lupoff's E. R. BURROUGHS MASTER OF ADVENTURE, pen and ink with brush on paper.
© E.R. Burroughs Inc./ Canaveral Press

CRANDALL, REED L. (1917-82)

One of the most recognized talents from the Golden Age of comic book art, Crandall actually started out to become a book illustrator. After getting side-tracked into the lucrative comic book field in 1941, he went on to lend his talents to hundreds of different characters and titles. During the 1960's Crandall's close friend Al Williamson asked him to help out on a few illustrations for the Canaveral Press hardcover edition of *John Carter of Mars* . This eventually led to over 40 other Burroughs illustrations being produced by Crandall, some of which never made it into print. Any of these detailed illustrations are highly collected by fans today.

Paintings
(very limited number of private commission works for Edgar Rice Burroughs themes)
[$2,000 $4,000 $6,000]

(watercolor fanzine covers, ERBDom, Spa Fon, etc.) $600 $1,200 $1,800
(monochrome paintings for various themes)
$1,000 $2,000 $3,000

Pen & Ink Illustrations.
(Canaveral Press Edgar Rice Burroughs Tarzan & John Carter covers)
$1,000 $1,500 $2,500
(Canaveral Press Edgar Rice Burroughs interior illustrations) $600 $900 $1,200
(Canaveral Press Burroughs illustrations in partnership with Al Williamson)
$1,500 $2,000 $2,500
(fanzine, usually Burroughs illustrations)
$400 $600 $800

CRISP, STEVE (1955-)
A British artist known for fantasy cover art and horror, with a strong presence in the UK paperback market.

Paintings (major works)
$2,000 $2,500 $3,000
Paintings (regular works)
$1,500 $2,000 $2,500
Paintings (preliminary works)
$400 $500 $600

D'ACHILLE, GINO (1935-)
American artist born in Rome, Italy, who in the 1960's from London created hundreds of paperback cover paintings, and HC SF works.

Paintings $750 $1,500 $3,000

DAMERON, NED (?)
An contemporary artist who had done many cover illustrations, some of his best work is for the Jack Vance titles for Underwood/Miller Press.

Paintings $1,000 $1,500 $2,500

DAVIES, GORDON C. (?)
One of the more interesting and accomplished English artists who began work in the 1950's with cult Paperback covers, was then given assignments for many of Robert Heinlein's paperback covers, and eventually went on to become highly respected throughout the field.

Paintings (early BEM 1950's)

$550	$750	$950

Paintings (Heinlein, and later air-brushed covers)

$600	$900	$1,250

DAVIS, ROGER (?)

An English artist who spent a very brief amount of time in the SF field in the 1950's. His intricate black and white scratchboard work for interior illustrations was beyond what most artists were willing to do for the pay they received from SF magazines.

Paintings	$400	$550	$750
Pen & Ink (scratchboard)	$90	$125	$225

DE SOTO, RAPHAEL (1904-87)

DeSoto was a prolific pulp cover artist who started out in 1930 working for Street and Smith. He eventually came to Popular Publications painting primarily covers for their mystery and adventure titles. De Soto was not thought of as a science fiction artist, but many of his covers had a strong science fiction element. He eventually became known for doing a great many of the *Spider* pulp covers, few of which seem to have survived today. Before his death in 1987 he produced a few recreations and special commissions for his fans.

Paintings (*Spider* & Fantasy)

[$3,000	$5,000	$7,000]

Pulp Cover Recreation Paintings

[$1,500	$2,500	$3,500]

DEAN, ROGER (1944-)

A very popular British artist who has designed futuristic album covers, and later went on to form Dragon's Dream and Paper Tiger press.

Paintings	$2,500	$4,000	$6,500

DEVITO, JOE (1957-)

A science fiction, horror, and fantasy author who began to work in the 1980's, noted for his continuing covers for the *Doc Savage* paperback series.

Paintings (SF and Fantasy)

$2,000	$4,000	$6,000

Paintings (*Doc Savage* paperback covers)

$1,500	$3,000	$4,500

DI FATE, VINCENT (1945-)

A science fiction artist who has worked in many levels of the industry, and won the Hugo for best artist in 1979. His style encompasses the best of the pulp art of the 1940's and contemporary trends. Mr. Di Fate has done much to champion the art of science fiction beyond his own artistic output, most recently noted as author of *Infinite Worlds*, the best cross-section history of SF art ever published. He was President of the Society of Illustrators for 1995-97. Published work includes *Di Fate's Catalog of Science Fiction Hardware* (Workman, 1980).

Paintings (major works)	$4,000	$5,000	$6,000
Paintings (regular works)			
	$2,500	$3,000	$4,000
Paintings (preliminary works)			
	$250	$450	$600
Pen & Ink Illustrations on Scratchboard			
	$200	$300	$500

Note: private sales have been made by the artist for major works at over $10,000 and $20,000 for individual paintings.

DILLION, LEO and DIANE (1933-)

A husband and wife team who have delivered masterful works for book covers over the years. Some of their finest works have been paintings for Harlan Ellison's books.

Paintings	$2,500	$5,500	$8,000
Paintings (non SF)	$1,000	$1,500	$2,500
Paintings (smaller 5x5")	$400	$800	$1,200
Pen & Ink Illustrations	$125	$250	$500

DIRGIN, S. R.

Bristish artist associated with *Fantasy Thrilling Science Fiction* cover paintings; examples are almost unknown.

Paintings	[$500	$1,000	$2,000]

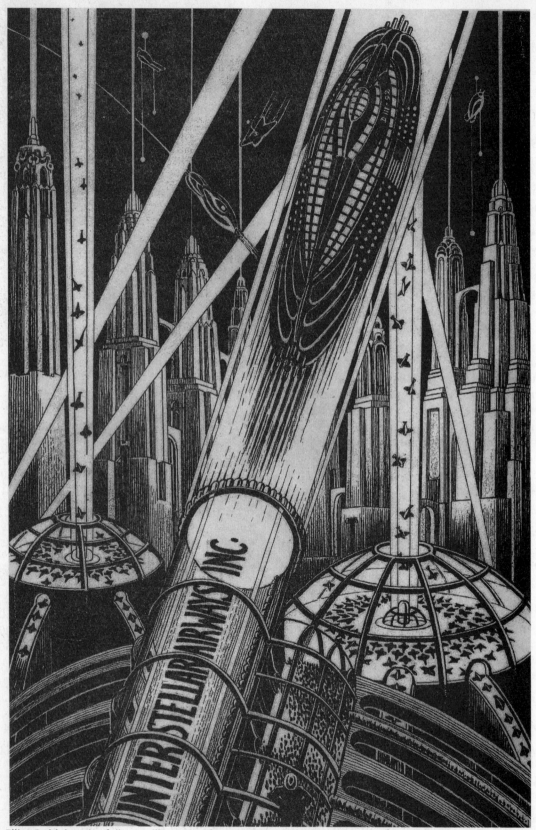

Elliot Dold, interior full page illustration from MIRACLE SCIENCE AND FANTASY STORIES #1 for April-May 1931, from the collection of Forrest J. Ackerman. © The Good Story Magazine Inc.

Elliot Dold, interior illustration for E.E. Smith's "Skylark of Valeron," from ASTOUNDING SF for 1/35, pen and ink on paper. © Street & Smith Publications

Elliot Dold, interior illustration for E.E. Smith's "Skylark of Valeron," from ASTOUNDING SF for 1/35, pen and ink on paper. © Street & Smith Publications

Elliot Dold, interior illustration for ASTOUNDING SF entitled "Negative Space," pen and ink on scratch board, from the collection of Forrest J. Ackerman. © Street & Smith Publications

DOLD, ELLIOTT (?)

Science Fiction artist for the early pulp titles. His most famous work was done for *Astounding Science Fiction* in the 1930's.

Pen & Ink (interior illustrations for famous authors)   [$150 $250 $400]

Pen & Ink (interior illustrations for special stories such as Campbell's "The Mightiest Machine" from *Astounding Stories* 1937)
[$750 $900 $1,200]

Pen & Ink (interior illustrations regular)
[$90 $125 $300]

Pen & Ink (non-science fiction illustrations)
$50 $100 $200

Note: Author and SF art historian Robert Weinberg remembers an early 1950's PilCon (Philadelphia) where a number of Dold originals were offered for sale at the convention auction on the final day. None of these originals were bought, and to this day the origin and whereabouts of these rare black and white originals remains a mystery. Two black and white originals from *Astounding Stories* were sold as private sales from the collection of FJA in the summer of 1999, for $750 and $1,000.

DOLGOV, BORIS (?)

Noted for his work with *Weird Tales*, this artist did several collaborations with Hannes Bok, signing under "Dolbokgov."

Paintings	$750	$1,500	$2,500
Pen & Ink Illustrations	$150	$250	$400
Pen & Ink Illustrations (under Dolbokgov with Bok)	$150	$300	$600

DOLLENS, MORRIS SCOTT (1920-)

A science fiction 'fan' artist, who later became better known with proessional magazine and book assignments.

Paintings (small, astronomy and space scenes)	$75	$150	$350
Paintings (magazine covers in the 1950's)	$125	$250	$500

DONNELL, A. J. (?)

An artist connected with the field because he was one of the original members of Fantasy Press. He was given many of the most important titles to illustrate, including Heinleins *Beyond This Horzion*, Weinbaum's *A Martian Odyssey*, and Williamson's *Darker Than You Think*.

Paintings (many are monotone)	$750	$1,250	$2,500
Pen & Ink illustrations	$90	$125	$250

DREANY, J (?)

An artist who did interior black and white illustrations for *Startling Stories* and *Thrilling Wonder Stories* in the late 1940's and 1950's.

Black & White Illustrations	$25	$50	$100

EASLEY, JEFF

An artist who was an original member of the in-house team of artists at TSR, and known for that association (see also Caldwell, Parkinson, Elmore) and Dungeons and Drangons (sword & socrery) works.

Paintings (major works)	$2,000	$3,500	$6,000
Paintings (regular finals)	$1,200	$1,400	$3,000

Paintings (preliminary works)	$75	$100	$150
Pen & Ink Illustrations	$75	$100	$150

EBEL, ALEX (1932-)

Ebel was an artist whose sophisticated use of inks and dyes turned out incredible cover paintings for various SF magazines during the 1950's. He also had a very controlled fine line delineation to his interior ink illustrations, and remains a collector favorite even today.

Paintings (mixed media)	$600	$1,000	$1,400
Pen & Ink Interiors	$200	$300	$400

EBERLE, JOSEPH R. (?)

An artist who entered the digest SF magazine market in the 1950's and did many interior illustrations for a number of different titles.

Black & White Illustrations	$25	$35	$45

EDWARDS, LES (1949-)

A British artist who was the winner of the 1990 and 1994 British Fantasy Society Award for best artist, known for gothic horror, 'splatter gore' illustration, movie concept work and literary genre paintings.

Paintings (major works)	$3,400	$3,800	$4,200
Paintings (regular finals)	$1,500	$1,750	$2,000
Paintings (preliminary works)	$150	$200	$250
Pen & Ink Illustrations	$500	$650	$800

EGGLETON, BOB (1960-)

Bob Eggleton is part of the current generation of 'supra-realist' artists who have had to compete with the imagry of the 1970's movies, and has come up with a style that both conjures up the best of these films and at times goes beyond them. He was a Hugo award winner for best artist for the years 1994, 1995, and 1996, and several Chesley Awards.

Paintings (major works)	$3,500	$4,000	$5,000

Paintings (regular finals)

$1,500	$2,000	$2,500

Paintings (preliminary works)

$150	$200	$250

Pen & Ink Illustrations $400 $600 $800

Prints: several limited edition prints are available through *Novagraphics*, no prices are available at this time.

ELLIS, DEAN (1920-)

A contemporary artist who has done many magazine and paperback covers during the 1960's and 1980's. Mr. Ellis is one of the best gadget artists of the 1960's through the 1980's, however he has ceased doing work for the SF field and will most likely not return.

Paintings (1960's) $1,500 $2,000 $3,000
Paintings (with emphasis on gadgets)
                        $1,750 $2,250 $3,750

ELMORE, LARRY

An American fantasy artist who started in the paperback cover field and has since gone on to become one of the original members of the in-house team of artists at TSR, and is known for that association (see Caldwell, Parkinson, Easley) and Dungeons and Dragons (sword and sorcery) works. There are few paintings by this artist on the market.

Paintings (major works)$4,000 $5,000 $6,000
Paintings (regular finals)$2,500 $3,000 $3,500

EMSHWILLER, EDMUND ALEXANDER (1925-90)

Ed Emshwiller is one of the most important artists to ever work in the field of science fiction. Selling his first painting in 1951 to *Galaxy* magazine, this artist would soon dominate the magazine and paperback field with his exceptional imagination and ability to express the most complex science fiction ideas visually. Matched only in the 1950's in popularity by Kelly Freas and Richard Powers, Emshwiller won many of the first Hugo's for professional artist (these awards were not extended to the SF artists until the early 1950's) and eventually went on to develop an avant garde career in film. His remaining years were spent

Ed Emshwiller, cover artwork for H.L. Gold's FIVE GALAXY NOVELS, a Doubleday Anthology, gouache and mixed media on board, privately sold for $750 in 1997. © Doubleday Books Inc.

teaching as Dean of the School of Film and Video at the California Institute of the Arts in Valencia.

Emshwiller's powers as an artist were such during the 1950's that he many times created what were called "concept" covers, where the idea was totally separate from any interior story in the magazine. Remembered for his attention to detail, marvellous use of color, and towering creative abilities collectors across the country are beginning to pay higher and higher prices for any and all Emsh originals.

The Emshwiller family has protected a number of paintings that were held within 'estate' property and to this day own a number of important early and mid-career paintings. Many of the most important early works are held within permanant collections and will not re-enter the market. Emsh did hundreds of interior black and white illustrations for the SF magazines and they surface with some frequency. There were also dozens and dozens of paintings that entered the fan

Ed Emshwiller, finished dust jacket cover artwork for Robert Heinlein's "Have Space Suit Will Travel," pen and ink on scratch-board, from the estate collection of Ed Emschwiller, private sale in 1997 for $500.
© Charles Scribners Sons

market in the 1950's and 1960's, and his paintings are to be discovered from a wide number of sources.

Paintings. (*Astounding, The Magazine of F.&S.F.*, for author's stories such as Heinlein, Asimov, etc.) [$1,750 $2,750 $4,750]

Paintings. (the concept covers, better *Astounding*, etc. covers. 1950's and very early 1960's) [$1,750 $2,500 $4,250]

Paintings (AceDouble covers from 1950-1955, possibly the most high demand by this artist) [$1,500 $3,000 $5,000]

Paintings (*Astounding, F.&S.F.* regular content covers) $900 $1,800 $2,750

Paintings (Hardcovers, sometimes monochrome or duo-tone paintings for Gnome Press, etc.) $800 $1,500 $2,500

Paintings (for Avalon Books, in monochrome)
$275	$350	$600

Preliminary paintings, small concept
watercolor works $150 $250 $350

Pen & Ink Illustrations (from 1949-54)
$100 $250 $450

(from 1955-60's) $50 $125 $200

(any illustration for Asimov, Heinlein or other major author from the 1950's)
$200 $400 $600

Note: the cover for IF SF for December 1958 sold at Sotheby's Sam Moskowitz auction in June of 1999 for $2,750.

Note: other individual sales include "Follow Me," (first Emsh *Astounding* cover) for $8,000; the F&SF cover for Robert Heinlein's "Starship Troopers" for $5,000; the black and white cover for the Scribners first edition of "Have Space Suit Will Travel" by Robert Heinlein for $500.

FABIAN, STEPHEN E. (1930-)

A fan artist during the 1960's, Stephen Fabian would go on to become a competent and thoughtful illustrator who held as one of his primary artistic beliefs that no illustration should ever give away any major part of the authors plot. His black and white work is considered stronger than his color work by many collectors.

Paintings	$500	$750	$2,000
Pen & Ink illustrations.	$150	$300	$450

FECK, LOU (1925-81)

A very prolific paperback artist who did his best covers during the 1970's for the SF field.

Paintings (Paperback covers 1970's)
$700 $1,500 $2,500

Henry Clay Ferguson, Jr., interior illustration from COSMOS, pen and ink on heavy paper, 1934, from the collection of Sam Moskowitz. © Fantasy Magazine/Julius Schwartz

COSMOS
Article by Jerry Weist; edited by Joseph Wrzos

In THE IMMORTAL STORM, his seminal history of science-fiction fandom (first begun in 1945, hardcover edition, 1954), Sam Moskowitz states that even in the 1940's COSMOS was already legendary within fandom. This unique round-robin sf "novel" was made possible solely through the Herculean efforts of a number of special individuals and circumstances which came together in sf fandom during the early 1930's.

Julie Schwartz, the remarkable editor for DC comics, who helped bring about the Silver Age of Comics and acted as editor for some of the most important DC Comics titles, began his career as a science-fiction fan. His early fan activity led to his editing and publishing some of the most important early sf fanzines, as noted by Moskowitz (in THE IMMORTAL STORM):

"Among those fans who had met and cultivated friendships at the gatherings of the Scienceers were Julius Schwartz and Mortimer Weisinger. Enlisting the aid of Allen Glasser - for they apparently doubted their brain-child, they circulated an announcement predicting the early appearance of a publication of interest to the science-fiction fan, editor and author which was to feature descriptive and biographical articles, news, bibliographical material and occasional fiction. The response - as hundreds of would-be publishers have since discovered - was far from sensational; but it was sufficient encouragement for the magazine to be issued. It was called *The Time Traveller*.

Soon after this Schwartz would move on to *Science Fiction Digest* and *Fantasy*

"YES," HODAR LEERED. "THE MILK WHICH YOU
JUST DRANK WAS POISONED. YOU ARE DONE
FOR, FAX GATOLA."

FO-PETA DID NOT HESITATE. HE SWUNG
UP THE HEAVY DISC. THE RULER COLLAPSED—

Henry Clay Ferguson, Jr., interior illustration from COSMOS, pen and ink on heavy paper, 1934, from the collection of Sam Moskowitz. © Fantasy Magazine/Julius Schwartz

Magazine, but in all three fanzines, the labor of one Conrad H. Ruppert would become paramount, as Moskowitz delineates (again in THE IMMORTAL STORM):

"To most present-day fans Conrad H. Ruppert is an all but unknown name, but his part in creating for fandom the finest set of periodicals it has ever produced is a story of unbelievable devotion to science fiction. He painstakingly set by hand every issue of *The Time Traveller* from then on, and every number of *Science Fiction Digest* and *Fantasy Magazine* up until the latter's third anniversary number. The fact that each of these rarely was less than 30,000 words in length and appeared on a regular monthly schedule gives the reader a rough notion of the amount of work involved. During this time, too, Ruppert hand-set Hornig's *Fantasy Fan* and the "COSMOS" supplements to *Fantasy Magazine* - all at below-production cost, out of sheer love of science fiction.

"IT IS UNCONTROLLABLE," SMILED
MEA-QUIN. "THE ANSWER TO THAT IS SIMPLE.
USE A BOMB OF GAMMA RAYS."

Henry Clay Ferguson, Jr., interior illustration from COSMOS, pen and ink on heavy paper, 1934, from the collection of Sam Moskowitz. © Fantasy Magazine/Julius Schwartz

Henry Clay Ferguson, Jr., interior illustration from COSMOS, pen and ink on heavy paper, 1934, from the collection of Sam Moskowitz. © Fantasy Magazine/Julius Schwartz

"Most legendary of all, however, was the novel "COSMOS," written by eighteen authors and issued with the magazine [*Fantasy Magazine*] in supplementary serial form. Each part ran five to ten thousand words, and the author line-up was as follows: A. Merritt, Dr. E.E. Smith, Ralph Milne Farley, Dr. David H. Keller, Otis Albert Kline, Arthur Burks, E. Hoffmann Price, P. Schuyler Miller, Rae Winters, John W. Campbell, Jr., Edmond Hamilton, Francis Flagg, Bob Olsen, J. Harvey Haggard, Raymond A. Palmer, Lloyd A. Eshbach, Abner J. Gelula and Eando Binder."

COSMOS was already a rare collector's item in 1954, when Moskowitz's history of sf fandom was published. However, contemporary fandom even then knew less about a special publisher's copy of COSMOS that had been assembled and illustrated by 1930's fan artist, Henry Clay Ferguson. Sam would tell friends that forty years later,

when Julie Schwartz allowed him to pick a few special items from his personal collection of science-fiction books before they were sold in the 1970's, he immediately went for the publisher's copy of COSMOS. This remarkable fan publication carried sixteen original drawings by Ferguson, laid in for the seven ½ x 6 inch format of the book, with an additional four original watercolor paintings. The block print cover for COSMOS was done by fan artist Hannes Bok. The labor that this single volume represents is unmatched by anything produced in contemporary fandom, whether it be science-fiction or comics fandom. Such, then, was life and leisure in the 1930's, conditions allowing young fans enough t-i-m-e to expend such a great effort on producing a single book.

Reproduced here are ten of the best black and white original drawings from Julie Schwartz's publisher's copy of COSMOS, offered so that fans today can witness the artistic creativity of a mostly long forgotten

Henry Clay Ferguson, Jr., interior illustration from COSMOS, pen and ink on heavy paper, 1934, from the collection of Sam Moskowitz. © Fantasy Magazine/Julius Schwartz

fan - Henry Clay Ferguson. His 1934 efforts represent a Golden Age of SF fandom now long gone, but one still remembered with reverence and respect by many of those now delving into the early history of the field.

FERGUSON, HENRY CLAY JR. (1914-)

An early fan artist who is most remembered for his classic illustrations for the publishers and limited edition copies of COSMOS. Ferguson also was featured in *Digest*, *Fantasy Magazine*, *Fantasy*, and eventually the pro-zine *Marvel Tales*.

Black and White illos (fanzines)
[$50 $100 $150]
Black and White illos (prozine)
[$50 $150 $250]

Henry Clay Ferguson, Jr., interior illustration from COSMOS, pen and ink on heavy paper, 1934, from the collection of Sam Moskowitz. © Fantasy Magazine/Julius Schwartz

Virgil Finlay, interior illustration for ASTROLOGY MAGAZINE, pen and ink on scratch board paper, private sale in 1995 for $1,000. © Popular Library Inc.

FINLAY, VIRGIL WARDEN (1914-71)

(Special Note: Sotheby's 1995 and 1996 Comic Art Auctions released two large collections of Finlay artwork into the market place. One collection focused on science fiction, and the other on astrology illustrations. While this temporally softened the market in prices, it should be stated that quality black and white illustrations and paintings have remained scarce to the market place. There is also an enormous gap between 1930's and mid 1940's paintings and the more recent 1950's paintings (such as *Fantastic Universe*) in both demand and price).

Large numbers of Finlay's artwork are known to exist, however the demand always continues to out-strip supply. Much like the example of why the movie-paper from *Forbidden Planet* continues to break records at auction when every dealer and collector is informed of the large numbers in existence, demand for this classic film continues unabated; and the same can be said for original artwork by Virgil Finlay. Long considered the most popular of all science fiction illustrators, this artists work remains in high demand today despite market fluctuations.

Paintings.
(*Weird Tales, Famous Fantastic Mysteries*, etc., 1937-44)   [$3,000 $7,500 $15,000]
(Note: exception when a mid 1940's *Famous Fantastic Mystery* of below average content failed to sell at Sotheby's in 1996 for $3,000)
(cover paintings from 1944-1949)
                              $2,500 $4,000 $7,000
(cover paintings to digest size titles from 1950-71) $1,500 $2,750 $3,750
(astrology, or non-science fiction works)
                              $500 $1,000 $1,500

Virgil Finlay, interior illustration for Ray Bradbury's "The Sound of Thunder," for PLANET STORIES for 1/35, pen and ink on scratch-board, sold privately in 1999 for $2,500. © Fiction House Publications

Virgil Finlay, artwork for "The Lilies," year unknown; estimate $3,500/4,000; sold for $4,675 in 10/92 (Sotheby's 2nd comic art auction). From the collection of Forrest J. Ackerman. © Virgil Finlay Estate

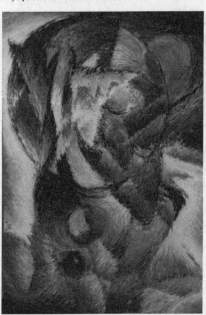

Virgil Finlay, original oil painting entitled "Love Lyrics," 1962; estimate $750/1,000; sold for $690 in 1993 (Sotheby's 3rd comic art auction). © Virgil Finlay Estate

Virgil Finlay, artwork for ASTROLOGY MAGAZINE, circa 1960's; estimate $600/900; sold for $1,035 in 1996 (Sotheby's 6th comic art auction). © Pines Publications Inc.

Virgil Finlay, interior illustration to unidentified SF Pulp title, pen and ink on scratch-board. © The Virgil Finlay Estate

Virgil Finlay, interior illustration for SCIENCE FICTION +, circa 1953 pen and ink on scratch-board, from the collection of Sam Moskowitz, private sale in 1998 for $300. © Hugo Gernsback Publications

(paintings for science fiction first edition hardcover titles from 1948-1959)

$2,500 $5,000 $7,500

(preliminary small watercolor and mixed media paintings for various covers and book cover works, usually ranging in size from 7" x 4" to 10" x 5 1/2") $600 $1,200 $1,800

Pen & Ink Illustrations

(special *Weird Tales*, early *Astounding SF* with special author illustrations (Lovecraft, Heinlein, etc.) from 1937-49)

[$1,200 $2,500 $5,000]

(interior illustrations for *Weird Tales* etc. from 1935-39) $1,200 $2,100 $3,250

(interior illustrations from 1940-47)

$800 $1,200 $1,800

(interior illustrations from 1948-70)

$400 $800 $1,000

(1940's through 1960's astrology illustrations)

$150 $350 $500

Note: over 70% of the activity in Finlay paintings changing hands has involved elaborate trades between collectors in the past three years.

FOGLIO, PHIL (1956-)

A well known and liked fan artist who won the Hugo's for best fan artist for the years 1977 and 1978, and later went on to do professional work.

Paintings	$400	$750	$800
Pen & Ink Illustrations	$50	$150	$300

FOSS, CHRISTOPHER (1946-)

One of the best of the contemporary English artists, Chris Foss developed some of the best and early air-brush covers for British paperback titles and soon came to define the "look" of an English paperback much as Frank Frazetta held sway over certian types of paperback covers in the United States.

Paintings (major works)	$3,000	$4,000	$6,000
Paintings (regular finals)			
	$2,500	$3,000	$3,500

FOSTER, JON

A very accomplished contemporary artist with a complex painting style.

Paintings	$1,750	$3,500	$5,000

FOSTER, ROBERT R. (?-?)

An artist who used super-realism and a suburb control of light within his paintings to create some of the classic paperback covers of the late 1960's and mid 1970's.

Paintings (Dell, Ballantine, etc.)			
	$900	$1,600	$3,250

FOX, LORRAINE (1922-76)

An artist who was very accomplished; she did very few illustrations for SF book titles and magazines.

Paintings (mixed media works)			
	***	***	***

FOX, MATTHEW (1906-)

Matt Fox was a self-taught artist who had a special yet strange style of drawing. He broke into the pulps in 1940 and eventually wound up working for various science fiction publishers. From 1943 to 1951 he produced several cover paintings and numerous interior illustrations for *Weird Tales* . He also worked in the comic

Frank Frazetta, cover painting for E.R. Burroughs THE MASTERMIND OF MARS, oil on board, sold at Christie's East for $82,500 in 1992.
© E.R. Burroughs Inc.

book field and did other magazine commercial illustration up through the 1960's. Very few of his originals and signed lithographs are know to exist.

Paintings (for *Weird Tales* covers)			
	[$2,500	$3,500	$4,500]
Pen & Ink Illustrations (for WT, FFM, and other magazine titles)			
	$250	$500	$750

Note: though some of Matt Fox's comic book covers, and some of his individual paintings and illustrations have been discovered, to date only one *Weird Tales* cover has ever been brought to light. His black and white artwork for *Weird Tales* is also extremely rare.

FRANCIS, RICHARD D. (?)

An artist who mostly did interior illustrations in the 1950's for *Galaxy, Amazing, Beyond, If,* and other titles.

Pen & Ink Illustrations	$50	$75	$125

Frank Frazetta, pencil concept production drawing for "Fire and Ice," 1982; estimate: $20,000/30,000; failed to sell at $19,000 (Sotheby's 2nd comic art auction for 10/92). © Frazetta Museum

FRAZETTA, FRANK (1928-)

(Special Note: It should be recognized that there is an enormous range in price to paintings by this artist based in the careful control of the release of the more important paintings into the public market by the Frazetta family. The acknowledged master-work and pivotal paintings are all still at the Frazetta museum and not one single Lancer *Conan* paperback cover has ever been sold privately or publicly. Because of this situation the upper end of the painting market has no comparable)

Paintings

(*Eerie, Creepy,* & early fantasy works for magazine covers during the 1960's)
[$20,000 $30,000 $40,000]
(1960's paperback Sword & Sorcery, Fantasy cover paintings) $30,000 $40,000 $60,000
(movie posters, MAD full page color works, record album covers, some oils & including watercolor works) $10,000 $15,000 $20,000

Specific sales at auction:
1) Sotheby's 1991 comic art auction, cover painting for *Vampirella* No. 1 (estimated $40,000/$50,000) sold for $77,000.00
2) Christie's East comic book auction for 1992, cover painting for Edgar Rice Burroughs *Mastermind/Fighting Man of Mars*, Nelson Doubleday Book Club Edition (estimate
3) Christie's East Comic Book auction for 1993, cover painting for (second version painted by Frazetta) Burroughs, *A Princess of Mars*, Doubleday Book Club Edition (estimate
4) Gurnsies [no data]
5) Sotheby's 1992 comic art auction, watercolor poster art for *The Night They Raided Minsky's*, Film/Poster work (estimated $50,000/$60,000) sold after auction for
$44,000
6) Sotheby's 1996 comic art auction, painting entitled "Savage World," original cover for *Monster Mania* No. 2 (estimated at $80,000/$100,000 sold at auction for $65,000.00

Specific failed sales at Public Auction:
1) Sotheby's 1992 comic art auction, painting entitled "Eternal Champion," (estimated at $60,000/$80,000) bidding stopped at below reserve $32,500.00
2) Sotheby's 1993 comic art auction, painting for "Battlestar Galactica," (estimated at $50,000/$60,000) bidding stopped at below reserve

Frank Frazetta, interior illustration for E.R. Burroughs TARZAN AND THE CASTAWAYS, entitled "He had me captured by an African Chief," pen and ink with brush on paper, sold for $50,000 in 1998.
© E.R. Burroughs Inc./ Canaveral Press

Pen and Ink Illustrations

(At this point in time 90% of the experts, dealers, and collectors acknowledge that the apex of Frazetta's talents as an artist came out in his masterpiece works for the Burroughs Canaveral Press illustrations from the period of 1962-65. These works are highly prized by fans and rarely enter the public market place as sales primarily take place privately between longtime collectors).

Canaveral Press E.R.Burroughs interior pen and ink illustrations

[$15,000 $25,000 $35,000]

Specific sales at auction:

Sotheby's 1996 comic art auction, original art from story entitled "Pellucidar," 1964, Canaveral Press, this is an unpublished plate that was never used (estimate $15,000/ $20,000) sold for $20,700

Sotheby's 1996 comic art auction, original for *Tarzan At The Earth's Core*, Canaveral Press, did not sell, bidding stopped at $10,000

(Doubleday Edgar Rice Burroughs illustrations) These works are usually slightly smaller than the Canaveral Press illustrations, they are inked works and do not make use of wash or brush work with as much detail.

$5,000 $8,000 $12,000

Frank Frazetta, artwork from PELLUCIDAR, an unpublished Canaveral Press illustration; estimate: $15,000/20,000; sold for $14,950 in 6/96 (Sotheby's 6th comic art auction). © ERB Inc.

(Ace paperback Burroughs illustrations)
  Most of these originals were done on tracing
  paper, and range in size from 5" x 3 1/2" to 7"
  x 4". $2,500 $4,000 $6,000
(note: a number of the more important Ace
  Burroughs frontice pieces by Frazetta entered
  the market and were completely sold out in
  1995, they originated from the collection and
  estate of Donald Wohlheim)
(published/unpublished watercolor and B&W
  illustrations from 1960-1988)
                                    $3,500 $6,000 $9,000
(Pen & Ink sketches - smaller than 7" x 10" in
  size) $700 $1,400 $2,400

(Frank Frazetta began in the mid-1980's and
  through the 1990's, sometimes by special
  commissions from Russ Cochran and other
  private collectors, to execute very detailed
  and subtle and powerful pencil works. These
  works should not be viewed as preliminary
  originals, but as very accomplished and
  developed works of art; the better examples
  are masterworks)
(large pencil examples from private
  commissions)   [$9,000 $14,000 $20,000]
(small pencil examples from private
  commissions) $3,000 $4,000 $5,000
(regular unpublished and published sketches
  from notebooks, etc.) $800 $1,400 $2,750

Frank Kelly Freas, interior illustration for Robert Heinlein's DOUBLE STAR, appearing in three installments in ASTOUNDING in 1956, pen and ink on scratch-board. Sold privately in 1999 for $650.
© Street & Smith Publications

FREAS, FRANK KELLY (1922-)

Evidence over the past five years indicates that Kelly Freas rises above the other two great paperback/magazine artists who dominated the 1950's (Ed Emsh-willer and Richard Powers) holds a very special place among science fiction fans' hearts. It is twice as likely that any given long time fan will sell their Powers or Emshwiller painting above one by Freas. This has caused a virtual drought within the period of 1950-55, considered by most historians as the very top period of Freas' creative output. Almost no *Astounding* or F&SF covers have entered the public market within the past three years, and the few that have were immediately bought.

Paintings

(*Astounding*, Gnome Press DJ covers, or covers related to major authors such as Asimov or Heinlein from the late 1940's to early 1950's)
[$3,000 $6,000 $10,000]

(regular late 1940's and early to mid 1950's *Astounding*, F&SF, *Super-Science, Planet Stories*, etc. covers) $2,000 $4,000 $6,000
(later 1960's paperback and SF covers)
$1,2000 $2,400 $3,200
(more recent 1970's paperback and SF covers)
$700 $1,000 $1,800
(preliminary paintings, usually 8" x 10" to 7" x 4 1/2" in size, from all periods)
$200 $400 $600
(covers to MAD magazine from 1950's, these are highly sought after and prized by collectors)   [$3,000 $5,000 $9,000]

Sotheby's Mad About Mad 1995, cover art to *More Trash from MAD* (1961), (estimated at $4,000/$6,000) sold at auction $4,310.00

Sotheby's Mad About Mad 1995, cover art to *The Fourth Annual Edition of More Trash From MAD*, (estimated at $3,000/$5,000) sold at auction for $4,310.00

(Note: early Freas MAD covers before No. 60 almost never enter the secondary market, thus causing the few examples to sell for very high prices)

Frank Kelly Freas, two interior illustrations for Robert Heinlein's DOUBLE STAR, appearing in three installments in ASTOUNDING in 1956, pen and ink on scratch-board. Sold privately in 1999 for $650 each.
© Street & Smith Publications

Frank Kelly Freas, two upright interior illustrations for "Sour Note On Palayate" from ASTOUNDING SCIENCE FICTION, circa late 1950's, pen and ink with brush on craft tint paper, part of a group sale from Sotheby's 1995 SF auction, approx. $200 each. © Street and Smith Publications

Pen & Ink Illustrations.
  (specific classic Asimov, Bradbury, Clarke, Heinlein, from the 1950's, or Hugo Novel black and white magazine illustrations)
              [$500 $1,000 $1,500]
  (regular 1950's *Astounding* and magazine illustrations)
              $200 $350 $600
  (more recent 1960's illustrations from magazines) $100 $250 $400

Note: over 50% of the movement of Freas paintings involve elaborate trades between long time collectors within the past five years.

FROUD, BRIAN (?)

A contemporary artist who does mixed media works that harken back to the style of Arthur Rackham and other great artists of the early 1900's.

Paintings (mixed media)$1,500 $2,000 $4,000

FUQUA, ROBERT (?) (TILLOTSON, JOSEPH WIRT)

An artist who did numerous covers in the 1930's and 1940's for pulp magazine titles. He signed his color work "Fuqua," and signed his black and white illustrations with both names, Fuqua and Joseph Tillotson.

Paintings (covers, 1930's and 1940's)
              $3,500 $5,500 $8,500
Paintings (backcover color works for *Amazing Stories* and *Fantastic Adventures*)
              $1,500 $2,000 $2,500
Pen & Ink Illustrations $400 $800 $1,200

Note: individual sales include: cover painting for *Amazing Stories* dated January 1944 selling for $14,300; and cover painting for *Amazing Stories* dated December 1936 selling for $9,775; both sales from 1992 & 1993 from Christie's East comic art auctions.

Jack Gaughan, interior plate for JACK GAUGHAN A PORTFOLIO, St. Louiscon 1969, illustrating "She" No. 3, 1968, ink on paper. © The Jack Gaughan Estate

Jack Gaughan, preliminary rough color for ACE DOUBLE SF TITLE, circa 1960's, mixed media on board, private sale in 1997 for $75. © Ace Books Inc.

GALLARDO, GERVASIO (1934-)

A Spanish artist who is best remembered for his classic covers for the Ballantine paperback line of Adult Fantasy titles.

Paintings	$800	$1,600	$3,250

GAUGHAN, JACK (1930-85)

Perhaps no other other artist was more popular and open to science fiction fans during the late 1950's and 1960's than Jack Gaughan. A prolific science fiction artist for both paperback titles and magazines.

Paintings (for better known authors, or special Hugo winning titles) $200 $500 [$800]

Paintings for standard SF magazine covers and Paperback titles $100 $300 $600

Preliminary Paintings, (many of these turned up at SF conventions for auction, or were traded by SF fans) $35 $65 $75

Pen & Ink illustrations (interiors for stories) $25 $75 $150

Note: there is a large amount of original

artwork by this artist in the market place. Very few of the Gaughan paintings for magazine covers and paperback titles were lost by publishers or the artist. This large number of originals keeps the market for this artist stable.

GEARY, CLIFFORD (?)

A childrens book artist who is remembered in SF fandom for doing just a few covers for Schribners titles, but what titles they were: Robert Heinlein's *Red Planet, Space Cadet, Farmer in the Sky, The Rolling Stones,* and *Starman Jones!*

Pen & Ink Illustrations for Heinlein Book Covers [$800 $1,600 $3,500]

GIANCOLA, DONATO (1967-)

One of the youngblood contemporary SF artists who has set new standards for others to follow. Giancola creates very defined, well crafted, and almost sculptural worlds with his paintings.

Paintings (1970's - major works)
$2,500 $3,500 $5,500
Paintings (regular finals)
$2,500 $3,000 $3,500

GIUNTA, JOHN (1920-1970)

An early New York SF fan artist Guinta started his career in the comic book field working in many different genres including science fiction and horror. He eventually started working for the various fantasy and science fiction pulps duing the 1940's and even contributed a few cover paintings for *Weird Tales* . He also worked in the comic book field and did other magazine commercial illustration up through the 1960's. Very few of his original and signed lithographs are known to exist.

Pen & Ink Illustrations $75 $150 $300
Cover Paintings (*Weird Tales*)
[$2,000 $3,000 $4,000]

GLADNEY, GRAVES (1907-76)

A pulp artist who is most remembered for his covers for *The Shadow* magazine. He also did some powerful covers for John W.

Campbell's *Astounding* and *Unknown.*

Paintings (*The Shadow*)
[$3,500 $4,500 $5,500]
Paintings (*Unknown, Astounding SF*)
[$2,500 $4,000 $6,500]

Note: a Graves Gladney Shadow painting dated April 15, 1940 sold at Sotheby's in 1994 for $5,750.

GOBLE, WARWICK WATERMAN (1862-1943)

An English artist who at the very beginning of science fiction was given the assignment of doing sixty-six illustrations for H.G. Well's magazine serializations for *The War of The Worlds.* None of these original works are known to have entered the American market. If they did their sale would be of great interest to many collectors.

Black & White Illustrations
(From *The War of the Worlds*)
[$3,500 $7,500 $10,000]

GRAEF, ROBERT A. (?-1951)

A pulp artist who worked for *Argosy* magazine in the 1920's and 1930's and did many of the important and early fantasy and SF related covers for authors like Fritz Leiber, Ray Cummings, O.A. Kline, etc.

Paintings (1920's through 1930's)
[$2,750 $5,000 $7,500]

GURNEY, JAMES (1958-)

An artist who first cut his professional teeth doing background work for Ralph Bakshi for Frazetta's *Fire and Ice* film. Later he moved on to magazine and paperback assignments (producing a few hundred in the SF field), and then broke through to another world of expression that made him famous with his Dinotopia paintings.

Paintings (SF magazine, pre-Dinotopia)
$5,000 $6,500 $8,000
Paintings (SF regular paintings)
$2,500 $3,000 $3,500
Paintings (preliminary works)
$150 $200 $250

Paintings (Dinotopia -major works)			
	$25,000	$30,000	$35,000
Paintings (Dinotopia-regular works)			
	$10,000	$12,500	$15,000
Paintings (Dinotopia-preliminary)			
	$700	$800	$1,000
Illustrations	$3,000	$3,500	$4,500

HARDY, DAVID A. (1936-)

British artist who was known for his space/landscape and space paintings, he did a number of covers for *F&SF* and *If*.

Paintings (1970's-1980's)	$250	$350	$550

Note: individual sales would include: two paintings from *Vision of Tomorrow* magazine selling for $690: and four paintings for *Vision of Tomorrow* selling for $690; both sales from Sotheby's 1995 SF auction.

HARRIS, JOHN (1948-)

The first British artist to be commissioned by NASA for their art program.

Paintings	$2,500	$3,000	$3,500

HARRISON, MARK (1951-)

An English artist with more than 350 covers for US & UK publications to his credit. Mark also was the 1991 winner of the British Science Fiction Award for best artist.

Paintings (major works)	$2,500	$2,750	$3,250
Paintings (regular finals)			
	$1,200	$1,400	$1,800
Paintings (preliminary works)			
	$100	$150	$200

HAY, COLIN (1947-)

A Scottish artist known for his covers for *Science Fiction Monthly*, and paperback book covers such as Le Guin's *The Lathe of Heaven*.

Paintings	$500	$1,000	$2,500

HERRING, MICHAEL (1947-)

English artist who likes to paint fantasy, adventure, and romance covers. His best known work in the US is for the Ballantine series of covers for the OZ books.

Paintings	$1,000	$2,000	[$3,500]

Laurence Herndon, cover painting for "The Land of the Hidden Men," from THE BLUE BOOK MAGAZINE for 5/31, oil on canvas, from the collection of Robert Lessor. © The Consolidated Magazines Corporation

HESCOX, RICHARD (1949-)

American SF artist who has done most of his work for DAW paperback titles. Richard is currently no longer active in the SF literary genre, since early 90's he has turned to personal works in the Brandywine fantasy style, published as prints (the originals are not for sale).

Paintings (1970's - 1980's major works)

$3,000	$4,000	$5,000

Paintings (regular finals)

$2,000	2,250	$2,500

Prints: there are small numbers of prints available at modest prices; no secondary market data is available at this time.

HICKMAN, STEVE (1949-)

Steve began his career with EC fandom and early fanzines such as SPA-FON, and he quickly ventured into SF and Sword and Sorcery fandom. An accomplished artist who soon began to do professional paperback and book cover illustrations, he has matured into one of the more important SF artists of the 1980's. It should also be noted that this artist works in two styles, one is 'harder edge' for SF book covers, and another more painterly, romantic "Brandywine" style for private commissions and personal projects. These latter works frequently and consistently comprise his best paintings.

Paintings (early to mid 80's, major)

$1,250	$1,500	$2,000

Paintings (early to mid 80's, regular)

$600	$700	$800

Paintings (late 80's to 90's, major)

$3,000	$3,500	$4,500

Paintings (late 80's to 90's, regular)

$1,500	$2,000	$2,500

Paintings (personal works, major)

$4,500	$5,000	$6,000

Paintings (personal works, regular)

$2,500	$3,000	$3,500

HILDEBRANDT, GREG AND TIM (1939-)

The Hildebrandt brothers have built a solid reputation during the past twenty years for unexcelled work directly related to Tolkein & Fantasy and Science Fiction illustration. They designed the original *Star Wars* one-sheet poster, and have recently done strong paintings for Marvel Card Sets related to *Stars Wars* and Marvel Super-Heroes.

(most Tolkein related paintings from the 1970's that are larger size in their format)
[$7,000 $15,000 $35,000]
(Tolkein related paintings from the 1970's that are medium sized in their format)
$5,000 $11,000 $18,000
(calendar paintings, paperback and hardcover paintings 1975 to present)
$3,500 $7,500 $15,000
(Marvel gum card super-hero paintings, ranging in size from 14" x 11" to 18" x 12")
$1,500 $3,000 $9,000
(*Star Wars* trading card paintings from the 1990's, in size from 7" x 10" to 14" x 10" to 28" x 20")
$2,000 $5,000 $9,000
(Preliminary cover concepts and other preliminary works)
$800 $2,400 $3,500

note: recent sales would include: Star Wars *Galaxy* magazine cover, painted in 1994, sold in 1995 for $8,000; *Stars Wars* comic covers for Dark Horse, created in 1997, sold in 1998 for $5,000 each; "The Unexpected Party" - Tolkein Centerfold from calendar, created in 1976 and sold in 1994 for $150,000; Boba Fett, Topps Trading card painting created in 1996, and sold in 1998 for $15,000.

HOLLAND, BRAD (1943-)

An American artist who does tour-de-force black and white illustrations, as well as very painterly color works for covers.

Paintings (1970's - 1980's)
$1,250 $2,250 $3,750
Pen & Ink Illustrations $500 $1,000 $1,500
(these works can be very complex)

HORNE, DANIEL

Paintings(major works) $3,000 $3,500 $4,000
Paintings(regular finals)
$1,500 $1,750 $2,000

HOWITT, JOHN NEWTON (1885-1958)

A well known landscape artist, portrait painter, and pulp artist who is best remembered for his *Terror Tales* and *Horror Stories* cover paintings.

Paintings (1920's-1930's)
[$5,000 $7,000 $12,000]

Note: a private sale was made of a *Terror Tales* cover painting, one of the only ever discovered, for $15,000. This cover was for the second issue of the pulp title.

HUNTER, ALAN

British artist remembered for his covers for *Nebula* and *New Worlds*.

Paintings (1950's) $100 $200 $400

HUNTER, MEL (1929-)

A popular 1950's science fiction cover and interior illustrator. Known for landscapes of the moon and other planets as well as outer space paintings. His originals are fairly uncommon.

Paintings (covers for The Magazine of F & SF, etc.) $400 $600 $1,000
Pen & Ink illustrations $50 $150 $300

INGELS, GRAHAM (1915-)

A noted comic book artist who started his comics career and brief pulp illustration association through Fiction House *Planet Comics* in 1943. He painted one cover and provided over a dozen interior illustrations for *Planet Stories* before going on to greater fame doing horror comic books for the EC Comics Publishing Group during the 1950's

Paintings (*Planet Stories*, 1940's)
[$2,000 $3,000 $4,000]
(none are known to exist)
Pen & Ink Illustrations (1950's)
[$400 $550 $650]
(none are known to exist)

JENSEN, BRUCE (1962-)

An artist who has pushed the design of his content into very fresh and original solutions for SF covers, doing some of the best graphic design and hardcover covers in the field.

Paintings (1980's-1990's)

$2,000	$4,000	$6,000

Pen & Ink Illustrations $400 $800 $1,200

JONES, EDDIE (1935-)

A British artist who is very popular and has done hundreds of covers for paperback titles and magazine covers.

Paintings (1970's - Present)

$150	$300	$750

Pen & Ink Illustrations $50 $75 $150

Note: individual sales would include: five paintings from 60's & 70's (including *Vision of Tomorrow* magazine covers 3, 4, 11) selling for $920; six paintings selling for $690; both sales at Sotheby's 1995 SF auction.

JONES, JEFFREY (1944-)

An American artist deeply influenced by Howard Pyle, Hal Foster, and Gustav Klimt. One of the original "Studio" artists, Jeff Jones has become one of the more sophisticated artists working within the Fantasy and SF field. Some of his paintings can be large in scale, and many of his best works are non-SF or non-Fantasy in their content.

Paintings (early 1970's paperback titles)

$750	$2,250	$3,750

Paintings (R.E. Howard paperback titles, Sword & Sorcery titles 1970's - present)

$1,500	$3,000	$5,000

Paintings (large fantasy works, special commissions)

[$4,000	$6,000	$9,000]

Paintings (card-series paintings based on Fantasy themes - most done in the late 1980's & 1990's)

$800	$1,400	$2,500

Watercolor Original Paintings

$600	$1,250	$2,500

Pen & Ink Illustrations (these can very wildly based on size and quality)

$750	$1,500	$2,750

Hunt, cover artwork for PACIFICON COMBOZINE issued in 1946 to commemorate the Fourth World SF Convention, pen and ink on paper, sold privately in 1999 for $500. © Pacificon Convention Committee

JONES, PETER (1951-)

A British SF cover artist who did an impressive number of paperback titles during the 1970's.

Paintings (1970's-Present) $750 $1,500 $2,500

JONES, ROBERT GIBSON (?)

A number of Jones paintings were given to fans who visited the offices of Ray Palmer during the 1940's, and a number also were donated to World Science Fiction Convention auctions, where they made their way into early collections.

(larger format paintings for *Amazing Stories, Fantastic Adventures,* from the 1940's and early 1950's) [$1,500 $2,500 $4,500]

(smaller format paintings, approximately 8" x 4 1/2" done for *Other Worlds* and other digest magazines) $800 $1,200 $1,500

Pen & Ink Illustrations.

(from all publications in 1940's to 1950's)

$50	$100	$300

JUSKO, JOE (?)

This popular comic artist has done a series of contemporary Burroughs acrylic paintings.

Paintings (Burroughs) $600 $1,200 $2,250

KALUTA, MICHAEL W. (1947-)

Michael Kaluta was influenced by such talents as Al Williamson and Roy Krenkel. Kaluta entered the field in 1970 contributing pen and ink illustrations for *Amazing Stories* and *Fantastic*. Soon after he developed into a full-fledged fantasy illustrator producing beautiful watercolor paintings for portfolios, magazine covers, album jackets, hardcover books, posters, etc. Recently he has ventured into the illustration of children's fantasy books.

Paintings (1970's -Present)
  $2,000 $3,000 $4,000
Watercolor Paintings $1,000 $2,000 $3,000
Pen & Ink Illustrations $400 $800 $1,250

KELLY, KEN (1946-)

Ken Kelly studied with Frank Frazetta and sold his first painting in 1969. He did a series of Fantasy covers for Warren Magazine titles such as *Creepy* and *Eerie*, and went on to illustrate for many paperback SF and Fantasy titles.

Paintings (1970's Warren Magazines)
  $1,250 $2,750 $3,750
Paintings (1970's-Present, SF & Fantasy)
  $1,500 $2,750 $4,500

KIDD, TOM (1955-)

An American artist who has developed a style that is very detail oriented and very Victorian, and who in his own way has reintroduced to SF fans the original "sense of wonder" many find lost in today's illustrators. This artist also signs his work with the pseudonym 'Gnemo', in a more expansive and extravagant style.

Paintings (1970's - Present)
  $2,000 $2,750 $3,500
Paintings (regular finals)
  $1,200 $1,800 $2,200

Paintings (preliminary works)
  $150 $200 $250
Paintings (Gnemo Project major works)
  $8,000 $12,000 $15,000
Paintings (Gnemo-regular works)
  $5,500 $6,500 $8,500

Prints: limited edition offset lithographic reproductions, both illustration works ($35) and Gnemo ($60) self-published.

KIRBY, JOSH (1928-)

British artist who began his work with commissions for *Authentic Science Fiction* magazine and soon began to do numerious paperback covers. Kirby works with gouache, acrylic, oil and watercolors in a very detailed style.

Paintings (1956-1966 magazine covers)
  $1,000 $2,000 $3,500
Paintings (larger format 1960's-Present for paperback titles) $1,500 $3,500 $5,000
Paintings (smaller format for paperback covers)
  $750 $1,250 $2,500

KIRK, TIM (1947-)

One of the best known and well liked of all the SF fan artists who has won the HUGO for best fan-artist in the years 1970, 1972-1974, and 1976. He has also done a number of important hardcover and softcover book illustrations as well as work for calendars and paperback and magazine covers.

Pen & Ink Illustrations (small works from 4"x4" to 12"x12" in scale, for fanzines and book covers, or commissions)
  $75 $150 $350
Pen & Ink Illustrations (cover designs, major B&W illustrations for stories in books and magazines) $150 $350 $750
Paintings (Tolkien 1975 calendar, magazine and paperback covers) $1,500 $2,500 $5,000

KRAMER, DAVE (?)

A contemporary artist with diamond precision realism built into his painting style.

Paintings $1,500 $3,000 $4,500

Roy Krenkel, title page decoration for E.R. Burroughs A FIGHTING MAN OF MARS Ace paperback edition, 1960's, pen and ink on paper, from the collection of Donald Wollheim, sold privately in 1995 for $500.
© Ace Books Inc./E.R. Burroughs Inc.

KRAMER, FRANK (?)

An artist who worked primarily for *Astounding* doing interior illustrations. Most of his work appeared in the 1940's.

Black & White illustrations

$50	$75	$150

KRENKEL. ROY GERALD, JR. (1918-83)

One of the great fantasy "doodlers" of this century, Krenkel started out assisting such talented comic book artists as Al Williamson, Wally Wood and Frank Frazetta on various jobs during the 1950's. He eventually became a major contributor to fanzines like *Amra* , and in 1962 was hired by Ace Books to provide cover paintings and fronticepiece pen and ink illustrations for their series of paperbacks reprinting stories by Edgar Rice Burroughs and Otis A. Kline. It was through Krenkel's association with Ace that eventually got Frazetta work there doing covers as well. Krenkel went on to produce illustrations for hardcover books, posters and prints before his untimely death in 1983.

Paintings.

(Ace Burroughs covers from 1962-66, specific classic examples, *Mastermind of Mars, Thuvia, Fighting Man of Mars, Out of Time's Abyss*)

[$6,000	$8,000	$11,000]

(Ace Burroughs covers of secondary importance and quality)

$3,500	$5,500	$7,500

(hardcover and paperback covers 1962-70)

$3,000	$4,000	$6,000

(paperback covers from 1971-79)

$2,500	$3,500	$4,500

Roy Krenkel, title page decoration for E.R. Burroughs ESCAPE ON VENUS Ace paperback edition, 1960's, pen and ink on paper, from the collection of Donald Wollheim, sold privately in 1995 for $400.
© Ace Books Inc./E.R. Burroughs Inc.

(preliminary watercolor & mixed media paintings) $700 $1,000 $1,300

Pen & Ink Illustrations.

(Ace Burroughs & O.A. Kline frontice illustrations from 1962-69)

$400 $800 $1,200

(Canaveral Press Burroughs from 1962-65)

$800 $1,200 $1,600

(note: R.G. Krenkel did exacting pencil preliminary works to all of his Ace E.R.B. and O.A.K. covers) $600 $900 $1,200

(pen and ink regular illustrations for fanzines, magazines, and paperbacks, from 1953-1975)

$400 $800 $1,200

(note: possibly no other fantasy artist in modern or early times did as many sketches for fans, fanzines, and personal artistic studies as R.G.K., virtually hundreds exist in quality from the average to sublime examples - "quality" is the key to value on these works, some are inked and some are pencil)

(larger scale 8" x 10" and above)

$150 $350 $550

(smaller 3" x 4" to 4" x 6" etc.)

$50 $200 $350

Julian Krupa, original illustration for an unidentified issue of AMAZING STORIES, 1939; estimate: $600/800; sold for $920 in 6/96 (Sotheby's 6th comic art auction). © The Ziff Davis Company

Julian Krupa, interior illustration for Hamling/Reinsberg's "War with Jupiter," from AMAZING STORIES for 5/39, pen and ink on paper. © The Ziff-Davis Company

KRUPA, JULIAN S. (1913-?)

An accomplished artist who worked in the 1930's and 1940's for the pulp magazine titles. Most of his black and white illustrations are done with brush. Many of his back cover paintings for *Amazing Stories* and *Fantastic Stories* still survive in the market.

Paintings (1930's and 1940's)
	$1,500	$2,500	$3,500

Paintings (1950's-1960's) $750 $1,000 $1,250
Brush and Ink Illustrations $150 $300 $450

KUKALIS, ROMAS (1956-)

A contemporary artist who has won the 1991 World Fantasy Award. His paintings feature very strong figure and color work. There have been recent advances in the prices for his paintings.

Paintings (major works)
	$1,750	$2,250	$3,500

Paintings (regular works)
	$1,400	$1,800	$2,200

Paintings (preliminary works)
	$150	$200	$250

Pencil Works $75 $100 $120

KYLE, DAVID

Long time SF fan - who began as a fan artist, and later in the 1930's & 1940's had many published illustrations in the pro-zines.

Black & White illustrations
$25	$50	$150

LANOS, HENRI (?)

A French artist who is best remembered for his illustrations for H.G. Wells "When the Sleeper Wakes" in *Graphic Magazine* at the turn of the century. His original works would be unknown to the market in the U.S.

Pen & Ink Illustrations
$3,000	$6,000	$9,000

LAWRENCE, STEPHEN (1886-1960)

(See LAWRENCE STERN STEVENS Listing)

LEHR, PAUL (1930-1998)

One of the few SF artists to develop a completely distinctive style incorporating SF illustration and abstract painting styles. Mr. Lehr left the illustration field in the late 1980's, opting for a series of personal works and crossing the line into fine arts exhibitions for his fantasy works.

Paintings.
(1958 through 1968 Heinlein, or Clarke paperback covers)
$900	$1,750	[$3,250]

(1958 through 1970 paperback cover paintings)
$900	$1,500	$2,500

(1971 to present paperback covers)
$500	$800	$1,500

Paintings (recent personal works -major)
$4,500	$5,500	$6,500

Paintings (recent personal works-regular)
$2,000	$2,500	$3,000

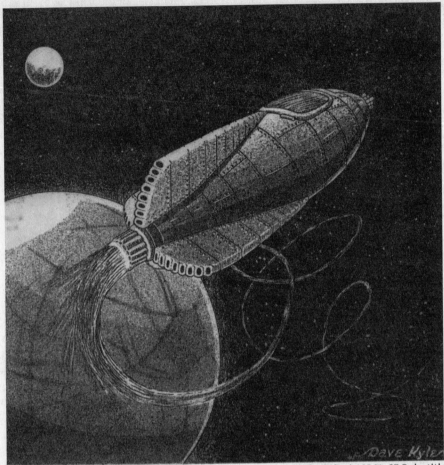

David Kyle, interior ilustration entitled "No Place to Go," from an unidentified 1930's SF Pulp title, pen and ink with white-out on board. © Dave Kyle Inc.

LEWIS, BRIAN MONCRIEFF (1929-78)

One of the two most prolific magazine cover artists during the 1950's in England. For a short time he dominated covers for *New Worlds*, *Science Fantasy* and *Science Fiction Adventures*.

Paintings $800 $1,200 $1,600

LEYDENFROST, ALEXANDER (1889-1961)

One of the most highly regarded commercial illustrators during the 1930's, he eventually dabbled in the field of science fiction producing a couple of classic cover paintings for *Planet Stories* and numerous interior illustrations. Along the way, his two sons, Harry and Bob Leydenfrost, also contributed black and white interiors for the pulps. His aliens and creatures were always top-notch, as was his solid ability at drawing anything with total realism. A few of his interior drawings have surfaced, but overall, they remain very rare in the marketplace.

Paintings (*Planet Stories*, and pulp covers)
[$2,500 $5,000 $7,500]
Pen & Ink Illustrations (almost unknown to the market) $800 $1,200 $1,600

LINDAHN, VAL(ENA) LAKEY (1951-)

A contemporary artist who does remarkably finished works for interior SF illustrations and is an accomplished painter in different mediums.

Paintings (watercolor, mixed media)
$1,000 $1,500 $2,500
Pen & Ink Illustrations $750 $1,000 $1,750

LOCKWOOD, TODD (?)

A contemporaty artist who blends the best of Emsh and Stanley Meltzoff in his painting style.

Paintings $1,000 $2,500 $4,000

LUDEKINS, FRED (?)

An artist remembered by SF fans primarily for his b&w illustrations for *The Saturday Evening Post* for Robert Heinlein's "Space Jockey."

Black & White Illustrations

                          $100 $200 $300

LUNDGREN, CARL (1947-)

A self taught artist who began his career in the counter-culture 1960's with the publication of *Tales From the Ozone* comics. Lundgren moved to New York in the 1970's and began a slow and deliberate development into one of SF's best current artists.

Paintings $2,500 $4,000 $6,500

MAITZ, DON (1953-)

One of the best of the contemporary artists who has produced dozens of classic covers for paperback covers during the 1970's, 1980's and 1990's. Mr. Maitz is a Hugo award and Chesley Award winner.

Paintings (early-mid 1980's-major works)
                  $4,000 $5,000 $6,000
Paintings (early-mid 1980's-regular)
                  $2,500 $3,500 $4,500
Paintings (early-mid 1980's-preliminary works)
                  $75 $100 $150
Paintings (late-80's -90's major works)
                  $8,000 $10,000 $12,000
Paintings (late 80's-90's regular works)
                  $5,500 $7,000 $8,500
Paintings (late 80's-90's preliminary works)
                  $150 $200 $350
Paintings (Card art, misc.)$900 $1,500 $2,500
Paintings (Card art-prelims)
                  $100 $150 $200

MATANIA, FORTUNINO (1881-1963)

A superb draftsman who specialized in historical paintings and drawings. Remembered mostly by SF collectors his incredible black and white illustrations for Edgar Rice Burroughs' *Pirates of Venus* and *Lost on Venus* serlialized stories featured in the English magazine *The Passing Show* from 1933 to 1934. Most of these originals reside in long-time collections within fandom and are rarely offered for sale.

Pen & Ink and Wash Illustrations
  (1930's) $1,500 $2,000 $3,000

MATTINGLY, DAVID B. (1956-)

One of the champions of photo-realism and the supra-real in his painting style, Mattingly worked in his early career within the film industry at Walt Disney Studios. One of the most popular and influential forces in recent SF paperback covers. Since 1996-97 Mattingly is primarily CGI, no longer taking commissions requiring hand-painted illustration.

Paintings for mid 1980's
  Paintings (major works)
                  $1,500 $2,000 $2,500
  Paintings (regular works)
                  $1,000 $1,250 $1,500
  Paintings (preliminary works)
                  $100 $150 $200
Paintings for late 1980's through 1990's
  Paintings (major works)
                  $2,000 $3,000 $3,750
  Paintings (regular works)
                  $1,500 $2,000 $2,250
  Paintings (preliminary works)
                  $150 $200 $250

McCALL, ROBERT THEODORE (1919-)

One of the most recognized of all science fictions artists, McCall did the artwork for many famous SF film posters including *2001: A Space Odessey*, *Star Trek - The Motion Picture* and *Meteor*. Also responsible for many space illustrations for U.S. Postal Stamps, this artist did a six-story high mural painting for the National Air and Space Museum, and he is also a Hall of Fame member.

Paintings $4,000 $8,000   [$12,000]

McCAULEY, HAROLD W. (1913-83)
A science fiction artist known for his good girl artwork. He also did a great deal of advertising art during his career. His earliest SF work is much less finished than his work from the 1950's.

Paintings (from the period of 1939-46)
                    $2,000 $3,500 $5,000
Paintings (for *Imagination*, etc. from 1947
   through 1960) $3,000 $6,000 $9,000
Pen & Ink Illustrations $100 $300 $400

Note: prices can vary widely on a McCauley painting depending on the subject matter.

McGOVERN, TARA (?)
Contemporary artist painting with acrylic; very fine delicate and masterful attention to detail.

Paintings $1,000 $2,000 $3,500

McQUARRIE, RALPH (?)
An artist who is best known for his ground breaking work for the *Star Wars* movie set designs and characterizations.

Pen & Ink Illustrations (preliminary pencil,
   and mixed media works for the movie *Star
   Wars*) $800 $2,500 $4,500
Paintings (preliminary works that are rough
   for *Star Wars*) $1,000 $1,750 $3,250
Paintings (more finished works that relate to
   Star Wars) $3,500 $7,000 $9,000

MELTZOFF, STANLEY (1917-)
Perhaps no other artist in the history of science fiction illustration has done so few works for the field, and yet been so highly regarded. This gifted painter has managed with just a few original Oils for important paperback covers to place himself at the top of every collectors list. Working for Signet Books during the 1950's, Meltzoff

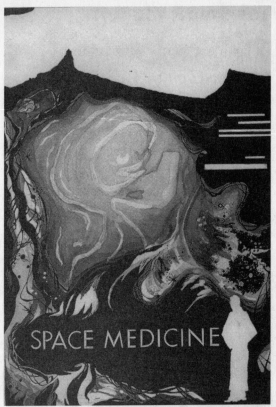

Frank D. McSherry, illustration entitled "Space Medicine," for an unidentified fan publication, pen and ink and mixed media on board.
© Frank D. McSherry

did the covers for Heinlein's *The Green Hills of Earth*, and Bester's *The Demolished Man*, among others.

Paintings (extremely rare to the market)
                  $4,000 $6,000 $8,000

Note: In the Winter of 1998/99 the paperback painting for the Signet edition of Robert Heinlein's *The Green Hills of Earth*, sold for a combination cash trade price of above $25,000.

MIGNOLA, MIKE (?)
An accomplished comic book artist who worked through the 1980's and 1990's and has developed a watercolor and ink painting style that is very sophisticated; recent SF themes are graced by this style.

Mixed Media Paintings $750 $1,500 $2,500

Ian Miller, interior illustration for "The Million Year Picnic," from Ray Bradbury's THE MARTIAN CHRONICLES
The Bantam trade Paperback Edition, 1979, pen and ink on paper, private sale in 1998 for $750.
© Bantam Books/ Doubleday & Company

MILLER, IAN (1946-)

A British artist who has developed an almost micro-detailed style which at the same time evokes fantasy and futuristic utopian visions. His original works (especially interior illustrations) can be quite small in scale.

Paintings (paperback and HC book covers)
$1,000	$1,500	$2,500

Pen & Ink Illustrations $350 $750 $1,500

MILLER, RON (1947-)

An American artist who has done both HC SF book covers, magazine illustrations and has worked as production illustrator for such films as *Dune* and *Total Recall*.

Paintings $1,750 $3,500 $6,500
Pen & Ink Illustrations $700 $1,250 $2,500

MINOR, WENDELL (1944-)

An American artist who works in a surrealist style.

Paintings $1,000 $2,000 $3,000

MOORE, CHRIS (1947-)

British paperback artist who has done many contemporary covers. Of special interest are the recent Philip K. Dick re-issues for which Moore did all of the covers.

Paintings (to mid 80's, major)
$2,000 $2,400 $2,800
Paintings (to mid 80's, regular)
$800 $1,000 $1,500
Paintings (above, preliminaries)
$100 $150 $200
Paintings (late 80's-90's, major)
$2,500 $3,000 $3,500
Paintings (late 80's-90's, regular)
$1,800 $2,000 $2,400
Paintings (above, preliminaries)
$150 $200 $250

MOREY, LEO (?-1965)

When Hugo Gernsback lost control of *Amazing Stories* in early 1929, he took his cover and interior artist Frank R. Paul with him to start his new magazines. The artist who immediately took control of *Amazing Stories* covers after Paul left was Leo Morey. Morey was an accomplished painter who has previously done covers for Gernsback's *Science & Invention* and continued to do SF pulp covers into the 1960's.

Paintings (SF covers are quite rare, though they do exist for *Amazing Stories*, etc.)
[$1,750 $3,500 $7,500]

Note: individual sales include a cover for *Amazing Stories* dated 12/1936 selling for $9,775 at Christie's East in 1993. In the Fall of 1998 the cover for *Amazing Stories* for April 1937 sold for $5,000.

MORRILL, ROWENA (1944-)

American artist who began her career with Ace Books and has become one of the top fantasy and SF cover artists during the 1980's and 1990's.

Paintings $3,000 $4,500 $6,000

MORRISSEY, DEAN

The illustration output for this artist since 1994 is replaced by major personal works created for self-written book projects.

Paintings (mid 80's early 90's, major)
$3,000 $3,500 $4,500
Paintings (mid 80's early 90's, regular)
$2,000 $2,500 $3,000
Paintings (personal works, Children's book illustrations, major) $8,000 $10,000 $15,000
Paintings (personal works, Children's book illustrations, regular) $3,000 $4,000 $4,500
Paintings (above, prelims)
$600 $700 $850

MORROW, GRAY (1934-)

An artist who broke into the comic book field doing fantasy stories in the 1950's and early on was influenced by other illuminated talents such as Al Williamson and Frank Frazetta. During the 1960's he became most popular contributing covers and interior illustrations for *Galaxy* and *IF* digests. A very prolific artist, Morrow has created hundreds of paintings for various hardcovers, magazines and paperbacks in the science fiction field. Possibly his most recognized contribution is over 100 cover

Leo Morey, cover artwork for COSMIC STORIES for 3/41, pen and ink with brush on board, private sale in 1999 for $1,000. © Cosmic Stories Inc.

paintings for Ace's *Perry Rodan* paperback series. He currently draws the syndicated "Tarzan" newspaper strip.

| Paintings | $500 | $800 | $1,200 |
| Pen & Ink Illustrations | $150 | $200 | $350 |

MUGNAINI, JOSEPH (1912-1992)

Mr. Muganini was one of the best known interior illustrators in the country, and is best known to SF fans for his brilliant covers and interior illustrations for Ray Bradbury's stories and books. Mugnaini's originals were seldom brought directly into SF fandom, and they have not been auctioned at WorldCons or traded from old time collections. The family estate still holds many important and historical originals.

| Paintings | [$3,500 | $5,500 | $7,500] |

Pen & Ink Illustrations

| | [$800 | $1,600 | $3,250] |

Pen & Ink Illustrations (for Bradbury books such as *The October Country, Farenheit 451, The Golden Apples of the Sun*, etc.)

| | [$1,000 | $2,000 | $4,000] |

Easton Press interiors (1970's)

| | $1,000 | $1,500 | $2,500 |

MURPHY, KEVIN (1968-)

One of the newer SF artists who has begun to work for Tor, Harper/Collins, DAW and other publishers.

| Paintings | $1,500 | $2,500 | $4,000 |

NAPOLI, VINCENT (?)

An artist noted for his interior illustrations for *Weird Tales, Thrilling Wonder Stories, Famous Fantastic Mysteries*, and other magazines during the 1930's through the 1950's.

| Pen & Ink Illustrations | $250 | $500 | $750 |

NAYLOR, RAYMOND (?)

An artist who made brief cover appearances for *Amazing Stories* and *Fantastic Adventures.*

Paintings	$75	$150	$350

NICHOLSON, JOHN

Brisish artist associated with the covers for *Tales of Wonder;* examples of his paintings are very scarce.

[$500 $1,000 $2,000]

NUETZELL, ALBERT A. (1901-1969)

An American artist who had a completely developed style when his son talked him into doing SF illustrations - a very accomplished painting style, with many unique design solutions for covers.

Paintings	$750	$1,500	$3,500

O'BRIAN, WILLIS (?)

The famed film animation master for *Lost World,* and *King Kong,* did remarkably detailed pencil studies for his film sets and design problems, a few of which have been known to show up in the marketplace - they are extremely rare.

Creation pencil works
[$4,000 $6,000 $10,000]
Lost World pencil works
[$5,000 $8,000 $15,000]
King Kong pencil works
[7,500 $15,000 $25,000]
Mighty Joe Young pencil works
[$2,500 $5,000 $7,500]

Note: a preliminary pencil work for *Mighty Joe Young,* was offered at Sotheby's in 1999 estimated at $4,000 to $6,000 and sold for $3,250.

ORBAN, PAUL (1896-1974)

One of the great interior illustrators for SF pulp titles during the 1930's through the 1950's. He did occasionally do cover paintings, but they are rare. His work was widly spread through SF fandom during the 1940's, but is now fairly hard to come by.

Joseph Mugnaini, interior illustration for Ray Bradbury's THE MARTIAN CHRONICLES Limited Edition Club printing, 1974, pen and ink on paper. © Doubleday Books/ Cardavon Press Inc.

Joseph Mugnaini, interior illustration for Ray Bradbury's THE MARTIAN CHRONICLES Limited Edition Club printing, 1974, pen and ink on paper. © Doubleday Books/ Cardavon Press Inc.

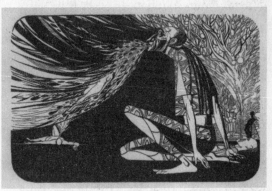

Joseph Mugnaini, interior illustration for Ray Bradbury's THE MARTIAN CHRONICLES Limited Edition Club printing, 1974, pen and ink on paper. © Doubleday Books/ Cardavon Press Inc.

Pen & Ink Illustrations	$250	$500	$800
Paintings (rare)	$600	$1,200	$1,800

Note: an interior illustration from *Startling Stories* circa 1940's, for a "Dr. Cyclops" story sold at Sotheby's Science Fiction auction in 1995 for $747.

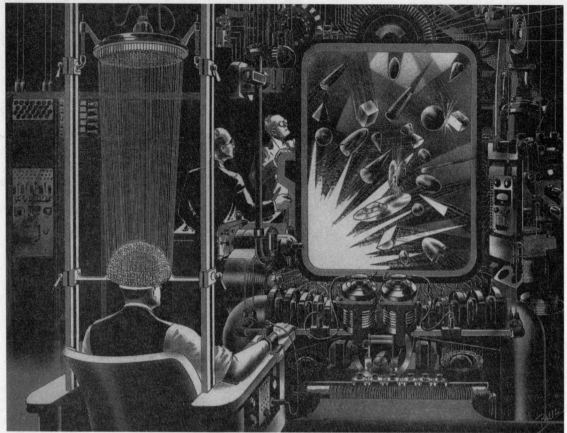

Frank R. Paul, interior illustration for SCIENCE FICTION +, pen and ink with airbrush on board, from the collection of Sam Moskowitz, sold privately in 1999 for $2,500. © Hugo Gernsback Publications

PARKHURST, H. L. (?-1950)

A cover artist for Fiction House pulps and other publications. His SF work was primarily covers for *Planet Stories*.

Paintings   [$2,000 $3,500 $5,000]

Note: a painting for a *Planet Stories* cover privately sold for $5,000 in 1996.

PAUL, FRANK R.
(1884-1963)

Paintings.
(specific note: Absoutely no paintings or black and white illustrations exist from Hugo Gernsback's *Science & Invention* or *Electrical Experimenter* from 1918-25, or any of the *Amazing Stories* years of 1926 through 1928. If any were to be discovered it would represent an historic find and new record prices would undoubltely be realized. In relation to

these facts only 3 known examples of Paul paintings exist from the first year that Hugo Gernsback edited *Science Wonder Stories* in 1929. Later paintings from the early 1930's to mid and late 1930's and the 1940's *Amazing Stories* and *Fantastic Adventures* back cover paintings and works on canvas for *Science Fiction Quarterly* and *Science Fiction*, were donated to World Science Fiction Conventions during the 1930's and 1940's and sold for a little at $7 to as much as $15. These paintings constitute most of the known surviving examples. The major early collectors of Paul were Sam Moskowitz, Forrest J. Ackerman, Darrell C. Richardson, and in more recent years Bob Lessor).

(*Science Wonder* cover paintings from the year 1929)   [$14,000 $25,000 $45,000]
Two examples from this period changed hands from private collections in 1996/1997 selling for $10,000 and $16,000.

Frank R. Paul, interior illustration for John Coleridge's "Mystery from the Stars," from FUTURE FICTION No. 1, pen and ink on paper, sold at Phil Weiss Auctions for $500 in 1999. © Future Fiction Inc.

(paintings from *Science Wonder*, and *Wonder Stories*, from 1930-35)

[$3,500 $5,500 $9,500]

(*Amazing Stories* and *Fantastic Adventures* back cover paintings. $2,750 $4,000 $8,500

(*Amazing Stories* and *Fantastic Adventures* back cover paintings with weaker examples of good SF content) $2,000 $3,000 $4,500

(Paul did a small number of oil paintings on canvas, rather than his traditional gouache on board, these paintings became covers for *Science Fiction*, and *Science Fiction Quarterly*, and appeared in the years 1939, 1940, 1941, and 1942)

(stronger examples) [$3,500 $5,500 $9,500]
(weaker examples) $2,000 $4,000 $5,500
(preliminary cover watercolor and gouache works for coverdesigns exist, usually 6" x 4" in size) $500 $1,000 $1,500

Public sales

Sotheby's 1995 Science Fiction art auction, original cover painting for *Science Fiction* No. 2 (oil on canvas example), June 1939, sold at auction for $6,900

Sotheby's 1995 Science Fiction Art auction; original back cover painting from *Amazing Stories*, 1940, gouache and watercolor on board, sold at auction for $10,350

Pen & Ink Illustrations

(pulp illustrations from 1929-1938)

$500 $800 $2,000

(pulp illustrations from 1939-1954, including work for *Science Fiction* +)

$275 $550 $1,000

(note: nearly 100% of the published work for *Science Fiction* +, and Hugo Gernsback's *Forecast* pamphlet which was sent to close friends and business associates as a New Years card for years from the years 1945 upward existed within the Sam Moskowitz collection.

Note: results from the Sam Moskowitz Sotheby's auction provide the following

CHRISTMAS 1957

Frank R. Paul, cover illustration for FORECAST 1958, pen and ink on board, sold privately from the collection of Sam Moskowitz in 1999 for $3,500. © Hugo Gernsback Publications

FUTURE
SPACELINER

Frank R. Paul, cover illustration for FORECAST for 1960, pen and ink with brush on illustration board, sold privately from the collection of Sam Moskowitz in 1999 for $2,500. © Hugo Gernsback Publications

Frank R. Paul, partial interior illustration (partial view) for an unidentified issue of SCIENCE WONDER STORIES, ink and brush on board, from the collection of Forrest J. Ackerman, sold at Sotheby's in 1995 for $1,725.
© Hugo Gernsback/ Science Wonder Publications

Frank R. Paul, interior illustration for "Exploration of Mars," from SCIENCE FICTION + for 3/53, pen and ink with airbrush on board, from the collection of Sam Moskowitz, sold privately for $800 in 1999. © Hugo Gernsback Publications.

numbers. The cover lot No. 551 for the original cover for *Science Wonder Quarterly* for Winter of 1930, estimated at $20,000 to $40,000 - sold for $77,750 to standing applause. This is the highest price ever paid for a Paul, and the auction environment should be taken into consideration. Other paintings included a watercolor interior illustration, lot 555, from *Science Fiction +* No. 4 selling for $9,775 and the painting for *Air Wonder Stories* from October 1929 selling for $23,000. The painting for lot 735, the cover painting for *Wonder Stories* from April of 1936 sold for $17,250 - a corner it seems has been turned on Paul paintings from which the market will never return. Black and white sales include a Paul/Tina back cover black and white illustration for *Science Fiction +* No. 4 selling for $1,840; a B&W Martian illustration from *Quip Magazine* selling for $2,875; a *Forecast* cover for 1962 selling at $1,035; a 1956 *Forecast* cover selling for $1,265.

Note: Prior to Sotheby's Moskowitz auction, Illustration House sold the back cover painting from *Fantastic Adventures* for February of 1940 for a selling price of $14,300 at auction.

PEDERSON, JOHN, JR. (?)

An artist who worked during late 1950's and 1960's specializing in astronomical scenes.

Paintings (for F &SF and Galaxy)
$600 $800 $1,200

PENNINGTON, BRUCE (1944-)

A British artist who started his SF career with Heinlein's cover painting for *Stranger in a Strange Land,* and he also illustrated a number of the important Bradbury British paperback titles.

Paintings $750 $1,500 $3,000

PEPPER, ROBERT (1938-)

An artist who created some of his most impressive work for record album covers, and did some of the more experimental work during the 1970's for SF paperback titles.

Paintings $800 $1,600 $3,250

Richard Powers, cover painting for Frederik Pohl's SLAVE SHIP, acrylic paint and mixed media on board, from the Powers Estate, private sale in 1997 for $2,500. © Ballantine Books Inc.

PFEIFFER, FRED (1940-95)

This artist took over the *Doc Savage* series from James Bama and also illustrated other paperback SF titles.

Paintings $700 $1,250 $2,250

PODWIL, JEROME (1938-)

This artist had his greatest effect on the SF field with covers between the 1960's and 1970's.

Paintings $600 $1,000 $1,400

POPP, WALTER (1920-)

Popular during the 1950's as both a magazine and paperback cover artist.

Paintings (1950's) $800 $1,600 $2,250

POTTER, JEFFREY KNIGHT (1956-)

A contemporary SF artist who has used his knowledge and interest in photography to do combination works that involve painting, pen and ink work, air-brush, and photography. It should be noted that this artist's output since 1994-95 has diminished due to increased movie industry work, and personal works.

Mixed Media Works in Color
                    $1,250 $1,500 $2,500
Mixed Media Works in Black and White
                    $1,000 $1,250 $1,500
Limited Edition Prints: self plublished, in limited edition of #'ed 100, series of 11 images, hand-prints from well known 'masters', at $150 @.

POWERS, RICHARD M. (1921-1996)

Powers became one of the most prolific and influential cover artists for the late 1950's through the 1960's, and sold large numbers of his early paintings at science fiction conventions through the late 1960's and early 1970's. The Powers estate has offered select paintings up through the 1990's through their agents, Worlds of Wonder. Though a large percentage of this artist's works survive in collections, few of the early 1950's works surface in the public market. Some private collectors are known to own from a dozen to over thirty paintings.

Paintings
(Ballantine covers to 1st editions from the early 1950's including covers to Clarke, Tenn, Sturgeon, Sheckley, or Signet 1950's Heinlein covers - example *Double Star* - or any special author covers)   [$1,500 $2,500 $4,500]
(1950's Ballantine, Berkley Medallion, Signet etc. covers) $800 $1,600 $3,000
(average Ballantine 1950's cover paintings)
                    $800 $1,400 $2,400
(late 1950's and through 1960's paperback covers) $500 $1,000 $1,750
Pen & Ink Illustrations. $500 $800 $1,200
(are extremely small in production numbers)

Richard Powers, original cover painting for Arthur C. Clarke's *Childhood's End*, paperback and HC editions, acrylic paint and mixed media on board, 1953. From the collection of David Hartwell, sold privately in 1996 for $5,000. © Ballantine Books Inc.

Note: individual sales include: cover painting for A.E. Van Vogt's *Away and Beyond* , paperback cover painting (measuring 12 x 7") selling for $1,495 at Sotheby's SF auction in 1995. The cover for Arthur C. Clarke's *Childhoods End* Ballantine paperback (and HC 1st Ed) painting sold privately in 1997 for $5,000. The cover for Pohl/Kornbluth *Wolfbane* (Ballantine cover painting) sold privately for $3,500.

POYSER, VICTORIA (?)
This artist from the late 1980's to current times has largely left the adult fantasy illustration field to pursue gallery representation and mainstream subject matter, along with children's book projects.

Paintings (major works)$1,000 $1,250 $1,500
Paintings (regular finals) $500 $600 $700

PUNCHATZ, DON IVAN (1936-)
A contemporary SF artist who has imbued his painting style with very poetic and emotional forms. Best known for his classic *Foundation* covers for Avon Books.

Paintings $1,250 $2,750 $5,500

QUINN, GERARD A. (1927-)
A well known and popular British artist who did the majority of his important work during the 1950's and 1960's.

Paintings $600 $1,250 $3,250

RANKIN, HUGH (1879-1957)
An artist for the early issues of *Weird Tales* magazine. None of his cover paintings are known to exist, though his work is highly collected.

Paintings (*Weird Tales*)[$2,000 $3,000 $5,000]
(Prices depend on what story was illustrated)
Pen & Ink illustrations $200 $600 $1,000
(Prices depend on what story was illustrated)

ROBERTS, TONY

A British SF artist who began to illustrate for covers during the 1970's.

Paintings (late 70's-late 80's, major)
$750 $1,000 $1,250

Paintings (late 70's-late 80's, regular)
$450 $500 $600

Paintings (late 80's-late 90's, major)
$1,000 $1,500 $2,000

Paintings (late 80's-late 90's, regular)
$700 $850 $1,000

ROGERS, HUBERT
(1898-1982)

This artist was highly regarded by John Campbell, Robert Heinlein, and many long time science fiction fans who would credit him with almost single-handily bringing the science fiction magazine covers out of the "racy" pulp era, and into the serious contemporary arena where cover illustrations were as creative and challenging as the fiction they portrayed. (note: Very few existing examples of this artists work survive in private collections in the United States. A great number of the most famous and best *Astounding* covers reside in a private museum collection in Canada, and will never surface on the public market)

Paintings

(*Astounding*, and other SF magazine covers featuring Van Vogt, Heinlein, or Asimov covers from 1939-52)

[$7,500 $10,000 $14,000]

(Magazine and Pulp covers from 1939-52 that feature regular or more average quality content) [$3,500 $6,000 $9,000]

(Monochrome or duo-color works done for Shasta, or other Hardcover books from the 1950's) [$2,000 $3,000 $5,000]

Pen & Ink Illustrations.

(hardcover, magazine illustrations featuring Asimov, Heinlein, Van Vogt or other important author or SF stories) [$250 $500 $800]

(hardcover, magazine pulp illustrations from 1939-52 featuring more average quality content) [$150 $300 $500]

Note: recent activity for Rogers originals would include the original painting on canvas for *Super Science Stories* for August

of 1942 selling at $15,000. The cover for *Astounding Science Fiction* for February 1939 selling into a private collection for $15,000, and the cover for *Astounding Science Fiction* for February of 1940 (to Robert Heinlein's "If This Goes On...,") selling for $25,000. All three sales took place between July of 1998 and February of 1999. This activity defines better than any other example where the Science Fiction Pulp market is headed for important artist's works that are scarce to begin with.

ROGERS, MARK

An American artist known primarily for his *Samurai Cat* illustrated series, featuring the exploits of Rogers' invented character, and his naughty pin-ups.

Paintings (Cat illos-major)
$200 $250 $300

Paintings (Cat illos-regular)
$100 $125 $150

Paintings (Cat-preliminarys)
$35 $45 $55

Paintings (Pin-up/etc.-major)
$600 $700 $800

Paintings (Pin-up/etc.-regular)
$300 $350 $400

ROMAS

A contemporary artist working with acrylic, with a very accomplished sense of light and color.

Paintings $2,000 $4,000 $6,000

ROSA, DOUG

An artist who did paperback covers for the "Doc Savage" series and SF covers during the 1960's.

Paintings $800 $1,600 $2,000

ROTSLER, WILLIAM
(194?- 1997)

One of the most beloved fan artists to ever illustrate fanzines, his simple almost "Feiffer style" characters covered the entire spectrum of SF fandom and then some.

William Rotsler, interior illustration from THE TATTOOED DRAGON & HIS ELECTRIC WHING-A-DING, 1964, mimeograph reproduction, pen and ink on paper. © Red Boggs Press

Black & White Illustrations

$25	$75	$150

RUDDELL, GARY (1951-)

A contemporary artist who has done cover work during the 1970's through the 1990's. Paintings late 1970's-mid 1980's.

Paintings (major works)

$1,250	$1,500	$2,000

Paintings (regular works)

$1,000	$1,250	$1,500

Pencil (preliminary works)

$100	$125	$150

Paintings late 1980's-through 1990's
Paintings (major works)

$2,500	$3,000	$3,500

Paintings (regular works)

$1,250	$1,500	$2,000

Paintings (preliminary works)

$150	$200	$250

RUTH, ROD (1912-)

A science fiction artist known for his work for the Ziff-Davis pulps, *Amazing Stories* and *Fantastic Adventures*. He also did much non-SF art, advertising art, and comic strip art.

Paintings	$800	$1,250	$1,500
Pen & Ink illustrations	$50	$100	$200

SANJULIAN, MANUEL (1941-)

Sanjulian began his career in comics, however he quickly developed into one of the more mature and remarkable painters of the 1970's.

Paintings	$2,500	$4,500	$7,500

John Schoenherr, unpublished illustration of John W. Campbell, pen on paper undated, private sale of $150 in 1997. © John Schoenherr

SAUNDERS, NORMAN B. (1907-1988)

Saunders began painting pulp and slick magazine covers during the 1930's and because of his great speed at the easel and a terrific sense of imagination and color, was in demand by many publishers. Although he only did a limited number of science fiction covers in the field, he went on to greater fame as the artist who painted the *Mars Attacks* gum card series in 1959. His art is very scarce in the marketplace.

Paintings for SF titles (30's-40's pulp)
[$5,500 $7,500 $11,500]

Paintings (small in scale) for the
Mars Attacks series   [$900 $1,750 $3,500]

Paintings (paperback and digest SF covers for 1940's & 1950's)   [$1,500 $2,500 $5,500]

Note: in November of 1994 the original Sanders cover painting from *Marvel Science Stories*, May 1939 was auctioned at Illustration House in New York for $9,000.

SCHNEEMAN, CHARLES, JR. (1912-72)

One of the gifted artists who worked for John W. Campbell during the Golden Age of *Astounding Stories*. His interior illustrations were as interesting as his very painterly covers.

Paintings (1940's through 1950's)
[$1,500 $2,500 $3,500]
Pen & Ink Illustrations $300 $500 $750

SHAPERO, HANNA

An American artist with low output for illustrations, her major works are mainly the result of private commissions.

Paintings (Cat Illos-major works)
$200 $250 $300
Paintings (Cat illos-regular finals)
$100 $125 $150
Paintings (pin-ups & misc-major)
$500 $650 $800
Paintings (pin-ups & misc-regular)
$300 $350 $400

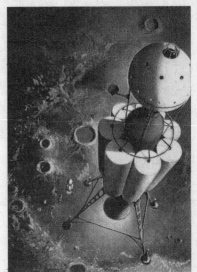

ex Schomburg, preliminary cover painting for SATELLITE SF for unused cover, circa late 1950's, gouache on board.
© Renown Publications

Alex Schomburg, preliminary cover painting for SATELLITE SF for unused cover, circa late 1950's, gouache on board.
© Renown Publications

Alex Schomburg, preliminary cover painting for SATELLITE SF for 10/58, gouache on board.
© Renown Publications

SCHOENHERR, JOHN (1935-)

One of the most highly regarded of all science fictions artists, John Schoenherr has crafted a style that to this day remains top-flight with a majority of SF fans and collectors. His most famous cover paintings were for Frank Herbert's *Dune* (in three variations, the magazine covers, the hardcover first edition, and the Ace paperback 1st edition cover), and some of the other classic *Analog* covers for other important SF authors. Though his original work is not rare, it is hoarded by collectors and few important pieces come onto the open market.

Paintings (*Analog* covers from the late 1950's and 1960's)	[$1,500	$2,500	3,500]
Paintings	$800	$1,000	$1,250
Pen & Ink Illustrations	$200	$400	$800

Note: a private sale was made in 1997 for the cover painting to the Ace paperback cover for *Dune* for $5,000.

SCHOMBURG, ALEX (1905-)

Many examples survive of this artists work during the 1950's, however it should be noted that the majority of these paintings traded hands between the years 1965 through 1980. Since this time the number of paintings to surface upon the public market has begun to decline, just as some of the greatest interest by private collectors started to kick in.

Paintings.

(Winston Press book cover paintings)			
	[$2,000	$4,000	$6,000]
(1939-1982 magazine and book covers with robots, aliens or creatures)			
	[$1,750	$3,500	$7,500]
(more average quality covers from 1930-82)			
	$1,500	$2,500	$4,000
(monochrome flyleaf design for Winston Press science fiction series, a classic example)			
	[$5,000	$7,000	$10,000]

Pen & Ink Illustrations.

(hardcover and magazine pulp illustrations from 1938-50)	$600	$1,200	$2,000
(hardcover and magazine digest illustrations from 1951-82)	$450	$700	$1,000

SCHULZ, ROBERT (1928-78)

One of the most talented painters of the early pulp illustrators, this artist continued with his career into the paperback titles of the 1950's and 1960's. His work is uncommon and does not turn up often.

Paintings (early 1950's paperback titles)			
	$1,000	$2,000	$3,000

1965 forecast

U.S.A.

NASA

UNMANNED SOFT
LUNAR LANDING

Christmas 1964

ALEX
SCHOMBURG

Alex Schomburg, cover artwork for FORECAST for 1965, pen and ink with airbrush on board, from the collection of Sam Moskowitz, sold privately in 1998 for $2,500. © Hugo Gernsback Publications

Alex Schomburg, preliminary color sketch for
unpublished cover to AMAZING STORIES,
circa 1926, gouache on paper.
© WaRP Graphics Inc./ The Alex Schomburg Estate

Alex Schomburg, preliminary color sketch for
unpublished cover to AMAZING STORIES,
circa 1926, gouache on paper.
© WaRP Graphics Inc./ The Alex Schomburg Estate

Alex Schomburg, interior illustration for Crossen's "The Hour of the Mortals," from STARTLING STORIES for
8/52, pen and ink on board. © The Standard Magazine Company

Paintings (mid 1950's to 1960's paperback titles) $1,500 $3,000 $4,500 (These works are more accomplished and more sought after by collectors)

SCOTT, HAROLD WINFIELD (1897-1977)

A popular pulp painter who did many cover paintings for John W. Campbell's *Unknown* .

Paintings (rare)   [$2,500 $3,500 $6,500]

SENF, CURTIS C. (1879-1948)

Curtis Senf was known for his work for *Weird Tales* magazine in the late 1920's and early 1930's. Most of his art is minor but he illustrated stories by many famous weird fiction authors, which increase the value for certain pieces.

Cover Paintings (very scarce)
[$4,000 $5,500 $7,000]
Pen & Ink illustrations $100 $300 $700 depending on the story illustrated

SEWELL, AMOS (1901-83)

Amos Sewell was an interior artist for horror pulps who later became famous as a *Saturday Evening Post* cover artist.

Pen & Ink Illustrations (for horror pulp titles) these originals are very scarce
[$400 $550 $700]

SHARP, HENRY (?)

A forgotten artist in today's market, Henry Sharp had a powerful dynamic style; his printed work showed considerably less than the finished originals. He worked primarly for Ziff-Davis doing B&W illustrations.

Black & White illustrations
$45 $65 $125

SHAW, BARCLAY (1949-)

This artist first established his reputation with a series of covers for Harlan Ellison's Ace paperback titles. He has continued to grow in stature in the SF field through the 1980's and 1990's.

Paintings, early to late 1980's
Paintings (major paintings)
$1,000 $1,250 $1,500
Paintings (regular paintings)
$500 $550 $600
Pencil preliminary works
$100 $125 $150
Paintings, late 1980's through 1990's
Paintings (major works)
$2,000 $2,500 $3,500
Paintings (regular works)
$2,000 $2,250 $2,500
Preliminary sketches $150 $200 $250

SIBLEY, DON (?)

An artist who did cover paintings and interiors for *Galaxy Science Fiction* during the 1950's.

Paintings $150 $250 $350
Black and White Illustrations
$10 $15 $25

SMITH, MALCOLM (1912-1966)

A prolific science fiction cover artist for the pulp titles and SF digest magazines.

Paintings (from the 1940's)
$2,000 $3,000 $4,000
Paintings (from the 1950's)
$1,000 $1,500 $2,000

SMITH, R.A. (?)

An artist who has a realistic style similiar to Bonestell, remembered for his illustrations to Arthur C. Clarke's *The Exploration of the Moon*.

Paintings $350 $750 $1,500

SOYKA, ED (1947-)

A current SF artist who uses elements of surrealist painting to achive unusual concepts for cover designs.

Paintings $1,000 $2,000 $3,000

Malcolm Smith, book cover for John W. Campbell's WHO GOES THERE?; second edition, goauche on board from 1951; from the collection of Mel Korsnak; sold in 1998 for $2,500. © Shasta Publishers Inc.

J. Allen St. john, interior illustration for Ziff-Davis publication, circa 1950's, pen and ink with brush on board, sold in 1996 for $2,500. © Ziff-Davis Publications

ST. JOHN, JAMES ALLEN (1872-1957)

Many of the early A.C. McClurg & Co. masterpiece original Edgar Rice Burroughs cover paintings are lost and feared destroyed, examples include *The Monster Men, Son of Tarzan, The Land That Time Forgot, The Mucker,* and other important early works. It must also be noted that several major paintings are permanently locked into the E.R.B. Inc. private estate & private collection, where they remain "not for sale" at any price. If these two realities were not enough together to make St. John paintings "rare," then it must finally be noted that many paintings that have remained in private Burroughs collections do just that - they remain there until the individual dies (at this point in time there is no record of any collector being buried with his or her St. John painting) causing further "stress" upon anyone seeking to own or purchase a great or average example by this acknowledged master of the fantasy field. Despite these facts, major paintings have changed hands over

the past ten years, and records are listed below along with the standard spreads.

Paintings. (sold between 1991-1998)
Note: inidvidual sales would include
Mastermind of Mars, Oil on board for front cover to dust jacket.Sold at San Diego Comic Convention, summer, 1993 for $45,000
Chessmen of Mars, Oil on board for front cover to dust jacket.
  Sold through Russ Cochran $60,000
Tarzan Lord of the Jungle, Oil on board for front cover to dust jacket.
  Sold privately in 1991 for $25,000
Tarzan and Jane, private commission by Vern Coriell from St. John in the 1950's, sold in 1996 for $90,000
At The Earth's Core, interior front illustration, painted in two colors, selling in 1996 for $35,000

Non-Burroughs works.
My Book House - In Shining Armor - cover painting sold in 1996 for $15,000

(Edgar Rice Burroughs hardcover front cover paintings from 1916 to 1943)
   [$25,000 $35,000 $70,000]

J. Allen St. John, interior plate illustration for E.R. Burroughs' TARZAN THE UNTAMED, oil on board, 1920, from the collection of John Coleman Burroughs'. © E.R.B. Inc.

J. Allen St. John, interior plate illustration for E.R. Burroughs' THE CHESSMAN OF MARS, oil on board, 1922, from the collection of Bradley Vinson. © E.R.B. Inc.

J. Allen St. John, interior plate illustration for E.R. Burroughs' SWORDS OF MARS, oil on board, 1936, from the collection of E.R.B. Inc. © E.R.B. Inc.

J. Allen St. John, interior illustration for "Warburton's Invention," for AMAZING STORIES for 9/44, pencil and charcoal on paper, from the collection of Robert Lessor. © The Ziff- Davis Company

J. Allen St. John, interior title plate illustration for E.R. Burroughs' AT THE EARTH CORE, oil on board, 1922, from the collection of Gerry de la Ree, sold privately in 1993 for $35,000. © E.R.B Inc.

(Edgar Rice Burroughs hardcover double wrap around dust jacket covers, examples include *Swords of Mars, Tarzan At The Earth's Core,* etc.) [$35,000 $55,000 $85,000]

(Non-Burroughs adventure and western front cover dust jacket paintings from 1915 through 1940) [$4,000 $6,000 $9,000]

(Burroughs pulp illustrated cover paintings for Blue Book, *Amazing Stories, Fantastic Adventures,* etc.) [$12,000 $16,000 $24,000]

(Non-Burroughs pulp cover paintings) [$3,000 $5,000 $10,000]

Black and White or three tone oil or gouache paintings for Edgar Rice Burroughs interior illustrations for book titles. [$5,000 $10,000 $20,000]

(Non-Burroughs, non-fantasy covers to western, romance, and other titles, oil on board or canvas) [$2,500 $5,000 $8,000]

Pen & Ink illustrations

(Pen and ink linear or charcoal on paper works, these differ from the gouache or interior paintings, examples would be interior illustrations for *Beasts of Tarzan*) [$7,500 $15,000 $20,000]

(Pen and ink and charcoal and paint on paper for E.R. Burroughs magazine interior illustrations from 1916-43) [$4,000 $6,000 $10,000]

James Steranko, interior plate for Harlan Ellison's REPENT HARLEQUIN! SAID THE TICKTOCKMAN An Illustrated Portfolio, 1978, pen and ink with brush on board. © Harlan Ellison/ Byron Preiss Visual Publications Inc.

(Non-Burroughs, hardcover and pulp interior illustrations from 1916-43)

$850 $1,250 $2,750

(preliminary pencil designs to E.R. Burroughs interior illustrations from 1916-43)

[$1,000 $1,200 $4,500]

STAHR, PAUL (1883-1953)

An accomplished illustrator who worked for all the major magazines before and after the first World War. In the 1920's he began to paint covers for *Argosy* which was then the best selling pulp magazine on the stands. It was during this period, and into the 1930's, that he produced numerous science fiction covers, including several illustrating stories of Edgar Rice Burroughs. During the 1950's he did a few select paperback covers. His paintings are scarce, but do occasionally turn up in the marketplace.

Paintings (Argosy covers)[$4,000 $6,000 $8,000]

STANLEY, ROBERT (?)

An artist who did SF cover paintings in the 1950's, very few examples of his work are known to exist in collections.

Paintings (1950's) $1,500 $2,500 $3,500

STARK, JAMES (?)

James Stark was the best of the Scottish artists famous for his cover for *Nebula Science Fiction*.

Paintings (1950's) $200 $300 $500

STERANKO, JAMES (1938-)

Extremely popular illustrator, designer, editor and magician who entered the comic book field during the 1960's, producing black and white stories for Marvel Comics. A collector himself of older pulp artists and illustrators work, Steranko began painting paperback covers in 1969 and during the next ten years painted over 50 covers, including 23 of which were done for the Pyramid/Jove Books reprinting of *The Shadow* . Today he edits and publishes his own magazine dealing with the movie and entertainment field. Steranko rarely lets go of any of his original art and has kept a tight hold on all of his *Shadow* cover paintings. However, during the 1970's he did release almost all of his tightly detailed pencil preliminaries for these paintings into the market. They were quickly bought up by fans and rarely change hands today.

Lawrence Stern Stevens, interior illustration for C.L. Moore's "Doorway Into Time," from FAMOUS FANTASTIC MYSTERIES, circa 1940's, pen and ink with white-out on illustration paper, sold privately in 1999 for $1,000.
© Popular Publications Inc.

Paintings (paperback covers and *Shadow*)

	[***]	
Pen & Ink illustrations $800	$1,600	$2,400
***Shadow* Cover Prelims** $600	$800	$1,000

STERNBACH, RICK (1951-)

An artist who has won the HUGO for best SF artist in 1977 and 1978. Sternbach specializes in astronomical scenes.

Paintings	$1,250	$2,500	$3,750

STEVENS, LAWRENCE STERN (1886-1960)

Lawrence Stern Stevens is the real name of the artist who did much science fiction artwork under the name of Lawrence. Many of the paintings attributed to Lawrence are the work of Stern Steven's son, Peter Stevens.

Paintings (1940's pulp magazine covers)

	$1,500	$3,000	$5,000
Paintings (1950's)	$750	$1,500	$3,000
Pen & Ink Illustrations (1940's pulp magazine			
titles)	$500	$700	$1,500

Pen & Ink illustrations

(1950's and up)	$300	$600	$1,200

These works depend on size and illustration content toward story or author.

Portfolios

There were two portfolios issued by *Famous Fantastic Mysteries Magazine* in the 1940's, depending on condition.

	$75	$100	$150

STEVENS, PETER (1920-)

The son of the artist Lawrence Stern Stevens. His work in the SF field appeared under the joint pen-name of Lawrence. Peter Stevens later became well known as an illustrator for the *Saturday Evening Post*.

Paintings	[$3,000	$4,000	$5,000]

Note: These paintings are very rare.

STONE, DAVID (?)

An artist who did interior B&W illustrations for *Galaxy Science Fiction* magazine in the 1950's.

Black & White Illustrations $10	$20	$35

Lawrence Stern Stevens, interior illustration for H.G. Wells' "The Island of Dr. Moreau" from FAMOUS FANTASTIC MYSTERIES, pen and ink on heavy paper, private sale in 1999 for $750. © All Fiction-Field

STOUT, WILLIAM (1949-)

An accomplished illustrator who has worked in all major markets including comic books, posters, calendars, record album jackets, paperbacks, hardcovers, and films. Stout works in ink, watercolors, and oils and excells in the subjects of horror, science fiction and especially dinosaurs. He's also a good cartoonist! Some of Stout's special works include illustrating *Dinosaur Tales* written by Ray Bradbury.

Paintings	$2,750	$3,500	$4,000
Pen & Ink Illustrations $600	$1,500	$2,750

some of these works can be very involved and with watercolor.

SUMMERS, LEO RAMON (1925-85)

A SF artist who began his professional career as art editor for the Ziff-Davis titles

Arthur Thompson, interior illustration from THE ATOM ANTHOLOGY, mimeograph reproduction, pen and ink on paper. © The C.A. Press

of *Amazing Stories* and *Fantastic Adventures.* After leaving Ziff-Davis in 1956 he continued to do SF paperback and magazine covers.

Paintings	$850	$1,400	$2,500
Pen & Ink Illustrations	$80	$160	$300

SWEET, DARRELL (1934-)
One of the freshest and best talents to enter the SF field in the 1970's, quickly becoming one of the favorite among science fiction readers.

Paintings	$2,500	$5,000	[$7,500]
Preliminary Works	$750	$1,250	$2,000

SZAFRAN, GENE (1941-)
An artist who was very prevalent during the SF new wave period of the late 1960's and 1970's. This artist's struggles with M.S. have kept him from returning to the field, and his early works are starting to become more scarce.

Paintings	$1,000	$2,000	[$3,000]

TAYLOR, RICHARD (?)
An artist who did fanzine illustration, and some excellent Arkham House dust jacket cover illustrations - his style was perfect for Lovecraft and the Arkham House authors.

Black & White Illustrations			
	$25	$50	$150
Arkham Covers (B&W)	$250	$350	$550

TERRY, WILLIAM E. (1921-)
A prolific science fiction artist for lesser digest titles and pulp magazines.

Paintings	$300	$400	$500
Pen & Ink illustrations	$25	$50	$100

THOMPSON, ARTHUR (fan artist name 'ATOM')
A popular SF fanzine artist who did exceptional work in the 1950's and 1960's.

Black & White illustrations (small)			
	$15	$25	$35
Black & White illustrations (larger)			
	$20	$45	$75

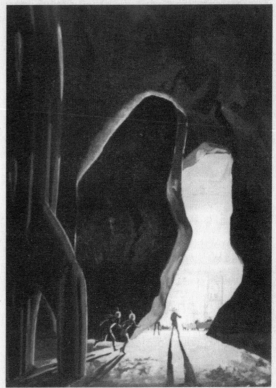

William Timmins, artwork for cover painting to ASTOUNDING SCIENCE FICTION, for 1940's Asimov *Foundation* installment; estimate: $700/1,000; sold for $805 in 6/96 (Sotheby's 6th comic art auction). © Street and Smith Publications

TILLOTSON, JOSEPH WIRT (1934-?)
A staff artist for Ziff-Davis who produced mainly black and white interior illustrations.

Black & White Illustrations			
	$25	$35	$75

TIMMINS, WILLIAM (?)
An artist who did some of the *Astounding* covers during the late 1940's and 1950's. His style was simple and effective, and he did some of the most important author covers during his tenure with *Astounding*.

Paintings	$800	$1,500	$2,500
Pen & Ink Illustrations	$50	$150	$200

TINKELMAN, MURRAY (1933-)
A very gifted artist who has worked in SF and Fantasy during the 1970's. His Lovecraft covers for Ballantine are some of the best work in the fantasy field. Many

collectors consider Mr. Tinkelman a modern equivalent of Howard Pyle.

Colored Ink works on Paper
$1,000 $2,000 $3,500

TSCHIRKY, L. ROBERT (?)

An artist who grew from SF Fandom during the 1950's and was involved with Prime Press, designing many of their covers.

Paintings(1950's- 1960's)
$500 $800 $1,400

TURNER, RONALD (1924-)

One of the most prolific paperback cover artists during the 1950's in England.

Paintings $750 $1,250 $1,750

UTPATEL, FRANK (1905-80)

This artist is known to most collectors for his striking cover designs for Arkham House book titles. An accomplished and inovative artist who sought different solutions for cover projects.

Paintings (can be color or monotone works)
$1,000 $2,000 $3,000
Pen & Ink and mixed media illustrations
$400 $600 $800

VALIGURSKY, EDWARD I. (1926-)

A prolific science fiction artist in the 1950's who did some work in the 1960's as well. This artist never signed his work. Many Ace paperback covers were done by Valigursky, including some of the most beautiful of the Ace/Double SF titles. Valigursky dominated the Ace line with Ed Emsh in the late 1950's.

Paintings (Ace/Double SF covers)
$1,500 $2,500 $3,500
Paintings (for paperback titles)
$1,000 $1,500 $2,000
Paintings (for *Digest* magazine SF titles)
$800 $1,000 $1,500

Note: at the summer 1999 PulpCon the cover for Harlan Ellison's Ace/Double title *Touch of Infinity* sold for $5,000.

VALLEJO, BORIS (1941-)

Boris started out with a career as a commercial illustrator during the 1960's.

After discovering the Warren black and white horror comic magazines he decided to try his hand at painting covers and sold successfully to Warren and Marvel. Later on he did quite a few covers for Marvel's *Savage Sword Of Conan* magazine, and eventually entered the science fiction and fantasy paperback cover field where he was heralded as the "next Frazetta." His work for the *Gor* series and ERB series of paperbacks remain very popular with fans.

Paintings (special sword and scorcery titles and the *Tarzan* Edgar Rice Burroughs series and some *John Carter* works.
$3,000 $4,500   [$9,000]
Paintings (for more regular content with SF)
$2,500 $3,000 $7,000

Note: individual sales would include: the cover painting for *Tarzan & The Castaways* Ballantine paperback edition, valued at $20,000; cover art to *Weird Tales of the Macabre* No. 2 selling at $3,250; painting for Buck Rogers based on TV show selling for $1,265.

VALLEJO, DORIAN (1968-)

The son of Boris Vallego, this extremely talented artist has done over 100 paperback and book covers during the late 1980's and 1990's and is sure to become more popular as time goes by. There is high interest in his earlier, more erotic works, and major sales to Japanese collectors in the late 1980's. This is contrasted to the mixed to relatively low interest in his more recent works, and poor showings at public auctions in the 1990's, esp. for *Star Trek* and movie related works, have led to major fluctuations in price.

Paintings (Mirage/Enchantment, personal works published in Vallejo art books - major paintings) $8,000 $11,000 $15,000
Paintings (Mirage/Etc.-regular works)
$3,500 $4,000 $4,500
Pencil Preliminary works (Mirage/Etc.)
$800 $1,000 $1,250
Paintings (late 1980's-90's paperback covers, *Star Trek/BattleTech*/movie - major works)
$6,000 $7,000 $8,500
Paintings (late 80's-90's PB covers, *Star*

Boris Vallejo, cover artwork for preliminary to STAR TREK II paperback cover, 1982; estimate: $1,000/1,500; sold for $1,265 in 1993 (Sotheby's 3rd comic art auction). © Paramount Pictures Inc.

H.R. Van Dongen, interior illustration for Jack Mann's "The Ninth Life," from A MERRITT'S FANTASY MAGAZINE for 4/50, sold privately in 1998 for $750. © Recreational Reading Inc.

Trek/BattleTech/movie -regular works)		
$1,750	$2,250	$2,750

VAN DONGEN, HENRY RICHARD (1920-)

During the John W. Campbell years of the 1950's for *Astounding Stories* this artist was among the most popular of all illlustrators for this magazine title, at times nearly as popular with fans as Kelly Freas.

Paintings.
(*Astounding* covers 1950 through 1955)

$750	$1,500	$2,250

(*Astounding* covers 1956 through 1965)

$500	$1,000	$1,800

(Magazine and paperback covers, 1950 through 1980)

$400	$950	$1,500

(Signet and early 1950's Heinlein covers)

$800	$1,600	$2,500

Pen & Ink illustrations
(*Astounding* from 1950 through 1955)

$75	$150	$250

(*Astounding* from 1956 through 1965)

$60	$150	$250

(Magazine and pulps from 1951 through 1960)

$50	$100	$175

VELEZ, WALTER

Paintings (major works -early mid-80's)

$1,000	$1,250	$1,500

Paintings (early mid-80's- regular)

$500	$600	$800

Paintings (book illo, late 80's-90's,)

$2,000	$2,500	$3,000

Paintings (book illo, 80's-90's, reg)

$1,000	$1,250	$1,500

Paintings (smaller card/game art)

$500	$650	$800

Hans Wesso, preliminary color study for unpublished THRILLING WONDER STORIES cover, circa 1939, pencil and colored pencil on board. From the collection of Forrest J. Ackerman.
© Standard Magazines Inc.

Hans Wesso, interior illustration for "The Seeker of Tommorow," from ASTOUNDING circa 1930's, from the collection of Donald Wollheim, sold in 1995 for $350. © Street & Smith Publications

VESTAL, HERMAN (?)

Herman Vestal was a Fiction House staff artist who did primarily black and white interior illustrations during the late 1940's and mid 1950's.

Black & White illustrations

$25	$35	$55

VIDMER, RENÉ

Paintings $35 $70 $140

WARD, LYND (1905-85)

An accomplished artist who was most famous for his wood-cut picture novels. He illustrated many famous books including special editions for *Frankenstein* and other Fantasy Titles.

Pen & Ink Illustrations (very scarce to the market) [$1,500 $2,500 $5,000]

WARHOLA, JAMES (1955-Present)

An artist who has worked for MAD

magazine as well as doing many contemporary SF paintings. His output since 1994-95 is primarily children's fantasy/illustrated books. He is currently back into limited assignments for adult, YA cover work. Since his uncle's death (Andy Warhol) he has received attention in verious media and public 'Warhol' related exhibitions, for familial art connection.

Paintings (late 70's -mid 80's)		
$2,000	$2,500	$3,000
Paintings (70's -mid 80's-regular)		
$1,000	$1,250	$1,500
Paintings (late 80's-90's, major)		
$5,500	$6,500	$8,000
Paintings (late 80's-90's, regular)		
$2,000	$2,500	$2,750
Paintings (late 80's-90's, prelim)		
$200	$250	$300

Prints & Portfolios: Visitor's *Night At Callahan's*, signed open edition is $75.

THRILLING WONDER STORIES

15¢

Hans Wesso, preliminary color study for unpublished THRILLING WONDER STORIES cover, circa 1939, pencil and colored pencil on board. From the collection of Forrest J. Ackerman. © Standard Magazines Inc.

WESSO, H. W. (1894-?)

One of the most important of the early pulp SF artists. This artist did many of the most interesting and important early covers for *Astounding Stories* in the period before John W. Campbell became editor.

Paintings (*Astounding Stories* covers, these are very scarce, there is only one known cover painting known to exist in private hands.
[$4,000 $8,000 $15,000]

Pen & Ink illustrations [$500 $1,000 $2,000]

Wesso illustrated many stories, E.E. Smith, early Campbell, and other important stories and authors drive the price up.

Note: two original colored pencil finished concept covers for *Thrilling Wonder Stories* were traded from the collection of FJA for an orignal Virgil Finlay painting in the summer of 1999.

WHELAN, MICHAEL (1950-)

(note: prices for Whelan's artwork have remained strong throughout the 1980's and 1990's, with many private purchases taking place between collectors and the artist directly. In some cases, as with the *John Carter of Mars* Edgar Rice Burroughs paintings, many of the originals are now in collectors hands. However with the Asimov *Foundation* paintings and other examples, many of the most historically important and desirable originals remain within Whelan's personal collection. It should also be noted that most of the originals remain within permanant collections; there is very little turn over in the secondary market for an artist so contemporary, and this is directly related to the high regard most collectors hold for this artist's work)

Paintings
  (paperback covers to Asimov's *Foundation* series I, II, and III, Heinlein book titles, Bradbury's *Martian Chronicles*, etc.)
$10,000 $15,000 $25,000
  (All Edgar Rice Burroughs paperback covers for Ballantine books) $7,000 $14,000 $20,000
  (hardcover, magazine, paperback covers, prints, from 1975 to present)
$3,500 $7,000 $12,000

(preliminary paintings in watercolor and mixed media) $800 $1,000 $1,500

Pen & Ink and Wash Black and White Illustrations
  (these works are rarer for Whelan because he seldom has time for anything other than cover paintings) $800 $1,600 $2,000

Note: recent private sales would include the cover to the Ballantine Edgar Rice Burroughs paperback cover for *Synthethic Men of Mars* at $22,000 and the cover to Isaac Asimov's *Foundation* paperback cover entitled "Trantorian Dream" for $25,000.00. The artist has recently ceased private sales of any of his paintings through his agents, Worlds of Wonder, and this could further cause prices for secondary paintings to rise.

WHITE, TIM (1952-)

Demand for original works and pricing has been depressed for this artist by lack of paintings on the market, and relatively low illustration output. Pricing therefore on this artist is more 'estimated.'

Paintings (late 70's-mid80's, major)
$1,500 $1,750 $2,000
Paintings (late 70's-mid80's, regular)
$800 $1,000 $1,200
Pen & Ink Illustrations (above years)
$500 $650 $800
Paintings (late 80's-90's, major)
$2,500 $2,750 $3,250
Paintings (late 80's-90's, regular)
$1,500 $1,750 $2,000
Paintings (above years, preliminary)
$100 $125 $150

WILSON, GAHAN (1930-)

This popular artist, who is best known for his color cartoons from within the pages of *Playboy* magazine, has always had a soft spot in his heart for horror and SF work. His illustrations have appeared in the *Magazine of F. & S.F.* and other titles.

Watercolor and Painted Covers
$1,500 $2,000 $3,500
Pen & Ink Illustrations $350 $500 $750

WOOD, WALLACE A.
(1927-81)

This popular and successful artist started out working in the comic book industry during the 1950's and eventually became known as one of the greatest science fiction comic book artists ever. His covers and stories for *Weird Science* and *Weird Fantasy*, published by EC Comics, remain his high-point of distinction. During the later 1950's to early 1960's, Wood branched outside the comics field, producing many wonderful illustrations and a few cover paintings for *Galaxy* and *If* digests. Most of these originals survived and are locked into permanent collections and rarely change hands.

Paintings (*Galaxy, Galaxy* Paperback covers, etc. from the 1950's) [$3,000 $4,000 $5,000] (these works are extremely scarce and 80% are locked into permanent collections)

Pen & Ink Illustrations $400 $800 $1,200
Pen & Ink and Wash illustrations
                            $500 $1,500 $2,000
Pen & Ink illustrations (for *Planet Stories*, very scarce).   [$750 $1,500 $2,250]

Note: individual sales would include: painting for *Galaxy* SF novel valued at $7,500; interior wash illustration from *Galaxy* valued at $1,750; interior black and white *Galaxy* illustration selling at $500.

YOULL, PAUL (1965-)

This artist is twin to Steve Youll, hence his early style is technically and expressively similar - but since the early 1990's, while maintaining technical similarites, the visual signature has become more distinct. Original artwork was not released into the market until the mid 1990's, therfore pricing is still in flux, and based on just a few sales.

Paintings (major works)
            $5,500 $7,500 $8,500
Paintings (regular finals)
            $3,500 $4,000 $5,000

Wally Wood, interior illustration for an unidentified issue of GALAXY magazine circa late 1950's, pen and ink with wash and brush work on paper. From the collection of Denis Kitchen, sold privately in 1995 for $3,000. © Galaxy Publishing Corporation

STEPHEN, YOULL (1965-)

Paintings (1990's major works)
            $5,500 $6,500 $7,500
Paintings (1990's regular finals)
            $3,000 $4,000 $5,000

PART VI

PULP MAGAZINES

ALL STORY, October 1912, featuring the first appearance of
"Tarzan of the Apes." Estimate: $4,000/6,000; sold for $17,250
(Sotheby's 9th comic art auction, June 1999). © The Frank A.
Munsey Company/ERB Inc.

SCIENCE FICTION AND PULP MAGAZINE LISTING

This listing is not complete, however it covers the major Pulp titles from the turn of the century, and attempts to cover some of the important early Science Fiction stories that appeared in magazines before the genre had its own title publications. This listing also includes a near complete Science Fiction Pulp and 1950's Digest listing with additional foreign titles. Also listed are the major Hero Pulps, Weird Tales, and other important titles to the genre.

Please check the credits page to confirm the Consultant list for this chapter. The author has taken careful consideration to contact many of the leading collectors, dealers, and enthusiasts before compiling this Pulp Price Guide. Some of the author's consultants have been with the market from its very beginning, such as Bob Madel who helped organize the 1937 Pre-World Con SF convention in Philadelphia and has been a collector and eventually major dealer from the 1930's onward. Other consultants like Robert Weinberg and Jim Steranko are accomplished authors and artists who have maintained a life long love of the Pulp Genre, and have given the author valuable input. Besides long time dealers and authors, the common fans have also given great input to this guide. Mark Trost and others have given the author specific focus on title availability and trends in pricing. Many of these people do not necessarily endorse the idea of a Pulp Price guide, however they have chosen to contribute important information in the hope that this guide will act as a historically correct source of information as well as a fundamental guide-line on how to price pulp magazines.

It is important to remember that "grading" on Pulp magazines has its own criteria separate from comic books. There is indeed such a thing as newsstand mint, or "file copies" found within the pulp world. However, because of the nature of how these magazines were made, with the majority of them having over-hanging covers (that would sometimes extend as far over as ¼ inch or more), and the quality of the paper stock used, the standards for grading are different.

The younger generations entering the Pulp market are drawn to the remarkable artwork on the covers, the colorful characters and ideas held within, yet they tend to "read less" the actual content of the magazines themselves. The original owners and collectors of these magazines read them (almost to pieces in some cases!) and it is important to remember that the majority of important Pulp magazine runs were put together during the great depression in America, when there were no hardcover Science Fiction books, no specialty Book Clubs, no Paperback (at least with any mass distribution, or overall availability) Books, no Television, or no high budget Science Fiction movies! In other words, if you wanted to be a fan of E.E. Smith, John Campbell, Otis Albert Kline, or any other number of Fantasy or Science Fiction authors, then you read and collected the Pulp magazines.

Because of this reality, finding very high grade Pulp runs is extremely difficult. The standards of acceptance on lower grades is also quite different than the Comic Book market (with some similarities in that really great Golden Age comic books with lower grades in unrestored condition are selling quite well, just as their cousins in the Pulp market do) and part of this is a generational difference. One very marked difference in both of these markets would be the brisk sales of rare Pulps and "in demand" titles with Xerox color covers. Many pulp collectors are content to own a very rare title or number with the Xerox cover, and will pay a decent percentage of the value for the otherwise coverless copy with facsimile cover. This reality again reinforces the reader vs. the "collector," who can only value a magazine by its condition and are not as concerned with its content. For these and other reasons this guide will use GOOD, VERY GOOD, and FINE as the three column divisions for value. Fine is used in the same sense as it is with Books, fine would imply "as new" with no tears, creases, or other flaws.

**FINE would imply brilliant colors, with no serious sun fading, tight spines with 90% of their original color intact, and interior paper that may be turning tan, but is no where near browning or in a brittle state. The covers would be flat and bright, registration of cover positions to spine turn could be slightly off.

Basically this example would look close to when it was originally delivered from the printer. Generally a Fine copy is permitted to have very minor flaws, such as minute overhang tears, chips, or cover split at spine, sometimes even one or two cover creases or minor spine damage. Some minor front9over wear is permissible. Cover can have sheen or not at this grade.

**VERY GOOD would imply some small chips, slight tears, folds, slight foxing and fraying to covers, some browning to interior covers and paper allowable, some fading to colors on covers and spine, yet still an intact fairly attractive example. Very good copies show some cover wear; edge tears up to ½"; small chips missing in overhang; several cover creases; minor spine damage, such at ¼" missing at top or bottom of spine; minor water damage; even clean tape repairs inside covers or on spine. Pulps are still in a collectible grade in this condition, except if there are many or all of the flaws listed.

**GOOD would imply the existence of slight missing chips, some folding, chipping to spine and cover edges should be marginal, fraying, darker paper, some soiling and foxing to covers. This grade could also include some amateur color touch to covers, provided full disclosure by the seller. It is important to remember that this grade to most long time pulp collectors (in special cases) is still acceptable, not just as a reading copy - but for limited value to a collector. Anyone in the field would be happy to own a copy of WEIRD TALES No. 1 or the October, 1912 ALL-STORY magazine with the first appearance of TARZAN OF THE APES in this condition, and indeed most surviving copies for these two rarities are about in this grade. Good copies are probably the most common because of the age and fragility of the pulps and are NOT considered to be a "collectible" grade overall. Copies show obvious wear; small pieces missing from covers and spine up to one inch; numerous creases and tears, especially in overhang; tan pages with brittle outside edges and flaking.

One more final word to newer collectors before this listing begins. The author has personally witnessed the storage designs of a number of important collections during the past three years in connection with consignments of large Pulp collections to Sotheby's auctions. With individuals as diverse as Fred Cook, Sam Moskowitz, and Frank McSherry, it is apparent that the old time first generation collectors had a very definite way of storing their Pulp Magazine collections. These periodicals were not set up-right like books, or paperback books; they were laid FLAT, in short stacks(usually in groups of twelve, for the volume year set), and they were not kept in plastic bags, or mylites, or mylar bags. These Pulp magazine collections were also kept in cellars - like fine wine - and they usually were kept out of direct sunlight, and of course in cool DRY cellars. Some of the older generation found that using mylites or bags would cut down on the problems of dust and extreme changes in temperature. This fundamental lesson should be remembered by the younger (condition conscious!) collectors as they begin to amass large Pulp collections. Treat these magazines like First Growth Bordeaux, and you will extend their lifetime, and your enjoyment of them to future generations. For after all, you will not drink them down eventually like wine, but you will absorb their wonderful artwork, read their remarkable stories, enjoy the thrill of new discoveries and obtaining "scarce" and impossible issues, and then in time they will be passed on to new owners.

A GENERAL INFORMATION NOTE
by Pulp Price Guide Advisor Jim Steranko

In the hierarchy of pulp collectibles, the low-end publications would include almost all romance, sports, railroad, and Western titles (except some of those noted here). Many of these titles sell at paper shows for under $5 each and are rarely collected seriously. The middle range collectibles include aviation, detecive, and science fiction themes, with such titles as *Argosy, Adventure,* and *Blue Book* at the bottom because they are still common and easy to find (except for earliest issues, they most often sell for under $15 each). Top-range collectibles include character pulps (such as *The Shadow* and *Spider*), weird menace titles (*Weird Tales, Terror Tales, Horror Stories,* etc.), and those with sexy, female covers (*Spicy Mystery, Spicy Detective, Spicy Adventure, Spicy Western* and several others). Ultra-pulp collectibles often consider special authors (such as L. Ron Hubbard, Tennesse Williams, Edgar Rice Burroughs, and others) or genuinely rare titles (such as *Gun Molls* and *Zeppelin Stories*).

Age is NOT a consideration (as in the older the magazine, the more expensive it is). Subject primarily determines pulp prices, with condition next, primarily that of the cover and spine.

Mel Korshak at 1950's Midwest Con about to auction off original Pulp artwork.

Long time science fans and authors Bob (Wilson) Tucker and Robert Bloch about to auction off a rare pulp original cover at a 1950's Midwest Con.

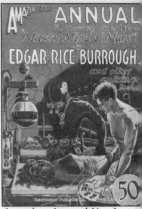

Air Stories
© Fiction House Pub.

Amazing Stories
© Ziff-Davis & Co.

Amazing Stories, 1927
© Hogo Gernsback Pub.

Amazing Annual No. 1
© Gernsback Pub.

	GOOD	VG	FINE		GOOD	VG	FINE
ACE G-MAN				1927-January-December	20.00	40.00	80.00
(With The Suicide Squad from May				1928-January-December	15.00	35.00	50.00
1939 through April 1943)				1928-Aug. (Buck Rogers CV)			
1936-39 All issues	25.00	40.00	50.00		125.00	250.00	600.00
1939-43 All issues	20.00	30.00	45.00	1929-1932 All issues	10.00	25.00	50.00

ACE G-MAN

(With The Suicide Squad from May 1939 through April 1943)

	GOOD	VG	FINE
1936-39 All issues	25.00	40.00	50.00
1939-43 All issues	20.00	30.00	45.00

ACE-HIGH MAGAZINE

	GOOD	VG	FINE
1921-33 All issues	10.00	20.00	35.00

ADVENTURE

	GOOD	VG	FINE
1910- Nov. (Vol. 1 No. 1)	100.00	200.00	350.00
1910-11 All issues	35.00	50.00	65.00
1912-19 All issues	35.00	55.00	75.00
1920-30 All issues	20.00	30.00	40.00
1931-40 All issues	10.00	15.00	20.00
1941-End All issues	6.00	10.00	15.00

AIR STORIES

	GOOD	VG	FINE
1927- August (No. 1)	25.00	55.00	120.00
1927-39 All issues	18.00	35.00	50.00

AIR WAR

(Featuring CAPTAIN DANGER.)

	GOOD	VG	FINE
1940-Fall (Vol. 1 No. 1)	25.00	35.00	55.00
1941-Win./Spr./Summer	16.00	30.00	45.00
1942-43 All issues	12.00	25.00	35.00

AMAZING STORIES

1926- April (Vol. 1 No. 1, the first magazine to feature Science Fiction exclusively, preceded only by *Weird Tales*)

	GOOD	VG	FINE
	125.00	250.00	500.00
1926- May-December	35.00	60.00	125.00

	GOOD	VG	FINE
1927-January-December	20.00	40.00	80.00
1928-January-December	15.00	35.00	50.00
1928-Aug. (Buck Rogers CV)			
	125.00	250.00	600.00
1929-1932 All issues	10.00	25.00	50.00

1933-January-December (this year was produced on cheaper paper, they are much harder to find in higher grades)

	GOOD	VG	FINE
	15.00	25.00	50.00
1934-38 All issues	10.00	20.00	35.00
1939-45 All issues	7.00	10.00	30.00
1946-49 All issues	7.00	10.00	20.00
1950-53 All Pulp issues	3.50	7.00	10.00
1954-59 All Digest issues	2.00	3.00	6.00

AMAZING STORIES SCIENCE FICTION NOVEL

*1957-March, Novel No. 1, special issue containing novelization of the movie *Twenty Million Miles To Earth*, with painted cover

	GOOD	VG	FINE
	25.00	50.00	75.00
1959-69 All Digest issues	1.25	2.50	5.00

Note: separate publication from *Amazing Stories*.

AMAZING STORIES ANNUAL

1927 -Featuring E.R.Buroughs "Master Mind of Mars" with Merritt and Wells (Vol. 1 No. 1) - extremely scarce in higher grades

	GOOD	VG	FINE
	150.00	500.00	1,500.00

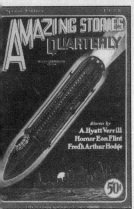

Amazing Quarterly
© Gernsback Pub.

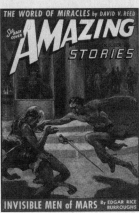

Amazing Stories
© Ziff-Davis & Co.

Amazing Stories
© Ziff-Davis & Co.

All-Story Weekly
© The Munsey Co.

	GOOD	VG	FINE		GOOD	VG	FINE

AMAZING STORIES QUARTERLY

	GOOD	VG	FINE
1928-Win-Fall (4 issues)	25.00	50.00	100.00
1929-Win-Fall (4 issues)	15.00	25.00	60.00
1930-34 (14 issues)	10.00	25.00	50.00

THE ALL-STORY MAGAZINE

	GOOD	VG	FINE
1905-10 All issues	7.00	15.00	25.00
1911-20 All issues	5.00	10.00	20.00
1921-28 All issues	5.00	10.00	15.00

Note: The *All-Story Magazine* was perhaps "the" most important early single general fiction Pulp title to feature SF and Fantasy stories before the advent of the Genre Titles of the late 1920's and 1930's. Authors as diverse as E.R. Burroughs, G.A. England, Ray Cummings, and others had important early novels and stories run within the pages of *The All-Story Magazine.*

*Any issues with SF and Fantasy themes can DOUBLE in value.

EDGAR RICE BURROUGHS NOVELS IN THE ALL-STORY MAGAZINE

THE MARS NOVELS:

A PRINCESS OF MARS
  (Appears as "Under The Moons of Mars")

1912- Feb.-July(6 issues)	125.00	200.00	350.00

THE GODS OF MARS

1913- Jan.-May (5 issues)	100.00	175.00	300.00

THE WARLORD OF MARS

1913-14-Dec./13-Mar./14	100.00	150.00	275.00

THUVIA, MAID OF MARS

1916- April 8,15,22	85.00	150.00	275.00

THE CHESSMEN OF MARS

1922- Feb.-April (7 issues)	75.00	100.00	175.00

THE TARZAN NOVELS:

TARZAN OF THE APES ("Tarzan of the Apes, A Romance of the Jungle," cover title with subtitle.)

1912 - October (complete novel in one issue, cover by Clinton Pette)

	4,000.00	6,000.00	14,500.00

Note:
The October 1912 copy of *The All-Story Magazine* is the single most valuable Pulp Magazine. Not only does E.R. Burroughs legendary and influential character Tarzan premier in this copy, but the unusual format of the entire novel being in one issue and the remarkable cover artwork contribute to this issue's desirability. Extremely scarce in unrestored FINE condition, it is estimated that only a few copies exist in FINE or better condition. Many experienced collectors also state that there are possibly only a dozen known copies in existence in any condition.

A good plus condition copy failed to sell at Sotheby's Book Auctions, and then later in 1995 at the first Sotheby's SF sale for $8,000. However, at the Sam Moskowitz science fiction auction on June 29, 1999, a very good copy with very minor restoration to a one inch square to the front cover, sold for $17,250.00 which sets a record for any pulp sold at public auction.

All-Story Magazine
© The Munsey Co.

All-Story Weekly
© The Munsey Co.

Argosy All-Story
© The Munsey Co.

Argosy Weekly
© The Munsey Co.

	GOOD	VG	FINE		GOOD	VG	FINE

Note: NEW STORY MAGAZINE (The second installment of the Tarzan series actually appeared in *The New Story Magazine,* and not *All-Story*. This title is recognized as an extraordinary RARE Burroughs pulp title, and very few collectors own copies in "any" condition above good)

THE RETURN OF TARZAN
1913-June/Dec. (7 issues) 200.00   275.00   450.00

THE BEASTS OF TARZAN
   (Appears in All-Story Cavalier Weekly)
1914-May/-Jun(5 issues) 100.00   175.00   250.00

THE SON OF TARZAN
1915-16-Dec./Jan (6 ish)   85.00   150.00   250.00

TARZAN AND THE JEWELS OF OPAR
1916-Nov./Dec. (5 issues)   75.00   125.00   250.00

INDIVIDUAL BURROUGHS NOVELS

THE CAVE GIRL
1913-July/Sept. (3 issues) 50.00   100.00   175.00
   (above first part appeared as "The Cave Girl")
1917-March/April (4 issues) 40.00   75.00   150.00
   (above second part appeared as "The Cave Man")

THE ETERNAL LOVER
1914-March 7 (1 issue)   100.00   150.00   300.00
   (above complete in one issue, appeared as "The Eternal Lover")
1915-Jan./Feb. (4 issues)   75.00   100.00   150.00
   (above appeared as "Sweetheart Primeval")

THE MAD KING
1914-March 21 (1 issue)
                         50.00   75.00   150.00

(appeared in one issue as "The Mad King")
1915-August (3 issues)
                         40.00   70.00   125.00
(appeared in three issues as "Barney Custer Of Beatrice")

Note: other early E.R. Burroughs novels appear in *All-Story*, the above figures can be reduced 30% for most of these appearances. It should also be noted that if single copies of the first installments of Burroughs issues are offered with cover artwork featuring the novel, the price can rise 50%.

ALL STORY DETECTIVE
(Featuring DOCTOR DEATH)
Began as NICKEL DETECTIVE
1932-34 All issues   25.00   50.00   100.00
1934-Aug./Sep./Oct./Jan. 150.00   250.00   500.00
   (Title changes to DOCTOR DEATH after January 1934 issue)

THE ANGEL DETECTIVE
1941-July (Vol. 1 No. 1)   30.00   50.00   100.00

ARGOSY-ALL-STORY, ARGOSY MAGAZINE
1922-35 All issues   5.00   10.00   15.00
1936-43 All issues   3.50   7.50   12.50

Argosy Weekly
© The Munsey Co.

Astounding Stories
© Clayton Pub.

Astounding Stories
© Street & Smith

Astounding Science Fiction
© Street & Smith

	GOOD	VG	FINE		GOOD	VG	FINE

EDGAR RICE BURROUGHS
NOVELS IN ARGOSY MAGAZINE

THE PIRATES OF VENUS
1932-Sept./Oct. (6 issues) 15.00 30.00 60.00

LOST ON VENUS
1933- Mar./April (7 issues) 15.00 30.00 60.00

CARSON OF VENUS
1938-Jan./Feb. (6 issues) 12.50 25.00 50.00

THE SYNTHETIC MEN OF MARS
1939-Jan./Feb. (6 issues) 15.00 30.00 75.00

TARZAN AND THE GOLDEN LION
1922-23-Dec./Jan. (7 issues)
                           12.50 25.00 50.00

TARZAN AND THE FORBIDDEN CITY
1938-Mar./Apr. (6 issues) 12.50 25.00 50.00
  (appeared as "The Red Star Of Tarzan")

TARZAN THE MAGNIFICENT
1936-Sept./Oct. (3 issues) 12.50 25.00 50.00
  (the first three part serial appeared in *Argosy*,
  the second part appeared in *The Blue Book
  Magazine*)

TARZAN AND THE GOLDEN LION
1922-23-Dec./Jan. (7 issues)
                           12.50 25.00 50.00

TARZAN AND THE ANT MEN
1924-Feb./Mar. (7 issues) 12.50 25.00 50.00

Note: Other important science fiction
authors seralized apperances would include
Otis Albert Kline, Ralph Milne Farley, Ray
Cummings, Murray Leinster, Eric North,
Victor Rosseau, and others. Prices can rise
50% from the normal colum listing for
issues containting stories by these authors.

ASTONISHING STORIES

1940-Feb. (Vol. 1 No. 1.) 20.00 30.00 60.00
1940-43 All issues   10.00 15.00 30.00

ASTOUNDING STORIES

1930-Jan. (Vol. 1 No. 1), this first issue is
  acknowledged as very scarce in higher grades,
  scarcer than *Amazing Stories* No. 1

	350.00	750.00	1,500.00
1930-February (No. 2)	150.00	350.00	700.00
1930-March (No. 3)	125.00	250.00	500.00
1930-April-Dec.	50.00	70.00	150.00
1931- All issues	35.00	110.00	200.00
1933 - Oct./Nov./Dec.	50.00	70.00	150.00 ·

Note: the first Street & Smith issues are
very scarce in condition.

1932-34 All issues	30.00	60.00	125.00

  (Becomes ASTOUNDING SCIENCE FICTION in
  March of 1938)

1935-1936 All issues	15.00	45.00	100.00
1937-41 All issues	12.50	25.00	40.00
1942-Bedsheet size	10.00	25.00	55.00
1943 -Jan./April Bedsheet	10.00	25.00	55.00
1943 -May/Oct. Pulp size	10.00	25.00	50.00
1943-47 All issues(Digest)	10.00	15.00	25.00

Note: first Digest size is November of 1943.

1948-49 All issues	5.00	10.00	20.00
1950-57 All issues (Digest)	1.00	2.00	5.00

  (Becomes ASTOUNDING (ANALOG) SCIENCE
  FACT & FICTION, Feb-60)
  (Becomes ANALOG SCIENCE FACT & FICTION,
  September 1960)

1958-64 All issues	1.00	2.00	4.50
1964-Present	.50	1.00	2.50

Astounding Science Fiction
© Street & Smith

Astounding Science Fiction
© Street & Smith

Authentic Science Fiction
No.51 © Avon Pub.

Avon Fantasy Reader
© Avon Pub.

	GOOD	VG	FINE		GOOD	VG	FINE

Note: All issues with stories by Robert Heinlein and L. Ron Hubbard from (1938-43) issues should be 50% and above in regular column listing prices.

AUTHENTIC SCIENCE FICTION SERIES
(British, Digest size)

	GOOD	VG	FINE
1951-52 All issues	3.50	7.00	14.00
1953-57 All issues	2.50	5.00	10.00

THE AVENGER

	GOOD	VG	FINE
1939-Sept. (Vol. 1. No. 1)	55.00	100.00	225.00
1939 (Vol. 1 Nos. 2-6)	25.00	40.00	75.00
1940-42 All issues	22.00	30.00	50.00
1943-44 All issues	10.00	20.00	35.00

Note: CLUES DETECTIVE MAGAZINE from Sept. '42 to May '43 featured appearances by The Avenger; the five issues bring the following range.

	GOOD	VG	FINE
	20.00	30.00	50.00

AVON FANTASY READER
(Digest Size, first 4 with square bound spines)

	GOOD	VG	FINE
1947-No date (No. 1)	9.50	20.00	40.00
1947-50 Nos. 2-18	7.50	15.00	25.00

AVON SCIENCE FICTION READER
(Digest Size)

	GOOD	VG	FINE
1951-52 Nos. 1-3	7.00	15.00	25.00

AVON SCIENCE FICTION AND

FANTASY READER
(Digest Size)

	GOOD	VG	FINE
1951-52 Nos. 1-2	8.00	12.50	25.00

BATTLE BIRDS
(Featuring CAPTAIN V)

	GOOD	VG	FINE
1942-Aug./Oct./Dec.	15.00	30.00	50.00
1943-Mar./May/July/Sept.	15.00	25.00	45.00

BATTLE STORIES

	GOOD	VG	FINE
1927-35 All issues	12.00	25.00	45.00

BEYOND (Digest Size)

	GOOD	VG	FINE
1953-55 All issues	3.50	7.00	15.00

BEYOND INFINITY
(Digest one-shot)

	GOOD	VG	FINE
1967-Nov./Dec. (#1)	4.00	8.00	20.00

BIG CHIEF WESTERN

	GOOD	VG	FINE
1941-42 Nos. 1 - 3	20.00	40.00	80.00

BILL BARNES AIR ADVENTURES

	GOOD	VG	FINE
1934-Vol. 1, No. 1 (Feb.)	75.00	150.00	275.00
1934-Vol. 1, No. 2 (Mar.)	55.00	95.00	235.00
1934-Vol. 1, nos. 3-6	45.00	75.00	135.00
1934-35-Vol. 2 & onward	35.00	70.00	125.00

(title changes to BILL BARNES AIR TRAILS with Oct. 1935 issue)

	GOOD	VG	FINE
1936-39 All issues	20.00	35.00	65.00

Note: Bill Barnes continued to appear from 1939 through 1943 in twenty-two issues of DOC SAVAGE. The issues are as

lack Book Detective

Black Mask

The Blue Book Magazine
© Consolated Mag.

The Blue Book Magazine
© Consolated Mag.

	GOOD	VG	FINE

follows: Sept./Oct./Nov./Dec. for 1939; Jan./Feb./Apr./May/July/Aug./Oct. for 1940; Feb./Oct./April for 1941; Jan./June/Oct. for 1942; Apr./May/June/Sept./Dec. for 1943.

BLACK ACES (very rare)

	GOOD	VG	FINE
1932-Jan.-July	30.00	60.00	100.00

BLACK BAT DETECTIVE
MYSTERIES (rare)

	GOOD	VG	FINE
1933-34 All issues	35.00	75.00	150.00

BLACK HOOD DETECTIVE/
HOODED DETECTIVE

	GOOD	VG	FINE
1941-42 All Issues	65.00	125.00	350.00

note: Very rare comic book to pulp crossover with only three issues.

THE BLACK BOOK DETECTIVE
(Featuring stories of THE BLACK BAT)

	GOOD	VG	FINE
1939-Vol.9/2,3; Vol.10/1	20.00	40.00	80.00
1940-V.10/2,3; V.11/1,2,3; V.12/1	15.00	35.00	70.00
1941-V.12/2,3; V.13/1,2,3; V.14/1	15.00	35.00	55.00
1942-44 All issues	12.50	20.00	40.00
1945-47 All issues	12.50	15.00	30.00
1948-53 All issues	7.00	10.00	20.00

THE BLACK MASK

	GOOD	VG	FINE
1920-April (Vol.1 No.1)	250.00	500.00	750.00
1920-May (Vol.1 No.2)	150.00	300.00	500.00
1920-24 All issues	35.00	50.00	100.00

	GOOD	VG	FINE
1925-35 All issues	25.00	40.00	75.00
1936-45 All issues	15.00	25.00	50.00
1946-51 All issues	10.00	15.00	25.00

Note: issues with E.S. Gardner, Dashiell Hammett (writing under his own name and the pseudonym of Peter Collinson), and Raymond Chandler can sell for at least triple their guide price, in some but not all cases. The 5-issue serialized "Maltese Falcon" (9/29-1/30) currently retails for $1,000 to $1,250.

THE BLUE BOOK MAGAZINE

	GOOD	VG	FINE
1900-10 All issues	10.00	15.00	25.00
1911-19 All issues	8.00	15.00	25.00
1920-39 All issues	7.00	15.00	25.00
1928-Jan. (St. John ERB CV)	35.00	75.00	125.00
1940-55 All issues	3.00	5.00	10.00

BLUE BOOK BURROUGHS
NOVELS:

JUNGLE TALES OF TARZAN,
  (appearing as "New Stories of Tarzan")

	GOOD	VG	FINE
1916-17 Sept.16-Aug.17	40.00	60.00	125.00

TARZAN, LORD OF THE JUNGLE

	GOOD	VG	FINE
1927-28 Dec.27-May28	30.00	40.00	75.00

TARZAN AND THE LOST EMPIRE

	GOOD	VG	FINE
1928-29 Oct.28-Feb.29	25.00	35.00	75.00

TARZAN AT THE EARTH'S CORE

	GOOD	VG	FINE
1929-30 Sept.29 Mar.30	20.00	40.00	75.00

TARZAN THE INVINCIBLE (appeared as "Tarzan Lord of the Jungle")

	GOOD	VG	FINE
1930-31 Oct.30-Apr.31	25.00	35.00	60.00

TARZAN: other titles include *TARZAN*

Captain Future
© Better Pub.

Captain Future
© Better Pub.

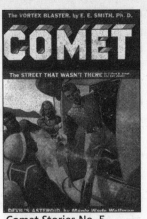
Comet Stories No. 5
© H.K. Pub.

Dare-Devil Aces
© Popular Pub.

	GOOD	VG	FINE

TRIUMPHANT 31/32, TARZAN AND THE LEOPARD MEN 32/33, TARZAN'S QUEST 35/36, TARZAN THE MAGNIFICENT 37/38.

	25.00	30.00	50.00

BLUE BOOK BURROUGHS NOVELS FOR JOHN CARTER OF MARS:

FIGHTING MAN OF MARS

1930- April-Sept.	20.00	40.00	75.00

SWORDS OF MARS

1934-35 Nov.34-Apr.35	25.00	35.00	70.00

Note: other Burroughs novels and stories appeared in *The Blue Book Magazine*, the above prices give an indication of value.

CAPTAIN COMBAT

1940- Nos. 1-3	25.00	50.00	75.00

CAPTAIN HAZARD

1938 Vol. 1 No. 1	70.00	125.00	200.00

CAPTAIN FUTURE

1940-Winter (Vol.1 No.1)	20.00	40.00	100.00
1940-44 All issues	16.00	30.00	50.00

Note: Captain Future also appeared in the following issues of STARTLING STORIES: Spr. 1945; Fall/Wint. 1946; Jan., May, Sept., Nov. 1950; Jan., March, May of 1951.

CAPTAIN SATAN

1938 Vol. 1/No.3(first issue)

	50.00	85.00	175.00

1938 Vol.1/No.4-Vol.2/No. 2

	25.00	60.00	125.00

Note: Stories written by William O'Sullivan; the run has five issues.

Note: also see STRANGE DETECTIVE MYSTERIES.

	GOOD	VG	FINE

CAPTAIN ZERO

1949-50 All 3 issues	22.00	30.00	55.00

CLUES (Clayton Publications)

1926-33 All Issues	15.00	30.00	50.00

CLUES (Street & Smith Publications)

1933-43 All issues	16.00	35.00	60.00

COMET STORIES

1940-Dec. (Vol.1 No.1)	15.00	30.00	60.00
1941-Jan.-July	12.50	20.00	50.00

COMPLETE STORIES

1924-37 All issues	12.00	25.00	50.00

COSMIC STORIES

1941-March, May, July	7.50	12.50	25.00

CRIME BUSTERS
(Includes authors such as Page, Dent, Gibson)

1938-39 All issues	20.00	45.00	75.00

DAN DUNN
(Written by James M Calvert Jr.) (rare)

1936- Vol. 1 Nos. 1, 2	35.00	75.00	175.00

Detective Fiction Weekly
© Red Star News

Detective Fiction Weekly
© Red Star News

Detective Magazine
© Popular Pub.

Detective Magazine
© Popular Pub.

	GOOD	VG	FINE

DAN TURNER-HOLLYWOOD DETECTIVE

	GOOD	VG	FINE
1942- Jan. (No. 1)	30.00	65.00	125.00
1942-50 All issues	25.00	40.00	65.00

DANGER TRAIL

	GOOD	VG	FINE
1926-30 All issues	12.00	25.00	45.00

DARE-DEVIL ACES

	GOOD	VG	FINE
1932-36 All issues	10.00	20.00	25.00
1939-41 All issues	7.00	10.00	15.00

DETECTIVE DIME NOVELS
(Featuring DR. THADDEUS C. HARKER)

	GOOD	VG	FINE
1940-Apr. (Vol. 1 No. 1)	20.00	40.00	60.00
1940- June/Aug (Nos. 2,3)			
	15.00	25.00	50.00

DETECTIVE FICTION WEEKLY
(Featuring Jimmie Dale, The Park Avenue Hunt Club, Satan Hall, Lester Leith and others)

	GOOD	VG	FINE
1925-31 All issues	5.00	8.00	12.50
(called FLYNNS DETECTIVE MAGAZINE.)			
1932-39 All issues	7.50	10.00	15.00
1940-51 All issues	4.00	8.00	12.50

DETECTIVE NOVELS
(Featuring THE CRIMSON MASK)

	GOOD	VG	FINE
1940-Aug./Oct./Dec.	15.00	25.00	55.00
1941-Feb./Apr./Jun./Aug./Dec.			
	15.00	25.00	50.00
1942-Apr./Aug./Dec.	12.50	25.00	50.00
1943-Apr./Aug./Dec.	12.50	25.00	50.00

	GOOD	VG	FINE
1944-April	12.50	25.00	50.00

DETECTIVE NOVELS
(Featuring JERRY WADE.)

	GOOD	VG	FINE
1939-June-Dec.	15.00	25.00	50.00
1940-Feb.-Dec.	15.00	25.00	50.00
1941-Feb.-Oct.	15.00	25.00	50.00
1942 Feb./June/Oct.	12.50	25.00	50.00
1943 Feb./June/Oct.	12.50	25.00	50.00
1944 February & June	12.50	25.00	50.00

DETECTIVE TALES

	GOOD	VG	FINE
1935-Aug. (Vol. 1 No. 1)	35.00	75.00	160.00
1935-39 All issues	20.00	45.00	90.00

Note: Bondage and yellow menace covers get a premium.

DIME DETECTIVE MAGAZINE
(Featuring Race Williams, Satan Hall, with Cornell Woolrich and other Black Mask-era authors)

	GOOD	VG	FINE
1931-36 All issues	25.00	75.00	135.00
1937-39 All issues	15.00	45.00	100.00
1939-41 All issues	12.50	35.00	80.00
1941-End All issues	10.00	20.00	35.00

DIME MYSTERY MAGAZINE

	GOOD	VG	FINE
1932-33 (started as DIME MYSTERY NOVEL)			
	30.00	40.00	50.00

Note: in October of 1933 became a horror orientated magazine.

	GOOD	VG	FINE
1934-35 All issues	45.00	75.00	150.00
1936-38 All issues	35.00	55.00	125.00

Double Detective
© Popular Pub.

Dusty Ayres
© Popular Pub.

Dynamic Science Stories
© Red Circle Pub.

Famous Fantastic Mysteries
© Popular Pub.

	GOOD	VG	FINE

Note: in July of 1938 changes again to mystery magazine format.

	GOOD	VG	FINE
1939-45 All issues	25.00	40.00	75.00

DOC SAVAGE MAGAZINE

	GOOD	VG	FINE
1933 Vol. 1, No. 1	250.00	500.00	1,000.00
1933 Vol. 1, No. 2	150.00	250.00	550.00
1933 All issues	85.00	175.00	325.00
1934-35 All issues	65.00	100.00	200.00
1936-38 All issues	35.00	60.00	125.00
1939-43 All issues	25.00	50.00	100.00
1944-48 All issues (Digest)	15.00	20.00	35.00
1949 (4 Pulp size issues)	50.00	75.00	150.00
1949 Vol.31/No 1(low dist.)	100.00	200.00	300.00

DOCTOR DEATH

	GOOD	VG	FINE
1935 Vol. 1 No. 1	150.00	250.00	450.00
1935 Vol. 1 Nos. 2 & 3	100.00	200.00	300.00

Note: ALL-STORY DETECTIVE for Aug./Sept. 1934 and Jan. 1935 have appearances of Doctor Death, these three issues bring the following range.

	150.00	250.00	500.00

DOCTOR YEN-SIN

	GOOD	VG	FINE
1936 Vol. 1 No. 1	125.00	200.00	350.00
1936 Vol. 1 Nos. 2 & 3	100.00	150.00	250.00

DOUBLE DETECTIVE
(Featuring the GREEN LAMA)

1940-Apr.-Dec.	35.00	50.00	100.00
1941-Feb.-Oct.	30.00	40.00	90.00
1943-March	30.00	50.00	70.00

DREAM WORLD (Digest size)

	GOOD	VG	FINE
1957-Vol. 1, Nos. 1-3	8.00	12.50	20.00

DUSTY AYERS AND HIS BATTLE BIRDS

1934 Vol. 5/No4(first ish)	85.00	135.00	275.00
1934 All issues	40.00	85.00	150.00
1935 All issues	40.00	85.00	175.00

DYNAMIC SCIENCE STORIES

1939-February/April-May	15.00	25.00	40.00

DYNAMIC SCIENCE FICTION

1952-54 All issues	4.00	6.00	15.00

EAGLES OF THE AIR
(very rare)

1929-30 All issues	35.00	75.00	165.00

EERIE MYSTERIES

1938-39 All 4 issues	60.00	125.00	225.00

EXCITEMENT

1930-31 All issues	20.00	40.00	85.00

FAMOUS FANTASTIC MYSTERIES

1939-Sept./Oct. (Vol.1 No.1)	20.00	30.00	50.00
1939-42 All issues	9.00	15.00	25.00
1943-47 All issues	5.50	10.00	20.00
1947-50 All issues	4.50	9.50	15.00

Note: Of the 55 issues, many carry A. Merritt stories, and host Virgil Finlay covers

Fantastic Adventures
© Ziff-Davis & Co.

Fantastic Adventures
© Ziff-Davis & Co.

Fantastic Story
© Better Pub.

Fantasy Mag. No.1
© Future Pub.

	GOOD	VG	FINE		GOOD	VG	FINE

- these issues can bring 20% to 30% more on grades of very good and fine.

FAMOUS SPY STORIES
(Featuring Anthony Hamilton stories by Max Brand)

	GOOD	VG	FINE
1940-Jan. (Vol. 1 No. 1)	20.00	40.00	85.00
1940-Mar. (Vol. 1 No. 2)	16.00	35.00	65.00

FANTASTIC ADVENTURES
(Bedsheets May 1939 to May 1940)

	GOOD	VG	FINE
1939-May (Vol. 1 No.1)	20.00	35.00	60.00
1939-40 July-May(Bd/Sht)	15.00	30.00	50.00
1940-43 All issues	9.00	15.00	25.00
1944-49 All issues	5.00	7.00	15.00
1950-52 All issues	2.50	4.50	10.00
1953-64 All issues(Digest)	1.00	2.00	5.00
1965-75 All issues (Digest)	.75	1.50	3.00

Note: All 1940's issues with J. Allen St. John covers, or E.R. Burroughs stories, are almost double prices on all grades.

FANTASTIC SCIENCE FICTION STORIES

	GOOD	VG	FINE
1952 All issues	10.00	15.00	25.00

FANTASTIC NOVELS

	GOOD	VG	FINE
1940-July (Vol.1 No. 1)	15.00	25.00	40.00
1940-42 All issues	10.00	15.00	25.00
1943-47 All issues	6.00	10.00	15.00
1948-51 All issues	4.00	6.00	12.00

Note: certain issues with A. Merritt, hosting Virgil Finlay covers can bring 20% to 30% more in all grades.

FANTASTIC STORY MAGAZINE

	GOOD	VG	FINE
1950-1955 All issues	3.50	5.00	10.00

FANTASTIC UNIVERSE SCIENCE FICTION
(Digest size for entire run)

	GOOD	VG	FINE
1953-1960 All issues	2.00	3.50	7.50

FANTASY (British)

	GOOD	VG	FINE
1938 Vol. 1 No. 1	25.00	50.00	75.00
1939 Two issues	15.00	35.00	60.00
1946-47 All issues	10.00	20.00	45.00

FANTASY BOOK
(first two issues bedsheet size)

	GOOD	VG	FINE
1947 Vol. 1 No. 1	10.00	20.00	30.00
1947 Vol. 1 No. 2	10.00	20.00	30.00
1948-50 All issues	4.50	7.50	15.00

FANTASY MAGAZINE
(Digest size)

	GOOD	VG	FINE
1953 All issues	7.50	12.50	25.00

FANTASY & SCIENCE FICTION
See THE MAGAZINE OF FANTASY & SF

FAR EAST ADVENTURE STORIES

	GOOD	VG	FINE
1930- Oct. (Vol. 1 No. 1)	30.00	85.00	175.00
1930-31 other 10 issues	20.00	55.00	100.00

FEAR!
(Digest)

	GOOD	VG	FINE
1960- July No. 1	7.50	15.00	25.00

Flash Gorgon
© King Features Inc.

Flynn's Weekly
© Red Star News Co.

Future Fantasy & Sci-Fi
© Columbia Pub.

Future with Sci-Fi
© Columbia Pub.

	GOOD	VG	FINE		GOOD	VG	FINE

FIGHT STORIES

	GOOD	VG	FINE
1928-38 All issues	16.00	25.00	40.00
1939-42 All issues	10.00	20.00	32.00

FIRE FIGHTERS
(very rare)

	GOOD	VG	FINE
1929-March-April	50.00	150.00	450.00

FROM UNKNOWN WORLDS

See UNKNOWN

FLASH GORDON STRANGE ADVENTURES MAGAZINE

	GOOD	VG	FINE
1936 (Vol. 1 No. 1)	200.00	450.00	750.00

Note: This one-shot pulp was formatted to look like a comic book with rounded spine, and center staples. However only its cover was comic-like in format, and also carried color interior illustrations. It is extremely rare in above Fine condition.

FLYERS (very rare)

	GOOD	VG	FINE
1929-30 All issues	30.00	60.00	125.00

FLYNN'S DETECTIVE FICTION WEEKLEY

	GOOD	VG	FINE
1920- September (No. 1)	45.00	85.00	175.00
1920-28 all issues	10.00	25.00	45.00
1929-42 all issues	7.00	16.00	25.00
1943-51 all issues	5.00	10.00	20.00

Note: This title was the rival of *Black Mask* and *Dime Detective* with many famous authors, including several Earle Stanley Gardner series and Cornell Woolrich stories.

FRONTIER STORIES

	GOOD	VG	FINE
1926-39 all issues	10.00	25.00	40.00
1940-53 all issues	6.00	16.00	25.00

FUTURE FICTION

	GOOD	VG	FINE
1939- Nov. (Vol. 1 No. 1)	10.00	20.00	35.00
(Becomes FUTURE COMBINED WITH SCIENCE FICTION Oct./1941)			
1940-43 All issues	10.00	15.00	30.00
FUTURE COMBINED WITH SCIENCE FICTION STORIES			
1950-54 All issues	2.50	3.50	7.00
1954-60 (Digest size)	1.50	3.50	6.00

GALAXY SCIENCE FICTION
(All issues Digest size)

	GOOD	VG	FINE
1950-Oct. (Vol. 1 No. 1)	7.50	15.00	35.00
1950-53 All issues	2.00	3.50	7.00
1954-64 All issues	1.50	3.00	5.50
1964-74 All issues	.75	1.50	2.50

GAMMA
(Digest size)

	GOOD	VG	FINE
1963-65 All issues	7.50	12.50	15.00

GALAXY SCIENCE FICTION NOVELS (Digest size)

	GOOD	VG	FINE
1950-60 All issues	2.50	5.00	10.00

Galaxy Novel No. 30

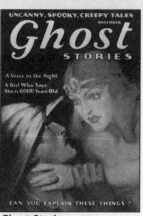

Ghost Stories
© Good Story Mag.

G-8 and His Battle Aces
© Popular Pub.

G-8 and His Battle Aces
© Popular Pub.

	GOOD	VG	FINE

Note: some issues with Wally Wood covers can bring 50% and more in higher grades.

GANGSTER STORIES/ GREATER GANGSTER STORIES

	GOOD	VG	FINE
1929-October (No. 1)	25.00	65.00	125.00
1929-1934 All issues	15.00	35.00	80.00

THE GHOST

	GOOD	VG	FINE
1940 Nos. 1-4	20.00	40.00	60.00

(title changes to...)

GREEN GHOST DETECTIVE

	GOOD	VG	FINE
1941- Vol. 2, Nos. 1-3	15.00	30.00	60.00

(The series continues, with THE GHOST appearing in...)

THRILLING MYSTERY

	GOOD	VG	FINE
1942- Sept./Nov.	15.00	25.00	50.00
1943- Mar./May/Fall/Wint.	15.00	25.00	50.00

GHOST STORIES

	GOOD	VG	FINE
1926-July (Vol. 1 No. 1)	60.00	100.00	175.00
1926-31 All issues	30.00	50.00	100.00

Note: When this title becomes bedsheet sized, higher grades are more difficult. The run is usually found in VG or below condition.

G-MEN MAGAZINE
(Featuring DAN FOWLER)

	GOOD	VG	FINE
1935-Oct. (Vol. 1 No. 1)	30.00	60.00	90.00

GOLDEN FLEECE

	GOOD	VG	FINE
1938-39 All 9 issues	30.00	50.00	85.00

G-8 AND HIS BATTLE ACES

	GOOD	VG	FINE
1933-Oct. (Vol. 1 No. 1)	125.00	175.00	300.00
1933 All issues	75.00	125.00	225.00
1934 All issues	75.00	125.00	200.00
1935-36 All issues	70.00	100.00	175.00
1937-39 All issues	50.00	75.00	125.00
1940-44 All issues	40.00	60.00	100.00

G-MEN DETECTIVE MAGAZINE
(Featuring DAN FOWLER)

	GOOD	VG	FINE
1935- Oct./ Vol. 1 No. 1	50.00	100.00	175.00
1935-38 All issues	20.00	40.00	70.00
1939-43 All issues	15.00	25.00	40.00
1944-53 All issues	7.50	15.00	25.00

THE GREEN LAMA

Note: appeared only in DOUBLE DETECTIVE MAGAZINE; see this listing.

GUN MOLLS

	GOOD	VG	FINE
1930-October (No. 1)	45.00	100.00	250.00
1930-32 all issues	25.00	55.00	125.00

HOPALONG CASSIDY

	GOOD	VG	FINE
1950-51 Vol. 1 Nos. 1-3	25.00	55.00	100.00

HORROR STORIES

	GOOD	VG	FINE
1935-Vol. 1 No. 1	75.00	175.00	250.00
1935-36 All issues	60.00	100.00	175.00
1937-45 All issues	40.00	75.00	150.00

Note: A small number of "File Copies" in Near Mint condition surfaced in the 1970's and entered some private collections, some of these copies have resurfaced on

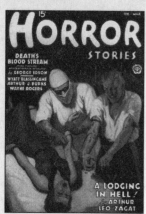

Horror Stories
© Popular Pub.

Imagination Sci-Fi
© Greenleaf Pub.

Imaginative Tales
© Greenleaf Pub.

Infinity Sci-Fi
© Royal Pub.

	GOOD	VG	FINE

the market. Otherwise, scarce in higher grades for all numbers.

IF, WORLDS OF SCIENCE FICTION
(All issues Digest size)

	GOOD	VG	FINE
1952-March (Vol. 1 No. 1)	7.50	15.00	25.00
1952-54 All issues	2.00	3.50	7.50
1955-65 All issues	1.00	2.00	5.00
1965-75 All issues	.75	1.50	2.50

IMAGINATION
(All issues are Digest size)

	GOOD	VG	FINE
1950-Oct. (Vol. 1 No. 1)	5.00	10.00	20.00
1950-55 All issues	1.50	3.50	7.50

(Becomes IMAGINATION SCIENCE FICTION in October of 1955)

1956-58 All issues	1.50	2.50	6.50

IMAGINATIVE TALES
(Digest size for all numbers)

	GOOD	VG	FINE
1954-58 All issues	2.50	5.00	10.00

INFINITY SCIENCE FICTION
(Digest size for all numbers)

	GOOD	VG	FINE
1955-58 All issues	1.50	3.00	7.00

JUNGLE STORIES
(Clayton Publications) (very rare)

	GOOD	VG	FINE
1939 All 3 issues	30.00	50.00	125.00

JUNGLE STORIES MAGAZINE

	GOOD	VG	FINE
1939 Vol. 1 No. 1	75.00	125.00	200.00
1939-43 All issues	25.00	45.00	95.00
1944-54 All issues	20.00	35.00	75.00

Note: All issues carried stories featuring KI-GOR.

KA-ZAR

	GOOD	VG	FINE
1936 Vol. 1 No. 1	75.00	120.00	200.00
1936 Vol. 1 No. 2	60.00	100.00	225.00

Becomes KA-ZAR THE GREAT

1937 Vol. 1 No. 3	100.00	150.00	175.00

KI-GOR
See Jungle Stories Magazine.

LARIAT STORY MAGAZINE

	GOOD	VG	FINE
1925-37 All issues	15.00	30.00	50.00
1938-50 All issues	10.00	20.00	35.00

THE LONE EAGLE

	GOOD	VG	FINE
1933-Sept. (Vol. 1 No. 1)	30.00	60.00	100.00
1933-Oct./Dec.	25.00	50.00	75.00
1934-37 All issues	15.00	30.00	50.00
1938-41 All issues	10.00	20.00	30.00

(title changes with August 1941 to THE AMERICAN EAGLE)

1941-43 All issues	7.00	15.00	20.00

THE LONE RANGER

	GOOD	VG	FINE
1937- April (Vol. 1 No. 1)	95.00	250.00	450.00
1937 All 6 issues	85.00	150.00	300.00

Fantasy and Sci-Fi
Mercury Pub.

Marvel Science Stories
© Red Circle Pub.

A. Merritt's Fantasy
© Popular Pub.

Miracle Science & Fantasy
© Good Story Mag.

	GOOD	VG	FINE

MAGAZINE OF FANTASY

	GOOD	VG	FINE
1940-Fall (Vol. 1 No. 1)	15.00	35.00	60.00

(Becomes MAGAZINE OF FANTASY & SCIENCE
FICTION with No.2.)

1950-54 All issues	2.50	5.00	10.00
1955-65 All issues	1.50	2.50	5.50
1965-present All issues	.75	1.50	3.00

MARVEL SCIENCE STORIES

1938-August (Vol. 1 No. 1)

	GOOD	VG	FINE
	20.00	30.00	60.00
1938-44 All issues	10.00	15.00	30.00

MARVEL SCIENCE STORIES

1950-51 All issues	3.50	5.50	10.00

Note: Early issues with Frank R. Paul covers
can bring 30% to 50% more in higher
grades.

THE MASKED DETECTIVE

1940- Fall (Vol. 1 No. 1)	25.00	50.00	75.00
1941 All issues	15.00	35.00	55.00
1942-43 All issues	10.00	30.00	45.00

A. MERRITT FANTASY

1949-50 five issues	7.50	15.00	30.00

MIND MAGIC

1931 4 issues	150.00	250.00	350.00

Note: title changes to MYSELF

1931 2 issues	150.00	250.00	350.00

MIRACLE STORIES

1931 2 issues	150.00	250.00	550.00

Note: Extremely RARE in VG+ or above,
most copies are found in good condition,
with the white cover paper with dust
soiling. Copies of Nos. 1 and 2 (in fine to
very fine condition), were auctioned off at
PulpCon in 1999 for $700.00 each.

MURDER STORIES (very rare)

	GOOD	VG	FINE
1931-July-October	45.00	100.00	225.00

MYSTERY ADVENTURE

1935-37 All 2 issues	65.00	150.00	300.00

NAVY STORIES (very rare)

1929-30 October-Oct.	35.00	75.00	175.00

NEBULA SCIENCE FICTION
(British, Digest size)

1952-59 All issues	3.50	6.50	12.00

NEW WORLDS
(British, first four issues large size,
others Digest)

1946- Vol. 1. No. 1	15.00	20.00	40.00
1946-48 All issues	9.50	15.00	30.00
1949-52 All issues	2.50	4.50	10.00
1953-59 All issues	2.00	3.50	9.50
1960-65 All issues	1.75	2.75	8.50

NICK CARTER MAGAZINE

1900's-1910 All issues	15.00	25.00	45.00

(These are Dime Novel format magazines)

New Worlds
© Nova Pub. Inc.

Nebula Science Fiction
© Nova Pub. Inc.

Operator # 5
© Popular Pub.

Operator #5
© Popular Pub.

	GOOD	VG	FINE

NICK CARTER, DETECTIVE

	GOOD	VG	FINE
1933- March Vol. (1 No. 1)	40.00	95.00	160.00
1933 All issues	30.00	60.00	125.00
1934 All issues	30.00	60.00	95.00
1935-36 All issues	20.00	50.00	85.00

(the following issues contain NICK CARTER Novelettes by Harrison Keith)

1934-May - through Dec.	30.00	60.00	95.00
1935 All issues	20.00	50.00	85.00
1936- Jan./Apr.	20.00	50.00	85.00

(NICK CARTER, Appeared in THE SHADOW for the following issues)

1944-June/July/Oct.	40.00	60.00	100.00

NORTH-WEST STORIES

1925-May (Vol. 1 No. 1)	25.00	50.00	75.00
1925-39 all issues	18.00	30.00	45.00
1940-53 all issues	12.00	25.00	35.00

NOVA SCIENCE FICTION NOVELS
(British, Digest size)

1953-54 All issues	4.00	6.00	12.00

THE OCTOPUS

1939- Vol.1 No.4	150.00	250.00	500.00

Note: This single issue Hero Pulp is highly desirable and had only a single issue appearance. This first issues numbering is the result of a continuation of Dr. YEN SIN title, so the company could save money on postal title permit.

(title changed to THE SCORPION.)

1939-April Vol. 1 No. 1	100.00	200.00	400.00

OPERATOR #5

	GOOD	VG	FINE
1934 Vol. 1 No. 1	150.00	200.00	350.00
1934-36 All issues	50.00	75.00	125.00
1937-39 All issues	35.00	55.00	100.00

Note: File copy sets were discovered in the mid-1970's, some of these runs entered private collections and have surfaced on the market. These file copies can bring higher prices.

ORBIT SCIENCE FICTION
(Digest size)

1953-54 All 8 issues	2.00	4.00	8.00

ORIENTAL STORIES

1930-Oct./Nov. (Vol.1 No.1)	150.00	200.00	400.00
1931-32 All other issues	80.00	150.00	275.00

(Becomes MAGIC CARPET with July 1933, Vol. 3 No. 2)

MAGIC CARPET
1933-34 All 3 issues	80.00	150.00	275.00

Note: Special issues featured Robert E. Howard stories.

ORIGINAL SCIENCE FICTION STORIES
see SCIENCE FICTION STORIES

OTHER WORLDS (Digest size)

1949- Nov. (Vol. 1 No. 1)	4.50	8.50	15.00
1950-57 All issues	2.50	3.50	7.50

(Becomes FLYING SAUCERS FROM OTHER

Planet Stories
© Fiction House Pub.

Planet Stories
© Fiction House Pub.

Planet Stories
© Fiction House Pub.

Planet Stories
© Fiction House Pub.

	GOOD	VG	FINE		GOOD	VG	FINE

WORLDS, June 1957)
1957 Final issues   1.50   4.00   8.00

OUT OF THIS WORLD ADVENTURE
1950 Vol. 1 Nos. 1,2   25.00   35.00   75.00

Note: Each issue contains a three story color COMIC BOOK insertion. The first issue contains two Joe Kubert stories with the lead story entitled "Lunar Station." The second issue contains one Kubert SF story. Obviously Avon was experimenting to see if any of their science fiction readers would cross over and buy their 1950's SF comic book titles.

THE PECOS KID WESTERN
1950-51 All 5 issues   7.50   10.00   12.50

PETER RICE (By Austin Gridley)
1933-Nov. (Vol. 1 No. 1)   35.00   75.00   150.00
1933-34 All issues   16.00   45.00   100.00
1935-36 All issues   15.00   40.00   80.00

PHANTOM
(British, large Digest size, 8½ by 5½")
1957-58 All 16 issues   5.00   7.50   20.00

THE PHANTOM DETECTIVE
1933-Feb. (Vol. 1 No. 1)   100.00   150.00   275.00
1933 All issues   40.00   85.00   150.00
1934-36 All issues   30.00   75.00   125.00
1937-41 All issues   25.00   60.00   100.00
1942-47 All issues   20.00   40.00   60.00
1948-53 All issues   10.00   20.00   45.00

PIRATE STORIES (rare)
1934-35 Nov.-July   30.00   60.00   120.00

PLANET STORIES
1939-Winter (Vol. 1 No.1)   55.00   100.00   175.00
1940-Spring/Summer/Fall   20.00   40.00   120.00
1941-44 All issues   30.00   45.00   90.00
1945-55 All issues   5.50   15.00   25.00

PLUCK AND LUCK
(not a pulp, part of dime detective series)
1887-1905 All issues   15.00   25.00   50.00
   (cover price 5 cents, covers can be found
   bright and white, interior paper is extremely
   hard to fine in near white condition)

POPULAR DETECTIVE
1934-Nov. (Vol. 1 No. 1)   35.00   75.00   150.00
1934-1939 All issues   15.00   30.00   65.00
1940-1953 All issues   10.00   20.00   40.00

PRISON LIFE (very rare)
1935-Sept.-Nov. All issues
                   35.00   85.00   175.00

PUBLIC ENEMY
(By Bryan James Kelley)
1935-Dec. (Vol. 1 No. 1)   25.00   50.00   75.00
1936 All 5 issues   20.00   35.00   50.00
   (title changed to FEDERAL AGENT)
1936-37 All 8 issues   20.00   30.00   40.00

Science and Invention
© Gernsback Pub.

Science and Invention
© Gernsback Pub.

Science and Mechanics
© Gernsback Pub.

Science and Invention
© Gernsback Pub.

	GOOD	VG	FINE		GOOD	VG	FINE

RAILROAD STORIES/MAGAZINE
(very common pulp title)

	GOOD	VG	FINE
1932-1954 All issues	3.00	6.00	10.00

RANGELAND ROMANCES

	GOOD	VG	FINE
1935-1955 All issues	1.00	3.00	5.00

RED MASK DETECTIVE
(Featuring THE MAN IN THE RED MASK)

	GOOD	VG	FINE
1941 Nos. 1,2	20.00	40.00	80.00
(title changes to RED HOOD DETECTIVE)			
1941 Vol. 1 No. 1	15.00	35.00	60.00
(also appears in MOVIE DETECTIVE)			
1942 Vol. 1 No. 1	15.00	35.00	50.00

RED STAR ADVENTURES

	GOOD	VG	FINE
1940 Vol. 1 No. 1	50.00	75.00	150.00
1940-41 Vol.1 Nos.2-4	35.00	55.00	100.00

Note: The character MATALA appeared in these issues.

RED STAR MYSTERY
(Featuring Don Diavolo)

	GOOD	VG	FINE
1940-June (Vol. 1 No. 1)	40.00	80.00	120.00
1940-Aug./Oct./Nov.	30.00	60.00	90.00

Note: Four issues starring "The Scarlet Wizard" by Clayton Rawson.

ROCKET STORIES (Digest Size)

	GOOD	VG	FINE
1953 All 3 issues	4.00	6.00	12.00

ROMANTIC DETECTIVE (rare)
1938-39 Feb.-Feb. All issues

	GOOD	VG	FINE
	30.00	65.00	150.00

SATELLITE SCIENCE FICTION
(Digest size)

	GOOD	VG	FINE
1956-59 All issues	2.50	5.50	8.00

SAUCY MOVIE TALES (rare)

	GOOD	VG	FINE
1935-38 April-Jan.	30.00	75.00	175.00

SCIENCE AND INVENTION
(Published by Hugo Gernsback, a non-Science Fiction slick magazine, it is however collected by Pulp and SF collectors for its content. Gernsback ran early science fiction stories, and from time to time featured SF theme covers.)

	GOOD	VG	FINE
1921-22 All issues	10.00	20.00	40.00
1922-Feb. (SF theme CV)	5.00	30.00	50.00
1923-24 All issues	7.50	15.00	30.00
1923-Feb. (SF theme CV)	5.00	30.00	50.00
1923-Aug. (the first magazine with the words "Scientific Fiction Number" on front cover, SF theme issue and cover, considered the first proto-type number before Amazing Stories No. 1 in 1926)	100.00	250.00	750.00
1924-25 All issues	7.50	15.00	30.00
1924-Aug. (SF theme CV)	10.00	30.00	50.00
1925-30 All issues	7.50	20.00	40.00

Note: Frank R. Paul and Howard V. Brown, two popular early SF artists, did many cover and interior illustrations for *Science & Invention*, their work is scattered throughout the run and certain covers by

Science Fiction +
© Gernsback Pub.

Science Fiction Quarterly
© Double Action Mag.

Scientific Detective
Monthly © Gernsback Pub.

Scientific Detective
Monthly © Gernsback Pub.

	GOOD	VG	FINE		GOOD	VG	FINE

them can bring higher prices.

(Becomes EVERYDAY SCIENCE AND
MECHANICS in late 1931)

EVERYDAY SCIENCE AND MECHANICS

	GOOD	VG	FINE
1931-44 All issues	7.50	15.00	20.00
1934-Feb. (Special cover and article on the filming of H.G.Wells "The Invisible Man")			
	15.00	25.00	50.00

SCIENCE-FANTASY
(British, large Digest size for early issues)

	GOOD	VG	FINE
1951-Wint (Vol. 1 No. 1)	5.50	10.00	25.00
1952-56 All issues	3.00	5.50	10.00
1956-65 All issues	2.75	4.50	9.50

SCIENCE FICTION

	GOOD	VG	FINE
1939-March (Vol. 1 No. 1)	15.00	25.00	50.00
1939-40 All issues	8.50	15.00	30.00
1941-43 All issues	7.50	15.00	30.00

SCIENCE FICTION ADVENTURES
(Digest size)

	GOOD	VG	FINE
1952-58 All issues	1.75	3.50	6.00

SCIENCE FICTION ADVENTURES
(British, Digest size)

	GOOD	VG	FINE
1958-63 All issues	3.00	5.00	10.00

SCIENCE FICTION +
(Magazine, 8½ by 11" slick format paper)

	GOOD	VG	FINE
1953 All 7 issues	2.50	7.50	15.00

SCIENCE FICTION QUARTERLY
(First series, Pulp size)

	GOOD	VG	FINE
1940-43 All issues	9.00	15.00	30.00

SCIENCE FICTION QUARTERLY
(Second series)

	GOOD	VG	FINE
1951-58 All issues	2.50	5.00	10.00

SCIENCE FICTION STORIES
(Digest size)

	GOOD	VG	FINE
1953-55 All issues	1.50	2.50	5.00
(Becomes ORIGINAL SCIENCE FICTION STORIES, Sept. 1955)			
1956-63 All issues	1.00	2.00	5.00

SCIENTIFIC DETECTIVE MONTHLY
(The rarest of all Gernsback publications, excluding *Amazing* Annual No. 1, rarely if ever found in fine condition)

	GOOD	VG	FINE
1930-Jan. (Vol. 1 No. 1)	70.00	100.00	250.00
1930-Feb./Mar./Apr./May	45.00	70.00	175.00
(Becomes AMAZING DETECTIVE TALES, June 1930)			
1930 last 5 issues	45.00	70.00	175.00
1930- March (No. 3)	50.00	100.00	200.00
(this issue has special Robot cover)			

SCIENCE WONDER QUARTERLY
see WONDER STORIES QUARTERLY

SCIENCE WONDER STORIES
see WONDER STORIES

The Shadow Detective Mag. © Street & Smith

The Shadow Magazine © Street & Smith

The Shadow Magazine © Street & Smith

The Shadow Magazine © Street & Smith

	GOOD	VG	FINE

SCOOPS
(Large format, on thin pulp paper, British)

	GOOD	VG	FINE
1934 All 20 issues	50.00	75.00	125.00

Note: Because of the paper that this title was printed on, high grade copies are extremely rare, very few sets known to exist in Very Fine or above.

THE SCORPION

	GOOD	VG	FINE
1939-April Vol. 1 No. 1	100.00	200.00	400.00

THE SECRET SIX

	GOOD	VG	FINE
1934 Vol. 1 No. 1	75.00	200.00	400.00
1934-35 Vol. 1 Nos.2-4	50.00	125.00	200.00

SECRET AGENT "X"

	GOOD	VG	FINE
1934- Feb. (Vol. 1 No. 1)	75.00	150.00	225.00
1934-37 All issues	55.00	100.00	150.00
1938-39 All issues	40.00	70.00	120.00

THE SHADOW

	GOOD	VG	FINE
1931 Vol. 1 No. 1	450.00	950.00	4,500.00
1931 Vol. 1 No. 2	350.00	600.00	1,250.00
1931-32 Vol. 1 Nos. 3-5	150.00	500.00	800.00
1932-35 All issues	100.00	200.00	400.00
1936-39 All issues	60.00	125.00	200.00
1940-43 All issues	50.00	100.00	150.00
1944-49 All issues(Digest)	25.00	45.00	65.00
1949 (Last 4 issues, for Winter, Spring, Summer, & Fall are all large Pulp size)			
	40.00	80.00	175.00

Note: The first issue of *The Shadow* is the most "in demand" of all the Hero Pulps, prices may vary on widely on this issue, it is also considered one of the RAREST of all early Pulp No. 1 titles, and extremely scarce in higher grades.

SHEENA, QUEEN OF THE JUNGLE

	GOOD	VG	FINE
1951 Vol. 1 No. 1	45.00	95.00	150.00

Note: Sheena appeared in *Jungle Stories* Vol. 5 No. 11, for Spring of 1954.

SHOCK MYSTERY TALES
(Digest - carry over from 8½ x 11" magazine title)

	GOOD	VG	FINE
1962 Vol. 2 #'s 1-4	7.50	20.00	35.00

SINISTER STORIES

	GOOD	VG	FINE
1940- Jan.-May all issues	30.00	75.00	150.00

THE SKIPPER
(By Wallace Brooker)

	GOOD	VG	FINE
1936-Dec. (Vol. 1 No. 1)	20.00	65.00	150.00
1937 All Issues	15.00	40.00	95.00

Note: The Skipper appears in *Doc Savage* for the following issues:

	GOOD	VG	FINE
1937-Nov./Dec.	35.00	60.00	125.00
1938-(ex. May) All issues	35.00	60.00	125.00
1939-(ex. Jan./Apr./Dec.)	25.00	50.00	100.00
1940-Feb./Mar./May/Sept.	25.00	50.00	100.00
1941-Dec.	25.00	50.00	100.00
1942-Feb./May/Jul./Sept./Nov.			
	25.00	50.00	100.00
1943-(ex. Apr., Nov.)	25.00	50.00	100.00

Shock Mystery Tales
© Culture Pub.

Spicy Detective Stories
© Culture Pub.

Spicy Mystery Stories
© Culture Pub.

Spicy Western Stories
© Culture Pub.

	GOOD	VG	FINE		GOOD	VG	FINE

SPACE SCIENCE FICTION
(Digest size)

	GOOD	VG	FINE
1952-53 All issues	1.50	2.50	6.00

SPACEWAY (Digest size)

	GOOD	VG	FINE
1953-70 All issues	2.00	4.00	7.00

SPEAKEASY STORIES
(very rare)

	GOOD	VG	FINE
1931-April-Aug.	25.00	50.00	100.00

SPEED STORIES (very rare)

	GOOD	VG	FINE
1931-32 Aug.-Jan.	35.00	80.00	200.00

SPICY ADVENTURE STORIES

	GOOD	VG	FINE
1934-36 All issues	65.00	125.00	225.00
1937-42 All issues	45.00	75.00	135.00

Note: Covers with Horror/Drugs/Bondage content can bring higher prices. Very high grades are scarce for this title. There are five issues that have Robert E. Howard stories, they go for 20 to 30% higher prices.

SPICY DETECTIVE STORIES

	GOOD	VG	FINE
1934-36 All issues	65.00	125.00	225.00
1937-42 All issues	45.00	75.00	150.00

Note: Covers with Drugs/Bondage content can bring higher prices. Very high grades are scarce for this title.

SPICY MYSTERY STORIES

	GOOD	VG	FINE
1934-39 All issues	65.00	125.00	225.00

	GOOD	VG	FINE
1940-42 All issues	50.00	75.00	150.00

Note: Covers with Horror/Drugs/Bondage content can bring higher prices. Very high grades are scarce for this title.

SPICY WESTERN STORIES

	GOOD	VG	FINE
1937-44 All issues	35.00	60.00	125.00

Note: Covers with Bondage content can bring higher prices. Very high grades are scarce for this title.

THE SPIDER

	GOOD	VG	FINE
1933-Oct. (Vol. 1 No. 1)	100.00	350.00	1,000.00
1933 Vol. 1 No. 2	75.00	250.00	500.00
1933-35 All issues	65.00	125.00	225.00
1936-39 All issues	50.00	100.00	150.00
1940-43 All issues	35.00	60.00	125.00
1943- Last issue (low dist.)			
	40.00	75.00	150.00

(the final issue was December of 1943)

Note: File copies were discovered in the mid 1970's for certain copies, some of these entered into collections and very few have been re-offered in the secondary market. File copies could demand up to 30 to 50% more in higher grades for all years.

STARTLING MYSTERY

	GOOD	VG	FINE
1940 All 3 issues	100.00	160.00	350.00

STARTLING STORIES

	GOOD	VG	FINE
1939-Jan. (Vol. 1 No. 1)	35.00	50.00	100.00
1939-March-Nov.	15.00	25.00	45.00
1940-45 All issues	10.00	20.00	40.00

Startling Stories
© Better Pub.

Strange Detective
Mysteries © Better Pub.

Strange Stories
© Better Pub.

Super Science Stories
© Popular Pub.

	GOOD	VG	FINE
1946-55 All issues	4.50	7.00	15.00

STRANGE DETECTIVE MYSTERIES

	GOOD	VG	FINE
1937-Oct. (Vol. 1 No. 1)	50.00	75.00	150.00
1937-39 All issues	35.00	50.00	100.00

1938 - with Vol. 1 No. 3 the title changed to CAPTAIN SATAN; then after five issues of CAPTAIN SATAN, the title reverts back to...

STRANGE DETECTIVE MYSTERIES

1940-42 All issues	20.00	35.00	75.00
1943-44 All issues	15.00	25.00	50.00

STRANGE STORIES

1939-Feb. (Vol.1 No. 1)	35.00	65.00	125.00
1939-41 All other issues	20.00	45.00	90.00

STRANGE TALES

1931-Sept. (Vol. 1 No. 1)	65.00	125.00	200.00
1931-33 All other issues	45.00	90.00	150.00

Note: Like the early Clayton *Astoundings*, these Pulps are extremely scarce in higher grades with white clean spines.

STIRRING SCIENCE STORIES

1941-42 All Issues	17.00	25.00	45.00

Note: The first three issues are Pulp size, the fourth issue was done larger than Pulp size, almost bedsheet size, 64 pages with saddle stiching. The publisher banded it as if it were a normal sized Pulp and thus they damaged most of the spines; very scarce thus.

	35.00	75.00	150.00

SUBMARINE STORIES
(very rare)

	GOOD	VG	FINE
1929-30 April-Sep.	35.00	75.00	175.00

SUPER DETECTIVE

1940-Oct. (Vol. 1 No. 1)	35.00	75.00	150.00
1940-50 All issues	12.00	25.00	45.00

Note: Early issues feature Indian manhunter Jim Anthony, Culture's answer to Doc Savage.

SUPER SCIENCE STORIES

1940-Mar. (Vol. 1 No. 1)	20.00	30.00	60.00
1940-43 All issues	10.00	20.00	40.00
1949-51 All issues	2.50	5.00	10.00

SUPER SCIENCE FICTION
(Digest size)

1956-59 All issues	2.50	5.00	10.00

Note: Many copies contain excellent Kelly Freas covers.

TAILSPIN TOMMY
(By Arnold Evan Ewart) (very rare)

1936-37- Vol. 1 Nos. 1,2.	20.00	65.00	150.00

TALES OF MAGIC AND MYSTERY

1927-Dec. (Vol. 1 No. 1)	100.00	250.00	500.00
1928 All 4 issues	75.00	150.00	300.00

Note: Scarce in higher grades. No. 4 should be priced as much as No. 1 because it features "Cool Air," by H.P. Lovecraft.

Tales of Wonder No. 11
© The Worlds Work

Terror Tales
© Popular Pub.

Terror Tales
© Popular Pub.

Thrilling Mystery
© Popular Pub.

	GOOD	VG	FINE

TALES OF WONDER (British)

	GOOD	VG	FINE
1937 Vol.1 No.1(winter)	30.00	50.00	100.00
1937 Vol.1 No.2(no date)	25.00	35.00	80.00
1938-39 All issues	20.00	35.00	70.00
1940-42 All issues	20.00	30.00	60.00

Note: Difficult in higher grades.

TALES OF TOMORROW
(British, Digest)

	GOOD	VG	FINE
1950-54 All issues	5.50	9.50	20.00

TEN DETECTIVE ACES

	GOOD	VG	FINE
1933 March, No. 1	35.00	60.00	120.00
1933-39 All issues	20.00	35.00	70.00
1940-49 All issues	12.00	25.00	40.00

Note: These issues of *Ten Detective*, carry stories of the character THE MOON MAN. Some issues feature tales by Lester Dent, the Doc Savage writer.

TEN STORY FANTASY

	GOOD	VG	FINE
1954 Only 1 issue	7.00	10.00	20.00

TERENCE X. O'LEARY'S
WAR BIRDS

	GOOD	VG	FINE
1935- Mar. (Vol. 1 No. 1)	135.00	200.00	375.00
1935 Nos. 2, 3	100.00	150.00	350.00

TERROR TALES

	GOOD	VG	FINE
1934-Sept. (Vol. 1 No. 1)	125.00	220.00	450.00
1934-37 All issues	100.00	125.00	225.00
1938-41 All issues	65.00	100.00	175.00

Note: File copies were discovered in the mid 1970's, and certain copies entered collections and have been available in the secondary market. These File copies can bring 50% more in higher grades.

THRILLING MYSTERY

	GOOD	VG	FINE
1935- Oct. (Vol. 1 No. 1)	40.00	85.00	175.00
1935-41 All issues	18.00	35.00	65.00

THRILLING WONDER STORIES
see WONDER STORIES

THE THRILL BOOK
(a bi-weekley)

	GOOD	VG	FINE
1919-March (Vol. 1 No. 1)	500.00	1,500.00	2,500.00
1919 Nos. 2-8	300.00	900.00	1,500.00

Note: Larger size than Pulp, almost bedsheet size.

	GOOD	VG	FINE
1919 All other issues	250.00	500.00	1,000.00

Note: Nos. 9-16 are Pulp size.

Note: Any copies of *The Thrill Book*, in any condition are rare, there are only a handful known to exist in conditions at strict Fine or above. Considered the scarcest and most desirable by long time pulp collectors of the early exotic Adventure titles. There was a complete set of 16 issues offered in 1999 for $20,000.00 in average very good to fine condition.

TWO COMPLETE SCIENCE
ADVENTURE BOOKS

	GOOD	VG	FINE
1950-54 All issues	3.00	5.00	10.00

Unknown Fantasy Fiction
© Street & Smith Co.

Unknown
© Street & Smith Co.

Utopia Grossband
© Paublo House

Vargo Statten
© Stuart Hardy Ltd.

	GOOD	VG	FINE		GOOD	VG	FINE

UNDERWORLD ROMANCES

	GOOD	VG	FINE
1931-32 All issues	30.00	65.00	150.00

UNKNOWN

	GOOD	VG	FINE
1939-Mar. (Vol.1 No.1)	35.00	75.00	125.00
1939-40 (to June 1940)	15.00	35.00	70.00
1940-43 (to Aug. 1941)	10.00	25.00	60.00

(Becomes UNKNOWN WORLDS, with October 1941, Bedsheet size)

	GOOD	VG	FINE
1941-43 (Oct. '41 Bedsheet)	10.00	25.00	60.00

FROM UNKNOWN WORLDS

	GOOD	VG	FINE
1948 -Anthology reprints	10.00	25.00	75.00

FROM UNKNOWN WORLDS (British, reprinted in boards with Cartier cover as Dust Jacket, 1952 Atlas Publishing. Scarce in Fine.)

	GOOD	VG	FINE
1952 Hardcover with dj	40.00	100.00	175.00

Note: The early 1939 and 1940 issues with Edd Cartier covers can bring 20% to 30% more. Also it should be noted that from August 1941 to the end of the run the cover format switched to a solid color "contents page" design format, unusual for a Pulp magazine, and less desirable to collectors.

UTOPIA GROSSBAND
(German SF Digest Size)

	GOOD	VG	FINE
1950's Nos. 1-200 up	3.50	7.50	15.00

VARGO STATTEN SCIENCE FICTION MAGAZINE
(British, begins with larger Digest size, and becomes regular Digest in three years)

	GOOD	VG	FINE
1954-56 All issues	5.50	10.00	20.00

VENTURE SCIENCE FICTION
(Digest size)

	GOOD	VG	FINE
1957-58 All issues	1.50	2.50	6.00

VICE SQUAD DETECTIVE

	GOOD	VG	FINE
1934- Vol. 1 No. 1	100.00	200.00	250.00

(Reported supressed shortly after printing, with only a few copies going into normal distribution)

WAR STORIES

	GOOD	VG	FINE
1928-36 All issues	15.00	30.00	50.00

WEB TERROR STORIES
(Digest horror title with Good Girl covers)

1962-65 Vol. 4 #'s 1-6, and Vol. 5 #'s 1, 2; issue No. 2 is Giant special size

	GOOD	VG	FINE
	7.50	15.00	25.00

WEIRD TALES

	GOOD	VG	FINE
1923-Mar. (Vol. 1 No. 1)	700.00	2,000	3,500.00

(Weird Tales No. 1 is almost never found in strict Fine condition, it is estimated that only seven strict Fine copies are known to exist)

	GOOD	VG	FINE
1923-Apr. (Vol. 2 No. 2)	900.00	1,200.00	2,000.00

1923-24 May '23 through May-June-July '24 are large Bedsheet size and extremely rare, almost unknown in strict Fine condition

	GOOD	VG	FINE
1923-24 Bedsheets	550.00	900.00	1,800.00
1924- May-June-July issues	700.00	1,500.00	2,000.00
1924-Nov./Dec.	300.00	500.00	700.00
1925-26 All ish(Reg/size)	200.00	250.00	400.00
1927-30 All issues	70.00	100.00	200.00

Weird Tales
© Weird Tales Inc.

Weird Tales
© Weird Tales Inc.

Weird Tales
© Weird Tales Inc.

Weird Tales
© Weird Tales Inc.

	GOOD	VG	FINE
1931-34 All issues	50.00	75.00	150.00
1935-39 All issues	30.00	45.00	100.00
1940-45 All issues	20.00	30.00	50.00
1946-53 " " to May 1953	10.00	15.00	30.00
1953-54 Digest size	15.00	20.00	40.00
1973-74 All 4 issues	5.00	8.00	15.00
1981-83 4 PB size issues	7.00	10.00	20.00
1984-Bedsheet size	35.00	60.00	100.00
1985-Bedsheet size with poor distribution			
	75.00	125.00	250.00

(*New Weird Tales*, edited by George Scithers, in Quarterly issues)

1988-1992	N/V	1.50	5.00

Note: Special author issues; R.E. Howard, Kline, Smigh, Lovecraft, and special cover issues; J.Allen St. John, Finlay, Brundage (on classic examples), can cause some prices to rise.

Note: First Lovecraft stories appear in Oct. 1923 ("Dagon"); Jan. 1924 ("Picture in the House"); Feb. 1924 ("The Hound"); Apr. 1924 ("The White Ape, & Nemesis"); and with H. Houdini for May/Jun/Jul. 1924 ("Imprisoned with the Pharaohs").

WESTERN DIME NOVELS
(Featuring the SILVER BUCK)

	GOOD	VG	FINE
1940-May (Vol. 1 No. 1)	10.00	20.00	30.00
(title changed to RED STAR WESTERN)			
1940-July/Sept.	10.00	15.00	20.00
(title changed to SILVER BUCK WESTERN)			
1940-41-Nov./Jan.	7.50	10.00	15.00

THE WHISPERER

	GOOD	VG	FINE
1936-39 All issues	35.00	75.00	125.00
1940-42 All issues	25.00	60.00	100.00

	GOOD	VG	FINE
note: The Whisperer appeared in *The Shadow* for the following issues.			
1937- Dec.	85.00	125.00	200.00
1938 All issues	85.00	125.00	200.00
1939 (ex. July/Dec.)	85.00	125.00	200.00
1940-May	75.00	100.00	150.00
note: The Whisperer appeared in one issue of *Crime Busters*.			
1939-June	25.00	50.00	75.00

WINGS

1928- Jan. (Vol. 1 No. 1)	20.00	45.00	90.00
1928-39 All issues	15.00	25.00	45.00
1940-53 All issues	10.00	20.00	30.00

THE WIZARD

1940-41 All issues	20.00	35.00	60.00

Note: Title changed to *Cash Gorman* for June of August of 1941.

WONDER STORIES
Note: For a historically correct progression of the way this run developed during Hugo Gernsback's years and afterwards, the titles are listed in the order of their appearance over time.

SCIENCE WONDER STORIES
(Bedsheet size)

1929-June (Vol. 1 No. 1)	35.00	60.00	125.00
1929-30 July-May	20.00	30.00	60.00
(Becomes combined with *Air Wonder* to make *Wonder Stories*)			

Science Wonder Stories
© Gernsback Pub.

Air Wonder Stories
© Gernsback Pub.

Wonder Stories
© Gernsback Pub.

Wonder Stories
© Gernsback Pub.

	GOOD	VG	FINE

AIR WONDER STORIES
(Bedsheet size)

| 1929-30 July-May | 25.00 | 45.00 | 80.00 |

(Becomes *Wonder Stories*, with June 1930 issue)

WONDER STORIES
(Regular Pulp size)

| 1930-31 only Nov.-Oct. | 15.00 | 20.00 | 40.00 |

Note: These years are much more difficult to find in Fine condition, because of normal overhanging pulp cover paper; the only time Gernsback would use such a format in his early years of publishing magazines.

| 1933-36- to Mar/Apr. | 12.00 | 16.00 | 32.00 |

(Gernsback ceases publication, becomes *Thrilling Wonder Stories*)

THRILLING WONDER STORIES
1936-August (1st New W.)

	GOOD	VG	FINE
	15.00	20.00	40.00
1936-37 All issues	9.50	15.00	30.00
1938-42 All issues	9.50	12.00	27.50
1939-June (10th annual issue)			
	18.00	25.00	40.00
1943-45 All issues	9.00	12.00	25.00
1946-50 All issues	4.00	8.00	15.00
1951-55 All issues	2.50	4.50	10.00

WONDER STORIES ANNUAL

| 1950-53 All issues | 2.50 | 5.50 | 10.00 |
| 1957,1963 All issues | 2.50 | 5.00 | 10.00 |

SCIENCE WONDER QUARTERLY

| 1929-30 Fall/Win/Spring | 20.00 | 35.00 | 75.00 |

(Becomes *Wonder Stories Quarterly* with Summer 1930 issue)

WONDER STORIES QUARTERLY

| 1930-33 All issues | 15.00 | 30.00 | 60.00 |

THE MYSTERIOUS WU FANG

| 1935 Vol. 1 No. 1 | 100.00 | 250.00 | 350.00 |
| 1935-36 All issues | 50.00 | 100.00 | 175.00 |

ZEPPELIN STORIES
(extremely scarce)

| 1929-April-Aug. | 250.00 | 650.00 | 1,500.00 |

Note: One of the rarest and most collectible of all pulp titles. Issue No. 3 (June of 1929) features the cover story "Gorilla of the Gas Bags," probably the most outrageous pulp cover ever published and the essence of the form.

ZOOM (very rare)

| 1931- April-Oct. All ish. | 35.00 | 85.00 | 200.00 |

The Frank McSherry Addam's Family "house of pulps." 1999.

Thrilling Wonder Stories © Better Pub.

Thrilling Wonder Stories © Better Pub.

Wonder Stories Quarterly © Gernsback Pub.

Wonder Stories Quarterly © Gernsback Pub.

Some of the authors who wrote for the pulps. Left to right: Philip Klass (William Tenn); Catherine; Judith Merril (behind piano); Ted Sturgeon (on top of the piano); L. Jerome "Jay" Stanton; Sam Merwin, Jr.; Groff Conklin; L. Sprague De Camp; Isaac Asimov; Fletcher Pratt. Photo by W.R. Cole.

PART VII

MONSTER MAGAZINES

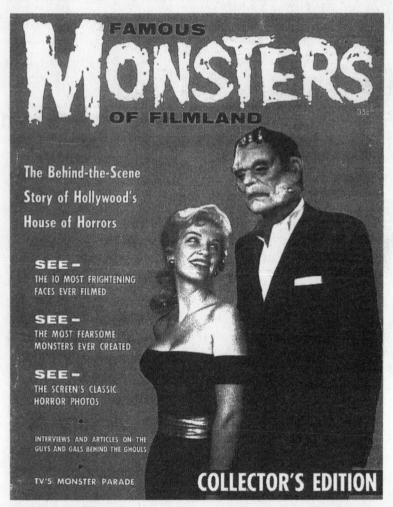

FAMOUS MONSTERS OF FILMLAND No. 1, Winter 1958, a fine copy in range from $500 to $700. © Warren Publications/DYNACOMM Inc.

Also please invite ROGER HILL, 4246 Cumberland,
and GREG TAYLOR, 3620 W 17 St, both Wichita.

I received invitations to visit over 1200 filmonster fans!
I AM COMING TO SEE YOU.
I expect to be there **WEDS, AUG 14** early morning

✓around noon

afternoon

evening between 5 & 7

Please inform anyone who needs informing NOW. Unless you receive further word from
me about 8 hours before I expect to arrive, everything should be going according to
schedule and I should turn up about the time predicted.
FLASH! SURPRISE! Wendayne ["Rocket to the Rue Morgue"] Wahrman--also known as
Mrs Ackerman--will be accompanying me! Two Ackermans for the price of none!!

PS--Personal to Jerry: If some mail for me arrives c/o *you,* will you be so good as to
    just hold onto it till I arrive? Thanx. Wd like to meet the Witches of Wichita,
    too, if you'll include them in your invitation. Also please invite Paula
    Tennery, 2105 El Rancho, Wichita.
                                   See you!

My SPECIAL
APPRECIATION
TO YOUR PARENTS!

4sJ
Sci-Fi
Esperanto

LOS ANGELES
AUG 1
4M
1963
CALIF.

JERRY WEIST
        1849 So 127 St E
                Wichita
                        KANS

MONSTER MAGAZINE AND MONSTER FANZINE
PRICE GUIDE LISTING

Collecting Monster Magazines and fanzines can be considered one of the most "cultish" parts of fandom. Often collectors of Monster Magazines have memories of having to listen to "older" more "mature" fans deride their enthusiasm for these most juvenile of publications. Within science fiction fandom of the 1950's the catch all phrase for Forrest J. Ackerman's *Famous Monsters of Filmland* was "Ackerman's Folly...." and to this day many long time science fiction collectors would consider these magazines not worth saving. What this older generation tends to forget however, is that during the Cold War and Eisenhower/A-Bomb years of the late 1950's - when EC comics had been thoroughly put into their grave and were gone forever - *Famous Monster of Filmland* introduced to a whole new younger generation the "sense of wonder" that many people felt when they first picked up issues of *Amazing Stories* or *Science Wonder Stories* back in 1926 through 1929. Many long time and serious fans first cut their fanish teeth on the Monster Magazines (the author of this guide included). And many young fans were introduced to comics fandom and later science fiction fandom within the pages of *Famous Monsters of Filmland,* and *Spacemen* from Ackerman's extensive articles about the film *Metropolis*, or articles by Bob Bloch, or from photos of Forry's own collection.

All of this is extraneous to the simple joy that is felt by the old time fan, who manages after years of searching to find that elusive issue of Larry Byrd's *Terror,* or that near mint copy of *FM* No. 6 that they have waited years to obtain. To quote from an anonymous SF fan of the 1950's "fans read.....fans collect....fans get together!" What was true forty years ago is still true today. Collecting Monster Magazines can be part of a larger interest that includes rare movie paper, or general interest in horror films, or it can simply be rewarding for its own benefits. Few collectors venture into serious Monster Fanzine collecting. However, for every collection of *Famous Monsters* there are likely to be found in the same boxes or on the same shelves copies of *Horrors of the Screen* or *Filmfax,* thus this Price Guide tries to cover as many bases as possible.

GRADING. Grading for this section follows the standard Good to Fine to Near Mint categories on a three column listing. Condition tends to be nearly as important for value with Monster Magazines as with comic books. Unlike pulp magazines where just finding a copy is sometimes considered a small victory, Monster Magazine collectors are most of the time looking for high grade copies. Condition does NOT play as important a role in Monster Fanzines where true rarity (only two copies known to exist, etc.) tends to dictate price.

The two features that preceed this Price Guide Chapter focus on two different areas of interest. John Ballantine is one of the premiere collectors of Monster Magazines and Fanzines in the World (some would argue that his collection is the greatest). We have interviewed him and taken photos of him in his home with his collection. In addition to this interview, the author has taken a trip down memory lane with "Mimeo-Daze," to his own days as publisher of a mimeograph Monster Fanzine, and wrote about what it is like to create and produce these obscure publications.

INTERVIEW WITH JOHN BALLANTINE
1/22/2000
By Brian Anthony
Questions Provided by Jerry Weist

Q: When did you buy your first Monster Magazine, where was it, and do you have any specific memories connected with this event?

JB: I was walking down Newhall Avenue in June of 1964. I was 11. My family had just arrived in California from Tuscon, Arizona; we'd been here about a week. I was walking past a Rexall store and just happened to pass the magazine rack and saw *Famous Monsters* #29, with the wild "Flesh Eaters" cover, and I remember going inside and picking it up and wondering what it was. I was always interested in monster movies, as was my sister and Dad, and would watch them on Saturday nights on the local Chiller Theater type show that we had back in the late fifties and early sixties. So I picked it up and looked at it and it really blew me away; all these movies pictured in there that I'd never seen on TV or had even known of. It was fifty cents so I bought it, took it home and immediately started looking through it. Suddenly I discovered the back issue department and thought to myself "Oh, this is issue #29, where are the other twenty-eight?" Most of them had sold out by then, but the few that were available I immediately sent for. Then I went back to that Rexall store every day for the next two weeks until issue #30 came out, and the 1965 *Yearbook*... so that got me started. I bought a subscription, then I noticed *Castle of Frankenstein* was also a magazine that was out at the time, and then *FM* came out with a small pocket-book, and all those wonderful Captain Company items in the back. So that got me started, and I collected on and off through the late sixties. Then I got interested in cars and girls, and put everything aside for about ten years. I didn't collect much through the seventies. Then in 1982 I was in Hollywood and stopped in a bookstore, because I had some time to kill, the Collector's Bookstore, and I remember buying some Golden Age comics from them in the mid 1960's. I used to collect *Captain America, Marvel Mystery Comics, Young Allies, Human Torch,* I really liked the Timelys. Even back then I was extremely quality conscious as I would only buy comics that were in near mint condition, and "Collector's" was an excellent source. So while in Collector's I saw a lot of magazines up on the wall and I asked to see a couple, and they happen to be *Famous Monsters.* They were *Famous Monsters* #4 and #6, which I was never able to obtain back in the 60's, and seeing them got me started all over again. What gorgeous covers! So I started buying them, again, in the early eighties. And pretty much over a six month period bought every issue "Collector's" had that I wanted.

Q: What were the prices like at this time, in the early eighties?

JB: Lets see, *FM* #4, I think I paid thirty-five dollars. Number 6 was around thirty, I got number 2 for twenty-five, and even into the teens they were only around twenty dollars apiece. And these were high grade copies. Today, a sharp #6 will sell for about six hundred dollars, or more, and that's assuming you can even find one. Now that's for a true near-mint copy, of which very few probably exist. I'd say between four to six hundred on a lot of the earlier *FM's*, which I believe is a bargain. For something as rare as a truly high grade, low number *FM*, to only have to pay four or five hundred dollars for it, well, you know what the comics go for. You'll pay four or five thousand for a high grade, early rare comic. So basically

I started collecting again at that point. I started picking up old *Castle of Frankenstein's* too, anything I could find locally here in LA. Then I saw an ad, I believe it was in a *Fangoria* magazine, a dealer in New York was selling this type of material, and that was Steve Dolnick. That was around 1986. So I wrote to him for his sales list, and noticed that he had other titles I'd never heard of like *Monster Parade, Monsters and Things,* and *World Famous Creatures.* I also noticed he had a FM #6 with a sticker, which I passed on because it was only a mid-grade copy. That particular issue is very controversial and is now believed to be a one-of-a-kind item, possibly the sticker having been placed there by some Florida youth back in 1960. Well, in a couple years time, from '85 through '88, I had assembled quite a collection. Then for various reasons, I stopped collecting for a few years. Then I started up again in '91 or '92, and that's when I started getting really serious. I started buying only high grade copies and I started being a completionist as well, and I also started learning about fanzines and researching what titles were available, where they came from, and who published them. Another dealer, Michael Pierce, knew quite a bit about fanzines, and between him and Steve Dolnick, I was able to get a lot of information. And I was just enthralled by these fanzines, all aspects of them. Their rarity and their unique covers and the different ways they were produced and assembled. Some titles, *Terror, Photon,* and *The Peter Cushing Journal,* had real photos mounted inside. So every extra penny I had I would sink into buying and searching out fanzines as well as prozines, and then I got into the foreign magazines: *Mad Movies, L'ecran Fantastique, Midi-Minuit Fantastique,* to name but a few. I was pretty well known to all dealers in the United States and many dealers overseas. I sold my projection TV to get money to buy magazines. I figured I could always get one of those anytime, but these magazines are not going to be around forever, at least not in this grade and this quantity and at this price. And I foresaw this correctly because at this point, for somebody trying to get started in collecting today, this amount and this quality of material, is almost impossible. And very expensive. Also, major collector's nowadays simply aren't selling. So I'm very glad that I pushed and pushed through the nineties to amass the collection that I have amassed. I had a lot of help from a lot of people, including Ron Borst and Michael Merrill. Ron Borst was a wealth of information, and he was there, right in the middle of the whole fanzine era. He was writing for *Garden Ghoul's Gazette, Gore Creatures, Photon,* and *Orpheus,* just to name a few. Michael was the first to tell me about issue #37 of *Midnight Marguee.* This specific issue has in incredible article entitled "Fanzines Of A Lifetime." It featured a very comprehensive listing of Fanzines and a wonderful article by Gary Svehla on the history of his *Gore Creatures/Midnight Marquee* fanzine, which as been going strong for 37 years now. I made a lot of friends who helped me look for things, and now with the internet I'm still looking. And finding things almost consistently. People are digging stuff out of their attics and basements, don't know what it is, and are putting it up on auction sites like ebay. Collectors are buying it, and a lot of it is at bargain prices, but some prices are astronomically high, as bidders compete for that rare issue. But the ultra rare items you still don't see. Some fanzines had print runs of only 20! And many, after being read, were probably thrown away at the time. Dealers don't have them, they're not on the internet sights, you don't see them for sale anywhere. So I'm very glad I was able to be such a completionist at that time. I would hardly ever pass up a mag I didn't have. I would somehow try to find the money, by borrowing it, or selling something, or talk my wife into putting something off so we could pick this rare fanzine, that I assured her would never be available again. It was very rare that I ever passed over something I didn't own. That was the reason I was able to amass such a complete collection.

Q: **What effect do you feel viewing these 1930's monster movies had on you as a child?**

JB: I just loved them. I was born in '53 and one of the earlist films I remember seeing, I was probably about five years old, was *From Hell It Came,* with the walking tree stump, and I remember it really scared me. Today it's laughable; it's almost hard to watch. And I remember *The Atomic Submarine, Giant From The Unknown* and *The Cyclops.*

There was just something about them I liked, I guess because they were scary, at least to a 6 year old kid. They just hit a chord. And I always wanted to see *The Thing From Another World.* It never played. And I remember waiting every Tuesday for the TV Guide to come out at the local Quonset Hut, so I could see if there was any possibility of any monster films being shown on TV that would be coming on. Some were on late, and I'd have to sneak out of bed to watch it. And *The Thing From Another World,* well I didn't see it until 1971. I remember seeing a picture in *Famous Monsters* #12, where they held a contest to see who could find a picture of *The Thing.* And now I have it on VHS and Laser Disc, and when it comes to DVD, well, I'll buy it again. With today's technoloby, I can watch it all daylong if I so choose.

Q: **Where you aware as a young child, the difference in quality between something like *Dracula,* or *Frankenstein,* and say, *I Was A Teenage Werewolf?***

JB: Well, I liked them both. I did know that the Universal's were the older pictures. And when *King Kong* was on the Million Dollar Movie I probably watched it seven times out of the seven days that it aired. I liked them all, including all the 1950's sci-fi and horror films. The Hammer films I didn't get into until the mid '60's. Probably the earliest Hammer film I saw was *The Evil of Frankenstein,* in 1964. And *First Men in the Moon* I remember seeing in Newhall right around that same time. I was always interested in films of that type. And even today, I like all genre films. Science Fiction, horror, fantasy, splatter, you name it. I like them all. And of course I like the mainstream films too, such as *Saving Private Ryan, Titanic* and *Apollo 13,* which are a few of my favorites. There's hardly anything you can name, even *Devil Bat's Daughter,* that I couldn't sit through and enjoy. There is really a wide scope of what I like when it comes to these films.

Q: As you began to develop an interest in these 'different' kinds of magazines, did your parents express any disapproval, or concern?

JB: Yes. My mom did. Back in '64, she thought I was warped and was worried about me, and threatened to throw everything out many times. I used to hide stuff in my closet because whenever she saw something new, she would ask, "Why are you interested in this? What is your obsession with this crap, I'm really worried about you!" That continued, but she was okay eventually, and let me keep the stuff. She didn't understand why I was interested in it, but it's the same story as a thousand other kids who grew up reading *Famous Monsters*.

Q: Did you have to 'defend' your interest, and how did you do so?

JB: I simply told her I liked these movies and magazines, and that I knew it wasn't real. It was something I enjoyed. I never was much at sports. Now that was something they would have approved of. I guess it was an escape for me, maybe it still is. I can come up to this room and pull out *Giant From The Unknown*, turn the lights out and be transported back to my childhood. For an hour and a half I don't have to worry about work, life or anything, it's just a nice escape for me. I enjoy it.

Q: When did you first notice that you were beginning a "collection?" Where there any initial events connected to this realization?

JB: Probably around '83 I started making a concerted effort to hunt down issues I needed to complete my set of *Famous Monsters, Castle of Frankenstein, Mad Monsters, ...* right around that time I was really serious about putting together a collection.

Q: If *Famous Monsters* was your favorite Monster Magazine, did you write to *FM* early on? Did you join the *FM Club*? Did you buy anyting from the Captain Company?

JB: I didn't joing the club, I don't know why. I never did write or correspond with anybody, and none of my friends were into this type of material at school. So I was kind of a one man show, I was just by myself, liking and buying these magazines. I didn't really have anyone to share it with at the time. As pertains to the Captain Company, I sent for a lot of stuff. I had the paint-by-numbers, the wallets, and a few things here and there whenever I had a little extra money. It always arrived. As did all the back issues. I even sent for *Wildest Westerns, Screen Thrills* and *Spacemen,* whatever I could get my hands on. Anything Warren. And of course I was into *Creepy* and *Eerie* too.

Q: When did you meet your first friend who was also interested in Monster Magazines, and did this first friend - or other early friends - cause your interests to widen into other areas?

JB: Well, that probably would have been around 1983. I was attending the monthly Comic Book and Science Fiction Convention, which was held at the Roosevelt Hotel on Wilshire, and I was hunting down back issues of *Famous Monsters*. As I walked in I noticed a dealer had a whole wall of monster mags for sale, as well as back issues of *Famous Monsters*. My eyes became as wide as saucers. I said to myself "Oh boy, I've hit pay dirt." There was another fellow standing there looking just as wide eyed. That fellow was Mike Yerkes and he happened to be another *Famous Monsters* collector, high grade, like me, and we just started talking. He mentioned he was good friends with Forry Ackerman and that I should come up to Forry's house with him, and meet Forry, and look through the "Garage Mahal." He had just bought a painting from Forry, the cover art from *Famous Monsters #4*, the Martian from

War of the Worlds, so he was real excited about that. And he also had quite a collection he was anxious to show me, because he didn't really meet anyone in all his years of liking this type of material that was really into it like I was. So we started a friendship, in '83, and we're still very good friends, he lives in Las Vegas and we talk every couple of weeks. He comes out every few months and hangs out with me; we still go to Forry's or hit the magazine stores. Anytime either one of us finds some little treasure we call the other, just like little kids would.

Q: When did you become aware of Monster Fanzines? How did this happen, and what were your early purchases?

JB: I remember seeing my first fanzine in *Famous Monsters* #23 way back in '64, which was the *Kaleidoscope* issue, by Don Shay, of *Cinefex* fame. And I also remember seeing *Horrors of the Screen*, about that same time. However I only saw pictures of them. The "Haunt Ad" section of *FM* ran ads about clubs and fanzines, but by the time I got into *Famous Monsters* the "Haunt Ads" were no more. So I never contacted anyone about buying a fanzine or joining a club. I wasn't really into fanzines until I started collecting again in '83. Now, the dealers were coming up with these fanzines, and I didn't know much about them, and really didn't know what they were. And they didn't know a lot about them either. But I bought them anyway because they were unique. I think the first fanzine I bought might have been Larry Byrd's *Terror* #5.

I don't know what I was expecting, but when I got it and saw that it was side stapled, I was a little bit dissapointed. I guess I expected it to look like a prozine and it didn't. It looked home-made. Then I got hold of a fanzine called the *Teratoid Guide*. The *Teratoid Guide* was a guide about fanzines and when I looked through it I went wild. There were just hundreds of fanzines in there with really cool names - *The Bela Lugosi Journal, Nightmare, Gruesome Creatures, Menace, Vampire's Crypt*, the list goes on. I was just blown away by the sheer number of fanzines listed in that guide. So then I started asking the dealers to find these fanzines for me. Michael Pierce, a dealer, at that time also collected fanzines. He knew about them, he'd been finding them and collecting them for some time. So I got a lot of information from him. He came out with a little sales catalog and had photographed some of his fanzines to put in the back of it. So I actually got to see many, and all at once, for the first time, and it was very exciting. I immediately fell in love with the fanzines which featured a Larry Byrd cover. I didn't own any of these and boy was I a man with a mission now! And Steve Dolnick, he was on a vendetta, using every resource he could think of to search for these fanzines.

Q: Did your exposure to Monster Fandom and fanzines cause you to move into other areas of collecting or reading or experiencing - such as seeking out older Silent Films and trying to view them - or finding early out of print books about the medium and reading them?

JB: Well, yes. It got me on to books, too. I started looking for out of print books, any book I could find on horror, science fiction and fantasy. At the time I only owned a couple of books, so I started looking for the books at the same time as the magazines. Then, the laser disc was just coming out in the early eighties. So for the first time, for a reasonable price you could own the film and it would also be a very high quality version of the film. So I started buying laser discs in '83 and '84, and continued buying them right up to today. I bought as many as I could afford, and if I couldn't afford a new copy I'd look for a used one, because I was buying a lot of magazines, which always took preference. So yes, it also got me started on collecting books and made me want to hunt down and own all my favorite movies of all these films I had seen in the pages of *FM* and in theatres and on TV.

Q: And you collected 8mm film?

JB: I collected a few even though I didn't have an 8mm projector. But I loved the box art, so if I saw an 8mm film I'd pick it up. Even today I don't own a projector. I still love the box art though, and I see them for sale on ebay and it's tempting to pick them up. They're very unique. Don't get me started.

Q: Forry Ackerman took a cross-country trip before a World Con to meet *FM* fans all over America in 1963. Did you meet him then?

JB: No, I did not meet him on his "Project 6000" tour. The first time I met Forry was in 1984. I was going to meet my friend Mike Yerkes there, but I arrived at Forry's at lunchtime on a weekday and Mike wasn't able to make it. It was just Forry and I. Long time Forry friend Ron Borst joined us for lunch at The Sizzler. I remember Ron telling me that he sells FM #1's at his shop in Hollywood for a couple hundred bucks apiece. Of course I went the following week to buy one. Well, I was at Forry's for a few hours and he gave me the run of the place, and was every bit as nice and pleasant a person as I had read he was. I remember buying a few magazines from him. He was selling at the time *House of Horror* which was a *Famous Monsters* spin-off mag, to halt the U.S. distribution of the English *House of Horror*. It was a mag that they only printed around four hundred copies of, so they had to distribute it in so many states, at so many news stands. He had about six or eight of them and was letting them go for about sixty five dollars apiece. I'd never seen it before, so it was very exciting to obtain a copy. But more importantly, when I was there he sold me a *Collector's Guide To Monster Magazines* that I didn't even know existed. That was the 1977 Michelucci guide. So looking through that was a real revelation for me, because for the first time, I was able to see all these magazines in numerical order, and all with publisher's info and dates, grouped together in one handy book. Little did I know I would be editing my own collector's guide, a decade later.

Q: When did you first become aware of "condition," and how quickly did you begin to want "perfect" or "Near Mint" copies of your fanzines, books, monster magazines, etc.?

JB: Well, I was always a condition fanatic all the way back to the early sixties and my comic collecting days. Of the comics I collected, I was very careful to pick out the highest-grade copies and then take extra good care of them. I wouldn't lend them out to friends, or roll them up and carry them around in my back pocket on my bike, as all my friends did. I handled them very carefully. When I ordered from the Captain Company I would never cut the magazines. I've never cut a coupon out of anything in my life. I'd hand write it out on a piece of paper, and I remember scotch taping the coins to a card and putting a little piece of paper around it. I always sent cash. I'd send it off and remember waiting for that postman everyday, eleven-thirty, eleven-forty-five, here he comes! Hoping there'd be something in the mailbox, the latest issue of *Famous Monsters*, or something from the Captain Company. Especially during the summer of '64.

Q: Did you collect the Aurora monster models?

JB: Yes, every one of them. Collected them all, built them all, painted them all, then sold them all for probably five dollars.

Q: As you grew older, was there any period during your life that you "left" your collection, or wanted to quit - or sell out?

JB: Yes. In 1970 I had amassed quite a collection of *Famous Monsters* magazines, and I also had all of my Golden Age comics, and I remember going down to Hollywood and selling them all for just a few hundred dollars so I could buy a new car. I wanted to buy a Camaro at the time so off they went! And some of those comics were in beautiful NM condition. I kept them in manila folders to keep them nice. I remember scrutinizing the condition of each and every magazine and comic even back then.

Q: What brought you back into collecting?

JB: Two words. Collector's Bookstore. Back in the 60's I was never able to locate the sold-out issues of *FM*. And the first 6, I had only see as little tiny black and white pictures in the back issue department of *FM* #7. I remember staring at them endlessly and wondering what was inside. Then there was the cover of the 1962 Yearbook, which featured the cover of *FM's* #1, 3, 5, and 6; a little larger in size, and in color. And of course the pocket book from '64 featured color covers of #3, 11 and 12. But there was nothing to prepare me for finally seeing, at long last, the "sold-out" *FMs*. To hold them in my hands full-size, and see those covers in vivid living color. I simply was bowled over and it brought it all back and got me started again. They were in very nice condition, and very inexpensive, so I was hooked, and started buying them again. I was able to purchase all the sold out issues. As an adult, I now knew I had the resources I lacked as a child. And it's led to this.

Q: Did you like the jokes and gags that permeated "*Famous Monsters*," or would you have preferred a more serious tone?

JB: I wish it was more serious. I did not like the jokes. I remember seeing a still of *King Kong*, fighting with a pterodactyl, and the caption read "Oh Fay can you see by the dawn's early light, that this pterodactyl has flown his last flight" that phrase has always stuck with me. I just thought the jokes were hokey, I really wanted it to be more serious. But I put up with the jokes, because the pictures were so incredible. That was one nice thing about *Castle of Frankenstein*, it was pretty much a serious film magazine.

Q: What were your favorite *FM* covers?

JB: My favorite *FM* covers? That's a tough one. I love #5, that's the Bela Lugosi experimental makeup test manimal from *The Island of Lost Souls*. Forry still has the original cover art for that one. I love #7, which is the Zacherley cover. And #9, *The Fall of the House of Usher*, which was also the first Basil Gogos cover. And #12 *Curse of the Werewolf*, with that vivid yellow background is one of my favorites. All the early ones I love, every single one, right up through #31. I remember when #32 came in the mail, and it was a photo of a plastic customized King Kong model, I thought, "where is our beautiful cover art?" Then #33 through #38 came out with some nice cover art, but I soon realized the magic was gone. Then #39 had a really yucky Japanese Frankenstein cover. Soon *FM* started reprinting articles and then I really got out of it.

Q: What were your favorite non-*FM* titles?

JB: *Castle of Frankenstein* was definitely my second favorite monster title, and I also liked *For Monsters Only* and collected it at the same time. I do have the *Mad Monsters* and *Horror Monsters* but I never saw those on the stands, I think they were pretty much gone by the time

I started collecting.

Q: What are your favorite monster fanzines?

JB: I'm a stop-motion animation enthusiast, a big Ray Harryhausen and Willis
The Animation Journal is one of my favorite fanzines. It ran nine issues and the
very, very rare. A very limited printing. It was very pleased to complete that run
tracking down the nine newsletters, which appeared between regular issues. Stev
and Bill Shrock were the editors. Other fanzines I like are *FXRH* (Special Effects
Harryhausen) done by Ernest Farino and Sam Calvin. *Closeup*, is another favorite wh
done by David Prestone. Also *Garden Ghoul's Gazette* is one of my favorites, that title
twenty-one issues. It then turned into *Cinefantastique*. Fred Clark changed the title be
everyone complained that the title was silly. However, I love the title. One of my crow
achievements was completing the *Garden Ghoul's* run. *Gore Creatures*, now know as *Midn*
Marquee Monsters, is another classic title, and no I haven't completed that run. Gary Sveh
is the editor. And least we forget *Photon* by Mark Frank, Ron Borst and Jim Wynorski. It
possibly the best of the fanzines. Another achievement, was completing the twenty-seven
issue *Photon* run. John Carpenter did a few fanzines back when he was a teenager. He did
Fantastic Films Illustrated, which was a three issue run. The first issue he hand colored each
and every individual cover in watercolor. Then he did *Phantasm Terror Thrills of the Film*.
He's gone on, of course, to be a very successful director. Gene Klein, famous rock star from
KISS, was into the fanzine scene in the sixties and did several of his own zines. They were
Cosmos, which then turned into *Cosmos Stiletto*, *Tinderbox*, and another called *Faun*. He also
did the original cover art to *Fantasy News #7*. At the time, he was notorious for his LOC's
(letter of comment), and let editors know exactly what he thought of their fanzines. And it
wasn't usually anything very nice, but everyone put up with him. And then of course he
became famous, and a mulit-millionaire with the rock group KISS. I know for a fact that
about seven or eight years ago he himself started to hunt down his old fanzines, evidently he
had thrown them all away. He contacted one specific dealer, trying to locate material he had
done in the sixties. Michael and John Burnas. One of their recent books that we all know
and love is *The Universal Horrors* by McFarland Press. One of their fanzines, *The Terror
Monster Club Journal*, well, evidently they didn't have any mimeo or hectograph or copying
equipment, so they hand typed each one individually on a typewriter and used carbon paper.
And friend Gary Dorst, who worked with them, hand drew the covers one at a time and hand
drew the inside pictures one at a time, for each issue. They'd do about fifteen or twenty of
these issues. They also put out *Chillers of the Screen*, and a follow up to that was simply called
Chiller.

Q: Why don't you use the word "mint" in grading your magazines?

JB: Well even today, I go out and buy magazines every Wednesday, just as I have for many,
many years. I never subscribe to magazines because they just don't arrive in top condition.
The trip through the mail takes its toll. I would rather pick them out myself. Well, when the
"Monster Mags" arrive at the store I visit weekly, "Creature Features In Burbank," who are
very careful about handling magazines, they may get say fifty copies. I'll go right over when
they receive that fifty copies and go through all fifty, and pull out the most perfect copy.
Sometimes I can't find that one perfect copy out of that fifty. This is for a number of reasons,
It can be a printing flaw, or maybe the cover is skewed, or sometimes the cover is rubbed
because the magazines all rub against each other when they're shipped from the printing
house. Then the distributor handles them. And let's not forget UPS. The results are dinged

things like that. Sometimes I go to 2 or 3 stands to find that
...lly bring it up to the register to pay for it and the cashier
...know how I am. But I always pull out the most perfect
... is with all magazines I purchase, even *Starlogs* and
...wless mint copy but very often I can't, and settle for a
...gine how impossible it is to find a flawless copy of say a
... definitely the most overused word in collecting.

...ading ever end?

...ecause no one in our lifetime will ever have perfect copies of
... to do the best you can and strive for near mint.

...ut that perfect copy that means so much?

...a just a perfectionist when it comes to this. Even when I go buy a laser disc,
... the seven or eight copies that are in the rack, and I make sure the one I buy
... a dinged corner. I do the same thing with books. I even grade the VHS's and
... buy to obtain the most perfect copy. I figure if I'm paying top dollar for my stuff, I
... it, before I buy it. I want the most bang for my buck. And it also keeps my grading
...s honed. I'm that way about all the material I buy for the collection. I make sure it's as
...op quality as possible. It's just one of my little quirks, I try not to lose sleep over it.

Q: Are there any women collectors within the ranks of monster magazine fandom?

JB: Not that I know of, it's pretty much a guy thing. My wife doesn't really understand it,
but she supports me and she's really good about helping me keep the collection going.

Q: Does she support it or tolerate it?

JB: She supports it and tolerates it. More so than most wives would. Because the amount
of money we spent on magazines and books and laser discs...well, we could have taken a lot
of vacations.

Q: What are some of your greatest moments as a collector? Your greatest finds and
discoveries?

JB: When I was looking for very early, high grade *Famous Monsters*, I was in a bookstore and
a guy came in with a perfect copy of *Famous Monsters* #12. I couldn't believe it. He pulled
it out of a manila envelope where it had been sitting for thirty-plus years. Never in plastic,
never saw the light of day, it was picked off a newsstand and put in this manila envelope, and
I was one of the first to see it unearthed. I bought that from him, and he also had a #13 and
#14. He didn't have any of the real early ones, but I just happened to be at the right place at
the right time when he walked in. Also, I'll never forget the day Steve Dolonick found me
a near perfect *FM* #6. Near flawless spine! Very tough issue to get high-grade. My #7 came
from the same source. Steve went to a lot of trouble to obtain them for me. Another
highlight was at a book fair in Burbank, about '93 or '94. I came upon a British *Screen Chills*
from 1957 a near mint copy, it was amongst a bunch of other film magazines. It was twelve
dollars, and it can go for about fifteen hundred in the condition it's in, maybe more. That
was very exciting, I was shaking when I picked it up and paid for it. I paid the dealer twelve
dollars, full asking price, and no I didn't try to haggle him down. I carefully sat it on the seat
of my car as I was driving home, I couldn't believe I had just purchased this beautiful
magazine for twelve dollars. I'm lucky I didn't wreck the car 'cause I kept looking down at it

to make sure it was still there. Another find was down in San Diego, at the San Diego Comc Con, I came upon a booth that had the Forry Ackerman 1960 Birthday Special Fanzine displayed on the wall, which I knew about and was looking for, and is extremely rare. Talk about stopping dead in my tracks! The price was high, but I wasn't leaving that stand without it, that was a nice prize. As recently as a year ago in Hollywood, I was in a bookstore and I saw a box up on the top shelf labeled monster magazines. Of course I asked to look through it. And there, amongst all the worn and tattered *FM's* sat a *Picture Goer* from England, a special all-horror issue from 1958, that I knew about from an article in *Scary Monsters* magazine. A nice, near mint copy, I think it was around seven dollars. And fanzine-wise, there are many many fanzine stories, having editors look high and low for their old copies for me. Steve Dolnick was very instrumental in helping me locate a lot of fanzines through editors, publishers, writers and contributors, him having them look through their attics, look through their basements, look through their mother's attics, everywhere trying to locate these old fanzines for me. We've come up with quite a few over the years.

Q: What is the most gratifying aspect of your collecting this material?

JB: It's finally finding that issue that you've been looking for for many years. One case in point would be a prozine I'd been looking for for over seven years called *Starblaster* #1, by S&J Publications. Evidently a very low print run with limited distribution, all the dealers knew I needed it, it was one of only 3 prozines I still needed, and everyone was looking for me. Couldn't find it anywhere, every time I went to San Diego I always had that magazine in the back of my mind, maybe I'd find a copy of it this year. That alone would make the trip worthwhile. And finally last year on ebay, I punched in "Starblaster" and up popped the magazine I was looking for, with a starting bid on only one dollar. And that's excactly what I paid for it and it's a near mint copy. That was extremely gratifying to find that magazine, which means nothing to most collectors because it's a typical low quality post-*Star Wars* magazine, but it was a prozine I didn't own so it was very important that I find it. And I would have paid almost anything for it in any condition.

Q: What is your advice to younger fans that are now beginning to collect monster magazines?

JB: It's a very gratifying and fun hobby. I enjoy it every day. However, its a little bit more difficult to get into today, just like it's more difficult to get into collecting posters or any type of film material. A lot of it's been eaten up, and more and more collectors are hanging onto it. But you need to keep bugging the dealers about what you need. The squeaky gear gets the grease. Go to all the conventions and talk to as many collectors as you can. Network. And don't be as concerned about condition as I am, or you won't have much of a collection. The really high-grade material, you have to know somebody to obtain it. It just isn't out there for sale very often. So you may need to lower you expectations as to the quality of the material you're going to collect. That's an important thing at this point. But, it's a big world out there and there's still plenty of mags and fanzines in hiding. I still find mags that I need almost weekly. You just never know. I find mags at conventions, swap meets, antique stores, at book fairs and on the internet. You just never know when something is going to pop up. You just have to keep looking.

MIMEO DAZE
by Jerry Weist

In 1958 I bought my first monster magazine with the second issue of *Famous Monsters of Filmland*. I pulled this jewel off the newsstand in the front of my father's grocery store, the 81 Super Market. This event would change my life forever. Harry Warner Jr., in his book about 1950's science fiction fandom *A Wealth of Fable*, states that science fiction fandom ...

> "..reacted to the appearance of the magazine as if Ackerman had set off an H-bomb during the guest of honor speech at a world-con. 'A half-assed thing with a farcical approach and a general air that left me sick' was Dick Lupoff's summary. 'As cheap and tawdry a publication as has ever appeared on American newsstands, with insipid stills and a text that with the greatest kindness can only be described as infantile,' Ed Wood advised. Yet teenagers and even younger people who bought the bulk of that first issue loved it. For them, it was the equivalent of the first issue of *Amazing Stories*."

Harry Warner Jr. couldn't have been more right in his observation, for a generation of young people during the height of the Cold War responded to *Famous Monsters* as if it were a bolt from the blue. As much as any serious student of science or academic type might have scorned the original *Amazing Stories* during the 1920's, with its garishly colored Frank R. Paul covers, science fiction fandom during the early 1960's liked to call *FM* "Ackerman's Folly." However, before moving any further it is appropriate to point out that Dick Lupoff's own fanzine *Xero* ran articles on comics during the 1960's. Lupoff himself must have faced a storm of protest, based on the average science fiction fans prejudice against comic books for the "All In Color For A Dime" series that ran in issues 1 through 10. And Ed Wood himself was a fan of the works of Edgar Rice Burroughs during the 1950's when it was popular to think that science fiction had matured through the golden years of John Campbell as editor of *Astounding Science Fiction* and into the late 1950's and early 1960's when the 'new wave' of SF was pressing more serious literary standards onto the field. And Ed Wood kept a complete set of FM with his science fiction magazines and fanzines.

For a 9 year old boy in Wichita, Kansas, who was isolated from the rest of the world and knew nothing of science fiction fandom and its history from the 1930's onward, *Famous Monsters of Filmland* represented a fantastic leap into worlds of imagination and creativity. For a young Jerry Weist who had been randomly collecting comic books and science fiction paperbacks (he did not read very many of them, and they were bought for the remarkable cover artwork by Emsh, Valigursky, Schultz, and other artists who he could not identify stylistically at the time), and the SF digest magazines, *Famous Monsters* brought focus. Here was a magazine that seemed to speak directly to him and featured stills and articles about the 1930's horror movies that he was staying up (without his parents knowledge, by sneaking out into the living room at 12:00 midnight and viewing the TV with the sound turned either off, or way down) late to watch. Wichita, Kansas had its own Monster Program with KSAS Fox-24's *Nightmare*, featuring The Host and Rodney. *Nightmare* began in January of 1958, and featured Tom Leahy who has been given little national attention in the historical works that deal with the SHOCK film package that was released to TV stations across America in the Fall of 1957. However, take the word of Wichita fans: The Host was nearly as good as Philadelphia's own Zacherley! With great make-up and props, and 'black-humor' that matched the best scripts of other TV hosts, Leahy would introduce each 1930's and 1940's

Forrest J Ackerman with FAMOUS MONSTERS fans in Wichita, Kansas. From left to right on the floor;
Steven Watters, Roger Hill. Seated on the divan from left to right; Steven Nimrod, Rick Showalter,
Jerry Weist, FJA, and a young lady who may be Paula Tennery (whom the author should remember,
since she met him one month later and traded her personal copy of FM #1 to the young Weist,
at the time the only issue missing from his collection).

horror movie with great effect and satire... "tonight's hoooooooooRRRRooooRRROwer classic is..." and the young viewers loved every minute of the mayhem.

It seems easy to look back now as we enter the year 2000 and view the illustrated fanzine section of Michael Pierce's excellent *Monsters Among Us* Price Guide and see the pictures of my early crude monster fanzines *Nightmare* and *Movieland Monsters* and say, "well I was young and perhaps I didn't know any better!" This article, however, will explore the simple fact that I was doing exactly what I wanted in 1962 when I started *Nightmare,* which was named after my favorite TV program. This article will also explain how mimeograph fanzines were produced.

My father, Norton Weist, was at this time owner of the 81 Super Market, a grocery store on the north side of Wichita, Kansas, and during his spare time he enjoyed nothing more than tending to his prized Giant Homer pigeons. These birds differed from both the wild pigeon, and the smaller pigeon that was bred for making long flights to carry messages during earlier times. The Giant Homer was bred for form and, like dog shows or horse shows, there were conventions where these birds were displayed. Prizes were awarded and like-minded breeders could get together to exchange breeding and feeding information and in general hang out with fellow enthusiasts. Because of my father's intense interest in breeding these birds (he owned over 5,000 of them, housed in five large long sheds) he also became involved with a club which for a short period of time convinced him to edit and print a small magazine for its organization. To do this he brought home the mimeograph machine from the grocery store and I was introduced at a young age on how to cut and print by the stencil process.

Thus was born another fanzine publisher. When I look at the copies that remain of *Nightmare* and *Movieland Monsters* with their yellow 'stock' covers, and white page interiors, I am swept back thirty five years to the time when they were made. By 1962 *Famous Monsters of Filmland* had published over sixteen issues. During this time there was also the *Famous Monsters Club*, and evidence within the pages of the magazine and in the FM letters column of other fanzines being produced by enthusiastic fans.

My father had enlisted my help in producing his pigeon magazines. From these work weekends I learned how to cut the stencil using a manual typewriter, especially paying attention to the fact that you had to use an even stroke when you typed. You could not type an "o" too hard, or it would cut a hole in the stencil! You had to clean the typewriter keys with a pointed pen - so that the dirty 'gum' held within the spaces of letters like "o," or "e," or "p," would not come out as solid blocks on the stencil. You had to be very careful and know where you were going with the written text so that you made as few mistakes as possible. Later, when electric typewriters became available it was very easy to set the pressure at about 4 to 6 and type very quickly with an 'even stroke.' You could use a correction fluid on the stencil itself if you made a mistake in typing, however this fluid (which was deep purple and smelled weird - and dried fast!) had its limitations and had to be used sparingly. You could use stencil lettering for titles, or design your own drawings, but this required patience, and you had to be very careful again not to "tear" the stencil surface or you would loose the whole page. To "draw" on a stencil required that you use a stiff underneath white wax paper stock - so that the special red stencil ball tipped pen could be used to draw on the image without cutting too deeply into the stencil itself. Some people could do this work with a regular ball point pen - others could not. The stencil itself was available in either standard or legal paper length. The advanced process for applying a grainy photograph to a stencil was never acquired by me back in 1962-63. After learning all the points of preparing a stencil for the mimeograph machine, one then had to learn how to mount the stencil on the machine!

With a finished stencil in hand the printer would carefully wrap the stencil around the drum of the mimeograph machine. This was done by fastening the top part down by matching the holes at the top of the stencil (paper stock) with the proper fasteners on the drum, and then wrapping the stencil around the drum, which had to be properly re-inked, or loaded with ink on the underside so that the stencil would stick down evenly. One could easily lose a whole stencil by mounting it wrong on the drum, causing wrinkles on the printed page or blotches in the printing process itself. I can remember cursing desperately after loosing a page with a great monster drawing on it by not wrapping it properly around the drum! This set back would require that you delicately pull the stencil back off the drum, and then try to remount it - or you pitched the whole effort into the trash and then had to re-type and re-cut the entire page! I notice now with my four year old son Ian that if I have shown him how to do something he immediately wants to try the task - without any help from dad! I'm afraid he has his father's genes, since I refused any advice from my father back in 1962 and paid the price with many lost pages of text to some monster fanzine when they went down the drum-drain to my inexperience.

Once you had the stencil properly loaded onto the mimeograph machine, you either hand cranked up the machine while slowly pumping up the ink load until it was just right, or you did this automatically if you were lucky enough to have an electric mimeograph machine that did not require the hand-cranked motion to move the drum around and around. I began my printing days with a hand-cranked mimeograph machine, and later moved on to the joys of the automatic electric machine. However there were trials with each machine! On the hand-cranked model you had better be smooth and sure, or you could lose pages. With the electric

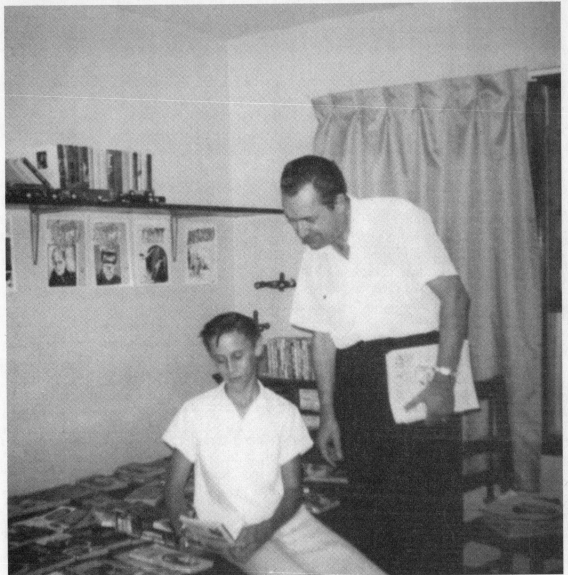

Forrest J Ackerman stands over a young Jerry Weist (Forry is holding a stack of MOVIELAND MONSTERS #2, the latest Weist Fanzine). On the wall are Larry Byrd Photo-off set covers to SCREEN WHIRL, GARDEN GHOULS GAZETTE, and DANTE'S INFERNO, extra covers given to the young collector by Byrd himself after a personal visit.

model you had better be well laid out, if something went amiss then the error could move toward a bigger printing problem by the sheer speed of the drum! If memory serves me right, you could print up to about 125 to 150 pages with a good quality stencil, and then you began to have tears at certain letters, or points on the page and quality would move down the more numbers you attempted. Once each page was done they were stacked to dry and again, if you had over inked the drum, you could have 'off-set' ink transferred onto the backsides of each stacked finished printed page! There was an "art" to using the mimeograph machine that required hours of work, and usually learning from your mistakes the hard way.

Imagine the ambitious fanzine editor who wanted multiple colors for each single page! Imagine the fanzine editors and publishers who wanted to use the special stencil methods for transferring photo-like images or more detailed drawings onto stencils, and the problems they

From the collection of John Ballantine. Photo © John Ballantine.

encountered with printing? Years later when I saw my first mid-1950's science fiction fanzines which were the result of more talented and adult producers I was totally amazed! Harlan Ellison knows the labors from which I speak! Ray Bradbury, Forrest J. Ackerman, Sam Moskowitz, Robert Silverberg, and a host of other people have all walked the road of the Mimeograph trail! Fantastic efforts such as Ellison's ambitious and thick *Dimensions*, with its multiple color overlays, strong design, and clarity of design. And its justified right hand margins! To get justified right hand margins required that the editor pre-type each page, then draw a line on the right hand side, and then using the slash mark "/" count their way to the end of each line. At the end of the process you then counted your /// slash marks at the end of each line, and got either one, or two, or three, etc., and you would graph out each page accordingly. You then could re-type this page on the stencil spacing out between words at the appropriate part the number of spaces you needed to end up with a justified right hand margin! Madness and labor until the bleak hours of the early morning! All for about 100 to 125 copies! Right! Who more than the special 75 to 100 fans would care at this point in time? However, justified right hand margins were a sign of sophistication, and they allowed the editor to produce a more professional looking magazine - alas *Dimensions* had justified right hand margins (and a wealth of other more mature features) and *Movieland Monsters* did not!

Once the pages were printed on both sides and ready, you then could lay out your finished product and collate by hand the entire issue. One at a time folks. If you had thirty five pages in your fanzine, and you printed 100 copies, then it was 100 passes times thirty five pages stacked into order. Then you stapled the finished issue together, and if you were lucky you had a photo-off set or special cover to wrap around the interior pages. If not, then it was mimeograph throughout. No photocopy machines in existence at the time! No thought even of the computer age with its laser printers please! No money from fans to go to off-set printing; these were the mimeo-days and it is no wonder that science fiction fandom created the phrase GAFIA (Get Away From It All). GAFIA usually meant withdraw from fandom activities (like publishing fanzines) to get back to a more normal life. But printing that next fanzine was usually too much fun, or too tempting, or too ego big for the fanish identity to resist that one more attempt at creativity.

I can remember all of these frustrations and small triumphs that took place in 1962 working with my first monster fanzines. They were horrible! The typing was bad, the spelling and punctuation were atrocities to the English language. The drawings were crude! But boy did I have fun! Dick Lupoff and Ed Wood would have looked at my fanzines and cried... "What has the Ackermonster wrought upon fandom? What foul denizens have arisen from this 'monster' fandom to haunt us?" Indeed. But we did grow up, and some of us graduated to *Squa Tront*, and many other worthy projects in later years.

I can still look back to this time and wish with nostalgic regret that I had attempted multiple color covers. I would have used bright GREEN ink for the *Creature From the Black Lagoon*, or bright BLUE ink for an outer space scene, or bright RED ink from some awful bloodsoaked monster. I wish I had spent more time seeking out other fans work, and I wish I had attempted more complicated illustrations. I can hear the soft click-click of the rotation of the mimeograph drum, or the electric faster phased printing machine. I can still smell the ink, and the paper, and the time - I can almost remember the smell of the days themselves - when we had all the time and energy in the world.

The author with TV Horror-Host Zacherley at the FM Con in Washington, D.C. Photo by Roger Hill.

	Good	Fine	Near Mint		Good	Fine	Near Mint

ADVENTURES IN HORROR
(Not a strict Monster Magazine - marginal)

(1) 1970, Oct./Dec. Stanley Publications, Theodore Hect editor, 8 1/2 x 11, 60 cents cover price, Horror fiction, illustrations, photo Horror features that experiment with Monsters and Sex, prozine. Not considered a strict Monster Magazine by collectors.

	20.00	35.00	50.00
(2)	10.00	20.00	30.00

(Becomes HORROR STORIES with issue No. 3 onward)

HORROR STORIES

(3-7) 1971, #'s 3,4,5,6,7, same format with Photo covers, some features get closer to Monster themes.   10.00   20.00   35.00

AFTER HOURS

(Vol. 1 No. 4) 1957 - James Warren Editor and Publisher, 8 1/2 by 11 format, cover price 35 cents, pro-zine Adult Magazine with limited distribution. The inside front cover with Monster Pic, pages 8-13 feature "Confessions of a SF Addict," an article by Forrest J. Ackerman, also there are SF cartoons, and pages 18-22 feature "Screamoscope," an article about the Monster Craze sweeping across America in the late 1950's due to Universal releasing 1930's and 1940's Horror films to TV stations. Very rare in top grades.
                                                 150.00   300.00   500.00

Note: Considered collectible because this magazine acted as a test for Warren, once he had met Forrest J. Ackerman - and was about to consider introducing *Famous Monsters Of Filmland*.

ALIEN

(nn) 1979, one-shot, Warren Publications, single issue feature of the movie.
                                10.00   20.00   35.00

ALIEN

(1-2) 1979, 20th Century Fox Publishers, "official poster magazine," 8 1/2 x 11, 1.50 cover price, prozine.   10.00   15.00   25.00

ALIENS
(Official Movie Book)

1986, one-shot, Starlog Publications, 8 1/2 x 11, prozine.   5.00   10.00   20.00

ALIENS (Official Movie Magazine)

1986, one shot, O'Quinn Studios Publications, 8 1/2 x 11, $2.95 cover price, prozine.
                                5.00   25.00   35.00

ALTERNATIVE CINEMA

(1-3) 1994, Tempe Press Publications, 8 1/2 x 11, $3.95 cover price, prozine.
                                2.50   5.00   15.00

AMAZING CINEMA (Fanzine)

(1-3) 1981, #'s 1,2,3, Don Dohler Publisher and Editor, 8 1/2 x 11, $2.50 cover price, excellent production and writing for this high quality fanzine.   3.00   7.00   10.00

(4) 1981, Special Ray Harryhausen interview issue.   10.00   15.00   25.00

AMAZING FORRIES (Crossover Fanzine-Prozine)

(nn) 1976 one-shot, published by FsJ as Metropolis Publications, James Warren

assisted in printing and publication of this one-shot; 8 1/2 x 11, 2.50 cover price, the cover features one of two 1959 Frank R. Paul re-creations that Forrest J. Ackerman personally commissioned from the artist - the cover is a re-creation with new additions from AMAZING STORIES No. 6, from 1926 (the first SF magazine that Ackerman bought as a young boy) - Ackerman had himself painted into the design of the cover. Inside features the life and times of 4sJ - from early SF fandom, through the 1950's and up to present, with many photos and different features. Considered a must by all FM collectors, the print run was limited and this magazine is now scarce in high grades.

25.00   50.00   80.00

ANIMATION JOURNAL (Fanzine)

(1-2) 1964, Bill Shrock editor and publisher, very crude early mimeo issues, 8 1/2 x 11, fanzine.

100.00   150.00   200.00

(3-4)   75.00   125.00   175.00

(5-6) 1965-1966, with issue No. 4 the cover illustrations become better drawn, designed, and the content become more developed; a classic early film-monster fanzine, scarce.

50.00   100.00   125.00

(7-9)   40.00   75.00   85.00

THE BELA LUGOSI JOURNAL (Fanzine)

(1-2) 1962-1963, Published and Edited by long time Lugosi fan Bill Obbagy, with photo off-set covers, this was an early serious attempt at coverage of the medium, rare and sought after by all collectors.

50.00   100.00   150.00

BIZARRE (Fanzine)

(1) 1972, Published by the Pit Company, off-set with photos, 8 1/2 x 11, cover price of 1.25, fanzine.   35.00   60.00   100.00

(2-4) 1973-74, Same format. 15.00 25.00   40.00

BLACK ORACLE (Fanzine)

(1) 1969, one-shot, Published by George Stover; Edited by Bill George, 5 1/2 x 4 1/4, no number on cover, fanzine.

15.00   20.00   30.00

(1) 1969, #1 of series, same cover as previous listing, with No. 1 March 1969, cover price of 25 cents, 5 1/2 x 4 1/4, the second #1 and continuing issues are published by George Stover and edited by Bill George, off-set with photos, fanzine, unique and rare.

20.00   40.00   50.00

(2-5)   10.00   15.00   25.00

(6-10)   5.00   10.00   15.00

JOURNAL OF FRANKENSTEIN

(1) 1959, Vol. 1 No. 1, Calvin Beck editor and publisher, 8 1/2 x 11 format, cover price 50 cents, prozine with limited distribution. This early Monster Magazine would be rarer, however upon the Publishers death a large number of perfect condition copies found their way into the market place.

25.00   50.00   75.00

CASTLE OF FRANKENSTEIN

(1) 1962, February (January is blackened out on cover.), Larry Ivie assistant editor, Calvin Beck editor and publisher, 8 1/2 x 11, 35 cents cover price.

Note: The White Mountain copy (this collector dated every magazine on the day

he bought it) is stamped November 14, 1961 - this magazine was released in 1961.
25.00 30.00 45.00

(2) No Date, again the White Mountain copy is noted as 10-18-1962 for a bought date. Larry Ivie becomes managing editor, same format. 15.00 25.00 35.00

(3,6,9,11,13) 1963-64, with Larry Ivie painted covers. 20.00 30.00 45.00

(4,5,7,8,9,12,15) 1966-67, at this point Bhob Stewart becomes acting editor, and designs most of the interior issues, same format. 15.00 25.00 35.00

(14, 16-25) 1971-1975, cover price moves from 50 cents with No. 17, to 60 cents and 75 cents with later issues.
10.00 15.00 25.00

CASTLE OF FRANKENSTEIN MONSTER ANNUAL (Fearbook)

(No#) 1967, same format, 50 cents cover price.
15.00 25.00 45.00

CHILDREN OF THE NIGHT
(Fanzine)

(1) 1975, Derek Jensen Editor & Publisher, 8 1/2 x 11, 2.00 cover price, photo off-set covers, excellent interior articles, one of the premier 1970's film-monster fanzines, high demand and low print runs combine to make this title very collectible.
25.00 50.00 100.00
(2) 2.50 cover price 15.00 40.00 60.00
(3) 3.00 cover price 10.00 25.00 45.00
(4-5) 10.00 15.00 25.00

CHILDREN OF THE NIGHT NEWSLETTER

(1-4) 1984 2.50 5.00 15.00

CHILLERS OF THE SCREEN
(Fanzine)

(1) 1964, John Brunas and Donald Shank combine to edit and publish this fanzine, 8 1/2 x 11, cover price of 25 cents, B&W off-set cover with hecto interior pages, early and scarce. 20.00 35.00 50.00
(Second issue called CHILLERS, very scarce.)
25.00 40.00 60.00

CHILLING MONSTER TALES

(1) 1966, August, one-shot, M.M. Publishing Company, 8 1/2 x 11, 50 cents cover price, B&W interior with pink-red tints used, 7 page interior Monster Gallery by artist Chic Stone, prozine. 12.00 25.00 40.00

CINEFAN (Fanzine)

(1-3) 1974-1983, Randall Larsen publisher and editor, 8 1/2 x 11, B&W photo off-set covers, quality artwork and articles, fanzine.
15.00 20.00 30.00

CINEFANTASTIQUE
(The Fanzine...)

(1) 1967, #1, Frederick Clarke as editor and publisher, a biweekly slim newsletter type film-fantastic-fanzine, B&W, 8 1/2 x 11, from humble beginnings - later to produce one of the most important film magazines - these early issues are sought after because of the association of editor Clarke and the later product. Scarce. 50.00 100.00 150.00
(2,3,4,5,7,20) 50.00 100.00 150.00
(#6, covers only) 100.00 150.00 200.00

CINEFANTASTIQUE

(1) 1970- Fall/Vol. 1 No. 1 - Frederick Clarke
editor/publisher, 8 1/2 by 11 format, cover
price $1, pro-zine with limited distribution.
One of the very early ground breaking
magazines to seriously cover fantastic films in
every genre, eventually setting the pace for
every quality publication in the 1970's.

	10.00	15.00	20.00

(2-3) 1971- Summer/Winter - Clarke editor/pub.,
same format, cover price $1, covers and
production become more professional.

available from publisher

(4-10) 1971/74 - Clarke Ed/Pub, format same,
cover stays at $1 till issue No. 10 which is $2,
production even more professional, some
interior color appearing.

available from publisher

(11-20) 1974/77 - Clarke Ed/Pub, format same,
cover price moves to $2.50 with #14, more
color added to interior, experiments with
"theme" issues about to begin.

available from publisher

(21-30) 1977/79 - Clarke Ed/Pub, format same,
CV price $2.50, issues #'s 24, 26, 28 are double
issue "theme" issues priced at $4.99.

available from publisher

(31-50) 1979/84 - Clarke Ed/Pub, format same,
CV price $2.95/3.95 to $4.50 by 1984.

available from publisher

#'s 31, 32, 40, 42, 44 (Blade Runner CV) & 44
(Star Trek CV), 46 (Thing CV) & 46 (Krull CV),
and 49.

	3.50	10.00	20.00

(51-75) 1984/90 - Clarke Ed/Pub, format size
same, cover price double issues are $8.95,
$4.50 price goes to $4.95.

From the mid 1970's through mid 1990's
CINEFANTASTIQUE , with very few exceptions,
is the dominating magazine for coverage,
interviews, special effects articles, for the
entire horror/fantastic/SF/comics film genre.
Superior production values, well researched
articles, and film coverage that becomes
international, sets this magazine apart form
most of its competitors - distribution however
remains limited.

available from publisher

#'s 52(Dune Double/Ish), 61(Psycho), 63-64(Star
Trek), 67(1950's Poster Art), 70(Vincent Price).

	3.50	10.00	20.00
(75-Present) 1990/99	2.50	5.00	8.00

Note: Most back issues are still available
through the publisher; you may contact
CFQ directly by calling their Back Issue
Department at 1-800-798.6515 or by calling
708-366-5566.

CINEFEX

(1) 1980 March - Vol. 1 No. 1, Don Shay editor
and publisher, 6 1/2 x 8 1/2, 2.95 cover price,
limited distribution prozine.

	35.00	60.00	100.00
(2-3) 1980, same format.			
	35.00	65.00	75.00
(9) 1981- 1982	35.00	50.00	75.00
(8)	25.00	35.00	45.00
(13,21,27)	15.00	25.00	35.00
(4,5,6,7,10,11,17,29,32,37)			
	15.00	20.00	30.00
(12,28,35,38)	10.00	15.00	20.00

Note: Back issues noted as "in print" are
available in VF + from the publisher,
contact Cinefex at 800-434-3339, or E-Mail
circulation@cinefex.com

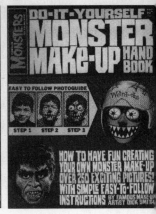

	Good	Fine	Near Mint		Good	Fine	Near Mint

CINEMACABRE (Fanzine)

(1) 1978 George Stove and John Parnum publishers and editors, 5 1/2 x 8 1/2, 2.00 and then 2.50 cover price, with color photo and painted covers, with limited distribution, fanzine.

	5.00	10.00	15.00
(2-4)	5.00	10.00	15.00
(5-7) runs to 1988	5.00	10.00	15.00

Note: This fanzine was continued from its original title of BLACK ORACLE.

CINEMAGIC

(1) 1972, Vol. 1 No. 1, Donald Dohler editor, Cinema Enterprises publisher, 8 1/2 x 11, prozine.

	15.00	20.00	25.00
(2-11) 1973-1974 format the same.	15.00	20.00	25.00

CINEMAGIC (Starlog Presents)

(1-6) 1979-1980, O'Quin Studios publishers, 8 1/2 x 11, 1.95 cover price, prozine.

	2.50	7.50	15.00
(7-20) 1980-up, format the same.	1.50	5.00	12.50
(21-present)	1.50	3.50	10.00

CINEMONSTERS (Fanzine)

(1-3) 1974-1975 Leonard Ciulla and Charles Sachetta editors and publishers, 8 1/2 x 11, 50 cents cover price, mimeograph fanzine, No. 3 a more serious effort, with improved cover artwork and cover price of 1.50, very low print runs.

	10.00	20.00	40.00

CINEWONDER (A Celebration of Fantasy on the Screen)

(1) 1981, one-shot, Jack Brent Publisher and Editor, 8 1/2 x 11, 2.00 cover price, professional design for B&W cover, limited distribution, fanzine.

	7.50	10.00	15.00

CLASSIC MOVIE MONSTERS (Fanzine)

(1-6) 1973-1976, Brian Gray Editor and Publisher, 8 1/2 x 11, 75 cents cover price, B&W covers, very limited print runs.

	5.00	15.00	25.00

CLOSEUP (Fanzine)

(1-3) 1975-1976, David Prestone publisher and editor, 8 1/2 x 11, 1.50 cover price, professional design photo off-set covers, slick cover stock, serious articles.

	10.00	20.00	30.00

CRACKED COLLECTOR'S EDITION: THOSE CRACKED MONSTERS

(nn) 1978-1984, one-shot printed numerous times through 1984, Major Magazines publishers, 8 1/2 x 11, 2.50 cover price, prozine.

	3.50	7.50	15.00

CRYPT OF HORRORS

(1-2) 1973-1974, Gary Heilman editor and publisher, 5 1/2 x 8 1/2 , 60 cents cover price, B&W covers, very limited print runs.

	15.00	30.00	40.00

(1) 1977, revised edition of same title, Gary Heilman, 8 1/2 x 11, 2.00 cover price, photo off-set cover, better production and printing.

	15.00	20.00	25.00

CULT MOVIES

(1) 1990, 8 1/2 x 11, 5.95 and 4.95 cover price, prozine.

	7.00	10.00	20.00

(2-6) 1991-up, format the same.

	Good	Fine	Near Mint			Good	Fine	Near Mint
	10.00	20.00	30.00					
(7-up) format same.	5.00	10.00	15.00					

and Weist would eventually pool their talents for *Squa Tront*!

CULT TIMES

(1-35) 1995-2000, edited by Richard Atkinson and published by Visual Imagination LTD, 8 1/4 x 11 1/4, 4.99 cover price, slick prozine devoted to media movies and TV, all issues are in print and available in VF+ from the publisher.   .75   2.50   5.00

Note: Contact the publisher at www.visimag.com for information on back issues.

DANTES INFERNO (Fanzine)

(1) 1963 Vol. 1 No. 1, one-shot, David Jones editor and publisher, 8 1/2 x 11, 30 cents cover price, B&W with off-set Larry Byrd cover design.   25.00   50.00   75.00

Note: The author would like to acknowledge a debt of gratitude to David Jones, who sometime in the Fall of 1964 sent a package of EC comic books to Wichita, Kansas. Upon receiving *Weird Science Fantasy* No. 24, *Panic* No. 6, *The Haunt of Fear* No. 13(1952), and *Weird Fantasy* No. 8, Jerry Weist called over new found friend Roger Hill (whom he had met at the Forrest J. Ackerman *FM* cross-country meeting held in Wichita in September of 1963) and two minds were "blown" at one time. Both young boys traded away their super-hero comics and immediately began to build complete EC collections. From Monster Fandom, to EC fandom, to SF fandom, and back to Comics Fandom, Hill

THE DARK SHADOWS QUARTERLY (Fanzine)

(1-11) 1980-1981, published and edited by the International Dark Shadows Society, 8 1/2 x 11, B&W covers - some off-set, 1.50 to 3.00 cover price, limited distribution. 10.00   20.00   35.00
(12-13) Summer-Fall 1982, large double issue.   15.00   30.00   50.00

Note: Very few collectors sales of any on these fanzines on record, prices could be higher or lower, depending upon demand.

DEEP RED (Fanzine)

(1-7) 1986-1989, Chas Balun Editor, Fantaco Publishers, 8 1/2 x 11, $2.50 - 3.95 - 4.95 cover prices, professional production and design, tremendous covers, this is a semi-prozine by anyone's standards, limited distribution.   5.00   10.00   15.00
(#0) format same.   20.00   25.00   40.00

DEMONS OF THE MIND (Fanzine)

(1) 1979, one-shot, Bob Tinnell, 8 1/2 x 11, 1.50 cover price, B&W off-set classic photo-montage cover, limited distribution.   7.50   15.00   30.00

DO-IT-YOURSELF MONSTER MAKE-UP HAND-BOOK (Famous Monsters of Filmland)

(nn) 1965, one-shot, Warren publications, edited and written and designed by Dick Smith, who

	Good	Fine	Near Mint		Good	Fine	Near Mint

shows step-by-step how to make a monster, 8 1/2 x 11, 50 cents cover price, prozine. James Warren was the only publisher to fully understand the "fun" element of Monsters with younger children - thus this magazine devoted to creating your own back yard monster was printed.   15.00   25.00   35.00

DRACULA CLASSIC

(nn) 1976, one-shot, Eerie Publications, 8 1/2 x 11, cover price 1.50, prozine.
7.50   15.00   25.00

DRACULA '79

(#5) 1979, one-shot, published under WARREN PRESENTS as No. 5, Warren Publications, 8 1/2 x 11, cover price 1.50, prozine.
5.00   15.00   25.00

DRACULA THE COMPLETE VAMPIRE

(nn) 1992, one-shot, Starlog Publications, 8 1/2 x 11, cover price 2.95, prozine.
2.50   7.50   15.00

DRACULINA

(1) 1985, October, Vol. 1 No. 1, Draculina Publishing, 8 1/2 x 11, cover price 3.25, prozine.   15.00   50.00   90.00
(2-5) Same Format   10.00   25.00   50.00
(6-12) Same Format   5.00   15.00   30.00
(7-up) Photo covers begin with issue #7, cover price now at 3.75.   2.50   5.00   10.00

DREADFUL PLEASURES (Fanzine)

(1-7) 1991-1995, Mike Accomando editor and publisher, a fanzine that visually embraces the Xerox culture with its production and design,

8 1/2 x 11, $2.00 cover price, limited print runs.
3.50   7.50   10.00

EEGAH
(See listing for MAGIC THEATER)

FAMOUS FANTASY FILMS (Fanzine)

(nn) 1965, one-shot, Philip B. Moshcovitz, 5 1/2 x 8 1/2, red tint color cover on glossy stock, 75 cents cover price, classic "Return of the Fly," photo-cover, this fanzine saw wide distribution within monster fandom, but still had limited distribution.
10.00   20.00   30.00

Note: Many copies of this fanzine have surfaced over the past few years.

FAMOUS FIENDS FROM FILMDOM (Fanzine)

(1-4) 1964, Mike Appel, 8 1/2 x 11, mimeograph covers and interiors, 25 cents cover price, the early issues have the early look, very limited distributed.
25.00   50.00   75.00

(Becomes SPECTRE with issue No. 5)

SPECTRE

(5-11) 1965-1966, #'s 5,6,7,8,9,10,11, same editorship, covers become photo-offset, but still retain the flavor of a 1960's monster fanzine, again limited print runs.
20.00   30.00   40.00
(12-25) 1966-1968   10.00   15.00   25.00

FAMOUS MONSTER FORRY ACKERMAN (Fanzine)

(#44 fake number) - 1960 -ND-one shot #44 on cover to celebrate Ackerman's 44th birthday. Larry Byrd and Ron Haydock produced this fanzine with off-set cover, and hectograph interior pages. Cover by Byrd, cartoons and features on Ack, inside off-set centerfold features Ray Bradbury in fanzine ad, of the 155 "Monster Birthday Club Members," names typed into the back pages (including Richard Nixon!) one would assume the print run was at this number, or slightly above - regardless, this is the RAREST of all FM Ackerman related fanzines.

$$100.00 \quad 200.00 \quad 350.00$$

Note: One of the most sought after of all FJA related FM items, very few copies went into monster or comics fandom, most of the copies would reside with science fiction fandom members, collectors take note! A perfect mint copy recently surfaced with the Sam Moskowitz SF fanzine collection - this copy obviously sent gratis by Forry to his old time friend from first fandom.

FAMOUS MONSTERS OF FILMLAND

(1) 1958 - No indication of Vol. or No. on cover or interior - Ackerman Ed/Warren Pub., 8 1/4 by 10 1/2 inches, cover price 35 cents, photo mock-up cover, square back spine with title and price on spine, the Magazine that started it all. Ironically Ackerman's two page excerpt of Kurtzman/Elder *Frankenstein* satire from *Humbug* Magazine most likely caused copycats to feature horror comics within each issue, the editorial tone, design, and cover content (excepting first two issues photo mock-up designs), were set in the very first issue for the successful formula that would eventually draw in thousands of fans all over America. This first issue is extremely scarce in conditions above a strict very fine, back cover tends to show wear and the blacks on front cover and "red" color at spine can also show wear, prozine. 200.00 550.00 1,500.00

(2) 1958 - Vol. 1 No. 2, 4sJ/Warren, CV price 35 cents, format is now 8 1/4 by 9 3/4, the second issue remained on the back issue list longer than many other early numbers, however it is rare in very fine or above.

$$100.00 \quad 200.00 \quad 350.00$$

(3) 1959 - April - 4sJ/Warren, CV price & format same, first Basil Gogos cover, extremely rare in higher grades, one of the first four issues to sell out in the back issue department by FM #12, also one of the most difficult early issues of FM to find in superior condition.150.00 300.00 500.00

(4) 1959 - August - 4sJ/Warren, pr/& format same, with "Ghoul's Eye" Willow Grover Amusement Park paste over on lower front cover, extremely scarce with this paste-over, the first issue of FM to sell out in the back issue department with FM #10, also very difficult in higher grades.

$$175.00 \quad 450.00 \quad 700.00$$

(4) 1959 - August - 4sJ/Warren, pr/& format same, without paste-over, Gogos cover, first issue to sell out. 150.00 375.00 600.00

(5) 1959 - Nov. 4sJ/Warren, format same, first cover painting by Albert Nuetzell, contents have now hit their stride, FM club members listed, also extremely rare in above Very Fine condition. 100.00 250.00 400.00

(6) 1960 - Feb. 4sJ/Warren, format same, with "M.T. Graves - Dungeon - WCKT/Miami" sticker bottom left, consider by many the

	Good	Fine	Near Mint		Good	Fine	Near Mint

rarest of all sticker variant FM issues, only one to two copies known to exist, 2nd Albert Nuetzell cover, also scarce in Near Mint condition.   ***   ***   ***

Note: only ONE copy is known to exist of this variant, and may not be done by Warren.

(6) 1960 - Feb. - 4sJ/Warren, format same, without sticker, rare in Near Mint.
    100.00   275.00   600.00

(7) 1960 - June - 4sJ/Warren, format same, there are three variant issues with lower left panel reading either 1) Tomorrow's Monsters, 2) Remember Roland? or 3) See Zacherley WOR-TV 9, there is no determined rarity of one cover label over another.
    75.00   175.00   350.00

(8) 1960 - Sept. - 4sJ/Warren, format same, cover painting by Albert Neutzell.
    50.00   150.00   325.00

(9)   40.00   100.00   200.00

(10) 1960/61 - 4sJ/Warren, format same, cover paintings mark the return of Basil Gogos for two of the classic all-time great FM covers. Issue No. 10 is first issue with Jack Davis "Fang Mail" heading drawing.
    30.00   85.00   200.00

(11) 1961 - April - 4sJ/Warren, format same, cover painting by Basil Gogos. More scarce than 9 or 10 in Very Fine and above conditions.
    40.00   175.00   450.00

(12) 1961 - June - 4sJ/Warren, format same, cover painting by Gogos, with this issue the Back Issue Department for the first time lists issues #'s 1, 3, 4, 5, as "sold out" and issues 2, 7, 8, are $1.00 each.   70.00   175.00   350.00

(13) 1961 - August, 4sJ/Warren, first 100 page issue, with square bound format and 50 cent cover price, Gogos *Frankenstein* cover,

because of square bound spine format, very tough in Near Mint.   45.00   120.00   275.00

(15)   45.00   165.00   250.00

(14,16) 1961/62 - 4sJ/Warren, format same, all three issues have Basil Gogos covers.
    40.00   125.00   250.00

(17-19) 1962, No. 19 is very hard with perfect square spine in Near Mint condition,
    40.00   100.00   225.00

(20) No. 20 is extremely rare in VF or above condition.   40.00   150.00   300.00

(21-22) 1963, cover price moves to 50 cents per issue, editor Ackerman persuaded publisher Warren and was able to prepare a photo filmbook for FM No. 25 that gave special attention to KING KONG.
    50.00   150.00   275.00

(23-24)   30.00   75.00   175.00

(25-26) 1963, square bound format is now standard, these two issues are slightly rarer in higher grades.   40.00   100.00   200.00

(27-28) 1964.   35.00   85.00   175.00

(29)   30.00   65.00   125.00

(30)   35.00   100.00   200.00

(32)   25.00   50.00   100.00

(38)   40.00   100.00   200.00

(31,33,37,48,51,92) 1965,1966, these issues now enter into the collectible area of where the Warren Warehouse find contributed massive multiple numbers that worked their way onto the market, mostly through the Koch brothers wholesale and retail mail order catalogues (dealer Gary Dolgolff also distributed back numbers of FM), still near mint copies can be rare, as these warehouse quantities were sometimes in VG+ to Fine minus at best with the early numbers, and the early numbers were limited in quantity.
    15.00   30.00   45.00

(35,42,44,45,69,90,91,93,99,120,135) format the same.   15.00   25.00   40.00

	Good	Fine	Near Mint		Good	Fine	Near Mint

(40,52,63,66,68,80,83-87,94-98,103,106,112,113) 1968, 1969, No. 52 has remained collectible because of the "Dark Shadows" cover and feature, and No. 56 has a classic Gogos Frankenstein cover with special Karloff features inside. 10.00 20.00 30.00

(56) 15.00 30.00 45.00

NOTE: FAMOUS MONSTERS had no issue #'s for 70 through 79, these numbers being used for issues of MONSTER WORLD by publisher Warren.

(70-79) see MONSTER WORLD.

(43,57,59,62,64,81,88,89,101,102,105,107,110, 111,116,119,121,122,124,126,127,130,134,140, 163,171,177,180,182,188)

 10.00 15.00 25.00
 5.00 10.00 20.00

(82) 1971, February, "Dark Shadows" special.
 25.00 50.00 100.00

(93) 1972, October, Luis Dominguez "Tales From the Crypt," cover - with no inside feature, back to square format for one issue.
 15.00 25.00 40.00

(100) 1973, August, square bound, 1.25 cover price, special 100th issue.
 15.00 25.00 40.00

(108) 1974, July, special KING KONG Photo Filmbook issue, Basil Gogos cover.
 15.00 25.00 40.00

(114) 35.00 65.00 100.00

(133,136-139,147,156,158,159,166,167,169,170, 172-175,179, 184-187,189,190,191)
 10.00 15.00 20.00

(141,143-146,148-155,157,160-162,164,165,168, 176,178,181,183)
 5.00 10.00 15.00

FAMOUS MONSTERS YEARBOOK

(nn) 1962, No. 1, Summer-Fall, cover price of 50 cents, very few lower grade copies available in Warren warehouse find, hard to find in above VF.
 50.00 100.00 225.00

(nn) 1964, second Yearbook, available in higher grades in Warren warehouse find.
 25.00 50.00 100.00

(nn) 1965, the third Yearbook, the last of the fairly scarce annuals.
 20.00 30.00 65.00

(nn's) 1966,1968,1969, the fourth, sixth, and seventh Yearbooks.
 10.00 15.00 25.00

(nn's) 1967, 5th YB. 15.00 25.00 40.00

(nn's) 1970,1971,1972, the eighth, ninth, and tenth Yearbooks, smaller print runs make these issues rarer. 15.00 30.00 50.00

FAMOUS MONSTERS PAPERBACK SPECIALS

(nn) 1967, 4 1/4 x 7 inch format, 50 cents cover price, the first paperback, rare.
 25.00 50.00 125.00

(nn) 1968 entitled SON OF FAMOUS MONSTERS, second paperback.
 25.00 40.00 100.00

(nn) 1969, entitled FAMOUS MONSTERS STRIKES BACK!, third title.
 25.00 35.00 75.00

FAMOUS MONSTERS GAME BOOK

(nn) 1969, one-shot, reprints *Creepy* No. 1 cover, all reprints, Warren Publications.
 10.00 20.00 35.00

	Good	Fine	Near Mint		Good	Fine	Near Mint

FAMOUS MONSTERS CONVENTION BOOK

(nn) 1974, distribution limited to mail order and convention attendance.

                25.00   50.00   75.00

(nn) 1975, distribution limited to mail order and convention attendance, this book is the scarcer of the two.   30.00   60.00   100.00

FAMOUS MONSTERS OF FILMLAND

(200,207) 1993, May, under new ownership (Dynacomm) and publishing rights Ray Ferry kicks off issue #200 at special Monster Convention held in Washington D.C. 8 1/2 x 11, $7.95 initial cover price, limited distribution, slick interior paper. Kelly Freas does the cover artwork and Forrest J. Ackerman is acting editor.

	15.00	30.00	40.00
(203)	25.00	50.00	75.00
(205)	20.00	35.00	50.00

(201,206,211-214,216/217,219,221,223,224)

                10.00   20.00   25.00

(202,204,208,209,210,215,218,222,225 and up)

                5.00   8.00   10.00

(220)   15.00   25.00   30.00

Note: After No. 210 Forrest J. Ackerman is no longer acting Editor, or connected in any way with the new FM.

FANDOM UNLIMITED

(1-3) 1971-1977, Randall Larson editor and publisher, 8 1/2 x 11, 2.00 cover price, B&W covers, limited print runs, fanzine.

                7.50   10.00   15.00

FANGTASTIC CREATURES (Fanzine)

(1-3) Limited press fanzine.

                20.00   30.00   50.00

FANTAGRAPHIC

(1) 1974, Wanda Butts Editor and Publisher, 8 1/2 x 11, 2.00 cover price, limited print run, fanzine.   5.00   10.00   15.00

FANGORIA (Starlog Presents)

(1) 1979, August, Vol. 1. No. 1, O'Quinn Studios-Starlog Press, 8 1/2 x 11, $2.95 cover price, *Fangoria* helped change the emphasis on other Monster Magazines to a more Media (the latest movies released) based, and more contemporary look to the format of these magazines, prozine.

                15.00   30.00   50.00

(2,3,6,7,18,21,44,57,65) in print

	5.00	10.00	20.00
(9)	20.00	40.00	75.00
(8,22,40,70) in print	7.50	15.00	20.00
(37) in print	10.00	15.00	30.00

(all other issues - 1985-present are available from prices ranging from $5.00 - $6.00 to $10.00 each from the publisher.)

Note: For "in print" copies, and all other back issues contact the publisher at Starlog Group, Inc. 475 Park Avenue South, New York, New York 10016.

FANTASCENE (Fanzine)

(1) 1977-1978, Robert Skotak editor and publisher, 8 1/2 x 11, $3.50 cover price, professional photo off-set covers, has the look of a prozine, but with limited distribution.

                15.00   25.00   35.00

	Good	Fine	Near Mint		Good	Fine	Near Mint

(2-3) 10.00 15.00 25.00

(4-) 5.00 10.00 15.00

FANTASTIC FILMS

(1-5) 1975 Blake Publishing/ Fantastic Films, 8 1/2 x 11, $2.50 cover price, prozine.

2.00 5.00 8.00

(6-25) 2.00 5.00 8.00

(26-46) 2.00 5.00 8.00

FANTASTIC KARLOFF

(nn) oneshot. 15.00 25.00 35.00

FANTASTIC LUGOSI

(nn) oneshot. 20.00 35.00 45.00

FANTASTIC MONSTERS

(1) 1962 - Vol. 1 No. 1, Ron Haydock/Jim Harmon editor publishers, 8 1/2 x 11 format, cover price 50 cents, with interior color and back cover Monster Fold Out. This magazine experienced troubles with its printer, and also experienced some trouble with distribution during its entire run, thus high grade copies can be hard to come by.

35.00 50.00 75.00

(2,3,5,7) 1962, same format.

25.00 35.00 45.00

(4,6) 1963, same format.

20.00 30.00 40.00

FANTASY FILM JOURNAL

(1-2) 1977-1978, Nostalgia Graphics Publishers, 8 1/2 x 11, $2.50 and $3.00 cover price, prozine.

15.00 30.00 50.00

FANTASTIC FILMS ILLUSTRATED

(1,2,3) Published by Carpenter.

60.00 120.00 175.00

FANTASY FILM JOURNAL
(Fanzine)

(1-7) 1972-1973, Charles Stanfield editor and publisher, 8 1/2 x 11, B&W covers, very limited print runs.

5.00 10.00 12.50

THE FANTASY JOURNAL
(Fanzine)

(1-6) 1962-1963, Jim Hollander editor and publisher, 8 1/2 x 11, B&W photo off-set covers, 75 cents cover price, early and great film-fan monster fanzine, limited print runs.

10.00 20.00 35.00

FANTASY MAGAZINE INDEX

(nn) oneshot by Winans. 15.00 25.00 40.00

FAVORITE WESTERNS OF FILMLAND

(See listing for WILDEST WESTERNS.)

FEAR OF DARKNESS (Fanzine)

(1-4) 1982-1984, Tim Mayer editor and publisher, 8 1/2 x 11, $1.50 cover price, B&W covers.

5.00 10.00 20.00

FEATURED CREATURES (Fanzine)

(1) 1994, #1, Clayton Sayre Editor and Publisher, 8 1/2 x 11 format, B&W covers.

5.00 10.00 20.00

FEMME FATALES

(1) 1992, Summer Vol. 1 No. 1, Frederick Clark
Publisher, 8 1/2 x 11, 4.95 cover price, prozine.

	Good	Fine	Near Mint
	10.00	20.00	40.00
(2-10) 1992-1994	7.50	10.00	20.00
(11-present)	5.00	7.50	10.00

FIENDISH DELIGHTS (Fanzine)

(nn) 1969, one-shot, Memory Lane Publishers, 8
1/2 x 11, 25 cents cover price, professional art
B&W off-set cover, a classic early effort,
limited print runs.　　15.00　30.00　50.00

FILMFAX

(1) 1986, Jan./Feb., Vol. 1 No. 1, #1 Space Patrol
Special, 8 1/2 x 11, 2.95 cover price, painted
cover for first issue. FILMFAX has answered
the prayers of film-monster and film fans for
a traditional, thoughtful, continuous
publication that dedicates itself to unusual
and horror films with serious historical
coverage. Edited and published by Michael
Stein, with a host of contributors over the
years, this magazine with its "noir" black and
white and single tint color covers has
remained popular and proven that there is
still a contemporary market for cult horror
magazines in the United States. Issue #'s 1-14
(with the exception of #4) are Out of Print
from the publisher (along with #'s 22 & 29)
and are highly collectible.

　　　　　　　　50.00　85.00　125.00

(2) 1986, April, color featured inside.

　　　　　　　　50.00　85.00　125.00

(3-5) 1986-1987, June/Oct.-Nov./and up, issue #5
with last painted cover.

　　　　　　　　10.00　20.00　30.00

Note: When #4 sells out at $20 from
Publisher above price range kicks in.

(6) 1987-1989, same format, photo covers

kick in with #6.	25.00	35.00	50.00
(4,9,11)	10.00	20.00	25.00
(7)	30.00	50.00	75.00
(8)	15.00	25.00	35.00
(15-and up)	5.00	10.00	15.00

Note: Most remaining numbers from #15
through the present are available from the
publisher at prices ranging from $6.00 to
$15.00 - they are file copy Near Mint.
Contact FILMFAX at filmfax@xsite.net or
call them at (847)-866-7155.

FILMS FANTASTIQUE (Fanzine)

(nn) 1976 one-shot issue, long time fan James
Van Hise who has been widely active in
Burroughs fandom was the editor, Nostalgia
World Publishers, 8 1/2 x 11, color tint cover
featuring classic scene from "The Day The
Earth Stood Still," small print runs, semi
fan/prozine.　　10.00　15.00　25.00

FORBIDDEN ZONE (Fanzine)

(1) 1993, one-shot, published by Jeff Smith, 3.00
cover price, 8 1/2 x 11, B&W photo off-set.
　　　　　　　　10.00　20.00　30.00

FOR MONSTERS ONLY

(Cover Design at CRACKED'S FOR MONSTERS
ONLY up to issue No. 8)

(1-5) 1965-1967, Major Magazines publishers,
Joe Kiernan editor, 8 1/2 x 11, 35 cents cover
price, the first five issues feature John Severin
cover paintings, with interior artwork by
Severin, features are mixed satire, and photo

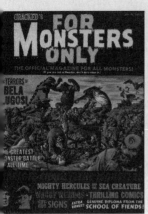

	Good	Fine	Near Mint		Good	Fine	Near Mint

articles, prozine.

	10.00	20.00	30.00

6-10) 1967-1972, same format, covers are now by Gray Morrow, Jeff Jones and other artists.

	5.00	15.00	25.00
ANNUAL 1967	15.00	25.00	40.00
ANNUAL 1987	10.00	15.00	20.00

FRIGHT (Fanzine)

(1) 1962 one-shot issue, Ron Haydock of *Fantastic Monsters* fame, and long time fan edited and designed this great fanzine, 5 1/2 x 8 1/2 with off-set cover, limited print run, highly desirable.

	40.00	75.00	150.00

FXRH (Special Visual Effects Created by Ray Harryhausen)

(1) 1971-1973, Ernie Farino and Sam Calvin combine efforts as editor and publisher for this specific focus fanzine, 8 1/2 x 11, B&W off-set covers, tremendous coverage and articles about the creative life of Ray Harryhausen, limited print runs, sought after by every serious film-monster magazine collector - rare, fanzine.

	75.00	150.00	250.00
(2)	50.00	100.00	150.00

(Becomes FXRH in title with issues 3 and 4.)

FXRH

(3) 1974-1976, same partnership to publish and edit, covers become single color background printing, more professional prozine look to last two issues, large print runs and a little greater distribution, available through Bud Plant for a period of time, fanzine.

	25.00	50.00	85.00
(4)	20.00	30.00	40.00

GARDEN GHOULS GAZETTE (Fanzine)

(1,2,3,) 1962, David Keil editor and publisher, Hectograph printing, most likely only 25 to 30 copies of the early issues, 3 to 6 pages per issue, 8/ 1/2 x 11, very primitive beginnings on the early numbers.

	100.00	200.00	300.00
(4-5)	50.00	100.00	200.00

(6,7,11,13-16) 1962, beginning with mixed hecto mimeograph printing, same format and editor.

	40.00	75.00	100.00

(9) 1962, same format, interview with Forrest J. Ackerman, Frankenstein cover.

	30.00	50.00	75.00

(8,10,12) 1962, same format, with mimeo covers and hecto interiors.

	30.00	50.00	75.00

(13) 1963, Larry Byrd steps in for a Hecto cover art design.

	40.00	75.00	100.00

(17-20) 1963-64, final issues edited by Keil, now featuring photo off-set covers by Larry Byrd, some of the finest early Monster fanzine covers ever released, all classic covers, with issue No. 16 Keil turns over the editorship to Gary Collins.

	15.00	35.00	60.00

(17-20) 1964-1965, with #17 format changes to more professional photo off-set covers featuring Photo covers of Chaney, Karloff, Lugosi, etc., No. 17 features Ron Borst reviews - interior design mixes photo off-set and mimeograph work.

	15.00	35.00	60.00

(21) 1966, Giant Issue, 39 pages, 40 cents cover price, photo off-set interior pages, with photo stencil design for some pages, "Skull" film insert, a great classic Monster fanzine.

	20.00	50.00	75.00

	Good	Fine	Near Mint		Good	Fine	Near Mint

GIALLAR (Fanzine)

(1-7) 1966-69, Randall Harris publisher & editor, B&W photo off-set.

	10.00	20.00	35.00

GORE CREATURES (Fanzine.)

(1) 1963, #1, small size, 5 1/2 x 8 1/2, mimeograph format, the first issue simply has the cover title, editors name and #1 on cover; this fanzine, which has developed over the years, and is now one of the finest semi-pro monster magazines in the business has been developed by Gary J. Svehla (who now works with his wife Susan). Because of the long running history of the magazine, and also because the very early issues are interesting in their own right GORE CREATURES is one of the most sought after of all early Monster Fanzines. Very limited print runs on the early issues, coupled with the fact that very few monster fans ordered them directly - with almost no cross over to SF fandom or comics fandom - means that they are truly RARE!

	250.00	500.00	750.00

(2-5) still retain smaller format, still retain linear mimeograph covers, 25 cents cover price.

	150.00	300.00	500.00

(6,7) covers are now B&W screen mimeograph in format, cover price 25 cents.

	100.00	200.00	300.00
(8,9,10)	75.00	150.00	200.00

(11,12) covers now have design elements and become more sophisticated, cover price moves up to 50 cents per issue.

	50.00	75.00	100.00
(13-15)	25.00	40.00	60.00

(16-25) linear, art covers, photo off-set images, Arkham House style designs, the magazine continues to evolve to its last issue No. 25 with the title of GORE CREATURES.

	10.00	20.00	30.00

(BECOMES MIDNIGHT MARQUEE WITH ISSUE No. 26.)

MIDNIGHT MARQUEE (Fanzine-semiprozine)

(26) first MM	15.00	25.00	30.00
(27-29)	10.00	20.00	30.00
(30,34,36)	5.00	10.00	15.00

(all other issues - present are available from the publisher at various prices.)

Note: To order recent back issues in VF+ contact Midnight Marquee Press, Inc. 9721 Britiany Lane, Baltimore, MD. 21234. or call 410-665-1198.

GOREZONE (From the Creators of Fangoria)

(1) 1988 April, Vol. 1 No. 1, O'Quinn Studios, 8 1/2 x 11, 3.95 cover price, prozine.

	7.50	15.00	25.00
(2-10)	3.50	7.50	10.00
(11-26)	2.50	5.00	10.00

GRUESOME CREATURES (Fanzine)

(1-2) 1962, Eugene Aiello, smaller format issues, B&W photo off-set covers, very rare and desirable.

	40.00	75.00	125.00
(3) same format.	40.00	65.00	100.00

HELP! For Tired Minds....

(1) 1960 Vol. 1 No. 1 - Harvey Kurtzman editor, James Warren Publisher. 8 1/2 x 11, cover price is 35 cents. Though NOT a Monster Magazine, in actuality a satire magazine by MAD creator Kurtzman, this magazine remains unlisted in other sources and is contained within this price guide list. Photo-fumeti format, with

	Good	Fine	Near Mint		Good	Fine	Near Mint

Arnold Roth, Jack Davis, and Harvey Kurtzman artwork. Kurtzman's last great effort as editor of a newsstand magazine.

35.00 75.00 175.00

(2) 1960, September, "Decadence Degenerated," 9 pager by Kurtzman.

30.00 50.00 75.00

(3-5) 1960, Oct.-Dec., No. 4 with Air Sickness Bag insert inside front cover.

25.00 35.00 50.00

(6-10) 1961, No. 6 with Ray Bradbury story, No. 8 with Bill Elder 5 page story, No. 10 with four page Bill Elder "Goodman Meets T*RZ*N."

15.00 20.00 35.00

(11-20) 1962-1963, No. 13 with classic "Goodman Goes Playboy," Kurtzman/Elder story - where Kurtzman slams the whole PLAYBOY world, shortly before he become part of it later with Little Annie Fanny; No. 14 with 7 page Elder story; No. 15 with 6 page Elder story "Goodman meets S*PERM*N; No. 16 with 5 page Elder story and 5 page Shelton Wonder Warthog story; No. 18 with 4 page Shelton Warthog story; No. 19 features Jack Davis and Kurtzman artwork; No. 20 with 6 page Shelton Story.

10.00 20.00 30.00

(21-26) 1964-1965, No. 22 with 2 pages of R. Crumb, and 5 page Shelton Warthog story; No. 23 with 5 page Shelton Warhog story and 3 pages of Gahan Wilson doing "The Monster Craze" cartoons; No. 24 associate editor Terry Gilliam persuades associate John Cleese to do 13 page Photo-story; No. 25 with six pages of R. Crumb artwork and 4 page Shelton Waryhog story; No. 26 with 5 page Shelton Warthog story.

7.50 15.00 25.00

ANNUAL October of 1964, 75 cents cover price, square bound

(nn) 10.00 20.00 30.00

HORROR OF PARTY BEACH

(nn) 1964, one-shot, Warren Publications, photo-fumeti comic book format with caption balloons, 8 1/2 x 11, 35 cents cover price, prozine. 5.00 15.00 25.00

HORROR FAN

(1) 1988 December, No. 1, Charlotte Magazine Publishers, 8 1/2 x 11, 2.95 cover price, prozine. 5.00 10.00 20.00

(2-4) 1988-89 3.50 7.50 10.00

HORROR MONSTERS PRESENTS BLACK ZOO

(nn) 1963, Fall - one shot, First Edition on cover, 8 1/2 x 11, 35 cents cover price.

15.00 30.00 40.00

HORROR MONSTERS

(1-nn) 1961, ND, No. #, "First Edition on cover," Charlton Publications, 8 1/2 x 11, 35 cents cover price, prozine. Painted covers for all issues. 25.00 40.00 75.00

(2) 1961, ND, Frank Di Marco is credited for covers on #'s 1,2,3. 20.00 30.00 50.00

(3-10) 1962, format the same.

15.00 25.00 40.00

HORRORS OF THE SCREEN
(Fanzine)

1962 - Spring/Vol. 1 No. 1 - Alexander Soma editor, 8 1/2 by 5 1/2, 50 cents price. Offset cover & interiors, one of the great early "scholarly" monster fanzines.

20.00 45.00 75.00

	Good	Fine	Near Mint		Good	Fine	Near Mint

1963 - June/Vol. 1. No. 2 - Alex Soma editor, format same as No. 1, 50 cents price.

15.00   35.00   50.00

1964 - Jan./Vol. 2 No. 2 - Alex Soma editor, format same, 75 cent price.

10.00   20.00   40.00

HAMMERS HALLS OF HORROR
(British)

(19-20) 1978, Top Sellers Publications, 8 1/2 x 11, with limited distribution in America, cover price for US $1.00 per issue, the only two issue in US release.   3.50   10.00   15.00

HOUSE OF HORROR
(Hammers, British)

(1) 1978, #1, Top Sellers Publications, 8 1/2 x 11, $1.00 cover price, prozine.

5.00   15.00   25.00

HOUSE OF HORROR

(1) 1978 April, No. 1, Warren Publications, released to secure copyright for title, with very limited distribution, less than 500 copies were printed - many never distributed in any way, one of the more obscure and rare of all Warren titles, similar in its scarcity to *Eerie* No. 1 photo off-set one-shot.

150.00   300.00   500.00

THE HOUSE THAT HAMMER BUILT
(British Fanzine)

(1-11) 1997-1999, Wayne Kinsey editor, published by Blackwell John Buckle, 8 1/4 x 11 1/2, cover price of L4/ $11.00 US, slick cover and interior paper stock, some color on inside, a brilliant series that should be rated as prozine, and not fanzine, no serious collector would want to be without these issues - order them while they last - and before they become very expensive as collectible out of print back issues.

3.50   7.50   11.00

Note: Contact the publisher at Blackwell John Buckle, Charles Street, Great Yarmouth, Norfold, ENGLAND, NR30 3LA (Tel 01493-844044). All back issues are available at this time.

IMAGI-MOVIES

(1-5) 1993, Frederick Clarke Publisher, 8 1/2 x 11, $4.95 cover price, prozine.

3.50   5.00   10.00

(6-present)   2.50   3.50   7.50

JAPANESE FANTASY FILM JOURNAL (Fanzine)

(1-2) 1968, Greg Shoemaker publisher & editor, 25 cents, B&W format, 8 1/2 x 11.

45.00   75.00   150.00

(3,4) 1969, format same.   40.00   60.00   100.00
(5-9) 1970-72, fmt. same.   35.00   50.00   75.00
(10) 1970's, format same.   20.00   30.00   50.00
(11,12) 1980's   10.00   20.00   30.00
(13-15) 1980's   10.00   15.00   20.00

JAPANESE GIANTS (Fanzine)

(1-5) 1978, Ed Godzisewski, B&W photo-off set.

30.00   50.00   85.00

(6) format same.   20.00   30.00   40.00
(7,8) format same. 15.00   20.00   30.00

	Good	Fine	Near Mint		Good	Fine	Near Mint

THE JOURNAL OF FRANKENSTEIN

(See listing for CASTLE OF FRANKENSTEIN.)

KALEIDOSCOPE (Fanzine)

1962 - Sept./Vol. 1 No. 1 - Donald Shay editor, 8 1/2 by 5 1/2, 50 cents price. Offset cover and interiors, only one issue published - fanzine.

	Good	Fine	Near Mint
	10.00	20.00	45.00

KARLOFF

(nn) 1969, one-shot, Cinefax Publications, 8 1/2 x 11, 1.00 cover price, prozine.

	15.00	30.00	50.00

KILLING MOON

(1-2) 1994, Draculina Publishers, 8 1/2 x 11, $3.25 cover price, prozine.

	3.50	7.50	15.00

LARRY IVIE'S MONSTERS AND HEROES

(1) 1967, Larry Ivie editor and publisher, 8 1/4 x 11, 35 cents cover price, painted Ivie covers, with B&W interior articles, Altron Boy starts, prozine.

	5.00	15.00	20.00

(2-7) 1968-1969, No. 2 with Altron Boy Origin story; No. 3 Creation of King Kong issue with 3 page Berni Wrightson feature; No. 4 Captain Marvel history also with Burroughs coverage; No. 5 Captain Midnight premiums shown, also history of Comic Book Conventions with photos; No. 6 with 4 pages of artwork by Al Williamson.

	5.00	15.00	20.00

LITTLE SHOPPE OF HORRORS (Fanzine)

(1) 1972, Richard Klemensen editor & publisher,

8 1/2 x 11, B&W photo off set.

	Good	Fine	Near Mint
	50.00	100.00	150.00
(2) 1973, format same.	45.00	85.00	125.00
(3) same format.	35.00	60.00	100.00
(4,6,7,) same.	25.00	35.00	50.00
(5) format same.	75.00	125.00	200.00
(8,10,11,) same.	15.00	25.00	35.00
(9) format same.	20.00	30.00	45.00
(12-14) same.	10.00	15.00	20.00

MAD MONSTERS

(1,5) 1961 - Charlton Publications, 8 1/2 x 11, 35 cents price, prozine. The first issue hosted a Steve Ditko cover and interior artwork for three page Monster Satire story.

	25.00	45.00	75.00

(2-4) 1961-62, same format, move to painted cover artwork.

	15.00	25.00	40.00

(6-10) 1963-64, same format.

	15.00	25.00	40.00

MAGIC THEATER (Fanzine)

(1,2,4,) 1976-77, Raymond Young publisher, 8 1/2 x 11, $1.00 cover price, photo offset, square bound on early issues, a very sought after fanzine title with excellent production and design.

	45.00	75.00	100.00
(3) 1977, format same.	50.00	100.00	125.00
(5) 1978, format same.	30.00	50.00	85.00
(6,7,8) 1979-80.	10.00	15.00	20.00

(Becomes EEGAH by title after No. 8)

EEGAH
(nn) 1988, one shot, Raymond Young.

	10.00	15.00	25.00

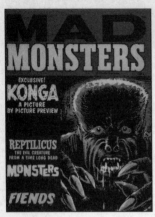

	Good	Fine	Near Mint		Good	Fine	Near Mint

MIDNIGHT MARQUEE
(Fanzine-semiprozine)

(see listing for GORE CREATURES, where the series begins)

MODERN MONSTER

(1) 1966, June - Vol. 1. No. 1, Jim Matthews publisher/ Gunther Collins editor, 8 1/2 x 11, 50 cents cover price, painted covers, prozine.

15.00   25.00   35.00

(BECOMES MODERN MONSTERS with second issue.)

MODERN MONSTERS

(2-4) 1966, June/August/Oct.-Nov. with issue #3 Larry Byrd become contributing artist and does the cover paintings for issues #3 and #4.

15.00   25.00   35.00

THE MOLE PEOPLE
(Universal Pictures)

(nn) 1964, one-shot, Warren Publications, 8 1/2 x 11, cover price 35 cents, square bound, photo-fumeti comic style with caption balloons, production by Russ Jones, prozine.

10.00   20.00   30.00

MONSTERAMA
(Forrest Ackerman's)

(1-2) 1991-1992, Fantagraphics/Gary Groth Publisher, Forrest J. Ackerman editor, short lived attempt to put Ackerman back at the helm of a Monster Magazine, 8 1/2 x 11, 2.75 cover price, slick paper, prozine.

5.00   10.00   20.00

MONSTERS ATTACK

(1-5) 1989-1990, Globe Publications, 8 1/2 x 11, $2.95 cover price, prozine.

3.50   7.50   15.00

MONSTER FANTASY

(1-4) 1975, April/June/Aug./Oct., Mayfiar Publications, 8 1/2 x 11, $1.25 cover price, prozine.

10.00   15.00   20.00

MONSTER HOWLS

(nn) 1966, one-shot, Humor-Vision Publications Inc., 8 1/2 x 11, 35 cents cover price, with John Severin artwork, prozine.

5.00   15.00   30.00

MONSTER INTERNATIONAL

(1-4) 1991, Kronos Publications, 8 1/2 x 11, $3.50 cover price, prozine.

3.50   7.50   15.00

(2)   10.00   20.00   30.00

MONSTER JOURNAL (Fanzine)

(2) 1962, August - Craig Stock editor and publisher, 8 1/2 x 11, 25 cents, mimeograph 13 page format, Manuel Lopes did cover artwork. One of the early consistent Monster fanzines, all issues are very scarce and are found in few collections.

25.00   50.00   75.00

(3-6) 1962-1963, #'s 3 Dec., 4 April, 5 Aug., 6 Dec.; No. 4 with Roger Hill color mimeo cover; #5.50 cents cover price; #6 "Robby the Robot" cover.

20.00   50.00   65.00

(7-9) 1964-1965, #'s 7 July with printing on both sides of paper and Multi Color cover;

(8) Oct., #9 Sept. marked "final issue" on cover, editor states he wants to write for more serious SF fanzine.

20.00   30.00   40.00

MONSTERLAND

(1) very common. 2.50 5.00 10.00
(2) 1985, New Media Publishers, 8 1/2 x 11, one
of the more recent attempts to put Forrest J.
Ackerman back into the editor's shoes of a
Monster Magazine, with good production and
covers for most of the run.

5.00 15.00 25.00
(3) 5.00 10.00 15.00

FORREST J. ACKERMAN'S MONSTERLAND
(MONSTERLAND continued as, after #4)

(7,15,17) same format 5.00 10.00 15.00
(all others) same format 5.00 8.00 10.00

MONSTERLAND FEARBOOKS

(1-2) 1988 10.00 25.00 40.00

MONSTER MADNESS

(1-3) 1972-1973, Marvel Comics Group Publisher,
Stan Lee listed as editor, 8 1/2 x 11, 60 cents
cover price, photo covers, and photo-fumeti
one page satire jokes featured throughout,
prozine. 5.00 10.00 15.00

MONSTERS AND THINGS

(1) 1959 - Jan./ Vol. 1 No. 1 - L.T. Shaw Ed, 8 1/2
by 11, 25 cents cover price, color covers, B&W
interior, combines fiction, comics, & some
Monster photos. Extremely rare in high
grades, prozine. 50.00 150.00 250.00
(2) 1959 - Apr./ Vol. 1 No. 2 - L.T. Shaw Ed,
format same, 25 cents cover price.
75.00 175.00 250.00

MONSTER MANIA

(1-3) 1966-67, Renaissance Productions
Publishers, 8 1/2 x 11, 35 cents cover price,
prozine. 15.00 25.00 35.00
(2) 1966, this issue carries the famous Frank
Frazetta wrap around cover for "The Lost
World." 15.00 25.00 35.00

MONSTERS OF THE MOVIES

(1-8) 1974-75, Marvel Comics Group Publisher,
Roy Thomas/Jim Harmon editors; 8 1/2 x 11,
$1.00 cover price, prozine.
5.00 10.00 15.00
ANNUAL, 1975, 1.25 cover price.
5.00 10.00 15.00

MONSTERS PRICE GUIDE

(1) 1974, Larry Kenton author and publisher,
early price guide, 8 1/2 x 11, black and white
covers, semi-prozine with limited distribution.
25.00 50.00 100.00
(2) 1975, Larry Kenton author and publisher,
second edition is slightly rarer than the first
number. 25.00 50.00 100.00

MONSTER PARADE

(1) 1958, No. 1 (listed inside as Vol. 2 No. 6),
September, Magnum Publications, Irwin Stein/
M.J. Shapiro-L. T. Shaw publisher and editors,
8 1/2 x 11, 35 cents cover price; square bound
spines to all four issues, combo photo/painted
cover for first issue - other issues with painted
covers, inside articles and fiction a mix of
horror stories, sex and filmMonster pix; one of
the rarest and most sought after of all early
FM copies, prozine.
125.00 300.00 600.00

	Good	Fine	Near Mint		Good	Fine	Near Mint

(2) 1958 November, same format as above, Matt Fox double page horror illustration, also feature on "Plan 9 From Outer Space."

75.00   150.00   300.00

(3) 1958 December, same format, 7 page comic Horror reprint "Magician of Death," artwork by Larry Ivie and Monster articles.

75.00   150.00   250.00

(4) 1959 March, same format, 7 page comic story by Lou Cameron "She Stalks at Sundown," inside ad for companion magazine MONSTERS AND THINGS.

75.00   125.00   250.00

MONSTERS TO LAUGH WITH

(1-3) 1964-1965, Marvel Comics Group Publisher, Stan Lee listed as editor; 8 1/4 x 11, 25 cents cover price, photo-fumeti single page satire joke pages for entire interior.

10.00   20.00   30.00

(BECOMES MONSTERS UNLIMITED With the Fourth issue.)

MONSTERS UNLIMITED
(4-7) 1965-1966, same format, publisher, and editor listing.

5.00   10.00   25.00

MONSTERSCENE

(1,3,9,) 1992, Gogo Entertainment Publications, a Monster Magazine with the focus on Basil Gogos famous FM covers and other paintings that graced Monster magazines through the years, 8 1/2 x 11, cover price $4.95, prozine.

10.00   20.00   30.00

(4)   20.00   35.00   50.00
(2,5-8,10-11)   10,00   15.00   20.00

THE MONSTER TIMES
(Newspaper fold over format)

(1) 1972 January, Vol. 1 No. 1, Monster Times Publishers, 8 x 12 or 12 x 16 format, 50 cents cover price, one of the more unusual publications, this fold over format magazine, read as an actual newspaper when opened up, on pulp paper for covers and interior paper, with slightly better paper cover stock and single to double tint color covers; this publication proved popular and ran many interesting fan-oriented articles and features through the years. Finding runs in very nice condition is now tough because of the way they were printed and produced.

5.00   10.00   15.00

(2-9,11-20) same format   5.00   10.00   15.00
(10) special EC issue   3.50   10.00   15.00
(21-48) 1974-1976   2.50   10.00   15.00

MONSTER TIMES SPECIALS

(nn) STAR TREK LIVES two one-shot issues, issued with color covers, 8 1/2 x 11 magazine format size, prozine.

5.00   10.00   20.00

THE MONSTER TIMES SPECIAL 'MONSTERS'
(nn) one-shot, the third MT special, Godzilla highlights, scarce.

20.00   45.00   70.00

MONSTER WORLD

(1-2) 1975, Mayfair Publications, 8 1/2 x 11, $1.75 cover price, prozine.

5.00   15.00   20.00

(Becomes with Third Issue...)

QUASIMODO'S MONSTER MAGAZINE
(3-8) 1976   5.00   15.00   20.00

	Good	Fine	Near Mint		Good	Fine	Near Mint

MONSTER WORLD

(1) 1964 November, Vol. 1 No. 1, Warren Publications, 4sJ Editor-In-Chief; Harry Chester production and layout; 8 1/2 x 11, square back spine, 35 cents cover price; with six page Wallace Wood/Russ Jones "The Mummy," comic story included. The first ten issues of Monster World replace the numbering for Famous Monsters in the Nos. 70-79.

	Good	Fine	Near Mint
	7.00	15.00	20.00
(5-10)	7.00	15.00	20.00
(2,4)	10.00	20.00	30.00
(3) limited quantities	15.00	40.00	60.00

Note: Most Monster Worlds had deep numbers in the Warren Warehouse find, and were available for years afterwards as back issues.

MOVIE CLUB

(1-4) 1993, Don Dohler editor and publisher, 8 1/2 x 11, cover price $3.50, prozine.

	2.50	5.00	10.00

MOVIE MONSTERS

(1-4) 1974-1975, Seabord Periodicals Inc. - Don Dohler editor, 8 1/2 x 11, $1.00 cover price, prozine with painted covers.

	5.00	10.00	15.00

MOVIE MONSTERS

(1-3) 1981, S. & J. Publications, 8 1/2 x 11, cover price 2.95, prozine.

	10.00	20.00	30.00

MOVIELAND MONSTERS (Fanzine)

(1) 1963, Vol. 1 No. 1 - Jerry Weist editor and publisher, 8 1/2 x 11, 20 cents cover price, mimeograph fanzine running at 6 pages with print run of approx. 40 copies.

	15.00	25.00	40.00

(2) 1963, July, same format.

	15.00	25.00	40.00

MOVIE PEOPLE (Fanzine)

(nn) 1975, one-shot, Susan Turner McGee editor and publisher, 8 1/2 x 11, photo off-set.

	10.00	20.00	30.00

NIGHTMARE (Fanzine)

(1) 1962, Vol. 1 No. 1 - Jerry Weist editor and publisher, 8 1/2 x 11, 30 cents cover price, mimeograph format with ink pad stencil colors used on cover; 6 page condensed version of H.G. Wells *Island Of Dr. Moreau* feature. Less than 50 copies run.

	20.00	30.00	50.00

(2) 1962, same format mimeo with 10 pages - 4 page rubber printed insert "The Daily Bat," as Broadsheet insert. The high point of this rarity is Blank Page with rubber stamp "A Picture of the Invisible Man, without anything on." Frankenstein Meets Wolfman cover.

	20.00	30.00	50.00

(3) 1963, #3 unfinished six page issue with combined title MACABRE AND NIGHTMARE, issued to Forrest J. Ackerman members and a few close friends, possible run at 25 copies.

	25.00	60.00	100.00

OFFICIAL THE MUNSTERS

(1) 1965, Vol. 1 No. 1, one-shot, Twin Hits Publications, 8 1/2 x 11, 50 cents cover price, Otto Binder teams with editor Roger Elwood, interior art, photos, games, fiction, painted cover art.

	35.00	65.00	100.00

	Good	Fine	Near Mint		Good	Fine	Near Mint

ORIENTAL CINEMA

(1-4) 1994, Draculina Publications, 8 1/2 x 11, 2.75 cover price, prozine.

3.50   7.50   15.00

ORIGINAL MONSTERS (Fanzine)

(1-6) 1969-70, Warren Stein editor & publisher, 50 cents cover price, 8 1/2 x 11, B&W photo off-set covers.   25.00   50.00   75.00
(7,8) format same.   15.00   30.00   50.00
(9) format same.   10.00   15.00   25.00
(10) format same.   5.00   10.00   15.00

OUTRÉ (Fanzine)

(1) 1963, Allen Kracalik editor and publisher, photo off-set Scarborough and Larry Byrd cover, EC type cover format. Rare.

15.00   20.00   30.00

OUTER LIMITS NEWSLETTERS (Fanzine)

(1-6, 6 1/2) 1978-79, published and edited by Paige Comics and Steve Streeter, $1.25 cover price.   40.00   75.00   100.00

THE OUTER LIMITS ILLUSTRATED REVIEW (Fanzine)

(1-2) 1977, Ted Rypel editor & publisher, $2.50 & $3.00 cover price, 8 1/2 x 11, photo off-set covers.   20.00   40.00   60.00

OUTRÉ (Filmfax Presents:)

(1) 1996, Michael Stein/Ted Okuda editors, Stein publisher, 8 1/2 x 11, $5.95 cover price, an extension of FILMFAX, the content ranging from genre artwork, to SF and other outside-based cinema articles, prozine.

in print   2.50   5.00   10.00
(3, 5, 6) in print   3.50   7.50   15.00
(2-11) in print   2.50   5.00   10.00

Note: The "in print" issues are available in VF+ from the publisher, contact them at (847)-866-7554 or by E-Mail at filmfax@xsite.com

PANIC (Fanzine)

(nn) 1963, one-shot, Wes Shank publisher & editor, 8 1/2 x 11, mimeograph pages, 35 cents cover price.   15.00   25.00   40.00

PHANTASM (Fanzine)

(nn) 1965, one-shot, John Carpenter editor & publisher, mimeograph pages, 8 1/2 x 11, scarce in any condition.

60.00   100.00   150.00

PHANTASMA (Cinema Beyond Reality)

(1-4) 1988-1990, Jack Brent and Gregg Boggia editors and publishers, 8 1/2 x 11, cover price $3.00, prozine.

7.50   10.00   20.00

PHOTO FIENDS (Fanzine)

(1-3) 1978-79, Timothy Paxton editor & publisher, 8 1/2 x 11, with photo off set photo covers, $1.00 cover price, fanzine.

7.50   15.00   25.00

PHOTON (Fanzine)

(1-2) 1963-64, Mark Frank editor and publisher, 8 1/2 x 11, 50 cents cover price, mimeograph covers and interiors. This fanzine had humble origins, however it would soon develop into

one of the premiere monster film fanzines with almost professional status. This has a lot to do with the very high demand for the very early numbers which are truly rare.

	200.00	400.00	500.00
(3) Mimeo format.	60.00	100.00	150.00
(4-6) Mimeo format.	45.00	65.00	100.00

(7) with more professional off-set B&W covers, 50 cents cover price, improved design, a more professional fanzine.

	25.00	40.00	60.00

(8-14,16) even better cover artwork, improved quality over all, now a top fanzine.

	25.00	50.00	85.00
(15,17,18)	20.00	35.00	50.00
(19,20)	15.00	25.00	35.00

(21-27) 1970's, now with photo covers, a fanzine that has evolved into near prozine status.

	10.00	20.00	30.00

PSYCHOTRONIC VIDEO

(1) 1989, Vol. 1 No. 1, Michael Weldon publisher, 8 1/2 x 11, 3.00 cover price, a unique magazine with one of the all time great titles, eventually hosting covers that stood out from the other magazines as both pop-art and new-wave in design.

	25.00	35.00	75.00
(2) in print	1.50	3.00	6.00
(3,5) in print	5.00	10.00	15.00
(4) in print	2.50	5.00	10.00
(6) Out of Print	10.00	20.00	30.00
(7-10) in print	1.50	3.00	5.00
(11) in print	2.00	4.00	6.00
(12) in print	5.00	10.00	20.00
(13) in print	2.50	5.00	10.00
(14-32-present) in print	1.50	3.00	5.00

Note: "In print" issues are available file copy VF from the publisher, call (914)-252-6803.

PURE IMAGES

(1-2) 1977, Greg Theakston editor and publisher, long time Monster/Comics/Kirby fan becomes active with this short run, 8 1/2 x 11, $4.00 cover price, semi-prozine.

	15.00	25.00	40.00
(3-4) 1986	5.00	10.00	20.00

QUANTUM (Fanzine)

(1) 1967, one-shot, Mark Frank editor & publisher, mimeograph pages, 8 1/2 x 11.

	50.00	100.00	150.00
(2) 1967, same.	75.00	125.00	200.00

RAY HARRYHAUSEN JOURNAL (Fanzine)

(1) 1973, one-shot, Ronald Fink editor & publisher, B&W off-set covers, 8 1/2 x 11.

	15.00	25.00	45.00

READY FOR SHOWING (Fanzine)

(1) 1965, one-shot, Leonard Minter editor & publisher, 50 cents cover price, 8 1/2 x 11, great quality fanzine.

	15.00	35.00	45.00

REMEMBER WHEN (Fanzine)

(1,2-7,10,11) 1971-75, Nostalgia Inc. publishers, these issues are not related to horror themes, 8 1/2 x 11, 65 cents cover price.

	2.50	5.00	10.00

(2,8,9,12,13) same format, the horror issues, photo off-set covers.

	10.00	15.00	25.00

	Good	Fine	Near Mint

THE ROBERT BLOCH FANZINE
(Fanzine)

(1-5) 1970's, Randall Larson editor & publisher, 8 1/2 x 11, one of the most popular, and one of the most active (pro) fans from 1940's and 1950's science fiction fandom is given his own fanzine! Such an honor must have given Robert "writers Bloch."

	Good	Fine	Near Mint
	2.50	7.50	15.00

SCARLET STREET (The Magazine of Mystery and Horror)

(1) 1991 January, Vol. 1 No. 1, Scarlet Street Publications, Jessie Lilley editor, 8 1/2 x 11, 3.95 and then 4.95 cover price, semi-pro and then prozine with specialty book store distribution. This magazine has filled a special niche in the magazine business, and has done an excellent job of focusing on the mystery/horror genre of film history with top notch articles that are always well researched; the first few issues are scarce for a contemporary magazine.

	Good	Fine	Near Mint
	100.00	200.00	300.00
(2,3) 1991 April-May	35.00	60.00	100.00
(4-5) 1991	10.00	25.00	35.00
(6-10) 1991-1992	5.00	10.00	15.00
(11-20) 1993	3.50	8.50	10.00
(21-present)	2.50	7.50	8.50

Note: Current copies are available from the publisher at back issue prices.

SCARY MONSTERS

(1-5) 1991, Dennis Druktenis publisher, 8 1/2 x 11, $3.50, then $3.95, then $4.95 cover price, prozine with great monster-fan oriented features and articles.

	Good	Fine	Near Mint
(1) 1991 October	4.00	6.00	10.00
(2-5) 1991-1992	3.50	6.00	10.00
(6-12) 1992-1993	3.50	6.00	10.00

SCARY MONSTERS MEMORIES YEARBOOKS
(nn) 1993	3.50	6.00	10.00
(nn) 1994	3.50	6.00	10.00

SCI-FI ENTERTAINMENT

(1-10) 1994-95, Sovereign Media Publishers, 8 1/2 x 11, slick paper throughout with heavy cover stock, 3.50 to 4.95 cover price, new movies based media magazine with slick layout and lots of color.

	Good	Fine	Near Mint
	1.50	5.00	7.50
(11-present)	1.50	3.50	6.00

Note: Back issues are available from the publisher.

SCI-FI UNIVERSE

(1-3) 1994, HG Publications, 8 1/2 x 11, $4.95 cover price, prozine.

	Good	Fine	Near Mint
	2.00	5.00	7.50
(4-up)	1.50	3.50	5.00

SCIENCE * FANTASY FILM CLASSICS (Featuring...)

(1-4) 1977-1978, SF Film Classics Publications, 8 1/2 x 11, $2.00 cover price, prozine that focused on Star Wars, Close Encounters, Star Trek, Battlestar Galactica in its only four issues.

	Good	Fine	Near Mint
	2.50	5.00	10.00

SCIENCE FICTION ILLUSTRATED

(1) 1977, One Shot, L/C Print Publications, 8 1/2 x 11, $2.95 cover price, prozine.

	Good	Fine	Near Mint
	5.00	15.00	25.00

SCIENCE FICTION HORROR & FANTASY

(1-2) 1977-1978, DW Publications, 8 1/2 x 11, $2.50 cover price, prozine.

	Good	Fine	Near Mint
	3.50	7.50	15.00

THE SCREAM FACTORY
(The Magazine of Horrors Past Present & Future)

(1-2) 1988, Deadline Publications, 8 1/2 x 11, beautiful art covers that remind collectors of early 1960's monster fanzines (the good titles!) for the first ten issues, great cult monster magazine; $4.95 cover price, semi-prozine with limited distribution.

	Good	Fine	Near Mint
	10.00	20.00	40.00
(3-8,10) 1989-1990	3.50	10.00	15.00
(9)	15.00	30.00	50.00
(11-14) 1991	2.50	5.00	12.50

SCREAM FACTORY PRESENTS, NIGHT OF THE LIVING DEAD

	Good	Fine	Near Mint
	3.50	7.50	15.00

SCREAM QUEENS ILLUSTRATED

(1) 1993, Market Square Publications, 8 1/2 x 11, cover price $5.95, the sexy woman on the cover monster magazine, prozine. Imagine, the first issue is scarce, in 'hot' demand.

	Good	Fine	Near Mint
	20.00	35.00	75.00
(2-up)	7.50	10.00	15.00

SCREEM

(1) 1992, Screemag Publications, 8 1/2 x 11, $3.95 cover price, "the magazine of beyond bad taste," monsters, prozine.

	Good	Fine	Near Mint
	15.00	25.00	40.00
(2-5)	3.50	7.50	10.00

SCREEN CHILLS (British)

(nn-1) 1957, Fall, one-shot, Pep Publications with Printers of Croydon. 8 x 10 1/2, stiff glossy covers, 1'6 net cover price. The exact historical story of this publication is hazy, however it would seem to predate FAMOUS MONSTERS No. 1 which appeared in America during a large snow storm that hit Philadelphia and New York City in January of 1958. Extremely rare to any known collection, in any grade - and especially scarce in Fine plus and above.

	Good	Fine	Near Mint
	375.00	750.00	1,250.00

SCREEN FACTS (Fanzine, limited newsstand dist. later issues)

(1) 1964, Alan G. Barbour editor and publisher, 5 3/4 x 8 1/2 inches, 50 cents cover price, early issues are fanzines, with low print runs, the format is slick hard paper covers with photo off-set covers, and interior plain stock - the early issues focus entirely on early serials, western, adventure, super-hero, science fiction, etc.

	Good	Fine	Near Mint
	5.00	10.00	25.00

(2,3,23/24, have monster covers)

	Good	Fine	Near Mint
(2-5) same format	10.00	15.00	25.00
(all other issues)	5.00	10.00	15.00

(23-24) special double issue, horror issue spotlight.

	Good	Fine	Near Mint
	10.00	15.00	25.00

SCREEN FACTS ALBUM Nos. 1 (Flash Gordon), 2 (Frankenstein), 3 (Dracula).
1971-72, 8 1/2 x 11, 75 cents cover price, fanzine.

	Good	Fine	Near Mint
	15.00	20.00	30.00

SCREEN MONSTERS

(1,3) 1981, Spring, and Fall, there was NO ISSUE NO. 2, SJ Publications, 8 1/2 x 11, $2.95 cover price, prozine.

	Good	Fine	Near Mint
	7.50	15.00	25.00

	Good	Fine	Near Mint		Good	Fine	Near Mint

SCREEN THRILLS ILLUSTRATED

(1) 1962, June, Vol. 1 No. 1 - Sam Sherman/F.J.Ackerman editors, published by Warren Publications, 8 1/2 x 11, 35 cents cover price, Basil Gogos cover painting.

    15.00   35.00   60.00

(2) 1962, Sept., Norman Edwards painted cover.

    15.00   25.00   40.00

(3-4)   15.00   25.00   40.00

(5-9) 1963-1965, with #5 cover price becomes 50 cents, photo covers. 10.00   15.00   20.00

(10) low distribution   20.00   45.00   75.00

SCREEN WHIRL (Fanzine)

(1-2) 1962, mimeograph pages and covers, 8 1/2 x 11, Ace Mask editor and publisher, 20 cents and 25 cents cover prices. Extremely rare first two issues.

    50.00   75.00   125.00

(3-5) 1963, with issue No. 3 editor Mask convinced talented fan artist Larry Byrd to do photo off-set covers, these covers are classics for this period, all issues scarce.

    30.00   50.00   85.00

Note: With issue No. 6 onward becomes VAMPIRE'S CRYPT.

VAMPIRE'S CRYPT (Fanzine)

(6-8) 1963, Same format, photo off-set Larry Byrd covers continue, page size increases, the covers become full page format and represent some of the classic Monster Fanzine covers of all time.   30.00   50.00   85.00

SFTV (Science Fiction TeleVision)

(1-7) 1984-1985, HJS Publications, 8 1/2 x 11, $2.75 cover price, the title says it all, prozine.

    3.50   7.50   15.00

SFTV COLOR POSTER BOOK

(1-3) 1978, $1.50 cover price.

    5.00   10.00   17.50

SHOCK TALES

(1) 1959, January - Vol. 1 No. 1, Myron Fass editor/publisher, 8 1/2 x 11, 35 cents cover price, the Vampire girl on cover photo is same as issue No. 2 of THRILLER. One of the rarest of all Monster Magazines, especially in Fine or better condition. 150.00 300.00 550.00

SHRIEK!

(1) 1965, May - Vol. 1 No. 1, Robin Bean/The House of Horror Publishers and editors, 8 1/2 x 11, 50 cents cover price, prozine.

    10.00   15.00   25.00

(2-4) 1966, Oct./Summer/Winter, format the same.   10.00   15.00   25.00

SLAUGHTER HOUSE

(1-5) 1988-1989, HCS Publications, 8 1/2 x 11 format, $2.95 cover price, prozine.

    5.00   7.00   10.00

SPACEMEN

(1) 1961 - July, Ackerman Ed, 8 1/2 by 11", 35 cents, Gogos cover, 4sJ's attempt to do a more serious science FilmFiction magazine, not part of warehouse find in multiple numbers, prozine.   40.00   100.00   200.00

(2) 1961 - Sept., Ackerman Ed, format CV price same, cover art by Bruce Minney. 25.00   60.00   150.00

(3) 1962 - April, Ackerman Ed, CV price & format same, letter column features David Kyle at early SF Con, Frank R. Paul *Amazing Stories*

	Good	Fine	Near Mint		Good	Fine	Near Mint

cover to H.G.Wells *War of the Worlds* shown.
40.00   100.00 225.00
(4-6) 1962/63 - Ackerman Ed, CV/pr & format
same, No. 6 features *Metropolis* article.
20.00   40.00   60.00
(7-8) 1963/64 - Ackerman Ed, CV/pr & format
same, No. 8 has March 1964 date stamped
over.   15.00   25.00   40.00
1965 ANNUAL - interior reprints with Wally
Wood painting on cover, available in
warehouse numbers. 20.00   40.00   60.00

SPACE MONSTERS (Fanzine)

(1) 1962, Vol. 1 No. 1, six pages, mimeograph
and rubber printer, 8 1/2 x 5 1/2 format, 25
cents price.   10.00   30.00   40.00

SPACE MONSTERS
(UFO Universe Presents, Prozine)

(1) 1990 February, Condor Publications, 8 1/2 x
11, $4.95 cover price, one-shot.
5.00   10.00   20.00

SPACE WARS

(1-14) 1977-1980, Countrywide Publications/SJ
Publications, 8 1/2 x 11, $1.95 cover price
prozine.   1.50   3.50   10.00
SPACE WARS HEROES (Ancient Astronaut
Special Edition)   1.50   3.50   7.50

SPFX (Fanzine)

(1) 1977, Jay Duncan and Ted A. Bohus editor &
publisher, photo off-set covers, very well
designed.   15.00   25.00   35.00
(2) 1978, format same.   20.00   35.00   50.00
(3-up) format same.   5.00   10.00   15.00

THE SPLATTER TIMES (Fanzine)

(1-3) 1983-84, Donald Farmer editor & publisher,
8 1/2 x 11.   10.00   20.00   40.00
(4-7) 1985-86, same format.
5.00   10.00   25.00

STAR BATTLES

(1-3) 1978-1979, SL&P Layouts Publications, 8 1/2
x 11, $1.75 cover price, prozine.
2.50   5.00   10.00

STAR BLASTER

(1-3) 1981, SJ Publications, 8 1/2 x 11, $2.95
cover price, prozine.   2.50   5.00   10.00

STAR BLASTER (British)

(1-2) 1983, Windsor Communications
Publications, 8 1/2 x 11, prozine.
2.50   7.50   15.00
STAR BLASTER SPECIAL
(1-5) 1986   2.50   10.00   15.00

STARBLAZER

(1-4) 1985, Liberty Publications, 8 1/2 x 11, $1.95
and $2.95 cover price, prozine.
2.50   5.00   10.00
STARBLAZER SPECIALS
(1-6) 1984-1986   2.50   5.00   10.00

STAR FORCE

(1-12) 1980-1982, SJ Publications, 8 1/2 x 11,
prozine.   2.50   5.00   10.00

STAR INVADERS

(1-5) 1984-1985, Liberty Publications, 8 1/2 x 11,
prozine.   1.00   3.50   7.50

	Good	Fine	Near Mint		Good	Fine	Near Mint

STARLOG

(1) 1976 August, Vol. 1 No. 1, O'Quinn Publications, 8 1/2 x 11, $1.50 original cover price, one of the first mainstream magazines to capitalize on newer films, and popular TV series - including Star Trek. To the dismay of older fans this trend would never be fully reversed, and old time titles such as *Castle Of Frankenstein* were headed for a permanent grave. The publishers maintained back issue stocks for year, and only a few issues are scarce.

	Good	Fine	Near Mint
	15.00	25.00	50.00
(2-8) 1977	2.50	5.00	10.00
(9)	5.00	10.00	25.00
(10-30)	1.50	3.50	7.50
(31-75)	1.25	2.50	6.00
(76-122)	1.00	2.00	3.50
(123,126) both issues feature Star Trek: The Next Generation.	7.50	15.00	30.00
(124-present)	.50	1.50	2.50

THE BEST OF STARLOG

(1-7) 1980-1986	2.50	5.00	10.00

STARLOG POSTER MAGAZINE

(1-10) 1983-1989	2.50	5.00	7.50

STARLOG SCRAPBOOK

(1-5) 1982-1987	2.50	5.00	7.50
(6) 1987	5.00	10.00	20.00

STARLOG SPECTACULAR

(1-7) 1990-up	2.50	5.00	7.50

STAR TREK
(general reference titles)

(nn's) 1970's, Various Publishers, there were numerous one-shot magazines published related to Star Trek, including Star Trek II Official Movie Magazine; Star Trek The Motion Picture; etc. These magazines had large print runs, and are generally not rare. The following range of price would apply to any one-shot titles.

	1.50	5.00	10.00

STAR TREK POSTER BOOK

(1-17) 1976-1978, Paradise Press Publications, 8 1/2 x 11, 1.00 cover price, very few pages, color on light weight paper, however each issue focused on a specific Star Trek episode, starting with No. 1 "The Cage," a simple formula that proved popular with Star Trek fans.

	2.50	15.00	25.00

STAR WARS OFFICIAL POSTER MONTHLY

(1-18) 1977-1978, Galaxy/Paradise Publications, 8 1/2 x 11, $1.50 cover price, slim color photo prozine.

	2.50	10.00	20.00

STAR WARS: RETURN OF THE JEDI
(1-4) 1983, same publisher.

	1.50	5.00	10.00

STAR WARS SPECTACULAR
(nn) 1977, one-shot, Warren Publications, 8 1/2 x 11, $2.95 cover price, prozine.

	2.50	10.00	20.00

STOP MOTION ANIMATION

(1-2) 1980-1982, Don & Pam Dohler publishers and editors, 8 1/2 x 11, $4.95 cover price, limited distribution, excellent contents and serious coverage.

	10.00	20.00	40.00

STRANGE UNKNOWN

(1-2) 1969, Tempest Publications, 8 1/2 x 11, 50 cents cover price, borderline horror-fiction magazine, not a monster film magazine, prozine.

	7.50	15.00	25.00

	Good	Fine	Near Mint		Good	Fine	Near Mint

SUSPENSE

(#4) 1959 September, Vol. 1 No. 4, Suspense Publications, 8 1/2 x 11, 35 cents cover price, horror-fiction borderline publication, with an early date - not a film-monster magazine, photo-cover, prozine.

50.00 150.00 250.00

TALES OF TERROR FROM THE BEYOND

(nn) 1964 Summer, one-shot, Charlton Publications, 8 1/2 x 11, 35 cents cover price, horror-fiction magazine, not a strict film-monster magazine, prozine.

10.00 15.00 35.00

TANA LEAFLET (Fanzine)

(1) 1973, one-shot, The Count Dracula Society, 8 1/2 x 11, photo off-set cover.

10.00 20.00 30.00

TERATOID GUIDE, THE (Fanzine)

(1-6) 1973-74, Claude D. Plum Jr., 8 1/2 x 11, 1.00 cover price.

5.00 10.00 15.00

TERROR (Fanzine)

(1-3) 1960-61, Larry Byrd editor and publisher, 8 1/2 x 11, 20 cents cover price, hecto color covers, one of the rarest and most sought after of all early monster fanzines. The editor was famous for his B&W cover work for other fanzines, and as early editor for "The Graveyard Examiner" in early issues of FM. The first three issues have Jack Davis-style EC horror cover themes; there are only a handful known to exist in any condition.

100.00 150.00 250.00

(4) 1962, with off-set covers and interior work, more professional in format, with some wider distribution, there are most likely three times the known numbers in existance for #'s 4 and 5 as there are with issues 1 through 3.

50.00 85.00 125.00

(5) format same. 25.00 35.00 50.00

TERROR (Fanzine)

(1-2) Mel Sobel editor & publisher.

	35.00	65.00	100.00
(3,9,)	15.00	30.00	45.00
(4-8,10)	10.00	20.00	30.00

3-D MONSTERS

(1) 1964, Vol. 1 No. 1, Fair Publishing LTD, 8 1/2 x 11, 50 cents cover price, interior first page has 3-D glasses attached by glue on top third of page, these glasses must be attached and intact for the magazine to rate Fine to Near Mint grades, interior pages black and white with only 15 tinted pages for 3-D, most are Aurora model kit environments in 3-D, prozine.

15.00 25.00 40.00

THRILLER

(1) 1962 Feb., Vol. 1 No. 1, Tempest Publications, 8 1/2 x 11, 35 cents cover, photo covers, prozine. Despite the later date of 1962, these three magazines are extremely rare in higher grades. Interior articles are sex/satire with use of modeled photos, some Monster Pix, Zacherley and early L.A. Vampirella TV host included in one article.

50.00 125.00 250.00

(2-3) 1962, May/July #'s 2,3, same format. Second issue with classic Vampire CV.

50.00 125.00 200.00

  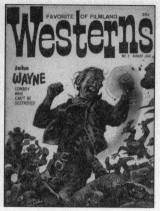 

	Good	Fine	Near Mint		Good	Fine	Near Mint

TOXIC HORROR

(1-5) 1989-1990, Starlog Publications, 8 1/2 x 11, $2.95 cover price, prozine. 3.50 7.50 15.00

TWO WORLDS (Fanzine)

(1-4) 1972-74, William McMichael, 8 1/2 x 11, 50 cents cover price.
    3.50 7.50 15.00

VIDEOOZE (Fanzine)

(1-6) 1991-1992, Bob Sargent editor & publisher, 8 1/2 x 11.
    3.50 7.50 15.00

VIDEO WATCHDOG

(1) 1990, #1, Tim & Donna Lucas Publishers, 8 1/2 x 11, cover price of $4.50, great standard TV oval cover design kept for all cover designs, a very interesting magazine, prozine.
    2.00 5.00 10.00
(2) original first printing, not the second printing.   25.00 35.00 50.00
(4) original 1st printing. 25.00 35.00 50.00
(3, 15, 22, 26-27, 32, 38, 41-42, 48-49)
    2.50 10.00 15.00
(1,2,4,10,11,13,16,19,25,41) available as back issues for 11.00 @.) 2.50 5.00 11.00
(all other issues to present are available as back issues for $8.00 @.) 1.50 3.50 8.00

Note: Back issues in VF+ are available from the publisher, contact 800-275-8395.

WEIRD WORLDS

(1-8) 1978-1982, Scholastic Publications, 8 1/2 x 11, semi-prozine. 3.50 7.50 15.00

WEREWOLVES AND VAMPIRES

(1) 1962, Vol. 1 No. 1, one shot, Charlton Publications, 35 cents cover price.
    20.00 30.00 60.00

FAVORITE WESTERNS OF FILMLAND

(1) 1960, May - Vol. 1 No. 1, Sam Sherman/James Warren editor and publisher, 8 1/2 x 11 format, cover price 35 cents, photo-cover for first issue, prozine. This first issue is extremely scarce in VF or above condition.
    40.00 75.00 150.00
(2) 1960, August, same format.
    35.00 50.00 80.00
(BECOMES WILDEST WESTERNS WITH THIRD ISSUE ONWARD.)

WILDEST WESTERNS

(3,5) 1960, October, same format, cover artwork by Jack Davis. 25.00 40.00 60.00
(4,6) 1961, Jan,May, Aug. - #4 with Jack Davis cover, #'s 5 and 6 with Basil Gogos covers.
    20.00 30.00 45.00

WONDER

(1) 1989, #1, Wonder Publications, Rod Bennett editor, 8 1/2 x 11, $2.95 cover price, first few issues have art covers, semi-prozine.
    20.00 60.00 100.00
(2,4)   20.00 35.00 50.00
(3,5-8)   2.50 5.00 10.00

WONDERAMA
(Forrest J. Ackerman's)

(1) 1993, one-shot, Pure Imagination Publishers, Ackerman editor, 8 1/2 x 11 square spine

	Good	Fine	Near Mint		Good	Fine	Near Mint

format, $7.95 cover price, semi-prozine,
limited distribution.

	2.50	10.00	20.00

WORLD OF BELA LUGOSI
(Fanzine)

(1-2) 1987, Garydon L. Rhodes editor &
publisher, 8 1/2 x 11.

	15.00	30.00	45.00
(3-7) 1989	10.00	20.00	30.00

WORLD FAMOUS CREATURES

(1) 1958 - Oct./ Vol. 1 No. 1 - Leon Howard Ed, 8
1/2 by 11, 35 cents, photos & monster articles,
comic satire involves MAD/Alfred Neuman,
scarce in higher grades, pro-zine.

	50.00	150.00	250.00

(2) 1958 - Dec., L. Howard Ed, format same, 35
cents, the rarest of four issues in higher
grades.

	75.00	200.00	300.00

(3-4) 1959 - Feb.-June, L. Howard Ed, format
same, 35 cents, John Severin art in both issues.

	50.00	125.00	225.00

THE WORLD OF FANDOM

(1) 1985, #1, PLAECO Publications, 8 1/2 x 11, 75
cents cover price, early covers use art and
photo's, semi-prozine at beginning.

	7.50	15.00	25.00
(2-6)	2.50	5.00	10.00

(7) with #6 and #7 now carries the subtitle "The
Important Magazine."
No. 7 special 15th anniversary edition.

	15.00	25.00	40.00
(8-13)	2.00	5.00	8.00

Becomes WORLD OF FANDOM with issue #14.

(14-23)	1.50	3.50	7.50

WORLDS OF HORROR

(1-2) 1989, Eclectic Publications, 8 1/2 x 11,
prozine.

	3.50	7.50	15.00

X POSÉ

(1-20) 1997-1999, David Richardson editor,
published by Visual Imagination LTD, 8 1/4 x
11 1/4, $4.99 cover price, slick color prozine
based on the TV series, and other like media.
All issues are in print.

	2.50	3.50	5.00

PART VIII

COMIC FANZINES AND UNDERGROUND COMIX

UNDERGROUND COMIC BOOKS, FANZINES, MAINSTREAM COMICS, GRAPHIC NOVELS & ALTERNATE PRESS COMICS LISTING WITH A SPECIAL CHAPTER ON SCIENCE FICTION FANZINES

Comics fandom is split about the importance of Underground comics and whether or not they have collectible value. One the one hand many of the original Underground artists had no desire to be a part of the mainstream comics when they began to create 'alternative press' comics as far back as the late 1950's, and there was no rallying cry among the artists when the first Underground guide was authored in the Summer of 1982 - - now over fifteen years ago. The author of this guide (and one of the original publishers of the guide along with Barbara Boatner) remembers that after Bill Griffith had done the original artwork for the cover of the book, this fellow artist and friend Art Spiegelman encouraged him to not turn the work over, and thus not support the new price guide.

Over fifteen years after that initial ground breaking and excellent reference source, the artists and collectors are still split over whether or not there should be a price guide. Many collectors have encouraged Bob Overstreet to list a small percentage of Underground comics, but the size of his book, and the fact that Underground comics never enjoyed traditional distribution, has kept them out of the Annual *Overstreet* guide.

This new listing contained as a separate chapther within the Comic Art Price Guide will attempt to serve collectors upon the following historial basis. First the author himself has been intimately involved with EC fandom, was present at the beginning of the undergound movement, and was involved as a small time distributor, collector, and personal friend to many of the early artists. In the author's opinion the three main historical developments within comics are symbolized by *Action Comics* No. 1, *Mad* No. 1, and then *Zap* No. 1: these three comic book titles represent the three main historical areas of development within comics. Other than funny animal, Disney, Romance, Crime & Horror and other genres, nothing fundamentally different has been marketed in America since the inception of four color comics in newspapers at the turn of the century, and EC either satirized the above mentioned exceptions or published serious titles (*Crime Suspecestories, Modern Love, Saddle Romances, Animal Fables, Tales From the Crypt*) that touched upon these areas of interest.

Whether or not any comics fan will acknowledge that Underground comics should be listed with regular comics or not the following goes without argument. Superman came from science fiction fandom. Without the 1930's fandom, and the development of Siegel and Shuster as young enthusiasts and readers of Edgar Rice Burroughs, H.G. Wells, and other authors of the fantastic, there would be no Golden Age of Comics as we now know it. After the Golden Age of comics EC comics gave rise to a new generation of editors, artists, and publishers and 'funny books' were never the same again. Within this very period of time when EC fandom was at full flower Underground comics got their true jump-off point beginning with the publication of *Mad* at the editorial helm of Harvey Kurtzman. Almost immediately a host of EC inspired *Mad* fanzines began to appear, and the authors and artists of many of these fanzines (Robert Crumb with *Foo*, Jay Lynch with *Jack High*, Skip Williamson with *Wild*, etc.) would go on to create the alternative press Underground comics. Underground comics came 'directly' from WITHIN comics fandom, they are not some alien virus foisted upon the medium!

The author will never forget the moment at the first Sotheby's auction when the newly formed A.C.G. grading committee refused to grade two groups of Underground comics stating that they were not comic books!

This prejudice has continued throughout the 1980's and 1990's, even though mainstream artists such as Berni Wrightson, Michael Kaluta, Wally Wood, Richard Corben, and a host of others were directly involved with publishing and creating artwork for Underground comics. As a matter of fact, the connnection between comics fanzines and Underground comics is also a direct 'overlap' area.

This chapter will list the "important" underground titles, and those titles that overlaped into fanzine formats. Also listed will be important science fiction and comics fanzines, alternative press comics, and newer graphic novels and comic books.

Undergound comics gave rise to self-published comic books. They encouraged the ownership of rights by the artists themselves and they created new areas of distribution before there was a Phil Seuling or any Direct Market. Before there were specialty comic books shops in America, there were head shops, and special book stores that displayed alternative press comic books. Mainstream artists such as Neal Adams and a host of others were encouraged by the Underground example to press the major publishers for the return of original artwork, and other various rights for artists that are now enjoyed by everyone and taken for granted in the current marketplace. The diversity of content (though they were criticized for their violent and sexual subject matter at the time) within Underground comics was as wide as the human experience: from environmental concerns, to human relationships, to the 1960's feminist movement, to science fiction and horror (sometimes in the pure H.P. Lovecraft vein), to satire, to political comics, to strict historical works. Underground comics sought out and succeded in expanding the focus of comic books unlike any other example within the history of the medium.

Information for dates and numbering was taken from the *Illustrated Checklist To Underground Comix*, Archival Press Inc, copyright 1979 Robert Weiner: photographs and historical dating information within this guide taken from the collections of Bill Desmond, Bhob Stewart, John Godin, Bruce Sweeney, Marc Von Arx, and other collectors. This early photo-UG-comix guide was the second important listing of collectible UG comics, following the original Shelby Kirch foldover 5 /2 x 8 /2 UG checklists. The author is also thankful for information provided from the collection of Arnie Schieman; from the collection of Jay Rogers; and from the collection of Peter Flynn. Information on comic book fanzines was provided by Bill Schelly from his own data-base listing and from Michael Cohen who was most helpful providing his own data-base listings for fanzines and their selling prices. The author would like to personally thank these individuals for their time and efforts.

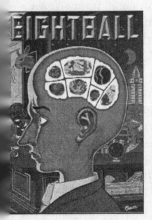

UNDERGROUND COMICS: A WORD ABOUT GRADING AND PRICING AND LISTINGS

The author has used the standard Good, to Fine, to Near Mint, catagories for the price spread on Underground and Newave comics. Collectors will see "radical" spreads on many of these comic prices and wonder how something can be ten times its value from Good to Near Mint. The market bears this out as the Underground Comic book market is still underdeveloped (possibly because of its exclusion from the *Overstreet Guide*, and for a number of other factors) and there are not large numbers of collectors as with Golden Age and Silver Age, or 1950's comic titles. Because of this there is practically "no" market for low grade copies, especially the mid 1970's UG comic titles.

Many old time collectors are shocked to find that dealers have little interest in their collection of 150 to 200 UG comic titles if they are in mixed condition. The difference between demand for 1950's horror and science fiction, or 1940's Golden Age Comics in lower grades compared to Underground comics bears this reality out. Because of this the PRICE RANGE from Good to Near Mint is sometimes extreme as the market now states that 'high-grade' copies are in some demand, and the lower grades are almost 'without demand.' The use of brackets [ ] would indicate that higher grades (for fanzines Fine and above) are extremely RARE, and prices with these brackets could go higher.

The author has chosen to identify Underground comics within the () marks, and he has also used the titles "Underground Comic," and "Independent," to draw the line between the UG comics distributed by Last Gasp, The Print Mint, and Rip Off Press and UG comics that were more "grass-roots" productions with scattered and random distribution. Fanzines, one-shot publications, related newspaper titles, and special books are also listed in this price guide if they were related to the artists or movement of Underground comics as well as the regular comic book fanzines. Thus, the collector can find listings for comic books, fanzines, hardcover editions, special one-shot publications, or any other publication related to the Underground movement herein.

AARDVARK (PAPERS)
1974- No. 1, newspaper covers
          5.00   7.50   15.00

AARDVARK (UG 5 1/2 x 8 1/2 format)
1971- No. 2, Holman cover 6.00   12.50   25.00

ABORTION EVE (UG, Regular)
Nanny Goat Publications, St. Sutton/Lyvely cover
   and artwork.   3.50   7.50   15.00

ABYSS (UG, No. 1 Fanzine crossover)
1973- No. 1, Wrightson cover
          7.50   15.00   35.00
1973- No. 2, Reg-UG size   5.00   10.00   17.50

ACE HOLE (UG, Portfolio, signed)
1974, Art Spiegelman, Ace Hole, Midget
   Detective, Noir/NYC/Satire.
1974- one shot, signed   25.00   50.00   [100.00]

AFTERWORLD (UG, Regular)
Rip Off Press, L. Blake artwork, four issues
only.
1975-76- Nos. 1-4   5.00   10.00   15.00

AIR PIRATES FUNNIES (UG, Regular)
Rip Off Press, Dan O'Neil, London, Halgren
and others take on the Walt Disney
Company, ... and lose. Dist. supressed,
issues somewhat rare.
1971- Nos. 1,2.   15.00   30.00   50.00

ALL CANADIAN BEVER
(UG, Regular)
Rip Off Press, Rand Holmes cover and
interior artwork, sex & guts.
1977- one shot.   10.00   15.00   25.00

ALL GIRL THRILLS (UG, Regular)
The Print Mint, Trina in one of her early UG
titles.
1975- one shot, No. 1   7.50   15.00   25.00

ALL STARS
(Fanzine, and the UG with No.2)
1965- No. 1, Ditko cover 10.00   25.00   45.00
1970- No. 2, 8 1/2 x 11, Griffin cover
         12.50   25.00   [50.00]

ALTERNATE MEDIA COMICS & STORIES (issued with fold-sheet)
Alternative Media, mimeograph printing,
very few pages, Shelton Art.

1970- one shot, with Alt/Media/Sht.
        25.00   45.00   [75.00]

ALL IN COLOR FOR A DIME
(mainstream hardcover book)
1970, Arlington House, no statement of first
   edition on copyright page, 8vo with red cloth
   boards, pictorial dust jacket, edited by Dick
   Lupoff & Don Thompson, the legendary
   articles from *Xero* bought into a hardcover
   eidtion.   25.00   75.00   125.00

ALTER EGO (Fanzine)
The seminal super-hero fanzine of all time.
Editors Roy Thomas and Jerry Bails brought
into focus for fans across the country
everything that was great and creative
about the Golden Age of comics, and the
then developing Silver Age of Comics. The
first two to three issues are extremely rare,
and are seldom available in 'any' condition.
(No. 1) 1961 March - Ditto-Master reproduction,
   copies sent only to fans who responded by
   mail, extremely rare.
        50.00   150.00   [250.00]
(Nos. 2,3) 1961 June/Nov. - same format as issue
   No. 1.   40.00   100.00   [175.00]
(Nos. 4,5) 1962 Oct./1963 March, the first two
   new format issues, with off-set printing, the
   first use of color and much wider distribution,
   these issues are still possible to find in larger
   fanzine collections.   20.00   50.00   85.00
(Nos. 6,7,8) 1964 March/Oct./1965 March - the
   mature issues, editor Roy Thomas in full
   command of production and editorial chores.
   These issues also received even wider
   distribution in fandom and are easier to find
   in high grades.   15.00   35.00   50.00
(9,10) 1965 August/-1969 The final issues of the
   original run, very widly distributed, including
   listings by Bud Plant Comics.
        10.00   25.00   35.00
(11) 1978 - one shot effort with Mike Friedrich,
   wide distribution.   5.00   15.00   25.00

AMAZING DOPE TALES
(UG, Regular)
Independent Press, Distributed through UG
channels, B&W cover, rare.
1967- one shot   25.00   50.00   125.00

AMAZING WORLD OF DC COMICS
(Fanzine, Pro-Published)
1974-78- Nos.1-17, all issues 7.50   15.00   30.00

AMERICAN FLYER FUNNIES
(UG, Regular)
The Print Mint, mixed title with several artists, covers Welz/Sutherland.
1971-72- Nos. 1,2.   7.50   15.00   22.50

AMERICAN SPLENDOR
(UG, 8 1/2 x 11 format)
Clevelands own Harvey Pekar began his comics with everyday life about collecting records, work, girlfriends, work, hanging out, and more work.
1976- No. 1, 2 pg. Crumb story 5.00 15.00   35.00
1977-80- Nos. 2,3,4,5. More Crumb
                  3.50   12.50   25.00
1980's - all issues   2.50   7.50   12.50

AMPUTEE LOVE (UG, Regular)
1974- Last Gasp, one shot 5.00   15.00   25.00

ANOMALY
(Fanzine for Nos. 1-3, then UG with No.4)
1969- No. 1, off-set, Kline Art,etc.
                  15.00   25.00   45.00
1970-71- Nos. 2,3, larger format
                  12.50   25.00   35.00
1973- No.4, Corben Cover (UG)
                  10.00   20.00   30.00

APEX TREASURY OF U.G. COMICS
1974- softcover pb anthology
                  12.50   25.00   37.50

ARCADE, THE COMICS REVUE
(UG /Mag)
1975- Nos. 1-4, Print Mint
                  5.50   15.00   35.00
1976- Nos. 5-7, Print Mint
                  3.50   7.50   15.00

ARMADILLO
(COMIC-TOONS, & COMICS for No. 2)
1969- Ripp Off Press, Franklin art
                  25.00   60.00   125.00
1971- ROP, not as rare, Franklin art
                  7.50   15.00   25.00

ARMAGEDDON (UG, Regular)
1970-73- Nos. 1,2,3. Last Gasp 3.50 7.50   15.00

ARTISTIC COMICS (UG, Regular)
1973-Golden Gate Publications, R. Crumb cover and sketchbook and comic pages, first

printing 75 cents cv.   5.00   15.00   25.00
1977-Kitchen Sink 2nd ed, 1.00 cv.
                  2.50   5.00   7.50

ARTSY FARTSY FUNNIES
(UG,one-shot history)
1974, Paranoia Press, Holland, 8 1/2 x 11 format, one of the first histories of the UG movement, authored by Patrick Rosenkranz & Hugo Van Baren, first printing is only printing.
                  7.50   25.00   45.00

AUSTIN COMIX (UG, Regular)
1976- one shot, J. Bates art.
                  7.50   15.00   22.50

AUSTIN ENQUIRER (UG Newspaper)
1977- October, Shelton Cv.
                  3.50   12.50   25.00

AUSTIN STONE (UG, Regular)
1975- Nos. 1,2. Garrett/Juke art
                  5.00   10.00   20.00

AUSTINTATIOUS (UG, 8 1/2 x 11 format, heavy paper covers)
1973- Bradley/Banman/Turner
                  7.50   15.00   35.00

AVENGING WORLD (UG, Regular)
1973- Steve Ditko Cover & art
                  7.50   15.00   25.00

BACKWATER BABIES
(UG, trade paperback)
1975- Last Gasp, G. Caldwell art
                  3.50   9.50   17.50

BADTIME STORIES (Fanzine)
1971-nn Wrightson C/Cv 12.50 25.00   50.00

BAEGLES LOONEY HEARTS CLUB
(UG, Regular)
1977-one shot with Beatles/Sgt/Pepper take off cover.   7.50   15.00   25.00

BAKERSFIELD KONTRY KOMICS
(UG, Regular)
1973- Last Gasp, Larry Welz
                  3.50   7.50   15.00

BALLOON VENDOR COMIX
(UG, Regular)
1971- ROP, Fred Schrier, glossy cover denotes 1st

printing. 7.50 12.50 25.00

BARBARIAN COMICS
(UG, Regular)
1972-74, Nos. 1-3, 50 cents on 1st.
3.50 7.50 15.00
1975- No. 4, 2.00 price on 1st ed.
5.00 10.00 25.00

BARBARIAN KILLER FUNNIES
(UG, Regular)
1974- No. 1, Comics & Co, 2.50 1st.
3.50 7.50 15.00

BARBARIAN WOMEN COMICS
(UG, Regular)
1975-77- Nos. 1, 2, 1.00 & 2.00 1st.
3.50 10.00 20.00

BAREFOOTZ FUNNIES
(UG, Regular)
1975-76 Nos. 1, 2, 75 cents on 1st Ed.
2.50 5.00 12.50

BARN OF FEAR (UG, Regular)
1977- No. 1, Alcala art, 1.00 on 1st Ed.
3.50 7.50 12.50

BATMANIA (Fanzine)
Bijo White Editor & Publisher, 8 1/2 x 11, hectograph, mimeo with off-set covers, the early 1960's fanzine all about Batman, scarce in all grades.
1964-66- Nos. 1-9, all issues
25.00 50.00 75.00
1967-up Nos. 10-17, all issues
20.00 35.00 55.00

BEER COMIX
(UG, Canadian, Regular)
1971- No. 1, 50 cents glossy covers 1st
5.00 15.00 25.00

BRIDGE CITY BEER COMIX
(title change)
1973- Nos. 2, 3. 50 cents 1st eds 3.50 17.50
35.00

BENT (UG, Regular)
1971, S. Clay Wilson-50 cents 1st
5.00 15.00 30.00

BERKLEY CON PROGRAM
(UG Convention Book)

1973- one shot, 5 1/2 x 8 1/2, all B&W matt paper for 1st printing 7.50 15.00 35.00

BEST OF BIJOU FUNNIES
(UG, paperback trade)
1975- Links, Crumb wraparound cv, 1st printing stated on copyright page. Reprints from Bijou.
7.50 25.00 50.00

BEST OF RIP OFF PRESS
(UG, paperback trade editions)
1972-74- 3.50 price 1st eds.5.00 15.00 35.00

BEYOND TIME AND AGAIN
(UG, Hardcover with dj, long format)
1976- Metzger Art, 1st ed15.00 35.00 [75.00]
1976- Signed edition 25.00 75.00 [125.00]

BICENTENNIAL GROSSOUTS
(UG, Regular)
1976-one shot, W. Stout cover
3.50 7.50 17.50

BIG APPLE COMIX (UG, Regular)
1975- W. Wood Art, 1.00 1st ed.
4.00 8.00 17.50

BIG ASS COMICS (UG, Regular)
1969- No. 1, 50 cents, gloss/p cv-1st
15.00 25.00 50.00
1971- No. 2, 50 cents, gloss/p cv-1st
12.50 20.00 35.00

BIG BABY (Raw-one-shot No. 5 book)
1986, Raw Books, illustrated board covers, no statement of printing on copyright page. Charles Burns artwork. 5.00 15.00 25.00

BIJOU FUNNIES (UG, Regular)
1968- No. 1, commonly called the "Overlap Edition," because interior pages (higher quality off-set paper stock) which are cut uneven are smaller by 1/4 to 1/2 inch than the cover - which overlaps the interior pages much like a pulp magaine, because of this Near Mint copies are almost unknown, extremely rare even as a Fine copy.
125.00 [375.00] [950.00]
1970- 2nd printing distributed through Print Mint, trimmed with pulp interior pages.
25.00 50.00 100.00
1969- No. 2, "Um Tut Sut," on copyright page for 1st edition. 17.50 50.00 125.00

1970- 2nd Ed. by The Print Mint,
7.50   17.50   35.00

1969- No. 3, 50 cents 1st Ed.
15.00   30.00   55.00

1970- No. 4, 50 cents 1st Ed.
15.00   30.00   50.00

1970-71- Nos. 5,6. 50 cents 1st Ed.
12.50   20.00   30.00

1972-73- Nos. 50 cents 1st Ed.
10.00   15.00   25.00

Note: Kitchen Sink Press takes over publication of 1st editions from No. 5.

BINKY BROWN MEETS THE VIRGIN MARY (UG, Regular)

1972- Justin Greens masterpiece work, noted by Film Great Fellini as "the greatest comic I have ever read," cover to cover an entire narrative. First edition is identified by bottom left panel to page 21 (centerfold page, right), having 'virgin mary' drawing printed behind the text - this back printing causes the reader to "not" be able to read the text, and was removed on later printings, gloss cover stock 50 cents cover price.   17.50   35.00   70.00

1974-77- 2nd & 3rd Eds.   3.50   7.50   15.00

BIRDLAND (UG-Newave comic)

(1-3) 1990's, Fantagraphics, Gilbert Hernandez enters the sex comic medium.
1.00   2.50   5.00

BIZARRE SEX (UG, Regular)

1972- No. 1 50 cents 1st Ed.
7.50   17.50   35.00

1972- Nos. 2-6, 50 cents/1.25
5.00   12.50   25.00

Note: No. 4, some copies carried an additional white page cover bound over, with the title and note..."Retailer: Remove this outer cover at your own risk!"   7.50   17.50   35.00

BLACK AND WHITE COMICS

(UG, Regular)

1973- Apex Novelties, matt/gloss cover to 1st edition, all Crumb comix.
7.50   20.00   40.00

BLASE (Fanzine UG/MAD)

Art Spiegelman Editor & Publisher, ditto/hectograph, very limited distribution.

1963-64- all issues   30.00   60.00   [125.00]

BLOWN MIND, THE

(UG, related comic)

1966- P. Yampolsky   25.00   75.00   125.00

BODE BROADS, THE (UG, Portfolio)

1977- Vaughn Bode Plates
17.50   35.00   75.00

BODE'S CARTOON CONCERT

(Regular PB Book Dist)

1973- Dell PB., color cv. 75 cents
7.50   17.50   35.00

BODE'S, VAUGHN - DEADBONE

(Hardcover trade & softcover)

1975- Northern Comfort Communications, issued with light red cloth boards, with color dust jacket, interior pages B&W art, 14.95 original price.   30.00   95.00   250.00

1976-2nd paper edition, 7.95.
12.50   25.00   45.00

BODE'S VAUGHN - CHEECH WIZARD

(UG Hardcover trade)

1976- Northern Comfort Communications, issued with tan cloth boards, with color dust jacket, interior pages B&W artwork, 14.95 original price.   40.00   125.00   275.00

1976-2nd paper edition, 7.95
12.50   25.00   45.00

BODE'S, VAUGHN - EROTICA

(UG, Hardcover trade)

1983- Last Gasp, first edition so stated on copyright page, issued with gloss cover boards, interior pages in full color.
20.00   40.00   80.00

BOGEYMAN COMICS

(UG, Regular, shorter height to size)

1969- SF CBkCo., 35 cents, matt cover.
10.00   25.00   45.00

1969- 50 cents 1st Ed, J.Lynch cover.
7.50   17.50   35.00

1970- 50 cents, stiff covers.
3.50   10.00   20.00

Note: In the 1970's multiple copies in mint surfaced for issue No. 3.

BOOK OF DREAMS

(UG, trade paperback)

1977- John Thompson Art, 3.95
10.00   20.00   35.00

BOOK OF RAZIEL, THE
(UG, Regular)
1969, Print Mint, 50 cents 1st Ed.
                 3.50   12.50   25.00

BRAIN FANTASY (UG, Regular)
1972-74, Nos. 1,2, 50 & 75 cents.
                 3.50   10.00   15.00

BREAKDOWNS
(Mainstream Hardcover)
(HC) 1977, The Belier Press, First printing so
   stated on copyright page, with Belier Press
   pasteover on verso of front free endpaper,
   slick illustrated board covers. Anthology of
   strips by Art Spiegelman.
            25.00   75.00   150.00

BRIDGE CITY REVIEW
(UG, Canadian Regular)
1976- No. 1, photo-cv, 1.00 price   7.50   15.00
   25.00

BUGLE AMERICAN (UG Newspaper)
1970- Covers by Kitchen, Mitchell.
                 5.00   12.50   17.50
1971- Kitchen, Poplaski, Lynch.
                 5.00   12.50   17.50
1972-77 Loft, Green, Other covers.
                 5.00   12.50   17.50

BURNT TOAST
(UG, 1/2 American Review)
1976- text with comix, 75 cents
            12.50   25.00   45.00

BUY THIS BOOK (UG, small paperback)
1965- Dan O'Neil, 1.00 price
              7.50   15.00   25.00

CALIFORNIA COMICS (UG, Regular)
1973-77- Nos. 1-3, .50/1.00/2.00
                 5.00   12.50   17.50

CAN O' BEANS
(UG, Independent, 8 1/2 x 11 format)
1972- Nos. 1,2, Scott/Clyde, 15 cents
            15.00   25.00   35.00
1972- No. 3, 50 cents price 1st Ed.
            35.00   75.00   95.00

Note: the first issue received very limited
distribution.

CAP'N RETRO (UG, Independent)

1977-78- Nos. 1-3. matt covers
            12.50   25.00   35.00

CAPT. GEORGE'S COMIC WORLD PRESENTS (Fanzine-reprints)
1969-1974- all issues   3.50   7.50   15.00

CAPTAIN GUTS (UG, Regular)
1969- No. 1, Larry Welz Art
            10.00   20.00   35.00
1969-71- Nos. 2,3, 50 cents 1st Ed.
            7.50   15.00   20.00

CAPTAIN JOINT COMICS
(UG, Independent)
1966- B. Beckman Art   12.50   25.00   45.00

CASCADE COMIX MONTHLY
(UG, related, news & interview zine)
1978-81- all issues   2.50   7.50   12.50

CEREBUS THE AARDVARK
(UG, Independent)
1977- No. 1, Dave Sim creates one of the most
   popular long running characters, the first
   issue has lower quality printing, matt reds.
            50.00   150.00   300.00
1980's- counterfeit editions entered the USA in
   5 to 7 cities almost on the same day and week
   during the 1980's - inside cover is glossy
   instead of matt, and there are additional
   printing errors on the cover.
            1.50   3.50   7.50
1970's- Nos. 2-6.   7.50   25.00   50.00
1980's- Nos. 7-19.   3.50   10.00   20.00
1980's- Nos. 20-40.   2.50   7.50   15.00
1980's-90's- Nos. 41-100.   2.00   5.00   7.50
1990's-Present (all issues)   .50   2.50   3.50

CHEECH WIZARD
(UG, Independent)
1967- small long format, matt paper, B&W
   cover, pulp paper covers.
            25.00   50.00   [100.00]

CHEECH WIZARD, THE COLLECTED
(UG, Regular)
1972- Co&Sons, 50 cents 1st Ed.
            7.50   17.50   35.00

CHICAGO MIRROR
(UG Newspaper in 8 1/2 x 11 Mag format)
1967- August No. 1, Green Cv.
            12.50   25.00   45.00
1968-Wint. No. 2, Green Cv.

| | 12.50 | 25.00 | 45.00 |

1968-Spring, No. 3, photo Cv.

| | 25.00 | 50.00 | 75.00 |

Note: In depth Nos. of 1 and 2 surfaced during the 1970's, however the No. 3 issue has always been rare and hard to find.

CHOICE MEATS (UG, Regular)
1971-72 Nos. 1,2, 50 cents 1st Ed.

| | 7.50 | 15.00 | 30.00 |

1972- No. 2, second cover 5.00   10.00   20.00

CLOUD COMIX (UG, Regular)
1971- No. 1, states 1st printing

| | 7.50 | 15.00 | 25.00 |

1972- No. 2, Skurski/Carbarga Art

| | 3.50 | 7.50 | 15.00 |

COCAINE COMIX (UG, Regular)
1975- No. 1, Stout Cv, 75 cents 1st Ed

| | 5.00 | 15.00 | 30.00 |

1980-81- Nos. 2,3, 1.50 cover price

| | 3.50 | 10.00 | 20.00 |

CO-EVOLUTION QUARTERLY
(UG related, C-Culture Magazine)
1976-1978- all issues with R. Crumb covers and
  interior art.   3.50   12.50   25.00

COLEMAN PORTFOLIO, JOE
(UG Portfolio)
1970's- one shot   7.50   20.00   35.00

COLLECTED UNCONSCIENCE OF ODD BODKINS (UG PB)
1973- Dan O'Neill, 3.95 1st Ed

| | 12.50 | 25.00 | 50.00 |

COLOR (UG, 5 1/2 x 8 1/2 format)
1971-nn, Print Mint, Moscoso art

| | 7.50 | 25.00 | 45.00 |

COMIC ART (Fanzine)
Legendary fanzine by Don and Maggie Thompson, mimeographed, 8 1/2 x 11, the first three issues with very small distribution, one of the most literate of the early comics fanzines - both editors had strong ties to SF fandom.
1961- No. 1- April   75.00   125.00   [250.00]
1961-62- Nos. 2,3,4. (small print/runs)

| | 50.00 | 100.00 | 150.00 |

1964-68 No. 5,6,7. mimeo 35.00   75.00   100.00

COMIC BOOK MARKETPLACE
(Fanzine)
Published and edited by Gary and Lisa Carter, early issues off-set, quickly attaining professional reproduction, color covers and interior color.
1991- No. 1, newsprint cover stock

| | 12.50 | 25.00 | 60.00 |

1991- Nos. 2-10 color introduced

| | 7.50 | 15.00 | 25.00 |

1991-94- Nos. 11-28 pro-quality

| | 5.00 | 12.50 | 20.00 |

1995-Present - most issues

| | 3.50 | 10.00 | 15.00 |

Note: a number of back issues are still available from the Publisher directly.

COMIC COLLECTORS NEWS
(Fanzine)
Malcom Willits & Jim Bradley Editors & Publisher, hold the distinction of publishing the first continous comics fanzine, mimeograph, copies almost unknown in the marketplace.
1947-48- Nos. 1-6   45.00   125.00   250.00
1949- all issues   35.00   100.00   125.00

COMICOLLECTOR, THE (Fanzine)
1961-63- Nos. 1-13 all issues

| | 12.50 | 25.00 | 35.00 |

COMIC CRUSADER (Fanzine)
Mike Royer and Martin Grime Publishers and Editors, 8 1/2 x 11 off-set.
1968-69 Nos. 2-6, 35cts/cv/pr

| | 10.00 | 25.00 | 35.00 |

1969-76 Nos. 7 up, all issues

| | 7.50 | 15.00 | 25.00 |

1970- No. 13 Steranko special Cv

| | 12.50 | 25.00 | 40.00 |

COMIC FANDOM MONTHLY
(Fanzine)
1971-72- Nos. 1-6, Digest size 7.50   15.00   30.00

THE COMIC READER
(Fanzine-newszine)
1962-63- Nos. 9-21 all issues 5.00   12.50   25.00
1964-67- Nos. 22-up all issues

| | 3.50 | 10.00 | 20.00 |

1969-75 - all issues   2.50   7.50   15.00
1976-Up - all issues   2.00   5.00   10.00

COMIX BOOK (UG Magazine format)
1974-76, Nos. 1-5, 1.00 price 1st Ed.

	Good	Fine	Near Mint
	2.50	7.50	17.50

COMIX UNLIMITED (UG Independent)
1975-76- Nos. 1,2, 60 & 30 cents

	7.50	17.50	35.00

COMMIE COMIX (UG Newspaper)
1971- extremely limited distribution in the Boston, Harvard Square area.

	75.00	125.00	[275.00]

COMMIES FROM MARS
(UG, Regular)
1973- No. 1, Kitchen Sink, 50 cents

	5.00	15.00	25.00

COMPLEAT FART, LEE MARRS
(UG, Regular)
1976- Kitchen Sink, 1.00 price

	3.50	7.50	12.50

CONCEPT (Fanzine)
1956-59- Nos. 1-6,Larry Ivie

	25.00	[50.00]	[75.00]

CONEN/ DR. STRENGE
(UG Magazine format)
1973- nn, stiff covers.

	7.50	20.00	40.00

CONSPIRACY CAPERS
(UG, Regular- one printing only)
1969- nn, Williamson covers,

	12.50	35.00	75.00

COOCHY COOTY MEN'S COMICS
(UG, Regular)
1970- No. 1, R. Williams, 50 cents

	7.50	15.00	25.00

CORBEN, BLOODSTAR
(UG Hardcover Independent)
1976- Morning Star Press, first printing stated on copyright page, issued in grey cloth boards, with color dust jacket, interior pages B&W artwork.

	35.00	75.00	175.00

CORBEN'S, RICHARD - FUNNY BOOK
(UG Hardcover trade)
1976- Nickelodeon Press, issued in black cloth boards, with color dust jacket, interior pages B&W and color artwork, 10.95 cover price.

	25.00	50.00	125.00

CORBEN, RICHARD - FLIGHTS INTO FANTASY (Ug, HC, Mainstream)
1981- Thumb Tack Books, no statement of printing on copyright page, large format with color and B&W artwork, 21.95 cover price, issued in brown cloth with dj.

	25.00	45.00	125.00

CORBEN, RICHARD - WEREWOLF
(UG HC trade)
1984-Catalan Communications, first printing stated on copyright page, hardcover, color interior pages, 12.95 cover price.

	15.00	30.00	50.00

CORN FED COMICS (UG, Regular)
1972-73- Nos. 1, 2, 50 cents 1st Eds.

	3.50	7.50	17.50

CORPORATE CRIME COMICS
(UG, Regular)
1977-79- Nos. 1, 2, 1.00 cover price

	3.50	7.50	15.00

COVER UP LOWDOWN
(UG, small format size)
1977- one shot, Kinney art

	3.50	7.50	15.00

R. CRUMB'S HEAD COMIX
(UG softcover mainstream distribution)
1968, The Viking Press, first edition stated with publication date on copyright page, softcover with stiff covers, 2.50 cover price.

	25.00	50.00	75.00

1968, The Viking Press, hardcover edition with dust jacket, extremely rare, and almost never found in high grades.

	150.00	350.00	[750.00]

1970, Ballantine first printing, larger format, 2.95 cover price.

	20.00	40.00	60.00

1988, Fireside reprint edition, small original format, 8.95 cover price.

	5.00	10.00	25.00

R. CRUMB'S FRITZ THE CAT
(UG softcover mainstream distribution)
1969, Ballantine Books, large format with stiff covers, first printing so stated on copyright page for October, 2.95 cover price.

	25.00	75.00	150.00

Note: later re-released by Ballantine in long single editions, each book covering one of the chapter stories from the original title.

FRITZ BUGS OUT

1972, Ballantine, long 2nd edition reprint, 1.00 cover price.

5.00   20.00   35.00

FRITZ THE NO-GOOD

1972, Ballantine, long 2nd edition reprint, 1.00 cover price.   5.00   20.00   35.00

R. CRUMB'S CARLOAD OF COMICS
(UG Paperback book)

1976- Belier Press 6.00 1st printing so stated on copyright page.

                12.50   45.00   75.00

R. CRUMB'S CARLOAD OF COMICS
(UG-promo comic)

1976- one shot, issued in color

                10.00   25.00   35.00

R. CRUMB (Alexander Gallery Hardcover limited Catalogue)

1993- R. Crumb A Retrospective- Alexander Gallery- blue cloth boards, with front cover paste-down illustration, includes B&W and full color process interior illustrations, issued No. 'ed with one dollar bills, the catalogues noted in pencil with serial No. of bill, many copies were destroyed after being bound, extremely recent - however extremely rare.

          250.00 350.00   500.00

R. CRUMB CHECKLIST
(Hardcover/Softcover trade)

1981- Fall, Boatner Norton Press- issued in brown cloth boards, with color illustrated dust jacket, authored by Donald M. Fiene, first edition so stated on copyright page, hardcover edition limited to 1,000 copies.

          75.00 150.00   225.00

1981- Softcover trade edition

          12.50   25.00   45.00

THE COMPLETE CRUMB
(Hardcover & Softcover trade, series)

1987- Volume One, The Early Years of Bitter Struggle- Fantagraphics, issued in hardcover signed and No. 'ed by R. Crumb in edition of 1,500 copies.   50.00 100.00 150.00

1988- Volume Two, Some More Early Years of Bitter Struggle- Fantagraphics, issued in hardcover boards with index card pastedown on inside front cover, signed and No. 'ed by Crumb in edition of 600 copies.

          40.00   75.00   125.00

1988- Volume Three, Starring Fritz The Cat- Fantagraphics, issued in hardcover signed and No. 'ed by Crumb in edition of 600 copies.

          35.00   60.00   120.00

1989- Volume Four, Mr. Sixties!- Fantagraphics, issued in hardcover signed and No. 'ed by R. Crumb in an edition of 600 copies, index card pastdown inside front cover.

          35.00   60.00   120.00

1990- Volume Five, Happy Hippy Comix- Fantagraphics, issued in hardcover signed and No. 'ed by R. Crumb with index card pastedown on inside front cover in edition of 600 copies.

          35.00   60.00   120.00

R. CRUMB SKETCHBOOK
(Hardcover Boxed editions)

1978- the 1974-78 YEARS, Zwei Tausend Eins, first edition so stated on copyright page, black cloth boards, with newsprint insert, boxed in grey cardboard.

          75.00 150.00   250.00

1981- 1966-67 YEARS, Zwei Tausend Eins, first edition so stated on copyright page, black cloth with color illustration on front cover, newspaper index insert, this edition with many full color page illustrations, boxed in grey cardboard.

        100.00 200.00   350.00

1984- July 1978 to Nov. 1983 YEARS, Zwei Tausend Eins, black cloth with green spine, first edition so stated on copyright page, boxed in grey cardboard.

          50.00   75.00   150.00

1986- the late 1967- to mid 1974 YEARS, Zwei Tausend Eins, black cloth with blue spine, red ink to pgs. 187-191, first edition so stated on copyright page, with newspaper insert index to artwork, boxed in grey cardboard.

          50.00 100.00   175.00

1989- Nov. 1983 to April 1987 YEARS, Zwei Tausend Eins, black cloth with grey corner ponts and grey spine, newspaper index insert, in grey cardboad box.

          50.00   75.00   150.00

1993- May 1987 to April 1991 YEARS, Zwei Tausend Eins, black cloth with red corner points and red spine, newspaper index text insert, in grey cardboard box.

          50.00   75.00   125.00

1993- Same as above, however issued with

special newspaper wrapped sheet cover which folds over and is sealed with two circular pieces of tape, the paper carried R. Crumb design motif- with this paper intact in fine.

75.00   125.00   250.00

R. CRUMB'S COMICS & STORIES
(UG, 5 1/2 x 8 1/2 format)
1969- Print Mint, with stiff covers

7.50   15.00   35.00

CUNT COMICS (UG, small format)
1969- No. 1, R. Hayes, one printing

25.00   50.00   100.00

CURSE OF THE MOLEMEN
(mainstream book)
1991, Kitchen Sink Press, illustrated boards, released in signed edition of 1,000 copies each signed and No. 'ed by artist Charles Burns, this is a colored version of the earlier BIG BABY book published by Raw Books.

10.00   20.00   30.00

DAN O'NEILL'S COMICS & STORIES
(UG, Regular)
1971- Nos. 1-3, 50 cents 1st Ed.

12.50   25.00   35.00

1975- Vol 2, Nos. 1, 2. 1.00 price

3.50   7.50   17.50

DAS KAMPF
(UG, loose sheets, long format)
1963- Self published by the artist while he was a student at Syracuse University, 100 loose sheets, off-set B&W, with 13 page hecto booklet stapled with inventory of titles, considered the RAREST of all early proto-type Underground comics. Very few copies got out, given to friends and associates by the artist, given NO distribution of any kind in the underground market, because of the nature of the loose pages, copies could turn up incomplete.   1,250   3,500   [5,000]
1977-Reprint, off-set format.

7.50   15.00   30.00

DEADBONE EROTICA
(UG paperback book)
1971- nn, Bantam Bks, 1.95

7.50   25.00   45.00

DEAD STORIES (UG, Independent)
1982- Mag/format, signed Byer

15.00   35.00   55.00

DEATH RATTLE (UG, Regular)
1972-73- Nos. 1-3. 50 cents 1st Ed.

5.00   10.00   20.00

DEEP 3-D COMIX
(UG, color Jaxon/Corbon story- Regular size)
1970- No. 1, Corben Cv, 75 cents 1st

10.00   25.00   40.00

1971- 2nd printing 1.00   3.50   7.50   15.00

DEMENTED PERVERT
(UG, Regular)
1971-72- Nos. 1,2, 50 cents 1st Ed

3.50   7.50   15.00

DESPAIR (UG comic)
(nn) No date, no copyright information listed on first edition, cover stock has gloss, printing gap can be viewed on lower left corner of some copies, the trimming can vary on individual issues. R.Crumb art throughout.

7.50   25.00   40.00

1971- 2nd printing, with c. info

3.50   7.50   15.00

1970's- later printings   1.50   3.50   7.50

DEVIANT SLICE FUNNIES
(UG, Regular)
1972-73- Nos. 1,2, 50 cents 1st Eds.

5.00   12.50   25.00

DIE GRETCHEN (UG, Independent)
1973- nn, 50 cents 1st Ed. 17.50   35.00   75.00

Note: Though rare, a number of these comics surfaced in near mint condition in the early 1970's.

DIRTY DUCK BOOK (UG, Regular)
1972- nn, Co & Sons, 50 cents 1st

5.00   15.00   30.00

DIRTY LAUNDRY COMICS
(UG, Regular)
1974- No. 1, 75 cents 1st Ed, Crumbs

7.50   15.00   30.00

1977-80's Nos. 2,3.   3.50   7.50   15.00

DR. ATOMIC (UG, Regular)
1972- No. 1, 50 cents 1st Ed 7.50   15.00   25.00
1970's- later printings have 75 and up

1.50   3.50   5.00

1973-76- Nos. 2,3,4. .50/.75/1.00 cv/pr

3.50   7.50   15.00

1979-81- Nos. 5,6. 1.25/1.50 cv/pr
3.50   7.50   12.50

DR. WERTHAMS COMICS & STORIES (UG, Independent)
1976-79- Nos. 1-4. 1.00/1.50 cv/pr
5.00   15.00   25.00
1976-79- 1-4 signed & #'d ed
12.50   25.00   50.00

DOOMSDAY (UG, Independent)
1973- No. 1, 50 cents 1st Ed.
25.00   50.00   100.00

DOPIN' DAN (UG, Regular)
1972-73- Nos. 1-3. .50/.50/.75 cv/pr
5.00   10.00   17.50

DOUGLAS COMIX (UG, Regular)
1972- nn, giveway, Spiegelman Cv
25.00   75.00   125.00

DRAWINGS BY S. CLAY WILSON
(UG, Mag/B&W/format)
1969-nn, flat cover stock, 2.00 1st Ed
45.00   125.00   [275.00]

DUTCH TREAT (UG, Regular)
1977- Kitchen Sink,1.00 1st Ed.
3.50   7.50   15.00

DYING DOLPHIN (UG, Regular)
1970- nn, Print Mint, 50 cents 1st Ed
5.00   15.00   25.00

EARTH ISLAND
(UG magazine with R. Crumb cover only)
1970- No. 1, Editorial Energy Center, 8 1/2 x 11, 50 cents cover price.   2.50   15.00   35.00

EAST VILLAGE, OTHER, THE
(UG Newspaper)
1967-68- Covers by Spain, Thompson, Spiegelman, Deitch, Bode.
1967-March 17; Apr. 19; May 1; Oct. 22: for 1968 Apr 9; June 7; Oct. 4; Oct. 11; Oct. 25 (Bode); Nov. 8; Nov. 15; Dec. 20.
12.50   25.00   40.00
1967- Oct. 4, R. Crumb Cover
25.00   75.00   [150.00]
1969-70- Covers by Hayes, Deitch, W. McCay, Spain, Bode, Spiegelman, Shelton, Yossarian, Tomlinson.
1969- Jan. 3; Jan. 24 (Bode); Mar. 1; Mar. 14 (Bode); Mar. 21; May 7; May 21; June 11, 18;

July 2; Oct. 15; Nov. 12; Dec. 3, 10, 17, 24; for 1970- Jan. 28; Mar. 24; Apr. 7, 28; May 5; Aug. 8; Oct. 13, 20; Dec. 27 (Bode).
12.50   25.00   40.00
1970- Feb. 11 & Mar. 16- R. Crumb
25.00   55.00   [100.00]
1971-72 Covers by Todd, Yossarian, Spain, Holland. For 1971 Jan. 12; Mar. 30; Apr. 20, 27; May 4; June 1, 23; Oct. 6, Nov. 3; Feb. 2.
10.00   20.00   35.00
1967-72 regular non-comix issues
7.50   12.50   25.00

Note: It is extremely rare for any of these Newspapers to turn up without having being previously folded in half, the Near Mint column would require no folds. The R. Crumb Cover issues, and special "comix" issued of EVO are sought after by collectors who want a more complete collection.

EAT IT (R. Crumb cookbook, trade paper)
1979- R. Crumb art, 1.95 1st Ed
7.50   25.00   35.00

THE COMPLETE EC CHECKLIST
(Fanzine-Checklist)
Fred Von Bernewitz, small mimeograph 8 1/2 x 5 1/2 format.
1955-nn-June (50 print run) 1st
50.00   100.00   [250.00]
1956, 2nd & 3rd printings
25.00   50.00   125.00

THE FULL EDITION OF THE COMPLETE EC CHECKLIST
Joe Vucenic, updated with all Pre-Trend EC titles included, Davis Cover.
1963-nn, yellow cvs/1.50 cv/pr
35.00   75.00   125.00
1974-2nd print/rpt/"Zombie Terror"
25.00   50.00   75.00

EC FAN ADDICT (EC Fanzine)
1967-68- Nos. 1-3. ditto & off-set
15.00   25.00   35.00

THE EC FAN BULLETIN
Bhob Stewart, Editor & Publisher, hectograph, 8 1/2 x 11. The first Comic Book fanzine.
1953- No. 1-Summer, Stewart/Cv
250.00   [500.00]   [950.00]
1953- No. 2-October, Spicer/Cv
150.00   [250.00]   [375.00]

Note: Only one or two copies are known to exist of the No. 1 issue.

EC LIVES (Fanzine)
1972-nn,B&W off-set/8 1/2 x 11
| | 20.00 | 40.00 | 80.00 |

EC PORTFOLIO (Fanzine-Portfolio)
1972 (One), Russ Cochran, large format 16 1/2 x 10 3/4, stiff covers, all white covers with EC logo embossed on front cover, limited printing.
| | 35.00 | 100.00 | 200.00 |

1972 (Two), Russ Cochran, large folio format, first color cover, square bound format for binding.
| | 30.00 | 100.00 | 175.00 |

1973 (Three), Russ Cochran, large folio, interior covers & cover with new coloring from Marie Severin.
| | 15.00 | 35.00 | 75.00 |

1973 (Four), Russ Cochran, large folio, continuing format.
| | 15.00 | 35.00 | 75.00 |

Note: These portfolios were published by Russ Cochran in cooperation with legendary EC publisher William M. Gaines. Russ went to NYC and obtained direct access to the original EC artwork that was stored in the Gaines Vault, thus giving the portfolios remarkable reproduction for the black and white stories. The Fan response was so positive, with the new Cochran/ Gaines partnership now established, that Russ could conceive the massive EC reprint boxed sets. These EC Boxed sets represent an historic change for comics fandom, thus these portfolios are remembered for blazing a new path in the comics market.

EIGHTBALL (UG-Newave comic)
1989- No. 1, August, Fantagraphics, Daniel Clowes artwork, 1st Ed, 2.00 cover price, 6 3/4 x 10 1/4 format.
| | 1.75 | 3.50 | 7.50 |

1990- Nos. 2-4, 2.00 cv/pr
| | 1.50 | 2.50 | 5.00 |

1991-92- Nos. 5-10, 2.25 cv/pr
| | 75 | 2.00 | 3.50 |

(Nos.11-present) format the same, most issues in print.

ELFQUEST (Independent)
FANTASY QUARTERLY, FEATURING ELFQUEST
1978-No. 1, Warp Graphics, matt cover stock, color cover, first printed appearance of Wendy Pini's characters, 1.00 cover price.

1978, No. 1
| | 25.00 | 45.00 | [65.00] |

ELFQUEST No. 1, 1.00 cv/pr/1st '79
| | 12.50 | 25.00 | 35.00 |

1978- No. 2, 1.00 cv/pr/1st Ed.
| | 10.00 | 20.00 | 27.50 |

1978-81-Nos. 3-10 1.00/1.50 cv/pr
| | 7.50 | 12.50 | 17.50 |

1981-85- Nos. 11-21, last mag sizes.
| | 3.50 | 5.50 | 7.50 |

EL PERFECTO (UG, Regular)
1973- nn, Print Mint, 50 cents 1st
| | 7.50 | 15.00 | 30.00 |

ENCLAVE (Fanzine UG/MAD)
1963- Nos. 1-5 (scarce) | 25.00 | 50.00 | [80.00] |

ETERNAL COMICS (UG, Regular)
1973- J. Thompson, 50 cents 1st Ed
| | 5.00 | 15.00 | 25.00 |

ETERNAL TALES
(UG, magazine format)
1972- nn, stiff paper cvs, 1.00 cv/pr
| | 12.50 | 25.00 | 50.00 |

ETERNAL TRUTH (UG, Regular)
1974- No. 1, 50 cents 1st Ed.
| | 5.00 | 10.00 | 20.00 |

EVERWUCHAWE (UG, Regular)
1973- nn, 50 cents 1st Ed. only
| | 15.00 | 35.00 | 75.00 |

Note: Though this comic is rare, a small number in VF/NM turned up in the early 1970's.

EXILE INTO CONSCIOUSNESS
(UG special portfolio, boxed)
1970 - Rip Off Press, limited to an edition of 1,000 copies, each signed and numbered by Jack Jaxon on the backside paste-down sheet, 11 1/4 x 8 1/4, boxed in intricate fold over box, loose interior pages, original price of 2.95. This edition became scarce by the late 1970's and is difficult in higher grades.
| | 50.00 | 125.00 | 250.00 |

EYE (Fanzine)
1965-69- Nos. 1,2. Bijou White
| | 25.00 | 50.00 | 75.00 |

E.Z.WOLF (UG, Regular)
1977- nn, T. Richards, 75 cents 1st
| | 5.00 | 10.00 | 17.50 |

E.Z. WOLFS ASTRAL OUTHOUSE
(UG, 5 1/2 x 8 1/2 format)
1977- nn, T. Richards, 75 cents

| | 5.00 | 10.00 | 15.00 |

FACTS O' LIFE SEX EDUCATION
FUNNIES (UG, Regular)
1972, Shelton Cv, 50 cents 1st Ed.

| | 7.50 | 15.00 | 25.00 |

FANBOY, ALFRED JUDSON'S
(UG, fanzine independent)
1976-79- nn, Xerox, 1.00 price

| | 12.50 | 25.00 | 50.00 |

FANFARE (EC Fanzine)
1959-nn-one shot single sheet

| | 25.00 | 35.00 | 45.00 |

1959- Nos. 1,2. Hecto/mimeo

| | 50.00 | 75.00 | [100.00] |

FANFARE (Fanzine)
1977-80- Nos. 1-4, Spicer Editor

| | 7.50 | 15.00 | 30.00 |

FAN FREE FUNNIES
(UG, Independent)
1973- Nos. 1-3. giveway/25 cents

| | 12.50 | 25.00 | 35.00 |

FANTAGOR
(Fanzine, then UG Regular)
1970- No. 1, Corben/Publisher 1.50/pr

| | 25.00 | 50.00 | 100.00 |

1970- No. 1 UG, Last Gasp, 50 cents

| | 7.50 | 17.50 | 35.00 |

1972- No. 2, Color, 1.00 1st Ed

| | 10.00 | 25.00 | 45.00 |

1972- Nos. 3,4, Corben, 75 cents 1st

| | 7.50 | 15.00 | 30.00 |

FANTASTIC EXPLOITS (Fanzine)
1969-79-Nos. 15-23, comic/reprints

| | 10.00 | 20.00 | 35.00 |

FANTASTIC FANZINE (Fanzine)
1969-70- Nos. 10-12.

| | 12.50 | 25.00 | 37.50 |

FANTASTIC FANZINE SPECIAL
(Fanzine)
1972-one shot

| | 10.00 | 20.00 | 30.00 |

FANTASY HERO (Fanzine)
1964- Nos. 3,4. Dubay/GGF/Pub

| | 20.00 | 50.00 | [85.00] |

FANTASY HERO'S HANGOUT
(Fanzine)
1964- No. 1, GGF/Bauman/Dubay

| | 17.50 | 35.00 | 60.00 |

FANTASY ILLUSTRATED (Fanzine)
Bill Spicer editor & publisher, the premier comics fanzine of the 1960's.
1963- No. 1, Winter, 9 1/2 x 6 1/2

| | 50.00 | 100.00 | 250.00 |

1964- Nos. 2-4. same format

| | 35.00 | 75.00 | 150.00 |

1966- No. 5, Spring Crandall/ERB/cv

| | 40.00 | 80.00 | 125.00 |

1966-68- Nos. 6-9. 8 1/2 x 11

| | 25.00 | 50.00 | 75.00 |

1969- No. 10 Special Bodé issue

| | 40.00 | 80.00 | 125.00 |

1970-73 Nos. 11-15, 8 1/2 x 11

| | 20.00 | 40.00 | 75.00 |

Note: Title change to Graphic Story Magazine with issue No. 9. Also the Editor continues his interests with fanzine publishing with FANFARE in the 1970's.

FARK COMIX (UG, Regular)
1969- nn, 50 cents 1st Ed

| | 17.50 | 35.00 | 75.00 |

FAT FREDDIES CAT, THE ADV. OF
(UG, 5 1/2 x 8 1/2 format)
1977-78- Nos. 1-4. 75 cents 1st

| | 5.00 | 12.50 | 25.00 |

FAT FREDDIES CAT
(UG, paperback book)
1977- one shot, 3.95 price

| | 7.50 | 17.50 | 35.00 |

FAT LIP FUNNIES
(UG, Independent)
1969- nn, matt yellow cv 1st Ed.

| | 27.50 | 55.00 | 125.00 |

1969- nn, orange & tan cvs also 1st

| | 27.50 | 55.00 | 125.00 |

FEDS AND HEADS (UG, Regular)
1968- Gilbert Shelton, first printed in Texas and then taken west for distribution, first printing has flat/matt surface cover, 35 cents price, scarce in higher grades and considered historically important.

| | 75.00 | 225.00 | [350.00] |

1969- 2nd Ed, Print Mint, 35 cents

| | 15.00 | 35.00 | 75.00 |

1970's- later printings, 50/75 cents

| | 3.50 | 7.50 | 9.50 |

FEELGOOD FUNNIES (UG, Regular)
1972, nn, RO/Press, 50 cents 1st Ed

| | 7.50 | 15.00 | 30.00 |

FELCH COMICS
(UG, small format, sex satire)
1975- No. 1, no price on Cv for 1st Ed

| | 12.50 | 25.00 | 35.00 |

FEVER DREAMS (UG, Regular)
1972- nn, Corben art, 50 cents 1st

| | 10.00 | 20.00 | 35.00 |

FIGHTING HERO COMICS (Fanzine)
G.B. Love Editor, the first comics fanzine devoted entirely to original fan hero comic stories, 8 1/2 x 11, 20 cents original cover price.
1963-Nos. 1-7, one printing

| | 15.00 | 35.00 | [75.00] |

1964- Nos. 8-11- all issues 12.50   50.00   60.00

FIRST KINGDOM (UG, Regular)
1974-75- No. 1-5, Katz, 1.00 1st Ed

| | 5.00 | 12.50 | 25.00 |

1976-78- No. 6-14, Katz 1.00/1.50

| | 3.50 | 7.50 | 12.50 |

FLAMED-OUT FUNNIES
(UG, Regular)
1975-76- Nos. 1,2. 75 cents 1st Eds

| | 5.00 | 12.50 | 25.00 |

FLAMING BALONEY
(UG, magazine format)
ND-Pekar/Dumm/Budget   5.00   15.00   25.00

FLAMING CARROT COMICS
(UG, Magazine & then Comic size)
1981- No. 1, Bob Burden, #ed by hand to 6,500
for 1st edition   25.00   45.00   60.00
1981- No. 1, #ed as proof copies

| | 35.00 | 75.00 | 125.00 |

1982-84- Nos. 2-6, 1.70 cv/pr

| | 7.50 | 15.00 | 30.00 |

1985-86- Nos. 7-12, 1.70 cv/pr

| | 5.00 | 10.00 | 20.00 |

1980's-present, all issues   3.50   7.50   9.50

FLESHAPODS FROM EARTH
(UG, Canadian)

1974- nn, 65 cents 1st/pr only

| | 10.00 | 25.00 | 40.00 |

FOG CITY COMICS (UG, Regular)
1977- No. 1, 1.00 1st Ed.   3.50   7.50   15.00

FOO! (Fanzine, Charles & Robert Crumb)
1958- No. 1-Sept. early Xerox printing, 6 1/2 x 9 format, done in response to Harvey Kurtzman's *Mad*, 15 cents cover price, extremely limited distribution (with original print runs of only 300 copies) to comics fandom (John Benson and a few EC fans heard of and ordered copies), possibly no more than 20 copies known to exist.

| | 375.00 | 950.00 | [1,500.00] |

1958- No. 2, Oct. off-set printing, "V-Vampires" satire cover signed C. Crumb, features Dracula satire, Fred Von Bernewitz letter, Mike Britt contro.

| | 350.00 | 750.00 | [1,250.00] |

1958- No. 3, Nov. off-set printing, "Khrushchev Visits U.S.!" and "Noah's Ark," by R. Crumb.

| | 350.00 | 750.00 | [1,250.00] |

1980- Facsimile Reprint, in envelope, in #ed edition of 800 copies.   25.00   75.00   125.00

FOOM (Fanzine-Pro/Published)
1973-78- Nos. 1-21 all issues 3.50   7.50   17.50

FORBIDDEN KNOWLEDGE
(UG, Regular)
1975- No. 1, 75 cent 1st Ed.   5.00   10.00   20.00

FOX COMICS, TALES OF THE
(UG, Independent)
1972, No. 1, matt/cv 50 cents 1st Ed.

| | 12.50 | 25.00 | 50.00 |

FRANK FRAZETTA SPECIAL
(Fanzine)
1964-one shot, Canadian   15.00   25.00   45.00

FRAZETTA (Fanzine)
1972-nn, one shot   12.50   25.00   35.00

FRAZETTA 100 DRAWINGS
(Fanzine)
1975-nn, one shot   15.00   35.00   55.00

THE FRAZETTA TREASURY
(Fanzine)
1975-nn, one shot, 8 1/2 x 11

| | 12.50 | 25.00 | 45.00 |

FRAZETTA, MAGIC OF FRANK
(Fanzine)
1980-one shot B&W   12.50   25.00   35.00

FREAK BROTHERS, THE FABULOUS FURRY
(UG, Regular)
1971- No. 1, Gilbert Shelton begins "the" most
popular Underground title after ZAP comics;
what WDC&S was to the 1950's the FreakBRO
comix were to the 1970's. Going through
multiple print runs, only the No. 1 and No. 2
first printings have been desirable in past
years. First edition for No. 1 is identified by
the tire being "black-dark-grey" as a 'solid'
color, with 50 cents cover price.
                    45.00 175.00 350.00
1972-74- 2nd & 3rd printings
                    3.50   10.00   20.00
1972- No. 2, verso/cv/B&W only
                15.00   30.00   60.00
1973-80- Nos. 3-6, 50/75/1.25 cv/pr
                7.50   15.00   25.00
1980's- Nos. 7 to present 2.50   7.50   15.00

FRESNO COMIX (UG, Regular)
1973- nn, giveway, one printing
                40.00   75.00 150.00

FRESNO FUNNIES
(UG, larger format)
1973- No. 1, signed copies 25.00   75.00 125.00
1975- No. 2, 75 cents 1st Ed
                12.50   25.00   35.00

FRITZ THE CAT, THE COMPLETE
(UG, trade paperback)
1978- Belier Press, reprints with some new
pencil material, 6.00 cover price, no statement
of printing on copyright page, heavy paper
wraps.   15.00   25.00   50.00

FRITZ THE CAT, THE LIFE AND DEATH OF (UG, paperback)
1993- Fantagraphics, 1st edition so stated on
copyright page, 9.95 cover price, reprints with
new cover art.   7.50   15.00   27.50

FRITZ THE CAT, R. CRUMB'S
(UG, Mainstream large paperback)
1969- Ballantine Books, first edition so stated on
copyright page, large 13 x 10 inch format,
2.95 cover price, stiff paper wraps, mass
distribution however still scarce in higher
grades.   35.00 150.00 350.00

FRITZ BUGS OUT
(UG, long format paperback)
1972- Ballantine, 1.00 cv/pr, reprints first chapter
printed in long format. 15.00   45.00   75.00

FRITZ THE NO-GOOD
(UG, long format paperback)
1972- Ballantine, 1.00 cv/pr, reprints third
chapter in long format PB.
                15.00   45.00   75.00

FUNNY AMINALS (UG comic)
1972 (No. 1) - Apex Novelties, 1st printing 50
cents with matt cover paper.
                7.50   15.00   40.00

FLASH GORDON
(Pulp magazine with color comics type
cover and interior illustrations) "The
Master of Mars."
1930's, no date or publisher information, 10 x 7
1/2, 10 cents cover price, comic type cover and
binding.   75.00 100.00 150.00

FUNNYWORLD (Fanzine)
1968-70- Nos. 10-12, 1.00 cv/pr
                25.00   45.00   75.00
1971-79- Nos. 13-21, all issues
                12.50   25.00   35.00

FOX RIVER PATRIOT (UG Newspaper)
Covers by Kitchen: for 1977- Oct., Nov. 9, 23;
Dec. 7, 21; for 1978- Feb. 6
.   7.50   15.00   27.50
1977-Aug. 25, R. Crumb. 15.00   30.00   50.00

FUNNY PAPERS, THE
(UG Newspaper)
With color covers, by R. Crumb, Bodé, and
Ted Richards.
1975- Feb./Mar./Apr.   7.50   15.00   35.00

GARBAGE COMIX (UG, Regular)
1973- No. 1, Krus/McDonald, 45 cents
                10.00   20.00   40.00

GAS COMIX (UG, Promotional)
1970- No. 1, gloss/cv, .05 cents cv/pr
                35.00   75.00 175.00
1970- No. 2, gloss/cv, .15 cents cv/pr
                35.00   75.00 175.00

Note: John Shelton, Franklin, & Texas artists
appear in one of the very best of the
'grass-roots' undergrounds; highly sought

after, and scarce.

GAY HEART THROBS (UG, Regular)
1976-81- Nos. 1,2,3. 1.00/2.00 cv/pr
| | 3.50 | 7.50 | 15.00 |

GHOST MOTHER COMICS
(UG, 5 1/2 x 8 1/2 format)
1968- No. 1, matt/cv, 35 cents 1st Ed.
| | 15.00 | 30.00 | [60.00] |

GIMMIE A BREAK COMIX
(UG, Independent)
1972- No. 2, no/cv/pr 1 printing only
| | 45.00 | 125.00 | 175.00 |

GIRLS AND BOYS
(UG, mini-Independents)
1979-1981- all issues, small mini comic hand made by artist Lynda Berry, with colored paper sheet covers, hand stamped designs, interior B&W Xerox comix, 1.00 each to the very few who ordered them, a total of approximately 20+ numbers, extremely scarce.
| | 15.00 | 30.00 | [50.00] |

GIRL FIGHT COMICS (UG, Regular)
1972-74- Nos. 1,2. 50 cents cv/pr
| | 7.50 | 15.00 | 22.50 |

GIVE ME LIBERTY (UG, Regular)
1976- nn, 75 cents 1st Ed   5.00   15.00   25.00
1976- Paperback edition   3.50   12.50   25.00
35.00

GLASS CITY GIGGLES
(UG, Independent)
1974-75- Nos. 1-4, giveway/one prnt.
| | 12.50 | 25.00 | 37.50 |

GOD NOSE
(UG, Magazine Format on 1st, then Comic Regular)
1964- Jack Jackson, self published in Austin Texas before he moved to San Francisco and began his Rock Poster & Comic career. Mimeographed pages, light pink colored cover paper, 8 1/2 x 11, no cover price, artwork by Jaxon, extremely limited distribution- only a few taken to West Coast by the artist.   350.00   750.00   [1,500]
1969- ROPress, 50 cents cv/pr
| | 15.00 | 25.00 | 50.00 |
1970's- later printings   3.50   7.50   9.50

GOOD JIVE COMIX (UG, Regular)
1972-73- Nos. 1,2. 50 cents cv/pr
| | 3.50 | 7.50 | 17.50 |

GOOGIEWAUMER COMICS
(UG, Regular)
1969- Print Mint, 50 cents 1st Ed   10.00   25.00
50.00

GOOSE LAKE GAGS
(UG, Independent)
1970- No. 1, 25 cts cv/pr one printing
| | 22.50 | 45.00 | 85.00 |

THE GOLDEN AGE (Fanzine)
1966-71- Nos. 2-7, all issues 7.50   15.00   25.00

GOPHER FREEDOM
(UG, Canadian Regular)
1975- No. 1, no/cv/pr one printing only
| | 12.50 | 25.00 | 45.00 |

GOSH WOW (Fanzine)
1967-69- Nos. 1,2,3. Bodé/etc.
| | 25.00 | 50.00 | 85.00 |

GOTHIC BLIMP WORKS
(UG, Newspaper)
1969- The East Village Other Newspaper responded to the popularity of the UG comics and issued this special comix newspaper, issues that are flat and unfolded are extremely rare, paper quality is low from pulp stock, 16 1/2 x 11 1/2, color covers, Crumb/Deitch/Lynch/ Spain/Bodé/Metzger & others. No. 1- Crumb cv.   35.00   95.00   [175.00]
1969- No. 2, Crumb/Cv scarcer #
| | 50.00 | 125.00 | [200.00] |
1969- Nos. 3-7, 35 cents cv/pr
| | 25.00 | 75.00 | [125.00] |
1969- No. 8, Crumb/Cv, scarcer #
| | 55.00 | 125.00 | [150.00] |

Note: *Gothic Blimp Works* had one printing, the 1st printing for each issue.

GRAPHIC FANTASY (Fanzine)
1982-83- Nos. 1,2,3.   7.50   12.50   25.00

GRAPHIC GALLERY
(Auction Catalogue-Independent)
Early listings of Original Comics artwork for sale by Russ Cochran, 8 1/2 x 11, B&W & occasional color, off-set reproduction.
1974-77- Nos. 1-7, all issues

5.00   15.00   25.00

GRAPHIC SHOWCASE (Fanzine)
1967- No. 1, Kaluta/Harper Clr/Cv

12.50   25.00   45.00

1969- No. 2, 8 1/2 x 11 c/cv 10.00   20.00   35.00

GREASER COMICS (UG, Regular)
1971-72- Nos. 1,2. 50 cents 1st Ed

5.00   10.00   17.50

GREAT MARIJUANA DEBATE
(UG, small format One Shot)
1972- nn, 10 cents cv/pr 1st Ed

20.00   40.00   80.00

GRIM WIT (UG, Regular)
1972- No. 1, Corben/Cv 50 cts 1st Ed

12.50   25.00   45.00

1973- No. 2, Corben, 1.00 cv/pr

10.00   20.00   35.00

GROSS OUT COMIX
(UG CX, INDEPENDENT)
1969- No. 'S 1,2., 50 & 35 cts/1ed Ed

25.00   65.00   125.00

GRUNT (UG, Promotional)
1972-73- Grunt Records, giveway promotional
comic, all color, slick paper stock. 7.50   25.00
45.00

GUNFIGHTER (UG, Independent)
1971-73- Nos. 1-3, 50 cts/1st Eds

12.50   25.00   65.00

1974- No. 4, 85 cents cover 1st Ed.

7.50   15.00   30.00

HAPPY ENDINGS COMICS
(UG, Regular)
1969, ROP, 50 cents 1st Ed.

10.00   20.00   40.00

HAROLD HEDD, COLLECTED ADVENTURES
(UG, Canadian)
1972, nn, lg/format 1.00 cv/pr 15.00 35.00   75.00

1973, No. 2, reg/cx/sz 75 cts/1st Ed 7.50   15.00
22.50

HATE! (UG, Newave, Regular)
1990-91- Nos. 1-4, 2.00 cv/pr

2.50   5.00   12.50

1992-95- Nos. 5-20, 2.95 cv/pr

1.50   3.50   5.00

HEAR THE SOUND OF MY FEET WALKING (UG, Paperback)
1969- 12 x 9, 3.95 cv/pr 1st Ed

12.50   25.00   50.00

1975- 2nd Ed. on cv/ 4.95 pr

7.50   15.00   25.00

HEAVY COMIX (UG, Independent)
1972- nn, B&W cv, 35 cts/1st Ed

20.00   40.00   80.00

HEAVY TRAGICOMIX
(UG, Regular)
1969- No. 1, Print Mint, 50 cts/1st Ed

10.00   20.00   40.00

THE HEY LOOK! BOOK! by Harvey Kurtzman
(fanzine, paperback)
1978, Glenn Bray, color Xerox interior pages
bound in red boards, released in a numbered
edition of 20 copies.   50.00   150.00   250.00

HEY LOOK! (Pro-PB & HC #ed)
1992, Kitchen Sink Press, the definitive version
with John Benson introduction, 9 1/4 x 6 1/4,
with illustrated boards, released in signed and
numbered edition of 500 copies signed by
Kurtzman.   20.00   50.00   75.00
(softcover trade edition) 7.50   15.00   25.00

HIGH ADVENTURE (UG, Regular)
1973- No. 1, 50 cts/cv/pr 1st Ed

7.50   15.00   25.00

HISTORY OF UNDERGROUND COMICS (UG, paperback history)
1974- Mark James Estern author, 8 1/2 x 11, off-
set, heavy color paper wraps, 319 #ed pages,
use of red color motif on interior illustrations
and captions. 1st printing so stated

15.00   35.00   75.00

1970's- 2nd printing so stated

12.50   25.00   50.00

1970's- 3rd printing so stated

7.50   15.00   25.00

HOME GROWN FUNNIES (UG comic)
1971, Kitchen Sink Press, no indication of first
printing on copyright page, however 2nd and
third printings so stated on separate line
beneath handwitten copyright on later
editions.   5.00   20.00   50.00
2nd edition   .50   5.00   10.00

HOO HAH! (EC Fanzine)
Ron Parker Editor & Publisher, first issues 8 1/2 x 5 1/2, mimeographed, later issues 8 1/2 x 11 with multi-color covers, considered the best of the first generation EC fanzines.

1955- No. 1 October/November
35.00 75.00 150.00
1955- Nos. 2,3. Dec./ Feb. 35.00 75.00 125.00
1956- Nos. 4,5,6,7. April-Oct.
25.00 50.00 100.00
1957-58- Nos. 8,9,10. 25.00 50.00 110.00

HOT STUFF (Fanzine)
1974-75- Nos. 1,2. Cl/Cvs 12.50 25.00 35.00

HOT STUFF (UG, Regular)
1974-77- Nos. 1-5, single printings
7.50 15.00 30.00

HYDROGEN BOMB FUNNIES
(UG, Regular)
1970- No. 1, 1.00 cv/pr 1st Ed
12.50 25.00 55.00

HORROR COMICS OF THE 1950's
(Nostalgia Press EC Hardcover)
1971, Nostalgia Press, no statement of printing on copyright page, large 14 1/4 x 10 1/4 format hardcover with dust jacket, issued at 19.95, one of the first serious reprint volumes to present EC comics. 50.00 125.00 [175.00]

IKE LIVES (UG, Independent)
1973- nn, 50 cts/cv/pr 1st Ed.
15.00 30.00 75.00

Note: A number of VF/NM copies surfaced in the mid 1970's.

I'LL BE DAMNED (Fanzine)
1968- No. 1-Fraz/Wrightson/Bode/etc 12.50 35.00 55.00

ILLUMINATIONS (UG, Regular)
1971- nn, 50 cts/cv/pr 1st Ed.
7.50 15.00 30.00

ILLUSTRATED CHECKLIST TO UNDERGROUND COMIX
(UG, checklist)
1979- Archival Press, 8 1/2 x 11, off-set pages, illustrated with photos, stiff paper wraps with color R. Crumb illustration wrap-around cover.
12.50 25.00 45.00

IMAGE OF THE BEAST, PHILIP JOSE FARMER'S (UG, Regular)
1973- Lst/Gsp, 75 cts/cv pr 1st Ed.
15.00 25.00 35.00

INFINITY (Fanzine)
1970-76- Nos. 1-6-Fraz/Krenk/Jones
12.50 25.00 45.00

INNER CITY ROMANCES
(UG, Regular)
1972-77- Nos. 1-4, 50 cents/1.00 pr
7.50 15.00 25.00

INSIDE COMICS (Fanzine, Large Dist.)
1974- Nos. 1,2,3. newsprint covers
3.50 12.50 25.00

INSECT FEAR (UG, Regular)
1969- No. 1, 50 cents cv/pr/1st Ed.
20.00 45.00 85.00
1970-72- Nos. 2,3, 50 cts/cv, 1st Ed.
7.50 15.00 27.50

IT AIN'T ME BABE (UG, Regular)
1970- Lst/Gsp, 50 cents, cv/pr, 1st Ed
12.50 25.00 35.00

JACK HIGH (Fanzine-UG/MAD)
1961-62- Nos. 1-8 (rare) 35.00 75.00 [125.00]

JESUS, THE NEW ADVENTURES OF
(UG, Regular)
1969- nn, 1st edition so stated c. page, stiff paper covers, high quality 60 lb off-set stock paper, 1.00 cv/pr. 25.00 45.00 75.00
1970's- 2nd print/ 50 cts, cv/pr
7.50 15.00 20.00

JESUS MEETS THE ARMED SERVICES
(UG, Regular)
1970, ROP, 50 cts/cv/pr, 1st Ed.
15.00 25.00 45.00

JESUS COMICS (title change)
1972- No. 3, 50 cts/cv/pr, 1st Ed.
10.00 20.00 30.00

JIZ (UG, small sex Satire issue)
1969- nn, uneven pages & heavy paper stock to first printing. 15.00 35.00 75.00

JOEL BECKS COMICS & STORIES
(UG, Regular)
1977- first printing on c. page

| | 3.50 | 7.50 | 15.00 |

JUNKWAFFEL (UG, Regular)
1971-72- Nos. 1-4, Bodé covers and artwork throughout, 50 cts/cv/pr, 1st Eds. The Print Mint. 7.50 25.00 40.00

KANNED KORN KOMIX
(UG, Independent)
1969, gloss/cv, 10 cts/pr, 1st Ed.
12.50 30.00 50.00

KAVER KOMIKS (UG, Independent)
1972- No. 1, 50 cts/cv/pr, 1st Ed.
20.00 40.00 85.00

KING BEE (UG, newspaper)
1969- No. 1, Donahue, one printing
35.00 75.00 [175.00}

Note: Copies of this UG Newspaper in flat perfect condition are very scarce.

KINGDOM OF HEAVEN IS WITHIN YOU, THE (UG, Regular)
1969- No. 1, 50 cts/cv/pr, 1st Ed.
12.50 30.00 60.00

KOAN COMICS (UG, Independent)
1969- No. 1, stiff/cvs one printing
35.00 75.00 150.00

KUAWY COMICS (UG, Regular)
1969- No. 1, J. Thompson 50 cts, 1st Ed
10.00 20.00 40.00

KURTZMAN, A TALK WITH
(Fanzine-Interview)
1966-nn, John Benson Editor & Publisher, 8 1/2 x 11, B&W format. 17.50 35.00 75.00

KURTZMAN COMICS (UG, Regular)
1976- nn, Kit/Sink 1.00 cv/pr, 1st
3.50 10.00 20.00

KURTZMAN'S WAR ART, HARVEY
1976?, Glenn Bray, color Xerox interior pages bound in black boards, with no identification on title page, no stamped title, in an edition of 20 to 30 copies each copy given away to close friends. This volume reprinted the top covers and stories from *Two-Fisted Tales*, and *Frontline Combat*. (nn) 50.00 150.00 250.00

KURTZMAN INDEX, THE ILLUSTRATED HARVEY (Fanzine-PB)

1976, Glen Bray, 9 1/4 x 6 1/4 paperback edition, first edition is only printing, a small press publication with distribution through Bud Plant & comic specialty stores.
35.00 100.00 225.00

L.A. COMICS (UG, Regular)
1971-73- Nos. 1,2, 50/75 cts, 1st Eds.
5.00 10.00 20.00

LAIR OF MADNESS
(UG, Independent)
1972-73- Nos. 1,2, 50 cts, 1st Eds.
12.50 25.00 35.00

LANGUAGE OF THE COMIX
(UG, lecture pamplet)
1974- one shot, Art Spiegelman lecture series, a giveway B&W pamplet used to highlight lecture. 7.50 17.50 35.00

LAUGH IN THE DARK (UG, Regular)
1971- No. 1, Deitch- 50 cts/cv, 1st Ed.
7.50 15.00 25.00

LEAN YEARS (UG, Regular)
1974- nn, 50 cts/cv/pr, 1st Ed.
5.00 10.00 20.00

LEFT FIELD FUNNIES (UG, Regular)
1972- No. 1, 50 cts/cv/pr, 1st Ed.
7.50 15.00 25.00

LEGION OF CHARLIES (UG, Regular)
1971- nn, 50 cts/cv/pr, 1st Ed.
10.00 20.00 30.00

LENNY OF LARADO
(UG, early format & regular)
1965- Joel Beck, one of the early pivotal UG classic titles, the 'green' Lenny is acknowledged as one of the two or three of the rarest of all UG comics, 8 1/2 x 11, printed off-set on green cover paper, 50 cents cover price. 1st "Green" edition.
350.00 [850.00] [1,750]
1965- 2nd, "Orange" cv, sm/fomat
175.00 [550.00] [1,000]
1967- 3rd, "White" matt/cv, Pnt/Mt
75.00 250.00 500.00

LIFE AND LOVES OF CLEOPATRA, THE
(UG, small format)
1969- nn, giveway 35.00 75.00 150.00

LIGHT COMITRAGIES
(UG, Regular, color)
1971- nn, 75 cts/cv/pr, 1st Ed.
15.00   30.00   50.00

LITTLE GREEN DINOSAUR, THE
(UG, Regular)
1972-73- Nos. 1,2, 50 cts/cv/pr 1st Ed.
5.00   10.00   20.00

LIVING IN THE U.S.A.
(UG, Independent)
1975- nn, lg/format, 1.25 cv/pr, 1st Ed.
12.50   25.00   45.00

LIZARD ZEN
(UG, Independent)
1973- R. Weiner Pub, hand-stapled small book
of Vaughn Bodé's work. 1st edition with no
tape to spine.   15.00   35.00   75.00

LOST CAUSE COMIX
(UG, Independent)
1976- nn, 75 cts/cv/pr, 1st Ed.
7.50   15.00   25.00

LOVE & ROCKETS
(UG-Newave comic)
1982- June, B&W small size, published by
Hernandez Brothers, in edition of 800 copies.
35.00   45.00   75.00
1982- No. 1, Fantagraphics, first Hernandez
Bros. issue, 2.95 cover price.
15.00   25.00   50.00
1982-84- Nos. 2-10   3.50   7.50   25.00
1980's- Nos. 11-30   2.50   6.50   15.00
1982-93- Nos. 31-41   2.00   5.50   9.50
1993-Present- all issues 1.50   3.50   5.75

LOVE AND ROCKETS
(UG Newave, paperback)
1987-PB, 1st ed. on c.pg- 9.95 cv/pr
7.50   25.00   45.00

LOVE & ROCKETS
(UG Newave paperback)
1987-Titan bks, signed by artist, No. 'ed
7.50   25.00   45.00

HEARTBREAK SOUP
(UG Newave paperback)
1987-Titan, signed by artist, No. 'ed
7.50   25.00   45.00

DUCK FEET (UG Newave paperback)

1988- Titan bks, signed Beto, #ed
7.50   25.00   45.00

MECHANICS (UG Newave paperback)
1988- Titan bks, signed by artist, #ed
7.50   25.00   45.00

MACHINES, THE (UG, Independent)
1967- small B&W matt covers,
35.00   75.00   175.00

MADISON AVENUE FUNNIES
(UG, Independent)
1971- No. 1, 45 cts/one printing
25.00   50.00   80.00

MAD FOR KEEPS
(mainstream hardcover)
1958, Crown Publishers, no statement of first
edition on copyright page, hardcover 10 3/4 x
8 1/2 with blue cloth boards, Alfred stamped
to front cover, pictoral dust jacket features
cover of MAD No. 30.   50.00   150.00   250.00

MAD FOREVER
(mainstream hardcover)
1959, Crown Publishers, same format and
points, cover by Wood. 50.00 150.00 225.00

A GOLDEN TRASHERY OF MAD
(mainstream hardcover)
1960, Crown Publishers, same format and
points, cover by Mingo. 50.00 150.00 200.00

THE RIDICULOUSLY EXPENSIVE
MAD (mainstream hardcover)
1969, World Publishing Company, first and only
printing, published at 9.95, the dust jacket
printed on very light paper stock, thus
extremely rare in VF or better condition.
50.00   125.00   175.00

THE MAD READER
(mainstream paperback)
1955, Ballantine Books No. 93, first edition so
stated on copyright page, extremely rare in
higher grades, the only MAD paperback
within the time of the EC MAD comic books,
just during transition between comics to the
magazine format.   15.00   50.00   75.00

MAD STRIKES BACK!
INSIDE MAD
UTTERLY MAD
THE BROTHERS MAD

SON OF MAD

1950's, Ballantine Books, same format, first
editions so stated on copyright page.
      7.50   20.00   35.00

WILLIAM M. GAINES' THE BEDSIDE MAD

1959, Signet Books, first edition so stated on
copyright page.   10.00   20.00   30.00

THE MAD WORLD OF WILLIAM M. GAINES (mainstream hardcover)

1972, Lyle Stuart Inc., no statement of first
edition on copyright page, 8vo with orange
cloth boards, title stamped in gold on spine,
photo-pictorial dust jacket by Don Martin.
      25.00   75.00   125.00

MAN, THE (UG, Independent)

1972- 8 1/2 x 11, gloss/cv 40 cts
      35.00   100.00   200.00
1972- 2nd PrintMint reg/cx/sz 50c
      7.50   15.00   25.00

MAN FROM UTOPIA

(UG, large format)
1972, Calitho Press, stiff covers, no price to
cover, 9 x 12 format, 1.50 price on copyright
page, first printing is only printing. Classic
Rick Griffin artwork.   15.00   30.00   75.00

MANHUNT COMIX (UG, Regular)

1973-74- Nos. 1,2, 50/75 cts/cv/pr
      7.50   12.50   25.00

MARCHING MARVIN

(UG, Magazine size format)
1967- nn, matt/cv-only printing
      45.00   175.00   375.00

Note: Limited copies (no more than 20) of
this rare underground surfaced in the mid
1970's in VF/NM condition.

MARVEL MANIA (Fanzine)

1969-70- Nos. 1-4, All   5.00   10.00   25.00

MEAN BITCH THRILLS (UG, Regular)

1967, nn-Spain, 50c/cv/pr, 1st Ed.
      10.00   25.00   35.00

MEEF COMIX (UG, Regular)

1972-73- Nos. 1,2, 50c/cv/pr, 1st Ed.
      7.50   15.00   30.00

MELOTOONS (UG, fanzine)

1972-76- Nos.1,2. 1.00 cv/pr
      10.00   20.00   35.00

MEDOCINO FUNNIES

(UG, Independent)
1975- No. 1, 1.25 cv/pr/1st Ed.
      10.00   20.00   40.00

MELOTOONS (Fanzine)

1969-70- Nos. 1,2, No. 2 R. Crumb
      12.50   25.00   35.00

MERTON OF THE MOVEMENT

(UG, Regular)
1972- nn, London-50c/cv/pr, 1st
      7.50   15.00   35.00

MICKEY RAT (UG, Regular)

1972- Nos. 1,2. 50c/cv/pr, 1st Eds.
      10.00   25.00   35.00

MIDDLE CLASS FANTASIES

(UG, Regular)
1973-76- Nos. 1,2, 50/1.00 cv/pr
      3.50   7.50   15.00

MINDWARP (UG, paperback)

1974- nn, 8 1/2 x 11, 3.50 cv/pr
      12.50   25.00   50.00

MR. A (Fanzine-by Pro-Steve Ditko)

1973-75- Nos. 1,2, Cl/Cvs   15.00   30.00   50.00

MR. NATURAL (UG, Regular)

1970- No. 1, gloss/cv, c. page states Apex
Novelties & Published by the SF Comic Bk Co,
with address.   25.00   75.00   175.00
1970's- up to 7 more printings
      2.50   7.50   12.50
1971- No. 2, 50c/cv/pr, 1st Ed15.00 30.00   50.00
1977- No. 3, K/Sink, 1.00 cv/pr, 1st
      7.50   15.00   25.00

MOM'S HOMEMADE COMICS

(UG, Regular)
1969- No. 1, matt/cv, high grade paper, self
published by Kitchen, 49c cv/pr for 1st Edition.
      25.00   50.00   100.00
1969- 2nd ed., Print Mint, 50c
      12.50   25.00   45.00
1970-71- Nos. 2,3, 50c/cv/pr 1st Eds.
      10.00   20.00   30.00

MOONCHILD COMICS

(UG, Independent)

1968-70- Nos. 1,2,3., B&W/matt/cvs
           12.50   25.00   50.00

MOONDOG (UG, Regular)
1969-71- Nos. 1-3, 50c/cv/pr, 1st Eds.
           7.50   15.00   30.00

MORSE'S FUNNIES
(UG, Ego-Boo Promotional)
1974-nn, B&W off-set, 8 1/2 x 11, first edition
with every other page blank, matt cover
paper.   75.00 250.00 500.00
1975-nn variant, more artists are added to
pages and printed on both sides for later
edition.   50.00 200.00 350.00

Note: This UG comic can be easily forged,
by clever photocopy work with older
paper. Buyers should beware of possible
fakes, and know the provenance of the
owner. Albert Morse was Robert Crumb's
personal lawyer for a number of years;
only friends and associates got many of the
original early copies.

MOTHER'S OATS COMICS
(UG, Regular)
1971- No. 1, 1st ed/Bk/cv 50c/pr
           12.50   27.50   60.00
1971-76- Nos. 2,3. 50c/75c/cv/pr
           7.50   15.00   25.00

MOTOR CITY COMICS (UG)
1969- No. 1, R. Crumb cover and interior
artwork, first printing with heavy flat stock
cover, with no Rip Off Press logo on the front
cover, trim size can vary with this first issue.
High grade file copies did surface in the mid
1970's of this rarer first edition.
           55.00 150.00 250.00
1970- No. 2, Rip Off Press, R. Crumb cover and
interior artwork, first edition with matt paper
cover, Rip Off Press cover logo hand lettered.
           7.50   25.00   40.00
(No. 2) the second and third states are
unconfirmed; an early variant exists with the
upper left logo blacked over (with no label
printed underneath), and another variant
with sticker applied over this black over print.
           2.50   10.00   15.00

MYRON MOOSE FUNNIES
(UG, Regular)
1971-73- Nos. 1,2, 50c/75c/pr, 1st Eds.
           7.50   15.00   30.00

NARD N' PAT (UG, Regular)
1974, Lynch- 50c/cv/pr, 1st 5.00   15.00   25.00

NATURE COMIX (UG, Canadian)
1970- Nos. 1,2, 50c/cv/pr, 1st Eds.
           12.50   25.00   35.00

NEAL ADAMS INDEX
(Fanzine-Index Listing)
1974-one shot, B&W art by Adams
           15.00   35.00   45.00

NET PROFIT (UG, Regular)
1974-nn, 50c/cv/pr, 1st Ed
           7.50   15.00   20.00

NEUROCOMICS, TIMOTHY LEARY
(UG, Regular)
1979- nn, 1.25 cv/pr, 1st Ed.
           10.00   20.00   30.00

NEWFANGLES
(Fanzine-fan/newszine-1 to 3 sheets)
Don & Maggie Thompson, small circulation
broadsheet with news about fans.
1967-71- Nos. 1-54, All issues
           3.50   5.50   7.50

NEW PLATZ COMIX (UG, Regular)
1973-77- Nos. 1-3, 50/75/1.25c
           5.00   10.00   20.00

NOPE (Fanzine-UG/MAD)
Jay Kinny Editor & Publisher, hecto with
color, 8 1/2 x 11, 25 cents for most issues,
very limited distribution, many copies went
to SF fans.
1965-66- Nos. 1-3.   25.00   45.00   75.00
1967-70- Nos. 4-10 all issues
           17.50   35.00   55.00

OCCULT LAFF-PARADE (UG, Regular)
1973- No. 1, Kinney-50c/cv/pr, 1st Ed.
           7.50   15.00   25.00

ODD (EC/MAD Fanzine)
1964-67- Nos. 7-12   12.50   25.00   45.00

O.K. COMIC COMPANY
(UG, newspaper format comics)
1970-73- Nos. 1-17, 25c/cv/pr/1st Ed.
           12.50   25.00   45.00

O.K. COMICS (UG, Regular)
1971-72- Nos. 1,2, 50c/cv/pr 1st Eds.

7.50   15.00   25.00

ON THE DRAWING BOARD
(formely The Comic Reader, title resumes)
1966-68- Nos. 51-68, all issues

5.00   12.50   25.00

OPHEMERA (Fanzine)
1977-nn Barks/Wood/etc.   7.50   15.00   30.00

PAIN (UG, Regular)
1977-nn, 1.00 cv/pr,1st Ed.   5.00   10.00   20.00

PANDEMONIUM EXPRESS FUNNIES
(UG, small Independent)
1974-75- Nos. 1-12, B&W, one painting

5.00   12.50   25.00

PANELOLOGIST PRESENTS (Fanzine)
1969-71- Nos. 1-8 all issues   5.00   15.00   25.00

PANELS (Fanzine)
1979-81- Nos. 1,2, Barks/Kurtz/etc.

6.50   15.00   35.00

PARAGON (Fanzine)
1969-71- Nos. 1-4, b&w&clr/ 1.00

7.50   15.00   35.00

PARANOIA (UG, Regular)
1972- nn, 50c cv/pr/1st Ed.   7.50   15.00   25.00

PEANUTS BOOKS
(mainstream paperbacks)
1960's, Holt Rinehart and Winston, stiff covers, single color covers, 8 x 5 1/4 format, 1.00 cover price for most editions, first edition so stated on copyright page, reprints of the popular newspaper strip by Charles Schulz. The first printings sold out almost immediately and these books went into multiple printings, the first editions in fine or better are rare, as copies were usually read to death.

PEANUTS

5.00   25.00   50.00

MORE PEANUTS

3.50   20.00   40.00

GOOD GRIEF, MORE PEANUTS - - GOOD OL'
CHARLIE BROWN - - SNOOPY - - YOU'RE OUT
OF YOUR MIND CHARLIE BROWN! - - BUT WE
LOVE YOU, CHARLIE BROWN - - PEANUTS
REVISITED - GO FLY A KITE, CHARLIE BROWN -

- PEANUTS EVERY SUNDAY - - IT'S A DOG'S
LIFE CHARLIE BROWN - - YOU CAN'T WIN
CHARLIE BROWN - - SNOOPY, COME HOME - -
YOU CAN DO IT, CHARLIE BROWN - - WE'RE
RIGHT BEHIND YOU, CHARLIE BROWN - - AS
YOU LIKE IT, CHARLIE BROWN - - SUNDAY'S
FUN DAY, CHARLIE BROWN - - YOU NEED
HELP, CHARLIE BROWN - - SNOOPY AND THE
RED BARON - - THE UNSINKABLE CHARLIE
BROWN - - YOU'LL FLIP, CHARLIE BROWN - -
YOU'RE SOMETHING ELSE, CHARIE BROWN.
(for all titles above)

2.50   15.00   25.00

PEOPLES COMICS, THE
(UG, Regular)
1972- No. 1, 50c cv/pr, 1st Ed.

10.00   25.00   35.00

1976- 2nd ed, Kitchen Sink

2.50   7.50   10.00

PHANTASMAGORIA (Fanzine)
1972-77 Nos. 1-5, Ken Smith   12.50   25.00   45.00

PHOTON (Fanzine)
1970-71- Nos. 1,2, Corben Art

12.50   25.00   50.00

PHUCKED UP PHUNNIES
(UG, early special edition)
1968- nn, self published under the artist Art Spiegelman's direction while at college and bound into his student yearbook; a few copies were left individually bound and given to close friends; one of the top seven rare 'grass-root' UG titles, extremely important because of Spiegelman's career. Glossy Paper large format.   175.00 [575.00]   [1,250]

PINK FLOYD (UG, Independent)
1974- nn, 25c sold at concerts

10.00   25.00   50.00

PLAYBOY'S LITTLE ANNIE FANNY
(mainstream hardcover)
1966, Playboy Press, first edition so stated on copyright page, large format 14 x 10 3/4 hardcover issued with dust jacket, lavish color reprints of the Kurtzman/Elder classics. Rare with a VF dust jacket. Condition rating would include dust jacket condition.

35.00   75.00   175.00

POGO BOOKS (mainstream paperbacks)
1950's, Simon & Shuster, first edition so stated on copyright page, 8 x 5 1/4 format,

with matt single color covers, reprints of the popular newspaper strip by Walt Kelly, each book listed in similar format.

	Good	Fine	Near Mint
POGO	15.00	35.00	75.00
I GO POGO	15.00	30.00	60.00
UNCLE POGO SO-SO STORIES			
THE POGO PAPERS	5.00	15.00	35.00
THE POGO STEPMOTHER GOOSE			
THE INCOMPLEAT POGO			
POGO PEEK-A-BOOK	5.00	15.00	35.00
POTLUCK POGO			
THE POGO SUNDAY BOOK			
THE POGO PARTY	5.00	15.00	35.00
POGO'S SUNDAY PUNCH			
POSITIVELY POGO			
THE POGO SUNDAY PARADE	15.00	15.00	35.00
G. O. FIZZICKLE POGO			
THE POGO SUNDAY BRUNCH	15.00	15.00	35.00

Note: Prices are for 'first-edition' copies, reprints command 1/2 to 1/3 of the listed price.

(Larger format titles)

	Good	Fine	Near Mint
TEN EVER-LOVIN' BLUE-EYED YEARS WITH POGO	15.00	40.00	80.00
SONGS OF THE POGO	10.00	25.00	50.00
POGOMOBILE	10.00	20.00	40.00

PORK (UG, small format sex satire)
1971-nn, S.ClayWilson, 50c, 1st Ed.
	15.00	35.00	45.00

POTRZEBIE (EC Fanzine)
Ted White Publisher & Editor, Larry Stark & Bhob Steward co-editors & contributions, mimeographed, all copies extremely scarce.
1954- No. 1-June/Bob Warner/Cv
	50.00	75.00	[175.00]
1954-55 Nos. 2,3,4. same format
	35.00	75.00	125.00
1955- No. 5 8 1/2 x 11 format
	35.00	75.00	150.00

PROFIT, THE (UG, booklet format)
1967- nn, Joel Beck, off-set paper stock, heavy orange paper covers, no price on cv, rare in higher grades. 75.00 150.00 250.00

PROJUNIOR (UG, Regular)
1971, nn, '23' artists noted on cover
	10.00	20.00	35.00

PROMETHEAN ENTERPRISES
(UG, related fanzine)
1969-71- Nos. 1,2,3, one print only
	15.00	35.00	75.00
1972- Nos. 4,5. one print only
	12.50	25.00	45.00

PSYCHOTIC ADVENTURES
(UG, Regular)
1972-74- Nos. 1-3, 50/50/75c, 1st Eds.
	7.50	15.00	25.00

PUDGE, GIRL BLIMP (UG, Regular)
1973-77- Nos. 1-3, 50/1.00/1.25c
	5.00	10.00	15.00

PURPLE CAT (UG, Regular)
1973- No. 1- Lynch, 50c cv/pr, 1st Ed.
	7.50	15.00	25.00

PURPLE WARP
(UG, small format Independent)
1972-73- Nos. 1-12, one printing each
	7.50	15.00	25.00

QUA BROT (EC Fanzine)
1985- No. 1, C/Cv-Krenkel/Fraz/etc.
	10.00	25.00	35.00

QUACK (UG, Regular)
1976-77- Nos. 1-6, 1.25c cv/pr, 1st Ed.
	3.50	7.50	15.00

QUAGMIRE COMICS (UG, Regular)
1970- No. 1, 50c cv/pr, 1st Ed.
	5.00	10.00	20.00

RADICAL AMERICA KOMIKS
(UG, Regular)
1969- Vol 3 No. 1, 50c cv/pr, the first printing has yellow toned shoes for Lestor Maddox on front cover. 12.50 35.00 75.00

RAW (UG/Newave publication)
(No. 1) 1980, Raw Books, stiff covers with 6 1/4 x 4 1/4 color pasteover to front cover, 1st printing only, original cover price 3.50.
	50.00	100.00	175.00
(No. 2) 1980, Raw Books, stiff covers, centerfold should have Mark Beyer Gum card set with gum enclosed, stiff covers, cover price of 4.00.
	30.00	75.00	125.00
(No. 3) ***
(No. 4) ***
(No. 5) 1983, Raw Books, stiff covers, "Maus"

Chapter Four insert to centerfold, cover price of 4.95, one printing only.

| | 15.00 | 35.00 | 75.00 |

(No. 6) 1984, Raw Books, stiff covers, "Maus" Chapter Five insert to centerfold, cover price of 5.00, first printing only.

| | 15.00 | 35.00 | 75.00 |

(No. 7) 1985, Raw Books, stiff covers, this issue with top right corner hand-torn off and mounted with tape on first page for every issue distributed, "Maus" Chapter Six to centerfold, cover price 6.00, first printing only.

| | 15.00 | 35.00 | 75.00 |

(No. 8) 1986, Raw Books, stiff covers, square back binding, "Maus" Chapter Seven mounted to centerfold, 7.95 cover price, first printing only.

| | 12.50 | 25.00 | 50.00 |

(Vol. 2 No. 1) 1989, Penguin Books, stiff covers, new format now 6 x 8 3/4, 201 pages, 14.95 cover price, mixed color and B&W interior pages, no insert, first printing only.

| | 10.00 | 15.00 | 25.00 |

(Vol.2 No. 2) 1990, stiff covers, same format and price, first printing only.

| | 10.00 | 15.00 | 25.00 |

(note: some issues of Vol. 2 No. 2 were distributed signed on the cover by all the artists)

| | 15.00 | 25.00 | 50.00 |

(Vol. 2 No. 3) 1991, Penguin Books, same format & price, first printing only.

| | 10.00 | 15.00 | 25.00 |

READ YOURSELF RAW

(nn) 1987, Raw Books/Pantheon Books, stiff covers, square back binding, with "Two-Fisted Painters" comic insert, and Mark Beyer trading cards insert to interior pages, 14.95 cover price, reprints from issues 1-3.

| | 12.50 | 25.00 | 50.00 |

REALITY (Fanzine)

1970-71- Nos. 1,2. Kaluta/Wrightson/Will

| | 12.50 | 25.00 | 45.00 |

REALM (UG, Regular)

1969-71- Nos. 1-7   3.50   7.50   17.50

REAL PULP COMICS (UG, Regular)

1971-73- Nos. 1,2, 50cts, 1st Eds.

| | 5.00 | 10.00 | 25.00 |

REAL WORLD COMIX

(UG, Independent, Magazine format)
1974-nn, one shot/one printing

| | 35.00 | 75.00 | 175.00 |

RED RAIDER (UG, Regular)

1977-nn, J.Jackson, 1.00, 1st Ed.

| | 5.00 | 10.00 | 17.50 |

RIP OFF COMIX

(UG, Regular & Larger Magazine format)
1977- Nos. 1,2, 75cts, 1st Eds.

| | 3.50 | 7.50 | 15.00 |

1978-82- Nos. 3-9, 75/1.00/1.50

| | 2.50 | 5.00 | 10.00 |

1983-Present-Nos. 10-up, 2.95/3.95

| | 1.50 | 3.50 | 7.50 |

ROCKETS BLAST - COMIC COLLECTOR, RBCC (Fanzine-Adzine)

Begun by G.B. Love, this fanzine is responsible in large part for the growth of fandom, comic book collecting, fanzine production, and the general welfare of comics fans through-out the 1960's and 1970's. During its long run many fine original covers and articles appeared along with all the ads for old comic books.

1961- No. 1-December, limited/Dist

| | 25.00 | 75.00 | [150.00] |

1962- Nos. 2-9, 35cts/cv/pr

| | 15.00 | 50.00 | 75.00 |

1962-64- Nos. 10-33 35/45cts cv/pr

| | 12.50 | 25.00 | 45.00 |

1963- RBCC Special 1,2.   15.00   35.00   60.00

1965-67- Nos. 34-54 all issues

| | 12.50 | 25.00 | 35.00 |

1969-76- Nos. 55- 130 all issues

| | 5.00 | 12.50 | 25.00 |

1977-80- Nos. 131-153 all issues

| | 3.50 | 10.00 | 20.00 |

Note: certian issues with Corben, Wrightson, Newton, and other special artist covers will demand higher prices.

ROWLF (UG, Regular)

1971-No. 1, Corben, 50cts, 1st Ed.

| | 7.50 | 17.50 | 35.00 |

ROXY FUNNIES (UG, Regular)

1971-No. 1, 50cts/cv/pr, 1st Ed.

| | 3.50 | 12.50 | 25.00 |

RUBBER DUCK TALES (UG, Regular)

1971-72- Nos. 1,2. 50cts/cv/pr, 1st Ed.

| | 3.50 | 7.50 | 15.00 |

SACRED & PROFANE

(UG, Large format)

1976-nn J.Green, 2.00 cv/pr, 1st
          7.50   17.50   35.00

SAN FRANCISCO COMIC BOOK
(UG, Regular)
1969-No. 1, .50cts/cv/pr, 1st Ed.
        25.00   50.00   150.00
1970-73- Nos. 2-,4, 50cts, 1st Ed.
        5.00   12.50   25.00

SAUCY SCI-FI COMICS
(UG, Independent)
1977- No. 1, B. Anthony, 15 cts/1st Ed.
        12.50   25.00   40.00

SCHIZOPHRENIA (UG, Regular)
1973, nn, Bodé, 75cts/1st Ed.
        10.00   25.00   50.00

SCHOOL IS HELL
(Mainstream paperback)
1987, Pantheon Books, first edition so stated on
  copyright page.   3.50   7.50   25.00

SCREAM DOOR (Fanzine)
1971- No. 1, Wrightson 12.50   25.00   35.00

S. CLAY WILSON TWENTY DRAWINGS (UG, Portfolio)
1967-Lawrence Kansas privately printed edition,
  with light grey cardboard wraps, individual
  B&W interior illustrations, extremely small
  number of copies given away to the artist's
  close friends & associates, very few distributed
  by The Print Mint, copies seldom survive in
  above very good condition, one of the rarest
  and most sought after of all Underground
  comics.   350.00 [950.00] [1,250]

Note: All copies exist with different
variation past-over cover illustrations.

SENSE OF WONDER (Fanzine)
1967-72- Nos. 5-12.   7.50   15.00   25.00

SERAPHIM
(EC Fanzine- formerly EC FAN ADDICT)
1969-70- Nos. 4,5.   12.50   25.00   35.00

SHORT ORDER (UG, Regular)
1973-74- Nos. 1,2, 50cts/75cts 1st Eds.
        3.50   7.50   17.50

SHOW AND TELL (UG, Regular)
1973-nn, J.Green, 50cts/1st Ed.
        4.00   12.00   25.00

SKULL COMICS (UG, Regular)
1970- No. 1, 50cts/1st Ed. 10.00   25.00   75.00
1970-72- Nos. 2-6. 50 cts, 1st Ed.
        3.50   7.50   17.50

SLOW DEATH FUNNIES (UG, Regular)
1970- No. 1, .50 cts (red border) 1st Ed.
        12.50   25.00   75.00
1970-77- Nos. 2-8, 50/75/1.00 cv/pr
        3.50   7.50   17.50

SLOW DEATH ANTHOLOGY
(UG, Trade Paperback)
1975-nn, 5.00 cv/pr, 1st/Ed   .
        10.00   25.00   45.00

SMILE (UG, Regular)
1970-72- Nos.1-3, 50cts/cv/pr
        3.50   7.50   12.50

SMUDGE (EC/MAD Fanzine)
1962- Nos. 1-4, Joe Pilati Ed.
        25.00   45.00   75.00

SNARF (UG, Regular)
1972- No. 1, 50cts/cv/pr, 1st/Ed.
        5.00   15.00   35.00
1972-75- Nos. 2-7, 50/65/75cts 1st
        3.50   7.50   12.50

SNATCH COMICS (UG, small format)
1968-No. 1, the first edition is one of the rarest
  of the mainstream UG comic titles, along with
  ZAP No. 1 in the Plymell printing: the first
  print can be identified by a heavy paper stock,
  uneven untrimmed interior pages to the right
  hand side and by the fact that the S. Clay
  Wilson double-page falls on pages 10/11, with
  25 cents cover price. 125.00 [350.00] [750.00]
1969-2nd printing 50cts/cv/pr
        15.00   35.00   50.00
1969-Nos. 2,3, 50cts/cv/pr, 1st Ed.   .
        25.00   45.00   65.00

SNATCH SAMPLER
(UG, small trade paperback, reprints)
1977-nn, 2.95 cv/pr, 1st Ed.
        15.00   25.00   50.00

SPACED (UG, Regular)
1974-76- Nos. 1-3, .75/1.00/2.00
        3.50   7.50   17.50

SPA-FON! (EC Fanzine)

Edited & Published by Rich Hauser, 8 1/2 x 11, off-set, later issues color.

1966- No. 1, paste-over cover to SF Outre
Fanzine cover.   35.00   75.00 [150.00]
1966-68 Nos. 2,3,4, off-set 25.00   50.00   75.00
1969- No. 5, C/Frazetta/Cv/Gaines/Intv.
                       50.00   75.00   135.00

SPASM
(UG, Regular)
1973-No. 1, J. Jones, 50cts/cv/pr, 1st Ed.
                        5.00   15.00   35.00

SPHINX COMICS, TALES FROM THE
(UG, Regular)
1972-73- Nos.2,3, 50cts/cv/pr, 1st Ed.
                        7.50   15.00   30.00

SPIFFY STORIES
(UG, Regular)
1969- No. 1, 50cts/cv/pr, 1st Ed.
                       15.00   30.00   75.00

SPIRIT, THE
(UG, Cross-over-Regular)
1973, K/Snk-Eisner, 50cts/1st Eds.
                        3.50   12.50   25.00

SQUATRONT
(EC Fanzine- Mike Britt issues)
1959-60- Nos. 1,2.   25.00   50.00   75.00

SQUA TRONT (EC fanzine)
Summer 1967 - Winter 1983, 8 1/2 x 11" off-set fanzine, Jerry Weist editor for Nos. 1-4, John Benson editor for Nos. 5-9.
(No. 1) 1967 September, first printing of 750 copies, first printing is square bound with stapled loose interior pages, 8 1/2 x 11, cover price of 75cents, offset cover and interior pages, a few copies issued with white title banner.   45.00   150.00 [225.00]
Second printing, edition of 1,500 copies, cover and interior pages are folded over with center staples, cover price the same but released at 1.50, with wider distribution with Bud Plant Comics.   20.00   50.00   75.00
(No. 2) 1968 September, first printing of 1,500 copies, first printing is identified by 75cents cover price on right top cover.
                       25.00   75.00 [125.00]
Second printing, edition of 2,000 copies, the cover price has been removed.
                       15.00   50.00   75.00
(No. 3) 1969 Summer, first printing can be

identified by the introduction and contents page only - there is black show-through from the "Squa Tront" title page showing through onto the contents page, the yellow paper used for this first fold in page is 'darker' than the second edition. First printing of 2,500 copies, 1.50 price.   10.00   50.00   75.00
Second Printing, 2,000 copies printed, the yellow paper used on the title page and contents page is a lemon color, lighter than the first eidtion, and there is practically no show-through from the black print. This fanzine remained In Print until the late 1980's.
                       10.00   15.00   35.00
(No. 4) 1970 Summer, first printing of 2,500 copies, the only way to identify the first printing is that the cover stock is more matt than the reprint edition which featured a more gloss cover stock.
                       15.00   50.00   75.00
Second Printing, 2,000 copies printed, the cover stock is high gloss.   10.00   25.00   50.00
(No. 5) 1974, first printing only printing, 3.00 cover price.   10.00   15.00   45.00
(No. 6) 1975, first printing of All Krigstein issue, 3.00 cover price.   10.00   15.00   35.00
(No. 7) 1977, first printing only printing, 4.00 cover price.   10.00   15.00   35.00
(No. 8) 1978, first printing only printing, 3.00 cover price.   10.00   15.00   25.00
(No. 9) 1983, first printing is only printing, 11.95 cover price.   10.00   15.00   25.00

SQUIRE (Fanzine- UG/MAD)
Skip Williamson, 8 1/2 x 11, hectograph/ditto with multi color, very limited distribution.
1961-62- Nos. 1,2,3.   30.00   60.00 [125.00]

STAR REACH (UG, Regular-Crossover)
1974- No. 1, 75cts/cv/pr/1st/Ed.
                        7.50   15.00   30.00
1975-77-Nos. 2-12, 1.00/1.25 cv/pr
                        3.50   7.50   15.00

STAR STUDDED COMICS (Fanzine)
Keltner/Saunders/Herndon- The Texas Trio Publishers & Editors, one of the early and "great" comics-hero fanzines, off-set & color covers.
1963-Nos. 1,2. 150/275 printed
                       25.00   50.00 [100.00]
1964-65- Nos. 3-7 all issues
                       20.00   45.00   [85.00]
1966-68- Nos. 8-15, all issues

| | 15.00 | 35.00 | [60.00] |

1969-72- Nos. 16-18, all issues

| | 10.00 | 20.00 | 40.00 |

ST. LOUIS BUG
(Fanzine-SFWorldcon/crossover small format)

1968- No. 1, Bodé B&W 12.50 25.00 [50.00]

STERANKO - HISTORY OF COMICS, THE
(Pro-Fanzine, large format)

1970- Volume one 25.00 50.00 [125.00]
1970- Volume two 25.00 50.00 [125.00]

STYX (Fanzine)
1973- No. 2, J.Jones Cv/Canadian
12.50 25.00 35.00

SUBVERT COMICS (UG, Regular)
1970-76- Nos., 1-3. 50cts/1.00 cv/pr
5.00 12.50 25.00

SUNDAY PAPERS
(UG Newspaper)
Covers by Shelton, London, Todd, Griffithy, Spiegelman, Murphy, Lynch, Gee, interior comix by other artists.
1972- all issues 7.50 20.00 35.00

SUPERMAN, THE STORY OF
(Fanzine, small format- 1st 3 printings)

SUPERMAN, THE FACTS BEHIND
(Fanzine, small format, 4th printing)
Ted White Editor & Publisher, post card sized, mimeographed, cover with four color overlays, 22 pages, extremely small print run, title changed with 4th printing.
1952-one shot- 1st printing
100.00 200.00 [500.00]
1953-54, 2nd/3rd/4th/prints
75.00 100.00 250.00

Note: it is estimated by John Benson in SQUA TRONT No. 5 that fewer than 50 copies ever found their way into distribution.

SWIFT PREMIUM COMICS
(UG mainstream paperback)
1971, April, Bantam Books, 8 1/4 x 5 1/4 1.95 paperback book, no statement of first edition on copyright page, one printing only.
7.50 25.00 50.00

TALES FROM THE BERKLEY CON
(UG, Regular)
1974-Vol 2 No. 2, R. Holmes, 50cts/cv
3.50 12.50 25.00

TALES FROM THE FRIDGE
(UG, Regualr)
1973- No. 1, EC/cv, 50cts/cv/pr/1st Ed.
5.00 15.00 30.00

TALES FROM THE LEATHER NUN
(UG, Regular)
1973- No. 1, 50cts/cv/pr, 1st Ed.
12.50 25.00 35.00

TALES FROM THE OZONE
(UG, Independent)
1969-No. 1, distributed at a Rock Concert, privately printed, with stiff cover paper stock, with one printing only, R. Crumb artwork, and cover art by Lundgren, 50 cents cover price.
50.00 [175.00] [350.00]
1972- No. 2, 50cts/cv/pr/1st/Ed
10.00 20.00 35.00

TALES FROM THE TUBE
(UG, Regular & Mag)
1973-No. 1, 8 1/2 x 11 fomat
12.50 45.00 [75.00]
1973-No. 1, comic format, 50cts/pr
7.50 15.00 35.00

TALES OF SEX AND DEATH
(UG, Regular)
1971-75- Nos. 1,2, 50/75cts/cv/pr, 1st Ed.
3.50 12.50 25.00

TALES OF THE TOAD (UG, Regular)
1970-No. 1, (& Other Stories),50cts/pr
10.00 25.00 45.00
1971-73- Nos. 2,3, 50cts/cv/pr, 1st Ed.
3.50 10.00 20.00

TASTY COMIX (UG, Regular)
1969-No. 1, flat cv/stock/ 50cts/pr
25.00 50.00 85.00
1970- No. 2, 3, 5cts/cv/pr, 1st Ed
7.50 15.00 25.00

TEENAGE HORIZONS OF SHANGRILA (UG, Regular)
1970-72, kitchen Sink, 50cts/cv/pr, 1st Ed.
4.00 8.00 16.00

THRILLING MURDER COMICS
(UG, Regular)
1971- No. 1, 50cts/cv/pr, 1st Ed.
| | 12.50 | 25.00 | 40.00 |

TITS AND CLITS (UG, Regular)
1972-77- Nos. 1-4, 50/1.00/1.25/cv/pr
| | 5.00 | 10.00 | 20.00 |

TOTAL EFFECT (UG, Independent)
1974- Nos. 1,2, 25/35/cts/cv/pr, 1st Ed.
| | 3.50 | 12.50 | 25.00 |

TRASHMAN (UG, Newspaper format)
1969-nn,UG Newspaper/ 25cts/cv/pr
| | 7.50 | 25.00 | 50.00 |

TRINA'S GIRLS/WOMEN
(UG, Regular)
1976-nn, 75cts/cv/pr,1stEd. 7.50 15.00 25.00

TRUCKING (UG, Regular)
1972- Nos. 1,2. 50cts/cv/pr, 1st Ed.
| | 10.00 | 20.00 | 35.00 |

TUFF SHIT COMICS (UG, Regular)
1972-nn, R.Williams/50cts/cv/pr, 1st Ed.
| | 7.50 | 15.00 | 30.00 |

TURNED ON CUTIES (UG, Regular)
1972-nn, 50cts/cv/pr, 1st Ed.
| | 7.50 | 15.00 | 25.00 |

2 (UG, Regular)
1975-nn, Wilson, 75cts/cv/pr, 1st Ed.
| | 12.50 | 25.00 | 35.00 |

2^2 (UG, Regular)
1976-nn, Wilson, 1.00/cv/pr, 1st Ed.
| | 10.00 | 20.00 | 30.00 |

TWO FOOLS (UG, Regular)
1976-nn-Richards,1.00/cv/pr, 1st Ed.
| | 3.50 | 7.50 | 15.00 |

UNCLE SAM TAKES LSD
(UG, Independent, Magazine format)
1972-nn, newspaper, stock cover.
| | 15.00 | 35.00 | 75.00 |

UNCLE SHAM (UG, Regular)
1970-71- Nos. 1,2. 50cts/cv/pr, 1st Ed.
| | 5.00 | 12.50 | 25.00 |

UNEEDA COMIX (UG, Regular)
1971- No. 1, Crumb,50cts/cv/pr, 1st Ed.
| | 12.50 | 25.00 | 50.00 |

UP FROM THE DEEP
(UG, Regular-color)
1971- No. 1, Corben, 1.00/cv/pr
| | 15.00 | 30.00 | 60.00 |

VIBRATORY PROVINCIAL NEWS
(UG, Independent)
1973-75 Nos. 1,2,3, small format
| | 6.50 | 20.00 | 40.00 |

VISUAL ADDICTION
(UG, Trade paperback)
1989- Last Gasp Publications, 19.95 cover price,
    color Robert Williams artwork.
| | 15.00 | 30.00 | 40.00 |

VOICE OF COMICDOM
(Fanzine/UG, Regular)
1970- No. 16, small fanzine
| | 15.00 | 25.00 | 50.00 |
1971- No. 17, UG, reg format
| | 12.50 | 25.00 | 40.00 |

WEIRD FANTASIES (UG, Regular)
1972- No. 1, 50cts/cv/pr/1st10.00 20.00 40.00

WEIRDO (UG, Magazine Format)
1979- No. 1, 1.25 cv/pr, 1st Ed.
| | 3.50 | 15.00 | 25.00 |
1980-83- Nos. 2-7, 1.75/2.50 cv/pr
| | 2.50 | 7.50 | 12.50 |
1984-85- Nos. 8-14, 2.50 cv/pr
| | 2.00 | 5.00 | 10.00 |
1986-93- Nos. 9-28, 2.50/4.95 cv/pr
| | 1.50 | 3.50 | 7.50 |

WEIRDOM (Fanzine/UG Regular)
1970-No. 13,Corben-fanzine12.50 30.00 65.00

WEIRDOM COMIX (UG, Regular)
1971-72- Nos. 14-15, Corben/50cts
| | 7.50 | 15.00 | 30.00 |

WHITE COMMANCHE (UG, Regular)
1977-nn, J.Jackson, 1.00/cv/pr, 1st Ed.
| | 5.00 | 12.50 | 25.00 |

WILD! (Fanzine UG/MAD)
Don Dohler Editor & Publisher, mimeo,
ditto/off-set covers, Jay Lynch, Skip
Williamson, & other UG artist cut their

teeth in this early fanzine, the character
Pro-Junior makes his first appearance -
extremely rare.
1960-61- Nos. 1-3 (scarce) 35.00   75.00 [125.00]
1962- Nos. 4-11 (scarce) 50.00 125.00 [175.00]

WITZEND (Fanzine)
1966- No. 1, Wood, off-set B&W
                          25.00   50.00 [125.00]
1967- Nos. 2-4, matt/cvs 2/tone/cvs
                          20.00   45.00   75.00
1968-70- Nos. 5-7, color/cvs 17.50 35.00   65.00
1971-76- Nos. 8-10, Pearson Ed.
                          12.50   30.00   50.00
1979-82- Nos. 11-13   10.00   25.00   35.00

WIMMIN'S COMIX (UG, Regular)
1972-76- Nos. 1-7, 50/75cts/cv/pr, 1st Ed.
                           3.50   7.50   15.00

WONDER WARTHOG
(UG Magazine-Mainstream)
1976- Nos. 1,2. reprints from early issues of
   Cartoons Comics Magazine, with original
   Shelton Covers, 50 cents cover price, scarce in
   VF or above condition. 17.50   35.00   75.00

WONDER WARTHOG, THE BEST OF
(UG, Regular)
1973-75- Nos. 1,2,3., 50/75cts/cv/pr
                           3.50   6.50   15.00

WONDERWORLD (Fanzine)
1973- Nos. 9,10, off-set   7.50   15.00   25.00

X-ARCHIE
(UG, Independent, small format)
1971- No. 1, stiff cv/paper/stock
                          15.00   30.00   45.00

XERO (Fanzine- see SF Fanzine Listing X)

XYZ (UG, Regular)
1972-nn, says 1st print/cpy-line
                          12.50   25.00   50.00

YANCY STREET JOURNAL (Fanzine)
Formely The Comic Caper, early all
Marvel/Timely fanzine, Dubay/Phals,
ditto/off-set.
1964-65- Nos. 3-8 ditto/mag/format
                          12.50   25.00   50.00
1965-66- Nos. 9-12, newszine format
                          10.00   20.00   35.00

YARROWSTALKS (UG Newspaper)
1967- Nos. 1,2.   10.00   20.00   45.00
1967- No. 3, R. Crumb Cv & art
                          50.00 150.00 [250.00]

Note: multiple copies became available in
the 1970's for Nos. 1 and 2, however the
No. 3 copy (especially flat- unfolded) is
extremely rare.

YELLOW DOG
(UG Newspaper format, then Regular)
(Nos. 1-12) 1968-1969, (note: issues 9/10 and
   11/12 are combination issues) The Print Mint,
   the first issue priced 15 cents in the Bay Area
   and 25 cents elswhere, other issues 25 cents
   cover prices, early issues contain R. Crumb,
   Joel Beck, R. Thompson, Gilbert Shelton.
   Generally found in sets, no one issue rarer
   than the other, now hard to find in VF or
   better. First editions identified by looking to
   copyright paragraph and confirming that
   there is no 5th Anniversary Limited edition
   line added.   3.50   15.00   35.00
(reprint set, usually found with yellow envelope,
   5th Ann. reprint)
(as set 1-12)   5.00   10.00   20.00
(No. 13/14) Print Mint, the first comic size
   format, first printing with heavy cover stock,
   50 cents cover price, wide distribution - with
   no way of telling later printings from first
   edition.   2.50   10.00   20.00
(No. 15) Print Mint, believed to have only one
   printing, the first with 50 cents cover price,
   scarcer even in the early 1970's, the reason for
   this rarity is unknown. 5.00   20.00   40.00
(No. 16) format the same, 1969, the only other
   scarce YD comic.   3.50   15.00   25.00
(Nos. 17-25) format the same, 1970's.
                            .50   5.00   8.50

YOUNG LUST (UG, Regular)
1970- No. 1, 50cts/flat/cv/stock
                          12.50   25.00   50.00
1971-77- Nos. 2-5, 50/75/1.00/pr
                           7.50   15.00   25.00

YOUNG LUST READER
(UG, Trade paperback)
1974- 3.95 cv/pr, 1st Ed. 15.00   25.00   45.00

YOUR HYTONE COMICS
(UG, Regular)
1971-nn, 50cts/matt/cv/stock
                          15.00   30.00   65.00

YUM YUM BOOK, R. CRUMBS THE
(UG, Hardcover Trade)
1975-Scrimshaw Press, no statement of printing on copyright page, red covered boards illustrated, with dust jacket, 6.95 cover price, full color high quality interior pages.

          25.00   50.00   75.00

Note: a number of copies were remaindered and saved during the 1970's.

ZAM (UG, small format)
1974-nn, 50cts/cv/pr/1st 12.50   25.00   45.00

ZAP COMICS (UG, Regular)
1967-No. 1, privately printed for artist R. Crumb by SF Poet Charles Plymell, and sold on the streets of San Francisco by Crumb out of a baby carriage. First printing copies exhibit an untrimmed cover, 25 cents cover price, on the back cover in blue ink "printed by Charles Plymell" on the lower corner, there were a number of high grade copies saved and then later released in the mid 1970's. The most important Underground comic book for the wide-spread effect that it had on other artists in SF and around the country, and the public at large.   350.00 [750.00]   [1,500]
1968-2nd print, 35 cents cover price, and "printed by Don Donahue" on the back cover.

      125.00 [350.00]   [550.00]
1968-3rd, Print/Mint, heavy cover stock paper, difficult to tell from 4th.

        50.00   75.00   100.00
1967- No. 0, actually printed after the No. 1 issue, because the original artwork had been lost, and artist R. Crumb had to deliver Xerox copies to the printer Don Donahue, this first edition can be identified by slightly larger untrimmed cover stock, heavy matt/cover stock paper, the interior pages on the upper right hand side are numbered 1,3,5,7,9, etc.

      150.00 [350.00]   [600.00]
1968- No. 2, heavy/matt/cv/stock/1st

        50.00   125.00   250.00
1968- No. 3, heavy/matt/cv/stock/1st

        40.00   100.00   175.00
1969- No. 4, heavy/cover/stock

        35.00   75.00   125.00
1970-73- Nos. 5,6, 50cts/cv/pr/1st

        25.00   50.00   75.00
1974-78- Nos. 7,8,9. 50/75cts/cv/pr

        15.00   35.00   50.00
1980's- Nos. 10-13, 1.25/2.50 cv/pr

         7.50   15.00   25.00

Note: On issues 2-4 the cover stock is more heavy than the later printings, comics almost have to be put side-by-side for comparision for the collector to become familiar with the differences but once noticed it is apparent.

ZIPPY STORIES (UG, small format)
1977- Nos. 1,2 - 95/75cts/cv/pr/1st

        12.50   25.00   35.00

ZIPPY (UG, Magazine format)
1993-95- Nos. 1-12, 3.50/3.95/cv/pr

         5.00   7.50   10.00

ZIPPY STORIES (UG, trade paperback)
1981-And/Or Press, 7.95 cv/pr

        15.00   25.00   45.00

FROM A TO ZIPPY
(UG, trade paperback)
1991-Penguin Press, 12.95 cv/pr

        12.50   25.00   35.00

ZIPPY'S HOUSE OF FUN
(UG, hardcover trade)
1995-Fantagraphics Books, first printing so stated on copyright page, with signed and #ed edition of 2,000 copies.

        40.00   80.00   120.00

ZOMBIE MYSTERY PAINTINGS
(UG, Hardcover trade)
1986-Blackthorne Publishing, issued in hardcover edition of 250 signed and #ed edition by artist Robert Williams.

        35.00   75.00   125.00

Need Cheaper Printing?

"A valuable and trusted resource"
Pete and Will Eisner
Poorhouse Press

"You've got a miracle worker in your production department"
Wendy Wolf, Senior Editor
HarperCollins

"Better prices, better people and better quality work...
I only wish I'd moved sooner."
Bud Plant
Bud Plant's Incredible Catalog

"Very valuable and would recommend him to anyone"
Cindy Marks, Production Director
Dark Horse Comics

"Great quality, on time, and at a great price"
Chris Oarr, Executive Director
Comic Book Legal Defense Fund

Want to see a sample of our work? You're holding one in your hands right now. Contact us at the numbers below for more information on printing high quality books, cards, catalogs. posters, specialty items, and promotional products.

BENCH PRESS, INC.

326 Main Road Chesterfield, MA 01012
Phone 413-296-0389 Fax 413-296-8095   E-mail khenell@massed.net
Jim Kitchen, President

A PUBLISHING RESOURCE SINCE 1984

PART IX

SCIENCE FICTION FANZINES

SCIENCE FICTION FANZINE LISTING

> "For some reason fans are born amateur journalists and produce large numbers of 'fanzines' - henceforth called 'fanmags' here for the very good reason that this one often runs out of 'i's. They vary in size from the minute '*Fanscient*' to mimeographed mountains, and in quality from '*Nekromantikon*' through good to ordinary. There is no such thing as a bad fanmag, because what's worth doing is worth doing badly."
>
> Walt Willis, from "The Prying Fan," *Slant* No. 5

As an introduction to this chapter we have obtained permission from author Dave Kyle to reprint his excellent personal history entitled "Phamous Phantasy Phan," which was originally published in the science fiction fanzine *Mimosa* No. 24. This short article conveys the flavor of early science fiction fandom, explores Kyle's involvment with the production of fanzines, and illuminates part of his cross-over interest between the worlds of science fiction and comics.

Interested readers are also encouraged to seek out *The Immortal Storm* by Sam Moskowitz, the Hyperion Press edition (available through the New England Science Fiction Society or Hyperion Press in Westport Connecticut). Readers are also directed to Harry Warner Jr.'s two books *All Our Yesterdays*, Advent Press, and *A Wealth of Fable*, SCIFI Press. Sam Moskowitz's book deals with SF fandom and fanzines up to and just after the 1939 WorldCon in New York. Mr. Warners' books both deal with 1940's and 1950's fandom and explore extensively the fanzine editors, publishers, and their history. The author would like to thank Harry Warner Jr. for input on pricing, Johnathen White for extensive advice on pricing, and Richard Newsome for special research and pricing on 1950's science fiction fanzines.

A SHORT COMMENT BY HARRY WARNER JR

Nobody is sure why science fiction stories spawned vast quantities of fanzines. Mystery fiction, sea stories, wild west yarns, and other genres didn't. I can't prove the truth of my suspicion: it happened because fans of science fiction couldn't easily use that interest to guide their lives. Mystery fiction lovers could become policemen or detectives or murderers. Those who liked sea stories could join the Navy. Western fiction fans could increase the population of Arizona or Nevada. But during the first half of the 20th century, compartively few young people could afford to go to college and become scientists, it wasn't practical to visit other planets, and no amount of amateur tinkering in the garage would produce a working time machine. They could, however, write about science fiction, its authors, the future, and publish those writings on hektographs and mimeographs, and fanzines were born.

A WORD ON CONDITION

Many science fiction fans are happy just to have copies of the numbers they want in good to very good condition. Harry Warner Jr. mentions in *A Wealth of Fable* that copies of Lee Hoffman's *Quandry* were already yellowing and chipping in the 1960's. It is indeed hard to find many of the 1930's and 1940's fanzines in top condition, but not impossible. However, new collectors would be encouraged to be satisfied with Very Good or Near Fine copies of many rare fanzines, as higher grades may be impossible.

[ ] = finding a copy in this condition would be unlikely; prices could be higher with these brackets.

THE ACOLYTE

One of the more well known 1940's fanzines, hecto and then mimeographed by Francis T. Laney and Duane W. Rimel, focusing on Lovecraft and Fantasy as well as fandom and sf themes Later issues include Samuel Russell as co-editor. Off-set covers began quite early and were exceptioal.   Many original Lovecraft letters and other poetry appeared in this fanzine, as well as verse and works by C.A.Smith, R.H.Barlow, W.Paul Cook, Manly Banister, Anthony Boucher, Fritz Leiber Jr., Bob Tucker, and others - its easy to see why this fanzine became so famous and popular within its own time.

	Good	Fine	Near Mint
1942-43- Vol. 1 Nos. 1-4	20.00	50.00	100.00
1943-44- Vol. 2 Nos. 1-4, real numbers of 5-8.	15.00	50.00	75.00
1945- Vol. 3 Nos. 1-4, real numbers of 9-12.	15.00	35.00	60.00
1946- Vol. 4 Nos. 1,2, Nos. 13-14.	15.00	30.00	50.00

Note: issues 1-6 are edited by Laney alone, with No. 8 Samuel Russell joins the editorial staff.

ALCHEMIST, THE

Hansen/Martin/Hunt Editors, 5 1/2 x 8 1/2, mimeo with color wood block print covers, color mimeo illos, Bob Tucker, Harry Warner Jr., & others contribute.

	Good	Fine	Near Mint
1940-41- all issues	7.50	15.00	25.00
1946- one shot issue	5.00	10.00	20.00

AD ASTRA

Published by Reinsberg, and Meyer, mimeographed, 8 1/2 x 11, very early and scarce.

	Good	Fine	Near Mint
1939- Nos. 1-4	25.00	50.00	75.00
1940- Nos. 5-6	20.00	50.00	60.00

AFTER TEN YEARS - A TRIBUTE TO STANLEY G. WEINBAUM

	Good	Fine	Near Mint
1945 (nn), one-shot, published by Gerry de la Ree.	25.00	50.00	100.00

THE ALCHEMIST

Published by Charles Ford Hansen, Lew Martin, and Roy Hunt, smaller format with some color covers.

	Good	Fine	Near Mint
1940-41- Vol. 1 Nos. 1-5	15.00	30.00	45.00
1946- Vol. 2 No. 1	10.00	20.00	35.00

ALGOL

Andrew Porter editor & publisher, beginning with mimeograph pgs & off-set covers, evolving into one of the leading SF newszines in fandom.

	Good	Fine	Near Mint
1965-68- early issues ditto, with off-set covers, 8 1/2 x 11 format, colored paper and illustrations. all issues	10.00	20.00	30.00
1970's- off-set with color cvs/	7.50	12.50	20.00
1977-78- off-set,Clr/process/cvs	5.00	10.00	20.00
1980's-present, becomes SCIENCE FICTION CHRONICLE (Newszine)			
1980's-Present all issues	2.50	7.50	12.50

ALIEN CRITIC, THE

Richard E. Geis editor & publisher, 8 1/2 x 11, mimeo with color paper covers, same great combination of talents from the SF Review.

	Good	Fine	Near Mint
1973-75- all issues	5.00	10.00	15.00

ALIEN CULTURE

Jim Leary editor, 8 1/2 x 11, mimeo, with off-set covers, only 3 issues.

	Good	Fine	Near Mint
1949- Nos. 1-3.	10.00	20.00	30.00

AMAZING WONDER TALES

Published by John Giunta who would later enter the comics field.

	Good	Fine	Near Mint
1938-Aug- Vol. 1 No. 1	35.00	75.00	150.00

AMERICAN FANTASY MAGAZINE

Published by James Taurasi, hecto with four pages, 8 1/2 x 11.

	Good	Fine	Near Mint
1938 Mar.- Vol. 1 No. 1	10.00	15.00	20.00

AMRA (A magazine about Conan the Cimmerian & his hyborean age, or so named because Conan once called himself that whilst a pirate.)

Edited by G.H. Scithers, the best of all Sword & Sorcery Fanzines, with a tremendous long run, remarkable cover and interior artwork by Larry Ivie, Roy Krenkel, G. Barr, R. Barrett, Eddie Jones, Jeff Jones, Gray Morrow, and others. A virtual who's who of fandom and professional SF & Fantasy authors contributing articles and poetry - all inspired by R.E. Howard. Format 10x7 inches, occasional duo-tone color covers, off-set interiors.

	Good	Fine	Near Mint
1955-59- as bulletin for the Hyborean Legion.	5.00	10.00	15.00
1959-60 Vol. 2 Nos. 1-11	5.00	25.00	35.00
1960-65 Vol. 2 Nos. 13-35	3.50	15.00	30.00
1965-80's Vol. 2 Nos. 36-70's	3.50	10.00	25.00

ARCTURUS (I)
Published by Kirshenblit, early issues average a dozen to twenty pages, mimeographed.

	Good	Fine	Near Mint
1935-36- Vol. 1 Nos. 1-5,8, there was no No.6 or No.7 issues.	7.50	15.00	25.00
1937 Vol. 2 No. 1	7.50	12.50	20.00
1937 Vol. 3 No. 1, this issue edited by Frederic Pohl.	15.00	25.00	35.00

ARCTURUS (II)
Produced by Rick Sneary & Tom Jewett, editors used rubber stamping, hecto and mimeograph for reproduction.

	Good	Fine	Near Mint
1947-50- Vol. 1 Nos. 1-4, note: No. 2 was bound with "Queer" No. 3.	5.00	12.50	20.00

THE ASTROID (I)
Produced by the Bay Street Science Club, one of the earliest SF fanzines, a bulletin issued by this club.

	Good	Fine	Near Mint
1930 Vol. 1 Nos. 1-3	50.00	100.00	[175.00]

ASTRA'S TOWER
Published by Marion Zimmer Bradley using hecto and mimeograph printing.

	Good	Fine	Near Mint
1947-50 Vol. 1 Nos. 1-5	15.00	35.00	55.00
A.T. LEAFLET 1952	2.50	5.00	15.00

ATOM ABROAD
Arthur Thompson, 8 x 10, mimeo format, with illustrations by the author, 90 page account of 1964 TAFF trip to U.S.A. by Thompson.

	Good	Fine	Near Mint
1965- one shot	10.00	25.00	35.00

BEST OF FANDOM - 1957
Twig Publications, 8 1/2 x 11, mimeo, forward by Robert Bloch, illustrated.

	Good	Fine	Near Mint
1957- one shot	10.00	20.00	25.00

BEYOND
Roscoe Wright editor/publisher, 8 1/2 x 11, mimeo blue inks on paper.

	Good	Fine	Near Mint
1943-46- Nos. 1-6	10.00	15.	25.00

THE HANNES BOK SKETCHBOOK FOLIO
NFFF publishers, 8 1/2 x 11, 16 pages off-set, distributed for NFFF, and for sale from Ed Meskys for $2.50, distributed at NyCon 3 in 1967.

	Good	Fine	Near Mint
1967- one shot.	12.50	25.00	45.00

BOK
Gerry de la Ree publisher, 8 1/2 x 11, off-set B&W, 76 page tribute to the late fantasy artist, in #'ed edition of 500 copies.

	Good	Fine	Near Mint
1974-	15.00	25.00	45.00

AND FLIGHTS OF ANGELS, by Emil Petaja
(The Life & Legend of Hannas Bok) Bokanalia Memorial Foundation, 8 1/2 x 11 B&W photo-off set from typewritten manuscript pages, illustrated, interior color and B&W photos, 156 numbered pages, pebble stock paper, stiff yellow paper wraps.

	Good	Fine	Near Mint
1968- one shot	15.00	30.00	50.00

CACTUS (Sweden/Norway)
Sture Sedolin/Roar Rigdahl co-editors. 8 1/2 x 12, mimeograph format.

	Good	Fine	Near Mint
1959- all issues	10.00	20.00	30.00

CENTAURI
Andy Anderson editor & publisher, 8 1/2 x 11, mimeo, with off-set covers.

	Good	Fine	Near Mint
1943-44- Nos. 1-4.	5.00	15.00	25.00

CINVENTION MEMORY BOOK
Stan Skirvin editor, Don Ford publisher, 8 1/2 x 11, mimeographed 96 numbered pages, illustrated with paste-down photos, heavy paper wraps with 3 inch metal binder, limited to 500 copies, original price of $1.00.

	Good	Fine	Near Mint
1950- May - one shot	20.00	40.00	60.00

CRY (CRY OF THE NAMELESS, THE)

Begun by Carr as bulletin for Seattle fan group, issue No. 17 Webber and Toskey join staff, stays club bulletin till issue No. 75, by 1955 Busbys are added to staff, fanzine continues to enlarge its page count into 1960s', 8 1/2 x 11, mimeo, occasonal off-set cover.

1950-52- 4 to 8 pp., bulletin.

	3.50	7.50	15.00
1953-54- all issues	5.00	10.00	20.00
1955-62- all issues	5.00	10.00	15.00
1963-70's - all issues	3.50	7.50	12.50

DAMN THING!, THE

T. Bruce Yerke editor, Ackerman fiancer, 8 1/2 x 11, color papers, green mimeo inks, Hornig, Bradbury, Knight, Ackerman, others contribute.

1940- Nov. Dec. Nos. 1,2. each with Bradbury fiction, the No. 2 issue with Ray Bradbury cover art.   15.00   30.00   [50.00]

1941- No. 3-. (Bradbury shorts)
            12.50   25.00   [35.00]

DEEPER THAN YOU THINK......

Joel Jay Reieman editor, Robert Weinberg Associate Editor, 8 1/2 x 11, B&W off-set with heavy paper covers by Edd Cartier. This fanzine focused on fantasy, Howard, and single theme issues.

1968-69- Nos. 1-3   7.50   15.00   25.00

DIABLERIE

Bill Watson, 8 1/2 x 11, mimeo with color, tipped in illustrations and photos in certain issues, E. Hoffman Price, Clyne, Bloch, and many others contribute to articles.

1944-45- Nos. 1-8   7.50   15.00   25.00

DIMENSIONS

Famed author Harlan Ellison continued his fanzine publishing days after successfully publishing *The Cleveland Science Fantasy Bulletin* for two more "mega" issues with *Dimensions* Nos. 14 and 15, and then a final FAPA issue mailing for No. 16. These 'fat'(over 60 and 80 pages for Nos. 14 and 15) fanzines, featured multi-color mimeograph artwork; articles and fiction by Poul Anderson, Theodore Sturgeon, Robert Bloch, Algis Budrys, Marion Zimmer

Bradley, David English, Gregg Calkins, Ray Palmer, Fletcher Pratt, Andre Norton - more pro names than would usually appear in a great issue of any SF pro-zine. Now quite rare, and very hard to find in higher grades (they were read to death), these few issues represent the very best that 1950's SF fandom could aspire to in fanzine production.

1954- Nos. 14, 15	35.00	70.00	150.00
1955- Nos. 16	20.00	40.00	75.00

DOUBLE:BILL

One of the best named (the editors were Bill Mallardi and Bill Bowers) and best produced fanzines of the early and mid 1960's. Mimeograph interior, very high quality illustrations, occasional off-set covers - a grand run.

1962- Vol. 1 Nos. 1,2.	5.00	10.00	17.50
1963- Vol. 1 Nos. 3-6.	7.50	12.50	25.00
1964-69 all other Nos.	7.50	15.00	30.00

EC'H-PI-EL SPEAKS (An

Autobiographical Sketch by HP Lovecraft) Gerry de la Ree, 8 1/2 x 11, typeset off-set pages, illustrated by Virgil Finlay, with burnt right hand page to title page, 500 copies #ed.

1972- 1st Edition- one shot
            10.00   25.00   45.00

ECLIPSE

Richard Kuhn, Lynn Bridges, Rudy Sayn, editors. Mimeo, with interior color mimeo and occasional paste-down photographs, Tucker articles.

1941-42- Nos. 1-5   12.50   25.00   40.00

THE ENCHANTED DUPLICATOR - Walt Willis

1954- 1st edition George Charters, with illustrations by Bob Shaw, 8 1/2 x 11 mimeographed in edition of 200 copies.
            75.00   150.00   [250.00]

1962- 2nd edition, Ted Johnstone/George Fields, with art by Eddie Jones.
            20.00   40.00   60.00

1971- 3rd edition, Katz/Brown, with illustrations by C. Ross Chamberlain.15.00   25.00   35.00

1972- 4th appearance serialized in *Amazing Stories* (see Pulp Guide)

1979- 5th edition for British WorldCon & Seacon
   edition.   10.00   15.00   25.00

1980- 6th appearance within *Warhoon* 28
   special Willish, in boards.
                     15.00   25.00   35.00

1981- 7th edition Gary Farber, 300-copy replica
                     10.00   15.00   25.00

1983- 8th edition, editions Dante, for
   ConStellation the 41st Worldcon
             5.00   10.00   15.00

ERB-DOM

From humble mimeograph beginnings,
Camille Cazedessus developed his fanzine
into quite the Burroughs magazine.
Eventually hosting color covers and
artwork by such greats as Reed Crandall,
Burne Hogarth, Russ Manning, J. Allen St.
John and Jeff Jones. In 1966 ERB-Dom
would win the Hugo for best fanzine.

1960-61- Nos. 1-3.   7.50   15.00   25.00

1960's - Nos. 1,2, reprints/pgs added
              5.50   12.50   25.00

1962-65 all Nos. (off-set cvs)
             3.50   10.00   20.00

1966-76 all issues   2.50   10.00   15.00

Note: Issue size was cut in half during the
50's, and then brought back up to 8 1/2 x
11 format.

EN GARDE

Al & Abby Lu Ashley editors & publishers,
tremendous creative screen color covers
(some of the most creative in 1940's
fandom), 8 1/2 x 11, mimeo interior pages.

1942- Nos. 1-4   12.50   25.00   [35.00]
1943-44- Nos. 5-12   10.00   20.00   30.00
1945-46- Nos. 13-17, 17 1/2
             7.50   15.00   25.00

EREBUS

Len Marlow editor & publisher, 8 1/2 x 11,
mimeo, with color, some creative stencil
covers, Larry Shaw & others contributed.

1943-44- Nos. 1-4   10.00   20.00   30.00

ESCAPE

Dick Wilson editor & publisher, 8 1/2 x 11,
mimeo, Kyle, Kornbluth, Speer, & others
contribute.

1939-40- Nos. 1-7   12.50   25.00   [35.00]

FAN

Walter Daugherty editor & publisher, 8 1/2
x 11, mimeograph format.

1945-46- all issues   10.00   20.00   35.00

FANART

Harry Jenkins editor/publisher, 8 1/2 x 11,
mimeograph, each illustration full page.
Second issue with solid red paper wraps.

1941- Nos. 1,2.   12.50   25.00   [50.00]

FANCYCLOPEDIA-Speer.

Author John Bristol Speer, with corrections
by Tucker, Ackerman, Rothman, published
by Forrest J Ackerman, NFFF/LASFS, 8 1/2 x
11 with red pepple surface wraps,
mimeographed yellow interior paper.

1944- 1st printing, 250 #ed copies
            25.00   75.00 [150.00]

Note: This Fancyclopedia works as a history
of fandom up to 1944.

FANCYCLOPEDIA II
(It's Eney's Fault)

Richard Eney, with assistance of
Boggs/Derry/Evans/Grennell/Pavlat/Rapp/
Tucker/Willis & others, 8 1/2 x 11 with
metal file binder, blue paper wraps,
mimeograph pages.

1959- 1st printing, 450 #ed copies
            15.00   30.00   60.00

FANCYCLOPEDIA II Additions And
Corrections - Richard Eney

1960- Richard Eney, mimeographed, many
   editions were bound in with the
   FANCYCLOPEDIA II and distributed.

1979- Mirage Press, a facsimile of the 1959
   edition, printed in an edition of 450 #ed
   copies.   10.00   15.00   25.00

FAN-DAGO

Frances T. Laney editor/publisher, 8 1/2 x
11, hecto with color covers.

1943-44- all issues   12.50   15.00   25.00
1945-51- all issues   7.50   12.50   20.00

FAN SLANTS

Mel Brown editor, mimeograph, 8 1/2 x 11
with off-set cover to No. 1

1943- Nos. 1-2   15.00   25.00   40.00

THE FANSCIENT

Donald B. Day editor & publisher. Who says good things don't come in small packages, this 5 1/4 x 4 1/2 inch B&W photo-off set fanzine had a remarkable run from 1947-51. With its excellent illustrations, its "Author-Author" series of articles, and its duo-color issues for No. 9 and Nos. 13-14 this 'zine pointed the way to the more sophisticated publications of the 1950's.

	Good	Fine	Near Mint
1947 - No. 1	10.00	20.00	40.00
1948-49- Nos. 2-8	7.50	15.00	30.00
1949-51- Nos. 9-11, 13/14	6.00	12.50	25.00

FANTASIA

Lou Goldstone editor, 8 1/2 x 11, mimeo, with woodblock color illustrations and covers.

	Good	Fine	Near Mint
1941- Nos. 1-3.	8.50	17.50	35.00

THE FANTASITE

Edited by Phil Bronson of Minnesota, mimeographed 8 1/2 x 11 format with color stencils used for interior illustrations, covers off-set, contirbutors include Ackerman, Tucker, Simak, de la Ree, Jacobi, Harry Warner Jr., Dickson & others.

	Good	Fine	Near Mint
1940-41 Vol. 1 Nos. 1-6	12.50	25.00	35.00
1942-44 Vol. 2 Nos. 1-6	10.00	20.00	30.00

FANTASY ADVERTISER

Gus Willmorth editor, 8 1/2 x 11, mimeo, articles and ads for pulps and books; by June of 1947 the popularity and high demand for issues caused the format change to 5 1/2 x 8 1/2 with photo-off set pages. Roy Squires becomes editor with January 1950 issue; in Summer of 1954 with No. 40 Ron Smith becomes editor and title merges with *Inside*. The final editorial change came in 1962 when John White took over.

	Good	Fine	Near Mint
1946-49- all issues	10.00	15.00	25.00
1950-51- all issues	7.50	12.50	20.00

SCIENCE FICTION ADVERTISER

(title change in 1952)

	Good	Fine	Near Mint
1952-54- all issues	5.00	10.00	15.00

INSIDE & SCIENCE FICTION

ADVERTISER

	Good	Fine	Near Mint
1955-1961- all issues	3.50	7.50	12.50
1962-present - all issues	2.50	5.00	10.00

FANTASY COMMENTATOR

A. Langley Searles editor & publisher, mimeographed, 8 1/2 x 11 format.

	Good	Fine	Near Mint
1943-45- all issues	15.00	25.00	35.00
1946-49- all issues	12.50	20.00	30.00
1950-55- all issues	10.00	15.00	25.00
1970's-90's- all issues	2.50	7.50	10.00

FANTASY DIGEST

Thaddeus Ditky editor, 8 1/4 x 5 1/4 and 8 1/2 x 11, hectograph, contributors include Moskowitz, Harry Warner Jr., Bob Tucker, Forrest J. Ackerman, scarce - there were only eight issues.

	Good	Fine	Near Mint
1939-40 All issues	12.50	25.00	45.00

FANTASY FAN, THE

Charles D. Hornig editor, printed by Conrad Rupert, small 6 x 9 format, colored slim paper wraps, extremtly rare especially in higher grades.

	Good	Fine	Near Mint
1933-35- Nos. 1-18	30.00	[50.00]	[75.00]

Note: Hugo Gernsback hired the 17 year fan-editor to edit *Wonder Stories*, all on the strength of his impression from viewing the fanzine in his office.

FANTASY MAGAZINE

Conrad Ruppert & Julius Schwartz co-editors, typeset with glossy cover stock covers featuring mono-tone color covers, 6 x 9 inches, Vol. 2 No. 5 is the first issue, a who's-who of early SF fandom, early, rare, and important.

	Good	Fine	Near Mint
1933 Vol. 2 No. 5 (first issue)	45.00	[75.00]	[150.00]
1933-34- all issues	35.00	[60.00]	[100.00]
1935-37- all issues	25.00	[50.00]	[75.00]
1938-39- all issues	25.00	[40.00]	[60.00]

FANTASY TIMES

James Taurasi editor, 8 1/2 x 11, mimeograph, from 4 to 20 pages per issue, holding a monthly schedule for years.

	Good	Fine	Near Mint
1941-47- all issues	2.50	7.50	15.00
1948-54- all issues	1.50	5.00	10.00

1954 - June No. 200 Paul off-set cv
                10.00   20.00   40.00

FFF'S (Fantasy Fiction Field) ILLUSTRATED NYCON REVIEW

1942, 1st edition with orange coated cover stock, 8 1/2 x 11, mimeographed interior, with paste-in original B&W photographs. A historical wrap up of the First WorldCon, with conference writeups by Loundes/Michel/Wollheim - extremely rare and important, the forerunner of later World/Con memory books.

1942- First Edition   50.00   150.00 [250.00]

FANTASY DIGEST

T. Dikty, 5 1/2 x 8 1/2, hecto, with color covers, some issues at end mimeograph.

1939-40- Nos. 1-8   12.50   25.00   45.00

FANTASY FICTION PICTORIAL

One shot, 8 1/2 x 11, hectograph fanzine, color throughout, one of the first fanzines to feature fan art, illustrations by Dollens, Giunta, Taurasi, Rothman, etc.

1939-Fall Vol. 1 No. 1   20.00   40.00   75.00

FANTASY NEWS

James Taurasi edits in 1938, William Sykora takes over in 1939. With an irregular schedule, this 2 to 3 page news fanzine lasted 182 issues, one of the first and longest running news-zines, 8 1/2 x 11, mimeographed.

1938-42- all issues   5.00   7.50   10.00

1939-1st Annish, Frank R. Paul off-set B&W cover, issued for the 1939 World Science Fiction Convention.   15.00   30.00 [60.00]

1943-49- all issues   3.50   5.00   7.50

FANTASY HERALD

Jack V. Baltadonis, five issues, 8 1/4 x 5 1/4, hectograph covers, some remarkable SF covers, the first issue is 8 1/2 x 11 sheet fold over four page fanzine, all issues rare.

1938-40 all issues   15.00   30.00   55.00

FANTASTIC WORLDS

Edward Ludwig editor, Sam Sackett asociate editor, off-set 5 1/2 x 8 1/2, contributions by Bloch, D.H. Keller, Tucker, Farmer, Willis, Ackerman.

1952-58- Nos. 1-8   10.00   20.00   30.00

Note: The Summer 1953, No. 4 issue carries a six page article with photos on Horror Movies by Robert Bloch.

FANTASY PICTORIAL

Bob Stein, hecto-color pages, 8 1/2 x 11, printed on office paper.

1938- Vol. 1 No. 1   15.00   25.00 [50.00]

FANTASY ILLUSTRATED

Bob Stein, Neotoric Press, color hectograph, 8 1/2 x 11, scarce.

1938- Vol. 1 No. 1   17.50   35.00 [60.00]

1940's later issues   10.00   20.00   30.00

FANTASY REVIEW (British)

Walter Gillings editor, 5 1/2 x 8 1/2, typeset off-set printing, illustrated, a news periodical.

1947-49- Nos. 1-15   7.50   15.00 [30.00]

Note: Name changes to *Science-Fantasy Review* after No. 15.

SCIENCE-FANTASY REVIEW

1949-50- Nos. 16-18   7.50   15.00 [30.00]

FANZINE READER'S REVIEW

Rick Sneary editor & publisher, hectograph 8 1/2 x 11, color/hecto covers.

1945-46- Nos. 1,2.   15.00   20.00 [30.00]

FIENDETTA

Charles Wells, with nominal assistance from Lee Hoffman, hectograph with color mimeo covers, 8 1/2 x 11, only two issues.

1952- Nos. 1,2.   15.00   25.00   35.00

FORECAST

Many SF fans would not consider Hugo Gernsback's New Years gift magazine to his close friends and associates a fanzine, however it was published in very limited quanities* and never received any kind of formal distribution. The small format (6 1/2 x 4 1/2) inches, the covers by Frank R. Paul and Alex Schomburg, and the diverse articles make this small magazine highly collectible; higher grade runs are quite rare. The magazine was issued in January of each year.

1950's issues   15.00   40.00   75.00

1960's issues 7.50 25.00 45.00

*Note: From "The Harp That Once Or Twice" by Walter A. Willis, *Quandry* No. 18, Lee Hoffman - March 1952... "Apparently Hugo Gernsback solves the Christmas Card problem the same way I did - issues of a special Christmas zine. I suppose you could even call it a fanzine."

FORGOTTEN SEA OF MARS - Michael D. Resnick

Published by Caz, as a free supplement to *ERB-dom* No. 12, edition of 1111 copies, 8 1/2 x 11, typed manuscript off-set repro with color wraps, illustrated by Neal MacDonald, Jr.

1965- 1st Edition 10.00 17.50 35.00

FRONTIER

Brazier & Klinbiel (No. 6) as editors, 8 1/2 x 11, hecto, with color use.

1940-42- Nos. 1-7 7.50 15.00 25.00

FUTURIA FANTASIA

Ray Bradbury's fabled early fanzines are now highly sought after by Bradbury collectors. Four issues only, with early Hannes Bok covers, the final issue featured a photo off-set cover. Bradbury was 18 years old when he began the fanzine; print runs were limited.

1939-40- Nos. 1-4. 250.00 350.00 [500.00]

FUTURIAN WAR DIGEST (nicknamed "Fido")

Edited by J. Michael Rosenblum, 8 1/2 x 11 to 10 x 8 format, B&W mimeograph format, issues varied between four and twenty pages, with many supplemental publications. British fanzine.

	Good	Fine	Near Mint
1940-41 Vol. 1 Nos. 1-12	10.00	20.00	30.00
1941-42 Vol. 2 Nos. 1-20	7.50	15.00	25.00
1942-43 Vol. 3 Nos. 1-8	7.50	15.00	25.00
1943-45 Vol. 4,5 Nos. 1-6,1-3	6.00	12.50	20.00

GOLDEN ATOM

Edited by Larry B. Farsaci, beginning as a mimeograph fanzine, in later years going to higher grade paper and typeset interiors with photo off-set covers. The early issues are scarce.

	Good	Fine	Near Mint
1939- Vol. 1 Nos. 1-3.	12.50	25.00	35.00
1940-43 Nos. 4-10	10.00	20.00	30.00
1950's as an occasional annual			
	7.50	15.00	25.00

THE GOON GOES WEST

editor, F.M. Busby, 8 1/2 x 11, mimeo, 167 numbered pages, tan covers, illustrated by Atom, the Adventures of John Berry, the 1959 Dentention Fan Guest of Honor.

1961- one shot 12.50 25.00 35.00

THE GORGON

Stanley Mullen editor, a fantasy based fanzine, 8 1/2 x 7 format, mimeograph interiors, silk screen covers.

1947-49- Vol. Nos. 1,2, all issues
5.00 15.00 25.00

GROTESQUE, THE

Ron Christenson editor, mimeo with some color, 8 1/2 x 11, Tucker, Warner, Shaw, Leinster, Ackerman all contribute.

	Good	Fine	Near Mint
1946- Nos. 1-4.	7.50	15.00	25.00
1948- all issues	5.00	10.00	20.00

HARLAN ELLISON, THE MAN, THE WRITER

(First Draft Publication of a Novel In Progress - Demon With A Glass Hand)

1968- one-shot, 165 copies printed and #ed, editors DeVore, Griffis, and Shapiro. Issued as a special for the Detroit Triple Fan Fair in 1968, where Harlan Ellison was guest of honor. Contains a near complete bibliography, a special piece "These Are My Dreams" by Ellison, and articles about Ellison's history in fandom and as a writer, with the First Draft Publication of *Demon With a Glass Hand*. Extremely rare and collectible.

1968- 50.00 100.00 [200.00]

HARLAN ELLISON: A BIBLIOGRAPHICAL CHECKLIST

Compiled by Leslie Kay Swigart, original price 3.00 in a #ed edition of 1000 copies, with photos and illustrations, 117 pages.

1973 15.00 30.00 60.00

HARP STATESIDE, THE - Walt Willis

Published in February 1957 by Walter Willis, Belfast, Northern Ireland, price 2/- or 35 cents, 8 1/2 x 11, mimeographed sheets, with green paper wraps, green tape to binding, 71 numbered pages, illustrated by Arthur Thomson.

75.00 150.00 [250.00]

Note: One of the most acclaimed single one-shot publications of the 1950's by the most widly read fan of that time. Harry Warner Jr. stated in *A Wealth Of Fable* that the last paragraph of page 32 where Willis writes …"Time went by and things got quieter and quieter until we seemed to be the only ones who were fully awake. As the dawn broke the three of us were quietly very happy and talked about how wonderful it had all been, and how much we were going to miss each other and how we must meet again some time. As for me, I was as happy as I'd ever been in my life. All the tension of the last few days was over, and to look forward to I had the prospect of four weeks of seeing America and after that a return to fandom without the worry and embarrasment that had spoiled it for so long. I had now been just seven days in America without even having had time to think about it, but now a feeling of utter exaltation swept over me to realise that I was sitting between Lee Hoffman and Max Keasler at the top of a Chicago skyscraper, watching the sun rise over Lake Michigan. Life can be wonderful. It was one of those moments that has to be broken while it's still perfect, and when the sun was fully up we went down to have breakfast." was almost a perfect summation of fandom at its best in the 1950's, and Willis' writing style at its finest.

HAUNTED

Samuel D. Russell edited two issues, 8 1/2 x 11, off-set covers, zine devoted to supernatural and horror litrature, Bloch and Fritz Leiber contribute.

1963-64 Nos. 1, 2. 10.00 20.00 30.00

HELIOS

First ish edited by Osheroff, all Nos. following by Sam Moskowitz. Format 5 1/2 x 4 inches to 8 1/2 x 5 1/2, off-set, hecto, and mimeo during its run, running from 8 to 32 pages.

1937-38 Nos. 1-7 10.00 15.00 25.00

HERO-PULP INDEX, THE - McKinstry & Weinberg

1970, 8 1/2 x 11, Xeroxed pages, tan heavy paper wraps, stated First Edition verso of title page, 250 copies printed.

1970- First Edition 10.00 17.50 35.00

HORIZONS

Harry Warner Jr. editor & publisher, 8 1/2 x 11, early issues hectograph with color, by September of 1942 moving to mimeograph reproduction. One of the longest running and best known SF fanzines by the BNF who never attended conventions!

1939-October Vol. 1 No. 1
25.00 50.00 [100.00]
1940- Nos. 2-6. 20.00 35.00 75.00

HPL: (A Tribute to Howard Phillips Lovecraft)

Meade & Penny Frierson, 8 3/4 x 11 1/4, typewritten then photo-offset, some type set pages, 144 pages, B&W illustrations by Arnold, Fabian, Kirk, Corbon, Coye, & others, articles by Bloch, Brennan, Long, E.H.Price, Leiber, Colin Wilson, Schiff, & others. Published in an edition of 1,000 copies 35 bound copies #ed on a special page.

1972- First Printing of 1000
10.00 25.00 45.00
1972- Bound #ed edition
20.00 45.00 100.00

HYPHEN

Walt Willis continued after Slant with Hyphen, this fanzine mimeographed and not as production heavy, however with all of the Willis writing style intact. Issues became irregular after 1960.

1952-53 All issues 15.00 30.00 60.00
1954-55 All issues 12.50 20.00 40.00
1956-60's All issues 7.50 15.00 25.00

THE IMMORTAL STORM- Sam Moskowitz

1951- November, 1st edition typing and mimeographing by Carr, Frahm, Weber, Johnson, Toskey, Macauley, Christoff, Kay & Henry Burwell: assembly and binding by Kay &

Hanry Burwell. With heavy tan wraps, metal button binder fastners, mimeographed pages 158 pgs, blue ink on yellow paper, reprinting the chapters from Fantasy Commentator, 8 1/2 x 11 format, scarce.

1951-1st edition.	50.00	75.00	[175.00]
1951-same as signed or inscribed	75.00	100.00	[250.00]

Note: With the publication of The Immortal Storm author Sam Moskowitz brought forth the first coherant history of science fiction fandom, beginning in the early 1930's and concluding with the Futurian Comeback just after the 1939 WorldCon. Jack Speer's "Up To Now" in the Number Two edition of Full Length Articles was the only previously printed attempt at a fan history. *The Immortal Storm* would inspire Harry Warner Jr. to continue the history of fandom with *All Our Yesterdays* and *A Wealth of Fable.*

THE INCOMPLEAT BURBEE

1958- April,1st printing, 8 1/2 x 11, mimeograph in edition of 150 copies, 68 distributed through FAPA.	12.50	25.00	35.00
1959- May, 2nd printing, 100 copies - published by Ron Ellik/Jim Caughran.	10.00	15.00	20.00
1974- May, 3rd printing, produced from 2nd printing stencils by Barry Gold.	5.00	10.00	12.50

INTERNATIONAL OBSERVER

Frederik Pohl, John Michel, Donald Wollheim editors. 8 1/2 x 11, color paper covers with silk-screen designs, mimeo pages, scarce.

1934-37- all issues	25.00	50.00	[75.00]

JOURNAL OF SCIENCE FICTION

Charles Freudenthal & Ed Wood editors, 5 1/2 x 8 1/2, off-set, the No. 4 issue a special ish on the 10th WorlCon held in Chicago, with photos, etc.

1951-53- Nos. 1-4	10.00	20.00	30.00

LETHE

Louis Smith/Riggs/Larry Smith editors, 6 1/2 x 9 1/2 first issue, then 8 1/2 x 11 format, remarkable color mimeograph work, fold

out illustrations, combination of silk screen with color mimeo for specific illos, scarce.

1944-46 Nos. 1,2,3,3 1/2.	12.50	25.00	40.00

LIGHT (Canada's Oldest Amateur Publication)

Leslie A. Croutch, Canadian publisher & editor, 8 1/2 x 11, mimeo and hecto format, some off-set covers, excellent interior illustrations.

1941- Nos. 1-4(#ed 108-111)	12.50	25.00	40.00
1942-43- all issues	10.00	20.00	30.00
1944-45- all issues	7.50	15.00	20.00
1946-52- all issues	5.00	10.00	15.00

Note: Numbering begins with 108, since this publication was formerly titled *Croutch News.*

LOCUS (News Bulletin)

Beginning with two 'trial issues' (Nos. 1,2) and a letter dated May 10th 1968, the editors Charlie Brown, Ed Meskys, and Dave Vanderwerf announced their attempt to cover fannish news "in a comprehensive and accurate way." Early issues were two to three pages mimeographed on colored green or yellow paper. By issues 9 and 10 Meskys and Vanderwerf have bowed out and Charlie & Marsha Brown are listed together. Lasting as a mimeographed Bulletin until No. 154, with No. 155 in June 21 of 1974 the Browns went off-set, and in later years the magazine grew and grew into the professional journal that it is today, many HUGO awards later

1968 (Nos. 1,2)	15.00	30.00	[50.00]
1960's-70's (Nos. 3-50)	3.50	5.00	10.00
1960's-70's (Nos. 50-154)	2.50	3.50	7.50
1970's (Nos. 154-200)	2.50	3.50	7.50
(Nos. 200-up)	3.50	5.00	10.00

Note: Many current back issues are available from the publisher, you may contact them at FAX (510)-339.8144 or Locus@locusmag.com

LOG OF THE U.S.S. ENTERPRISE, THE

Elyse Pines editor, Poison Pen Press, 8 1/2 x 11, mimeo on one-sided sheets, heavy paper wraps with brass pen binders, illustrated. A short synopsis of the first three years of the voyage of the Enterprise.

1970- one shot   17.50   35.00   50.00

THE NEW H.P. LOVECRAFT BIBLIOGRAPHY

Anthem Press Chapbook, Edited by Jack L. Chalker, 8 1/2 x 11, mimeo, with color mimeo cover, tipped in paste-over stating edition of 110 on verso of title page, each issue #ed by hand stamp.

1962- one shot   17.50   35.00   50.00

LUNA

Published by Franklin M. Dietz, single copies 15 cents, 8 1/2 x 11, B&W & color mimeo with dramatic off-set covers.

1962-1970 Nos. 1-8   5.00   10.00   17.50

MAD

Why publisher and editor Dick Ryan didn't sue Harvey Kurtzman and EC publications is unknown!! B&W mimeo, 8 1/2 x 11, soon to use color mimeo on covers and interiors. Lasting only 5 issues, the final No. 5 issue was special Willis Tribute with Lee Hoffman cover and color bleeds to interior printing. EC fans take note, this fanzine has nothing whatsoever to do with comics - it's pure SF.

1951-52 Nos 1-4   12.50   25.00   35.00

1952- No. 5 special Willis issue.
                        20.00   30.00   50.00

MASQUE

One of fandoms most famous fan-artists produced and edited this great fanzine, 8 1/2 x 11 with combined elements of mimeograph and hectograph (for color illustration effects), certain issues had paste-down design elements, color silk-screen intro's to gallery illustrations, and more.

1948-50 Nos. 1-6.   12.50   25.00   40.00

METEOR, THE

Robert Madle editor/publisher, 5 1/2 x 8 1/2, hectograph with color, 4 to 8 pages, 3 issues only, extremely scarce.

1938- Nos. 1-3.   15.00   30.00   [45.00]

MICRO

Donald Cantin edited & published this 6 x 4 inch mini; masking tape to spines, color

paper and mimeograph covers, three issues only.

1953 Nos. 1-3.   7.50   15.00   25.00

P. SCHUYLER MILLER, A CANTICLE FOR

Sam Moskowitz author, Chamberlain/Katz assistants, 8 1/2 x 11, mimeo 11 numbered pages, in edition of less than 300 copies, off-set photo cover.

1975- one shot   7.50   15.00   30.00

THE MUTANT

editor Fred Pohl mimeographed this small 5 1/4 x 4 inch first issue, rare.

1939-April Vol. 1 No. 1 25.00   35.00   75.00

THE MUTANT

Editor & publisher Gergen put out three mimeographed issues.

1942- all three issues 12.50   17.50   22.50

THE MUTANT

With editors Singer/Rapp/Young/ Groover/Metchette/James. Mimeographed 8 1/2 x 11 format.

1948-49- all issues   10.00   15.00   20.00

NEKROMANTIKON, THE

Manly Banister, legendary fanzine, hand set type, zinc half-tones used for interior color illustrations, pro-quality fiction, the editor eventually sent his press to Walt Willis in Ireland and gave up with exhaustion after the fifth issue, emphasis is on Weird Tales fiction.

1950-51- Nos. 1-5.   25.00   50.00   85.00

NEW FANDOM

Sam Moskowitz editor, with final two issues edited by Taurasi. Bright silk screen color covers, printed over colored wraps, interiors mimeo, 12 x 9 to 11 x 8 1/2, scarce, fold over covers prevent any higher grade copies from surviving.

1938-41- Nos. 1-9   25.00   35.00   [75.00]

NORMAL LOVECRAFT, THE

Gerry de la Ree, B&W off-set, 8 1/2 x 11, illustrated, 600 copies #ed.

1973- First Printing #ed 10.00 25.00   45.00

NOVAE TERRAE (British)

Published by Chapter 22 of the SF League, Nuneaton, England.

One of the rarer and more famed of the early English fanzines, featuring early writing by Forrest J. Ackerman (HonMem), Ted Carnell, Arthur C. Clarke, William F. Temple, and others. Edited by Maurice Hanson. Early issues of the first volume were sewn bound, B&W mimeo for Vol. No. 1 and then moving to a standard 'blue' mimeo ink for the later issues, Frank Debby and Harry Turner did a series of simple dramatic cover illustrations for the magazine.

	Good	Fine	Near Mint
(Vol.1 Nos.1-12) 1936-37	35.00	70.00	[150.00]
(Vol.2 Nos.1-12) 1937-38	25.00	50.00	[100.00]
(Vol.3 Nos.1-5) 1938-39	25.00	40.00	[80.00]

ODD

Ray Fisher editor & publisher, 8 1/2 x 11, mimeograph in all early issues, eventually in the 1960's off-set with a high circulation of 1,000 copies for special convention issues.

	Good	Fine	Near Mint
1950-60- all issues	12.50	20.00	30.00
1960-70- all issues	10.00	15.00	20.00

OUTRÉ

Editor Francis Litz, mimeograph, with color paper covers, 8 1/2 x 11, also early 1939 issues are hectograph with color covers.

	Good	Fine	Near Mint
1939-40- Nos. 1-4.	7.50	15.00	25.00

PACIFICON COMBOZINE

(4th WorldCon Commerative Issue)

Various editors, combines a number of fanzines to be distributed at the 4th WorldCon in Los Angeles in 1946, 8 1/2 x 11, mimeo, heavy paper wraps.

	Good	Fine	Near Mint
1946- one shot	25.00	35.00	60.00

PARADOX

Frank Wilimczyk editor/publisher, 8 1/2 x 11, mimeo, with color-mimeo covers, the first issue was hectographed.

	Good	Fine	Near Mint
1942-44- all issues	7.50	15.00	25.00

PEACE AND OLAF STAPLEDON

(An editorialized Report)

Sam Moskowitz, 8 1/2 x 11, pale blue paper wraps, mimeographed 12 pages, based on Moskowitz's report of the Olaf Stabledon visit to US.

	Good	Fine	Near Mint
1950-Spring-one shot	10.00	25.00	[50.00]

PEON

Charles Riddle editor & publisher, early issues with mimeograph covers with some color, excellent cover artwork, contributions by Peeples, Rotsler, Bloch, Boucher, E.E. Evans, Silverberg, E.H. Price, Lee Hoffman, Blish, Bixby, Carr, ect., a long run and a great fanzine!

	Good	Fine	Near Mint
1948- July Vol. 1 No. 1	17.50	35.00	50.00
1948- Sept. Vol 1 No. 2	15.00	30.00	45.00
1948-49- all issues	12.50		

THE PLANETOID

1932 Dec. (Vol. 1 No. 1) The first fanzine by Bob Tucker, a 6 x 7" sheet folded over to 6 x 3 1/2" bulletin. People will realistically ask "how can you 'price' a periodical such as this?" The author states flatly that 'history' is history, and Tucker is important history. To quote from Planetoid , "About 700 planetoids have been discovered in the space between Mars and Jupiter. This sheet makes the 701st, but we aren't on Mars.........YET!" How can you not price such a rarity! Hoy Ping Pong indeed.

Good	Fine	Near Mint
25.00	50.00	[75.00]

PHANTASY WORLD

Feb. 1936 - April 1937, issues 1,2 (9 x 7 1/2), No. 3 (8 1/2 x 11), both mimeographed and hectographed fanzine, edited by David Kyle, extremely rare, issues one through three herald the first comic book features in any fanzine.

	Good	Fine	Near Mint
1936- Nos. 1-3	100.00	150.00	[250.00]

PHILCON MEMORY BOOK

Various publications included: Burroughs Bulletin; Canadian Fandom; Gorgon; Fanscient; Shangri-L'Affairs; and others, 8 1/2 x 11, mimeo with a few hecto and off-set pages, illustrated, duo-color cover wraps.

	Good	Fine	Near Mint
1947- 1st edition	17.50	35.00	55.00

PLUTO

Marvis & Vincent Manning editors, 8 1/2 x 11, color mimeo, multi-color use throughout, justified right hand columns, low print runs.

| 1940-41- Nos. 1-6 | 15.00 | 30.00 | 45.00 |

PROPER BOSKONIAN, THE

Various editors, 8 1/2 x 11, mimeographed, with heavy paper wraps, free to NESFA members and with limited distribution.

| 1970's- all issues | 7.50 | 15.00 | 20.00 |

PSYCHOTIC

If there was no cult-of-personality before Walt Willis in the early 1950's, then Richard E. Geis would have certainly taken up the yoke for American fans. Eventually publishing a fanzine with his name for the title. Early issues of *Psychotic* were hectograph, 8 1/2 x 11, by 1967 with No. 21 off-set covers were appearing.

1953- Nos. 1-6	12.50	25.00	35.00
1954- Nos. 7-12	10.00	15.00	25.00
1955- Nos. 13-20	8.50	15.00	22.50

PSYCHOTIC (in revived format.)

1967- No. 21* (Ron Cobb Cv)			
	15.00	20.00	30.00
1967-68- Nos. 22-25	10.00	15.00	25.00

(Becomes SCIENCE FICTION REVIEW.)

*Note: As the editorial states: "I've heard of publishing late, but this is ridiculous. How long has it been? Eleven Years? Twelve Years? When I went GAFIA, man, I WENT GAFIA." And so, R.E. Geis returned.

QUANDRY

Edited and published by Lee Hoffman who in her 13th Annish wrote "It's a great world, this fandom, full of really swell people." One of the most famed of all 1950's SF fans, Lee's creative drive eventually attracted contributions from Bob Tucker, Walt Willis (whose column "The Harp That Once Or Twice," would garner fame beyond the pages of *Quandry*) and other well known 1950's fans. It should also be noted that Hoffman controlled the circulation with later issues when it became impossible to print enough copies to meet demand, the printings remained small.

| 1950-51 (Nos. 1-8) | 20.00 | 35.00 | [75.00] |
| 1951 (Nos. 9-12) | 17.50 | 30.00 | 50.00 |

(No. 13) 100/pg Annish, a classic.

	35.00	70.00	150.00
1952 (Nos. 14-23)	15.00	25.00	35.00
(No. 24) Bob Tucker Special Issue.			
	30.00	50.00	75.00
1952-53 (Nos. 25-26,29-30)			
	15.00	20.00	30.00
(No. 27-28) Partial section of Willis second American trip "The Harp Stateside," with "Phan Photo" insert.	25.00	50.00	75.00

Note: Nos. 27-28 contains first appearance of the memorable SF fan quote "I hope the hotel doesn't sue."

RICHARD E. GEIS

Is Published by Richard E. Geis, 8 1/2 x 11, mimeo, the more 'personal' Geis.

| 1972- Nos. 1-4 | 10.00 | 20.00 | 30.00 |

RHODOMAGNETIC DIGEST

Bluemson editor issues 1-7; Moore issues 8-11; Dan Fabun thereafter, 6 x 9, typeset interiors, color plate illustrations, mixed media color covers.

| 1949- Nos. 1-3. | 15.00 | 25.00 | 45.00 |
| 1950-53- all issues | 10.00 | 15.00 | 30.00 |

SCIENCE ADVENTURE STORIES

Ossie Train editor, 5 1/2 x 8 1/2, hecto with color, extremely rare.

| 1938- Nos. 1,2. | 17.50 | 35.00 | [75.00] |

SCIENCE FANTASY BULLETIN

Harlan Ellison editor from 1952 through 1953. First four issues titled *Bulletin of The Cleveland SF Society,* this local fanzine was soon developed into one of the leading SF fanzines of the early 1950's by editor Ellison.

1952 (Nos. 1-5 are numbered 12-16)			
	15.00	30.00	50.00
1952-53- Nos. 6-13	25.00	50.00	75.00

SCIENCE-FANTASY MOVIE REVIEW

Walter Marconette, 5 1/2 x 8 1/2, hectograph with color illustrations, the first two issues are 4 page fold-overs, extremely rare in any condition.

1938- Nos. 1, 2.	25.00	[35.00]	[65.00]
1938- No. 3 (Flash Gordon)			
	35.00	[75.00]	[150.00]

1938- No. 4 (King Kong) 75.00 [150.00] [275.00]

1938- No. 5 (Mighty Joe Young)
35.00 [85.00] [150.00]

Note: These small early fanzines can qualify as the grandfathers of movie and horror-fanzines which would come twenty years later; the focus is on fantasy films.

SCIENCE FICTION

Sept./May 1932/33, 8 1/2 x 11 mimeographed fanzine, less than 50 to 100 printed, edited by Jerome Siegel, only four to five full sets known to exist.

No. 3, with the "Reign of the Superman", first appearance of the concept that would lead to the Superman character

| 3 | 1,500 | [2,500] | [5,000] |
| Nos. 1-2, 4-5 | 1,000 | [2,000] | [3,500] |

Note: A heavily restored set of Nos. 1-5 sold at Sotheby's auctions in 1997 for $19,950 with buyers premium. Two additional sets also sold in the summer of 1999 at Phil Weiss auctions, the first set with two issues missing covers and three copies personally inscribed by Jerry Seigel sold for $5,500 the condition was good plus; the second set had better condition, was missing the No. 1 issue, covers intact with no signature to any issues and sold for $6,800.

SCIENCE FICTION DIGEST

Maurice Ingher/Conrad Ruppert, typeset and professional printed, thin paper wraps on cover, pulpish interior paper, contributions by Schwartz, Ackerman, Eshback, Weisinger, Palmer & others, extremely important, rare and scarce in higher grades.

1932- Nos. 1-4. 45.00 [100.00] [175.00]

1933- all issues 25.00 50.00 [75.00]

Note: Becomes *Fantasy Magazine* after Vol. 2 No 4.

SCIENCE FICTION FORUM

Editors Lester del Rey and Damon Knight, heavily populated with pro articles and fiction, or soon-to-be professional SF writers, 8 1/2 x 11, mimeograph, colored paper covers, thick 50 page issues.

1957-59- all issues 12.50 25.00 35.00

SCIENCE FICTION NEWS

Dan McPhail, first two issues hand typed, thereafter carbon typed copies, by 1934 size and number of pages is larger but carbon copies still used, illustrations were sometimes original pencil drawings, covers were hecto illustrated, because of this format copies are extremely rare. editor McPail built one of the largest SF fanzines collections in America during his lifetime.

1931-32- all issues 15.00 30.00 50.00

1933-36- all issues, carbons
12.50 22.50 35.00

1936- all issues in printed format
10.00 15.00 20.00

SCIENCE FICTION REVIEW

Richard E. Geis editor & publisher, 8 1/2 x 11, mimeo with a few off-set covers.

1953-1955- all issues 15.00 20.00 30.00

SCIENCE FICTION REVIEW

Richard E. Geis editor & publisher, 8 1/2 x 11, mimeo with colored papers and covers, artists include Bodé, Fabian, Kinny, Gaughan, Kirk, Rostler, Austin, Adkins, Barr & others. Fandoms best and brightest, articles by a great cross-section of fans & pros.

1969-73- all issues 7.50 12.50 25.00

Note: Becomes *The Alien Critic.*

SCIENCE FICTION REVIEW

Started up again by Geis, off-set on cheaper paper, 8 1/2 x 11, same format.

1976-77 - all issues 2.50 7.50 15.00

SCIENTIFANTASY

A small 1/4 size off-set zine, noted for its "Galaxy Excozela" comic book strip by John Grossman, which ran for each issue in 2 or 3 page format, very professional articles and illustrations. Editors are Bill Kroll/John Grossman.

1948-49 Nos. 1-4 12.50 25.00 45.00

SCIENTIFICTION, THE BRITISH FANTASY REVIEW

Walter Gillings, typeset printed format, 5 1/2 x 8 1/2, B&W, some photos.

1937-38- all issues   10.00   15.00   30.00

THE SF DEBATER
Established in the Summer of 1938 as a fanzine devoted to criticism with the community of fandom, edited by John Baltadonis & Milton Rothman. Hectograph color covers, 8 1/4 x 5 1/4 format, scarce.

1938-40 all issues   15.00   25.00   45.00

SF HORIZONS
Edited by Harry Harrison and Brian Aldiss, lasting only two issues. 8 1/4 x 5 1/4, 50 cents, color tinted covers, extremely strong content with an excellent interview with William Burroughs in No. 2, Aldiss, Blish, Harrison all contribute.

1964-65 Nos. 1, 2.   5.00   12.50   25.00

SHANGRI-LA (name changes to) SHANGRI-L'AFFAIRES
One of the most famous, and long running SF fanzines, with many different editors, at one point in time every issue featured a different editor. Originally a club Bulletin of LASFS .

1940-45 Nos. 1-22   7.50   25.00   45.00
1945-1952 Nos. 23-40   5.00   12.50   25.00
1950's continuing numbers
                       3.50   10.00   20.00

SLANT
The legendary fanzine by the most famous overseas fan of the 1950's: Walt Willis. Willis represented a turning point in SF fandom when he began his early issues, printed on impossibly complicated terms, with hand set type and original color wood and lino-cut covers by James White. Begun in November of 1948, by issue No. 5 in the Spring of 1951 Walt had begun his articles for Lee Hoffman's *Quandry* entitled "The Harp That Once Or Twice," and nothing was ever to be the same again in fandom. Copies of the first issue were circulated in Europe only, and the single copy to be mailed to America went to Forrest J. Ackerman. All copies are extremely scarce.

1948- Vol. 1 No. 1   150.00 [350.00] [500.00]
1949-50- Nos. 2,3.   50.00 100.00 [200.00]
1950-53- Nos. 4-7.   50.00   75.00 150.00

SMITH, CLARK ASHTON, THE TALES OF (A Bibliography)
1951- November -Thomas Cockcroft publisher, typeset, printed in an edition of 500 copies, paper wraps.   15.00   35.00   [75.00]

CLARK ASHTON SMITH, IN MEMORIAM:
Jack Chalker & Associates, Mirage Press, 8 1/2 x 11, mimeo with illustrations, 98 numbered pages, in an edition of approximately 450 copies #ed on front cover and inside back page, heavy paper wraps; with introduction by Ray Bradbury.

1963- August - one shot   25.00   50.00   75.00

SOL (itude)
Dave Ish publisher and editor, 8 1/2 x 5 1/2, 10 cents price, mimeograph with multiple color covers in later issues.

1951-52 Nos. 1-4.   10.00   15.00   25.00
1952-August No. 5 (special Willish)
                      20.00   30.00   50.00
1952- Nos. 6-9.   7.50   12.50   25.00

SPACE
James Taurasi editor, 5 1/2 x 8 1/2, mimeograph one pg. foldover, rare.

1938- Fall Vol. 1 No. 1
                      15.00   25.00   [50.00]

SPACE MAGAZINE
Clyde T. Hanback editor, published by the American Rocketry Society, 7 1/2 x 5 1/2, off-set with some photo covers.

1949-52 Nos. 1-5   12.50   25.00   35.00

SPACESHIP
No SF fan would have believed in April of 1949 when the first amaturish issue of Spaceship appeared that this title would evolve by 1952 into the literate & well designed classic that it quickly became - but then who knew that Bob Silverberg from Brooklyn would also evolve into one of the most important SF authors of the 1960's onward? Mimeographed, early issues are small at 8 1/2 x 5 1/2, and in very small runs, early issues also include Saul Diskin as co-editor.

1949- Vol. 1 Nos. 1-4   15.00   30.00   60.00
1950-51- Nos. 5-11   15.00   25.00   50.00

1951-52- Nos. 11-15, 8 1/2 x 11

                     15.00   30.00   60.00

Nos. 12-28, Silverberg as ed. alone

                     15.00   35.00   75.00

SPACETALES

Tom Ludowitz editor & publisher, mimeo 8 1/2 x 11 with off-set covers.

1941- Nos. 1-5   12.50   25.00   40.00

SPACETEER

Co-edited by Lin Carter & Bill Paxton, 8 1/2 x 11, mimeo, duo-color covers, artwork by Lin Carter.

1947-49- all issues   15.00   25.00   50.00

SPACE TRAILS

K.J. Krueger editor, 4 1/4 x 7 1/4, off-set, type set pages, one shot issue features Wilson Tucker's "Prison Planet," complete with photo-bio on back cover.

1947-Summer Vol. 1 No. 1

                     10.00   12.50   35.00

SPACEWARP

Arthur Rapp editor & publisher, 8 1/2 x 11, color mimeo & color hecto covers, occasional interior color.

1947-48- Nos. 1-18 10.00   20.00   30.00

1949-1952 all issues   7.50   15.00   25.00

SPACEWAYS

Harry Warner Jr.'s fanzine, 8 1/2 x 11 format, early issues with illustrated covers, mimeograph with colored paper covers.

1938- Vol. 1 No. 1 original*

                     17.50   35.00 [100.00]

1940-April No. 1 (2nd printing)

                     10.00   20.00   30.00

1939- Nos. 2-8   10.00   25.00   50.00

1939-42 Nos. 9-30   7.50   15.00   25.00

*Note: The first printing of *Spaceways* No. 1 has light orange colored paper, the second printing has a grey-tone colored paper, and inside the front cover printed with a rubber stamp is "second printing April 1940."

STARDUST
(The Magazine Unique)

William Lawrence Hamling editor,

professional typeset printing on high quality paper, mono-tone color covers on colored paper, fiction by Williamson, Williams, Willy Ley, articles by Ackerman, Hornig, etc.

1940- Nos. 1-5   17.50   35.00   50.00

STAR TREK (An Analysis Of A Phenomenon In Science Fiction)

Harrison/Dyckoff editors, SC Enterprises publishers, NY, 8 1/2 x 11, off-set with coated paper and grey tone cover, 75 cents cover price.

1968- one shot   20.00   50.00   75.00

STELLAR

Edited by Ted White, Larry Stark as listed editor for Nos. 8 and 9, mimeograph with color papers and inks, excellent interior illustrations and fiction.

1955-56 Nos. 1-11 10.00   20.00   35.00

THE THING

Published by Burton Crane & Helen Wesson, 8 1/2 x 11, mimeo, color interior titles, No. 2 with off-set cover, from San Francisco.

1946- Nos. 1-3.   7.50   15.00   30.00

THE TIMEBINDER

E. Everett Evans editor & publisher, 8 1/2 x 11 mimeograph, with color paper covers with standard logo design.

1944-46 - Nos. 1-8 12.50   25.00 [35.00]

TIME TRAVELLER, THE

Allen Glasser editor & Publisher, recognized as one of the first true science fiction fanzines, extremely rare in any grade. Early issues had contributions by Schwartz and Weisinger.

1932-33- Nos. 1-9   45.00 [75.00] [150.00]

TOWARD TOMORROW

James Kepner editor & publisher, 8 1/2 x 11, mimeo, with some off-set interior plates and covers, colored papers, varied content.

1944-45 Nos. 1-4.   7.50   15.00   30.00

TRUMPET

One of the great cross-over fanzines from

SF fandom, editor Tom Reamy featured Burroughs, Star Trek, Comics by Barr and other artists, as well as important articles from mainstream SF authors. Professional off-set throughout and eventually with color covers for Nos. 7-10.

	Good	Fine	Near Mint
1965 Nos. 1-3	15.00	25.00	50.00
1966-67 Nos. 4-6	10.00	20.00	40.00
1968-69 Nos. 7-10	7.50	10.00	25.00

UNKNOWN & UNKNOWN WORLDS, AN INDEX TO

Printed by Sirius Press, forward by Robert Bloch, 8 1/2 x 11, typeset, photo off-set, with stiff heavy paper illustrated cover wraps, red plastic binders, the first printing with hand correction of 1933 date to "1939" on the first page of the Bloch forward.

1955- one shot	12.50	25.00	45.00

UP TO NOW- Jack Speer (a history of fandom as Jack Speer sees it)

1939-June-Fall, issued first in FAPA, reprinted with yellow wraps for distribution at the 1939 WorldCon, 8 1/2 x 11, mimeograph pages, 36 un-numbered pages, the first published history of science fiction fandom, extremely rare in any condition.

1939- FAPA mailing form	75.00	150.00	[225.00]
1939- Yellow Wraps/39'NyCon ed.			
	50.00	100.00	[175.00]

VARIANT

Allison Wilson editor/publisher, 8 1/2 x 11, mimeograph, illustrated.

1947- Nos. 1, 2, 4.	7.50	15.00	30.00
1947- No. 3 (Convention Issue)			
	10.00	25.00	35.00

VOICE OF THE IMAGI-NATION or VOM

Edited by Forrest J. Ackerman and Morojo, mimeographed with the famous typewritter script of 4-S-J, by issue No. 9 featuring photo off-set covers. The longest running effort by Ackerman with any fan publication.

1939- Nos. 1-4	15.00	30.00	[75.00]
1940-42- Nos. 5-20	12.50	25.00	40.00
1942-50- Nos. 21-50	10.00	15.00	25.00

WARHOON

Richard Bergeron editor/publisher, early issues ditto reproduction, later issues mimeograph, 8 1/2 x 11, first five issues in 1952, then a hiatus of six years - after No. 6 begins to quickly become one of the top SF fanzines.

1952- Nos. 1-5 (Dist. SAPS)	7.50	15.00	20.00
1960's- all issues	5.00	10.00	25.00
Special 600 pg + Willis reprint ish. bound in			
green boards.	20.00	45.00	75.00

A WARNING! (pamplet, issued at 1st New York WorldCon)

Four page pamplet issued by Dave Kyle and snuck into the New York WorldCon for circulation, with "BEWARE Of The Dictatorship," on the first page. This warning clearly states that SF fandom should be open to "everyone" and that Democratic values should prevail in the FAN-WARS of 1936-42 between different NY, NJ and PA SF fan clubs. Extremely scarce (since Moskowitz, who represented New Fandom & was in conflict with the Futurians who he felt would disrupt the 1939 WorldCon, personally saw to it that any copies 'found' would be destroyed) in any condition, and saved by very few fans in 1939. Printed on thin yellow-orange paper, 6 x 4 1/2 inches.

1939-July 2 (nn)	75.00	[175.00]	[375.00]

Note: Harry Warner Jr. states... "This was an extremely important document in early fandom and even the history of pulp magazine science fiction, because it worsened the split between the two main factions in New York City fandom and when the Futurians became editors of several prozines, they bought material from one another and none of their opponets ever became major pro writers. I'm sure that very few copies survive (I have one somewhere, hand delivered to me by hitchiking Futurians shortly after that famous first worldcon)."

WHISPERS

Stuart David Schiff published the best contemporary 'Arkham'-based horror and fantasy fanzine of the 1970's and 1980's.

Starting out with B&W photo off-set format, eventually including square bound spines with color covers. The best 'Weird Tales' type fanzine of the modern era, crammed with great art and articles.

	Good	Fine	Near Mint
1973 July Vol. 1 No. 1	20.00	30.00	50.00
1973-74 Nos. 2-4	15.00	25.00	35.00
1974-87 Nos. 5-24, exist as double issue Nos.	10.00	20.00	40.00

THE WILLIS PAPERS
A. Vincent Clarke, editor, 8 1/2 x 11, mimeo-B&W, heavy paper cover wraps, printed in an edition of 150 copies hand numbered.

	Good	Fine	Near Mint
1959-61- one shot	12.50	25.00	45.00

WIZARD OF VENUS (Souvenir of the 22nd WorldCon)
Story Adapted by Dale Broadhurst, illustrations by Mike Royer, a comic book adaptation of the Burroughs story, off-set, heavy paper cover wraps, 9 x 6 1/2, B&W, 36 numbered pages.

	Good	Fine	Near Mint
1964- Summer, one-shot	7.50	15.00	35.00

XERO
One of the great 1960's SF fanzines, edited by Pat and Dick Lupoff. This mimeograph fanzine would begin with issue No. 1 (No. 3 was actually titled *Xero Comics*) to feature articles by different fans entitled "All In Color For A Dime," which explored the Golden Age of Comics history. By issue No. 3 the copyright paragraph on the first page stated "*Xero* continues to appall an already reeling fandom at the behest of Pat & Dick Lupoff," and while it may have appalled SF fandom - it now remains in the history books with comics fandom as one of the most important fanzines ever. Because of this cross-over interest *Xero* is very expensive and in demand.

	Good	Fine	Near Mint
1960- Nos. 1,2.	45.00	95.00	[175.00]
1961- Nos. 3,4,5- 3,5 Comic/Cvs	30.00	60.00	[150.00]
1961-63- Nos. 6-10	25.00	45.00	[125.00]

YANDRO (EISFA From Nos. 1-35)
Robert & Juanita Coulson Editors/publishers, 8 1/2 x 11, mimeograph on colored papers throughout its run, one of fandom's longest running zines. Initally titled EISFA (Eastern Indiana SF Association), a club zine.

	Good	Fine	Near Mint
1953-55- all issues	7.50	15.00	30.00
1956-63- all issues	5.50	12.50	17.50
1964-70's- all issues	3.50	10.00	15.00
1980-90's- all issues	1.50	5.00	7.50
1959-Yandro Calander, illustrated	5.00	15.00	25.00

ZENITH
Edited by Harry E. Turner, 8 x 10 1/2, mimeo with pale blue cover stock covers, some limited use of color.

	Good	Fine	Near Mint
1941-42- Nos. 1-3 & 5.	7.50	15.00	25.00
1942- Feb. No. 4 (contains Arthur C. Clark's "The Awakening")	15.00	25.00	50.00

ZOMBIE, LE
Bob Tucker editor and publisher, mimeo at 8 1/2 x 11 format, from December 1938 through July of 1948, one of the longest running fanzines by one of SF fandom's most important fans. Eventually Tucker would began a more active life as pro-author, but he has always considered himself an SF fan first.

	Good	Fine	Near Mint
1938-39- Nos. 1-20	20.00	40.00	[75.00]
1940-48- Nos. 21- 63	10.00	20.00	35.00

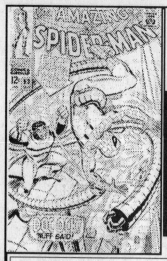

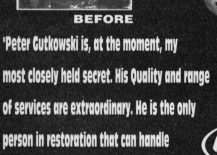

ORIGINAL ART

TRH GALLERY
SPECIALIZING IN VINTAGE COMIC BOOK AND COMIC STRIP ORIGINAL ART.

@ D.C. Comics

@ D.C. Comics

TOM HORVITZ
TRH GALLERY
18324 CLARK ST. #223
TARZANA CA. 91356
1-818-757-0747 phone
1-818-757-0859 fax
trhgallery@earthlink.net email
TRHGALLERY.COM website

One of the largest websites devoted to buying and selling comic art.

@ Marvel Comics

@ D.C. Comics

@ Marvel Comics

@ Darkhorse Comics

Enjoy The Last Laugh!

*Got comic art to sell?
Get your best estimate,
then talk to us at Greg
Manning Auctions.
You'll like what you hear.*

The reason why Greg Manning
Auctions, Inc., buys more original
comic book art than anyone else in
the business is because we pay more
than anyone else. Period. End of
story. But don't just take our word
for it. Put us to the test.

If you have cover art, interior
pages (color or black and white),
complete books or entire
collections to sell, get as many
estimates as you like from as many
dealers as you can. Then bring us
their best offer. And watch us top it.

When you sell to Greg
Manning, you're dealing with the
leader in collectibles auctions and
sales, the largest publicly-traded
collectibles auction house. You can
expect great service. And the last
laugh will be all yours, all the way
to the bank.

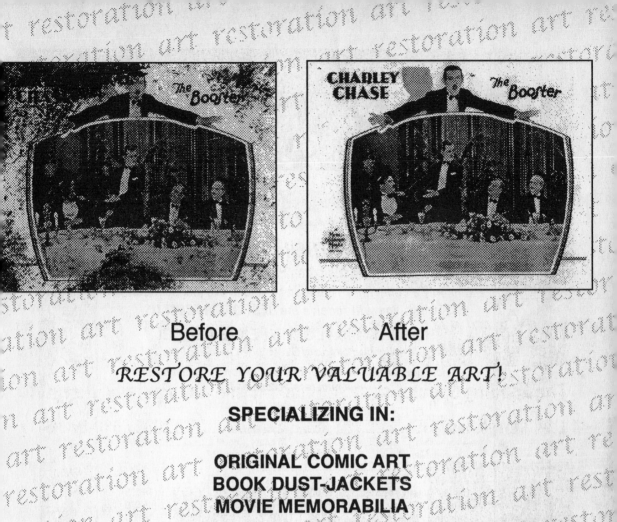

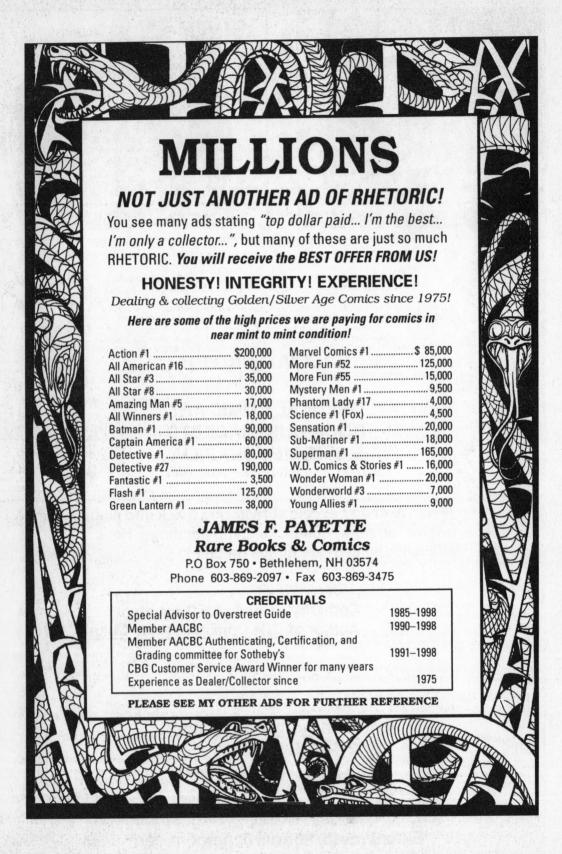

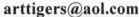

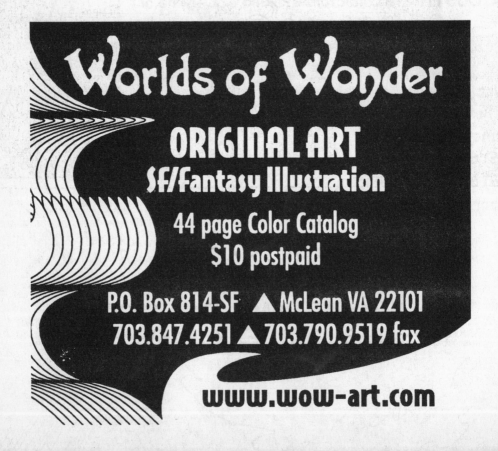

ORIGINAL
UNDERGROUND COMIX
ART

1967   to   1978

*PRIME EXAMPLES ALWAYS WANTED,
ART AVAILABLE FOR EXHIBITION.

ERIC SACK
2011 Old York Road
JENKINTOWN, PA. 19046
(215)-885-7070   FAX (215)885-6103